Pattern Recognition Principles

APPLIED MATHEMATICS AND COMPUTATION

A Series of Graduate Textbooks, Monographs, Reference Works

Series Editor: ROBERT KALABA, University of Southern California

No. 1 MELVIN R. SCOTT
Invariant Imbedding and its Applications to Ordinary Differential Equations: An Introduction, 1973

No. 2 JOHN CASTI and ROBERT KALABA
Imbedding Methods in Applied Mathematics, 1973

No. 3 DONALD GREENSPAN
Discrete Models, 1973

No. 4 HARRIET H. KAGIWADA
System Identification: Methods and Applications, 1974

No. 5 V. K. MURTHY
The General Point Process: Applications to Bioscience, Medical Research, and Engineering, 1974

No. 6 HARRIET H. KAGIWADA and ROBERT KALABA
Integral Equations Via Imbedding Methods, 1974

No. 7 JULIUS T. TOU and RAFAEL C. GONZALEZ
Pattern Recognition Principles, 1974

In Preparation

No. 8 HARRIET H. KAGIWADA, ROBERT KALABA, and SUEO UENO
Multiple Scattering

Pattern Recognition Principles

JULIUS T. TOU

Center for Information Research
University of Florida, Gainesville

RAFAEL C. GONZALEZ

Department of Electrical Engineering
University of Tennessee, Knoxville

1974

Addison-Wesley Publishing Company
Advanced Book Program
Reading, Massachusetts

London · Amsterdam · Don Mills, Ontario · Sydney · Tokyo

CODEN: APMCC

First printing, 1974
Second printing, with revisions, 1977
Third printing, 1979
Fourth printing, 1981

ISBN 0-201-07587-3

Library of Congress Cataloging in Publication Data

Tou, Julius T., 1926–
Pattern recognition principles.

(Applied mathematics and computation)
1. Pattern perception. I. Gonzalez, Rafael C., joint author. II. Title.
Q327.T68 001.53′4 74-13092

ISBN 0-201-07586-5

American Mathematical Society (MOS) Subject Classification Scheme (1970):
68A45, 68A30, 90D35, 68A35, 93C40

FGHIJKLM-HA-8987654

Printed in the United States of America

To our wives

LISA TOU and CONNIE GONZALEZ

CONTENTS

SERIES EDITOR'S FOREWORD

Execution times of modern digital computers are measured in nanoseconds. They can solve hundreds of simultaneous ordinary differential equations with speed and accuracy. But what does this immense capability imply with regard to solving the scientific, engineering, economic, and social problems confronting mankind? Clearly, much effort has to be expended in finding answers to that question.

In some fields, it is not yet possible to write mathematical equations which accurately describe processes of interest. Here, the computer may be used simply to simulate a process and, perhaps, to observe the efficacy of different control processes. In others, a mathematical description may be available, but the equations are frequently difficult to solve numerically. In such cases, the difficulties may be faced squarely and possibly overcome; alternatively, formulations may be sought which are more compatible with the inherent capabilities of computers. Mathematics itself nourishes and is nourished by such developments.

Each order of magnitude increase in speed and memory size of computers requires a reexamination of computational techniques and an assessment of the new problems which may be brought within the realm of solution. Volumes in this series will provide indications of current thinking regarding problem formulations, mathematical analysis, and computational treatment.

Pattern recognition cuts across many areas—medical diagnosis, language translation, and statistics, to name a few. This work provides an introduction to the basic methods and ideas and should stimulate even further development in an already burgeoning field.

ROBERT KALABA

PREFACE

This textbook was written to provide engineers, scientists, and students involved in data analysis and information processing activities with a comprehensive, well-organized, and up-to-date account of basic principles and available techniques for the analysis and design of pattern processing and recognition systems.

Initial efforts in the study of automatic pattern recognition may be traced to the early 1950's when the digital computer first became a potential information processing tool. Some of the first efforts in pattern recognition were attempts to program computers for automatic decision making, and to develop specialized hardware to read patterns such as printed alpha-numeric characters. In the late 1950's, Rosenblatt introduced the Perceptron algorithm which was an early model for information storage and organization in the brain. During this period, major approaches to the pattern recognition problem were based primarily upon statistical decision theory and threshold logic principles. Research in pattern recognition system design gained momentum during the 1960's as the use of computers multiplied and the need for faster and more efficient communication between man and machine became evident. To make use of computer language theory and its associated processing capabilities, the syntactic approach was introduced as a supplement to analytical techniques in solving certain pictorial pattern recognition problems.

Pattern recognition concepts have become increasingly recognized as an important factor in the design of modern computerized information systems. Interest in this area is still growing at a rapid rate, having been a subject of interdisciplinary study and research in such varied fields as engineering, computer science, information science, statistics, physics, chemistry, linguistics, psychology, biology, physiology, and medicine. Each of these fields emphasizes certain aspects of the problem, ranging from the modeling of physiological processes to the development of analytical techniques for automatic decision making. The bulk of the material dealing with pattern recognition theory and applications has been widely scattered in various technical journals, conference proceedings, advanced monographs, and some textbooks which focus attention on certain specific approaches to the pattern recognition problem. Consequently, it is a rather difficult task, particularly for a newcomer to this interdisciplinary field, to learn the range of principles underlying this subject matter. This text attempts to put between the covers of one book available basic analytical techniques and fundamental principles, and to organize them in a coherent and unified manner. Thus, the present volume is intended to be of use both as textbook and as reference work. To the student, it presents in step-by-step fashion a discussion of basic theories and important techniques. For the practicing engineer or scientist, it provides a ready source of reference in systematic form.

As background to the text, it is assumed that the reader has adequate introductory preparation in computer programming, statistics, matrix theory, and mathematical analysis. In presenting the material, emphasis is placed on the development of fundamental results from basic concepts. Numerous examples are worked out in the text and exercises of various types and complexity are included at the end of each chapter. Some of these problems permit the reader to clarify for himself the points discussed in the text through actual practice in problem solution. Others serve as supplement and extensions of the material in the text.

This book is primarily the outgrowth of lecture notes for courses taught by the authors at the University of Florida and the University of Tennessee. Earlier versions of these notes had been prepared in 1962 for a one-quarter course at Northwestern University. Later, the material was also taught at the Ohio State University. The material has been extensively tested in various levels of coverage in senior- and graduate-level courses in electrical engineering and in computer science curricula. The suggestions and criticisms of students in these courses resulted in extensive revisions of the original manuscript.

We are indebted to a number of individuals who, directly or indirectly, assisted in the preparation of the text. In particular, we wish to extend our appreciation to Professors W. H. Chen, J. M. Googe, J. F. Pierce, M. G. Thomason, C. C. Li, K. S. Fu, and to Dr. R. C. Kryter, Dr. P. H. Swain, Mr. S. D. Blazier, Mr. C. W. Swonger, Dr. Neil Wald, and to Mr. G. C. Guerrant. Thanks are also due to Mrs. Mary Bearden, Mrs. Grace Searle, Mrs. Debra Dillingham, and to the secretarial staffs of the Universities of Florida and Tennessee for typing numerous versions of the manuscript. In addition, we express our appreciation to the Office of Naval Research, the Army Research Office, the National Aeronautics and Space Administration, the Oak Ridge National Laboratory, and the National Science Foundation for their sponsorship of our research activities in information processing and pattern recognition.

JULIUS T. TOU

RAFAEL C. GONZALEZ

NOTATION

The following is a list of the principal symbols used in this book.

Symbol	Explanation
$\mathbf{x} = \begin{pmatrix} x_1 \\ x_2 \\ \vdots \\ x_n \end{pmatrix}$	vector; also, pattern or pattern vector. Lowercase bold letters, **a**, **b**, **x**, **y**, **z**, **w**, . . . , are used throughout to denote vectors
$\mathbf{x} = \begin{pmatrix} x_1 \\ x_2 \\ \vdots \\ x_n \\ 1 \end{pmatrix}$	augmented vector
$\mathbf{x}' = (x_1, x_2, \ldots, x_n)$	transposed vector
$\mathbf{x}_j$	subscripted vector
$\lVert\mathbf{x}\rVert = \left[\sum_{j=1}^{n} x_j^2\right]^{1/2}$	Euclidean norm or magnitude of vector **x**
$\lvert\mathbf{x}\rvert = \begin{pmatrix} \lvert x_1\rvert \\ \lvert x_2\rvert \\ \vdots \\ \lvert x_n\rvert \end{pmatrix}$	a vector whose components are the absolute value of the components of **x**
$\mathbf{A}, \mathbf{B}, \mathbf{C}, \mathbf{X}, \ldots$	matrices
$\lvert\mathbf{A}\rvert$	determinant of **A**

Symbol	Explanation
n	dimensionality of pattern vectors
E^n	n-dimensional Euclidean space
N	number of patterns
ω_i	ith pattern class
M	number of pattern classes
N_i	number of patterns in ω_i
$\mathbf{w}$	weight vector; also, coefficient vector
$\mathbf{w}_i$	weight vector of class ω_i
$\mathbf{w}'\mathbf{x} = \sum_{j=1}^{n} w_j x_j$	dot or inner product of vectors $\mathbf{w}$ and $\mathbf{x}$
$\|\mathbf{w}'\mathbf{x}\|$	absolute value of the scalar $\mathbf{w}'\mathbf{x}$
$d(\mathbf{x})$	decision or discriminant function
$d_i(\mathbf{x})$	decision function of class ω_i
$d_i(\mathbf{x}) = \mathbf{w}_i'\mathbf{x}$	linear decision function
$p(\omega_i)$	*a priori* probability of class ω_i; a scalar quantity describing the probability of occurrence of class ω_i
$p(\mathbf{x}) = p(x_1, x_2, \ldots, x_n)$	probability density function of $\mathbf{x}$
$p(\mathbf{x}/\omega_i)$	probability density function of $\mathbf{x}$ when $\mathbf{x}$ comes from ω_i, sometimes denoted by $p_i(\mathbf{x})$
$p(\omega_i/\mathbf{x})$	conditional density function of class ω_i
$\int_{\mathbf{x}} d\mathbf{x} = \int_{x_1}\int_{x_2}\cdots\int_{x_n} dx_1\,dx_2\cdots dx_n$	multiple integral
$E\{f(\mathbf{x})\} = \int_{\mathbf{x}} f(\mathbf{x})p(\mathbf{x})\,d\mathbf{x}$	expected value of $f(\mathbf{x})$

Symbol	**Explanation**
$\mathbf{m} = E\{\mathbf{x}\} = \int_{\mathbf{x}} \mathbf{x} p(\mathbf{x})\, d\mathbf{x} = \begin{pmatrix} \int_{\mathbf{x}} x_1 p(\mathbf{x})\, d\mathbf{x} \\ \vdots \\ \int_{\mathbf{x}} x_n p(\mathbf{x})\, d\mathbf{x} \end{pmatrix} = \begin{pmatrix} E\{x_1\} \\ \vdots \\ E\{x_n\} \end{pmatrix}$	mean vector; also, expected value of $\mathbf{x}$
$\mathbf{m}_i$	mean vector of class ω_i
$\mathbf{C} = E\{(\mathbf{x} - \mathbf{m})(\mathbf{x} - \mathbf{m})'\} = \int_{\mathbf{x}} (\mathbf{x} - \mathbf{m})(\mathbf{x} - \mathbf{m})' p(\mathbf{x})\, d\mathbf{x}$	covariance matrix
$\mathbf{C}_i$	covariance matrix of class ω_i
$N(\mathbf{m}_i, \mathbf{C}_i)$	abbreviated notation of normal or Gaussian density for class ω_i. This density function is completely characterized by the parameters $\mathbf{m}_i$ and $\mathbf{C}_i$
$K(\mathbf{x}, \mathbf{x}_j)$	potential function of sample $\mathbf{x}_j$
$G = (V_N, V_T, P, S)$	grammar: V_N is set of nonterminals, V_T is set of terminals, P is set of productions, and S is the start or sentence symbol
$G = (V_N, V_T, P, Q, S)$	stochastic grammar: V_N, V_T, P, and S are as above, and Q is a set of probabilities associated with the productions of P
$G = (V_N, V_T, P, R, S)$	tree grammar: V_N, V_T, and S are as above, P is a set of tree productions, and R is a ranking function
G_i	grammar of class ω_i
$L(G)$	language generated by grammar G
k	iteration index

Symbol	Explanation
$C_r^q = \dfrac{q!}{r!(q-r)!}$	binomial coefficient
$\exists$	there exists
$\in$	belongs to or is in
$\notin$	does not belong to
$\forall$	for all
δ_{ij}	Kronecker delta function: $\delta_{ij} = 0$ if $i \neq j$, and $\delta_{ij} = 1$ if $i = j$

1

INTRODUCTION

Several years ago the Sunday *New York Times* asked this question: "Will a full week of shorter trading hours bring happiness to brokerage firms whose back offices are jammed with paper work?" and reported the following item: "A professor of psychology at Harvard University warned that by the year 2000 the limit of man's mind to absorb information may be reached. 'We may already be nearing some kind of limit for many of the less gifted among us,' he said, 'and those still able to handle the present level of complexity are in ever-increasing demand.'" Certainly the daily press has little doubt that information is exploding.

In recent years our very complex and technologically oriented society has created a situation in which more people and organizations have become concerned with handling information and fewer with handling materials. The need for improved information systems has become more conspicuous, since information is an essential element in decision making, and the world is generating increasing amounts of information in various forms with different degrees of complexity. One of the major problems in the design of modern information systems is automatic pattern recognition, which forms the theme of this book.

1.1 THE INFORMATION-HANDLING PROBLEM

The advancement of material civilization and modern science has created the information problem confronting our society. People in a primitive society are not faced with such a problem. In fact, the level of development of a society may be measured by the amount of information and knowledge that it generates. Without information civilization, as we know it, would not exist. In order to solve the social problems of our times, we must first solve the information problem. One of the major critical challenges that our society will face in the 1970's and 1980's is the explosion of information, which will continue at an accelerated pace.

The information explosion problem is clearly illustrated by a brief glance at the following statistics. In 1830 about 300 technical and scientific journals were in circulation. Today there are over 60,000 journals and 2.5 million articles per year throughout the world in over 50 languages. Each year approximately 80,000 new book titles are published throughout the world. Each year about 20 billion checks pass through the banks, each check being handled four to five times. The nation's major banks process 25 million transactions per day. The U.S. Post Office Department is facing a severe mail problem. Today the U.S. postal system processes some 27,000 pieces of mail per second or 84 billion pieces per year, and this figure is expected to reach 116 billion by 1980. Several years ago, the Postmaster General told a congressional subcommittee, "Frankly, your Post Office Department is in a race with catastrophe."

The U.S. federal offices currently maintain files for more than 200 million fingerprints and 150 million social security accounts. In 1940 there were only 15 million income tax returns. In 1973 the Internal Revenue Service processed over 100 million income tax returns and another 360 million related documents. By 1980 the IRS anticipates processing 137 million tax returns. Furthermore, the problem of volume is compounded by the fact that American tax returns are the product of a complex law and reflect the ever-growing variety of financial transactions.

Medicine is facing a problem of information explosion similar to that confronting many other segments of society today. Physicians are beginning to feel incapable of handling effectively the tremendous flood of information that must be processed in medical research and patient care. For proper diagnosis and treatment, a physician must interview and examine the patient, conduct laboratory and other studies, and record the information obtained. He must select, collate, and compare these data with his own previously gained experience and derive a diagnosis which identifies the ailment. In both diagnosis and treatment, a doctor is constantly analyzing and processing information toward realizing the goals of medicine. If he could routinely access and store clinical data in a medical information system without undue effort on his part, he could then take advantage of the speed and analytical capabilities of the system to extend his professional abilities. In terms of patient care, a physician should be able to retrieve previous medical history or treatment immediately in a form that he can use effectively. In evaluating an unusual illness, he may wish to retrieve a table of statistical analyses involving hundreds to thousands of cases for signs and symptoms or laboratory findings in patients with a given diagnosis. Clinical laboratories need automated systems to read X-ray films, to recognize cellular specimens, to screen electrocardiograms from mass heart tests, and to aid in medical diagnosis. Hospitals need automated information systems to store patient records, to retrieve medical histories, to monitor patient scheduling, and to handle patient care. Medical information systems will provide the physician with a tool to extend his insight and capabilities in medicine.

Industry is confronted with a pressing need for better information flow between businesses. Executives and managers need to know more about the various functions within their company, more about their own operations and the markets they are serving, and they need timely information in order to make the best decision in a rapidly changing business environment. Information systems find increasingly important use in policy decision making, both in government and in business. Managerial decision making will always involve human judgment, but new concepts and computer-oriented techniques have been developed that both suggest and evaluate a greater variety of options than any manager could ever seriously consider. The added feature of risk analysis enables a manager to measure the degree of risk involved in each of a variety of strategies. Information systems will provide the manager with a clearer insight as to the implications of his decisions.

It is fortunate that the digital computer, one of the most important technological advances of twentieth century, stepped into the widening information gap. The computer, just past its thirtieth birthday, has come of age, progressing from a scientific curiosity to an essential part of human life in a remarkably short time. No single technological development in history has had a greater immediate impact upon man and the way he lives. In many respects, computers have erased time, altered the ordinary boundaries and relationships that affect our lives and our organizations, and accelerated the rate of change. Just imagine what would happen if computers were suddenly pulled out of service. Airline travel would be chaotically disrupted, banks would bulge with unprocessed papers, industrial systems would grind to a halt, and much in our lives that we now take for granted would suddenly vanish.

The banking industry has witnessed many changes since the "bank holiday" of 1933. These changes have created the so-called banking revolution. The electronic digital computer, although not the cause of this revolution, was the instrument for its acceleration. The banking revolution was the banks' recognition of the retail market—the needs of the individual—rather than primarily the needs of business, large corporations, and businessmen. The revolution resulted in increased emphasis on personal checking accounts, installment loans, credit cards, and various types of savings media with different interest rates. The revolution also created a "paper explosion" problem. The volume of checks cleared by the banking system has increased over 15 times in the last 30 years. By the late 1950's the resulting proliferation of paper to shuffle and checks to process was threatening to choke the nation's banks. At that point digital computers came to the rescue. They enabled bankers to process great volumes of paper at a rapid rate and a reasonable cost, thus providing the banks with better opportunities to continue to grow. Furthermore, the computer serves as a powerful management tool. The growth and the accelerated turnover of funds have forced the banks to search continuously for new markets and more customers to serve, resulting in even faster growth. In fact, the advent of the computer permitted the acceleration of the banking revolution. It is the information system which made the revolution necessary.

Tax administration problems are among the most severe that are caused by the paper storm. The IRS looks forward to the development of machines and systems that will provide greater speed, increased information storage and retrieval facilities, and efficient character recognition capability. What is needed is a sophisticated tax information system which will not only provide real-time and random-access capability, but also, by a remote display network, make relevant information available to any IRS field office, literally at the push of a button. This will not only enable remote field offices to answer taxpayers' questions promptly, but also minimize requests to taxpayers for information previously furnished.

It appears that we are entering an era in which man and his information systems, in a new partnership, can undertake much more complex tasks than ever before. The new partnership will make society more productive and human life more satisfying. One of the major problems in the design of fully automated modern information systems is automatic pattern recognition, which has been an area of research and study by many diverse groups. These include research workers in engineering, computer science, information theory, physics, statistics, psychology, biology, physiology, medicine, and linguistics. Each group emphasizes certain aspects of the problem. This book attempts to discuss fundamental principles underlying the design of automatic pattern recognition systems.

1.2 BASIC CONCEPTS OF PATTERN RECOGNITION

Recognition is regarded as a basic attribute of human beings, as well as other living organisms. A pattern is the description of an object. We are performing acts of recognition every instant of our waking lives. We recognize the objects around us, and we move and act in relation to them. We can spot a friend in a crowd and recognize what he says; we can recognize the voice of a known individual; we can read handwriting and analyze fingerprints; we can distinguish smiles from gestures of anger. A human being is a very sophisticated information system, partly because he possesses a superior pattern recognition capability.

According to the nature of the patterns to be recognized, we may divide our acts of recognition into two major types: the recognition of concrete items and the recognition of abstract items. We recognize characters, pictures, music, and the objects around us. This may be referred to as sensory recognition, which includes visual and aural pattern recognition. This recognition process involves the identification and classification of spatial and temporal patterns. On the other hand, we can recognize an old argument, or a solution to a problem, with our eyes and ears closed. This process involves the recognition of abstract items and can be termed conceptual recognition, in contrast to visual or aural pattern recognition. In this book, we are concerned with the first type of pattern recognition. Examples of spatial patterns are characters, fingerprints, weather maps, physical objects, and pictures. Temporal patterns include speech waveforms, electrocardiograms, target signatures, and time series.

Recognition of concrete patterns by human beings may be considered as a psychophysiological problem which involves a relationship between a person and a physical stimulus. When a person perceives a pattern, he makes an inductive inference and associates this perception with some general concepts or clues which he has derived from his past experience. Human recognition is in reality a question of estimating the relative odds that the input data can be associated with one of a set of known statistical populations which depend on our past experience and which form the clues and the *a priori* information for recognition. Thus, the problem of pattern recognition may be regarded as one of discriminating the input data, not between individual patterns but between populations, via the search for features or invariant attributes among members of a population.

The study of pattern recognition problems may be logically divided into two major categories:

1. The study of the pattern recognition capability of human beings and other living organisms.

2. The development of theory and techniques for the design of devices capable of performing a given recognition task for a specific application.

The first subject area is concerned with such disciplines as psychology, physiology, and biology. The second area deals primarily with engineering, computer, and information science.

In this book we are concerned with the computer, information science, and engineering aspects of the design of automatic pattern recognition systems. In simple language, pattern recognition can be defined as the categorization of input data into identifiable classes via the extraction of significant features or attributes of the data from a background of irrelevant detail. Weather prediction can be treated as a pattern recognition problem. The received input data are in the form of weather maps. The system interprets these maps by extracting the significant features and makes a forecast based on these features. Medical diagnosis can also be considered as a pattern recognition problem. The symptoms serve as the input data to the recognition system, which identifies the disease by analysis of the input data. A character recognition system is a pattern recognition system which receives optical signals as the input data and identifies the name of the character. In a speech recognition system, the name of the spoken word is identified on the basis of the received acoustic waveforms. Table 1.1 describes several classification tasks, together with the corresponding input data and output responses.

TABLE 1.1

Task of Classification	Input Data	Output Response
Character recognition	Optical signals or strokes	Name of character
Speech recognition	Acoustic waveforms	Name of word
Speaker recognition	Voice	Name of speaker
Weather prediction	Weather maps	Weather forecast
Medical diagnosis	Symptoms	Disease
Stock market prediction	Financial news and charts	Predicted market ups and downs

The subject of pattern recognition spans a number of scientific disciplines, uniting them in the search for a solution to the common problem of recognizing members of a given class in a set containing fuzzy elements from many pattern classes. A pattern class is a category determined by some given common attributes. A pattern is the description of any member of a category representing a pattern class. When a set of patterns falling into disjoint classes is available, it is desired to categorize these patterns into their respective classes through the use of some automatic device. The reading and processing of canceled checks exemplifies a pattern recognition problem. Such tasks can be readily performed by human workers; however, a machine can achieve much greater speed. On the other hand, some recognition tasks are of such a nature that they can hardly be performed by human beings alone. An example of such a recognition problem is the detection of the sound of a submarine in the midst of other marine signals and noise through the analysis of subaquatic sound.

An obvious but simple-minded solution to a pattern recognition problem is to perform a number of simple tests on the individual input patterns in order to extract the features of each pattern class. Such tests should be sufficient to distinguish between permissible input patterns that belong to different classes. Consider, for instance, the following four Chinese characters:

天 下 為 公

These simple characters may be recognized by performing tests on the existence of a vertical stroke, a horizontal stroke, a single dot, an open bottom, an open top, and a dot sequence, and by counting the number and sequence of strokes. As a second example, consider the following five English letters:

C O I N S

These letters can be classified by making tests on the existence of such features as a lake, a single bay, a double bay, a vertical line, and a short line. A functional block diagram illustrating the pattern recognition concept described above is shown in Fig. 1.1.

The foregoing intuitive concept seems to make the design of an automatic pattern recognition system rather simple. However, there is no general theory to determine which of all possible tests on the real world should be applied to the input patterns. Too few or poorly chosen tests will not characterize the input patterns sufficiently to permit categorization into their respective pattern classes. Too many tests, on the other hand, will needlessly increase the complexity of the calculations involved in the subsequent analysis. Nor is any general rule available which might provide clues concerning how to

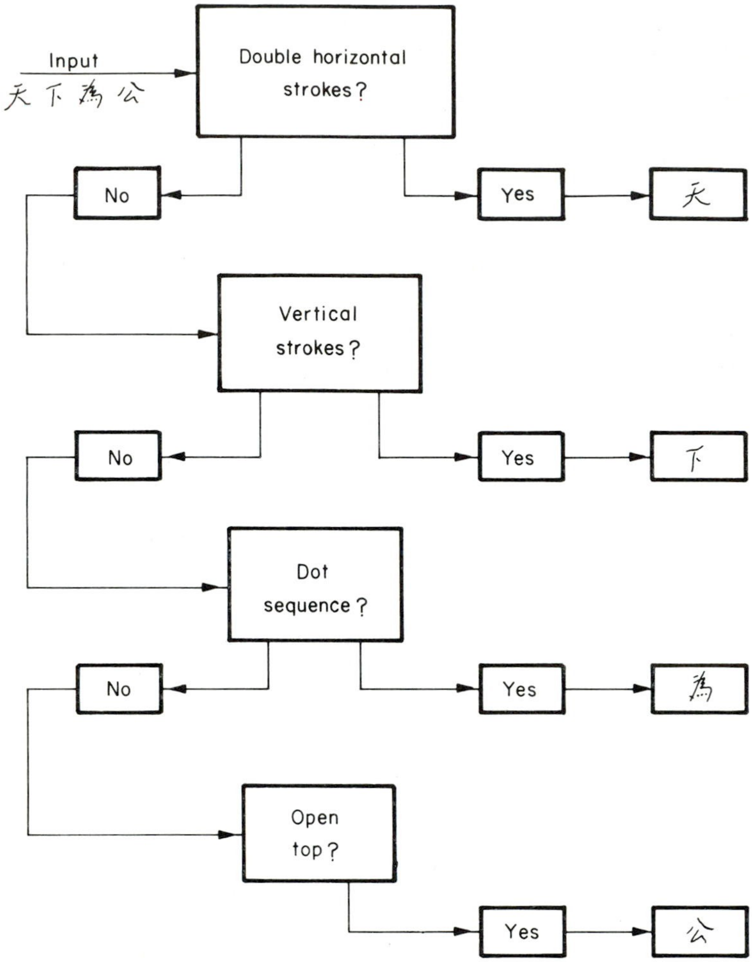

Figure 1.1. A simple question-answer scheme for classifying characters

find any such set of tests. This approach relies too heavily on the past experience and engineering intuition of the designer, and consequently does not lead to satisfactory solutions to many pattern recognition problems that arise in practice. More powerful approaches can be conceived by careful study of the problems involved in the process of pattern recognition. These problems are examined and analyzed in this book.

A hierarchical relation exists between patterns and pattern classes. In Fig. 1.2, the alphanumeric characters and Chinese characters are patterns, and character is a pattern class. Alphabets and numerals are patterns if alphanumeric character is considered as the pattern class. Printed and handwritten A's, for example, are patterns belonging to English letter A, which is a pattern class. In many information systems, we need a machine to recognize various fonts of printed letters and numerals, and different styles of handwritten letters and numerals. In this case, there are 62 pattern classes representing 26 upper-case letters, 26 lower-case letters, and 10 numerals. The different fonts and styles of a particular letter or numeral form the patterns in that pattern class.

Consider the character recognition problem. A specified letter or numeral, no matter how it is printed or written, retains some common attributes which are used as the means for identification. The letter or numeral is identified and classified according to the observed attributes. Thus, the basic functions of a pattern recognition system are to detect and extract common features from the patterns describing the objects that belong to the same pattern class, and to recognize this pattern in any new environment and classify it as a member of one of the pattern classes under consideration.

1.3 FUNDAMENTAL PROBLEMS IN PATTERN RECOGNITION SYSTEM DESIGN

The design of an automatic pattern recognition system generally involves several major problem areas. The first one is concerned with the representation of input data which can be measured from the objects to be recognized. This is the sensing problem. Each measured quantity describes a characteristic of the pattern or object. Suppose, for example, that the patterns in question are alphanumeric characters. In this case, a grid measuring scheme such as the one shown in Fig. 1.3(a) can be effectively used in the sensor. If we assume that the grid has n elements, the measurements can be arranged in the form of a *measurement* or *pattern vector*:

$$\mathbf{x} = \begin{pmatrix} x_1 \\ x_2 \\ \vdots \\ x_n \end{pmatrix} \tag{1.3–1}$$

where each element x_i is, for example, assigned the value 1 if the ith cell

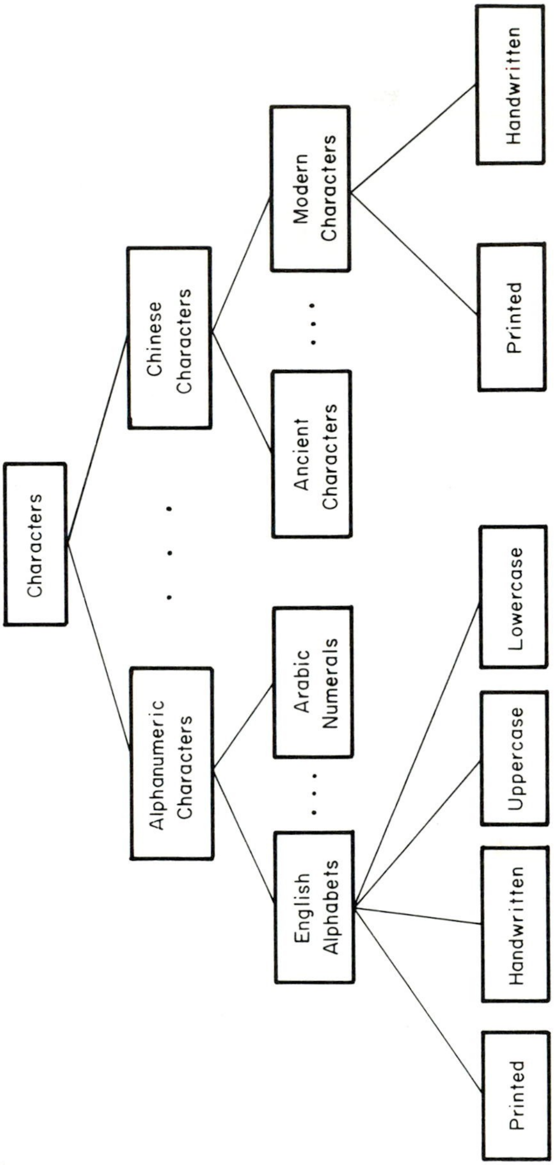

Figure 1.2. Hierarchical relation between patterns and pattern classes

contains a portion of the character, and is assigned the value 0 otherwise. In the following sections, we will refer to pattern vectors simply as patterns when the meaning is clear.

pattern vector = pattern

$$\mathbf{x} = \begin{pmatrix} x_1 \\ x_2 \\ \vdots \\ x_n \end{pmatrix} \quad x_i = 0 \text{ or } 1$$

(a)

$$\mathbf{x} = \begin{pmatrix} x_1 \\ x_2 \\ \vdots \\ x_n \end{pmatrix} \quad x_i = f(t_i)$$

(b)

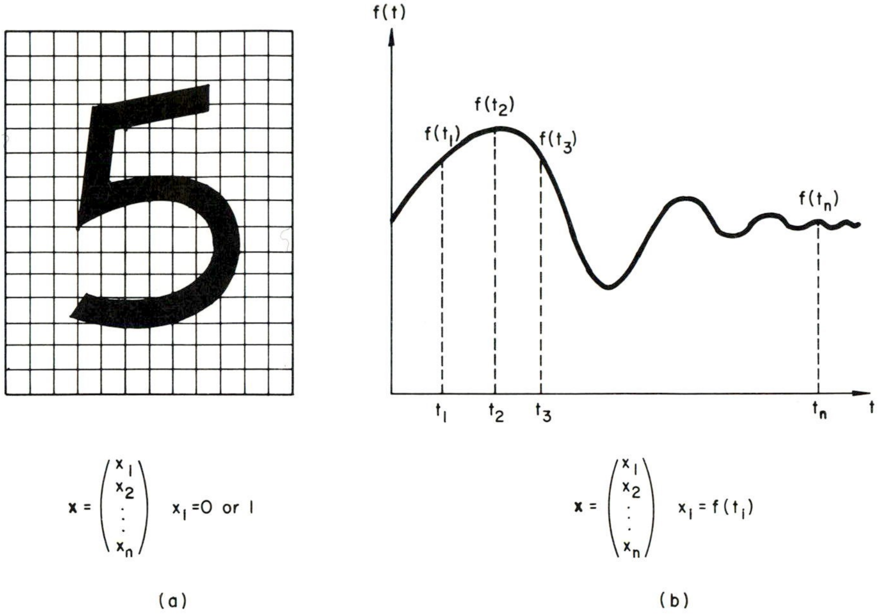

Figure 1.3. Two simple schemes for the generation of pattern vectors

A second example is shown in Fig. 1.3(b). In this case, the patterns are continuous functions (such as acoustic signals) of a variable t. If these functions are sampled at discrete points $t_1, t_2, \ldots, t_n$, a pattern vector may be formed by letting $x_1 = f(t_1)$, $x_2 = f(t_2), \ldots, x_n = f(t_n)$.

Pattern vectors will be denoted by lower-case boldface letters, such as $\mathbf{x}$, $\mathbf{y}$, and $\mathbf{z}$. As a matter of convention, these vectors will be assumed throughout to be column vectors, as indicated in Eq. (1.3–1). The equivalent notation, $\mathbf{x} = (x_1, x_2, \ldots, x_n)'$, where the prime (') indicates transposition, will be used interchangeably, particularly in a line of text.

The pattern vectors contain all the measured information available about the patterns. The measurements performed on the objects of a pattern class may be regarded as a coding process which consists of assigning to each pattern characteristic a symbol from the alphabet set $\{x_i\}$. When the measurements yield information in the form of real numbers, it is often useful to think of a pattern vector as a point in an n-dimensional Euclidean space. The set of patterns belonging to the same class corresponds to an ensemble of points scattered within some region of the measurement space. A simple example of this is shown in Fig. 1.4 for two pattern classes, denoted by ω_1 and ω_2.

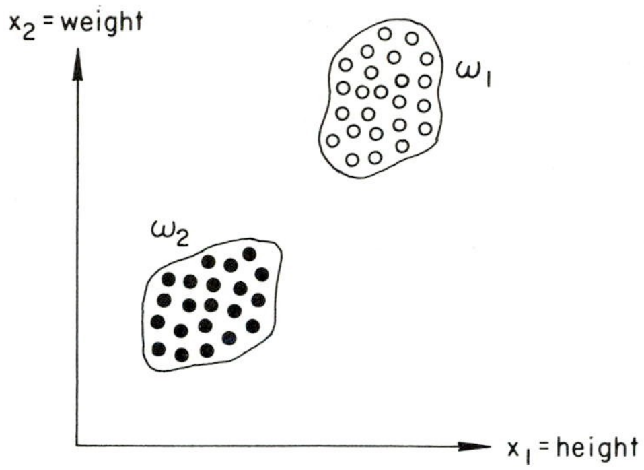

Figure 1.4. Two disjoint pattern classes

In this illustration, classes ω_1 and ω_2 are assumed to be sets of professional football players and jockeys, respectively. Each "pattern" is characterized by two measurements: height and weight. The pattern vectors are, therefore, of the form $\mathbf{x} = (x_1, x_2)'$, where x_1 represents height and x_2 represents weight. Each pattern vector may be viewed as a point in two-dimensional space. As shown in Fig. 1.4, these two classes form disjoint sets because of the nature of the measurements. In practical situations, however, one is not always able to specify measurements that will result in neatly disjoint sets. For instance, there would be considerable overlap in the classes of professional football and basketball players if height and weight were the criteria chosen for discrimination.

The second problem in pattern recognition concerns the extraction of characteristic features or attributes from the received input data and the reduction of the dimensionality of pattern vectors. This is often referred to as the preprocessing and feature extraction problem. In speech recognition, for example, we may discriminate vowels and vowel-like sounds from fricative and certain other consonants by measuring the distribution of energy over frequency in the spectra. The commonly used features for speech recognition are the duration of sound, the ratios of energy in various frequency bands, the location of spectral peaks, or formants, and the movement of these peaks in time.

The features of a pattern class are the characterizing attributes common to all patterns belonging to that class. Such features are often referred to as intraset features. The features which represent the differences between pattern classes may be referred to as the interset features. The elements of intraset features which are common to all pattern classes under consideration carry no discriminatory information and can be ignored. The extraction of features has been recognized as an important problem in the design of pattern recognition systems. If a complete set of discriminatory features for each pattern class can be determined from the measured data, the recognition and classification of patterns will present little difficulty. Automatic recognition may be reduced to a simple matching process or a table look-up scheme. However, in most pattern recognition problems which arise in practice, the determination of a complete set of discriminatory features is extremely difficult, if not impossible. Fortunately, we can often find some of the discriminatory features from the observed data. These features may be used to advantage in the simplification of the automatic recognition process. For instance, we may reduce the dimensionality of the measurement vectors through a transformation, with minimum loss of information, as discussed in Chapter 7.

The third problem in pattern recognition system design involves the determination of optimum decision procedures, which are needed in the identification and classification process. After the observed data from patterns to be recognized have been expressed in the form of pattern points or measurement vectors in the pattern space, we want the machine to decide to which pattern class these data belong. Assume that the machine is to be designed to recognize M different pattern classes, denoted by $\omega_1, \omega_2, \ldots, \omega_M$. Then the pattern space can be considered as consisting of M regions, each of which encloses the pattern points of a class. The recognition problem can now be viewed as that of generating the decision boundaries which separate the M pattern classes on the basis of the observed measurement vectors. Let the decision boundaries be defined, for example, by decision functions, $d_1(\mathbf{x}), d_2(\mathbf{x}), \ldots, d_M(\mathbf{x})$. These functions, which are also called discriminant functions, are scalar and single-valued functions of the pattern $\mathbf{x}$. If $d_i(\mathbf{x}) > d_j(\mathbf{x})$ for $i, j = 1, 2, \ldots, M$, and $j \neq i$, the pattern $\mathbf{x}$ belongs to pattern class ω_i. In other words, if the ith decision function, $d_i(\mathbf{x})$, has the largest value for a pattern $\mathbf{x}$, then $\mathbf{x} \in \omega_i$. Such an automatic classification scheme using a decision-making process is illustrated conceptually in the block diagram of Fig. 1.5, in which DFG denotes decision function generator.

The decision functions can be generated in a variety of ways. When complete *a priori* knowledge about the patterns to be recognized is available, the decision functions may be determined with precision on the basis of this information. When only qualitative knowledge about the patterns is available, reasonable guesses of the forms of the decision functions can be made. In this case the decision boundaries may be far from correct, and it is necessary to design the machine to achieve satisfactory performance through a sequence of adjustments. The more general situation is that there exists little, if any, *a priori* knowledge about the patterns to be recognized. Under these circumstances pattern-recognizing machines are best designed using a training or learning procedure. Arbitrary decision functions are initially assumed, and through a sequence of iterative training steps these decision functions are made to approach optimum or satisfactory forms. Classification of patterns by decision functions can be approached in a variety of ways. In this book we will study several deterministic and statistical algorithms for the generation of these functions.

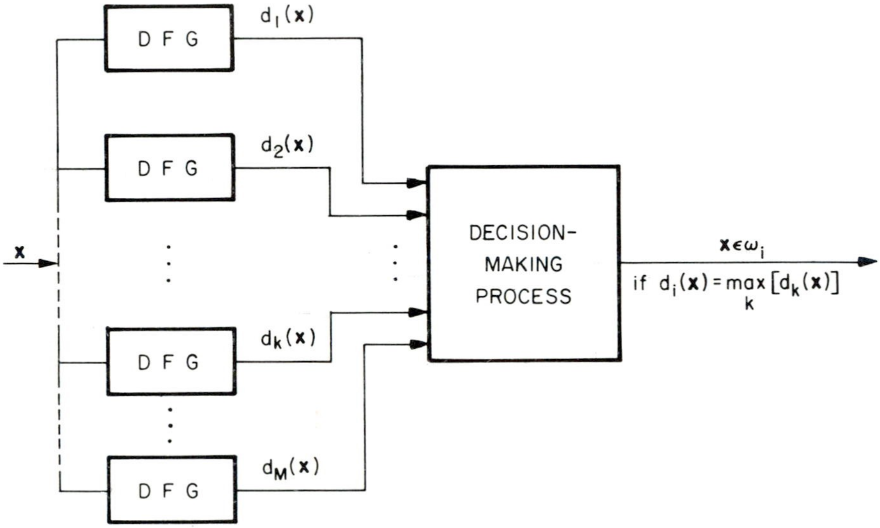

Figure 1.5. Block diagram of a pattern classifier

Solving the preprocessing and feature extraction problem and the optimum decision and classification problem generally involves a set of parameters that must be estimated and optimized. This gives rise to the parameter estimation problem. Furthermore, it is conceivable that both the feature extraction process and the decision-making process may be considerably improved by making use of contextual information in the patterns. Contextual information can be measured by contingent probabilities, language statistics, and neighboring variations. In some applications, contextual information is indispensable in achieving accurate recognition. For instance, fully automatic speech recognition is possible only when contextual and linguistic information is available to supplement the information of the speech sound wave. Similarly, in the recognition of cursive handwritten characters and the classification of fingerprints, contextual information is extremely desirable. When we wish to design a pattern recognition system which is resistant to distortions, flexible under large pattern deviations, and capable of self-adjustment, we are confronted with the adaptation problem.

The foregoing, brief discussion of the major problems involved in pattern recognition suggests a functional block diagram, as shown in Fig. 1.6, to provide a conceptual description of an adaptive pattern recognition system. This block diagram illustrates a natural and convenient breakdown of the functions which a pattern recognition system is expected to perform. The functional blocks are constructed for convenience in analysis and are not intended to produce isolation of interactive operations between blocks. Although the distinction between optimum decision and preprocessing or feature extraction is not essential, the concept of functional breakdown provides a clear picture for the understanding of the pattern recognition problem.

The patterns to be recognized and classified by an automatic pattern recognition system must possess a set of measurable characteristics. When these measurements are similar within a group of patterns, the latter are considered to be members of the same pattern class. The objective of a pattern recognition system is to determine, on the basis of the observed information, the pattern class responsible for generating a set of measurements similar to the observed data. Correct recognition will depend on the amount of discriminating information contained in the measurements and the effective utilization of this information. If all possible characteristics can be measured and unlimited time is available for processing the measured information, a brute-force technique may be applied to achieve quite adequate pattern recognition. In usual practice, however, restrictions in time, space, and cost dictate the development of realistic approaches.

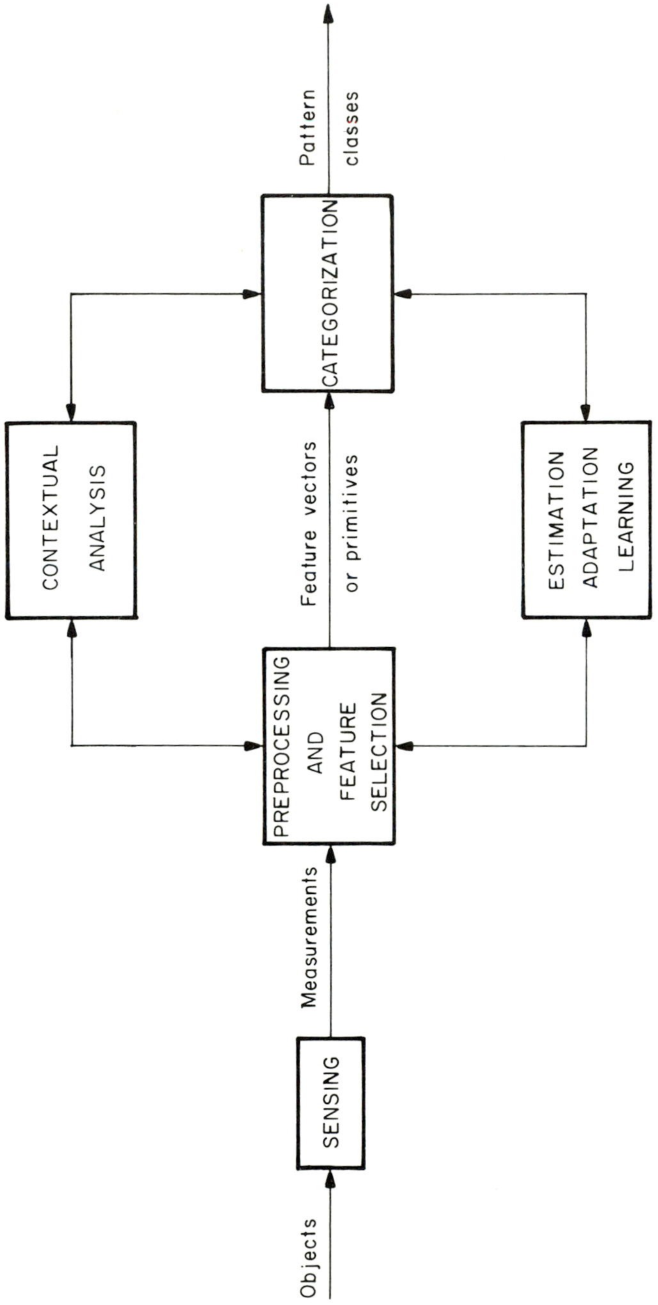

Figure 1.6. Functional block diagram of an adaptive pattern recognition system

1.4 DESIGN CONCEPTS AND METHODOLOGIES

The design concepts for automatic pattern recognition are motivated by the ways in which pattern classes are characterized and defined. Our experience suggests several basic possibilities. When a pattern class is characterized by a roster of its members, the design of a pattern recognition system may be based on the membership-roster concept. When a pattern class is characterized by common properties shared by all of its members, the design may be based on the common-property concept. When a pattern class exhibits clustering properties in the pattern space, the design may be based on the clustering concept. These three basic design concepts are discussed in the following paragraphs.

1. Membership-roster concept

Characterization of a pattern class by a roster of its members suggests automatic pattern recognition by *template matching*. The set of patterns belonging to the same pattern class is stored in the pattern recognition system. When an unknown pattern is shown to the system, it is compared with the stored patterns one by one. The pattern recognition system classifies this input pattern as a member of a pattern class if it matches one of the stored patterns belonging to that pattern class. For instance, if letters of different fonts are stored in the pattern recognition system, such letters may be recognized by the membership-roster approach as long as they are not distorted by noise due to smear, bad inking, porous paper, or the like. Clearly, this is a simple-minded method. However, this concept can lead to the design of inexpensive recognition schemes which serve the purpose in certain applications. The membership-roster approach will work satisfactorily under the condition of nearly perfect pattern samples.

2. Common-property concept

Characterization of a pattern class by common properties shared by all of its members suggests automatic pattern recognition via the detection and processing of similar features. The basic assumption in this method is that patterns belonging to the same class possess certain common properties or attributes which reflect similarities among these patterns. The common properties, for example, can be stored in the pattern recognition system. When an unknown pattern is observed by the system, its features are extracted and sometimes coded and then are compared with the stored features. The recognition scheme will classify the new pattern as belonging to the pattern class with similar features. Thus, the main problem in this approach is to determine common properties from a finite set of sample patterns known to belong to the pattern class to be recognized.

It appears that this concept excels the membership-roster approach in many respects. The storage requirement for the features of a pattern class is much less severe than that for all the patterns in the class. Since features of a pattern class are invariant, comparison of features allows variation in individual patterns. On the other hand, significant pattern variations cannot be tolerated in template matching. If all the features of a class can be determined from sample patterns, the recognition process reduces simply to *feature matching*. However, it is extremely difficult, if not impossible, to find the complete set of discriminating features for a pattern class, as was previously mentioned. Utilization of this concept, therefore, often necessitates the development of feature selection techniques which are optimum in some sense. Several methods for feature selection are discussed in Chapter 7. The common-property concept is also fundamental in pattern recognition by means of formal language theory, as will be seen below.

3. Clustering concept

When the patterns of a class are vectors whose components are real numbers, a pattern class can be characterized by its clustering properties in the pattern space. The design of a pattern recognition system based on this general concept is guided by the relative geometrical arrangement of the various pattern clusters. If the classes are characterized by clusters which are far apart, simple recognition schemes such as the minimum-distance classifiers discussed in Chapter 3 may be successfully employed. When the clusters overlap, however, it becomes necessary to utilize more sophisticated techniques for partitioning the pattern space, such as the methods discussed in Chapters 4 through 6. Overlapping clusters are the result of a deficiency in observed information and the presence of measurement noise. Hence, the degree of overlapping can often be minimized by increasing the number and the quality of measurements performed on the patterns of a class.

The basic design concepts for automatic pattern recognition described above may be implemented by three principal categories of methodology: heuristic, mathematical, and linguistic or syntactic. It is not uncommon to find a combination of these methods in a pattern recognition system.

1. Heuristic methods

The heuristic approach is based on human intuition and experience, making use of the membership-roster and common-property concepts. A system designed using this principle generally consists of a set of ad hoc procedures developed for specialized recognition tasks. An example of this approach was given in Section 1.2 in connection with the problem of character recognition, where the classification of a pattern (character) was based on the detection of features such as the number and sequence of particular strokes. Although the heuristic approach is an important branch of pattern recognition system design, little can be said about generalized principles in this area since each problem requires the application of specifically tailored design rules. It follows, therefore, that the structure and performance of a heuristic system will depend to a large degree on the cleverness and experience of the system designers.

2. Mathematical methods

The mathematical approach is based on classification rules which are formulated and derived in a mathematical framework, making use of the common-property and clustering concepts. This is in contrast with the heuristic approach, in which decisions are based on ad hoc rules. The mathematical approach may be subdivided into two categories: deterministic and statistical.

The deterministic approach is based on a mathematical framework which does not employ explicitly the statistical properties of the pattern classes under consideration. An example of the deterministic approach is the iterative learning algorithms discussed in Chapter 5.

The statistical approach is based on mathematical classification rules which are formulated and derived in a statistical framework. As will be seen in Chapter 4 and 6, the design of a statistical pattern classifier is generally based on the Bayes classification rule and its variations. This rule yields an optimum classifier when the probability density function of each pattern population and the probability of occurrence of each pattern class are known.

3. Linguistic (syntactic) methods

Characterization of patterns by primitive elements (subpatterns) and their relationships suggests automatic pattern recognition by the linguistic or syntactic approach, making use of the common-property concept. A pattern can be described by a hierarchical structure of subpatterns analogous to the syntactic structure of languages. This permits application of formal language theory to the pattern recognition problem. A pattern grammar is considered as consisting of finite sets of elements called variables, primitives, and productions. The rules of production determine the type of grammar. Among the most studied grammars are regular grammars, context-free grammars, and context-sensitive grammars. The essence of this approach lies in the selection of pattern primitives, the assembling of the primitives and their relationships into pattern grammars, and analysis and recognition in terms of these grammars. This approach, which is discussed in Chapter 8, is particularly useful in dealing with patterns which cannot be conveniently described by numerical measurements or are so complex that local features cannot be identified and global properties must be used.

Attention will be focused in this book on methods 2 and 3. Although, as mentioned earlier, the heuristic approach is important, little can be said, in general, concerning it. It should be pointed out, however, that a sound understanding of the other methods is essential background for the design of a system based on an intuitive approach.

Once a specific design method has been selected, one is still faced with the actual design and implementation problem. In most cases, representative patterns from each class under consideration are available. In these situations, *supervised* pattern recognition techniques are applicable. In a supervised learning environment, the system is "taught" to recognize patterns by means of various adaptive schemes. The essentials of this approach are a set of *training* patterns of known classification and the implementation of an appropriate learning procedure.

In some applications, only a set of training patterns of unknown classification may be available. In these situations, *unsupervised* pattern recognition techniques are applicable. As mentioned above, supervised pattern recognition is characterized by the fact that the correct classification of every training pattern is known. In the unsupervised case, however, one is faced with the problem of actually learning the pattern classes present in the given data. This problem, also known as *learning without a teacher*, is discussed in some detail in Chapter 3.

It is important to keep clearly in mind that learning or training takes place only during the design (or updating) phase of a pattern recognition system. Once acceptable results have been obtained with the training set of patterns, the system is applied to the task of actually performing recognition on samples drawn from the environment in which it is expected to operate. Of course, the quality of the recognition performance will be largely determined by how closely the training patterns resemble the actual data with which the system will be confronted during normal operation.

1.5 EXAMPLES OF AUTOMATIC PATTERN RECOGNITION SYSTEMS

The last decade has witnessed considerable interest and rapid advances in research and development in automatic pattern recognition and machine learning. Examples of automatic pattern recognition systems exist in abundance. Successful attempts have been made to design or program machines to read printed or typewritten characters, to screen electrocardiograms and electroencephalograms, to recognize spoken words, to identify fingerprints, and to interpret photographs. Other applications include recognition of handwritten characters and words, general medical diagnosis, classification of seismic waves, detection of targets, weather prediction, and identification of faults and defects in mechanical devices and manufacturing processes. In this section we consider several illustrative examples of areas in which pattern recognition concepts have been successfully applied.

Character recognition

A practical example of automatic pattern classification is found in optical character recognition devices such as the machines that read the code characters on ordinary bank checks. The stylized character set found on most U.S. checks today is the familiar American Bankers Association E-13B font character set. As shown in Fig. 1.7, this set consists of 14 characters which have been purposely designed on a 9×7 zone grid in order to facilitate their reading. The characters are usually printed in ink which contains very finely ground magnetic material. If the character is being read by a magnetic device, the ink is magnetized before the reading operation in order to accentuate the presence of the characters and thus facilitate the reading process.

The characters are typically scanned in a horizontal direction with a single-slit reading head which is narrower but taller than the character. As the head moves across the character, it produces an electrical signal which is conditioned to be proportional to the rate of increase of the character area under the head. Consider, for example, the waveform associated with the number zero in Fig. 1.7. As the reading head moves from left to right, the area seen by the head begins to increase, thus producing a positive derivative. As the head begins to leave the left "leg" of the zero, the area under the head starts to decrease, producing a negative derivative. When the head is in the middle zone of the character, the area remains constant, producing a zero derivative. This pattern repeats itself as the head enters the right leg of the character, as shown in the figure. The design of the characters is seen to be

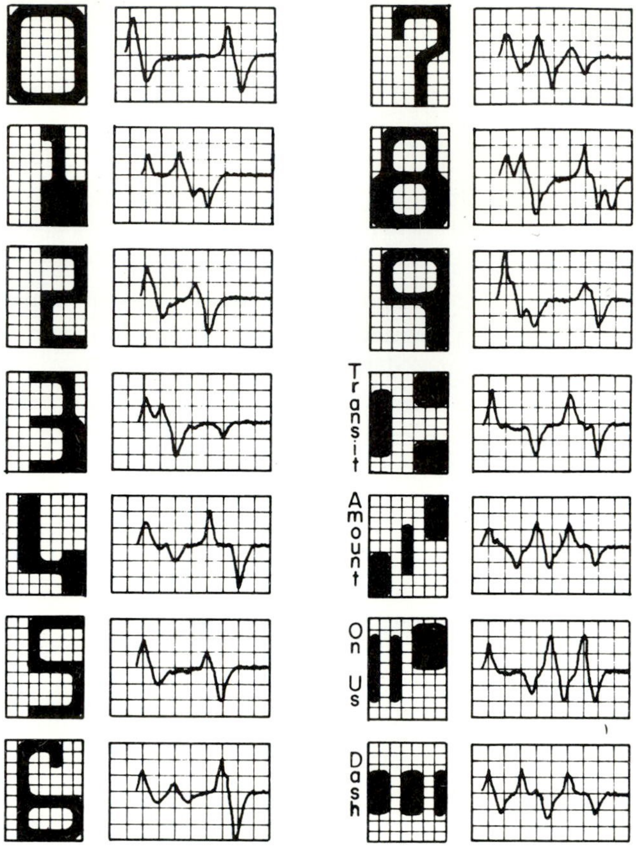

Figure 1.7. American Bankers Association E-13B font character set and corresponding waveforms

such that the waveform of each character is distinct from all others. It is noted that the peaks and zeros of each waveform occur approximately on the vertical lines of the background grids on which these waveforms are displayed in the figure. The E-13B characters have been designed so that sampling the waveforms *only* at these points yields enough information for their proper classification. The character reader has only these points in storage for each of the 14 characters. When a character comes in for classification, the system matches its waveform against the prestored waveforms and classifies the character according to the closest match. This scheme makes use of the membership-roster or common-property concepts. Most stylized font character readers on the market today operate on this principle.

Machines capable of recognizing a variety of fonts have also been commercially implemented. The Input 80 system (Fig. 1.8) developed by Recognition Equipment Incorporated, for example, reads typed, printed, and hand-printed information directly from source documents at rates of up to 3600 characters per second. The vocabulary of this system is modular and can be tailored to the requirements of specific applications. A single-font system can read any one of a wide selection of type fonts, while a multifont system can read simultaneously a variety of different type fonts chosen by the user from a list of available fonts. Up to 360 distinct characters can be recognized by a single machine. A system can also be structured so that it will read hand-printed numbers and selected hand-printed letters and symbols in conjunction with the reading of machine-printed data.

Basically, the REI Input 80 system works as follows. A combination of vacuums and air jets feeds pages into a system of belts and rollers, which

Figure 1.8. REI's Input 80 Model A character recognition system. The components shown are, in clockwise direction, as follows: Recognition unit, programmed controller, input/output typewriter, line printer, recognition unit, magnetic tape units, and page processor unit. Courtesy of Recognition Equipment Incorporated, Dallas, Texas

transports them into the reading mechanism. As pages move through the reader, a high-speed oscillating mirror focuses a beam of high-intensity light on the characters to be read, sweeping across a line of printed data at a speed of 300 in./sec. A second, synchronized mirror picks up light images representing different portions of a character, and these images are projected onto the "Integrated Retina"—an integrated reading device with 96 photodiodes incorporated in a single slice of silicon $1\frac{1}{2}$ in. long. This device is the "eye" of the system. The Integrated Retina electronically reduces each character to a matrix 16 cells high by 12 cells wide, normalizes the characters, and makes adjustments for size variations, at speeds of up to 3600 characters per second. The Retina also classifies each cell in every character into one of 16 different shades of gray.

Data from the reading device are transmitted to the recognition unit, where gray levels from each cell in a character image are compared with those from 24 adjacent cells in a video enhancement circuit. The resulting data are then thresholded to form a 1-bit black-white image. This cleans up the character images, filling weak strokes, ignoring smudges, and sharpening contrast with dirty backgrounds. The system recognizes machine-printed characters by making a determination of the least amount of mismatch between the character being read and one of the characters stored in its vocabulary within the recognition unit. The system also determines that an adequate gap exists between the minimum mismatch character and the second least mismatched character in the vocabulary of the system. This classification concept will be discussed in Chapter 3.

Recognition of hand-printed characters is accomplished by a different type of logic. Rather than being compared with prestored patterns, hand-printed characters are analyzed as combinations of common features, such as curved lines, vertical and horizontal lines, corners, and intersections. Classification of a character is then based on the particular features present in the character, as well as the relative interconnection of these features. The components of this character recognition system are shown and identified in Fig. 1.8.

Automatic Classification of Remotely Sensed Data

The relatively recent national interest in the quality of the environment and in earth resources has created numerous areas of applications for pattern recognition technology. Among these areas, the automatic classification of remotely sensed data has received the greatest attention. Because of the large volumes of data generated by multispectral scanners located aboard aircraft, satellites, and space stations, it has become necessary to search for automated means to process and analyze this information. The applications of remotely sensed data are varied. Among the areas of current interest are land use, crop inventory, crop-disease detection, forestry, monitoring of air and water quality, geological and geographical studies, and weather prediction, plus a score of other applications of environmental significance.

As an example of automatic multispectral data classification, consider Fig. 1.9(a),† which shows a color photograph of the ground taken from an aircraft. The area shown is a small section of a flight path covering several miles in central Indiana. The objective is to gather enough data to train a machine to recognize automatically different types of ground cover (classes), such as light and dark soil areas, river and pond water, and a variety of green vegetation conditions.

A multispectral scanner responds to light in selected wavelength bands. The scanner used in the flight path mentioned above responded to light in the 0.40–0.44, 0.58–0.62, 0.66–0.72, and 0.80–1.00 micron (10^{-6} meter) wavelength bands. These ranges are in the violet, green, red, and infrared bands, respectively. A ground region scanned in this manner produces four images—one image in each color range. Each point in the region, therefore, is characterized by four color components. The information for each point can be expressed in the form of a four-dimensional pattern vector, $\mathbf{x} = (x_1, x_2, x_3, x_4)'$, where x_1 is a shade of violet, x_2 a shade of green, and so forth. A collection of patterns for each soil-cover class constitutes a training set for that class. These training patterns can then be used to design a pattern classifier.

A Bayes classifier for normally distributed patterns (see Section 4.3) has been designed using the multispectral data obtained in the flight path described above. Figure 1.9(b) shows a computer printout of results obtained by applying this classifier to automatically classify the multispectral data obtained from the small region shown in Fig. 1.9(a). The arrows indicate some features of interest. Arrow 1 is at the corner of a field of green vegetation, and arrow 2 is a river. Arrow 3 shows a small hedgerow between two areas of bare soil, which was accurately identified on the printout. A tributary which was correctly identified is indicated by arrow 4. Arrow 5 is a very small pond that is almost indistinguishable on the color photograph. When

† Following page 26

the original image is compared with the results of machine classification, it is clear that these results correspond closely to what a human interpreter would identify by eye.

Biomedical applications

As was indicated in Section 1.1, the medical field is presently facing a serious information-handling problem. Pattern recognition concepts have been applied with varied degrees of success to the automatic screening of medical diagnostic tools such as X-rays, electrocardiograms, and electroencephalograms, and to the analysis and interpretation of patient questionnaires. A problem which has also received a great deal of attention is the automatic analysis and classification of chromosomes.

The interest in automatic chromosome analysis arises from the fact that the capability for automated cytogenetic analysis would increase the feasibility of using chromosome studies for a wide variety of clinical diagnostic purposes. In addition, it would make possible the performance of large-scale prospective population studies to determine the health significance of many small variations in the chromosome pattern whose effect is currently unknown. Also, the ability to study large populations would permit a variety of other useful medical studies, such as routine cytogenetic characterization of the antenatal and newborn population for preventive or remedial medical intervention, routine screening of special occupationally or environmentally exposed groups for increased chromosome aberrations induced by damaging agents, and the monitoring of new chemicals and pharmaceuticals for chromosome-damaging potential.

Figure 1.10 shows a typical Giemsa-stained preparation of a human blood cell in the metaphase stage of mitosis. The most tedious and time-consuming task in analyzing such an image is the coding process, in which each chromosome must be individually classified by a doctor or trained laboratory assistant. Some typical categories of classification are indicated in the figure.

Numerous methods for computer classification of chromosomes have been proposed. One approach which is particularly effective for the classification of chromosomes such as the ones shown in Fig. 1.10 is based on the syntactic pattern recognition concepts discussed in Chapter 8. The essence of this approach is as follows. Pattern primitives, such as long arcs, short arcs, and semistraight segments, which characterize the chromosome boundaries are defined. When combined, these primitives form a string or symbol sentence which can be associated with a so-called pattern grammar. There is one grammar for each type (class) of chromosome. In order to recognize a particular chromosome, the computer tracks its boundary and produces a string of primitives. The tracking algorithms are generally heuristic proce-

(a) 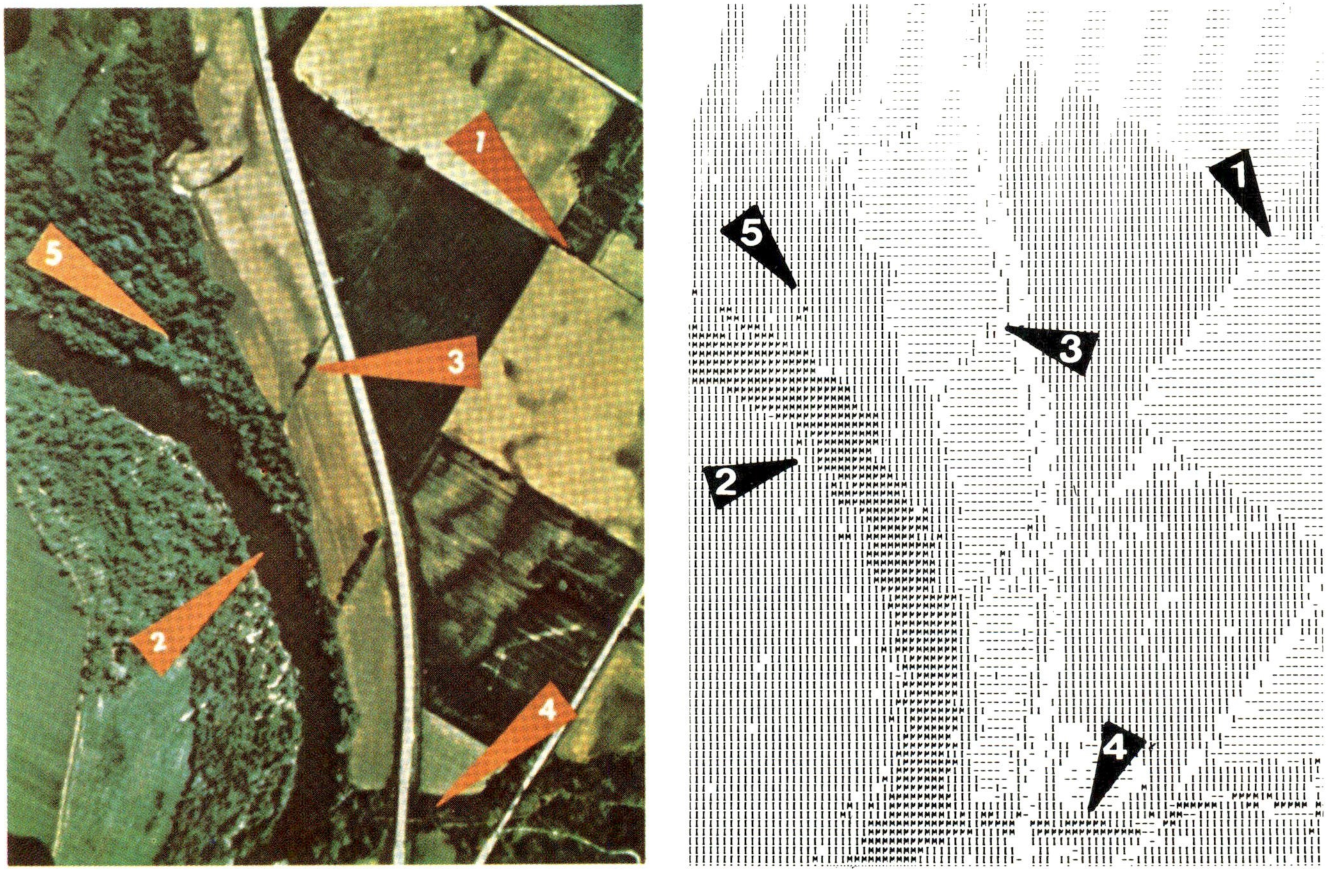 (b)

Figure 1.9. (a) Color photograph of region as seen from an aircraft. (b) Printout of machine classification results. Courtesy of the Laboratory for Applications of Remote Sensing, Purdue University, Lafayette, Indiana

ISBN 0-201-07586-5

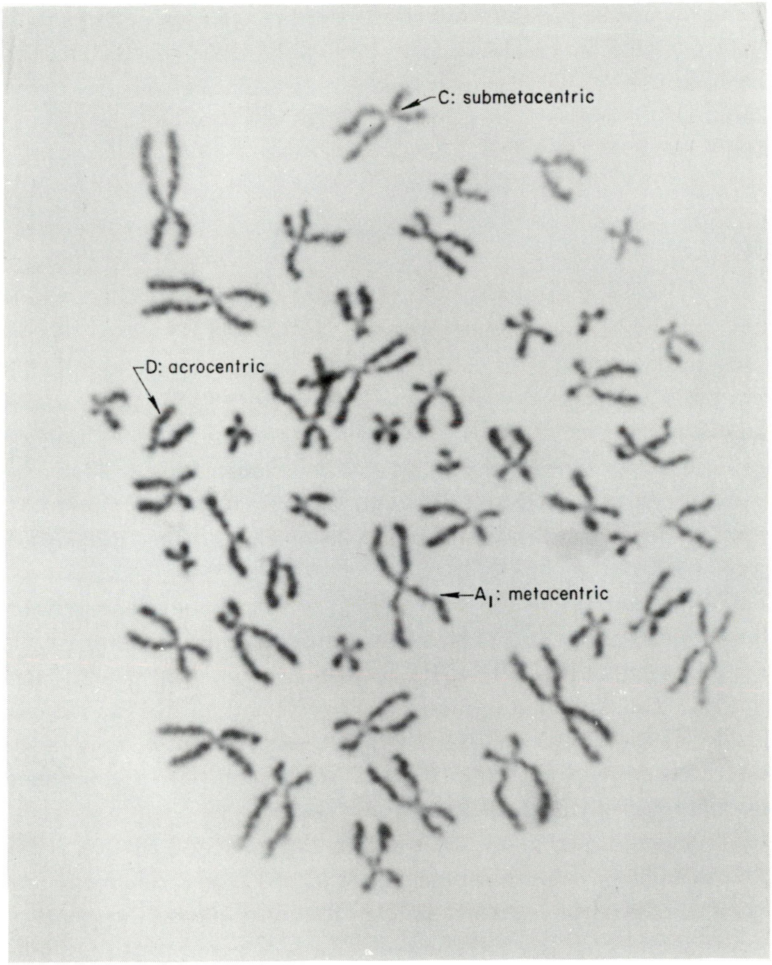

Figure 1.10. Giemsa-stained preparation of a human blood cell, showing chromosome structures. Courtesy of Dr. Niel Wald, Graduate School of Public Health, University of Pittsburgh, Pittsburgh, Pennsylvania

dures which are designed to handle such eventualities as adjacent and overlapping chromosomes. The resulting string is then fed into a recognizer, which determines whether the string is a valid symbol sentence of some grammar. If this process results in a unique grammar, the chromosome is classified into the class associated with that grammar. If the process is ambiguous or unsuccessful, the chromosome is rejected and further processing is carried out by a human operator.

Although the automatic chromosome recognition problem has not been solved in general, the present syntactic pattern recognition systems represent an important step in that direction. We will return to this recognition scheme in Section 8.5, where a particular chromosome grammar is considered in detail.

Fingerprint recognition

As was mentioned in Section 1.1, government agencies maintain files of more than 200 million fingerprints. The Identification Division of the Federal Bureau of Investigation, for example, operates the largest file of fingerprints in the world—over 160 million. This division receives up to 30,000 search requests daily. To accommodate this volume, some 1400 technicians and clerks are required to perform the meticulous tasks of classification and subsequent search for a match.

The FBI has been interested for a number of years in developing automatic systems to identify fingerprints. An example of efforts in this area is the prototype system, called FINDER, developed by the Calspan Corporation for the FBI. This system automatically detects and locates unique features in a print. The features read are not the grosser structures, such as arches, loops, or whorls, used in primary classification but rather minutiae—the endings and forks of ridges shown in Fig. 1.11.

A block diagram of the system is shown in Fig. 1.12. Briefly, FINDER operates as follows. The operator loads standard fingerprint cards into the automatic handler, which moves and accurately positions the prints under the "eye" of the system—the scanner. Each fingerprint is digitized into a 750×750 point matrix where each point is one of 16 shades of gray. The scan is accomplished under the control of the general-purpose computer. An example of a scanned section of a print is shown in Fig. 1.13.

The data from the scanner are fed into the ridge-valley filter, a high-speed, parallel, two-dimensional processing algorithm that sequentially examines each point of the 750×750 matrix. The output of this algorithm is an enhanced binary image, as shown in Fig. 1.14. This algorithm also records the ridge direction at each point in the fingerprint for subsequent processing.

Figure 1.11. Minutiae—the ridge endings (squares) and bifurcations (circles)—used by the FINDER system for fingerprint identification. Courtesy of Mr. C. W. Swonger, Calspan Corporation, Buffalo, New York

Over some portions of most fingerprints, sufficiently clear ridge structure cannot be developed to read minutiae reliably. These areas are treated in the pre-editor, which excludes them from further consideration as sources

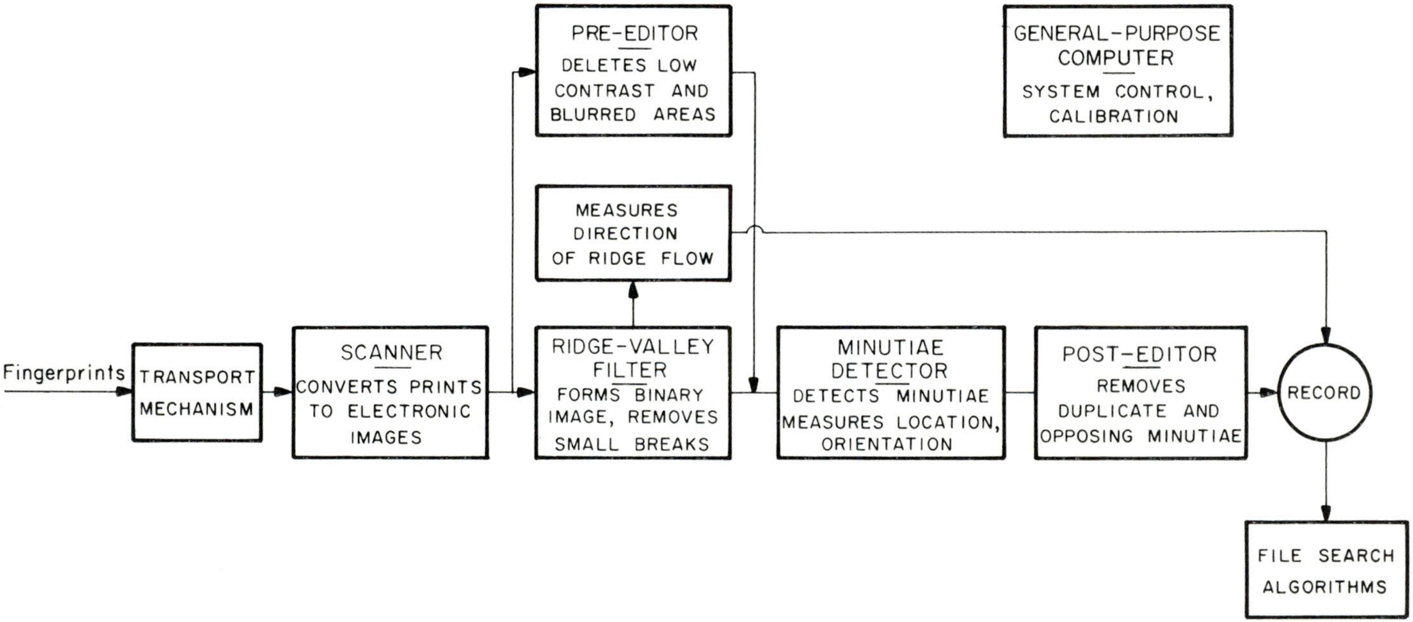

Figure 1.12. Block diagram of the FINDER fingerprint recognition system. Courtesy of Mr. C. W. Swonger, Calspan Corporation, Buffalo, New York

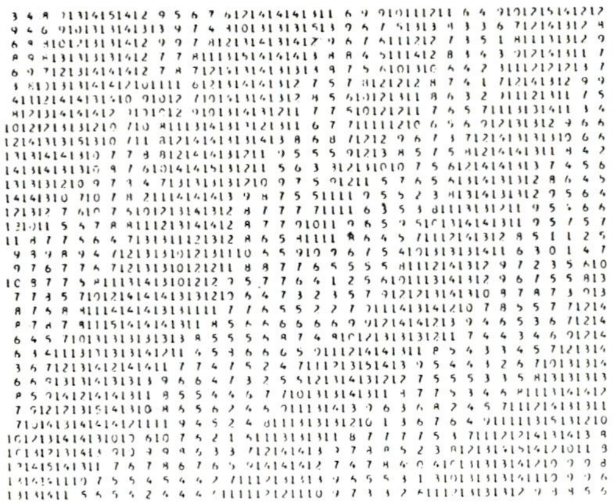

Figure 1.13. Printout of a section of scanner output. In this numerical representation black is 0 and white 15. Courtesy of Mr. C. W. Swonger, Calspan Corporation, Buffalo, New York

Figure 1.14. Result of applying ridge-valley filter to the data of Fig. 1.13. In this representation black points are shown as z's. Courtesy of Mr. C. W. Swonger, Calspan Corporation, Buffalo, New York

of legitimate minutiae. Tests are made for whiteness, for blackness, and for insufficient ridge structure or contrast to allow reliable detection.

The next step in processing is the actual detection of minutiae. This is accomplished by an algorithm which follows synchronously behind the ridge-valley filter. It detects tentative minutiae and records their precise locations and angles.

The results of the minutiae finder are fed into the posteditor. First, the area and perimeter of the detected minutiae are compared to thresholds that are characteristic of true minutiae to eliminate obviously false data. Duplicate minutiae are then merged. If a particular minutia is detected more than once, the one having the greatest length is retained. By use of a chaining technique, only the minutiae neighboring the one being considered are included in the search, greatly reducing processing time. Next, opposing and canceling minutiae such as result from a gap in the ridge structure are removed. The minutiae list is now culled of minutiae whose form and quality factors are below certain thresholds. The final stages in the postediting process determine whether a minutia is part of a cluster of minutiae or whether the minutia angle is significantly different from the local ridge structure orientation. The cluster test discards groups of minutiae such as result from a scar on the finger. If more than a specific number of minutiae are found near the minutia being analyzed, the latter is deleted as false. If the minutia passes this test, the logic performs an anomalous-angle test, using a grid of ridge direction data collected during preprocessing. Depending on the deviation from the average ridge angle, the minutia is either accepted, rejected or, if it is slightly out of line, adjusted to the average of the surrounding ridge angles.

Finally, approximately 2500 bits of data defining the minutiae surviving all the postediting tests are recorded on magnetic tape for eventual electronic comparison against minutiae for prints on file.

Application of pattern recognition methods to nuclear reactor component surveillance

This final illustration deals with a relatively new area of application of pattern recognition concepts. Among the many safety features incorporated in the design of nuclear power plants are numerous detection mechanisms for monitoring the integrity of a plant. A particular device that has gained wide acceptance in the monitoring field is the neutron noise monitor. This device, although originally designed to measure neutron level, produces a signal which is also influenced by mechanical vibrations in a reactor. One of the principal objectives for having such a monitor in a nuclear reactor is to detect, as early as possible, any internal vibration modes which are not characteristic of normal operating conditions.

A topic of considerable interest in the field of noise (neutron, acoustic, thermal, etc.) analysis today is the development of total surveillance systems which are at least partially automatic and which have the capability of adapting to normal changes in conditions. Monitoring systems produce large volumes of information which, to be useful, must be processed on a regular basis. Although this does not presently pose any real difficulties, since, as of this writing, there are less than 50 operating nuclear power plants in the United States, the Atomic Energy Commission has estimated that by the year 2000 there will be more than 1000 nuclear plants in this country alone. Clearly, some methods must be found to automatically process the information produced by the numerous monitoring systems which will be integral parts of these plants. Although pattern recognition research in this area is still in its infancy, a clear indication of its potential has already been established. The following paragraphs briefly describe these findings.

Figure 1.15 shows the basic components of an automated monitoring system. Sensors in the nuclear power plant produce noise signals which are conditioned and preprocessed and then are fed into a pattern recognition system. The output of this system is a decision concerning the status of the plant. In the case under discussion, the plant is the high-flux isotope reactor (HFIR) located at the Oak Ridge National Laboratory. The measurements derived from this plant are neutron noise observations, taken on an average of three times per day. A fuel cycle (time between fuel element reloadings) is typically 22 days at full power. The preprocessor computes the power spectral density (PSD) of these measurements in the range from 0 to 31 Hz

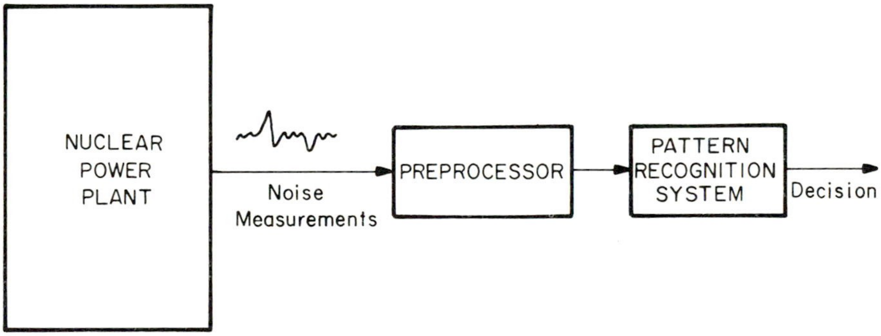

Figure 1.15. Basic components of an automatic noise analysis system

at 1-Hz intervals. Each observation, therefore, may be expressed in the form of a 32-dimensional pattern vector, $\mathbf{x} = (x_1, x_2, \ldots, x_{32})'$, where x_1 is the PSD amplitude at 0 Hz, x_2 the amplitude at 1 Hz, and so forth. The problem is then to design a pattern recognition system capable of automatically analyzing these patterns.

The data for two HFIR fuel cycles are shown in three-dimensional perspective in Figs. 1.16(a) and (b). The x-axis in these figures represents increasing time in the fuel cycle, the y-axis the 32 components of each pattern, and the z-axis the normalized PSD amplitude. The data shown are representative of normal operating conditions. It will be noted that there is close overall similarity between these two data sets.

The HFIR pattern recognition system extracts features typical of normal operation from the processed neutron noise measurements. Basically, what this involves is the detection of clusters of pattern vectors by iterative

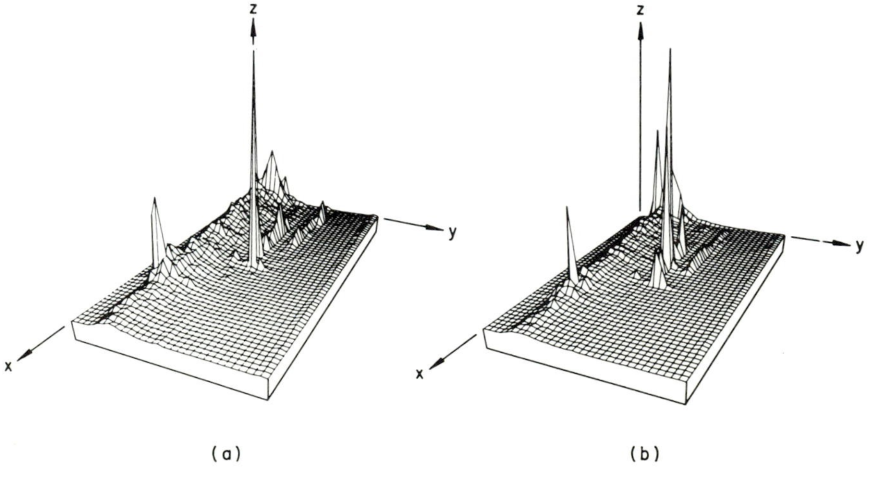

Figure 1.16. Typical normal neutron power spectral densities for the HFIR. Highest peak in each figure has value of 1. True values may be obtained by multiplying the plot values by appropriate scale factors. The scale factor in (a) is 1.831×10^{-4}; in (b), 2.881×10^{-4}. From R. C. Gonzalez, D. N. Fry, and R. C. Kryter, "Results in the Application of Pattern Recognition Methods to Nuclear Reactor Core Component Surveillance," *IEEE Trans. Nucl. Sci.*, vol. 21, No. 1, February 1974

applications of a cluster-seeking algorithm (these concepts are discussed in Chapter 3). The data cluster centers and associated descriptive parameters, such as cluster variances, can then be used as templates against which measurements are compared at any given time in order to determine the status of the plant. Significant deviations from the pre-established characteristic normal behavior are flagged as indications of an abnormal operating condition. Figures 1.17(a) and (b), for example, show a pattern of behavior which can be easily detected as being quite different from the normal operating conditions. These data have been correlated with a broken guide bearing in a mechanical assembly near the reactor core. Although this condition did not represent an immediately dangerous situation, these results are indicative of the potential value of incorporating pattern recognition methods as an integral part of a total plant surveillance system. Additional details on this subject can be found in the paper by Gonzalez, Fry, and Kryter [1974].

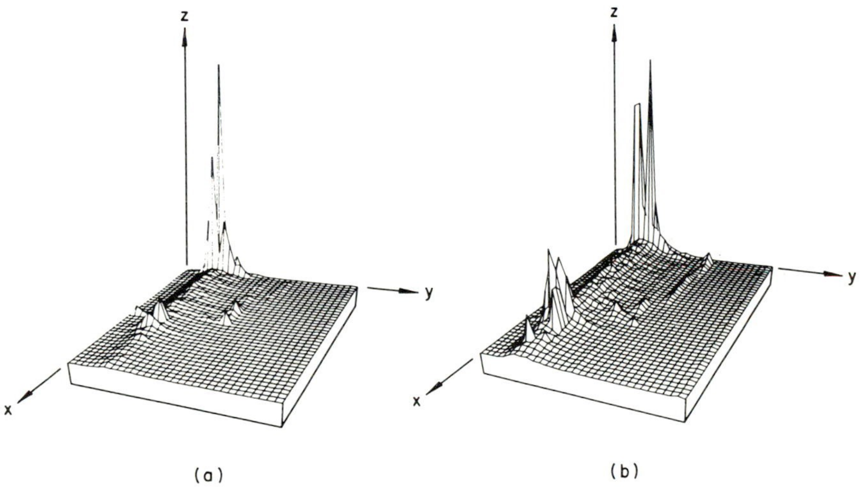

Figure 1.17. Abnormal measurements in the HFIR. The scale factor in (a) is 5.555×10^{-4}; in (b), 2.832×10^{-4}. From R. C. Gonzalez, D. N. Fry, and R. C. Kryter, "Results in the Application of Pattern Recognition Methods to Nuclear Reactor Core Component Surveillance," *IEEE Trans. Nucl. Sci.*, vol. 21, No. 1, February 1974

1.6 A SIMPLE PATTERN RECOGNITION MODEL

We conclude this introductory chapter with a simple mathematical model for automatic pattern recognition which illustrates some basic notions. A simple scheme for pattern recognition consists of two basic components: sensor and categorizer. The sensor is a device which converts a physical sample to be recognized into a set of quantities $\mathbf{x} = (x_1, x_2, \ldots, x_n)'$ which characterize the sample. The categorizer is a device which assigns each of its admissible inputs to one of a finite number of classes or categories by computing a set of decision functions.

The pattern recognizer is said to have made an error whenever it assigns to class ω_j a physical sample actually belonging to a class other than ω_j. A pattern recognizer R_1 is said to be better than pattern recognizer R_2 if the probability that R_1 will make an error is less than the probability that R_2 will make an error. The output of the sensor is $\mathbf{x} = (x_1, x_2, \ldots, x_n)'$, where n measurements of each physical sample are assured. The measurement vector $\mathbf{x}$ is assumed to belong to one of M pattern classes, $\omega_1, \omega_2, \ldots, \omega_M$.

We assume that the *a priori* probabilities for the occurrence of each class are equal, that is, it is just as likely that $\mathbf{x}$ comes from one class as from another. Let $p(\mathbf{x}/\omega_i) = p_i(\mathbf{x})$ be the probability density function of $\mathbf{x}$ when $\mathbf{x}$ is from class ω_i. Then the probability that a measurement vector $\mathbf{x}$ actually came from class ω_j is given by

$$p_j = \frac{p(\mathbf{x}/\omega_j)}{\sum_{k=1}^{M} p(\mathbf{x}/\omega_k)}$$

The probability that $\mathbf{x}$ did not come from class ω_j is

$$1 - p_j = 1 - \frac{p(\mathbf{x}/\omega_j)}{\sum_{k=1}^{M} p(\mathbf{x}/\omega_k)}$$

which is the probability of error.

A decision function is a function $d(\mathbf{x})$ which assigns each $\mathbf{x}$ to exactly one of the M classes. An optimal decision function is the function $d^\circ(\mathbf{x})$, for which the probability of error is smallest for each possible value of $\mathbf{x}$. The value of j for which $1 - p_j$ is smallest is also the value of j for which $p(\mathbf{x}/\omega_j)$ is largest. Thus, the optimal decision function $d^\circ(\mathbf{x})$ assigns $\mathbf{x}$ to class ω_i if and only if

$$p(\mathbf{x}/\omega_i) > p(\mathbf{x}/\omega_j) \qquad \forall\, j \neq i$$

or

$$\frac{p(\mathbf{x}/\omega_i)}{p(\mathbf{x}/\omega_j)} > 1 \qquad \forall j \neq i$$

When $p(\mathbf{x}/\omega_i) = p(\mathbf{x}/\omega_k)$ and $p(\mathbf{x}/\omega_i) > p(\mathbf{x}/\omega_j)$, $j = 1, 2, \ldots, M$, $j \neq i \neq k$, the optimal decision function $d^\circ(\mathbf{x})$ can assign $\mathbf{x}$ to either ω_i or ω_k. For a given value of $\mathbf{x}$, the categorizer determines the optimal decision function.

Now, we assume that the measured values are normally distributed with equal covariance matrices:

$$\mathbf{C} = \begin{pmatrix} c_{11} & c_{12} & \cdots & c_{1n} \\ c_{21} & c_{22} & \cdots & c_{2n} \\ \vdots & & & \\ c_{n1} & c_{n2} & \cdots & c_{nn} \end{pmatrix}$$

where c_{ij} is the covariance between the ith and the jth components of the measurement vector $\mathbf{x}$, and c_{ii} is the variance of the ith component of $\mathbf{x}$. Since the expression for normal $p(\mathbf{x}/\omega_i)$ is

$$p(\mathbf{x}/\omega_i) = \frac{1}{(2\pi)^{n/2}|\mathbf{C}|^{1/2}} \exp[-\tfrac{1}{2}(\mathbf{x} - \mathbf{m}_i)'\mathbf{C}^{-1}(\mathbf{x} - \mathbf{m}_i)]$$

where $\mathbf{m}_i$ is the mean vector, the ratio of two conditional probability densities, $p(\mathbf{x}/\omega_i)$ and $p(\mathbf{x}/\omega_j)$, is

$$\frac{p(\mathbf{x}/\omega_i)}{p(\mathbf{x}/\omega_j)} = \exp\{-\tfrac{1}{2}[(\mathbf{x} - \mathbf{m}_i)'\mathbf{C}^{-1}(\mathbf{x} - \mathbf{m}_i) - (\mathbf{x} - \mathbf{m}_j)'\mathbf{C}^{-1}(\mathbf{x} - \mathbf{m}_j)]\}$$

Since the covariance matrix is symmetrical, this conditional probability ratio reduces to

$$\frac{p(\mathbf{x}/\omega_i)}{p(\mathbf{x}/\omega_j)} = \exp[\mathbf{x}'\mathbf{C}^{-1}(\mathbf{m}_i - \mathbf{m}_j) - \tfrac{1}{2}(\mathbf{m}_i + \mathbf{m}_j)'\mathbf{C}^{-1}(\mathbf{m}_i - \mathbf{m}_j)]$$

By defining

$$r_{ij}(\mathbf{x}) = \ln \frac{p(\mathbf{x}/\omega_i)}{p(\mathbf{x}/\omega_j)}$$

we have the recognition function given by

$$r_{ij}(\mathbf{x}) = \mathbf{x}'\mathbf{C}^{-1}(\mathbf{m}_i - \mathbf{m}_j) - \tfrac{1}{2}(\mathbf{m}_i + \mathbf{m}_j)'\mathbf{C}^{-1}(\mathbf{m}_i - \mathbf{m}_j)$$

The optimal recognition function is determined by forming the $M(M - 1)$ quantities of $r_{ij}(\mathbf{x})$ for all i and j, $i \neq j$, and picking the largest of these quantities. If $r_{kj}(\mathbf{x})$ is the largest, $\mathbf{x}$ is said to belong to class ω_k. On the basis of the above analysis, the optimal recognition scheme is as shown in Fig. 1.18.

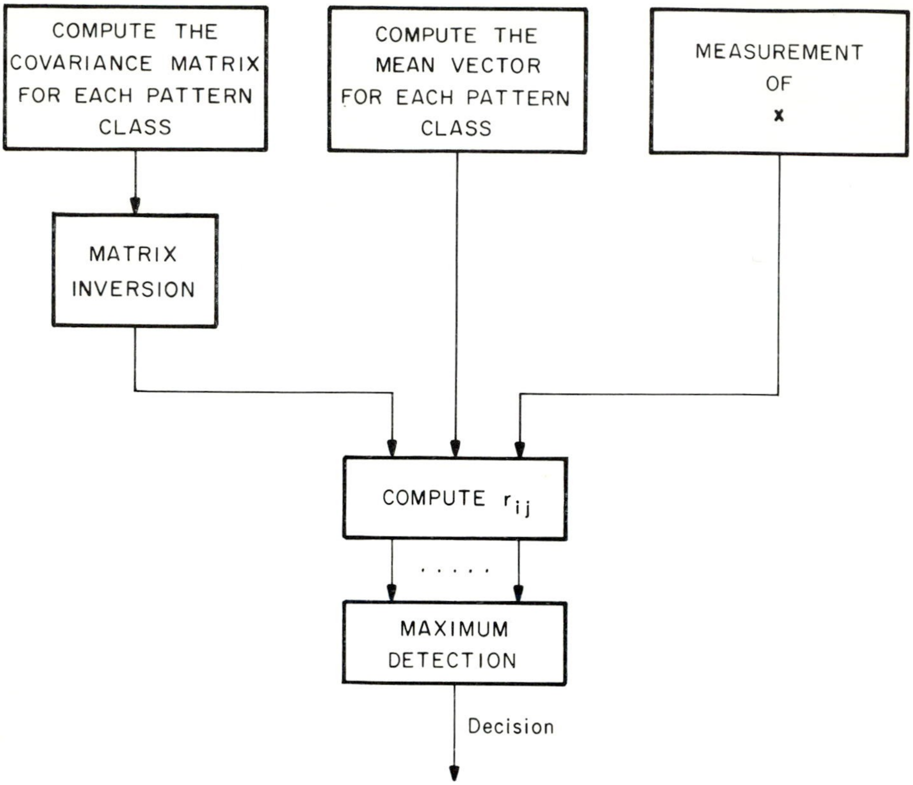

Figure 1.18. A simple recognition scheme

It is noted that the equation

$$r_{ij}(\mathbf{x}) = \mathbf{x}'\mathbf{C}^{-1}(\mathbf{m}_i - \mathbf{m}_j) - \tfrac{1}{2}(\mathbf{m}_i + \mathbf{m}_j)'\mathbf{C}^{-1}(\mathbf{m}_i - \mathbf{m}_j) = 0$$

describes a hyperplane in the n-dimensional space which divides the space into two parts for the two-class case:

$$r_{ij} > 0 \quad \text{for} \quad \mathbf{x} \in \omega_i$$

$$r_{ij} < 0 \quad \text{for} \quad \mathbf{x} \in \omega_j$$

Hence, $r_{ij} = 0$ forms the decision boundary between the ith and the jth pattern classes. The following chapter presents a comprehensive discussion of decision functions and decision boundaries.

2

DECISION FUNCTIONS

2.1 INTRODUCTION

The principal function of a pattern recognition system is to yield decisions concerning the class membership of the patterns with which it is confronted. In order to accomplish this task, it is necessary to establish some rules upon which to base these decisions. One important approach to this problem is the use of decision functions. As a way of introduction to this relatively simple concept, consider Fig. 2.1, where two hypothetical pattern classes are shown. It is seen in this figure that the two pattern populations can be conveniently separated by a line.

Let $d(\mathbf{x}) = w_1x_1 + w_2x_2 + w_3 = 0$ be the equation of a separating line where the w's are parameters and x_1, x_2 are the general coordinate variables. It is clear from the figure that any pattern $\mathbf{x}$ belonging to class ω_1 will yield a positive quantity when substituted into $d(\mathbf{x})$. Similarly, $d(\mathbf{x})$ becomes negative upon substitution of any pattern from ω_2. Therefore, $d(\mathbf{x})$ can be used as a *decision* (or *discriminant*) *function* since, given a pattern $\mathbf{x}$ of unknown classification, we may say that $\mathbf{x}$ belongs to ω_1 if $d(\mathbf{x}) > 0$, or to ω_2 if $d(\mathbf{x}) < 0$. If the pattern lies on the separating boundary, we obtain the indeterminate condition $d(\mathbf{x}) = 0$. As will be seen in the following sections, these concepts need not be restricted to two classes. In addition, they can be easily extended to encompass the more general case of nonlinear boundaries in any finite-dimensional Euclidean space.

The success of the foregoing pattern classification scheme depends on two factors: (1) the form of $d(\mathbf{x})$, and (2) one's ability to determine its coefficients.

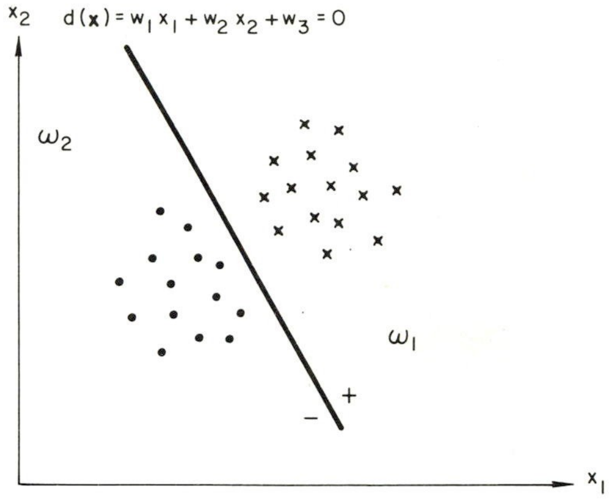

Figure 2.1. A simple decision function for two pattern classes

The first problem is directly related to the geometrical properties of the pattern classes under consideration. It is not difficult to visualize situations in which boundaries that are considerably more complicated than the linearly separable example discussed above might be necessary to separate the given pattern populations. If the dimensionality of the patterns is higher than three, our powers of visualization are no longer of assistance in determining these boundaries. Under these conditions, the only reasonable recourse is a strictly analytical approach. Unfortunately, unless some *a priori* information is available, the only way to establish the effectiveness of a chosen decision function is by direct trial.

Once a certain function (or functions if more than two classes are involved) has been selected, the problem becomes the determination of the coefficients. As will be seen in subsequent chapters, several adaptive and training schemes can be brought to bear on this problem. It will be shown that, if the pattern classes under consideration are separable by the specified decision functions, it is possible to utilize sample patterns in order to determine the coefficients which characterize these functions.

2.2 LINEAR DECISION FUNCTIONS

The simple two-dimensional linear decision function introduced in Section 2.1 can be easily generalized to the n-dimensional case. Thus, a general linear decision function is of the form

$$d(\mathbf{x}) = w_1x_1 + w_2x_2 + \cdots + w_nx_n + w_{n+1}$$
$$= \mathbf{w}_0{}'\mathbf{x} + w_{n+1} \qquad (2.2\text{–}1)$$

where $\mathbf{w}_0 = (w_1, w_2, \ldots, w_n)'$. This vector is referred to as the *weight* or *parameter* vector.

It is a widely accepted convention to append a 1 after the last component of *all* pattern vectors and express Eq. (2.2–1) in the form

$$d(\mathbf{x}) = \mathbf{w}'\mathbf{x} \qquad (2.2\text{–}2)$$

where $\mathbf{x} = (x_1, x_2, \ldots, x_n, 1)'$ and $\mathbf{w} = (w_1, w_2, \ldots, w_n, w_{n+1})'$ are called the *augmented* pattern and weight vectors, respectively. Since the same quantity is equally appended to all patterns, the basic geometrical properties of the pattern classes are not disturbed. Whether or not a pattern or weight vector has been augmented can usually be determined from the context. We will normally refer to $\mathbf{x}$ and $\mathbf{w}$ in Eq. (2.2–2) simply as pattern and weight vectors, respectively.

In the two-class case a decision function $d(\mathbf{x})$ is assumed to have the property

$$d(\mathbf{x}) = \mathbf{w}'\mathbf{x} \begin{cases} > 0 & \text{if } \mathbf{x} \in \omega_1 \\ < 0 & \text{if } \mathbf{x} \in \omega_2 \end{cases} \qquad (2.2\text{–}3)$$

When we have more than two classes, denoted by $\omega_1, \omega_2, \ldots, \omega_M$, we consider the following multiclass cases.

Case 1. Each pattern class is separable from the other classes by a single decision surface. In this case there are M decision functions with the property

$$d_i(\mathbf{x}) = \mathbf{w}_i{}'\mathbf{x} = \begin{cases} > 0 & \text{if } \mathbf{x} \in \omega_i \\ < 0 & \text{otherwise} \end{cases}, \quad i = 1, 2, \ldots, M \qquad (2.2\text{–}4)$$

where $\mathbf{w}_i = (w_{i1}, w_{i2}, \ldots, w_{in}, w_{i,n+1})'$ is the weight vector associated with the ith decision function.

Example: A simple example of multiclass Case 1 is shown in Fig. 2.2(a). It is noted that each class is separable from the rest by a single decision boundary. For instance, if a specific pattern $\mathbf{x}$ belongs to class ω_1, it is clear from the geometry of Fig. 2.2(a) that $d_1(\mathbf{x}) > 0$ while $d_2(\mathbf{x}) < 0$ and $d_3(\mathbf{x}) < 0$.

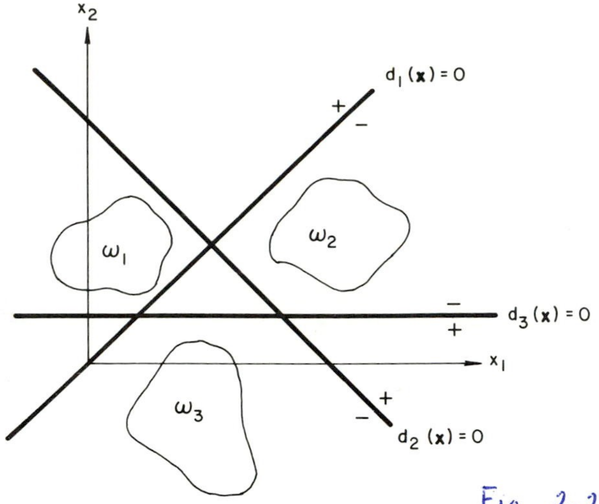

Fig 2.2 (a)

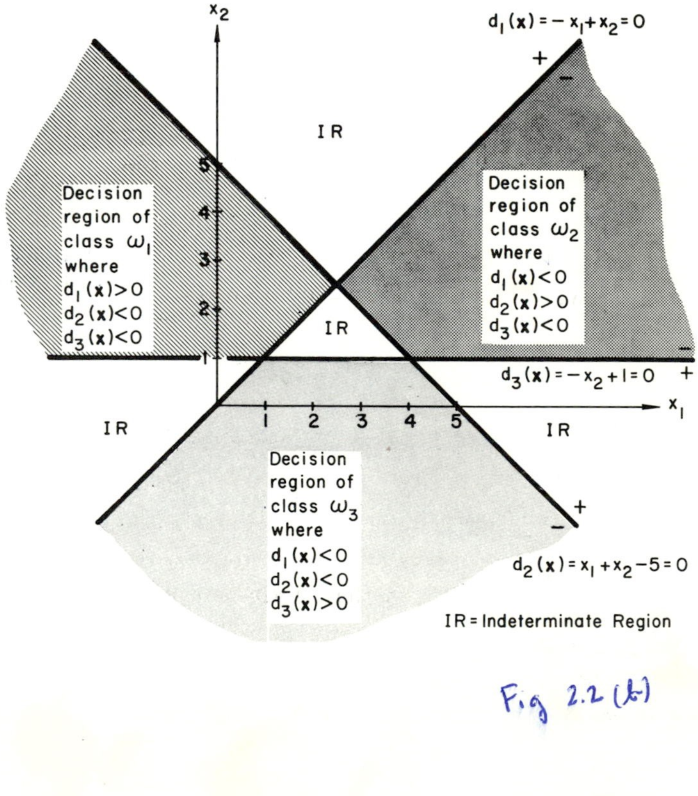

Fig 2.2 (b)

The boundary between class ω_1 and the other classes is given by the values of $\mathbf{x}$ for which $d_1(\mathbf{x}) = 0$.

As a numerical illustration assume that the decision functions of Fig. 2.2(a) are

$$d_1(\mathbf{x}) = -x_1 + x_2, \qquad d_2(\mathbf{x}) = x_1 + x_2 - 5, \qquad d_3(\mathbf{x}) = -x_2 + 1$$

The three decision boundaries are, therefore,

$$-x_1 + x_2 = 0, \qquad x_1 + x_2 - 5 = 0, \qquad -x_2 + 1 = 0$$

Now, any pattern for which $d_1(\mathbf{x}) > 0$ while $d_2(\mathbf{x}) < 0$ and $d_3(\mathbf{x}) < 0$ is automatically assigned to class ω_1. Therefore, the region corresponding to class ω_1 consists of the area determined by the positive side of line $-x_1 + x_2 = 0$ and the negative side of lines $x_1 + x_2 - 5 = 0$ and $-x_2 + 1 = 0$. This region is shown in Fig. 2.2(b). We see that, although class ω_1 occupies a relatively small area, the actual *decision* region where a pattern would be assigned to this class is infinite in extent. Similar comments hold for the other two classes.

It is interesting to note that, if $d_i(\mathbf{x})$ is greater than zero for more than one value of i, a decision cannot be reached using this classification scheme. This is also true if $d_i(\mathbf{x}) < 0$ for all i. As shown in Fig. 2.2(b), this particular example has four indeterminate regions in which one of these conditions would occur.

Classification of an unknown pattern into one of the three classes characterized by the above decision functions is straightforward. For example, suppose that it is desired to classify the pattern $\mathbf{x} = (6, 5)'$. Substituting this pattern into the three decision functions yields

$$d_1(\mathbf{x}) = -1, \qquad d_2(\mathbf{x}) = 6, \qquad d_3(\mathbf{x}) = -4$$

Since $d_2(\mathbf{x}) > 0$ while $d_1(x) < 0$ and $d_3(\mathbf{x}) < 0$, the pattern is assigned to class ω_2.

Case 2. Each pattern class is separable from every other individual class by a distinct decision surface, that is, the classes are pairwise separable. In this case there are $M(M-1)/2$ (the combination of M classes taken two at a time) decision surfaces. The decision functions here are of the form $d_{ij}(\mathbf{x}) = \mathbf{w}'_{ij}\mathbf{x}$ and have the property that, if $\mathbf{x}$ belongs to class ω_i, then

$$d_{ij}(\mathbf{x}) > 0 \quad \text{for all} \quad j \neq i \tag{2.2–5}$$

These functions also have the property that $d_{ij}(\mathbf{x}) = -d_{ji}(\mathbf{x})$.

It is not uncommon to find problems involving a combination of Cases 1 and 2. These situations require fewer than the $M(M-1)/2$ decision surfaces which would be needed if all the classes were only pairwise separable.

Example: Figure 2.3(a) illustrates three pattern classes separable under Case 2 conditions. We see that no class is separable from the others by a single decision surface. Each boundary shown is capable of separating just two classes. For example, although the boundary $d_{12}(\mathbf{x}) = 0$ cuts through class ω_3, it effectively separates only ω_1 and ω_2.

For the purpose of illustration, let us assume the following numerical values:

$$d_{12}(\mathbf{x}) = -x_1 - x_2 + 5, \qquad d_{13}(\mathbf{x}) = -x_1 + 3, \qquad d_{23}(\mathbf{x}) = -x_1 + x_2$$

The decision boundaries are again determined by setting the decision functions equal to zero. The decision regions, however, are now given by the positive sides of multiple decision boundaries. For example, the region of class ω_1 is determined by values of $\mathbf{x}$ for which $d_{12}(\mathbf{x}) > 0$ and $d_{13}(\mathbf{x}) > 0$. The value of $d_{23}(\mathbf{x})$ in this region is irrelevant since $d_{23}(\mathbf{x})$ is not related to class ω_1.

The subscripts 2 and 3 are not "1".

The regions corresponding to the three decision functions given above are shown in Fig. 2.3(b), where the condition $d_{ij}(\mathbf{x}) = -d_{ji}(\mathbf{x})$ has been used to determine the regions of the various classes. For instance, since $d_{12}(\mathbf{x}) = -x_1 - x_2 + 5$ we have that $d_{21}(\mathbf{x}) = x_1 + x_2 - 5$, and it follows that the positive side of the boundary $d_{12}(\mathbf{x}) = 0$ is on the negative side of the boundary $d_{21}(\mathbf{x}) = 0$. As in Case 1, we see that the decision regions are infinite in extent, and also that there exists an indeterminate region in which the conditions of Case 2 are not satisfied.

Suppose that it is desired to classify the pattern $\mathbf{x} = (4, 3)'$. Substitution of this pattern into the above decision functions yields

$$d_{12}(\mathbf{x}) = -2, \qquad d_{13}(\mathbf{x}) = -1, \qquad d_{23}(\mathbf{x}) = -1$$

It follows automatically that $d_{21}(\mathbf{x}) = 2$, $d_{31}(\mathbf{x}) = 1$, $d_{32}(\mathbf{x}) = 1$; that is,

$$d_{3j}(\mathbf{x}) > 0 \quad \text{for} \quad j = 1, 2$$

Therefore, using (2.2–5), we assign the pattern to class ω_3.

LINEAR SEPARABLE

Case 3.   There exist M decision functions $d_k(\mathbf{x}) = \mathbf{w}_k'\mathbf{x}$, $k = 1, 2, \ldots, M$, with the property that, if $\mathbf{x}$ belongs to class ω_i,

$$d_i(\mathbf{x}) > d_j(\mathbf{x}) \quad \text{for all} \quad j \neq i \qquad (2.2\text{–}6)$$

note no comparison to zero.

Can this condition be satisfied given when $\vec{x} \neq \vec{w}_i$?

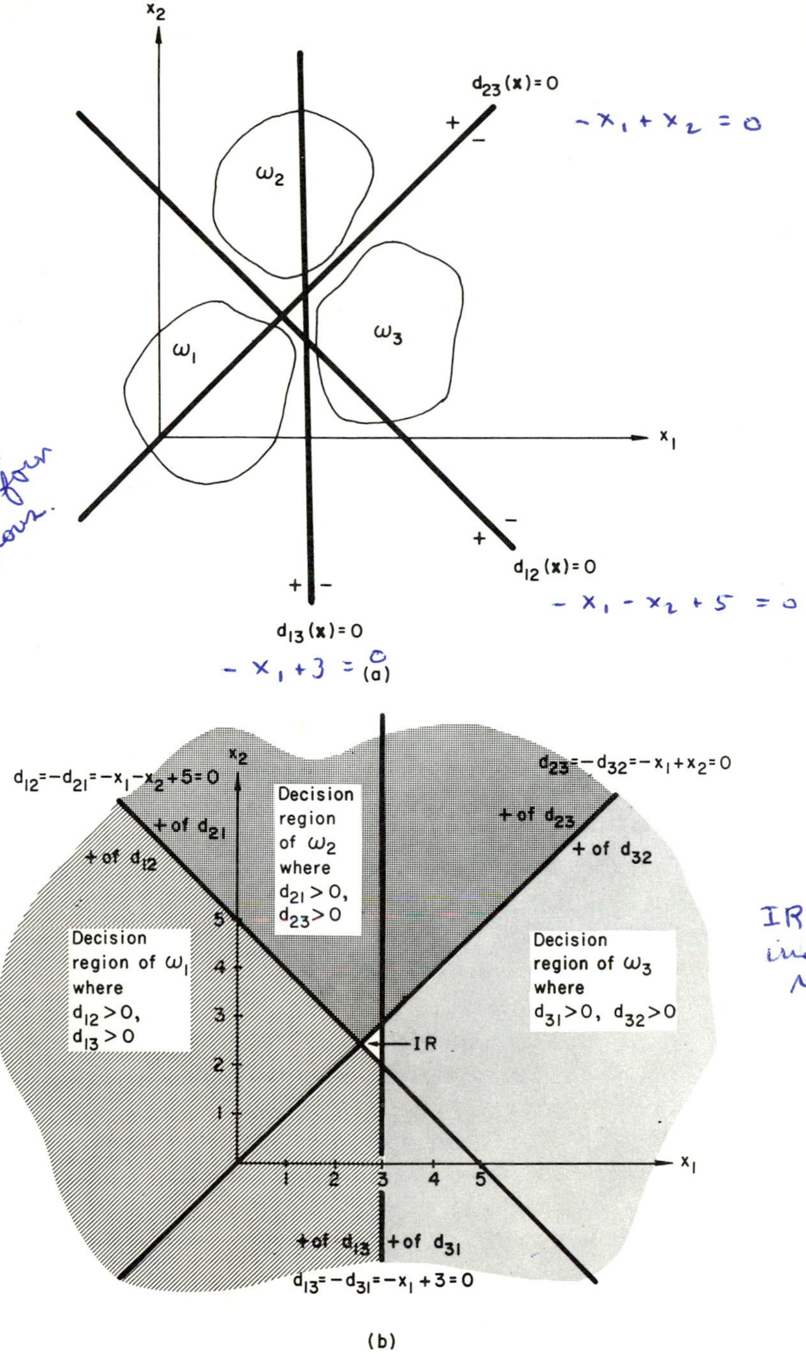

Figure 2.3. Illustration of multiclass Case 2

Try an example with four regions.

IR = indeterminate region

This is a special instance of Case 2 since we may define

$$\begin{aligned} d_{ij}(\mathbf{x}) &= d_i(\mathbf{x}) - d_j(\mathbf{x}) \\ &= (\mathbf{w}_i - \mathbf{w}_j)'\mathbf{x} \\ &= \mathbf{w}_{ij}'\mathbf{x} \end{aligned} \tag{2.2-7}$$

where $\mathbf{w}_{ij} = \mathbf{w}_i - \mathbf{w}_j$. It is easily verified that, if $d_i(\mathbf{x}) > d_j(\mathbf{x})$ for all $j \neq i$, then $d_{ij}(\mathbf{x}) > 0$ for all $j \neq i$, that is, if the classes are separable under Case 3 conditions, they are automatically separable under Case 2. The converse, however, is in general not true.

Example: Before illustrating Case 3, let us first note that the boundary between classes ω_i and ω_j is given by values of $\mathbf{x}$ for which $d_i(\mathbf{x}) = d_j(\mathbf{x})$ or (what is the same thing) $d_i(\mathbf{x}) - d_j(\mathbf{x}) = 0$. Therefore, we see that the values of $d_i(\mathbf{x})$ and $d_j(\mathbf{x})$ combine to give the equation of the surface separating ω_i and ω_j.

A simple example of Case 3 is shown in Fig. 2.4(a) for $M = 3$. For the patterns of class ω_1 we require that $d_1(\mathbf{x}) > d_2(\mathbf{x})$ and $d_1(\mathbf{x}) > d_3(\mathbf{x})$. This is equivalent to the requirement that the patterns of this class lie on the positive side of the surfaces $d_1(\mathbf{x}) - d_2(\mathbf{x}) = 0$ and $d_1(\mathbf{x}) - d_3(\mathbf{x}) = 0$. In general, we require that the patterns of class ω_i lie on the positive side of the surfaces $d_i(\mathbf{x}) - d_j(\mathbf{x}) = 0$, $j = 1, 2, \ldots, M$, $j \neq i$. As before, the positive side of $d_i(\mathbf{x}) - d_j(\mathbf{x}) = 0$ is on the negative side of $d_j(\mathbf{x}) - d_i(\mathbf{x}) = 0$.

As a numerical illustration consider the decision functions

$$d_1(\mathbf{x}) = -x_1 + x_2, \qquad d_2(\mathbf{x}) = x_1 + x_2 - 1, \qquad d_3(\mathbf{x}) = -x_2$$

The boundaries between the three classes are determined as follows:

$$\begin{aligned} d_1(\mathbf{x}) - d_2(\mathbf{x}) &= -2x_1 + 1 = 0 \\ d_1(\mathbf{x}) - d_3(\mathbf{x}) &= -x_1 + 2x_2 = 0 \\ d_2(\mathbf{x}) - d_3(\mathbf{x}) &= x_1 + 2x_2 - 1 = 0 \end{aligned}$$

To find the decision region corresponding to class ω_1, we find the region for which $d_1(\mathbf{x}) > d_2(\mathbf{x})$ and $d_1(\mathbf{x}) > d_3(\mathbf{x})$. This region corresponds to the positive side of the lines $-2x_1 + 1 = 0$ and $-x_1 + 2x_2 = 0$, as shown in Fig. 2.4(b). The region for class ω_2 is determined by the positive sides of the lines $2x_1 - 1 = 0$ and $x_1 + 2x_2 - 1 = 0$. Finally, the region of ω_3 is given by the positive sides of $x_1 - 2x_2 = 0$ and $-x_1 - 2x_2 + 1 = 0$. It

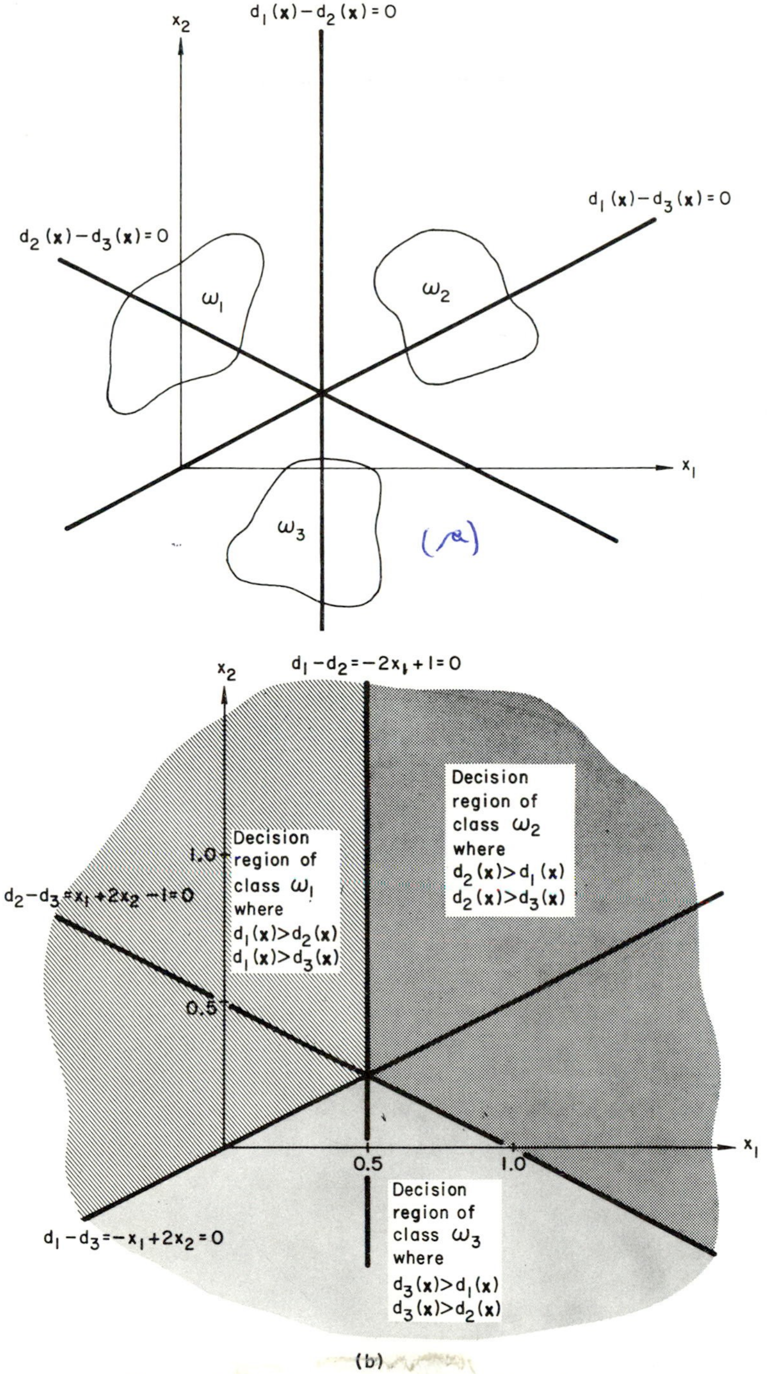

Figure 2.4. Illustration of multiclass Case 3

is interesting to note that under Case 3 conditions there are no indeterminate regions except parts of the boundaries themselves.

As an example of the classification process, consider the pattern $\mathbf{x} = (1, 1)'$. Substituting this pattern into the above decision functions yields

$$d_1(\mathbf{x}) = 0, \qquad d_2(\mathbf{x}) = 1, \qquad d_3(\mathbf{x}) = -1$$

Since

$$d_2(\mathbf{x}) > d_j(\mathbf{x}) \quad \text{for} \quad j = 1, 3$$

the pattern is assigned to class ω_2. ●

If the pattern classes in a given situation are classifiable by any of the linear decision function cases discussed above, the classes are said to be *linearly separable*. The reader should keep clearly in mind that the basic problem, after a set of decision functions (linear or otherwise) has been specified, is to determine the coefficients. As was previously mentioned, these coefficients are normally determined by using the available sample patterns. Once the coefficients of each decision function have been established, these functions may be used as the basis for pattern classification, as indicated in Chapter 1.

2.3 GENERALIZED DECISION FUNCTIONS

It is not difficult to show that decision boundaries can always be established between pattern classes which do not share identical pattern vectors. The complexity of these boundaries may range from linear to very nonlinear surfaces requiring a large number of terms for their description. Often in practical applications the pattern classes are not truly separable within economic or technical constraints, and it then becomes desirable to seek approximations to decision functions. One convenient way to generalize the linear decision function concept is to consider decision functions of the form

$$\begin{aligned} d(\mathbf{x}) &= w_1 f_1(\mathbf{x}) + w_2 f_2(\mathbf{x}) + \cdots + w_K f_K(\mathbf{x}) + w_{K+1} \\ &= \sum_{i=1}^{K+1} w_i f_i(\mathbf{x}) \end{aligned} \tag{2.3–1}$$

where the $\{f_i(\mathbf{x})\}$, $i = 1, 2, \ldots, K$, are real, single-valued functions of the pattern $\mathbf{x}$, $f_{K+1}(\mathbf{x}) = 1$, and $K + 1$ is the number of terms used in the expansion. Equation (2.3–1) represents an infinite variety of decision functions, depending on the choice of the functions $\{f_i(\mathbf{x})\}$ and on the number of terms used in the expansion.

In spite of the fact that Eq. (2.3–1) could represent very complex decision functions, it is possible to treat these functions as if they were *linear* by virtue of a straightforward transformation. In order to show this, we define a vector $\mathbf{x}^*$ whose components are the functions $f_i(\mathbf{x})$, that is,

$$\mathbf{x}^* = \begin{pmatrix} f_1(\mathbf{x}) \\ f_2(\mathbf{x}) \\ \vdots \\ f_K(\mathbf{x}) \\ 1 \end{pmatrix} \tag{2.3–2}$$

Using Eq. (2.3–2), we may express (2.3–1) as

$$d(\mathbf{x}) = \mathbf{w}'\mathbf{x}^* \tag{2.3–3}$$

where $\mathbf{w} = (w_1, w_2, \ldots, w_K, w_{K+1})'$.

Once evaluated, the functions $\{f_i(\mathbf{x})\}$ are nothing more than a set of numerical values, and $\mathbf{x}^*$ is simply a K-dimensional vector which has been augmented by 1, as discussed in Section 2.2. Therefore, Eq. (2.3–3) represents a linear function with respect to the new patterns $\mathbf{x}^*$. Clearly, if we transform *all* the original patterns $\mathbf{x}$ into the patterns $\mathbf{x}^*$ by evaluating the functions $\{f_i(\mathbf{x})\}$ for all $\mathbf{x}$, the problem has been effectively transformed into a linear representation. The implication of all this is simply that we may restrict all further discussion to linear decision functions without loss of generality. Any decision function of the form shown in Eq. (2.3–1) can be treated as linear by virtue of Eqs. (2.3–2) and (2.3–3).

The above manipulations are useful only for mathematical expendiency. Nothing is really changed, as can be seen by comparing Eqs. (2.3–1) through (2.3–3). If the $\mathbf{x}$ patterns are n-dimensional, the $\mathbf{x}^*$ patterns are K-dimensional (excluding the appended 1), where K may be considerably greater than n. Thus, although the decision functions can be considered as linear in the K-dimensional space, they retain their general nonlinear properties in the n-dimensional space of the original patterns.

One of the most commonly used types of generalized decision functions is that in which the functions $\{f_i(\mathbf{x})\}$ are of polynomial form. In the simplest case these functions are linear; that is, if $\mathbf{x} = (x_1, x_2, \ldots, x_n)'$, then $f_i(\mathbf{x}) = x_i$, with $K = n$. Under this condition we obtain $d(\mathbf{x}) = \mathbf{w}'\mathbf{x} + w_{n+1}$.

At the next level in complexity are the second-degree, or quadratic, functions. In the two-dimensional case $\mathbf{x} = (x_1, x_2)'$, and these functions are of the form

$$d(\mathbf{x}) = w_{11}x_1^2 + w_{12}x_1x_2 + w_{22}x_2^2 + w_1x_1 + w_2x_2 + w_3 \qquad (2.3\text{–}4)$$

which may be expressed in the linear form $d(\mathbf{x}^*) = \mathbf{w}'\mathbf{x}^*$ by defining $\mathbf{x}^* = (x_1^2, x_1x_2, x_2^2, x_1, x_2, 1)'$ and $\mathbf{w} = (w_{11}, w_{12}, w_{22}, w_1, w_2, w_3)'$.

The general quadratic case is formed in a similar manner by considering all combination of the components of $\mathbf{x}$ which form terms of degree two or less, that is, if the patterns are n-dimensional,

$$d(\mathbf{x}) = \sum_{j=1}^{n} w_{jj}x_j^2 + \sum_{j=1}^{n-1} \sum_{k=j+1}^{n} w_{jk}x_jx_k + \sum_{j=1}^{n} w_jx_j + w_{n+1} \qquad (2.3\text{–}5)$$

In this equation, the first function on the right-hand side consists of n terms, the second function of $n(n-1)/2$ terms, and the third function of n terms. Hence, the total number of terms is $(n+1)(n+2)/2$, which is equal to the total number of parameters or weights. Comparing Eq. (2.3–5) with the general form given in Eq. (2.3–1) reveals that all terms $f_i(\mathbf{x})$ from which $d(\mathbf{x})$ is derived are of the form

$$f_i(\mathbf{x}) = x_p^s\, x_q^t$$

$$p, q = 1, 2, \ldots, n; \qquad s, t = 0, 1 \qquad (2.3\text{–}6)$$

Equation (2.3–6) suggests a general scheme for the generation of polynomial decision functions of any finite degree. To form an rth-order polynomial function we let the functions $f_i(\mathbf{x})$ be of the form

$$f_i(\mathbf{x}) = x_{p_1}^{s_1}\, x_{p_2}^{s_2} \cdots x_{p_r}^{s_r}$$

$$p_1, p_2, \ldots, p_r = 1, 2, \ldots, n; \qquad s_1, s_2, \ldots, s_r = 0, 1 \qquad (2.3\text{–}7)$$

Since terms of the form shown in Eq. (2.3–7) contain all powers of r or less, it is possible to express polynomial decision functions in the following recursive form:

$$d^r(\mathbf{x}) = \left(\sum_{p_1=1}^{n} \sum_{p_2=p_1}^{n} \cdots \sum_{p_r=p_{r-1}}^{n} w_{p_1p_2\ldots p_r} x_{p_1}x_{p_2} \cdots x_{p_r} \right) + d^{r-1}(\mathbf{x}) \qquad (2.3\text{–}8)$$

where r indicates the degree of nonlinearity, and $d^0(\mathbf{x}) = w_{n+1}$. This relationship provides a convenient method for the generation of decision functions of any finite degree.

Example: As a simple illustration, let us consider the use of Eq. (2.3–8) to generate the quadratic function given in Eq. (2.3–4). In this case $r = 2$ and $n = 2$, so we have

$$d^2(\mathbf{x}) = \sum_{p_1=1}^{2} \sum_{p_2=p_1}^{2} w_{p_1p_2}x_{p_1}x_{p_2} + d^1(\mathbf{x})$$

where $d^1(\mathbf{x})$ is the linear function

$$d^1(\mathbf{x}) = \sum_{p_1=1}^{2} w_{p_1}x_{p_1} + d^0(\mathbf{x}) = w_1x_1 + w_2x_2 + w_3$$

Carrying out the indicated summation results in

$$\begin{aligned} d^2(\mathbf{x}) &= w_{11}x_1^2 + w_{12}x_1x_2 + w_{22}x_2^2 + d^1(\mathbf{x}) \\ &= w_{11}x_1^2 + w_{12}x_1x_2 + w_{22}x_2^2 + w_1x_1 + w_2x_2 + w_3 \end{aligned}$$

which agrees with Eq. (2.3–4). Higher-order functions are generated in the same manner. ●

As might be suspected, the number of terms needed to describe a polynomial decision function grows quite rapidly as a function of r and n. It is not difficult to show that, for the n-dimensional case, the number of coefficients in a function of the rth degree is given by

$$N_w = C_r^{n+r} = \frac{(n+r)!}{r!n!} \tag{2.3–9}$$

where C_r^{n+r} is the combination of $n + r$ things taken r at a time.

Table 2.1 illustrates the number N_w of coefficients for various values of r and n. It should be noted that, although N_w grows quite rapidly as a function of r and n, all the terms given by the general expansion of Eq. (2.3–8) need not always be used. For example, in forming a second-degree decision function one may choose to leave out all terms which are linear in the components of $\mathbf{x}$.

With reference to Eq. (2.3–5), if we let

$$\begin{aligned} w_{jj} &= a_{jj}, & j &= 1, 2, \ldots, n \\ w_{jk} &= 2a_{jk}, & j, k &= 1, 2, \ldots, n;\ j \neq k \\ w_j &= b_j & j &= 1, 2, \ldots, n \\ w_{n+1} &= c \end{aligned}$$

TABLE 2.1. *Tabulation of N_w for Various Values of r and n*

n \ r	1	2	3	4	5	6	7	8	9	10
1	2	3	4	5	6	7	8	9	10	11
2	3	6	10	15	21	28	36	45	55	66
3	4	10	20	35	56	84	120	165	220	286
4	5	15	35	70	126	210	330	495	715	1,001
5	6	21	56	126	252	462	792	1,287	2,002	3,003
6	7	28	84	210	462	924	1,716	3,003	5,005	8,008
7	8	36	120	330	792	1,716	3,432	6,435	11,440	19,448
8	9	45	165	495	1,287	3,003	6,435	12,870	24,310	43,758
9	10	55	220	715	2,002	5,005	11,440	24,310	48,620	92,378
10	11	66	286	1,001	3,003	8,008	19,448	43,758	92,378	184,756

then Eq. (2.3–5) may be expressed in a compact form as

$$d(\mathbf{x}) = \mathbf{x}'\mathbf{A}\mathbf{x} + \mathbf{x}'\mathbf{b} + c \tag{2.3–10}$$

in which

$$\mathbf{A} = (a_{jk}) \tag{2.3–11}$$

and

$$\mathbf{b} = \begin{pmatrix} b_1 \\ b_2 \\ \vdots \\ b_n \end{pmatrix} \tag{2.3–12}$$

The properties of matrix **A** determine the shape of the decision boundary. When **A** is the identity matrix, the decision function describes a hypersphere. When **A** is positive definite, the decision function describes a hyperellipsoid with axes in the directions of the eigenvectors of **A**. When matrix **A** is positive semidefinite, the decision boundary is a hyperellipsoidal cylinder, the cross sections of which are lower-dimension hyperellipsoids with axes in the directions of the eigenvectors of **A**, corresponding to nonzero eigenvalues. When matrix **A** is negative definite, the decision boundary is a hyperhyperboloid.

There are, of course, other methods for generating decision functions. A more detailed treatment of the theoretical foundation of multivariate functions and their construction is given in Section 2.7.

2.4 PATTERN SPACE AND WEIGHT SPACE

It has been previously stated that a decision function for a two-class problem is assumed to have the property $d(\mathbf{x}) > 0$ for all patterns of one class, while $d(\mathbf{x}) < 0$ for all patterns of the other class. Assume for a moment that each class contains two two-dimensional patterns, $\{\mathbf{x}_1{}^1, \mathbf{x}_2{}^1\}$ and $\{\mathbf{x}_1{}^2, \mathbf{x}_2{}^2\}$, where the superscripts indicate classes ω_1 and ω_2, respectively. If the classes are linearly separable, the problem is to find a vector $\mathbf{w} = (w_1, w_2, w_3)'$ so that

$$\begin{aligned} w_1 x_{11}^1 + w_2 x_{12}^1 + w_3 &> 0 \\ w_1 x_{21}^1 + w_2 x_{22}^1 + w_3 &> 0 \\ w_1 x_{11}^2 + w_2 x_{12}^2 + w_3 &< 0 \\ w_1 x_{21}^2 + w_2 x_{22}^2 + w_3 &< 0 \end{aligned} \tag{2.4–1}$$

In other words, $\mathbf{w}$ is the solution to the set of linear inequalities determined by all patterns of both classes.

If the augmented patterns of one of the classes are multiplied by -1, the expressions in (2.4–1) may be written in the form

$$\begin{aligned} w_1 x_{11}^1 + w_2 x_{12}^1 + w_3 &> 0 \\ w_1 x_{21}^1 + w_2 x_{22}^1 + w_3 &> 0 \\ -w_1 x_{11}^2 - w_2 x_{12}^2 - w_3 &> 0 \\ -w_1 x_{21}^2 - w_2 x_{22}^2 - w_3 &> 0 \end{aligned} \tag{2.4–2}$$

where the patterns of ω_2 have been multiplied by -1. In this manner, the problem may be interpreted as that of finding a $\mathbf{w}$ such that all inequalities are greater than zero. Clearly there is no difference between expressions (2.4–1) and (2.4–2) since the same $\mathbf{w}$ will satisfy both sets on inequalities. Both formulations will be used in subsequent discussions.

The inequalities of (2.4–1) or (2.4–2) simply indicate that $\mathbf{w}$ must be a vector whose components establish a decision boundary between ω_1 and ω_2. To gain further insight into the geometrical properties of a solution vector $\mathbf{w}$, it is convenient to consider the difference between the pattern space and the weight space.

The *pattern space* is the n-dimensional Euclidean space containing the pattern vectors, as shown in Fig. 2.5(a) for the hypothetical case associated

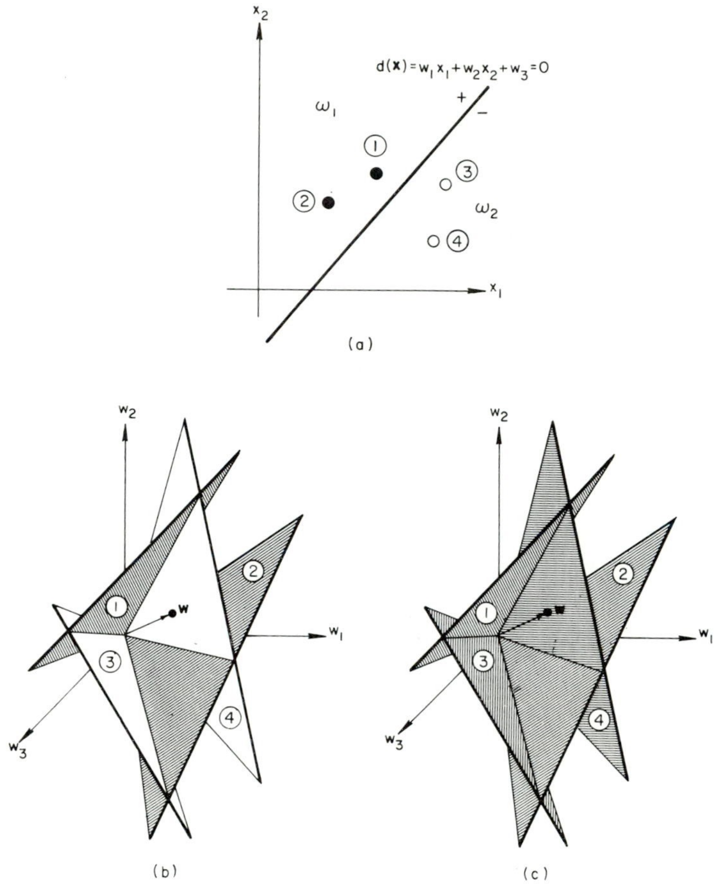

Figure 2.5. Geometrical illustration of the pattern space and the weight space. (a) Pattern space. (b) Weight space corresponding to inequalities (2.4–1). (c) Weight space corresponding to inequalities (2.4–2). Shaded areas indicate positive side of planes

with expressions (2.4–1). The coordinate variables are $x_1, x_2, \ldots, x_n$. In this space, **w** is viewed as the set of coefficients which determine a decision surface.

The *weight space* is the $(n + 1)$-dimensional Euclidean space in which the coordinate variables are $w_1, w_2, \ldots, w_{n+1}$. In this space *each* inequality represents the positive or negative side of a hyperplane which passes through the origin. This can be seen from expressions (2.4–1), where, for example, setting the first inequality equal to zero yields $w_1x_{11}^1 + w_2x_{12}^1 + w_3 = 0$, which is recognized as the equation of a plane passing through the origin of the weight space. A solution to the set of inequalities given in expressions (2.4–1) is any vector $\mathbf{w}$ which lies on the positive side of all planes determined by the patterns of class ω_1, and on the negative side of all planes determined by the patterns of class ω_2. A solution to the inequalities of (2.4–2) is any vector $\mathbf{w}$ which lies on the positive side of all planes, since the augmented patterns of class ω_2 have been multiplied by -1. Both cases are shown in Figs. 2.5(b) and (c), where the encircled numbers identify the patterns and their corresponding planes in the weight space. It is noted that the solution vector is the same in both cases, and that the solution region is bounded by a cone. In the general case we call the bounding surface a *convex polyhedral cone*. The total number of cones in addition to the solution cone (if it exists) depends on the number of patterns and their dimensionality, as will be seen in Section 2.5.2.

From the foregoing discussion we see that the general problem associated with the use of linear decision functions is the solution of a set of linear inequalities, where each inequality is determined by a pattern vector. In Chapters 5 and 6 attention is focused on several approaches to this problem.

2.5 GEOMETRICAL PROPERTIES

In this section we discuss several important geometrical properties of linear decision functions. Starting with the properties of hyperplanes, we introduce the concept of pattern dichotomies as a simple measure of the discriminatory power of decision functions. This concept is then used in the definition of dichotomization capacity.

2.5.1 Hyperplane Properties

In the two-class problem, as well as in multiclass Cases 1 and 2 discussed in Section 2.2, the equation of the surface separating the pattern classes is obtained by letting the decision functions be equal to zero. In other words, in the two-class case the surface between the two pattern populations is given by the equation

$$d(\mathbf{x}) = w_1x_1 + w_2x_2 + \cdots + w_nx_n + w_{n+1} = 0 \qquad (2.5\text{–}1)$$

In Case 1 the equation of the boundary between ω_i and the remaining classes is given by

$$d_i(\mathbf{x}) = w_{i1}x_1 + w_{i2}x_2 + \cdots + w_{in}x_n + w_{i,n+1} = 0 \qquad (2.5\text{–}2)$$

Similarly, in Case 2 the boundary between ω_i and ω_j is given by

$$d_{ij}(\mathbf{x}) = w_{ij1}x_1 + w_{ij2}x_2 + \cdots + w_{ijn}x_n + w_{ij,n+1} = 0 \qquad (2.5\text{–}3)$$

In Case 3 letting the individual decision functions be equal to zero does *not* yield the equation of the separating surface. In general, the equation of the decision surface between classes ω_i and ω_j is given by

$$\begin{aligned} d_{ij}(\mathbf{x}) = d_i(\mathbf{x}) - d_j(\mathbf{x}) &= (w_{i1} - w_{j1})x_1 + (w_{i2} - w_{j2})x_2 + \cdots \\ &\quad + (w_{in} - w_{jn})x_n + (w_{i,n+1} - w_{j,n+1}) \\ &= 0 \end{aligned} \qquad (2.5\text{–}4)$$

From Eqs. (2.5–1) through (2.5–4) we see that the boundaries given by these equations are of the same form, differing only in the values of the coefficients. For this reason, it will be advantageous in the following discussion to drop the subscripts temporarily and express these decision surfaces in the general form

$$\begin{aligned} d(\mathbf{x}) &= w_1x_1 + w_2x_2 + \cdots + w_nx_n + w_{n+1} = 0 \\ &= \mathbf{w}_0'\mathbf{x} + w_{n+1} = 0 \end{aligned} \qquad (2.5\text{–}5)$$

where $\mathbf{w}_0 = (w_1, w_2, \ldots, w_n)'$. It is noted that the vector $\mathbf{x}$ has not been augmented since, as will be seen below, the coefficient w_{n+1} plays an important role in the geometrical interpretation of Eq. (2.5–5).

Equation (2.5–5) is recognized as the equation of a line when $n = 2$, and as the equation of a plane when $n = 3$. When $n > 3$, Eq. (2.5–5) is the equation of a *hyperplane*. Since linear decision boundaries will play a central role in this chapter as well as subsequent ones, it is essential that the geometrical properties of hyperplanes be clearly understood.

Consider Fig. 2.6, in which a "hyperplane" is schematically shown. Let $\mathbf{u}$ be a unit normal to the hyperplane at some point $\mathbf{p}$ and oriented to the positive side of the hyperplane. From purely geometrical considerations the equation of the hyperplane may be written as

$$\mathbf{u}'(\mathbf{x} - \mathbf{p}) = 0 \qquad (2.5\text{–}6a)$$

or

$$\mathbf{u}'\mathbf{x} = \mathbf{u}'\mathbf{p} \qquad (2.5\text{–}6b)$$

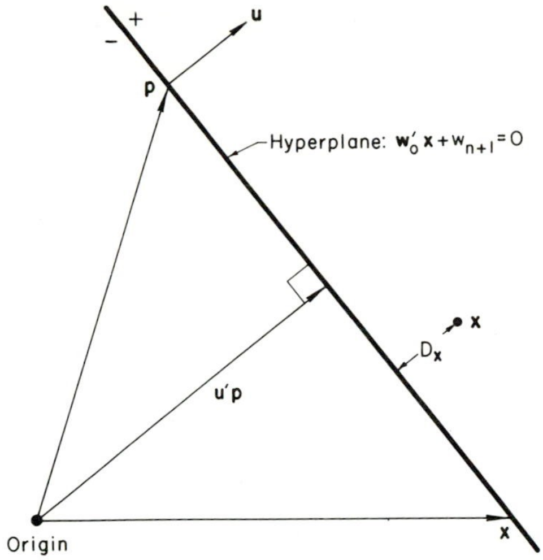

Figure 2.6. Some geometrical properties of hyperplanes

Dividing Eq. (2.5–5) by $\|\mathbf{w}_\circ\| = \sqrt{w_1^2 + w_2^2 + \cdots + w_n^2}$ results in the equation

$$\frac{\mathbf{w}_\circ'\mathbf{x}}{\|\mathbf{w}_\circ\|} = -\frac{w_{n+1}}{\|\mathbf{w}_\circ\|} \tag{2.5–7}$$

Comparing Eqs. (2.5–6b) and (2.5–7), we see that the unit normal to the hyperplane is given by

$$\mathbf{u} = \frac{\mathbf{w}_\circ}{\|\mathbf{w}_\circ\|} \tag{2.5–8}$$

Also,

$$\mathbf{u}'\mathbf{p} = -\frac{w_{n+1}}{\|\mathbf{w}_\circ\|} \tag{2.5–9}$$

It is seen by comparing Fig. 2.6 and Eq. (2.5–9) that the absolute value of $\mathbf{u}'\mathbf{p}$ represents the normal distance from the origin to the hyperplane. Denoting this distance by D_u, we obtain

$$D_u = \frac{|w_{n+1}|}{\|\mathbf{w}_\circ\|} \tag{2.5–10}$$

Examination of Fig. 2.6 also reveals that the normal distance $D_{\mathbf{x}}$ from the hyperplane to an arbitrary point $\mathbf{x}$ is given by

$$\begin{aligned} D_{\mathbf{x}} &= |\mathbf{u}'\mathbf{x} - \mathbf{u}'\mathbf{p}| \\ &= \left|\frac{\mathbf{w}_\circ{}'\mathbf{x}}{\|\mathbf{w}_\circ\|} + \frac{w_{n+1}}{\|\mathbf{w}_\circ\|}\right| \\ &= \left|\frac{\mathbf{w}_\circ{}'\mathbf{x} + w_{n+1}}{\|\mathbf{w}_\circ\|}\right| \end{aligned} \tag{2.5–11}$$

The unit normal $\mathbf{u}$ indicates the orientation of the hyperplane. If any component of $\mathbf{u}$ is zero, the hyperplane is parallel to the coordinate axis which corresponds to that component. Therefore, since $\mathbf{u} = \mathbf{w}_\circ/\|\mathbf{w}_\circ\|$, it is possible to tell by inspection of the vector $\mathbf{w}_\circ$ whether a particular hyperplane is parallel to any of the coordinate axes. We also see from Eq. (2.5–10) that if $w_{n+1} = 0$ the hyperplane passes through the origin.

2.5.2 Dichotomies

One measure of the discriminatory power of decision functions is the number of ways in which they can classify a given set of patterns. For example, consider Fig. 2.7, which shows a set of four two-dimensional patterns, $\mathbf{x}_1, \mathbf{x}_2, \mathbf{x}_3, \mathbf{x}_4$. Each line in the figure corresponds to a different classification of the patterns into two classes. For example, line 1 separates the group into pattern $\mathbf{x}_1$ and patterns $\mathbf{x}_2, \mathbf{x}_3, \mathbf{x}_4$. Since we can assign $\mathbf{x}_1$ to ω_1 or ω_2, we see that line 1 produces two possible classifications. In this case the total number of two-class groupings or *dichotomies* is 14. It is interesting to compare this number with the 2^4 ways in which we can group four patterns into two classes. Clearly 2 of these 16 dichotomies are not linearly implementable.

The number of linear dichotomies of N points in an n-dimensional Euclidean space is equal to twice the number of ways in which the points can be partitioned by an $(n - 1)$-dimensional hyperplane. It can be shown that, if the points are well distributed, the number of linear dichotomies for N n-dimensional patterns is given by

$$\mathscr{D}(N, n) = \begin{cases} 2\sum_{k=0}^{n} C_k^{N-1}, & N > n+1 \\ 2^N, & N \leqslant n+1 \end{cases} \tag{2.5–12}$$

where $C_k^{N-1} = (N-1)!/(N-1-k)!k!$. A set of N points in an n-dimen-

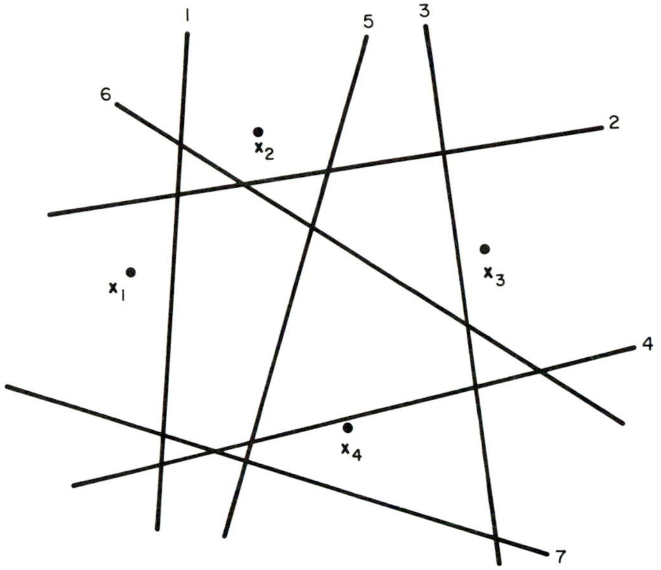

Figure 2.7. Linear dichotomies of four well-distributed patterns in two dimensions

sional space is said to be *well distributed*† if no subset of $n + 1$ points lies on an $(n - 1)$-dimensional hyperplane. For example, N points in two dimensions are well distributed if no three points lie on a line (or one-dimensional hyperplane).

Values of $\mathscr{D}(N, n)$ for various combinations of N and n are shown in Table 2.2. Notice the dramatic growth of $\mathscr{D}(N, n)$ for moderately increasing N and n.

It is interesting to associate Eqs. (2.5–12) with the number of convex polyhedral cones in the weight space representation discussed in Section 2.4. Consider Fig. 2.5(c) again. Any vector $\mathbf{w}$ inside one of the convex cones corresponds to a *unique* classification of the given patterns. Since there are $\mathscr{D}(N, n)$ linear dichotomies (assuming that the patterns are well distributed), we conclude that there must be an identical number of convex polyhedral cones in the weight space configuration of N n-dimensional patterns.

The preceding discussion can be easily extended to include the generalized decision functions discussed in Section 2.3. Since the net effect of these

† The term *in general position* is also often used in the literature.

TABLE 2.2. *Evaluation of* $\mathscr{D}(N, n)$

$N \backslash n$	1	2	3	4	5	6
1	2	2	2	2	2	2
2	4	4	4	4	4	4
3	6	8	8	8	8	8
4	8	14	16	16	16	16
5	10	22	30	32	32	32
6	12	32	52	62	64	64
7	14	44	84	114	126	128
8	16	58	128	198	240	254
9	18	74	186	326	438	494
10	20	92	260	512	764	932
25	50	602	4,650	15,662	100,670	379,862
50	100	2,452	39,300	463,052	4,276,820	32,244,452
100	200	9,902	323,600	7,852,352	150,898,640	2,391,957,152
200	400	39,802	2,627,200	129,409,702	5,073,927,280	164,946,662,302

functions is to produce patterns of new dimensionality, we need merely substitute for n the dimensionality of the transformed patterns. For example, suppose that we have 10 patterns in two dimensions and that these sample patterns are well distributed. Then the number of dichotomies is $\mathscr{D}(10, 2) = 92$. If we use a second-degree polynomial decision function, the dimensionality of the new patterns is given by $n = N_w - 1 = 5$, which results in $\mathscr{D}(10, 5) = 764$ dichotomies.

Since we are using the number of dichotomies as a measure of classification power, it should be evident that, the greater the number of implementable dichotomies for a given N, the better our chances are of finding a solution to the given inequalities. This, of course, agrees with the fact that the chances of dichotomizing two sets of patterns increase as the nonlinearity of the attempted decision boundary is increased.

2.5.3 Dichotomization Capacity of Generalized Decision Functions

Consider for a moment the generalized decision functions of Eq. (2.3–1), which are characterized by $K + 1$ adjustable weights or parameters. Given N transformed, well-distributed patterns, there are 2^N dichotomies, $\mathscr{D}(N, K)$ of which are linearly implementable with respect to the K-dimensional space of the transformed patterns. The probability $p_{N,K}$ that a dichotomy chosen at random will be linearly implementable is given by

$$p_{N,K} = \frac{\mathscr{D}(N, K)}{2^N} = \begin{cases} 2^{1-N} \sum_{j=0}^{K} C_j^{N-1} & \text{for } N > K + 1 \\ 1 & \text{for } N \leqslant K + 1 \end{cases} \tag{2.5–13}$$

In other words, if the number of patterns is less than or equal to $K + 1$, we are assured that, regardless of the way in which we group the given patterns, they will be linearly separable in the K-dimensional pattern space.

The probability $p_{N,K}$ possesses some additional interesting properties. In order to examine these properties it is convenient to let $N = \lambda(K + 1)$ and to plot $p_{N,K}$ versus λ. Clearly we can always select λ so that, whatever the value of K, $\lambda(K + 1)$ will equal N. The plot of $p_{\lambda(K+1),K}$ versus λ is shown in Fig. 2.8. Notice the marked threshold effect that occurs at $\lambda = 2$ for large values of K. We also note that, at this value of λ, $p_{2(K+1),K} = \frac{1}{2}$ for all values of K.

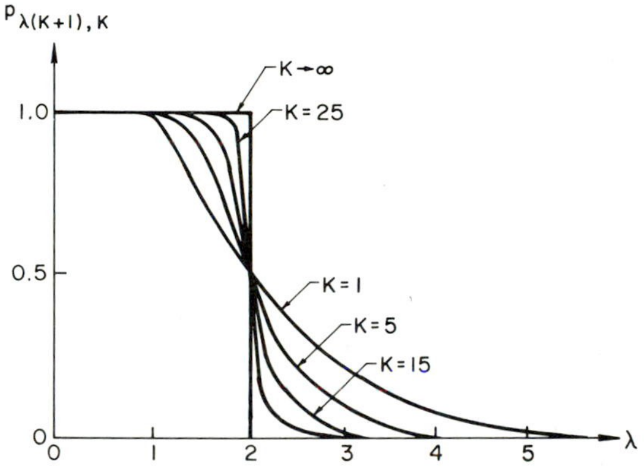

Figure 2.8. Plot of $p_{\lambda(K+1),K}$ versus λ for various values of K

Careful examination of the threshold phenomenon at $\lambda = 2$ shows that, for large values of K, we are almost guaranteed the ability to totally classify $N = 2(K + 1)$ well-distributed patterns with a generalized decision function of $K + 1$ parameters. On the other hand, if N is greater than $2(K + 1)$, we see that the probability of achieving a dichotomy declines sharply for similarly large values of K.

The foregoing considerations lead us to define the *dichotomization capacity* of generalized decision functions as

$$C_K = 2(K + 1) \tag{2.5–14}$$

We see that the capacity, as defined here, is equal to twice the number of degrees of freedom (adjustable parameters) of the generalized decision functions given in Eq. (2.3–1). This concept will occur again in Chapter 5 in connection with certain important deterministic algorithms.

Tabulated below for comparison are the dichotomization capacities of some decision functions for n-dimensional patterns.

Decision Boundary	*Dichotomization Capacity*
Hyperplane	$2(n + 1)$
Hypersphere	$2(n + 2)$
General quadratic surface	$(n + 1)(n + 2)$
rth-order polynomial surface	$2C_r^{n+r}$

2.6 IMPLEMENTATION OF DECISION FUNCTIONS

Two reasonable questions at this point are: (1) Exactly how does one determine decision functions, and (2) how are these functions implemented to form a pattern classifier? The answer to the first question will encompass much of the material in this book. Fortunately, a fairly complete answer to the second question can be given within the span of this section.

The implementation phase of a pattern classifier based on the decision functions previously discussed consists simply of choosing an acceptable method for mechanizing these functions. In many applications, the entire pattern recognition system is implemented in a computer. In other applications where a computer is available only during the design phase, or where very high speed of computation or other specialized requirements are essential factors, it may be necessary to utilize specialized circuitry to do the job.

A schematic diagram of a multiclass pattern classifier based on the generalized decision functions previously discussed is shown in Fig. 2.9. For simplicity, the discussion is limited here to multiclass Case 3. The other two cases can be implemented with a similar system. The preprocessor in this case simply mechanizes Eq. (2.3–1). The box following the preprocessor evaluates the decision functions $d_i(\mathbf{x}^*) = \mathbf{w}_i'\mathbf{x}^*$, for $i = 1, 2, \ldots, M$, where M is the number of classes. The next stage is a maximum selector. It selects the largest vector product and assigns the unknown pattern to the corresponding class.

A very inexpensive but computationally effective hardware implementation of linear decision functions is shown in Fig. 2.10. As is indicated in this figure, the admittance of each resistor is equal to a decision function weight.

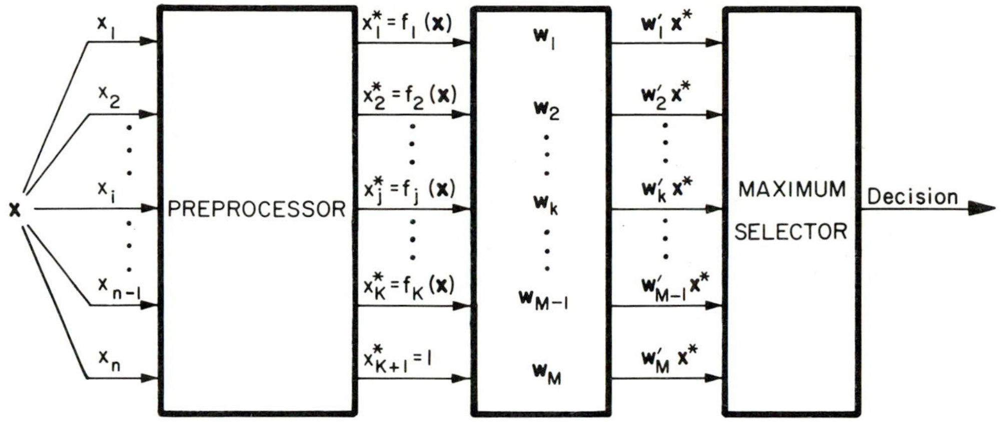

Figure 2.9. Schematic diagram of a multiclass pattern classifier

If we let the vector components represent voltages, we see that the form of the current leaving the jth resistor of the ith bank is given by $I_{ij} = w_{ij}x_j$. There is one bank of resistors for each pattern class. Since these currents are added at the node shown, it is evident from the figure that the current leaving the ith bank is equal to the dot product $\mathbf{w}_i'\mathbf{x}$. The output of each resistor bank is fed into a maximum selector, where the largest decision function value is detected and a corresponding classification made.

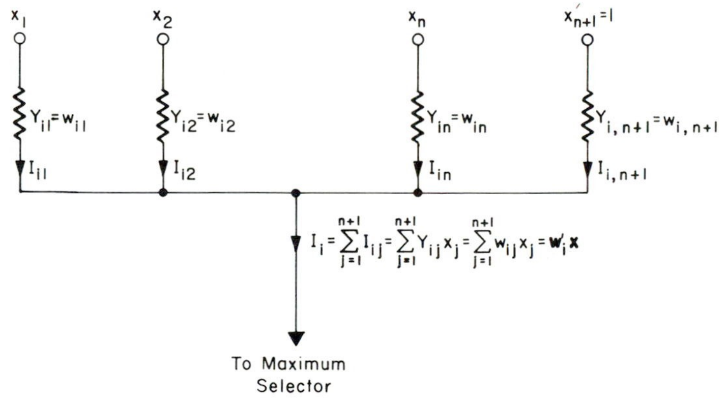

Figure 2.10. Implementation of the vector product $\mathbf{w}_i'\mathbf{x}$. There are M resistor banks, one for each class

In the two-class case the resistor-bank/maximum-selector combination assumes a form commonly known as a *threshold gate.* The schematic of a threshold gate is shown in Fig. 2.11. The gate is capable of responding in only two ways. One response corresponds to the condition $\mathbf{w}'\mathbf{x} > T$, while the other corresponds to $\mathbf{w}'\mathbf{x} \leqslant T$, where T is a nonnegative threshold. These two responses are conventionally denoted by 1 and -1, respectively. Since we are dealing with two classes, only one set of coefficients is needed. We observe that a threshold gate is, in effect, a two-class pattern classifier since it implements all the conditions necessary for classification, except preprocessing.

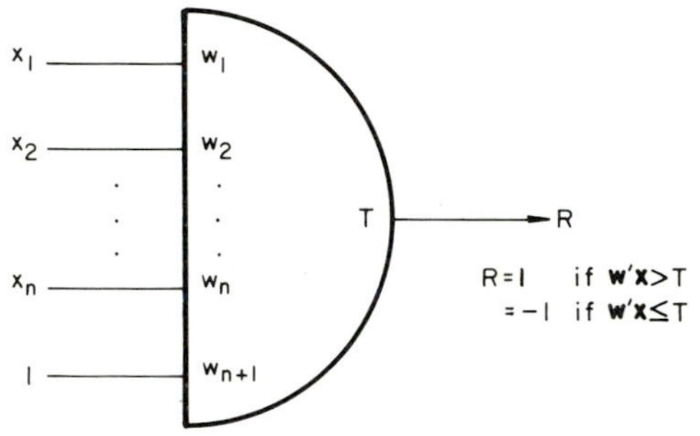

Figure 2.11. Schematic diagram of a threshold gate

Threshold gates are easily obtainable from several electronic component manufacturers. In addition to representing a useful tool in the design of pattern recognition systems, threshold gates possess properties which make them attractive from a digital computer designer's point of view. The interested reader will find the literature on this subject well documented (see, e.g., Winder [1962, 1963, 1968]).

2.7 FUNCTIONS OF SEVERAL VARIABLES

Multivariate functions play a central role in the study and design of pattern recognition systems. The purpose of this section is to provide a brief treatment of the theoretical foundation and construction of these functions. The following discussion is first limited to functions of one variable. The resulting concepts are then extended to the multivariate case.

2.7.1 Definitions

The *inner product* of two functions $f(x)$ and $g(x)$ in the interval $[a, b] = a \leqslant x \leqslant b$ is defined as

$$(f, g) = \int_a^b f(x)g(x)\, dx \tag{2.7–1}$$

The inner product of a function $f(x)$ with itself:

$$(f, f) = \int_a^b f^2(x)\, dx \tag{2.7–2}$$

is called the *norm* of $f(x)$. A function whose norm is unity is said to be *normalized.* A function is easily normalized by dividing it by the square root of its norm.

Two functions, $f(x)$ and $g(x)$, are *orthogonal* with respect to the weighting function $u(x)$ in the interval $[a, b]$ if

$$\int_a^b u(x)f(x)g(x)\, dx = 0 \tag{2.7–3}$$

Several examples of orthogonal functions will be given in Section 2.7.3.

A system of functions $\phi_1(x), \phi_2(x), \ldots$, any two of which are orthogonal in $[a, b]$, is called an *orthogonal system.* For such a system of functions, we have the familiar *orthogonality condition*

$$\int_a^b u(x)\phi_i(x)\phi_j(x)\, dx = A_{ij}\delta_{ij} \tag{2.7–4}$$

where

$$\delta_{ij} = \begin{cases} 1 & \text{if} \quad i = j \\ 0 & \text{if} \quad i \neq j \end{cases} \tag{2.7–5}$$

and A_{ij} is a factor dependent on i and j. Since the right-hand side of Eq. (2.7–4) is zero except when $i = j$, it is common practice to express A_{ij} simply as A_i or A_j. If $A_i = 1$ for all i, the system of functions is called an *orthonormal system* and we have the *orthonormality condition*

$$\int_a^b u(x)\phi_i(x)\phi_j(x)\, dx = \delta_{ij} \tag{2.7–6a}$$

It is common practice to absorb $u(x)$ in the orthonormal functions, in which case Eq. (2.7–6a) can be expressed in the form

$$\int_a^b \phi_i(x)\phi_j(x)\, dx = \delta_{ij} \tag{2.7–6b}$$

where $\phi_i(x)$ and $\phi_j(x)$ in Eq. (2.7–6b) represent $\sqrt{u(x)}\, \phi_i(x)$ and $\sqrt{u(x)}\, \phi_j(x)$ from Eq. (2.7–6a). If the formulation shown in Eq. (2.7–6b) is used, care must be exercised to include the square root of the weighting term in each orthonormal function. It should be evident that Eq. (2.7–4) can also be expressed in this simplified form by absorbing $u(x)$ in the orthogonal functions.

If a system of functions $\phi_1^*(x), \phi_2^*(x), \ldots$ is orthogonal in the interval $[a, b]$, an orthonormal system in the same interval may be obtained by means of the relation

$$\phi_i(x) = \sqrt{\frac{u(x)}{A_i}}\, \phi_i^*(x) \tag{2.7–7}$$

where A_i is obtained from Eq. (2.7–4) with $i = j$, that is,

$$A_i = \int_a^b u(x)\phi_i^{*2}(x)\, dx \tag{2.7–8}$$

It is easy to show that the functions $\{\phi_i(x)\}$ are orthonormal since

$$\int_a^b \phi_i(x)\phi_j(x)\, dx = \frac{1}{A_i}\int_a^b u(x)\phi_i^*(x)\phi_j^*(x)\, dx$$

$$= \frac{1}{A_i}(A_i\delta_{ij}) = \delta_{ij}$$

where the last step follows from the fact that the functions $\{\phi_i^*(x)\}$ are orthogonal.

A set of functions $\{f_1(x), f_2(x), \ldots, f_m(x)\}$ is said to be *linearly independent* if no coefficients $c_1, c_2, \ldots, c_m$, which are not all equal to zero, exist such that the relation

$$c_1 f_1(x) + c_2 f_2(x) + \cdots + c_m f_m(x) = 0 \qquad (2.7\text{–}9)$$

holds for all x. The functions of an orthogonal system are linearly independent.

Finally, we call a system of functions *complete* if any piecewise continuous function can be approximated in the mean arbitrarily closely by a linear combination of functions of the system. All the functions discussed below satisfy this condition.

2.7.2 Construction of Multivariate Functions

Suppose that we have a complete system of orthonormal functions of one variable, $\phi_1(x), \phi_2(x), \ldots,$ over the interval $a \leqslant x \leqslant b$. Then a complete system of orthonormal functions of two variables, x_1 and x_2, may be constructed as follows (Courant and Hilbert [1955]):

$$\begin{aligned} \varphi_1(x_1, x_2) &= \phi_1(x_1)\phi_1(x_2) \\ \varphi_2(x_1, x_2) &= \phi_1(x_1)\phi_2(x_2) \\ \varphi_3(x_1, x_2) &= \phi_2(x_1)\phi_1(x_2) \\ \varphi_4(x_1, x_2) &= \phi_2(x_1)\phi_2(x_2) \\ \varphi_5(x_1, x_2) &= \phi_1(x_1)\phi_3(x_2) \\ &\vdots \end{aligned} \qquad (2.7\text{–}10)$$

It is easily shown that the functions $\varphi_1, \varphi_2, \ldots$ are orthonormal over the square region $a \leqslant x_1 \leqslant b$, $a \leqslant x_2 \leqslant b$, that is,

$$\int_a^b \int_a^b u(x_1, x_2)\varphi_i(x_1, x_2)\varphi_j(x_1, x_2)\, dx_1\, dx_2 = \delta_{ij} \qquad (2.7\text{–}11)$$

It is noted that the above construction rule consists simply of taking pairs of functions from the one-variable set and multiplying them together after proper substitution of the variables x_1 and x_2. The order in which the one-variable functions are taken is immaterial, as long as the order of the variables indicated in Eq. (2.7–10) is preserved.

When dealing with multivariate functions, it is convenient to express the orthonormality condition in vector form as follows:

$$\int_{\mathbf{X}} u(\mathbf{x})\varphi_i(\mathbf{x})\varphi_j(\mathbf{x})\, d\mathbf{x} = \delta_{ij} \qquad (2.7\text{–}12)$$

where, for n variables, $u(\mathbf{x}) = u(x_1, x_2, \ldots, x_n)$, $\varphi_i(\mathbf{x}) = \varphi_i(x_1, x_2, \ldots, x_n)$, and $\int_{\mathbf{x}}$ denotes the multiple integral

$$\int_{x_1=a}^{b} \int_{x_2=a}^{b} \cdots \int_{x_n=a}^{b}$$

Extension of the above procedure to the general n-variable case is straightforward. All that is required is to multiply together groups of n functions from the one-variable set after proper substitution of the variables $x_1, x_2, \ldots, x_n$. If the original functions are orthonormal in the interval $a \leqslant x \leqslant b$, the resulting n-variable functions $\varphi_1, \varphi_2, \ldots$ are orthonormal over the hypercube $a \leqslant x_j \leqslant b$, $j = 1, 2, \ldots, n$. For example, the functions of a multivariate set with $n = 4$ are formed as follows:

$$\begin{aligned}
\varphi_1(\mathbf{x}) &= \phi_1(x_1)\phi_1(x_2)\phi_1(x_3)\phi_1(x_4) \\
\varphi_2(\mathbf{x}) &= \phi_1(x_1)\phi_1(x_2)\phi_1(x_3)\phi_2(x_4) \\
\varphi_3(\mathbf{x}) &= \phi_1(x_1)\phi_1(x_2)\phi_2(x_3)\phi_1(x_4) \\
\varphi_4(\mathbf{x}) &= \phi_1(x_1)\phi_1(x_2)\phi_2(x_3)\phi_2(x_4) \\
\varphi_5(\mathbf{x}) &= \phi_1(x_1)\phi_2(x_2)\phi_1(x_3)\phi_1(x_4) \\
&\vdots
\end{aligned} \tag{2.7-13}$$

where, as above, $\varphi_i(\mathbf{x}) = \varphi_i(x_1, x_2, x_3, x_4)$. Some orthonormal sets of functions useful in pattern recognition work are discussed in the next section.

2.7.3 Orthogonal and Orthonormal Systems of Functions

In this section attention is focused on orthogonal and orthonormal polynomial functions. The motivation for using these functions in pattern recognition is twofold. First, they are easy to generate. Second, they satisfy the Weierstrass approximation theorem, which states that any function which is continuous in a closed interval $a \leqslant x \leqslant b$ can be uniformly approximated within any prescribed tolerance over this interval by some polynomial.

Legendre Polynomials

The orthogonal Legendre polynomial functions $P_0(x)$, $P_1(x)$, $P_2(x), \ldots$ can be derived from the following recursive relation:

$$(k + 1)P_{k+1}(x) - (2k + 1)xP_k(x) + kP_{k-1}(x) = 0, \quad k \geqslant 1 \quad (2.7\text{–}14)$$

where $P_0(x) = 1$ and $P_1(x) = x$. These functions are orthogonal in the interval $-1 \leqslant x \leqslant 1$.

The first few Legendre polynomials are

$$P_0(x) = 1, \qquad P_1(x) = x, \qquad P_2(x) = \tfrac{3}{2}x^2 - \tfrac{1}{2}$$

$$P_3(x) = \tfrac{5}{2}x^3 - \tfrac{3}{2}x, \qquad P_4(x) = \tfrac{35}{8}x^4 - \tfrac{15}{4}x^2 + \tfrac{3}{8}$$

where $P_0(x)$ and $P_1(x)$ are given, and $P_2(x)$, $P_3(x)$, and $P_4(x)$ are generated using Eq. (2.7–14).

These functions are orthogonal with respect to the weighting function $u(x) = 1$. To obtain an orthonormal system we use Eq. (2.7–8) as follows:

$$A_k = \int_{-1}^{1} P_k^2(x)\, dx$$

It can be shown after some algebraic manipulations (see Courant and Hilbert [1955]) that

$$A_k = \frac{2}{2k + 1}$$

Therefore, using Eq. (2.7–7) with $\phi_k^*(x) = P_k(x)$, the orthonormal Legendre polynomials are given by

$$\phi_k(x) = \sqrt{\frac{u(x)}{A_k}}\, P_k(x)$$

$$= \sqrt{\frac{2k + 1}{2}}\, P_k(x), \quad k = 0, 1, 2, \ldots \qquad (2.7\text{–}15)$$

Laguerre Polynomials

The Laguerre polynomials may be generated using the recursive relation

$$L_{k+1}(x) - (2k + 1 - x)L_k(x) + k^2L_{k-1}(x) = 0, \quad k \geqslant 1 \qquad (2.7\text{–}16)$$

where $L_0(x) = 1$ and $L_1(x) = -x + 1$. These polynomials are orthogonal in the interval $0 \leqslant x < \infty$ with respect to the weighting function $u(x) = e^{-x}$.

The first few Laguerre polynomials are

$$L_0(x) = 1, \qquad L_1(x) = -x + 1, \qquad L_2(x) = x^2 - 4x + 2$$

$$L_3(x) = -x^3 + 9x^2 - 18x + 6, \qquad L_4(x) = x^4 - 16x^3 + 72x^2 - 96x + 24$$

where $L_0(x)$ and $L_1(x)$ are given, and the others are determined from Eq. (2.7–16).

By using Eq. (2.7–8) to determine A_k, and substituting into Eq. (2.7–7) with $\phi_k^*(x) = L_k(x)$, it can be shown that the orthonormal Laguerre polynomials are given by the relation

$$\phi_k(x) = \frac{\exp(-x/2)\, L_k(x)}{k!}, \quad k = 0, 1, 2, \ldots \tag{2.7–17}$$

Hermite Polynomials

The Hermite polynomials are generated by means of the recursive relation

$$H_{k+1}(x) - 2xH_k(x) + 2kH_{k-1}(x) = 0, \quad k \geqslant 1 \tag{2.7–18}$$

where $H_0(x) = 1$ and $H_1(x) = 2x$. These functions are orthogonal with respect to $u(x) = \exp(-x^2)$, and their interval of orthogonality is $-\infty < x < \infty$, a fact that makes them very useful since it eliminates worry about the range of the variables.

The first few Hermite polynomials are

$$H_0(x) = 1, \qquad H_1(x) = 2x, \qquad H_2(x) = 4x^2 - 2$$

$$H_3(x) = 8x^3 - 12x, \qquad H_4(x) = 16x^4 - 48x^2 + 12$$

where $H_0(x)$ and $H_1(x)$ are given, and the others are determined from Eq. (2.7–18).

By using Eq. (2.7–8) to determine A_k, and substituting into Eq. (2.7–7), it can be shown that the orthonormal Hermite polynomials are given by the relation

$$\phi_k(x) = \frac{\exp(-x^2/2)\, H_k(x)}{\sqrt{2^k k!\, \sqrt{\pi}}}, \quad k = 0, 1, 2, \ldots \tag{2.7–19}$$

Example: The construction of multivariate functions using any of the polynomials discussed above is straightforward. For instance, suppose that we want to construct five Legendre orthogonal functions of three variables. From the discussion in Section 2.7.2 we have

$$\varphi_1(\mathbf{x}) = \phi_1(x_1)\phi_1(x_2)\phi_1(x_3) = 1$$

$$\varphi_2(\mathbf{x}) = \phi_1(x_1)\phi_1(x_2)\phi_2(x_3) = x_3$$

$$\varphi_3(\mathbf{x}) = \phi_1(x_1)\phi_2(x_2)\phi_1(x_3) = x_2$$

$$\varphi_4(\mathbf{x}) = \phi_2(x_1)\phi_1(x_2)\phi_1(x_3) = x_1$$

$$\varphi_5(\mathbf{x}) = \phi_1(x_1)\phi_2(x_2)\phi_2(x_3) = x_2x_3$$

where $\phi_1(x) = P_0(x)$ and $\phi_2(x) = P_1(x)$. Of course, there are an infinite number of other combinations which could have been chosen to construct these five functions. ●

The systems of functions discussed above will often be used as a basis for expanding decision functions as described in Section **2.3**. Given a set of m orthonormal functions $\varphi_1(\mathbf{x}), \varphi_2(\mathbf{x}), \ldots, \varphi_m(\mathbf{x})$, we may express a set of decision functions $d_1(\mathbf{x}), d_2(\mathbf{x}), \ldots, d_M(\mathbf{x})$ as a linear combination of the $\varphi(\mathbf{x})$'s with unknown coefficients, that is,

$$d_i(\mathbf{x}) = \sum_{j=1}^{m} w_{ij}\varphi_j(\mathbf{x}) \qquad (2.7\text{–}20)$$

Each orthonormal function $\varphi_j(\mathbf{x})$ is related to its corresponding orthogonal function $\varphi_j^*(\mathbf{x})$ by a weighting function $u(\mathbf{x})$ and the A_k factors given by Eq. (2.7–7) for the one-variable case. Assume, for example, that the function $\varphi_1(\mathbf{x})$ is formed from one-variable orthonormal functions as follows:

$$\varphi_1(\mathbf{x}) = \phi_1(x_1)\phi_1(x_2)\cdots\phi_1(x_n)$$

Using Eq. (2.7–7), we obtain for $\varphi_1^*(\mathbf{x})$

$$\varphi_1^*(\mathbf{x}) = \sqrt{\frac{A_1}{u(x_1)}}\,\phi_1(x_1)\sqrt{\frac{A_1}{u(x_2)}}\,\phi_1(x_2)\cdots\sqrt{\frac{A_1}{u(x_n)}}\,\phi_1(x_n)$$

$$= \frac{\sqrt{A_1^n}}{\sqrt{u(\mathbf{x})}}\,\varphi_1(\mathbf{x})$$

where $u(\mathbf{x}) = u(x_1)u(x_2)\cdots u(x_n)$. We can see from this equation that the term $1/\sqrt{u(\mathbf{x})}$ will appear in the same form in all functions $\varphi_j^*(\mathbf{x})$. If Eq. (2.7–20) is expressed in terms of orthogonal functions, it is evident from the above discussion that

$$d_i(\mathbf{x}) = \frac{1}{\sqrt{u(\mathbf{x})}} \sum_{j=1}^{m} c_{ij}\varphi_j(\mathbf{x}) \tag{2.7–21}$$

where the A_1's have been absorbed in the coefficients c_{ij}. Since the term $1/\sqrt{u(\mathbf{x})}$ is a positive factor common in all $d_i(x)$, it may be dropped from these decision functions without affecting their basic classification properties. Then

$$d_i(\mathbf{x}) = \sum_{j=1}^{m} c_{ij}\varphi_j(\mathbf{x}) \tag{2.7–22}$$

Comparing Eqs. (2.7–20) and (2.7–22), we see that the only difference between using orthonormal and using orthogonal functions for the expansion of decision functions lies in the coefficients. However, since these coefficients are unknown and must be determined to fit a given problem, it is possible in many cases to use orthogonal and orthonormal functions interchangeably without adverse effects in classification performance. We will use orthogonal functions for numerical problems because they are simpler to compute. The reader should keep in mind that the above considerations apply only to functions used for decision making. The basic difference between these two types of functions must be carefully observed in theoretical developments.

2.8 CONCLUDING REMARKS

The basic purpose of this chapter has been to present the theoretical foundation of decision functions and their application to pattern classification. Within this framework, the essential points necessary for a mathematical and geometrical understanding of these concepts have been developed and illustrated.

Decision functions have played a central role in the development of pattern recognition theory, as will be evident in the following chapters. Their significance lies not only in the fact that they provide a workable and meaningful tool, but also in the fact that they can usually be generated by utilizing representative patterns from each class. This "trainable" property is of considerable importance when we think of pattern recognition as a significant branch of artificial intelligence.

The next four chapters are related in one way or another to the problem of determining decision functions. Although these chapters will in many instances be radically different in the approaches taken, their basic aim is the same—to develop techniques which can be used to generate, from training patterns, functions that can serve as the basis for automatic decision making.

REFERENCES

Early references on linear decision functions are Highleyman [1961], Widrow [1962], and Nilsson [1965]. A fairly comprehensive survey of decision functions is given by Ho and Agrawala [1968]. Additional material on generalized decision functions can be found in Cover [1964], Nilsson [1965], and Specht [1967].

The concept of dichotomies and their use in the definition of dichotomization capacity have been studied by Koford [1962], Brown [1963], and Winder [1962, 1963, 1968]. The material of Section 2.7 is based on the book by Courant and Hilbert [1955].

PROBLEMS

2.1 (a) Give a specific decision function capable of correctly classifying the patterns shown in the following figure.

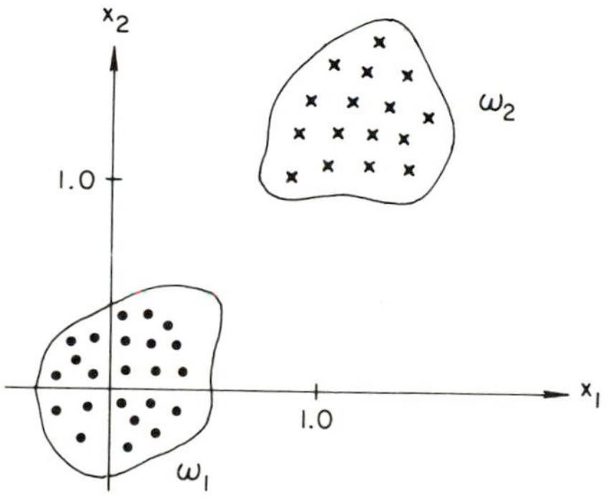

(b) Sketch $d(\mathbf{x})$ versus x_1 and x_2 for $x_1 \geqslant 0$, $x_2 \geqslant 0$.

2.2 Prove that the conditions $d(\mathbf{x}) > 0$ when $\mathbf{x} \in \omega_1$ and $d(\mathbf{x}) < 0$ when $\mathbf{x} \in \omega_2$ follow directly from the conditions $d_1(\mathbf{x}) > d_2(\mathbf{x})$ when $\mathbf{x} \in \omega_1$ and $d_1(\mathbf{x}) < d_2(\mathbf{x})$ when $\mathbf{x} \in \omega_2$.

2.3 Suppose that in a ten-class pattern recognition problem three classes individually satisfy Case 1 and the remaining classes satisfy Case 2 (see Section 2.2). What is the minimum number of decision functions required for this problem?

2.4 The following decision functions are given for a three-class problem:

$$d_1(\mathbf{x}) = -x_1, \qquad d_2(\mathbf{x}) = x_1 + x_2 - 1, \qquad d_3(\mathbf{x}) = x_1 - x_2 - 1$$

(a) Assume that these functions were determined under multiclass Case 1 and sketch the decision boundaries and regions for each pattern class.

(b) Assuming Case 2 conditions and letting $d_{12}(\mathbf{x}) = d_1(\mathbf{x})$, $d_{13}(\mathbf{x}) = d_2(\mathbf{x})$, and $d_{23}(\mathbf{x}) = d_3(\mathbf{x})$ above, sketch the decision boundaries and regions for multiclass Case 2.

(c) Assuming finally that $d_1(\mathbf{x})$, $d_2(\mathbf{x})$, and $d_3(\mathbf{x})$ were determined under Case 3 conditions, sketch the decision boundaries and regions for each class.

2.5 Starting with $d^0(\mathbf{x}) = w_3$, use Eq. (2.3–8) to derive a polynomial decision function of the third degree. Assume that $n = 2$.

2.6 Figure 2.5(c) was derived from four two-dimensional patterns which were assumed to be linearly separable.

(a) Draw a corresponding figure for four one-dimensional patterns which are linearly separable.

(b) How is the figure of part (a) altered if, instead of the condition $d(\mathbf{x}) > 0$ for linear separability, we require $d(\mathbf{x}) > T$, where T is a nonnegative threshold?

2.7 Refer to Fig. 2.7 and identify the two dichotomies which are not linearly implementable.

2.8 Advance an argument which shows that, as long as two pattern classes do not share any common patterns, it is always possible to find a decision surface which will correctly dichotomize the classes, regardless of the way in which the patterns are arranged.

2.9 Given two pattern classes, each containing five three-dimensional, distinct patterns, assume that all patterns are well distributed. It is desired to construct a polynomial decision function which can separate the two classes, *regardless* of the geometrical arrangement of the patterns, as long as they are well distributed. What is the minimum number of coefficients required?

2.10 For a group of five well-distributed patterns in two dimensions, what is the probability that any two-class grouping will be linearly separable?

3

PATTERN CLASSIFICATION BY DISTANCE FUNCTIONS

3.1 INTRODUCTION

In this chapter we begin the study of pattern classifiers by considering one of the simplest and most intuitive approaches to the problem: the concept of pattern classification by distance functions. The motivation for using distance functions as a classification tool follows naturally from the fact that the most obvious way of establishing a measure of similarity between pattern vectors, which we also consider as points in Euclidean space, is by determining their proximity. For example, in Fig. 3.1 we may intuitively arrive at the conclusion that **x** belongs to class ω_i solely on the basis that it is closer to the patterns of this class.

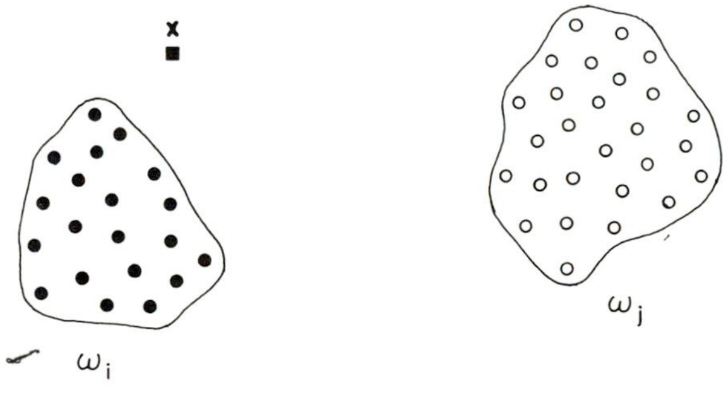

Figure 3.1. Patterns classifiable by proximity concept

The method of pattern classification by distance functions can be expected to yield practical and satisfactory results only when the pattern classes tend to have clustering properties. This can be appreciated by comparing Figs. 3.1 and 3.2. In the first figure we see that there would be little difficulty in classifying $\mathbf{x}$ into ω_i because of its proximity to this class, as mentioned above. In Fig. 3.2, however, although the two pattern populations are perfectly disjoint, one would in general be hard-pressed to arrive at a justification for classifying $\mathbf{x}$ into either class based on a measure of the proximity of this pattern to a class.

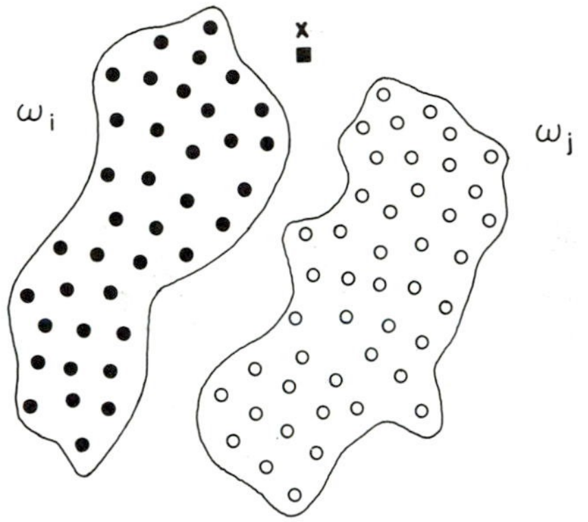

Figure 3.2. Patterns not easily classifiable by proximity concept

The above concepts are generalized and developed in a mathematical framework in the following sections. Since the proximity of an unknown pattern to the patterns of a class will serve as a measure for its classification, the term *minimum-distance pattern classification* will be used to characterize this particular approach. Since clustering properties play an important role in the performance of classifiers based on a distance concept, several cluster-seeking algorithms are also developed in this chapter.

3.2 MINIMUM-DISTANCE PATTERN CLASSIFICATION

Pattern classification by distance functions is one of the earliest concepts in automatic pattern recognition. This simple classification technique is an effective tool for the solution of problems in which the pattern classes exhibit a reasonably limited degree of variability. In this section, the properties and mechanization of minimum-distance classifiers are investigated in detail. We first consider classes which can be characterized by single prototype patterns. The resulting concepts are then extended to the multiprototype case. Finally, the general classification properties of this approach are discussed, and bounds on classification performance are established.

3.2.1 Single Prototypes

In some situations, the patterns of each class tend to cluster tightly about a typical or representative pattern for that class. This occurs in cases where pattern variability and other corruptive influences are well behaved. A typical example is the problem of reading bank checks by machine. The characters in the checks are highly stylized and are usually printed in magnetic ink to facilitate the measurement process. In a situation such as this, the resulting measurement vectors (patterns) of each character class will be almost identical since the same characters in different checks are identical for all practical purposes. Under these conditions, minimum-distance classifiers can constitute a very effective approach to the classification problem.

Consider M pattern classes and assume that these classes are representable by prototype patterns $\mathbf{z}_1, \mathbf{z}_2, \ldots, \mathbf{z}_M$. The Euclidean distance between an arbitrary pattern vector $\mathbf{x}$ and the ith prototype is given by

$$D_i = \|\mathbf{x} - \mathbf{z}_i\| = \sqrt{(\mathbf{x} - \mathbf{z}_i)'(\mathbf{x} - \mathbf{z}_i)} \tag{3.2–1}$$

A minimum-distance classifier computes the distance from a pattern $\mathbf{x}$ of unknown classification to the prototype of each class, and assigns the pattern to the class to which it is closest. In other words, $\mathbf{x}$ is assigned to class ω_i if $D_i < D_j$, for all $j \neq i$. Ties are resolved arbitrarily.

Equation (3.2–1) may be expressed in a more convenient form. Squaring all terms of this equation yields

$$\begin{aligned} D_i^2 = \|\mathbf{x} - \mathbf{z}_i\|^2 &= (\mathbf{x} - \mathbf{z}_i)'(\mathbf{x} - \mathbf{z}_i) \\ &= \mathbf{x}'\mathbf{x} - 2\mathbf{x}'\mathbf{z}_i + \mathbf{z}_i'\mathbf{z}_i \\ &= \mathbf{x}'\mathbf{x} - 2(\mathbf{x}'\mathbf{z}_i - \tfrac{1}{2}\mathbf{z}_i'\mathbf{z}_i) \end{aligned} \tag{3.2–2}$$

Choosing the minimum D_i^2 is equivalent to choosing the minimum D_i since all distances are positive. From Eqs. (3.2–2), however, we see that since the term $\mathbf{x}'\mathbf{x}$ is independent of i in all D_i^2, $i = 1, 2, \ldots, M$, choosing the minimum D_i^2 is equivalent to choosing the maximum $(\mathbf{x}'\mathbf{z}_i - \frac{1}{2}\mathbf{z}_i'\mathbf{z}_i)$. Consequently, we may define the decision functions

$$d_i(\mathbf{x}) = \mathbf{x}'\mathbf{z}_i - \tfrac{1}{2}\mathbf{z}_i'\mathbf{z}_i, \quad i = 1, 2, \ldots, M \tag{3.2–3}$$

where a pattern $\mathbf{x}$ is assigned to class ω_i if $d_i(\mathbf{x}) > d_j(\mathbf{x})$ for all $j \neq i$.

Observe that $d_i(\mathbf{x})$ is a linear decision function; that is, if z_{ij}, $j = 1, 2, \ldots, n$, are the components of $\mathbf{z}_i$, and we let

$$\begin{aligned} w_{ij} &= z_{ij}, \quad j = 1, 2, \ldots, n \\ w_{i,n+1} &= -\tfrac{1}{2}\mathbf{z}_i'\mathbf{z}_i \end{aligned} \tag{3.2–4}$$

and

$$\mathbf{x} = \begin{pmatrix} x_1 \\ x_2 \\ \vdots \\ x_n \\ 1 \end{pmatrix}$$

then we may express Eq. (3.2–3) in the familiar linear form

$$d_i(\mathbf{x}) = \mathbf{w}_i'\mathbf{x}, \quad i = 1, 2, \ldots, M \tag{3.2–5}$$

where $\mathbf{w}_i = (w_{i1}, w_{i2}, \ldots, w_{i,n+1})'$.

The decision boundary of a two-class example in which each class is characterized by a single prototype is shown in Fig. 3.3. It is left as an exercise at the end of this chapter to show that the linear decision surface separating every pair of prototype points $\mathbf{z}_i$ and $\mathbf{z}_j$ is the hyperplane which is the perpendicular bisector of the line segment joining the two points. We see, therefore, that minimum-distance classifiers are a special case of linear classifiers, in which the decision boundaries are constrained to have this property. Since a minimum-distance classifier categorizes a pattern on the basis of the closest match between the pattern and the respective class prototypes, this approach is also known as *correlation* or *cluster matching*.

3.2.2 Multiprototypes

Suppose that instead of being representable by a single prototype pattern each class is characterized by several prototypes, that is, each pattern of class ω_i tends to cluster about one of the prototypes $\mathbf{z}_i^1, \mathbf{z}_i^2, \ldots, \mathbf{z}_i^{N_i}$, where N_i is the number of prototypes in the ith pattern class. Under these conditions we can design a classifier similar to the one discussed in the preceding

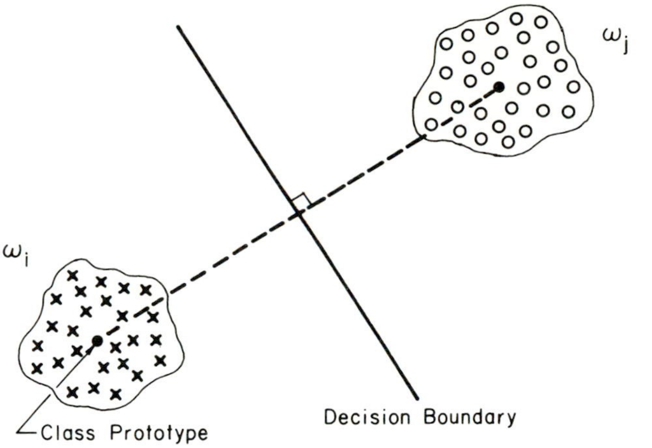

Figure 3.3. Decision boundary of two classes characterized by single prototypes

section. Let the distance function between an arbitrary pattern $\mathbf{x}$ and class ω_i be denoted by

$$D_i = \min_l \|\mathbf{x} - \mathbf{z}_i^l\|, \quad l = 1, 2, \ldots, N_i \tag{3.2-6}$$

that is, D_i is the smallest of the distances between $\mathbf{x}$ and each of the prototypes of ω_i. As before, the distances D_i, $i = 1, 2, \ldots, M$, are computed and the unknown is classified into ω_i if $D_i < D_j$ for all $j \neq i$. Ties are resolved arbitrarily.

Following the development in Section 3.2.1 results in the decision functions

$$d_i(\mathbf{x}) = \max_l \{(\mathbf{x}'\mathbf{z}_i^l) - \tfrac{1}{2}(\mathbf{z}_i^l)'\mathbf{z}_i^l\}, \quad l = 1, 2, \ldots, N_i \tag{3.2-7}$$

where, as before, $\mathbf{x}$ is placed in class ω_i if $d_i(\mathbf{x}) > d_j(\mathbf{x})$, for all $j \neq i$.

The decision boundaries for a two-class case in which each class contains two prototypes are illustrated in Fig. 3.4. Observe that the boundaries between classes ω_i and ω_j are piecewise linear. Since we could have defined this as a single-prototype, four-class problem, the sections of the boundaries are the perpendicular bisectors of the lines joining the prototypes of different classes. This is in agreement with the decision boundaries of single-prototype classifiers, which are a special case of Eqs. (3.2–6) and (3.2–7).

In the same manner that Eq. (3.2–3) was a special case of linear classifiers, Eq. (3.2–7) is a special case of a more general form of *piecewise-linear* classi-

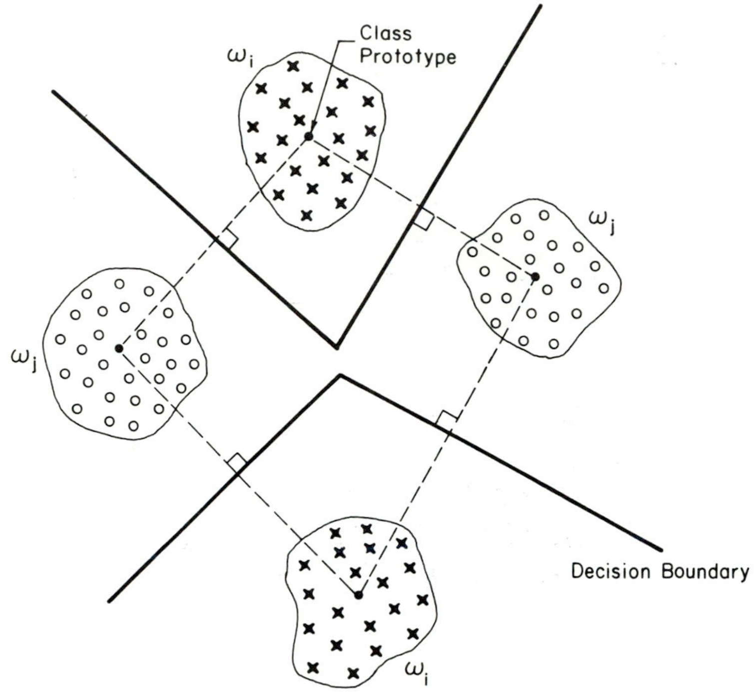

Figure 3.4. Piecewise-linear decision boundaries for two classes, each of which is characterized by two prototypes

fiers. The decision functions of these classifiers are of the following form:

$$d_i(\mathbf{x}) = \max_l \{d_i^l(\mathbf{x})\}, \quad i = 1, 2, \ldots, M; \quad l = 1, 2, \ldots, N_i \tag{3.2–8}$$

where $d_i^l(\mathbf{x})$ is given by

$$\begin{aligned} d_i^l(\mathbf{x}) &= w_{i1}^l x_1 + w_{i2}^l x_2 + \cdots + w_{in}^l x_n + w_{i,n+1}^l \\ &= (\mathbf{w}_i^l)'\mathbf{x} \end{aligned} \tag{3.2–9}$$

Unlike the decision functions of Eq. (3.2–7), these functions are not constrained to be of the form shown in Fig. 3.4.

The reader will recall from Chapter 2 that one of the basic problems in the design of pattern classifiers is the determination of the decision function parameters. As was previously indicated, general iterative algorithms exist which can be used in the calculation of linear decision function parameters; these algorithms will be discussed in Chapters 5 and 6. Unfortunately, no truly general algorithm is yet known for the piecewise-linear case of Eqs. (3.2–8) and (3.2–9). It is noted, however, that the special case of Eq. (3.2–6) or (3.2–7) can be easily implemented if the pattern classes are characterized by a reasonably small number of prototypes.

3.2.3 Extension of Minimum-Distance Classification Concepts

Although the ideas of small numbers of prototypes and familiar Euclidean distances are geometrically attractive, they are not limiting factors in the definition of the minimum-distance classification concept. In order to explore further the general properties of this scheme, let us consider a set of sample patterns of *known* classification $\{\mathbf{s}_1, \mathbf{s}_2, \ldots, \mathbf{s}_N\}$, where it is assumed that each pattern belongs to one of the classes $\omega_1, \omega_2, \ldots, \omega_M$. We may define a *nearest neighbor* (NN) classification rule which assigns a pattern $\mathbf{x}$ of unknown classification to the class of its nearest neighbor, where we say that $\mathbf{s}_i \in \{\mathbf{s}_1, \mathbf{s}_2, \ldots, \mathbf{s}_N\}$ is a nearest neighbor to $\mathbf{x}$ if

$$D(\mathbf{s}_i, \mathbf{x}) = \min_l \{D(\mathbf{s}_l, \mathbf{x})\}, \quad l = 1, 2, \ldots, N \tag{3.2–10}$$

where D is any distance measure definable over the pattern space.

We may call this scheme the 1-NN rule since it employs only the classification of the nearest neighbor to $\mathbf{x}$. There is no reason, however, why we could not define a q-NN rule which consists of determining the q nearest neighbors to $\mathbf{x}$, and using the *majority* of equal classifications in this group as the classification of $\mathbf{x}$. Comparing Eqs. (3.2–10) and (3.2–6), we see that the 1-NN rule is nothing more than the multiprototype case discussed in the preceding section if we choose D to be a Euclidean distance measure.

An interesting comparison between the 1-NN and the q-NN rules may be derived with the aid of Fig. 3.5. Assume that the patterns of both classes shown are equally likely to occur and that the patterns of ω_i and ω_j are uniformly distributed over the disks R_i and R_j shown. Then, for N samples, the probability that exactly α of these samples belong to class ω_i is given by

$$p_i = \frac{1}{2^N} C_\alpha^N \tag{3.2–11}$$

where $C_\alpha^N = N!/\alpha!(N - \alpha)!$ is the number of ways in which the N samples can be divided into two classes containing α samples and $N - \alpha$ samples, respectively, and 2^N gives the total number of ways in which N samples can be divided into two classes. The probability p_j that α of the N samples belong to class ω_j is clearly equal to p_i.

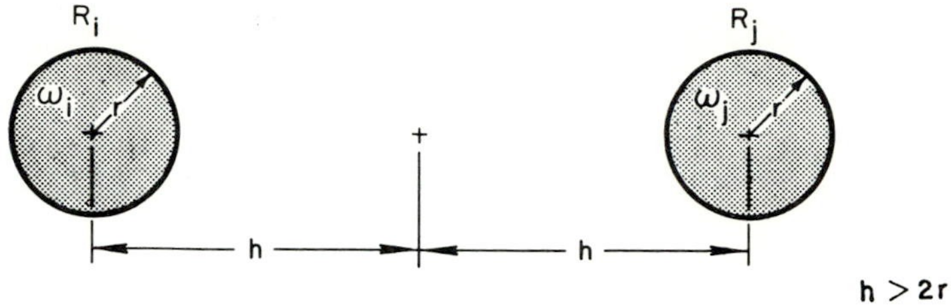

Figure 3.5. Two pattern classes distributed uniformly over identical regions

Suppose that a given unknown pattern $\mathbf{x}$ belongs to ω_i. Then, the 1-NN rule will commit an error only if the nearest neighbor to $\mathbf{x}$ belongs to ω_j and, consequently, lies in R_j. But, if $\mathbf{x}$ comes from ω_i and its nearest neighbor lies in R_j, *all* patterns must lie in R_j, as is evident from the geometry of Fig. 3.5. Thus, the probability of error of the 1-NN rule is in this case equal to the probability that all patterns belong to ω_j, which is obtained by letting $\alpha = N$ in Eq. (3.2–11), that is,

$$p_{e_1} = \frac{1}{2^N} \tag{3.2–12}$$

The probability of error of the q-NN rule may be similarly obtained. This rule assigns an unknown pattern to the class of the majority of its q closest neighbors. Since we are considering two classes, the value of q is assumed to be an odd integer, so that a majority will always result.

Suppose that a pattern $\mathbf{x}$ comes from ω_i and is, therefore, contained in R_i. Then, the q-NN rule will commit a classification error only if there are $(q - 1)/2$ or fewer patterns in R_i. Under this condition it will not be possible to arrive at the majority of more than the $(q - 1)/2$ nearest neighbors from R_i required for correct classification of $\mathbf{x}$ into class ω_i. The probability of this happening, which is in fact the probability of error of the q-NN rule, is obtained by summing the probabilities that there are $0, 1, 2, \ldots, (q - 1)/2$ samples in R_i. Therefore, the probability of error of the q-NN rule is, from Eq. (3.2–11),

$$p_{e_q} = \frac{1}{2^N} \sum_{\alpha=0}^{(q-1)/2} C_\alpha{}^N \tag{3.2–13}$$

Comparing p_{e_1} and p_{e_q}, we see that, in this case, the 1-NN rule has a strictly lower probability of error than any q-NN rule ($q \neq 1$).

From this example we may generalize and say that, given M pattern classes, the 1-NN rule is superior to the q-NN rule ($q \neq 1$) if all the distances between patterns of a class are smaller than any distance between patterns of different classes.

It can also be shown that in the large-sample case ($N \to \infty$), and under some mild conditions, the error probability of the 1-NN rule satisfies the following bounds:

$$p_B \leqslant p_{e_1} \leqslant p_B \left(2 - \frac{M}{M-1} p_B\right) \tag{3.2–14}$$

where p_B is the Bayes probability of error. As will be discussed in the next chapter, the Bayes probability of error is the lowest achievable on an average basis.

We see from expression (3.2–14) that the error probability of the 1-NN rule is at most twice the Bayes probability of error. This equation provides the theoretical lower and upper bounds of this classification rule. The drawback in practice is the fact that to achieve the bounds shown above it is necessary to store a large set of samples of known classification. In addition, the distances from each pattern to be classified to all the stored samples must be computed for classification. This represents a serious computational difficulty for large sample sets.

3.2.4 A Design Example

A widely used application of minimum-distance pattern classification is found in specialized character recognition devices such as the machines which read the code characters on ordinary bank checks, as discussed in Chapter 1. The purpose of this example is to discuss in some detail the principles of operation of these machines and to use these concepts to demonstrate the steps followed in the design of a simple pattern recognition system which utilizes the methods developed thus far.

The basic principle involved in recognizing stylized font characters is feature matching, which was briefly explained in Section 1.5. The matching process may be implemented as a minimum-distance classifier. Because of the high stylization and good quality of the characters, we have in effect a fourteen-class problem in which each class is characterized by a single prototype. The design of the characters guarantees adequate separation between the prototypes. Let the vectors $\mathbf{z}_i$, $i = 1, 2, \ldots, 14$, denote the stored points in the waveform of each of the characters, and the vector $\mathbf{x}$ represent the points in the waveform of an input character to be classified. If we consider only the values of the waveforms at the nine interior vertical lines of the grids shown in Fig. 1.7, each of these patterns will be characterized by a nine-dimensional vector. For a pattern $\mathbf{x}$ of unknown classification, it is a straightforward procedure to assign $\mathbf{x}$ to the class of the prototype to which it is closest. This procedure makes use of the minimum-distance classification concept.

It was shown in Eqs. (3.2–4) and (3.2–5) that the single-prototype problem is expressible in the form of linear decision functions. In practice, this fact is exploited by implementing these decision functions with the simple resistor matrix of Fig. 2.10, thus increasing the classification speed of stylized font readers.

Although most stylized font readers on the market today operate on the principle described above, it will be instructive to consider the same problem and design a simple computerized character recognition system. The purpose of this discussion is not to consider design details and alternatives but, rather, to use a familiar problem in order to illustrate systematically the typical methodology followed in designing a pattern recognition system.

The first consideration in the design is the selection of a measurement device which will convert each character into a quantitative pattern. Although the scheme presented above is perhaps the most efficient measurement method, let us consider the alternative technique shown in Fig. 3.6(a). This method, which is frequently used in more complex machines capable of reading a variety of fonts such as typed characters, works as follows. Each character is illuminated and projected by a system of lenses (only one is shown) onto a photocell matrix. Each photocell or element of the matrix is activated only if sufficient light shines on its surface. If we call an active cell output "0" and a nonactive cell output "1," it is clear that the result of this measurement operation is a binary matrix for each character. This matrix is in effect a binary image of a character which is composed of 0's for the white projected areas and 1's for the black projected areas.

If we choose a photocell matrix identical to the matrix grid arrangement shown for each character in Fig. 1.7, it is clear that each character will be converted into a 9×7 binary matrix. Each matrix may in turn be converted into a 63-dimensional vector by, for example, considering the first

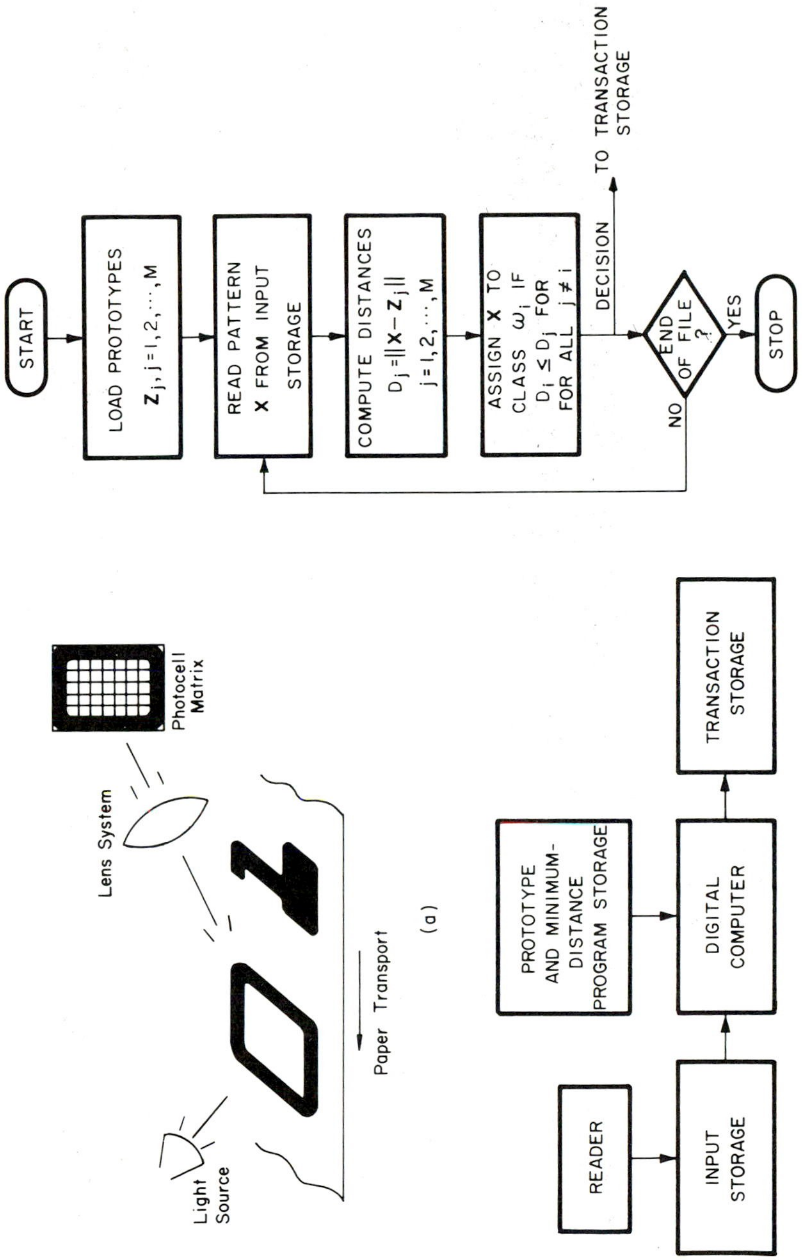

Figure 3.6. Stylized character recognition system. (a) Optical reader. (b) Computer system. (c) Basic software flowchart

row of the matrix as the first seven components of the vector, the second row as the next seven, and so forth. Of course, this is not necessary, but for the sake of notational consistency it will be assumed that all pattern matrices are expressed in vector form.

The next typical step in the design deals with selecting an appropriate set of pattern features. This step may be skipped here since we are dealing with a simple problem in which each class is characterized by a single prototype. Methods of feature selection which are applicable to a large family of more complex problems will be considered in Chapter 7.

Finally, we must consider the design of the pattern classifier itself. In this case this simply involves the development of a mechanism with the ability to compute the distances from a given pattern to all prototypes and to select the smallest of these distances for classification.

A basic computer system implementation of the minimum-distance classifier is shown in Fig. 3.6(b). The character reader, as mentioned above, supplies a pattern vector for each character read. The input storage device shown is simply a buffer. It may consist typically of a magnetic tape or disk unit which is used for storing the result of the reading phase for later processing in the computer. The prototypes and minimum-distance programs are normally stored externally on a disk, magnetic tape, cards, or other convenient medium. A flowchart of the program is shown in Fig. 3.6(c). This program is brought into the machine only when it is desired to use the computer for processing characters. Finally, the results of the recognition phase are stored for future transactions such as billing, account deductions, and interbank accounting.

The system of Fig. 3.6 may be implemented on any reasonably equipped general-purpose computer since the storage and processing requirements are obviously not very demanding. In practice, the procedure normally followed in implementing a character recognition system is to structure the system in the form of special-purpose hardware in order to gain processing speed.

3.3 CLUSTER SEEKING

It is evident from the preceding sections that the ability to determine characteristic prototypes or cluster centers in a given set of data plays a central role in the design of pattern classifiers based on the minimum-distance concept. In this section we consider various cluster-seeking methods in some detail. The methods discussed constitute a cross section of representative approaches to the cluster-seeking problem. It is worth mentioning at the onset, however, that cluster seeking is very much an experiment-oriented "art" in the sense that the performance of a given algorithm is not only dependent on the type of data being analyzed, but is also strongly influenced by the chosen measure of pattern similarity and the method used for identifying clusters in the data. These concepts, which are discussed in the following section, also provide a foundation for unsupervised pattern recognition systems, as discussed in Section 3.4.

3.3.1 Measures of Similarity

The idea of a data cluster has thus far been considered on a rather informal basis. To define a data cluster, it is necessary to first define a measure of similarity which will establish a rule for assigning patterns to the domain of a particular cluster center. In the preceding sections we considered the Euclidean distance between two patterns $\mathbf{x}$ and $\mathbf{z}$:

$$D = ||\mathbf{x} - \mathbf{z}|| \tag{3.3-1}$$

as a measure of their similarity—the smaller the distance, the greater the similarity. All the algorithms developed in this chapter will be based on this concept. There are, however, other meaningful distance measures which are sometimes useful. For example, the *Mahalanobis distance* from $\mathbf{x}$ to $\mathbf{m}$

$$D = (\mathbf{x} - \mathbf{m})'\mathbf{C}^{-1}(\mathbf{x} - \mathbf{m}) \tag{3.3-2}$$

is a useful measure of similarity when statistical properties are being explicitly considered. In Eq. (3.3–2) $\mathbf{C}$ is the covariance matrix of a pattern population, $\mathbf{m}$ is the mean vector, and $\mathbf{x}$ represents a variable pattern. These concepts are discussed in detail in the next chapter.

Measures of similarity need not be restricted to distance measures. For example, the nonmetric similarity function:

$$s(\mathbf{x}, \mathbf{z}) = \frac{\mathbf{x}'\mathbf{z}}{||\mathbf{x}||\,||\mathbf{z}||} \tag{3.3-3}$$

which is the cosine of the angle between the vectors $\mathbf{x}$ and $\mathbf{z}$, is maximum when $\mathbf{x}$ and $\mathbf{z}$ are oriented in the same direction with respect to the origin. This measure of similarity is useful when cluster regions tend to develop along principal axes, as shown in Fig. 3.7. We see in this figure, for example, that pattern $\mathbf{z}_1$ is more similar to $\mathbf{x}$ than pattern $\mathbf{z}_2$ since $s(\mathbf{x}, \mathbf{z}_1)$ is greater than $s(\mathbf{x}, \mathbf{z}_2)$. It should be noted, however, that the use of this similarity

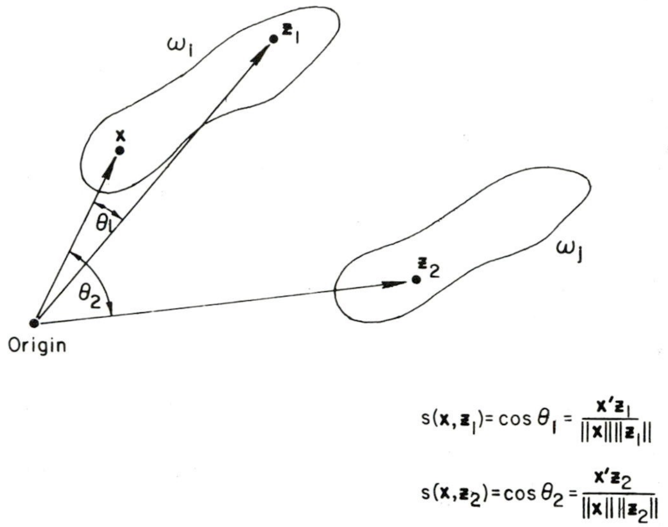

Figure 3.7. Illustration of a similarity measure

measure is governed by certain qualifications, such as sufficient separation of cluster regions with respect to each other as well as with respect to the coordinate system origin.

When the patterns under consideration are binary valued with 0, 1 elements, the similarity function of Eq. (3.3–3) may be given an interesting non-geometrical interpretation. We say that a binary pattern $\mathbf{x}$ possesses the ith attribute if $x_i = 1$. Then the term $\mathbf{x}'\mathbf{z}$ in Eq. (3.3–3) is simply the number of attributes shared by $\mathbf{x}$ and $\mathbf{z}$, while $\|\mathbf{x}\|\,\|\mathbf{z}\| = \sqrt{(\mathbf{x}'\mathbf{x})(\mathbf{z}'\mathbf{z})}$ is the geometric mean of the number of attributes possessed by $\mathbf{x}$ and the number possessed by $\mathbf{z}$. In this case the similarity function $s(\mathbf{x}, \mathbf{z})$ is, therefore, seen to be a measure of common attributes possessed by the binary vectors $\mathbf{x}$ and $\mathbf{z}$.

A binary variation of Eq. (3.3–3) which has received attention in information retrieval, nosology (classification of diseases), and taxonomy (classification of plants and animals) is the so-called *Tanimoto measure,* which is given by

$$s(\mathbf{x}, \mathbf{z}) = \frac{\mathbf{x}'\mathbf{z}}{\mathbf{x}'\mathbf{x} + \mathbf{z}'\mathbf{z} - \mathbf{x}'\mathbf{z}} \tag{3.3–4}$$

It is left as an exercise for the reader to give an interpretation of this measure.

The similarity measures presented in this section are by no means unique; they are simply typical. As was previously mentioned, the following discussion is based on the Euclidean similarity measure given in Eq. (3.3–1) because of its simple interpretation in terms of the familiar concept of proximity. This measure is also consistent with the methods of pattern classification discussed in Section 3.2.

3.3.2 Clustering Criteria

After a measure of pattern similarity has been adopted, we are still faced with the problem of specifying a procedure for partitioning the given data into cluster domains. The clustering criterion used may represent a heuristic scheme, or it may be based on the minimization (or maximization) of a certain performance index.

The heuristic approach is guided by intuition and experience. It consists of specifying a set of rules which exploit the chosen measure of similarity in order to assign patterns to a cluster domain. The Euclidean distance measure of Eq. (3.3–1) readily lends itself to this approach because of its familiar interpretation as a measure of proximity. However, since the proximity of two patterns is a *relative* measure of similarity, it is usually necessary to establish a threshold in order to define degrees of acceptable similarity in the cluster-seeking process. The algorithms discussed in the next two sections illustrate this approach.

The performance-index approach is guided by the development of a procedure which will minimize or maximize the chosen performance index. One of the most often used indices is the sum of the squared errors index, given by

$$J = \sum_{j=1}^{N_c} \sum_{\mathbf{x} \in S_j} \|\mathbf{x} - \mathbf{m}_j\|^2 \qquad (3.3\text{–}5)$$

where N_c is the number of cluster domains, S_j is the set of samples belonging to the jth domain, and

$$\mathbf{m}_j = \frac{1}{N_j} \sum_{\mathbf{x} \in S_j} \mathbf{x} \qquad (3.3\text{–}6)$$

is the sample mean vector of set S_j. In Eq. (3.3–6), N_j represents the number of samples in S_j. The index of Eq. (3.3–5) represents the overall sum of the squared errors between the samples of a cluster domain and their corresponding mean. An algorithm based on this performance index is discussed in Section 3.3.5.

There are, of course, numerous performance indices in addition to the example given above. Other common indices are the average squared distances between samples in a cluster domain, the average squared distances between samples in different cluster domains, indices based on the scatter matrix concept, and minimum- and maximum-variance indices, plus a score of other performance measures which have been used throughout the years.

It is not uncommon to find a cluster-seeking algorithm that represents a combination of the heuristic and performance index approaches. The Isodata algorithm discussed in Section 3.3.6 is such a combination. In view of our earlier comments on the state of the art in cluster seeking, this is not surprising since the performance of a particular cluster-seeking algorithm is dictated largely by the cleverness of its designers in extracting valuable information from the data being analyzed.

3.3.3 A Simple Cluster-Seeking Algorithm

Suppose that we have a set of N sample patterns $\{\mathbf{x}_1, \mathbf{x}_2, \ldots, \mathbf{x}_N\}$. Let the first cluster center $\mathbf{z}_1$ be equal to any of the sample patterns, and select an arbitrary nonnegative threshold T. For convenience, we may choose $\mathbf{z}_1 = \mathbf{x}_1$. Next, we compute the distance D_{21} from $\mathbf{x}_2$ to $\mathbf{z}_1$ (see Eq. (3.2–1)). If this distance exceeds T, a new cluster center, $\mathbf{z}_2 = \mathbf{x}_2$, is started. Otherwise, we assign $\mathbf{x}_2$ to the domain of cluster center $\mathbf{z}_1$. Suppose that $D_{21} > T$ so that $\mathbf{z}_2$ is established. In the next step, the distances D_{31} and D_{32} from $\mathbf{x}_3$ to $\mathbf{z}_1$ and $\mathbf{z}_2$ are computed. If both D_{31} and D_{32} are greater than T, a new cluster center, $\mathbf{z}_3 = \mathbf{x}_3$, is created. Otherwise, we assign $\mathbf{x}_3$ to the domain of the cluster center to which it is closest. In a similar fashion, the distance from each new pattern to *every* established cluster center is computed and thresholded, and a new cluster center is created if all of these distances exceed T. Otherwise, the pattern is assigned to the domain of the cluster center to which it is closest.

The results of the foregoing procedure depend on the first cluster center chosen, the order in which the patterns are considered, the value of T, and, of course, the geometrical properties of the data. These effects are illustrated in Fig. 3.8, where three different cluster center arrangements have been obtained for the same data simply by varying T and the starting point.

Although this algorithm has some obvious limitations, it constitutes a quick, simple way to establish some rough properties of a given set of data. Also, since it requires only one pass through the sample set to establish the cluster domains for a specific value of T, it is computationally attractive. In practice, however, this procedure normally requires extensive experimentation with

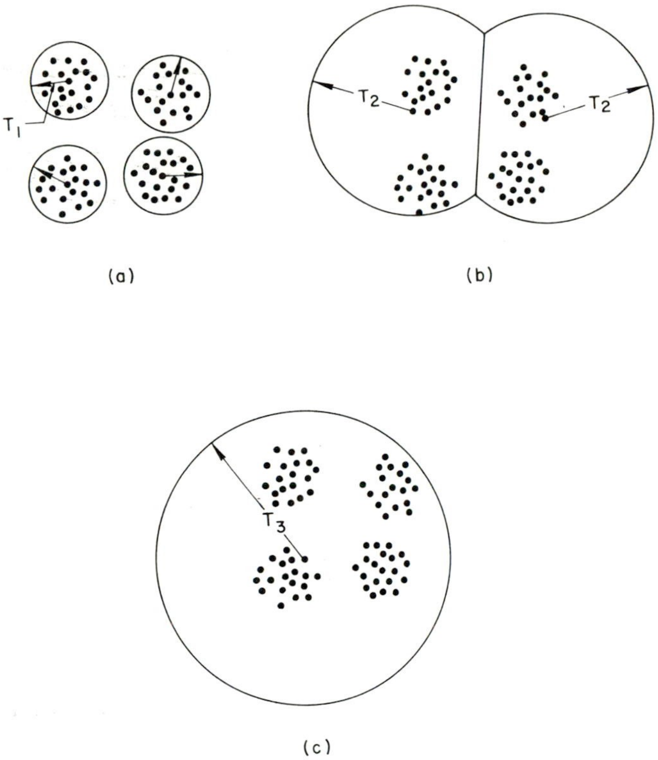

Figure 3.8. Effects of the threshold and starting points in a simple cluster-seeking scheme

various values of the threshold and different starting points in order to gain useful insight into the geometrical distribution of the samples. Since the samples are usually of high dimensionality, which prevents visual interpretation of the results, this information is obtained primarily by comparing the distance between cluster centers and the numbers of samples contained in the resulting domains after each pass through the data. The closest and farthest points in each domain from the cluster center and the variance of these domains are also useful parameters. The information thus obtained in each pass through the data can be used to advantage in selecting the new value of T and the starting point for the next pass. This procedure may be expected to yield useful results in situations where the data exhibit characteristic "pockets" which are reasonably well separated with respect to the chosen values of the threshold.

3.3.4 Maximin-Distance Algorithm

The *maximin* (maximum-minimum)-*distance algorithm* is another simple heuristic procedure based on the Euclidean distance concept. This algorithm is similar in principle to the scheme presented in Section 3.3.3, with the exception that it first identifies the cluster regions which are farthest apart. The procedure is best illustrated by an example.

Consider the ten two-dimensional samples shown in Fig. 3.9(a). It is desired to use the maximin-distance algorithm to obtain an idea of the number of cluster domains present. The explanation of the algorithm is simplified if we consider the tables shown in Fig. 3.9(b). One table contains the samples; the other, a list of cluster center assignments developed during execution of the algorithm. The latter table is initially empty. Then, in the first step, we arbitrarily let $\mathbf{x}_1$ become the first cluster center, designated by $\mathbf{z}_1$ in Fig. 3.9(b). The numbers over the arrows in this figure indicate the steps in which the cluster center assignments took place.

Next, we determine the farthest sample from $\mathbf{x}_1$, which in this case is $\mathbf{x}_6$, and call it cluster center $\mathbf{z}_2$. In the third step we compute the distance from each remaining sample to $\mathbf{z}_1$ and $\mathbf{z}_2$. For every pair of these computations we save the minimum distance. Then, we select the maximum of these minimum distances. If this distance is an appreciable fraction of the distance between cluster centers $\mathbf{z}_1$ and $\mathbf{z}_2$ (say, at least one half of this distance), we call the corresponding sample cluster center $\mathbf{z}_3$. Otherwise the algorithm is terminated. If we use this criterion in the present example, it is easily seen by inspection that sample $\mathbf{x}_7$ becomes cluster center $\mathbf{z}_3$.

In the next step we compute the distance from each of the three established cluster centers to the remaining samples and save the minimum of every group of three distances. Then, we again select the maximum of these minimum distances. If this distance is an appreciable fraction of the "typical" previous maximum distances, the corresponding sample becomes cluster center $\mathbf{z}_4$. Otherwise the algorithm is terminated. A useful measure of the typical previous distances is the average of these distances. If this criterion is used in the present example, and we require that the new maximum distance be at least one half of the average, we see from Fig. 3.9(a) that the new maximum distance, which happens to be the distance between $\mathbf{x}_1$ and $\mathbf{x}_3$, will not satisfy this condition. The algorithm is therefore terminated at this

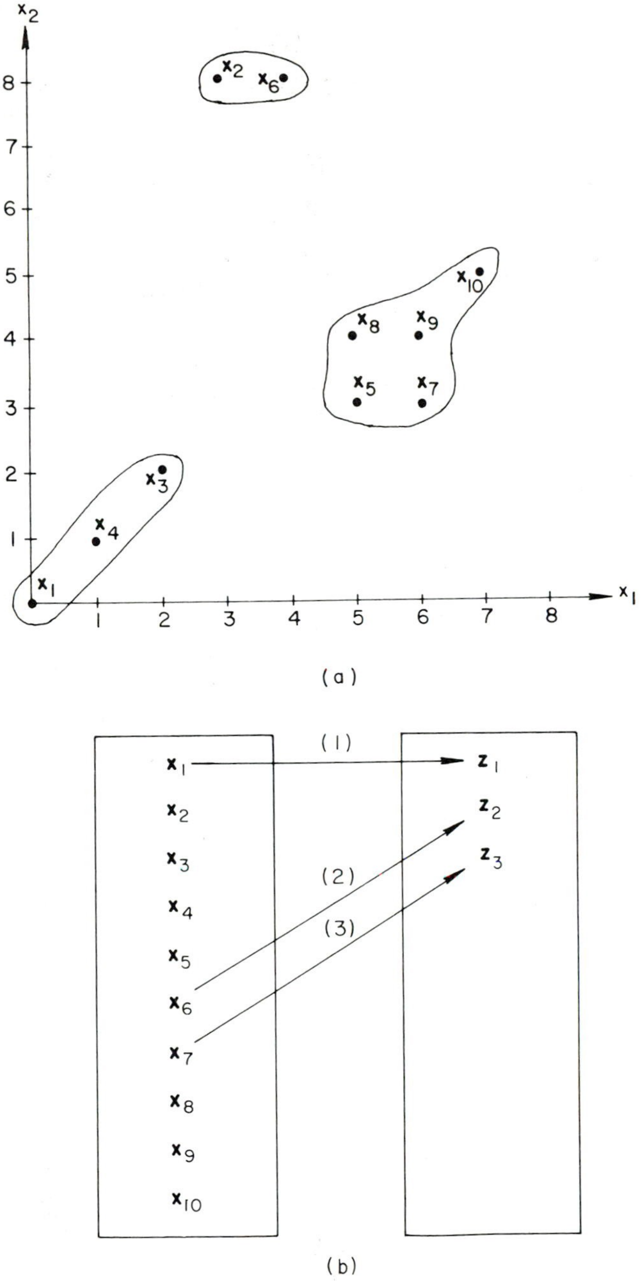

Figure 3.9. (a) Sample patterns used in illustrating the maximin-distance algorithm. (b) Sample and category tables

step. In the general case, the above procedure is repeated until the new maximum distance at a particular step fails to satisfy the condition for the creation of a new cluster center.

In this simple example we have obtained three cluster centers, $\mathbf{x}_1$, $\mathbf{x}_6$, and $\mathbf{x}_7$. To assign the remaining samples to the domain of these centers we simply assign each sample to its nearest cluster center. Thus, from Fig. 3.9(a) we obtain the cluster domains $\{\mathbf{x}_1, \mathbf{x}_3, \mathbf{x}_4\}$, $\{\mathbf{x}_2, \mathbf{x}_6\}$, and $\{\mathbf{x}_5, \mathbf{x}_7, \mathbf{x}_8, \mathbf{x}_9, \mathbf{x}_{10}\}$. These results agree with the cluster domains that we would intuitively expect to get from these data. To obtain a more representative cluster center for each group, we may take the sample mean for each set, using Eq. (3.3–6). These means can then be used as the new cluster centers.

3.3.5 *K*-Means Algorithm

The simple algorithms derived in Sections 3.3.3 and 3.3.4 are basically intuitive procedures. The algorithm presented below, on the other hand, is based on the minimization of a performance index which is defined as the sum of the squared distances from all points in a cluster domain to the cluster center. This procedure, often called the K-means algorithm, consists of the following steps.

Step 1. Choose K initial cluster centers $\mathbf{z}_1(1), \mathbf{z}_2(1), \ldots, \mathbf{z}_K(1)$. These are arbitrary and are usually selected as the first K samples of the given sample set.

Step 2. At the kth iterative step distribute the samples $\{\mathbf{x}\}$ among the K cluster domains, using the relation,

$$\mathbf{x} \in S_j(k) \quad \text{if} \quad \|\mathbf{x} - \mathbf{z}_j(k)\| < \|\mathbf{x} - \mathbf{z}_i(k)\| \tag{3.3–7}$$

for all $i = 1, 2, \ldots, K$, $i \neq j$, where $S_j(k)$ denotes the set of samples whose cluster center is $\mathbf{z}_j(k)$. Ties in expression (3.3–7) are resolved arbitrarily.

Step 3. From the results of Step 2, compute the new cluster centers $\mathbf{z}_j(k+1)$, $j = 1, 2, \ldots, K$, such that the sum of the squared distances from all points in $S_j(k)$ to the new cluster center is minimized. In other words, the new cluster center $\mathbf{z}_j(k+1)$ is computed so that the performance index

$$J_j = \sum_{\mathbf{x} \in S_j(k)} \|\mathbf{x} - \mathbf{z}_j(k+1)\|^2, \quad j = 1, 2, \ldots, K \tag{3.3–8}$$

is minimized. The $\mathbf{z}_j(k+1)$ which minimizes this performance index is simply the sample mean of $S_j(k)$. Therefore, the new cluster center is given by

$$\mathbf{z}_j(k+1) = \frac{1}{N_j} \sum_{\mathbf{x} \in S_j(k)} \mathbf{x}, \quad j = 1, 2, \ldots, K \tag{3.3-9}$$

where N_j is the number of samples in $S_j(k)$. The name "K-means" is obviously derived from the manner in which cluster centers are sequentially updated.

Step 4. If $\mathbf{z}_j(k+1) = \mathbf{z}_j(k)$ for $j = 1, 2, \ldots, K$, the algorithm has converged and the procedure is terminated. Otherwise go to Step 2.

The behavior of the K-means algorithm is influenced by the number of cluster centers specified, the choice of initial cluster centers, the order in which the samples are taken, and, of course, the geometrical properties of the data. Although no general proof of convergence exists for this algorithm, it can be expected to yield acceptable results when the data exhibit characteristic pockets which are relatively far from each other. In most practical cases the application of this algorithm will require experimenting with various values of K as well as different choices of starting configurations.

Example: As a simple numerical illustration of the K-means algorithm, consider the samples shown in Fig. 3.10. Following the above procedure yields:

Step 1. Let $K = 2$ and choose $\mathbf{z}_1(1) = \mathbf{x}_1 = (0, 0)'$, $\mathbf{z}_2(1) = \mathbf{x}_2 = (1, 0)'$.

Step 2. Since $||\mathbf{x}_1 - \mathbf{z}_1(1)|| < ||\mathbf{x}_1 - \mathbf{z}_i(1)||$ and $||\mathbf{x}_3 - \mathbf{z}_1(1)|| < ||\mathbf{x}_3 - \mathbf{z}_i(1)||$, $i = 2$, we have that $S_1(1) = \{\mathbf{x}_1, \mathbf{x}_3\}$. Similarly, the remaining patterns are closer to $\mathbf{z}_2(1)$, so $S_2(1) = \{\mathbf{x}_2, \mathbf{x}_4, \mathbf{x}_5, \ldots, \mathbf{x}_{20}\}$.

Step 3. Update the cluster centers:

$$\begin{aligned}\mathbf{z}_1(2) &= \frac{1}{N_1} \sum_{\mathbf{x} \in S_1(1)} \mathbf{x} \\ &= \tfrac{1}{2}(\mathbf{x}_1 + \mathbf{x}_3) \\ &= \begin{pmatrix} 0.0 \\ 0.5 \end{pmatrix}\end{aligned}$$

$$\mathbf{z}_2(2) = \frac{1}{N_2} \sum_{\mathbf{x} \in S_2(1)} \mathbf{x}$$

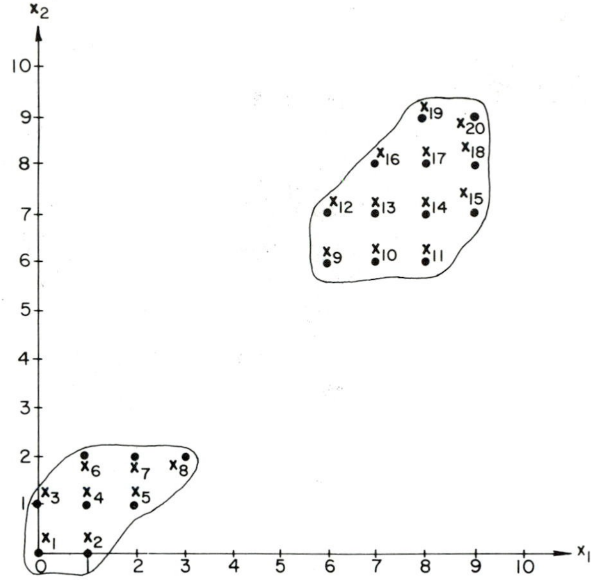

Figure 3.10. Sample patterns used in illustrating the K-means algorithm

$$= \tfrac{1}{18}(\mathbf{x}_2 + \mathbf{x}_4 + \cdots + \mathbf{x}_{20})$$

$$= \begin{pmatrix} 5.67 \\ 5.33 \end{pmatrix}$$

Step 4. Since $\mathbf{z}_j(2) \neq \mathbf{z}_j(1)$, $j = 1, 2$, we return to Step 2.

Step 2. With the new cluster centers we obtain $||\mathbf{x}_l - \mathbf{z}_1(2)|| < ||\mathbf{x}_l - \mathbf{z}_2(2)||$, for $l = 1, 2, \ldots, 8$, and $||\mathbf{x}_l - \mathbf{z}_2(2)|| < ||\mathbf{x}_l - \mathbf{z}_1(2)||$ for $l = 9, 10, \ldots, 20$. Therefore, $S_1(2) = \{\mathbf{x}_1, \mathbf{x}_2, \ldots, \mathbf{x}_8\}$ and $S_2(2) = \{\mathbf{x}_9, \mathbf{x}_{10}, \ldots, \mathbf{x}_{20}\}$.

Step 3. Update the cluster centers:

$$\mathbf{z}_1(3) = \frac{1}{N_1} \sum_{\mathbf{x} \in S_1(2)} \mathbf{x}$$

$$= \tfrac{1}{8}(\mathbf{x}_1 + \mathbf{x}_2 + \cdots + \mathbf{x}_8)$$

$$= \begin{pmatrix} 1.25 \\ 1.13 \end{pmatrix}$$

$$\mathbf{z}_2(3) = \frac{1}{N_2} \sum_{\mathbf{x} \in S_2(2)} \mathbf{x}$$

$$= \tfrac{1}{12}(\mathbf{x}_9 + \mathbf{x}_{10} + \cdots + \mathbf{x}_{20})$$

$$= \begin{pmatrix} 7.67 \\ 7.33 \end{pmatrix}$$

Step 4. Since $\mathbf{z}_j(3) \neq \mathbf{z}_j(2)$ for $j = 1, 2$, we return to Step 2.

Step 2 yields the same results as in the previous iteration: $S_1(4) = S_1(3)$ and $S_2(4) = S_2(3)$.

Step 3 also yields the same results.

Step 4. Since $\mathbf{z}_j(4) = \mathbf{z}_j(3)$ for $j = 1, 2$, the algorithm has converged, yielding these cluster centers:

$$\mathbf{z}_1 = \begin{pmatrix} 1.25 \\ 1.13 \end{pmatrix}, \qquad \mathbf{z}_2 = \begin{pmatrix} 7.67 \\ 7.33 \end{pmatrix}$$

These results agree with what we would expect from inspection of the given data. ●

3.3.6 Isodata Algorithm

The *Isodata*† algorithm presented in this section is similar in principle to the K-means procedure in the sense that cluster centers are iteratively determined sample means. Unlike the latter algorithm, however, Isodata represents a fairly comprehensive set of additional heuristic procedures which have been incorporated into an interactive scheme. The word "heuristic" should be kept clearly in mind as the reader progresses through the following discussion, since many of the steps which will be presented have been incorporated into the algorithm as a result of experience gained through experimentation.

Before executing the algorithm it is necessary to specify a set N_c of initial cluster centers, $\mathbf{z}_1, \mathbf{z}_2, \ldots, \mathbf{z}_{N_c}$. This set, which need not necessarily be equal

† The term "*Isodata*" is derived from *I*terative *S*elf-*O*rganizing *D*ata *A*nalysis *T*echniques *A*, the A being added to make the word pronounceable.

in number to the desired cluster centers, can be formed by selecting samples from the given set of data.

For a set of N samples, $\{\mathbf{x}_1, \mathbf{x}_2, \ldots, \mathbf{x}_N\}$, Isodata consists of the following principal steps.

Step 1. Specify the following process parameters:

K = number of cluster centers desired;

θ_N = a parameter against which the number of samples in a cluster domain is compared;

θ_s = standard deviation parameter;

θ_c = lumping parameter;

L = maximum number of pairs of cluster centers which can be lumped;

I = number of iterations allowed.

Step 2. Distribute the N samples among the present cluster centers, using the relation

$$\mathbf{x} \in S_j \quad \text{if} \quad \|\mathbf{x} - \mathbf{z}_j\| < \|\mathbf{x} - \mathbf{z}_i\|, \quad i = 1, 2, \ldots, N_c; \quad i \neq j$$

for all $\mathbf{x}$ in the sample set. In this notation, S_j represents the subset of samples assigned to cluster center $\mathbf{z}_j$.

Step 3. Discard sample subsets with fewer than θ_N members; that is, if for any j, $N_j < \theta_N$, discard S_j and reduce N_c by 1.

Step 4. Update each cluster center $\mathbf{z}_j$, $j = 1, 2, \ldots, N_c$, by setting it equal to the sample mean of its corresponding set S_j; that is,

$$\mathbf{z}_j = \frac{1}{N_j} \sum_{\mathbf{x} \in S_j} \mathbf{x}, \quad j = 1, 2, \ldots, N_c$$

where N_j is the number of samples in S_j.

Step 5. Compute the average distance $\bar{D}_j$ of samples in cluster domain S_j from their corresponding cluster center, using the relation

$$\bar{D}_j = \frac{1}{N_j} \sum_{\mathbf{x} \in S_j} \|\mathbf{x} - \mathbf{z}_j\|, \quad j = 1, 2, \ldots, N_c$$

Step 6. Compute the overall average distance of the samples from their respective cluster centers, using the relation

$$\bar{D} = \frac{1}{N} \sum_{j=1}^{N_c} N_j \bar{D}_j$$

Step 7. (a) If this is the last iteration, set $\theta_c = 0$ and go to Step 11. (b) If $N_c \leqslant K/2$, go to Step 8. (c) If this is an even-numbered iteration, or if $N_c \geqslant 2K$, go to Step 11; otherwise, continue.

Step 8. Find the standard deviation vector $\boldsymbol{\sigma}_j = (\sigma_{1j}, \sigma_{2j}, \ldots, \sigma_{nj})'$ for each sample subset, using the relation

$$\sigma_{ij} = \sqrt{\frac{1}{N_j} \sum_{\mathbf{x} \in S_j} (x_{ik} - z_{ij})^2}, \quad i = 1, 2, \ldots, n; \quad j = 1, 2, \ldots, N_c$$

where n is the sample dimensionality, x_{ik} is the ith component of the kth sample in S_j, z_{ij} is the ith component of $\mathbf{z}_j$, and N_j is the number of samples in S_j. Each component of $\boldsymbol{\sigma}_j$ represents the standard deviation of the samples in S_j along a principal coordinate axis.

Step 9. Find the maximum component of each $\boldsymbol{\sigma}_j$, $j = 1, 2, \ldots, N_c$, and denote it by $\sigma_{j\,\max}$.

Step 10. If for any $\sigma_{j\,\max}$, $j = 1, 2, \ldots, N_c$, we have $\sigma_{j\,\max} > \theta_s$ *and*

(a) $$\bar{D}_j > \bar{D} \quad \text{and} \quad N_j > 2(\theta_N + 1)$$

or

(b) $$N_c \leqslant K/2$$

then *split* $\mathbf{z}_j$ into two new cluster centers $\mathbf{z}_j^+$ and $\mathbf{z}_j^-$, delete $\mathbf{z}_j$, and increase N_c by 1. Cluster center $\mathbf{z}_j^+$ is formed by adding a given quantity γ_j to the component of $\mathbf{z}_j$ which corresponds to the maximum component of $\boldsymbol{\sigma}_j$; $\mathbf{z}_j^-$ is formed by subtracting γ_j from the same component of $\mathbf{z}_j$. One way of specifying γ_j is to let it be equal to some fraction of $\sigma_{j\,\max}$, that is, $\gamma_j = k\sigma_{j\,\max}$, where $0 < k \leqslant 1$. The basic requirement in choosing γ_j is that it be sufficient to provide a detectable difference in the distance from an arbitrary sample to the two new cluster centers, but not so large as to change the overall cluster domain arrangement appreciably.

If splitting took place in this step, go to Step 2; otherwise continue.

Step 11. Compute the pairwise distances D_{ij} between all cluster centers:

$$D_{ij} = \|\mathbf{z}_i - \mathbf{z}_j\|, \quad i = 1, 2, \ldots, N_c - 1; \quad j = i + 1, \ldots, N_c$$

Step 12. Compare the distances D_{ij} against the parameter θ_c. Arrange the L smallest distances which are less than θ_c in ascending order:

$$[D_{i_1j_1}, D_{i_2j_2}, \ldots, D_{i_Lj_L}]$$

where $D_{i_1j_1} < D_{i_2j_2} < \cdots < D_{i_Lj_L}$ and L is the maximum number of pairs of cluster centers which can be lumped together. The lumping process is discussed in the next step.

Step 13. With each distance $D_{i_lj_l}$ there is associated a pair of cluster centers $\mathbf{z}_{i_l}$ and $\mathbf{z}_{j_l}$. Starting with the smallest of these distances, perform a pairwise lumping operation according to the following rule:

For $l = 1, 2, \ldots, L$, if neither $\mathbf{z}_{i_l}$ nor $\mathbf{z}_{j_l}$ has been used in lumping in this iteration, merge these two cluster centers using the following relation:

$$\mathbf{z}_l^* = \frac{1}{N_{i_l} + N_{j_l}} [N_{i_l}(\mathbf{z}_{i_l}) + N_{j_l}(\mathbf{z}_{j_l})]$$

Delete $\mathbf{z}_{i_l}$ and $\mathbf{z}_{j_l}$ and reduce N_c by 1.

It is noted that only pairwise lumping is allowed and that a lumped cluster center is obtained by weighting each old cluster center by the number of samples in its domain. Experimental evidence indicates that more complex lumping can produce unsatisfactory results. The above procedure makes the lumped cluster centers representative of the true average point of the combined subsets. It is also important to note that, since a cluster center can be lumped only once, this step will not always result in L lumped centers.

Step 14. If this is the last iteration, the algorithm terminates. Otherwise go to Step 1 if any of the process parameters requires changing at the user's discretion, or go to Step 2 if the parameters are to remain the same for the next iteration. An iteration is counted every time the procedure returns to Step 1 or 2.

Example: Although the Isodata algorithm does not lend itself readily to manual calculations, the principles involved in its operation may be demonstrated by considering the simple sample distribution shown in Fig. 3.11.

In this case $N = 8$ and $n = 2$. Suppose that we initially let $N_c = 1$, $\mathbf{z}_1 = (0, 0)'$, and specify the following parameters:

Step 1.

$$K = 2, \qquad \theta_N = 1, \qquad \theta_s = 1, \qquad \theta_c = 4, \qquad L = 0, \qquad I = 4$$

If no *a priori* information on the data being analyzed is available, these parameters are arbitrarily chosen and then adjusted during successive iterations through the algorithm.

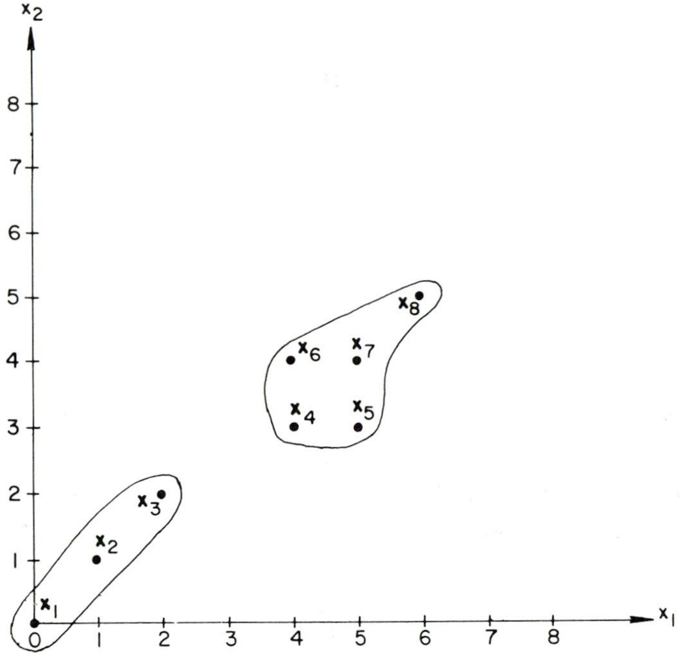

Figure 3.11. Sample patterns used in illustrating the Isodata algorithm

Step 2. Since there is only one cluster center,

$$S_1 = \{\mathbf{x}_1, \mathbf{x}_2, \ldots, \mathbf{x}_8\}$$

and $N_1 = 8$.

Step 3. Since $N_1 > \theta_N$, no subsets are discarded.

Step 4. Update the cluster centers:

$$\mathbf{z}_1 = \frac{1}{N_1} \sum_{\mathbf{x} \in S_1} \mathbf{x} = \begin{pmatrix} 3.38 \\ 2.75 \end{pmatrix}$$

Step 5. Compute $\bar{D}_j$:

$$\bar{D}_1 = \frac{1}{N_1} \sum_{\mathbf{x} \in S_1} \|\mathbf{x} - \mathbf{z}_1\| = 2.26$$

Step 6. Compute $\bar{D}$. In this case,

$$\bar{D} = \bar{D}_1 = 2.26$$

Step 7. Since this is not the last iteration and $N_c = K/2$, go to Step 8.

Step 8. Find the standard deviation vector for S_1:

$$\boldsymbol{\sigma}_1 = \begin{pmatrix} 1.99 \\ 1.56 \end{pmatrix}$$

Step 9. The maximum component of $\boldsymbol{\sigma}_1$ is 1.99; hence, $\sigma_{1\,\max} = 1.99$.

Step 10. Since $\sigma_{1\,\max} > \theta_s$ and $N_c = K/2$, we split $\mathbf{z}_1$ into two new clusters. Following the procedure described in Step 10, suppose that we let $\gamma_j = 0.5\sigma_{j\,\max} \approx 1.0$. Then,

$$\mathbf{z}_1^+ = \begin{pmatrix} 4.38 \\ 2.75 \end{pmatrix}, \qquad \mathbf{z}_1^- = \begin{pmatrix} 2.38 \\ 2.75 \end{pmatrix}$$

For convenience these two cluster centers are renamed $\mathbf{z}_1$ and $\mathbf{z}_2$, respectively. Also, N_c is increased by 1. Go to Step 2.

Step 2. The sample sets are now

$$S_1 = \{\mathbf{x}_4, \mathbf{x}_5, \mathbf{x}_6, \mathbf{x}_7, \mathbf{x}_8\}, \qquad S_2 = \{\mathbf{x}_1, \mathbf{x}_2, \mathbf{x}_3\}$$

and $N_1 = 5$, $N_2 = 3$.

Step 3. Since both N_1 and N_2 are greater than θ_N, no subsets are discarded.

Step 4. Update the cluster centers:

$$\mathbf{z}_1 = \frac{1}{N_1} \sum_{\mathbf{x} \in S_1} \mathbf{x} = \begin{pmatrix} 4.80 \\ 3.80 \end{pmatrix}, \qquad \mathbf{z}_2 = \frac{1}{N_2} \sum_{\mathbf{x} \in S_2} \mathbf{x} = \begin{pmatrix} 1.00 \\ 1.00 \end{pmatrix}$$

Step 5. Compute $\bar{D}_j$, $j = 1, 2$:

$$\bar{D}_1 = \frac{1}{N_1} \sum_{\mathbf{x} \in S_1} \|\mathbf{x} - \mathbf{z}_1\| = 0.80, \qquad \bar{D}_2 = \frac{1}{N_2} \sum_{\mathbf{x} \in S_2} \|\mathbf{x} - \mathbf{z}_2\| = 0.94$$

Step 6. Compute $\bar{D}$:

$$\bar{D} = \frac{1}{N} \sum_{j=1}^{N_c} N_j \bar{D}_j = \frac{1}{8} \sum_{j=1}^{2} N_j \bar{D}_j = 0.85$$

Step 7. Since this is an even-numbered iteration, condition (c) of Step 7 is satisfied. Therefore, go to Step 11.

Step 11. Compute the pairwise distances:

$$D_{12} = ||\mathbf{z}_1 - \mathbf{z}_2|| = 4.72$$

Step 12. Compare D_{12} to θ_c. In this case, $D_{12} > \theta_c$.

Step 13. From the results of Step 12, we see that no lumping of cluster centers can take place.

Step 14. Since this is not the last iteration, we are faced with the decision of whether or not to make an alteration in the parameters. Since, in this simple example, (1) we have obtained the desired number of clusters, (2) their separation is greater than the average spread indicated by the standard deviations, and (3) each cluster subset contains a significant percentage of the total number of samples, we arrive at the conclusion that the cluster centers are representative of the data. Therefore, we return to Step 2.

Steps 2–6 yield the same results as in the previous iteration.

Step 7. None of the conditions in this step is satisfied. Therefore, we proceed to Step 8.

Step 8. Compute the standard deviation of sets $S_1 = \{\mathbf{x}_4, \mathbf{x}_5, \mathbf{x}_6, \mathbf{x}_7, \mathbf{x}_8\}$ and $S_2 = \{\mathbf{x}_1, \mathbf{x}_2, \mathbf{x}_3\}$:

$$\boldsymbol{\sigma}_1 = \begin{pmatrix} 0.75 \\ 0.75 \end{pmatrix}, \qquad \boldsymbol{\sigma}_2 = \begin{pmatrix} 0.82 \\ 0.82 \end{pmatrix}$$

Step 9. In this case $\sigma_{1\,\max} = 0.75$ and $\sigma_{2\,\max} = 0.82$.

Step 10. The conditions for splitting are not satisfied. Therefore, we proceed to Step 11.

Step 11. We obtain the same result as in the previous iteration:

$$D_{12} = ||\mathbf{z}_1 - \mathbf{z}_2|| = 4.72$$

Step 12. We obtain the same result as in the previous iteration.

Step 13. We obtain the same result as in the previous iteration.

Step 14. Nothing new has been added in this iteration, except the computation of the standard deviation vectors. Therefore, we return to Step 2.

Steps 2–6 yield the same results as in the previous iteration.

Step 7. Since this is the last iteration, we set $\theta_c = 0$ and go to Step 11.

Step 11.

$$D_{12} = ||\mathbf{z}_1 - \mathbf{z}_2|| = 4.72$$

as before.

Step 12. We obtain the same result as in the previous iteration.

Step 13. From the results of Step 12, we see that no lumping can take place.

Step 14. Since this is the last iteration, the algorithm is terminated. ●

It should be clear, even from the above simple example, that the application of Isodata to a set of moderately complex data requires, in general, extensive experimentation before one can arrive at meaningful conclusions. However, by properly organizing the information obtained in each iteration, it is possible to gain considerable insight into the structure of the data. This information can be used to guide the adjustment of the process parameters during execution of the algorithm, as will be discussed in the following section.

3.3.7 Evaluation of Clustering Results

The principal difficulty in evaluating the results of clustering algorithms is inability to visualize the geometrical properties of a high-dimensional space. Although the examples presented in the preceding sections were limited to two dimensions in order to illustrate fundamentals, the reader must keep in mind that the dimensionality encountered in most pattern recognition problems is usually much higher. Therefore, to be able to properly interpret the results of a cluster-seeking procedure, we must resort to schemes which will allow at least partial insight into the geometrical properties of the resulting cluster domains. Several interpretation techniques are discussed below.

A very useful interpretation tool is the distance between cluster centers. This information is best presented in a table such as the hypothetical numerical example shown in Table 3.1. Several important pieces of information may be deduced by examining this table. The most obvious is that cluster center $\mathbf{z}_5$ is significantly removed from the other four cluster centers. We see also that the distances between cluster centers $\mathbf{z}_1$ and $\mathbf{z}_2$, as well as $\mathbf{z}_1$ and $\mathbf{z}_4$, are relatively the same in comparison with the close and widely separated cluster centers.

TABLE 3.1. *Example of a Distance Table for Interpreting Clustering Results*

Cluster Centers	$\mathbf{z}_1$	$\mathbf{z}_2$	$\mathbf{z}_3$	$\mathbf{z}_4$	$\mathbf{z}_5$
$\mathbf{z}_1$	0.0	4.8	14.7	2.1	50.6
$\mathbf{z}_2$		0.0	21.1	6.1	48.3
$\mathbf{z}_3$			0.0	15.0	36.7
$\mathbf{z}_4$				0.0	49.3
$\mathbf{z}_5$					0.0

A distance table is, of course, an insufficient basis for arriving at meaningful conclusions. It is customary to list the number of samples in the domain of each cluster center as an aid in interpreting the results of a distance table. For example, we note from Table 3.1 that cluster center $\mathbf{z}_5$ is far removed from the other cluster centers. If it is known that this cluster center is associated with numerous samples, we would accept it as a valid description of the data. However, if only one or two samples are in the domain of $\mathbf{z}_5$, we might dismiss this cluster center after further study as representative of noise samples. It is possible, of course, that a sample which is very distinct from all others represents a significant event. This can be determined only by carefully studying the data under consideration.

Cluster membership information can also be used for merging purposes. If two cluster centers are relatively close, and one of the centers is associated with a much larger number of samples, it is often possible to merge the two cluster domains.

The variances of a cluster domain about its mean can be used to infer the relative distribution of the samples in the domain. This information can also be advantageously displayed in terms of a variance table, such as the hypothetical numerical example shown in Table 3.2, where we have assumed for simplicity

TABLE 3.2. *Example of a Variance Table for Interpreting Clustering Results*

Cluster Domains	Variances			
	σ_1	σ_2	σ_3	σ_4
S_1	1.2	0.9	0.7	1.0
S_2	2.0	1.3	1.5	0.9
S_3	3.7	4.8	7.3	10.4
S_4	0.3	0.8	0.7	1.1
S_5	4.2	5.4	18.3	3.3

that the samples are four-dimensional. As before, the notation S_i is used to indicate the ith cluster domain. It is assumed that each variance component is along the direction of one of the coordinate axes. Several properties of the sample populations may be inferred from this table. For example, since domain S_1 has very similar variances, it can be expected to be roughly spherical in nature. Cluster domain S_5, on the other hand, is significantly elongated about the third coordinate axis. A similar analysis can be carried out for the other domains. This information, coupled with the distance table and sample numbers, can be of significant value in interpreting clustering results.

There are, of course, numerous other quantitative measures of clustering properties. It is also useful, for example, to know the closest and farthest points from the cluster center in each domain. The average distance between cluster centers can be used to augment the information present in a distance table. The covariance matrix of each sample set can also be of value, although it is difficult to interpret in high-dimensionality problems and can add computational difficulties to an iterative algorithm.

When using measures of clustering performance such as the ones discussed above, the information should be presented in such a way that it lends itself to quick interpretation. Since this information is often used to guide the selection of parameters during the course of an iterative algorithm such as Isodata, for example, it is customary to incorporate the calculation and display of a selected set of performance measures in the body of these procedures. It is evident from the nature of cluster-seeking algorithms that they are best implemented in the form of an interactive scheme where the results of each iteration through the data are displayed in such a manner that the user can guide the execution of the algorithm by the selection of its parameters.

3.3.8 Graph-Theoretic Approach

The cluster-seeking algorithms discussed in the preceding sections are derived on the basis of similarity measures making use of a distance measure. These algorithms prove to be useful when the given sample patterns are characterized by numerical values expressed in terms of vectors. The clusters are determined in such a way that the intraset distance among each cluster is kept to a minimum, and the interset distances between two clusters are made as large as possible. This is the basic concept.

An alternative approach to cluster seeking is to make use of some basic notion in graph theory. In this approach, a *pattern graph* is first constructed from the given sample patterns, which form the nodes of the graph. A node j is connected to a node k by an edge, if the patterns corresponding to these two nodes are similar or are related. Pattern $\mathbf{x}_j$ and pattern $\mathbf{x}_k$ are said to be similar if the similarity measure $s(\mathbf{x}_j, \mathbf{x}_k)$ is greater than a prespecified threshold T. The similarity measure may be used to generate a similarity matrix $\mathbf{S}$, whose elements are 0 or 1. The similarity matrix provides a systematic way to construct the pattern graph. Since cliques of a pattern graph form the clusters of the patterns, cluster seeking can be accomplished by detecting the cliques of the pattern graph. Several clique detection algorithms and programs have been introduced in the literature. The reader is referred to papers by Bonner [1964], Jardine and Sibson [1968], Harary [1969], Augustson and Minker [1970], Zahn [1971], and Osteen and Tou [1973]. This graph-theoretic approach can also be applied to cluster seeking for sample patterns which are characterized not by numerical measures, but by relations, thus covering a broad spectrum of clustering problem.

3.4 UNSUPERVISED PATTERN RECOGNITION

Cluster seeking may be viewed as a problem in unsupervised pattern recognition. Suppose that we are given a set of patterns without any information whatsoever as to the number of classes present in the group. The unsupervised learning problem may be stated as that of identifying the classes in the given set of patterns. If we are willing to accept cluster centers as a method of representation, one obvious way of characterizing a given set of data is by cluster identification.

The application of cluster-seeking algorithms to unsupervised learning is, in principle, straightforward. Suppose that we are given a set of patterns $\{\mathbf{x}_1, \mathbf{x}_2, \ldots, \mathbf{x}_N\}$ of unknown classification. These patterns may be submitted to one or more of the algorithms previously discussed in an effort to identify representative cluster centers. The resulting cluster domains may then be interpreted as different pattern classes. Once this has been accomplished, these classes can be used to determine decision functions by means of one or more of the training algorithms to be discussed in Chapters 5 and 6. Alternatively, the cluster centers identified in the unsupervised learning phase may be used as the basis for a minimum-distance classifier.

It is clear from the above comments that the design of an unsupervised pattern recognition system will, in general, require a great deal of intuition and experimentation. This, of course, is in agreement with the problem of identifying clusters in a given set of data of unknown characteristics.

3.5 CONCLUDING REMARKS

The material in this chapter exemplifies the principal concepts underlying the idea of distance-based pattern classifiers. Minimum-distance classifiers are developed starting with single prototypes and are then extended to a scheme which, given enough capability to store a large number of patterns of known classification, can approximate the theoretical optimum performance of a Bayes classifier.

Cluster seeking and prototype determination play central roles in the design of minimum-distance classifiers. The algorithms developed in Section 3.3 are illustrative of how significant clusters may be identified in a given set of data. Two approaches are followed in the development of these algorithms. The first is the heuristic approach, which is based on intuition and experience. The second approach is based on the minimization or maximization of a chosen performance index. This approach is, in general, more elegant and lends itself easily to the development of iterative procedures. Examples of both approaches were given in Section 3.3. All algorithms presented in this chapter are based on a Euclidean distance measure of pattern similarity. This choice is in agreement with the familiar concept of proximity, as well as with the classification approach established in Section 3.2.

The unsupervised learning problem arises when the classification of a given set of sample patterns is not known. The application of cluster-seeking algorithms to unsupervised learning follows naturally from the fact that an obvious approach to the problem of identifying groups of similar patterns in a given set of data is to search for clusters in these data. Once identified, these cluster domains may be considered as pattern classes and used in the design of pattern classifiers by means of the methods presented in this chapter and the following ones.

REFERENCES

Early references on minimum-distance classifiers are the books by Nilsson [1965] and Tou [1969a]. A reference on piecewise-linear classifiers, in addition to Nilsson [1965], is Duda and Fossum [1966]. The extension given in Section 3.2.2 is based on the work of Cover and Hart [1967].

The cluster-seeking problem has been treated in numerous ways by a variety of authors. Additional measures of pattern similarity and clustering criteria can be found in the book by Duda and Hart [1973], which also covers several cluster-seeking algorithms, and in the paper by Rogers and Tanimoto [1960]. The maximin-distance algorithm presented in Section 3.3.4 is based on the algorithm by Batchelor and Wilkins [1969]. The K-means algorithm has been investigated in considerable detail by MacQueen [1967]. The Isodata algorithm presented in Section 3.3.6 is based on the work of Ball and Hall [1965a, 1965b]. An interesting application of the Isodata algorithm to nuclear reactor component surveillance can be found in the paper by Gonzalez, Fry, and Kryter [1974]. Additional references on cluster-seeking algorithms are the books by Patrick [1972] and Fukunaga [1972]. These books are particularly strong in the statistical approach to cluster seeking. An excellent set of procedures for handling binary patterns can be found in the paper by Bonner [1964].

Additional reading on the unsupervised learning problem is available in the books by Duda and Hart and by Fukunaga, as well as in the papers by Spragins [1966], Cooper and Cooper [1964], and Cover [1969].

PROBLEMS

3.1 Show that the decision boundary of a minimum-distance classifier for two pattern classes characterized by the single prototypes $\mathbf{z}_1 = (z_{11}, z_{12}, \ldots, z_{1n})'$ and $\mathbf{z}_2 = (z_{21}, z_{22}, \ldots, z_{2n})'$, respectively, is a hyperplane which is the perpendicular bisector of the line joining $\mathbf{z}_1$ and $\mathbf{z}_2$.

3.2 Consider three disjoint pattern classes in a two-dimensional Euclidean space. Sketch the decision boundaries of a minimum-distance classifier for these three classes.

3.3 Interpret the Tanimoto similarity measure given in Eq. (3.3–4).

3.4 Given a set of samples $S = \{\mathbf{x}_1, \mathbf{x}_2, \ldots, \mathbf{x}_N\}$, show that the cluster center $\mathbf{z}$ which minimizes the sum of the squared distances from every sample in S to $\mathbf{z}$ (see Eq. 3.3–8) is the sample mean

$$\mathbf{z} = \frac{1}{N} \sum_{j=1}^{N} \mathbf{x}_j$$

3.5 Apply the cluster-seeking algorithm given in Section 3.3.3 to the data set $\{(0, 0)', (0, 1)', (5, 4)', (5, 5)', (4, 5)', (1, 0)'\}$.

3.6 Repeat Problem 3.5 using the maximin-distance algorithm.

3.7 Repeat Problem 3.5 using the K-means algorithm.

3.8 Repeat Problem 3.5 using the Isodata algorithm. Start the procedure with one cluster center.

4

PATTERN CLASSIFICATION BY LIKELIHOOD FUNCTIONS

4.1 INTRODUCTION

In this chapter we begin a study of the statistical approach to pattern recognition. As the name implies, this approach takes into account the statistical properties of pattern classes in order to arrive at a classification scheme.

As is true in most fields which deal with measuring and interpreting physical events, statistical considerations become important in pattern recognition because of the randomness under which pattern classes are normally generated. For instance, consider the problem of classifying electrocardiogram signals (ECG's) into two classes: normal and abnormal. The sample patterns for these two classes would be obtained by gathering numerous ECG's which have been labeled by a physician as either normal or abnormal. Clearly, these samples would form a statistical distribution since, for example, there would be great variability or randomness among the ECG's labeled as normal. This randomness would be due to the varied physical characteristics of different patients, the electrical noise present in the measurement devices, and a score of other variables ever present in all biological experiments.

This chapter introduces the reader to the formulation of pattern recognition problems in a statistical framework. By means of statistical considerations it is possible to derive a classification rule which is optimal in the sense that, on an average basis, its use yields the lowest probability of committing classification errors. This statistically optimal classification rule is a generally accepted standard against which the performance of other classification algorithms is often compared.

4.2 PATTERN CLASSIFICATION AS A STATISTICAL DECISION PROBLEM

The decision-making process in pattern recognition may be treated as a statistical game played by the classifier of the pattern recognition system against nature. This process is analogous to a two-person zero-sum game with nature acting as player A and the pattern classifier acting as player B. A zero-sum game is a game in which one player's gain is equal in magnitude to the other player's loss. Among the strategies used are the Bayes strategy, the minimax strategy, and the Neyman-Pearson strategy. The job of the classifier is to find an optimal decision which minimizes the average risk or cost.

A game is characterized by a set of rules having a certain formal structure which governs the behavior of certain individuals or groups called the *players*. A game G in the normal form is a triplet (Y, Z, L), where Y and Z are arbitrary spaces and L is a bounded numerical function defined on the Cartesian product space $Y \times Z$ of pairs (y, z) with $y \in Y$ and $z \in Z$. The elements y and z are called *strategies* for players A and B, respectively, and the function L is referred to as the *pay-off* or *loss function*. The game G is played as follows. Player A chooses $y \in Y$, and player B chooses $z \in Z$. If player A loses, he pays player B the amount $L(y, z)$. If player A wins, he receives the amount $L(y, z)$.

A game

$$G = (Y, Z, L) \tag{4.2–1}$$

is called finite if both Y and Z contain a finite number of elements. If G is a finite game with

$$Y = (y_1, y_2, \ldots, y_M) \tag{4.2–2a}$$

and

$$Z = (z_1, z_2, \ldots, z_N) \tag{4.2–2b}$$

then $Y \times Z$ is the set of pairs

$$Y \times Z = [(y_1, z_1), (y_1, z_2), \ldots, (y_1, z_N), \ldots, (y_M, z_1), (y_M, z_2), (y_M, z_N)] \tag{4.2–3}$$

The M by N matrix $\mathbf{L} = (L_{ij})$ with elements

$$L_{ij} = L(y_i, z_j) \tag{4.2–4}$$

is called the *pay-off* or *loss matrix* of game G. Each element of this matrix specifies the loss associated with a pair of actions by the players; that is, L_{ij} is the loss if player B chooses strategy z_j when player A has chosen strategy y_i. As a matter of convention, a positive loss represents a true loss and a zero or negative loss represents a gain.

In this section we review elementary decision theory as an extension of the theory of two-person zero-sum games. As indicated above, the decision-making process in pattern recognition may be considered as a game against nature. We may imagine that nature is player A and that the classifier is player B. We call the strategies of A the states of nature, which will be denoted by ω_i. The states of nature correspond to pattern classes. The strategies of the classifier are decisions concerning the states of nature. The set Y, therefore, contains the possible pattern classes, while the set Z contains the possible decisions that the classifier can make in a particular game. In the following discussion it will be assumed that the number of decisions is equal to the number of possible classes.

Each time that the game is played, nature selects a strategy ω_i according to the probability $p(\omega_i)$, which is called the *a priori* probability of class ω_i. This is simply the probability of occurrence of class ω_i. The outcome of nature's move is a sample pattern $\mathbf{x}$. In other words, we do not know which class nature has chosen. All the information that we have is a sample $\mathbf{x}$. The job of the classifier is to determine, on the basis of this information, which class $\mathbf{x}$ came from. The classifier's move, therefore, consists of some decision which indicates what class it "thinks" nature has selected.

There are two main differences between an ordinary game and this game which the classifier plays against nature. This type of game is often referred to as a statistical game. First, nature is not an "intelligent opponent" who deliberately tries to pick her strategies to maximize our loss. We may imagine that nature selects strategies based on the probabilities $p(\omega_i)$, $i = 1, 2, \ldots, M$, and sticks to these strategies even though they may not be the best ones in the game theory sense. Second, there is the possibility of "spying" on nature. We may perform experiments in order to gain insight into the techniques used by nature in selecting her strategies. The result of an experiment is a set of patterns which may be used to design the classifier.

Suppose that, in a game between nature and the classifier, nature selects class ω_i and produces a pattern $\mathbf{x}$. The probability that $\mathbf{x}$ comes from ω_i

is written as $p(\omega_i/\mathbf{x})$. If the classifier decides that $\mathbf{x}$ came from ω_j when it actually came from ω_i, it incurs a loss equal to L_{ij}. Since pattern $\mathbf{x}$ may belong to any of the M classes under consideration, the expected loss incurred in assigning observation $\mathbf{x}$ to class ω_j is given by

$$r_j(\mathbf{x}) = \sum_{i=1}^{M} L_{ij} p(\omega_i/\mathbf{x}) \tag{4.2–5}$$

which is often referred to as the *conditional average risk* or *loss* in decision theory terminology.

The classifier has M possible categories to choose from for each pattern given by nature. If it computes the quantities $r_1(\mathbf{x}), r_2(\mathbf{x}), \ldots, r_M(\mathbf{x})$, for each $\mathbf{x}$, and assigns each pattern to the class with the smallest conditional loss, it is clear that the total expected loss with respect to all decisions will also be minimized. The classifier which minimizes the total expected loss is called the *Bayes classifier*. From a statistical point of view, the Bayes classifier represents the optimum measure of performance.

Using Bayes' formula,

$$p(\omega_i/\mathbf{x}) = \frac{p(\omega_i)p(\mathbf{x}/\omega_i)}{p(\mathbf{x})} \tag{4.2–6}$$

we may express Eq. (4.2–5) in the form:

$$r_j(\mathbf{x}) = \frac{1}{p(\mathbf{x})} \sum_{i=1}^{M} L_{ij} p(\mathbf{x}/\omega_i) p(\omega_i) \tag{4.2–7}$$

where $p(\mathbf{x}/\omega_i)$ is called the *likelihood function* of class ω_i. Since $1/p(\mathbf{x})$ is a common factor in the evaluation of $r_j(\mathbf{x})$, $j = 1, 2, \ldots, M$, it may be dropped from Eq. (4.2–7). The expression for the average loss then reduces to

$$r_j(\mathbf{x}) = \sum_{i=1}^{M} L_{ij} p(\mathbf{x}/\omega_i) p(\omega_i) \tag{4.2–8}$$

When $M = 2$, we have that for an observation $\mathbf{x}$, if strategy 1 is chosen, then

$$r_1(\mathbf{x}) = L_{11} p(\mathbf{x}/\omega_1) p(\omega_1) + L_{21} p(\mathbf{x}/\omega_2) p(\omega_2) \tag{4.2–9}$$

and, if strategy 2 is chosen,

$$r_2(\mathbf{x}) = L_{12} p(\mathbf{x}/\omega_1) p(\omega_1) + L_{22} p(\mathbf{x}/\omega_2) p(\omega_2) \tag{4.2–10}$$

As indicated above, the Bayes classifier assigns a pattern $\mathbf{x}$ to the class with the lowest value of r. Thus, $\mathbf{x}$ is assigned to class ω_1 if $r_1(\mathbf{x}) < r_2(\mathbf{x})$; that is, if

$$L_{11}p(\mathbf{x}/\omega_1)p(\omega_1) + L_{21}p(\mathbf{x}/\omega_2)p(\omega_2) < L_{12}p(\mathbf{x}/\omega_1)p(\omega_1) + L_{22}p(\mathbf{x}/\omega_2)p(\omega_2) \tag{4.2–11}$$

or, equivalently, if

$$(L_{21} - L_{22})p(\mathbf{x}/\omega_2)p(\omega_2) < (L_{12} - L_{11})p(\mathbf{x}/\omega_1)p(\omega_1) \tag{4.2–12}$$

It is generally assumed that $L_{ij} > L_{ii}$. Under this assumption, expression (4.2–12) leads to the condition that if

$$\frac{p(\mathbf{x}/\omega_1)}{p(\mathbf{x}/\omega_2)} > \frac{p(\omega_2)}{p(\omega_1)} \frac{(L_{21} - L_{22})}{(L_{12} - L_{11})} \tag{4.2–13}$$

then $\mathbf{x}$ is assigned to ω_1. The left-hand side term in (4.2–13) is often referred to as the *likelihood ratio*:

$$l_{12}(\mathbf{x}) = \frac{p(\mathbf{x}/\omega_1)}{p(\mathbf{x}/\omega_2)} \tag{4.2–14}$$

which is the ratio of two likelihood functions. Hence, the Bayes decision rule for $M = 2$ is as follows:

1. Assign $\mathbf{x}$ to class ω_1 if $l_{12}(\mathbf{x}) > \theta_{12}$.
2. Assign $\mathbf{x}$ to class ω_2 if $l_{12}(\mathbf{x}) < \theta_{12}$.
3. Make an arbitrary decision if $l_{12}(\mathbf{x}) = \theta_{12}$.

Here θ_{12}, often called the threshold value, is given by

$$\theta_{12} = \frac{p(\omega_2)}{p(\omega_1)} \frac{(L_{21} - L_{22})}{(L_{12} - L_{11})} \tag{4.2–15}$$

Example: Consider a simple classification scheme for categorizing the signal from a noisy channel as 0 or 1, as shown in Fig. 4.1. Each input is 0 or 1, and the outcome of the experiment is x, which is contaminated by Gaussian noise with mean zero and variance σ^2. Determine the optimal decision rule.

Let ω_1 be the hypothesis that 0 was sent, and ω_2 be the hypothesis that 1 was sent. We are required to decide upon ω_1 or ω_2 on the basis of an observation of x. Intuitively, the decision rule would be that, for $x < 0.5$, x is a 0 and, for $x > 0.5$, x is a 1. Let us verify whether intuition provides the correct answer.

Let $p(0)$ and $p(1)$ be the *a priori* probabilities that 0 and 1 were sent, respectively. Let the loss matrix be given by

$$\mathbf{L} = \begin{array}{c} \\ \omega_1 \\ \omega_2 \end{array} \begin{array}{c} \begin{array}{cc} a_1 & a_2 \end{array} \\ \begin{pmatrix} 0 & L_{12} \\ L_{21} & 0 \end{pmatrix} \end{array}$$

where a_1 and a_2 are the decisions that 0 and 1 were sent, respectively. Also, L_{12} is the loss incurred in taking action a_2 when the true class is ω_1, and L_{21} is the loss from taking action a_1 when ω_2 is true. It is clear from this

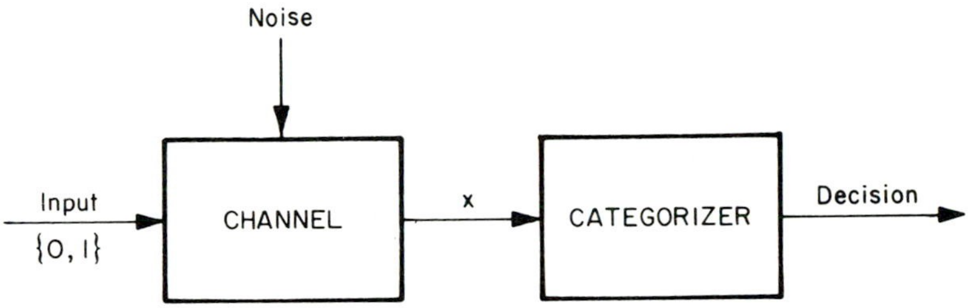

Figure 4.1. A simple classification problem

matrix that correct decisions are assigned zero loss. The Bayes decision rule decides that 0 was sent if $l_{12}(\mathbf{x}) > \theta_{12}$, where $\theta_{12} = L_{21}p(1)/L_{12}p(0)$. Since the noise is of mean zero and variance σ^2, the probability density of the received signal, given that 0 was sent, is

$$p(x/\omega_1) = \frac{1}{\sqrt{2\pi}\,\sigma} \exp\left(-\frac{x^2}{2\sigma^2}\right)$$

and the probability density of the received signal, given that 1 was sent, is

$$p(x/\omega_2) = \frac{1}{\sqrt{2\pi}\,\sigma} \exp\left(-\frac{(x-1)^2}{2\sigma^2}\right)$$

Thus, the likelihood ratio is

$$l_{12}(x) = \exp\left(\frac{1-2x}{2\sigma^2}\right)$$

and we choose class ω_1 if

$$\exp\left(\frac{1-2x}{2\sigma^2}\right) > \theta_{12} \quad \text{or if} \quad x < \tfrac{1}{2} - \sigma^2 \ln \theta_{12}$$

In other words, the Bayes decision rule says that a 0 was sent if

$$x < \tfrac{1}{2} - \sigma^2 \ln \frac{L_{21}p(1)}{L_{12}p(0)}$$

These results agree with intuition only if $\sigma^2 = 0$ or $\theta_{12} = 1$. ●

In the general multiclass case we have that a pattern $\mathbf{x}$ is assigned to class ω_i if $r_i(\mathbf{x}) < r_j(\mathbf{x})$ for $j = 1, 2, \ldots, M$, $j \neq i$; in other words, $\mathbf{x}$ is assigned to class ω_i if

$$\sum_{k=1}^{M} L_{ki}p(\mathbf{x}/\omega_k)p(\omega_k) < \sum_{q=1}^{M} L_{qj}p(\mathbf{x}/\omega_q)p(\omega_q), \quad j = 1, 2, \ldots, M; \quad j \neq i \tag{4.2–16}$$

By using an argument similar to the one used in the two-class case, we could express Eq. (4.2–16) in terms of likelihood ratios and appropriate thresholds.† However, the general multiclass case is best explained by using a specific type of loss function. In most pattern recognition problems, the loss is nil for correct decisions, and it is the same for all erroneous decisions. Under these conditions, the loss function may be expressed as

$$L_{ij} = 1 - \delta_{ij} \tag{4.2–17}$$

where $\delta_{ij} = 1$ when $i = j$ and $\delta_{ij} = 0$ when $i \neq j$. This equation indicates a normalized loss of unity for incorrect classifications and no loss for correct classification of a pattern. Substituting Eq. (4.2–17) into Eq. (4.2–8) yields

$$\begin{aligned} r_j(\mathbf{x}) &= \sum_{i=1}^{M} (1 - \delta_{ij})p(\mathbf{x}/\omega_i)p(\omega_i) \\ &= p(\mathbf{x}) - p(\mathbf{x}/\omega_j)p(\omega_j) \end{aligned} \tag{4.2–18}$$

The Bayes classifier assigns a particular pattern $\mathbf{x}$ to class ω_i if

$$p(\mathbf{x}) - p(\mathbf{x}/\omega_i)p(\omega_i) < p(\mathbf{x}) - p(\mathbf{x}/\omega_j)p(\omega_j) \tag{4.2–19}$$

or

---

† The interested reader can show that the general form of the likelihood ratio is $l_{ij}(\mathbf{x}) = p(\mathbf{x}/\omega_i)/p(\mathbf{x}/\omega_j)$ and that the corresponding threshold for each pair of values (i, j) is $\theta_{ij} = p(\omega_j)(L_{ji} - L_{jj})/p(\omega_i)(L_{ij} - L_{ii})$.

$$p(\mathbf{x}/\omega_i)p(\omega_i) > p(\mathbf{x}/\omega_j)p(\omega_j), \quad j = 1, 2, \ldots, M; \quad j \neq i \qquad (4.2\text{–}20)$$

From the discussion on decision functions given in Chapter 2, it is noted that the Bayes decision rule of Eq. (4.2–20) is really nothing more than the implementation of the decision functions:

$$d_i(\mathbf{x}) = p(\mathbf{x}/\omega_i)p(\omega_i), \quad i = 1, 2, \ldots, M \qquad (4.2\text{–}21)$$

where a pattern $\mathbf{x}$ is assigned to class ω_i if for that pattern $d_i(\mathbf{x}) > d_j(\mathbf{x})$ for all $j \neq i$. This is the multiclass Case 3 discussed in Section 2.2.

An expression that is equivalent to Eq. (4.2–21) but does not require explicit knowledge of $p(\mathbf{x}/\omega_i)$ or $p(\omega_i)$ is obtained upon substitution of Eq. (4.2–6) into Eq. (4.2–21). Performing this substitution yields

$$d_i(\mathbf{x}) = p(\omega_i/\mathbf{x})p(\mathbf{x}), \quad i = 1, 2, \ldots, M \qquad (4.2\text{–}22)$$

However, since $p(\mathbf{x})$ does not depend on i, it may be dropped, yielding the decision functions:

$$d_i(\mathbf{x}) = p(\omega_i/\mathbf{x}) \qquad (4.2\text{–}23)$$

Equations (4.2–21) and (4.2–23) provide two alternative, yet equivalent, approaches to the same problem. Since estimation of the *a priori* probabilities $p(\omega_i)$, $i = 1, 2, \ldots, M$, normally presents no difficulties,† the basic difference between these two formulations lies in the use of $p(\mathbf{x}/\omega_i)$ versus $p(\omega_i/\mathbf{x})$. The rest of this chapter will be focused on the problems of describing and estimating the densities $p(\mathbf{x}/\omega_i)$. Most of Chapter 6 will deal with algorithms for estimating the densities $p(\omega_i/\mathbf{x})$, and the relative advantages and disadvantages of the two approaches will be discussed in that chapter.

The foregoing discussion leads to realization of the recognition scheme shown in Fig. 4.2. This special case of the Bayes classifier, which assigns zero loss to correct classifications and equal loss to incorrect classifications, possesses the property that the optimal decision minimizes the probability of error in classification. Because of this important property, and also because the loss assignments are very meaningful, this special case is a frequently used formulation in pattern recognition. Unless otherwise stated, all further discussions of Bayes classifiers in this book will be implicitly restricted to this case.

The design of a Bayes classifier using Eq. (4.2–21) requires knowledge of the *a priori* probabilities and densities of each class as well as the costs of

---

† In supervised pattern recognition, knowledge about the classes under consideration simplifies the task of assigning a probability of occurrence to each class.

decision. However, when these quantities are not available, it is still possible to reach optimal statistical decisions. When the *a priori* probabilities are not available or cannot be estimated directly, the *minimax criterion* offers an alternative approach to the problem. The basic idea underlying the minimax criterion is to choose a decision rule which will minimize the average loss under the worst possible conditions. In this manner one can be certain of having covered any adverse eventualities which may result from lack of knowledge of the *a priori* probabilities. When neither the *a priori* probabilities nor the loss assignments are known, the *Neyman-Pearson criterion* may be employed.

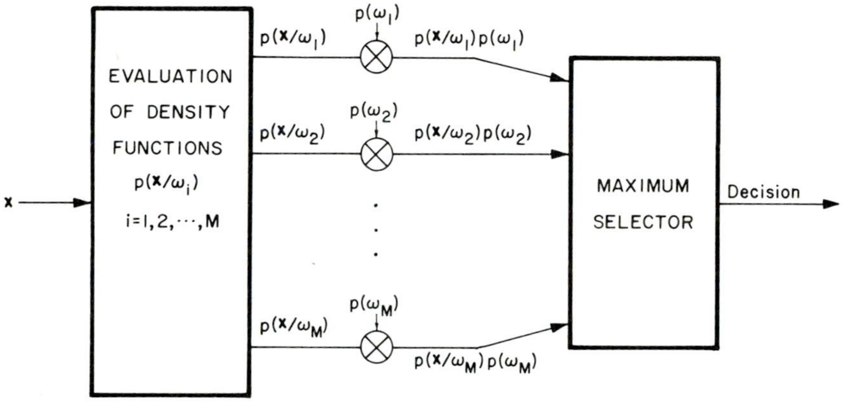

Figure 4.2. A Bayes classifier

Although the three criteria mentioned above are certainly different, derivation of the minimax and Neyman-Pearson decision rules would reveal that the basic likelihood ratio test is the same for all three cases. The only factor that changes with the decision criterion chosen is the form of the threshold. Although both the minimax and Neyman-Pearson criteria have been extensively investigated in many fields, the Bayes criterion has found much wider acceptance in pattern recognition. This is due to the fact that in most pattern recognition problems it is possible to specify the *a priori* probabilities as well as the losses. In the next section a particular form of Bayes classifier is discussed in detail.

4.3 BAYES CLASSIFIER FOR NORMAL PATTERNS

When it is known or it is reasonable to assume that the probability density functions $p(\mathbf{x}/\omega_i)$ are multivariate normal (Gaussian), the Bayes classifier derived in the preceding section results in some interesting and familiar decision functions. Because of its analytical tractability, the multivariate normal density function has received considerable attention. Furthermore, it represents an appropriate model for many important practical applications. By way of introduction, we begin the discussion with the univariate normal density function for a single random variable x:

$$p(x) = \frac{1}{\sqrt{2\pi}\,\sigma} \exp\left[-\frac{1}{2}\left(\frac{x-m}{\sigma}\right)^2\right] \tag{4.3–1}$$

which is completely specified by two parameters, the mean m and the variance σ^2. These two parameters are defined, respectively, by

$$m = E\{x\} = \int_{-\infty}^{\infty} x p(x)\, dx \tag{4.3–2}$$

and

$$\sigma^2 = E\{(x-m)^2\} = \int_{-\infty}^{\infty} (x-m)^2 p(x)\, dx \tag{4.3–3}$$

where $E\{\cdot\}$ denotes the expected value. Since the normal density function is characterized by these two parameters, it is often written as $p(x) \sim N(m, \sigma^2)$ for simplicity. Normally distributed samples tend to cluster about the mean, with a dispersion proportional to the standard deviation σ. About 95% of the samples drawn from a normal population will fall within the range $m - 2\sigma$ to $m + 2\sigma$.

Now, let us consider M pattern classes governed by the multivariate normal density functions

$$p(\mathbf{x}/\omega_i) = \frac{1}{(2\pi)^{n/2}|\mathbf{C}_i|^{1/2}} \exp[-\tfrac{1}{2}(\mathbf{x}-\mathbf{m}_i)'\mathbf{C}_i^{-1}(\mathbf{x}-\mathbf{m}_i)], \qquad i = 1, 2, \ldots, M \tag{4.3–4}$$

where each density is completely specified by its mean vector $\mathbf{m}_i$ and covariance matrix $\mathbf{C}_i$, which are defined as

$$\mathbf{m}_i = E_i\{\mathbf{x}\} \tag{4.3–5}$$

and

$$\mathbf{C}_i = E_i\{(\mathbf{x} - \mathbf{m}_i)(\mathbf{x} - \mathbf{m}_i)'\} \tag{4.3–6}$$

where $E_i\{\cdot\}$ denotes the expectation operator over the patterns of class ω_i. In Eq. (4.3–4), n is the dimensionality of the pattern vectors and $|\mathbf{C}_i|$ indicates the determinant of matrix $\mathbf{C}_i$.

The covariance matrix $\mathbf{C}_i$ is symmetric and positive semidefinite. The diagonal element c_{kk} is the variance of the kth element of the pattern vectors. The off-diagonal element c_{jk} is the covariance of x_j and x_k. When the elements x_j and x_k are statistically independent, $c_{jk} = 0$. The multivariate normal density function reduces to the product of the univariate normal densities, when all the off-diagonal elements of the covariance matrix are zero.

The multivariate normal density function is completely determined by $n + \frac{1}{2}n(n + 1)$ parameters, which consist of the elements of the mean vector and the independent elements of the covariance matrix. Sample patterns taken from a normal population tend to fall in a single cluster with its center determined by the mean vector and its shape defined by the covariance matrix. Equation (4.3–4) points out that the loci of points of constant density are hyperellipsoids with the principal axes in the directions of the eigenvectors of the covariance matrix and the lengths of these axes determined by the eigenvalues.

According to Eq. (4.2–21), the decision function for class ω_i may be chosen as $d_i(\mathbf{x}) = p(\mathbf{x}/\omega_i)p(\omega_i)$. Because of the exponential form of the normal density function, however, it is more convenient to work with the natural logarithm of this decision function. In other words, we may use the form

$$d_i(\mathbf{x}) = \ln [p(\mathbf{x}/\omega_i)p(\omega_i)] = \ln p(\mathbf{x}/\omega_i) + \ln p(\omega_i) \tag{4.3–7}$$

which is totally equivalent to Eq. (4.2–21) in terms of classification performance since the ln is a monotonically increasing function.

Substituting Eq. (4.3–4) into Eq. (4.3–7) yields

$$d_i(\mathbf{x}) = \ln p(\omega_i) - \frac{n}{2} \ln 2\pi - \tfrac{1}{2} \ln |\mathbf{C}_i| - \tfrac{1}{2}[(\mathbf{x} - \mathbf{m}_i)'\mathbf{C}_i^{-1}(\mathbf{x} - \mathbf{m}_i)],$$

$$i = 1, 2, \ldots, M \tag{4.3–8}$$

Since the term $(n/2) \ln 2\pi$ does not depend on i, it can be eliminated from the expression; $d_i(\mathbf{x})$ then becomes

$$d_i(\mathbf{x}) = \ln p(\omega_i) - \tfrac{1}{2} \ln |\mathbf{C}_i| - \tfrac{1}{2}[(\mathbf{x} - \mathbf{m}_i)'\mathbf{C}_i^{-1}(\mathbf{x} - \mathbf{m}_i)], \quad i = 1, 2, \ldots, M \tag{4.3–9}$$

Equations (4.3–8) and (4.3–9) represent the Bayes decision functions for normal patterns. The reader should keep in mind the assumption of zero loss for correct classifications and equal loss for misclassifications which lead to these decision functions.

The decision functions of Eqs. (4.3–8) and (4.3–9) are hyperquadrics since, as can be seen by inspection, no terms higher than the second degree in the components of $\mathbf{x}$ appear in these equations. Clearly, then, the best that a Bayes classifier for normal patterns can do is to place a general second-order decision surface between each pair of pattern classes. If the pattern populations are truly characterized by normal densities, however, no other surfaces will yield better results on an average basis.

If all covariance matrices are equal, $\mathbf{C}_i = \mathbf{C}$, for $i = 1, 2, \ldots, M$, it can easily be shown that by dropping the terms independent of index i, Eq. (4.3–9) becomes

$$d_i(\mathbf{x}) = \ln p(\omega_i) + \mathbf{x}'\mathbf{C}^{-1}\mathbf{m}_i - \tfrac{1}{2}\mathbf{m}_i'\mathbf{C}^{-1}\mathbf{m}_i, \quad i = 1, 2, \ldots, M \tag{4.3–10}$$

which represents a set of linear decision functions.

If in addition $\mathbf{C} = \mathbf{I}$, where $\mathbf{I}$ is the identity matrix, and $p(\omega_i) = 1/M$, $i = 1, 2, \ldots, M$, then

$$d_i(\mathbf{x}) = \mathbf{x}'\mathbf{m}_i - \tfrac{1}{2}\mathbf{m}_i'\mathbf{m}_i, \quad i = 1, 2, \ldots, M \tag{4.3–11}$$

The reader will recognize Eq. (4.3–11) as the decision functions of a minimum-distance pattern classifier for single prototypes, where the prototype of each class is its mean vector. It follows from Eq. (4.3–10) that the decision boundary between classes ω_i and ω_j is given by

$$\begin{aligned} d_i(\mathbf{x}) - d_j(\mathbf{x}) &= \ln p(\omega_i) - \ln p(\omega_j) + \mathbf{x}'\mathbf{C}^{-1}(\mathbf{m}_i - \mathbf{m}_j) \\ &\quad - \tfrac{1}{2}\mathbf{m}_i'\mathbf{C}^{-1}\mathbf{m}_i + \tfrac{1}{2}\mathbf{m}_j'\mathbf{C}^{-1}\mathbf{m}_j = 0 \end{aligned} \tag{4.3–12}$$

From the foregoing discussion it is evident that, when the covariance matrices are equal, the decision surface given by Eq. (4.3–12) is linear in the variables, describing a hyperplane. When the covariance matrices are different, the surface is the sum of linear and quadratic terms, describing a hyperquadratic. It can be shown that linear and quadratic decision functions are theoretically optimal, with different values for the coefficients, for a number of types of probability density functions in addition to normal density functions. Interest in linear and quadratic discriminant functions stems also from considering them as first-order and second-order approximations to arbitrary likelihood ratios, since in many realistic situations they represent a practical approach that can easily be realized in hardware or by computation.

Example: Consider the patterns shown in Fig. 4.3. It will be shown in Section 4.6 that the mean vectors and covariance matrices may be estimated by using the following relations:

$$\mathbf{m}_i = \frac{1}{N_i} \sum_{j=1}^{N_i} \mathbf{x}_{ij}$$

and

$$\mathbf{C}_i = \frac{1}{N_i} \sum_{j=1}^{N_i} \mathbf{x}_{ij}\mathbf{x}_{ij}' - \mathbf{m}_i\mathbf{m}_i'$$

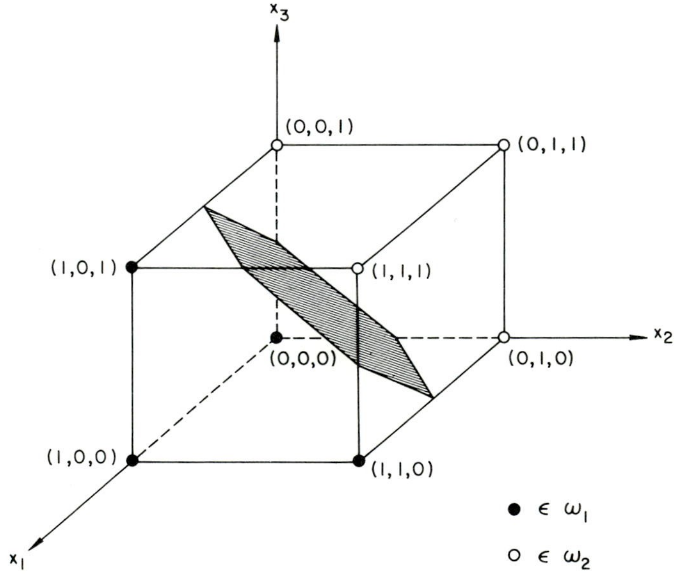

Figure 4.3. Patterns of the illustrative example and their Bayes decision boundary

where N_i denotes the number of patterns in class ω_i, and $\mathbf{x}_{ij}$ represents the jth pattern in the ith class.

Applying these equations to the patterns of Fig. 4.3 yields

$$\mathbf{m}_1 = \frac{1}{4}\begin{pmatrix} 3 \\ 1 \\ 1 \end{pmatrix}, \qquad \mathbf{m}_2 = \frac{1}{4}\begin{pmatrix} 1 \\ 3 \\ 3 \end{pmatrix}$$

$$\mathbf{C}_1 = \mathbf{C}_2 = \frac{1}{16}\begin{pmatrix} 3 & 1 & 1 \\ 1 & 3 & -1 \\ 1 & -1 & 3 \end{pmatrix}$$

Since the covariance matrices are equal in this case, the Bayes decision functions for this example are given by Eq. (4.3–10). If we assume that $p(\omega_1) = p(\omega_2) = \frac{1}{2}$, the $\ln p(\omega_i)$ term may be dropped, yielding

$$d_i(\mathbf{x}) = \mathbf{x}'\mathbf{C}^{-1}\mathbf{m}_i - \tfrac{1}{2}\mathbf{m}_i'\mathbf{C}^{-1}\mathbf{m}_i$$

where

$$\mathbf{C}^{-1} = \begin{pmatrix} 8 & -4 & -4 \\ -4 & 8 & 4 \\ -4 & 4 & 8 \end{pmatrix}$$

Carrying out the expansion yields

$$d_1(\mathbf{x}) = 4x_1 - \tfrac{3}{2}$$

and

$$d_2(\mathbf{x}) = -4x_1 + 8x_2 + 8x_3 - \tfrac{11}{2}$$

The decision surface is given by the equation

$$d_1(\mathbf{x}) - d_2(\mathbf{x}) = 8x_1 - 8x_2 - 8x_3 + 4 = 0$$

A section of this surface is shown in Fig. 4.3. Note that it effectively dichotomizes the two classes.

It should be pointed out that, although things worked out very well in this example, the Bayes classification rule is a statistical concept and, consequently, should not in general be expected to yield optimal results for small sample sets. ●

4.4 ERROR PROBABILITIES

Having discussed the Bayes classifier for normal patterns, we will now study the probability of error associated with this classification scheme. Consider two pattern classes, ω_i and ω_j, for which the pattern vectors are characterized by multivariate normal density functions

$$p(\mathbf{x}/\omega_i) = \frac{1}{(2\pi)^{n/2}|\mathbf{C}|^{1/2}} \exp[-\tfrac{1}{2}(\mathbf{x} - \mathbf{m}_i)'\mathbf{C}^{-1}(\mathbf{x} - \mathbf{m}_i)] \qquad (4.4\text{–}1)$$

and

$$p(\mathbf{x}/\omega_j) = \frac{1}{(2\pi)^{n/2}|\mathbf{C}|^{1/2}} \exp[-\tfrac{1}{2}(\mathbf{x} - \mathbf{m}_j)'\mathbf{C}^{-1}(\mathbf{x} - \mathbf{m}_j)] \qquad (4.4\text{–}2)$$

with equal covariance matrices. In view of the exponential form of the density functions, we can simplify the analysis by taking the logarithm of the likelihood ratio. Let

$$u_{ij} = \ln l_{ij}(\mathbf{x}) = \ln p(\mathbf{x}/\omega_i) - \ln p(\mathbf{x}/\omega_j) \qquad (4.4\text{–}3)$$

Then it follows from Eqs. (4.4–1) and (4.4–2) that

$$u_{ij}(\mathbf{x}) = \mathbf{x}'\mathbf{C}^{-1}(\mathbf{m}_i - \mathbf{m}_j) - \tfrac{1}{2}(\mathbf{m}_i + \mathbf{m}_j)'\mathbf{C}^{-1}(\mathbf{m}_i - \mathbf{m}_j) \qquad (4.4\text{–}4)$$

When a zero-one loss function is chosen, the condition for a pattern $\mathbf{x}$ to belong to class ω_i in the sense of minimum probability of misclassification is

$$u_{ij}(\mathbf{x}) > \alpha \qquad (4.4\text{–}5)$$

where α is the logarithm of the threshold

$$\theta = \frac{p(\omega_j)}{p(\omega_i)} \qquad (4.4\text{–}6)$$

The probability of misclassifying a pattern when it comes from class ω_j is $p(u_{ij} > \alpha/\omega_j)$, and the probability of misclassifying a pattern when it comes from class ω_i is $p(u_{ij} < \alpha/\omega_i)$.

Since $u_{ij}(\mathbf{x})$ is a linear combination of the components of $\mathbf{x}$ which is normally distributed, u_{ij} is also characterized by a normal distribution. Thus, from Eq. (4.4–4) the expected value of u_{ij} with respect to class ω_i is

$$E_i\{u_{ij}\} = \mathbf{m}_i'\mathbf{C}^{-1}(\mathbf{m}_i - \mathbf{m}_j) - \tfrac{1}{2}(\mathbf{m}_i + \mathbf{m}_j)'\mathbf{C}^{-1}(\mathbf{m}_i - \mathbf{m}_j) \qquad (4.4\text{–}7)$$

which may be reduced to

$$E_i\{u_{ij}\} = \bar{u}_{ij} = \tfrac{1}{2}r_{ij} \tag{4.4–8}$$

where

$$r_{ij} = (\mathbf{m}_i - \mathbf{m}_j)'\mathbf{C}^{-1}(\mathbf{m}_i - \mathbf{m}_j) \tag{4.4–9}$$

This expression is often referred to as the *Mahalanobis distance* between two densities $p(\mathbf{x}/\omega_i)$ and $p(\mathbf{x}/\omega_j)$. If $\mathbf{C}$ is the identity matrix, r_{ij} represents the squared distance between the means of $p(\mathbf{x}/\omega_i)$ and $p(\mathbf{x}/\omega_j)$.

Since the variance of u_{ij} is defined by

$$\text{Var}_i\{u_{ij}\} = E_i\{(u_{ij} - \bar{u}_{ij})^2\} \tag{4.4–10}$$

it follows from Eqs. (4.4–4) and (4.4–8) that

$$\text{Var}_i\{u_{ij}\} = E_i\{(\mathbf{m}_i - \mathbf{m}_j)'\mathbf{C}^{-1}(\mathbf{x} - \mathbf{m}_i)(\mathbf{x} - \mathbf{m}_i)'\mathbf{C}^{-1}(\mathbf{m}_i - \mathbf{m}_j)\} \tag{4.4–11}$$

which may be simplified to

$$\text{Var}_i\{u_{ij}\} = r_{ij} \tag{4.4–12}$$

Thus, for $\mathbf{x} \in \omega_i$, u_{ij} is distributed according to $N(\frac{1}{2}r_{ij}, r_{ij})$. Similarly, for $\mathbf{x} \in \omega_j$, we have that the corresponding u_{ij} is distributed according to $N(-\frac{1}{2}r_{ij}, r_{ij})$. Therefore,

$$\begin{aligned} p(u_{ij} > \alpha/\omega_j) &= \int_{\alpha}^{\infty} \frac{1}{\sqrt{2\pi r_{ij}}} \exp\left[-\frac{(u_{ij} + \frac{1}{2}r_{ij})^2}{2r_{ij}}\right] du_{ij} \\ &= 1 - \Phi\left(\frac{\alpha + \frac{1}{2}r_{ij}}{\sqrt{r_{ij}}}\right) \end{aligned} \tag{4.4–13}$$

and

$$\begin{aligned} p(u_{ij} < \alpha/\omega_i) &= \int_{-\infty}^{\alpha} \frac{1}{\sqrt{2\pi r_{ij}}} \exp\left[-\frac{(u_{ij} - \frac{1}{2}r_{ij})^2}{2r_{ij}}\right] du_{ij} \\ &= \Phi\left(\frac{\alpha - \frac{1}{2}r_{ij}}{\sqrt{r_{ij}}}\right) \end{aligned} \tag{4.4–14}$$

where Φ is defined as

$$\Phi(\zeta) = \int_{-\infty}^{\zeta} \frac{1}{\sqrt{2\pi}} \exp(-y^2/2)\, dy \tag{4.4–15}$$

The probability of error is given by

$$p(e) = p(\omega_i)p(u_{ij} < \alpha/\omega_i) + p(\omega_j)p(u_{ij} > \alpha/\omega_j) \tag{4.4–16}$$

Making use of Eqs. (4.4–13) and (4.4–14), we obtain

$$p(e) = p(\omega_i)\Phi\left(\frac{\alpha - \frac{1}{2}r_{ij}}{\sqrt{r_{ij}}}\right) + p(\omega_j)\left[1 - \Phi\left(\frac{\alpha + \frac{1}{2}r_{ij}}{\sqrt{r_{ij}}}\right)\right] \tag{4.4–17}$$

When the *a priori* probabilities are equal,

$$p(\omega_i) = p(\omega_j)$$

θ is unity, and $\alpha = 0$. The probability of error is then

$$p(e) = \tfrac{1}{2}\Phi(-\tfrac{1}{2}\sqrt{r_{ij}}) + \tfrac{1}{2}[1 - \Phi(\tfrac{1}{2}\sqrt{r_{ij}})] \tag{4.4–18}$$

$$= \frac{1}{2}\int_{(1/2)\sqrt{r_{ij}}}^{\infty} \frac{1}{\sqrt{2\pi}}\exp(-y^2/2)\,dy + \frac{1}{2}\left(1 - \int_{-\infty}^{(1/2)\sqrt{r_{ij}}} \frac{1}{\sqrt{2\pi}}\exp(-y^2/2)\right)dy$$

$$= \int_{(1/2)\sqrt{r_{ij}}}^{\infty} \frac{1}{\sqrt{2\pi}}\exp(-y^2/2)\,dy \tag{4.4–19}$$

Thus, the function that relates the Mahalanobis distance to the error probability is the univariate normal density with zero mean and unit variance. The relationship between $p(e)$ and r_{ij} is plotted in Fig. 4.4. It is observed that $p(e)$ is a monotonically decreasing function of r_{ij}. The error probability is less than 5% when $r_{ij} = 11$.

The above analysis may be extended to evaluate the error probability associated with the linear decision functions discussed in Chapter 2, when the patterns in each of the two classes are normally distributed. The linear classifier assigns an unknown pattern $\mathbf{x}$ to class ω_i if $\mathbf{w}'\mathbf{x} > \theta$, and to class ω_j otherwise. Since pattern $\mathbf{x}$ comes from a multivariate normal population and $\mathbf{w}'\mathbf{x}$ is a linear function of $\mathbf{x}$, $\mathbf{w}'\mathbf{x}$ is characterized by a univariate normal probability density, with mean and variance determined as follows.

The mean of $\mathbf{w}'\mathbf{x}$ is given by

$$E\{\mathbf{w}'\mathbf{x}\} = \mathbf{w}'E\{\mathbf{x}\} \tag{4.4–20}$$

The variance for $\mathbf{w}'\mathbf{x}$ is, by definition,

$$\sigma^2 = E(\mathbf{w}'\mathbf{x} - \mathbf{w}'E\{\mathbf{x}\})^2 \tag{4.4–21}$$

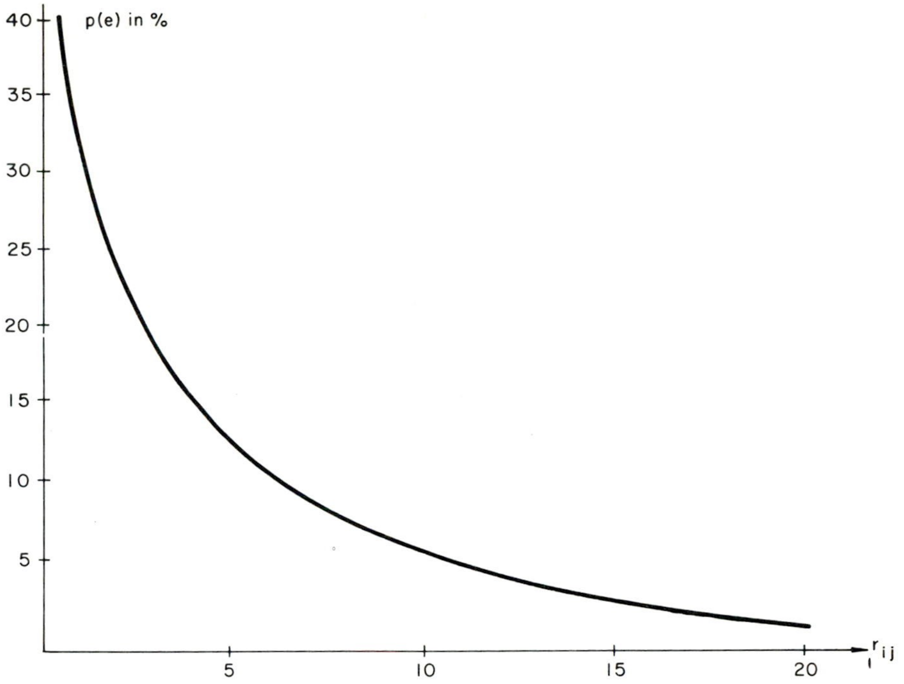

Figure 4.4. Probability of error versus the Mahalanobis distance

which may be written as

$$\sigma^2 = E\{\mathbf{w}'(\mathbf{x} - E\{\mathbf{x}\})(\mathbf{x} - E\{\mathbf{x}\})'\mathbf{w}\}$$

$$= \mathbf{w}'\mathbf{C}\mathbf{w} \tag{4.4-22}$$

where $\mathbf{C}$ is the covariance matrix. Thus, for $\mathbf{x} \in \omega_i$, $\mathbf{w}'\mathbf{x}$ is distributed according to $N(\mathbf{w}'\mathbf{m}_i, \mathbf{w}'\mathbf{C}_i\mathbf{w})$; and, for $\mathbf{x} \in \omega_j$, it is distributed according to $N(\mathbf{w}'\mathbf{m}_j, \mathbf{w}'\mathbf{C}_j\mathbf{w})$. The probability of error is given by

$$p(e) = p(\omega_i)p(\mathbf{w}'\mathbf{x} < \theta/\omega_i) + p(\omega_j)p(\mathbf{w}'\mathbf{x} > \theta/\omega_j) \tag{4.4-23}$$

where

$$p(\mathbf{w}'\mathbf{x} < \theta/\omega_i) = \int_{-\infty}^{\theta} \frac{1}{\sqrt{2\pi\mathbf{w}'\mathbf{C}_i\mathbf{w}}} \exp\left[-\frac{(\mathbf{w}'\mathbf{x} - \mathbf{w}'\mathbf{m}_i)^2}{2\mathbf{w}'\mathbf{C}_i\mathbf{w}}\right] d(\mathbf{w}'\mathbf{x})$$

$$= \Phi\left(\frac{\theta - \mathbf{w}'\mathbf{m}_i}{\sqrt{\mathbf{w}'\mathbf{C}_i\mathbf{w}}}\right) \tag{4.4–24}$$

and

$$p(\mathbf{w}'\mathbf{x} > \theta/\omega_j) = \int_\theta^\infty \frac{1}{\sqrt{2\pi\mathbf{w}'\mathbf{C}_j\mathbf{w}}} \exp\left[-\frac{(\mathbf{w}'\mathbf{x} - \mathbf{w}'\mathbf{m}_j)^2}{2\mathbf{w}'\mathbf{C}_j\mathbf{w}}\right] d(\mathbf{w}'\mathbf{x})$$

$$= 1 - \Phi\left(\frac{\theta - \mathbf{w}'\mathbf{m}_j}{\sqrt{\mathbf{w}'\mathbf{C}_j\mathbf{w}}}\right) \tag{4.4–25}$$

The above equations are analogous to Eqs. (4.4–13) and (4.4–14). By substitution, we obtain the error probability as

$$p(e) = p(\omega_i)\Phi\left(\frac{\theta - \mathbf{w}'\mathbf{m}_i}{\sqrt{\mathbf{w}'\mathbf{C}_i\mathbf{w}}}\right) + p(\omega_j)\left[1 - \Phi\left(\frac{\theta - \mathbf{w}'\mathbf{m}_j}{\sqrt{\mathbf{w}'\mathbf{C}_j\mathbf{w}}}\right)\right] \tag{4.4–26}$$

which is analogous to Eq. (4.4–17) defining the probability of error for a Bayes classifier.

From the foregoing error probability analysis, we may determine the dichotomy weight vector on the basis of a minimax criterion. If equal *a priori* probabilities, $p(\omega_i) = p(\omega_j) = \frac{1}{2}$, are assumed, the error probability of Eq. (4.4–26) may be written as

$$p(e) = \tfrac{1}{2}[1 - \Phi(y_i)] + \tfrac{1}{2}[1 - \Phi(y_j)] \tag{4.4–27}$$

where

$$y_i = \frac{\mathbf{w}'\mathbf{m}_i - \theta}{\sqrt{\mathbf{w}'\mathbf{C}_i\mathbf{w}}} \tag{4.4–28}$$

and

$$y_j = \frac{\theta - \mathbf{w}'\mathbf{m}_j}{\sqrt{\mathbf{w}'\mathbf{C}_j\mathbf{w}}} \tag{4.4–29}$$

In Eq. (4.4–27), use is made of the relationship

$$\Phi\left(\frac{\theta - \mathbf{w}'\mathbf{m}_i}{\sqrt{\mathbf{w}'\mathbf{C}_i\mathbf{w}}}\right) = 1 - \Phi\left(\frac{\mathbf{w}'\mathbf{m}_i - \theta}{\sqrt{\mathbf{w}'\mathbf{C}_i\mathbf{w}}}\right) \tag{4.4–30}$$

It follows from Eq. (4.4–27) that the error probability $p(e)$ is minimized when $\Phi(y_i)$ and $\Phi(y_j)$ are maximized. Since the error function $\Phi(y)$ is single-valued and monotonically increasing, $p(e)$ is minimized when y_i and y_j are maximized. It is noted that y_i and y_j are related through the choice of weight vector $\mathbf{w}$ and threshold θ. The optimization may be formulated as the maximization of y_j subject to a fixed value of y_i.

From Eqs. (4.4–28) and (4.4–29), we obtain

$$\theta = -\,y_i\sqrt{\mathbf{w}'\mathbf{C}_i\mathbf{w}} + \mathbf{w}'\mathbf{m}_i \qquad (4.4\text{–}31)$$

and

$$y_j = \frac{-\,\mathbf{w}'(\mathbf{m}_j - \mathbf{m}_i) - y_i\sqrt{\mathbf{w}'\mathbf{C}_i\mathbf{w}}}{\sqrt{\mathbf{w}'\mathbf{C}_j\mathbf{w}}} \qquad (4.4\text{–}32)$$

Since y_j is a function of $\mathbf{w}$, to maximize y_j the derivative $dy_j/d\mathbf{w}$ must be zero. A more rigorous justification, including a sufficiency condition, is given by Anderson and Bahadur [1962].

Differentiating Eq. (4.4–32) with respect to $\mathbf{w}$ yields

$$\frac{dy_j}{d\mathbf{w}} = -\left[\mathbf{w}'(\mathbf{m}_j - \mathbf{m}_i) + y_i(\mathbf{w}'\mathbf{C}_i\mathbf{w})^{1/2}\,\frac{d}{d\mathbf{w}}\,(\mathbf{w}'\mathbf{C}_j\mathbf{w})^{-1/2}\right]$$
$$-\,(\mathbf{w}'\mathbf{C}_j\mathbf{w})^{-1/2}\,\frac{d}{d\mathbf{w}}\left[\mathbf{w}'(\mathbf{m}_j - \mathbf{m}_i) + y_i(\mathbf{w}'\mathbf{C}_i\mathbf{w})^{1/2}\right] \qquad (4.4\text{–}33)$$

It can readily be shown that

$$\frac{d}{d\mathbf{w}}\,(\mathbf{w}'\mathbf{C}_j\mathbf{w})^{-1/2} = -\,(\mathbf{w}'\mathbf{C}_j\mathbf{w})^{-3/2}\mathbf{w}'\mathbf{C}_j$$

$$\frac{d}{d\mathbf{w}}\,[\mathbf{w}'(\mathbf{m}_j - \mathbf{m}_i)] = (\mathbf{m}_j - \mathbf{m}_i)'$$

$$\frac{d}{d\mathbf{w}}\,[y_i(\mathbf{w}'\mathbf{C}_i\mathbf{w})^{1/2}] = y_i(\mathbf{w}'\mathbf{C}_i\mathbf{w})^{-1/2}\mathbf{w}'\mathbf{C}_i$$

Thus, Eq. (4.4–33) becomes

$$\frac{dy_j}{d\mathbf{w}} = [\mathbf{w}'(\mathbf{m}_j - \mathbf{m}_i) + y_i(\mathbf{w}'\mathbf{C}_i\mathbf{w})^{1/2}](\mathbf{w}'\mathbf{C}_j\mathbf{w})^{-3/2}\mathbf{w}'\mathbf{C}_j$$
$$-\,(\mathbf{w}'\mathbf{C}_j\mathbf{w})^{-1/2}[(\mathbf{m}_j - \mathbf{m}_i)' + y_i(\mathbf{w}'\mathbf{C}_i\mathbf{w})^{-1/2}\mathbf{w}'\mathbf{C}_i] \qquad (4.4\text{–}34)$$

Now, for the minimax criterion with equal *a priori* probabilities, the two kinds of errors are made equally likely. This is equivalent to saying that $y_i = y_j$. When this condition is used, Eq. (4.4–32) yields

$$\mathbf{w}'(\mathbf{m}_j - \mathbf{m}_i) = -\,y_i[(\mathbf{w}'\mathbf{C}_j\mathbf{w})^{1/2} + (\mathbf{w}'\mathbf{C}_i\mathbf{w})^{1/2}] \qquad (4.4\text{–}35)$$

Substituting Eq. (4.4–35) in Eq. (4.4–34), simplifying, and equating the result to zero yields

$$y_i(\mathbf{w}'\mathbf{C}_j\mathbf{w})^{-1}\mathbf{w}'\mathbf{C}_j + (\mathbf{w}'\mathbf{C}_j\mathbf{w})^{-1/2}[(\mathbf{m}_j - \mathbf{m}_i) + y_i(\mathbf{w}'\mathbf{C}_i\mathbf{w})^{1/2}\mathbf{w}'\mathbf{C}_i] = 0$$

from which we obtain

$$\mathbf{w} = -\frac{1}{y_i}\left[\frac{\mathbf{C}_j}{(\mathbf{w}'\mathbf{C}_j\mathbf{w})^{1/2}} + \frac{\mathbf{C}_i}{(\mathbf{w}'\mathbf{C}_i\mathbf{w})^{1/2}}\right]^{-1}(\mathbf{m}_j - \mathbf{m}_i) \tag{4.4–36}$$

Equation (4.4–36) may be written as

$$\mathbf{w} = -\frac{1}{y_i}\left[\frac{(\mathbf{w}'\mathbf{C}_j\mathbf{w})^{1/2}(\mathbf{w}'\mathbf{C}_i\mathbf{w})^{1/2}}{(\mathbf{w}'\mathbf{C}_j\mathbf{w})^{1/2} + (\mathbf{w}'\mathbf{C}_i\mathbf{w})^{1/2}}\right]\left[\frac{(\mathbf{w}'\mathbf{C}_j\mathbf{w})^{1/2}\mathbf{C}_i + (\mathbf{w}'\mathbf{C}_i\mathbf{w})^{1/2}\mathbf{C}_j)}{(\mathbf{w}'\mathbf{C}_j\mathbf{w})^{1/2} + (\mathbf{w}'\mathbf{C}_i\mathbf{w})^{1/2}}\right]^{-1}(\mathbf{m}_j - \mathbf{m}_i) \tag{4.4–37}$$

It is noted that $\mathbf{w}$ can be replaced by $s\mathbf{w}$ for any positive scalar constant s and the equation will still be valid. We will choose s so that

$$\frac{1}{y_i}\left[\frac{(\mathbf{w}'\mathbf{C}_j\mathbf{w})^{1/2}(\mathbf{w}'\mathbf{C}_i\mathbf{w})^{1/2}}{(\mathbf{w}'\mathbf{C}_j\mathbf{w})^{1/2} + (\mathbf{w}'\mathbf{C}_i\mathbf{w})^{1/2}}\right] = 1 \tag{4.4–38}$$

Thus, the desired weight vector may be determined from the following implicit equation:

$$\mathbf{w} = \left[\frac{(\mathbf{w}'\mathbf{C}_j\mathbf{w})^{1/2}\mathbf{C}_i + (\mathbf{w}'\mathbf{C}_i\mathbf{w})^{1/2}\mathbf{C}_j}{(\mathbf{w}'\mathbf{C}_j\mathbf{w})^{1/2} + (\mathbf{w}'\mathbf{C}_i\mathbf{w})^{1/2}}\right](\mathbf{m}_i - \mathbf{m}_j) \tag{4.4–39}$$

Combining Eqs. (4.4–28) and (4.4–38) yields the threshold as

$$\theta = \mathbf{w}'\mathbf{m}_i - \frac{(\mathbf{w}'\mathbf{C}_j\mathbf{w})^{1/2}(\mathbf{w}'\mathbf{C}_i\mathbf{w})}{(\mathbf{w}'\mathbf{C}_j\mathbf{w})^{1/2} + (\mathbf{w}'\mathbf{C}_i\mathbf{w})^{1/2}} \tag{4.4–40}$$

From Eqs. (4.4–39) and (4.4–40) we may determine the weight vector and the threshold for a linear dichotomizer which minimizes the probability of error.

4.5 A FAMILY OF IMPORTANT PROBABILITY DENSITY FUNCTIONS

The general form of a family of important probability density functions is given by the relation†

† For the sake of clarity, class membership is not incorporated in the present notation. To take class membership into account we would express Eq. (4.5–1) as

$$p(\mathbf{x}/\omega_i) = K_n|\mathbf{W}_i|^{1/2}f[(\mathbf{x} - \mathbf{m}_i)'\mathbf{W}_i(\mathbf{x} - \mathbf{m}_i)]$$

$$p(\mathbf{x}) = K_n|\mathbf{W}|^{1/2}f[(\mathbf{x} - \mathbf{m})'\mathbf{W}(\mathbf{x} - \mathbf{m})] \tag{4.5–1}$$

where K_n is a normalizing constant, $\mathbf{W}$ is a weight matrix which is real, symmetric, and positive definite, $\mathbf{m}$ is the mean vector, and n is the dimensionality of $\mathbf{x}$. This density function is integrable in the $\mathbf{x}$-space. It is ellipsoidally symmetric since the contours of constant probability are hyperellipsoids. If $\mathbf{W} = [\alpha\mathbf{I}]^2$, where α is a scalar and $\mathbf{I}$ is the identity matrix, $p(\mathbf{x})$ becomes a spherically symmetric density function given by

$$p(\mathbf{x}) = K_n\alpha f[\alpha^2(\mathbf{x} - \mathbf{m})'(\mathbf{x} - \mathbf{m})] \tag{4.5–2}$$

The normal probability density function

$$p(\mathbf{x}) = \frac{1}{(2\pi)^{n/2}|\mathbf{C}|^{1/2}} \exp[-\tfrac{1}{2}(\mathbf{x} - \mathbf{m})'\mathbf{C}^{-1}(\mathbf{x} - \mathbf{m})] \tag{4.5–3}$$

belongs to the class of density functions defined by Eq. (4.5–1). By comparison we note that

$$K_n = (2\pi)^{-n/2}, \qquad \mathbf{W} = \mathbf{C}^{-1}$$

$$f[\cdot] = \exp[-\tfrac{1}{2}(\mathbf{x} - \mathbf{m})'\mathbf{C}^{-1}(\mathbf{x} - \mathbf{m})] \tag{4.5–4}$$

The Pearson Type II density function is a symmetric function given by

$$p(\mathbf{x}) = \begin{cases} h(\mathbf{x}) & \text{over region } R \\ 0 & \text{elsewhere} \end{cases} \tag{4.5–5}$$

where

$$h(\mathbf{x}) = \frac{\Gamma(\frac{1}{2}n + k + 1)}{\pi^{n/2}\Gamma(k + 1)} |\mathbf{W}|^{1/2}[1 - (\mathbf{x} - \mathbf{m})'\mathbf{W}(\mathbf{x} - \mathbf{m})]^{-k} \tag{4.5–6}$$

R denotes the interior of the hyperellipsoid,

$$(\mathbf{x} - \mathbf{m})'\mathbf{W}(\mathbf{x} - \mathbf{m}) = 1 \tag{4.5–7}$$

and Γ is the gamma function.

The weight matrix in Eq. (4.5–6) is given by

$$\mathbf{W} = \frac{1}{n + 2(k + 1)} \mathbf{C}^{-1}, \quad k \geqslant 0 \tag{4.5–8}$$

where $\mathbf{C}$ is the covariance matrix. The parameter k determines the shape of the density function. When $k = 0$ the Pearson Type II density reduces to a uniform density. When $k = \frac{1}{2}$ it is an inverted hypersemiellipsoid, and when $k = 1$ it describes an inverted hyperparaboloid. As k approaches infinity, the Pearson Type II density becomes the normal density.

The Pearson Type VII density function also belongs to the class of functions defined by Eq. (4.5–1). This density function is given by

$$p(\mathbf{x}) = \frac{\Gamma(k)}{\pi^{n/2}\Gamma(k - \frac{1}{2}n)} |\mathbf{W}|^{1/2}[1 + (\mathbf{x} - \mathbf{m})'\mathbf{W}(\mathbf{x} - \mathbf{m})]^{-k}, \quad k > \frac{n}{2} \tag{4.5–9}$$

The weight matrix is given by

$$\mathbf{W} = \frac{1}{2k - (n + 2)} \mathbf{C}^{-1}, \quad k > (n/2 + 1) \tag{4.5–10}$$

The limiting function as k approaches infinity is also a normal density in this case. For the purpose of comparison, Fig. 4.5 shows one-variable plots of the normal, Pearson Type II, and Pearson Type VII densities. In the figure the densities have been normalized to have the same peak value.

When the probability density functions of any two pattern classes are symmetric, multivariate, and monotonically decreasing, it can be shown that the Bayes decision boundary between the two classes is either a hyperplane or a hyperquadric, depending on the weight matrix. This fact was demonstrated in the Section 4.3 for normal densities. The reader will recall from that discussion that the covariance matrices determine whether the decision boundary between two normal pattern populations is a hyperquadric or a

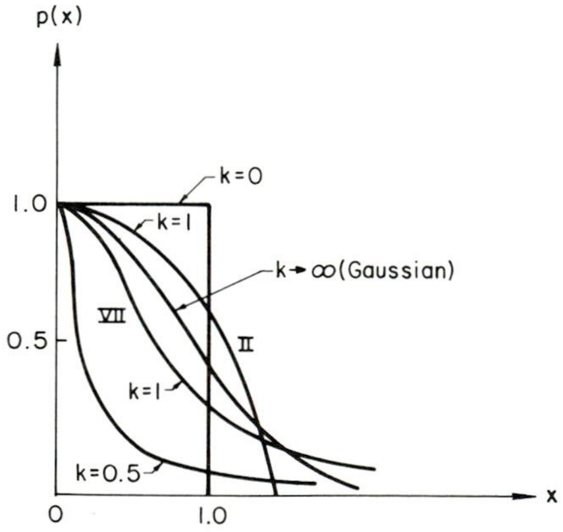

Figure 4.5. Symmetric univariate density functions

hyperplane. The following example illustrates how these two types of decision boundaries are obtained with Pearson Type VII density functions.

Example: Suppose that two pattern classes ω_1 and ω_2 are governed by Pearson Type VII density functions with equal values of k, that is,

$$p(\mathbf{x}/\omega_1) = \frac{\Gamma(k)}{\pi^{n/2}\Gamma(k - \frac{1}{2}n)} |\mathbf{W}_1|^{1/2}[1 + (\mathbf{x} - \mathbf{m}_1)'\mathbf{W}_1(\mathbf{x} - \mathbf{m}_1)]^{-k}$$

$$p(\mathbf{x}/\omega_2) = \frac{\Gamma(k)}{\pi^{n/2}\Gamma(k - \frac{1}{2}n)} |\mathbf{W}_2|^{1/2}[1 + (\mathbf{x} - \mathbf{m}_2)'\mathbf{W}_2(\mathbf{x} - \mathbf{m}_2)]^{-k}$$

It is desired to find the Bayes decision boundary between the two classes.

From Eq. (4.2–21),

$$d_1(\mathbf{x}) = p(\mathbf{x}/\omega_1)p(\omega_1), \qquad d_2(\mathbf{x}) = p(\mathbf{x}/\omega_2)p(\omega_2)$$

The equation of the decision boundary is

$$d_1(\mathbf{x}) - d_2(\mathbf{x}) = 0$$

from which we have

$$p(\mathbf{x}/\omega_1)p(\omega_1) = p(\mathbf{x}/\omega_2)p(\omega_2)$$

at the boundary.

Assuming that $p(\omega_1) = p(\omega_2)$ and substituting the Pearson Type VII density functions for $p(\mathbf{x}/\omega_1)$ and $p(\mathbf{x}/\omega_2)$ yields the following relation:

$$|\mathbf{W}_1|^{1/2}[1 + (\mathbf{x} - \mathbf{m}_1)'\mathbf{W}_1(\mathbf{x} - \mathbf{m}_1)]^{-k} = |\mathbf{W}_2|^{1/2}[1 + (\mathbf{x} - \mathbf{m}_2)'\mathbf{W}_2(\mathbf{x} - \mathbf{m}_2)]^{-k}$$

or

$$\sqrt[2k]{|\mathbf{W}_1|}[1 + (\mathbf{x} - \mathbf{m}_2)'\mathbf{W}_2(\mathbf{x} - \mathbf{m}_2)] = \sqrt[2k]{|\mathbf{W}_2|}[1 + (\mathbf{x} - \mathbf{m}_1)'\mathbf{W}_1(\mathbf{x} - \mathbf{m}_1)]$$

Letting $K_1 = \sqrt[2k]{|\mathbf{W}_1|}$ and $K_2 = \sqrt[2k]{|\mathbf{W}_2|}$ for simplicity, we obtain as the equation of the decision boundary

$$K_1(\mathbf{x} - \mathbf{m}_2)'\mathbf{W}_2(\mathbf{x} - \mathbf{m}_2) - K_2(\mathbf{x} - \mathbf{m}_1)'\mathbf{W}_1(\mathbf{x} - \mathbf{m}_1) + (K_1 - K_2) = 0$$

which is clearly a quadratic function.

The matrices $\mathbf{W}_1$ and $\mathbf{W}_2$ are proportional to the covariance matrices $\mathbf{C}_1$ and $\mathbf{C}_2$, as indicated in Eq. (4.5–10). If the covariance matrices are equal, we have that $\mathbf{W}_1 = \mathbf{W}_2 = \mathbf{W}$ and $K_1 = K_2$. In this case,

$$(\mathbf{x} - \mathbf{m}_2)'\mathbf{W}(\mathbf{x} - \mathbf{m}_2) - (\mathbf{x} - \mathbf{m}_1)'\mathbf{W}(\mathbf{x} - \mathbf{m}_1) = 0$$

However, since the term $\mathbf{x}'\mathbf{W}\mathbf{x}$ is now class independent, it may be dropped from the decision-making process. The simplified decision boundary then becomes

$$2\mathbf{x}'\mathbf{W}(\mathbf{m}_1 - \mathbf{m}_2) + \mathbf{m}_2'\mathbf{W}\mathbf{m}_2 - \mathbf{m}_1'\mathbf{W}\mathbf{m}_1 = 0$$

which is the equation of a hyperplane. As was true in the case of normal densities, the covariance matrix also plays a central role in the decision boundaries obtained with Pearson Type VII densities. ●

4.6 ESTIMATION OF PROBABILITY DENSITY FUNCTIONS

It is evident from the discussion in the preceding sections that estimation of the densities $p(\mathbf{x}/\omega_i)$ is the most important problem in the implementation of a Bayes pattern classifier. In this section attention is focused on several basic approaches which may be employed to obtain estimates of these densities using sample patterns.

4.6.1 Form of the Probability Density Function

Before proceeding with the development of methods for estimating probability density functions, it is important to provide some motivation for choosing a particular type of density function over another. The entropy concept provides a meaningful criterion upon which a discussion of this type can be based. The principle of maximum entropy states that, if the probability density function characterizing a random variable is not known, the probability density function which maximizes the entropy of the random variable subject to any known constraints is a logical choice. Application of this principle leads to the minimum-bias solution, since any other function would show a bias toward the information available from the known data. The maximum-entropy probability density function is particularly easy to determine when all known constraints are in the form of averages, such as means or variances for the probability density function.

The population entropy for patterns governed by probability density function $p(\mathbf{x})$ is

$$H = -\int_{\mathbf{x}} p(\mathbf{x}) \ln p(\mathbf{x}) \, d\mathbf{x} \tag{4.6–1}$$

To simplify the notation we again omit class membership. As before, if we are considering class ω_i, $p(\mathbf{x})$ represents $p(\mathbf{x}/\omega_i)$. Assume that the *a priori* information about the random variable $\mathbf{x}$ is given by

$$\int_{\mathbf{x}} p(\mathbf{x})\, d\mathbf{x} = 1 \tag{4.6–2a}$$

and

$$\int_{\mathbf{x}} b_k(\mathbf{x}) p(\mathbf{x})\, d\mathbf{x} = a_k, \quad k = 1, 2, \ldots, Q \tag{4.6–2b}$$

We wish to determine $p(\mathbf{x})$ so that the entropy is maximized subject to the constraints defined in Eqs. (4.6–2a) and (4.6–2b). Introducing the Lagrange multipliers $\lambda_0, \lambda_1, \ldots, \lambda_Q$, we form the synthetic function

$$H_1 = -\int_{\mathbf{x}} p(\mathbf{x}) \left[\ln p(\mathbf{x}) - \sum_{k=0}^{Q} \lambda_k b_k(\mathbf{x})\right] d\mathbf{x} - \sum_{k=0}^{Q} \lambda_k a_k \tag{4.6–3}$$

where $a_0 = 1$ and $b_0(\mathbf{x}) = 1$ for all $\mathbf{x}$.

Taking the partial derivative of H_1 with respect to $p(\mathbf{x})$ yields

$$\frac{\partial H_1}{\partial p(\mathbf{x})} = -\int_{\mathbf{x}} \left\{\left[\ln p(\mathbf{x}) - \sum_{k=0}^{Q} \lambda_k b_k(\mathbf{x})\right] + 1\right\} d\mathbf{x} \tag{4.6–4}$$

Equating the integrand to zero and solving for $p(\mathbf{x})$, we obtain the probability density:

$$p(\mathbf{x}) = \exp\left[\sum_{k=0}^{Q} \lambda_k b_k(\mathbf{x}) - 1\right] \tag{4.6–5}$$

In Eq. (4.6–5) the $Q + 1$ parameters $\lambda_0, \lambda_1, \ldots, \lambda_Q$ are to be chosen to fit the *a priori* information about $\mathbf{x}$ which is given in Eqs. (4.6–2a) and (4.6–2b).

From Eq. (4.6–5) it can readily be shown that, when the random variable is known to be nonzero only in a finite interval, a uniform density would be chosen. If any real values of the random variable are permitted and the mean and variance are considered as the only meaningful characteristics, a normal density would be chosen. Once the form of the probability function is selected, the next step is to estimate the parameters of these densities. The above analysis points out that when the mean and the variance of $\mathbf{x}$ are the only known characteristics a normal density is a satisfactory assumption from the entropy point of view. Since this is a problem of considerable practical significance, attention is focused in the next two sections on estimation of the mean vector and covariance matrix of a sample population.

Example: As an illustration, assume that the *a priori* information about the random variable x is $\alpha < x < \beta$ and $\int_0^\infty p(x)\,dx = 1$. Then, from Eq. (4.6–5), $p(x) = \exp(\lambda_0 - 1)$. Since $\int_\alpha^\beta \exp(\lambda_0 - 1)\,dx = 1$, $\exp(\lambda_0 - 1) = 1/(\beta - \alpha)$ and

$$p(x) = \begin{cases} \dfrac{1}{\beta - \alpha} & \text{for} \quad \alpha < x < \beta \\ 0 & \text{otherwise} \end{cases}$$

which describes a uniform density function within the specified interval.

Now, let us assume that the *a priori* information about x is $x \geqslant 0$, $\int_0^\infty p(x)\,dx = 1$, and $\int_0^\infty xp(x)\,dx = m$. Then, from Eq. (4.6–5), $p(x) = \exp(\lambda_0 - 1 + \lambda_1 x)$. Since

$$\int_0^\infty \exp(\lambda_0 - 1 + \lambda_1 x)\,dx = 1 \quad \text{and} \quad \int_0^\infty x \exp(\lambda_0 - 1 + \lambda_1 x)\,dx = m$$

solving for λ_0 and λ_1 yields

$$\exp(\lambda_0 - 1) = \frac{1}{m} \quad \text{and} \quad \lambda_1 = -\frac{1}{m}$$

Hence

$$p(x) = \begin{cases} \dfrac{1}{m} \exp\left(-\dfrac{x}{m}\right) & \text{for} \quad x \geqslant 0 \\ 0 & \text{otherwise} \end{cases}$$

If the *a priori* information about x is

$$-\infty < x < \infty, \qquad \int_{-\infty}^{\infty} p(x)\,dx = 1, \qquad \int_{-\infty}^{\infty} xp(x)\,dx = m, \qquad \int_{-\infty}^{\infty} x^2 p(x)\,dx = \sigma^2$$

then, from Eq. (4.6–5), we have

$$p(x) = \exp(\lambda_0 - 1 + \lambda_1 x + \lambda_2 x^2)$$

and from the given *a priori* information we obtain

$$\int_{-\infty}^{\infty} \exp(\lambda_0 - 1 + \lambda_1 x + \lambda_2 x^2)\, dx = 1$$

$$\int_{-\infty}^{\infty} x \exp(\lambda_0 - 1 + \lambda_1 x + \lambda_2 x^2)\, dx = m$$

$$\int_{-\infty}^{\infty} x^2 \exp(\lambda_0 - 1 + \lambda_1 x + \lambda_2 x^2)\, dx = \sigma^2$$

Solving for λ_0, λ_1, and λ_2 yields the probability density function

$$p(x) = \frac{1}{\sqrt{2\pi}\,\sigma} \exp\left[\frac{-(x-m)^2}{2\sigma^2}\right]$$

which describes a normal density function. ●

4.6.2 Estimation of the Mean Vector and Covariance Matrix

It was shown in Section 4.5 that some important probability density functions, of which the normal density is a special case, are completely specified by their mean vectors and covariance matrices. When the form of a density is known within a set of parameters, the estimation problem is referred to as parametric estimation. This is an area which has received a great deal of attention in the statistical literature, and we will enter it only to discuss a method for estimating the mean vector and covariance matrix of a pattern population.

Assume that a pattern population is characterized by the probability density function $p(\mathbf{x})$. The mean vector of this population is defined as

$$\mathbf{m} = E\{\mathbf{x}\} = \int_{\mathbf{x}} \mathbf{x} p(\mathbf{x})\, d\mathbf{x} \tag{4.6–6}$$

where $\mathbf{x} = (x_1, x_2, \ldots, x_n)'$ and $\mathbf{m} = (m_1, m_2, \ldots, m_n)'$.

If we approximate the expected value by the sample average, the mean vector may be expressed as

$$\mathbf{m} = E\{\mathbf{x}\} \approx \frac{1}{N} \sum_{j=1}^{N} \mathbf{x}_j \tag{4.6–7}$$

where N is the number of samples.

The covariance matrix is given by

$$\mathbf{C} = \begin{pmatrix} c_{11} & c_{12} & \cdots & c_{1n} \\ c_{21} & c_{22} & \cdots & c_{2n} \\ \vdots & \vdots & & \vdots \\ c_{n1} & c_{n2} & \cdots & c_{nn} \end{pmatrix} \tag{4.6–8}$$

with the element c_{lk} of $\mathbf{C}$ being defined as

$$c_{lk} = E\{(x_l - m_l)(x_k - m_k)\} = \int_{-\infty}^{\infty}\int_{\infty}^{\infty} (x_l - m_l)(x_k - m_k)p(x_l, x_k)\, dx_l\, dx_k \tag{4.6–9}$$

where x_l, x_k and m_l, m_k are the lth and kth components of $\mathbf{x}$ and $\mathbf{m}$. The covariance matrix may be expressed in the following vector form:

$$\begin{aligned} \mathbf{C} &= E\{(\mathbf{x} - \mathbf{m})(\mathbf{x} - \mathbf{m})'\} \\ &= E\{\mathbf{xx}' - 2\mathbf{xm}' + \mathbf{mm}'\} \\ &= E\{\mathbf{xx}'\} - \mathbf{mm}' \end{aligned} \tag{4.6–10}$$

Approximating again the expected value by the sample average yields

$$\mathbf{C} \approx \frac{1}{N} \sum_{j=1}^{N} \mathbf{x}_j\mathbf{x}_j' - \mathbf{mm}' \tag{4.6–11}$$

It has been shown (Anderson [1958]) that, if $N > n$ and the samples are drawn from a normal population, the estimate of $\mathbf{C}$ given by Eq. (4.6–11) possesses an inverse $\mathbf{C}^{-1}$ with probability 1.

The estimates of the mean vector and covariance matrix may be expressed in a recursive form. Suppose that we wish to add one more sample to the mean vector estimate obtained with N samples. Denoting the new estimate by $\mathbf{m}(N + 1)$, we obtain

$$\begin{aligned} \mathbf{m}(N + 1) &= \frac{1}{N + 1} \sum_{j=1}^{N+1} \mathbf{x}_j \\ &= \frac{1}{N + 1}\left(\sum_{j=1}^{N} \mathbf{x}_j + \mathbf{x}_{N+1}\right) \\ &= \frac{1}{N + 1}(N\mathbf{m}(N) + \mathbf{x}_{N+1}) \end{aligned} \tag{4.6–12}$$

where $\mathbf{m}(N)$ is the estimate obtained with N samples. The procedure is started with $\mathbf{m}(1) = \mathbf{x}_1$. This recursive expression may be used both to calculate and to update the mean vector.

A similar expression may be obtained for the covariance matrix. Letting $\mathbf{C}(N)$ represent the estimate for N samples, we obtain

$$\mathbf{C}(N) = \frac{1}{N}\sum_{j=1}^{N} \mathbf{x}_j\mathbf{x}_j' - \mathbf{m}(N)\mathbf{m}'(N) \tag{4.6–13}$$

Adding one sample yields

$$\begin{aligned}\mathbf{C}(N+1) &= \frac{1}{N+1}\sum_{j=1}^{N+1} \mathbf{x}_j\mathbf{x}_j' - \mathbf{m}(N+1)\mathbf{m}'(N+1)\\ &= \frac{1}{N+1}\left(\sum_{j=1}^{N} \mathbf{x}_j\mathbf{x}_j' + \mathbf{x}_{N+1}\mathbf{x}_{N+1}'\right) - \mathbf{m}(N+1)\mathbf{m}'(N+1)\\ &= \frac{1}{N+1}(N\mathbf{C}(N) + N\mathbf{m}(N)\mathbf{m}'(N) + \mathbf{x}_{N+1}\mathbf{x}_{N+1}')\\ &\quad - \frac{1}{(N+1)^2}(N\mathbf{m}(N) + \mathbf{x}_{N+1})(N\mathbf{m}(N) + \mathbf{x}_{N+1})'\end{aligned} \tag{4.6–14}$$

This expression provides a convenient method for estimating or updating the covariance matrix, starting with $\mathbf{C}(1) = \mathbf{x}_1\mathbf{x}_1' - \mathbf{m}(1)\mathbf{m}'(1)$ and $\mathbf{m}(1) = \mathbf{x}_1$. We see from this condition that $\mathbf{C}(1) = \mathbf{0}$, the zero matrix.

4.6.3 Bayesian Learning of the Mean Vector and Covariance Matrix

If we can specify appropriate probability densities for the unknown mean vectors and covariance matrices, we may design an iterative procedure for calculating the estimates by making use of the training sample patterns. In the following discussions the probability density function $p(\mathbf{x}/\omega_i)$ is taken as a normal density with mean vector $\mathbf{m}_i$ and covariance matrix $\mathbf{C}_i$. Assume that $\mathbf{C}_i$ is specified and $\mathbf{m}_i$ is an unknown parameter $\boldsymbol{\theta}$ which is characterized by a normal density with initial mean vector $\mathbf{m}_i(0)$ and initial covariance matrix $\mathbf{K}(0)$. Then we have

$$p(\boldsymbol{\theta}/\omega_i) \sim N[\mathbf{m}_i(0), \mathbf{K}(0)] \tag{4.6–15}$$

The effect of the uncertainty in the mean vector is to increase the covariance matrix for $\mathbf{x}$ from $\mathbf{C}_i$ to $\mathbf{C}_i + \mathbf{K}(0)$. The initial covariance matrix $\mathbf{K}(0)$ is a measure of uncertainty. Thus the initial density function for $\mathbf{x}$ is

$$p(\mathbf{x}/\omega_i, \boldsymbol{\theta}) \sim N[\mathbf{m}_i(0), \mathbf{C}_i + \mathbf{K}(0)] \tag{4.6–16}$$

Using Bayes' formula:

$$p(\boldsymbol{\theta}/\omega_i, \mathbf{x}_1, \ldots, \mathbf{x}_N)$$
$$= \frac{p(\mathbf{x}_N/\omega_i, \boldsymbol{\theta}, \mathbf{x}_1, \mathbf{x}_2, \ldots, \mathbf{x}_{N-1})p(\boldsymbol{\theta}/\omega_i, \mathbf{x}_1, \mathbf{x}_2, \ldots, \mathbf{x}_{N-1})}{p(\mathbf{x}_N/\omega_i, \mathbf{x}_1, \mathbf{x}_2, \ldots, \mathbf{x}_{N-1})} \tag{4.6–17}$$

we may compute the *a posteriori* density function for $\boldsymbol{\theta}$ from the *a priori* density function and the information obtained from the training sample patterns.

After the presentation of the first training sample pattern $\mathbf{x}_1$, we can write the *a posteriori* density function for the mean vector as

$$p(\boldsymbol{\theta}/\omega_i, \mathbf{x}_1) = \frac{p(\mathbf{x}_1/\omega_i, \boldsymbol{\theta})p(\boldsymbol{\theta}/\omega_i)}{p(\mathbf{x}_1/\omega_i)} \tag{4.6–18}$$

which reduces to a normal density, since the product of $p(\mathbf{x}_1/\omega_i, \boldsymbol{\theta})$ and $p(\boldsymbol{\theta}/\omega_i)$ forms a normal density. Substituting Eqs. (4.6–15) and (4.6–16) into Eq. (4.6–18), we obtain

$$p(\boldsymbol{\theta}/\omega_i, \mathbf{x}_1) \sim N[\mathbf{m}_i(1), \mathbf{K}(1)] \tag{4.6–19}$$

where

$$\mathbf{m}_i(1) = \mathbf{K}(0)[\mathbf{K}(0) + \mathbf{C}_i]^{-1}\mathbf{x}_1 + \mathbf{C}_i[\mathbf{K}(0) + \mathbf{C}_i]^{-1}\mathbf{m}_i(0) \tag{4.6–20}$$

and

$$\mathbf{K}(1) = \mathbf{K}(0)[\mathbf{K}(0) + \mathbf{C}_i]^{-1}\mathbf{C}_1 \tag{4.6–21}$$

The probability density function for $\mathbf{x}$, given $\mathbf{x}_1$, is normal and is given by

$$p(\mathbf{x}/\omega_i, \boldsymbol{\theta}, \mathbf{x}_1) \sim N[\mathbf{m}_i(1), \mathbf{C}_i + \mathbf{K}(1)] \tag{4.6–22}$$

since the sum of two statistically independent normal vectors is normal with mean equal to the sum of the means and covariance matrix equal to the sum of the covariance matrices.

After presenting the second training sample pattern $\mathbf{x}_2$, we can write the *a posteriori* density function for the mean vector as

$$p(\boldsymbol{\theta}/\omega_i, \mathbf{x}_1, \mathbf{x}_2) = \frac{p(\mathbf{x}_2/\omega_i, \boldsymbol{\theta}, \mathbf{x}_1)p(\boldsymbol{\theta}/\omega_i, \mathbf{x}_1)}{p(\mathbf{x}_2/\omega_i, \mathbf{x}_1)} \tag{4.6–23}$$

Upon substitution of Eqs. (4.6–19) and (4.6–22) this function reduces to

$$p(\boldsymbol{\theta}/\omega_i, \mathbf{x}_1, \mathbf{x}_2) \sim N[\mathbf{m}_i(2), \mathbf{K}(2)] \tag{4.6–24}$$

where

$$\mathbf{m}_i(2) = \mathbf{K}(1)[\mathbf{K}(1) + \mathbf{C}_i]^{-1}\mathbf{x}_2 + \mathbf{C}_i[\mathbf{K}(1) + \mathbf{C}_i]^{-1}\mathbf{m}_i(1) \tag{4.6–25}$$

and

$$\mathbf{K}(2) = \mathbf{K}(1)[\mathbf{K}(1) + \mathbf{C}_i]^{-1}\mathbf{C}_i \tag{4.6–26}$$

represent, respectively, the new mean vector and the covariance matrix for the unknown parameter $\boldsymbol{\theta}$. The probability density function for $\mathbf{x}$, given $\mathbf{x}_1$ and $\mathbf{x}_2$, is still normal; thus

$$p(\mathbf{x}/\omega_i, \boldsymbol{\theta}, \mathbf{x}_1, \mathbf{x}_2) \sim N[\mathbf{m}_i(2), \mathbf{C}_i + \mathbf{K}(2)] \tag{4.6–27}$$

After the presentation of N training sample patterns $\mathbf{x}_1, \mathbf{x}_2, \ldots, \mathbf{x}_N$, the *a posteriori* density function for the mean vector is derived from Eq. (4.6–17) as

$$p(\boldsymbol{\theta}/\omega_i, \mathbf{x}_1, \mathbf{x}_2, \ldots, \mathbf{x}_N) \sim N[\mathbf{m}_i(N), \mathbf{K}(N)] \tag{4.6–28}$$

where

$$\begin{aligned}\mathbf{m}_i(N) &= \mathbf{K}(N-1)[\mathbf{K}(N-1) + \mathbf{C}_i]^{-1}\mathbf{x}_N \\ &\quad + \mathbf{C}_i[\mathbf{K}(N-1) + \mathbf{C}_i]^{-1}\mathbf{m}_i(N-1) \\ &= N\mathbf{K}(0)[N\mathbf{K}(0) + \mathbf{C}_i]^{-1}\hat{\mathbf{m}}_i + \mathbf{C}_i[N\mathbf{K}(0) + \mathbf{C}_i]^{-1}\mathbf{m}_i(0)\end{aligned} \tag{4.6–29}$$

and

$$\begin{aligned}\mathbf{K}(N) &= \mathbf{K}(N-1)[\mathbf{K}(N-1) + \mathbf{C}_i]^{-1}\mathbf{C}_i \\ &= \mathbf{K}(0)[N\mathbf{K}(0) + \mathbf{C}_i]^{-1}\mathbf{C}_i\end{aligned} \tag{4.6–30}$$

In Eq. (4.6–29) $\hat{\mathbf{m}}_i$ is the sample mean vector for pattern class ω_i and is given by

$$\hat{\mathbf{m}}_i = \frac{1}{N}\sum_{j=1}^{N} \mathbf{x}_j \tag{4.6–31}$$

Equation (4.6–29) points out that the Bayesian estimated mean vector is equal to the weighted sum of the *a priori* mean vector and the sample mean vector. The probability density function for $\mathbf{x}$, given $\mathbf{x}_1, \mathbf{x}_2, \ldots, \mathbf{x}_N$, is

$$p(\mathbf{x}/\omega_i, \boldsymbol{\theta}, \mathbf{x}_1, \mathbf{x}_2, \ldots, \mathbf{x}_N) \sim N[\mathbf{m}_i(N), \mathbf{C}_i + \mathbf{K}(N)] \tag{4.6-32}$$

The property of reproducible distribution simplifies the learning of the mean vector on the basis of training sample patterns.

It can be readily shown that, when $\mathbf{x}$ is of unit dimension, by letting $\alpha = K(0)/C_i$ the Bayesian estimated mean and variance are

$$m_i(N) = \frac{N\alpha}{1 + N\alpha}\hat{m}_i + \frac{1}{1 + N\alpha}m_i(0) \tag{4.6-33}$$

and

$$K(N) = \frac{1}{1 + N\alpha}K(0) \tag{4.6-34}$$

The preceding discussions lead to the following remarks: When the initial covariance for the unknown mean is large, the Bayesian estimated mean $m_i(N)$ weights the initial mean lightly and the sample mean heavily. For large α, the *a priori* mean and covariance have only little influence, and the feature function parameters are determined almost exclusively by the training sample patterns. When the initial covariance for the unknown mean is small, the Bayesian estimated mean tends to change slowly from the initial mean, even if the sample mean vector differs from it a great deal. These two remarks point out that the constant α may be regarded as a measure of our confidence in the initial mean $m_i(0)$.

If the covariance matrix is unknown, we want the pattern recognition machine to learn this matrix. For class ω_i, if zero mean is assumed, the probability density function for pattern vector $\mathbf{x}$ is given by

$$p(\mathbf{x}/\boldsymbol{\theta}_i) = (2\pi)^{-n/2}|\mathbf{C}_i|^{-1/2}\exp(-\tfrac{1}{2}\mathbf{x}'\mathbf{C}_i^{-1}\mathbf{x}) \tag{4.6-35}$$

where $\mathbf{C}_i$ is a random function.

It will be convenient to work in terms of the inverse covariance matrix, $\mathbf{P}_i = \mathbf{C}_i^{-1}$. The probability density function then becomes

$$p(\mathbf{x}/\boldsymbol{\theta}_i) = (2\pi)^{-n/2}|\mathbf{P}_i|^{1/2}\exp(-\tfrac{1}{2}\mathbf{x}'\mathbf{P}_i\mathbf{x}) \tag{4.6-36}$$

In applying Bayes' formula:

$$p(\boldsymbol{\theta}_i/\mathbf{x}_1) = \frac{p(\mathbf{x}_1/\boldsymbol{\theta}_i)p(\boldsymbol{\theta}_i)}{p(\mathbf{x}_1)} \tag{4.6-37}$$

we select a reproducing *a priori* density function for normal $p(\mathbf{x}/\boldsymbol{\theta}_i, \omega_i)$ with unknown $\mathbf{C}_i$ as the Wishart density function:

$$p(\mathbf{P}_i) = \begin{cases} C_{n,\nu_0} \left|\dfrac{\nu_0 \boldsymbol{\Phi}_0}{2}\right|^{(\nu_0-1)/2} |\mathbf{P}_i|^{(\nu_0-n-2)/2} \exp[-\frac{1}{2} \operatorname{tr}(\nu_0 \boldsymbol{\Phi}_0 \mathbf{P}_i)] & \text{on } S \\ 0 & \text{otherwise} \end{cases} \tag{4.6–38}$$

where S is the subset of the Euclidean space of dimension $\frac{1}{2}n(n+1)$, $\mathbf{P}_i$ is positive definite and symmetric:

$$\mathbf{P}_i = \begin{pmatrix} p_{11} & p_{12} & \cdots & p_{1n} \\ p_{21} & p_{22} & & p_{2n} \\ \vdots & \vdots & & \vdots \\ p_{n1} & p_{n2} & \cdots & p_{nn} \end{pmatrix} \tag{4.6–39}$$

with $p_{ij} = p_{ji}$, and the normalizing constant is given by

$$C_{n,\nu_0} = \frac{1}{[\pi^{n(n-1)/4}] \left[\prod_{\alpha=1}^{n} \Gamma\left(\dfrac{\nu_0 - \alpha}{2}\right)\right]} \tag{4.6–40}$$

The symmetric matrix $\mathbf{P}_i$ has $\frac{1}{2}n(n+1)$ distinct elements.

By assigning a Wishart density to the *a priori* density function of $\mathbf{P}_i$, we obtain the reproducing property. In Eq. (4.6–38), $\boldsymbol{\Phi}_0$ is a positive definite matrix which reflects the initial knowledge of $\mathbf{P}_i$, and ν_0 is a real number greater than n which reflects the confidence about the initial estimate $\boldsymbol{\Phi}_0$.

We consider a model for $p(\mathbf{x}_N/\boldsymbol{\theta}_i, \omega_i)$ where each pattern class has a normal density function with mean vector zero and covariance matrix $\mathbf{C}_i$, one for each pattern class.

Suppose that we have computed the probability density function:

$$p(\boldsymbol{\theta}_i/\mathbf{x}_1, \ldots, \mathbf{x}_{N-1}; \omega_i)$$

and observe an additional learning sample $\mathbf{x}_N$; we then want the new probability density function:

$$p(\boldsymbol{\theta}_i/\mathbf{x}_1, \ldots, \mathbf{x}_N; \omega_i)$$

to have the same parametric description as before. With a reproducing *a priori* density $p(\boldsymbol{\theta}_i)$, the structure of the classifier will remain the same; only the parameters involved in the computation of the likelihood function:

$$p(\mathbf{x}_N/\mathbf{x}_1, \ldots, \mathbf{x}_{N-1}; \omega_i)$$

will change with N.

Since

$$p(\mathbf{x}/\mathbf{P}_i) = (2\pi)^{-n/2}|\mathbf{P}_i|^{1/2} \exp(-\tfrac{1}{2}\mathbf{x}'\mathbf{P}_i\mathbf{x})$$

and the measurements $\mathbf{x}_1, \ldots, \mathbf{x}_N$ are independent,

$$\begin{aligned} p(\mathbf{x}_1, \ldots, \mathbf{x}_N/\mathbf{P}_i) &= \prod_{j=1}^{N} (2\pi)^{-n/2}|\mathbf{P}_i|^{1/2} \exp[-\tfrac{1}{2}\mathbf{x}'(j)\mathbf{P}_i\mathbf{x}(j)] \\ &= (2\pi)^{-nN/2}|\mathbf{P}_i|^{N/2} \exp[-\tfrac{1}{2} \operatorname{tr} (N\mathbf{P}_i\overline{\mathbf{x}\mathbf{x}'})] \qquad (4.6\text{–}41) \end{aligned}$$

where

$$\overline{\mathbf{x}\mathbf{x}'} = \frac{1}{N} \sum_{j=1}^{N} \mathbf{x}(j)\mathbf{x}'(j)$$

and we have used the fact that

$$\mathbf{x}'(j)\mathbf{P}_i\mathbf{x}(j) = \operatorname{tr} [\mathbf{P}_i\mathbf{x}(j)\mathbf{x}'(j)]$$

Here $\mathbf{x}\mathbf{x}'$ denotes the matrix outer product and results in a symmetric matrix of rank 1.

Since

$$p(\mathbf{P}_i/\mathbf{x}_1, \ldots, \mathbf{x}_N) = \frac{p(\mathbf{x}_N/\mathbf{x}_1, \ldots, \mathbf{x}_{N-1}/\mathbf{P}_i)p(\mathbf{P}_i)}{p(\mathbf{x}_1, \ldots, \mathbf{x}_N)} \qquad (4.6\text{–}42)$$

we obtain from Eqs. (4.6–38) and (4.6–42)

$$\begin{aligned} p(\mathbf{P}_i/\mathbf{x}_1, \ldots, \mathbf{x}_N) = K &\left\{ C_{n,\nu_0} \left| \frac{\nu_0\mathbf{\Phi}_0}{2} \right|^{(\nu_0-1)/2} |\mathbf{P}_i|^{(\nu_0-n-2)/2} \exp[-\tfrac{1}{2} \operatorname{tr} (\nu_0\mathbf{\Phi}_0\mathbf{P}_i)] \right\} \\ &\times \{(2\pi)^{-nN/2}|\mathbf{P}_i|^{N/2} \exp[-\tfrac{1}{2} \operatorname{tr} (N\mathbf{P}_i\overline{\mathbf{x}\mathbf{x}'})]\} \qquad (4.6\text{–}43) \end{aligned}$$

where K is a constant.

We do not need to include the denominator of Eq. (4.6–42) since it only normalizes the density considered as a function of $\mathbf{P}_i$. By collecting terms which are functions of $\mathbf{P}_i$, we can easily see that the *a posteriori* density function is again Wishart:

$$p(\mathbf{P}_i/\mathbf{x}_1, \ldots, \mathbf{x}_N) = K|\mathbf{P}_i|^{(\nu_N-n-2)/2} \exp[-\tfrac{1}{2} \operatorname{tr} (\nu_N\mathbf{\Phi}_N\mathbf{P}_i)] \qquad (4.6\text{–}44)$$

where

$$\nu_N = \nu_0 + N \tag{4.6–45}$$

and

$$\mathbf{\Phi}_N = \frac{\nu_0 \mathbf{\Phi}_0 + N\mathbf{x}\mathbf{x}'}{\nu_0 + N} = \frac{1}{1 + (N/\nu_0)} \mathbf{\Phi}_0 + \frac{1}{1 + (\nu_0/N)} \mathbf{x}\mathbf{x}' \tag{4.6–46}$$

The *a posteriori* probability has parameter $\mathbf{\Phi}_N$, which reflects the weight attached to $\mathbf{\Phi}_0$ and $\mathbf{x}\mathbf{x}'$ by taking a weighted sum with multipliers ν_0 and N, respectively. Parameter $\mathbf{\Phi}_N$ represents the weighted average of the prior knowledge about $\mathbf{P}_i$, $\mathbf{\Phi}_0$, and the sample information contained in $\mathbf{x}\mathbf{x}'$.

4.6.4 Functional Approximation of Probability Density Functions

In Sections 4.6.2 and 4.6.3 we discussed special cases of the estimation of parameters of a probability density function whose form is assumed to be known. Often, this assumption is not valid and it becomes necessary to estimate the density function directly.

Let $\hat{p}(\mathbf{x})$ represent an estimate of $p(\mathbf{x})$ where, as before, $p(\mathbf{x})$ represents $p(\mathbf{x}/\omega_i)$. We wish this estimate to minimize the mean-square error function, defined as

$$R = \int_{\mathbf{x}} u(\mathbf{x})[p(\mathbf{x}) - \hat{p}(\mathbf{x})]^2 \, d\mathbf{x} \tag{4.6–47}$$

where $u(\mathbf{x})$ is a weighting function. Let us expand the estimate $\hat{p}(\mathbf{x})$ in the series

$$\hat{p}(\mathbf{x}) = \sum_{j=1}^{m} c_j \varphi_j(\mathbf{x}) \tag{4.6–48}$$

where the c_j are coefficients to be determined, and the $\{\varphi_j(\mathbf{x})\}$ are a set of specified basis functions. Section 2.7 contains a discussion of how these functions may be formed. The well-known Fourier series expansion is a special case of Eq. (4.6–48) in which the basis functions are sinusoidal in nature.

Substituting Eq. (4.6–48) into (4.6–47) yields

$$R = \int_{\mathbf{x}} u(\mathbf{x})[p(\mathbf{x}) - \sum_{j=1}^{m} c_j \varphi_j(\mathbf{x})]^2 \, d\mathbf{x} \tag{4.6–49}$$

We wish to determine the coefficients c_j which minimize the error function R. A necessary condition for the minimum of R is

$$\frac{\partial R}{\partial c_k} = 0, \quad k = 1, 2, \ldots, m \tag{4.6–50}$$

Carrying out the partial differentiation yields

$$\sum_{j=1}^{m} c_j \int_{\mathbf{x}} u(\mathbf{x})\varphi_j(\mathbf{x})\varphi_k(\mathbf{x})\, d\mathbf{x} = \int_{\mathbf{x}} u(\mathbf{x})\varphi_k(\mathbf{x})p(\mathbf{x})\, d\mathbf{x} \tag{4.6–51}$$

We recognize the right-hand side of Eq. (4.6–51) as the definition of the expected value of the function $u(\mathbf{x})\varphi_k(\mathbf{x})$. In agreement with our previous discussion, the expected value may be approximated by the sample average, yielding

$$\int_{\mathbf{x}} u(\mathbf{x})\varphi_k(\mathbf{x})p(\mathbf{x})\, d\mathbf{x} \approx \frac{1}{N} \sum_{i=1}^{N} u(\mathbf{x}_i)\varphi_k(\mathbf{x}_i) \tag{4.6–52}$$

Substituting this approximation into Eq. (4.6–51) results in the relation

$$\sum_{j=1}^{m} c_j \int_{\mathbf{x}} u(\mathbf{x})\varphi_j(\mathbf{x})\varphi_k(\mathbf{x})\, d\mathbf{x} = \frac{1}{N} \sum_{i=1}^{N} u(\mathbf{x}_i)\varphi_k(\mathbf{x}_i) \tag{4.6–53}$$

If the basis functions $\{\varphi(\mathbf{x})\}$ are chosen to be orthogonal with respect to the weighting function $u(\mathbf{x})$, then, by the definition of orthogonality given in Eq. (2.7–4),

$$\int_{\mathbf{x}} u(\mathbf{x})\varphi_j(\mathbf{x})\varphi_k(\mathbf{x})\, d\mathbf{x} = \begin{cases} A_k & \text{if} \quad j = k \\ 0 & \text{if} \quad j \neq k \end{cases} \tag{4.6–54}$$

Substituting Eq. (4.6–54) into (4.6–53) results in the following relation for the evaluation of the coefficients:

$$c_k = \frac{1}{NA_k} \sum_{i=1}^{N} u(\mathbf{x}_i)\varphi_k(\mathbf{x}_i), \quad k = 1, 2, \ldots, m \tag{4.6–55}$$

If the basis functions $\{\varphi_k(\mathbf{x})\}$ are orthonormal, $A_k = 1$ for all k. Also, since the terms $u(\mathbf{x}_i)$ are independent of k and are thus distributed equally over all coefficients, they often can be eliminated from the approximation without impairing the discriminatory power of the coefficients. Under these conditions, we then have that

$$c_k = \frac{1}{N} \sum_{i=1}^{N} \varphi_k(\mathbf{x}_i), \quad k = 1, 2, \ldots, m \tag{4.6–56}$$

Once the coefficients have been determined, the density function $\hat{p}(\mathbf{x})$ is formed, using Eq. (4.6–48).

By means of the procedure used in Section 4.6.2, Eq. (4.6–56) may be expressed in a convenient recursive form. If we let $c_k(N)$ represent a coefficient obtained with N samples, the coefficient obtained with one more sample is given by

$$c_k(N+1) = \frac{1}{N+1} \sum_{i=1}^{N+1} \varphi_k(\mathbf{x}_i)$$

$$= \frac{1}{N+1} [Nc_k(N) + \varphi_k(\mathbf{x}_{N+1})] \tag{4.6–57}$$

where $c_k(1) = \varphi_k(\mathbf{x}_1)$. When Eq. (4.6–57) is used, only the previously determined coefficients $c_k(N)$ need be employed to determine the new coefficients, thus simplifying the computational procedure.

The successful application of Eqs. (4.6–48) and (4.6–55) or (4.6–56) requires that two basic considerations be taken into account. First, it should be kept clearly in mind that the quality of approximation for a chosen set of basis functions depends on the number m of terms taken. Since we presumably do not know $p(\mathbf{x})$, it is not possible to test the quality of $\hat{p}(\mathbf{x})$ by direct comparison. However, since the purpose of calculating $\hat{p}(\mathbf{x})$ is to design a Bayes classifier, we should be concerned only with the recognition performance of this classifier. This can certainly be measured by direct experimentation with the training set. If the performance of the classifier for a given $\hat{p}(\mathbf{x})$ is poor, more basis functions should be included to see whether improving the quality of $\hat{p}(\mathbf{x})$ enhances the classification performance. This procedure is continued until "saturation," in the sense that adding new terms has little or no effect, occurs, or until the number of terms exceeds an acceptable value.

A second important consideration is the choice of basis functions. For example, if $p(\mathbf{x})$ is sinusoidal in nature and we choose to expand $\hat{p}(\mathbf{x})$ in a polynomial series, it is clear that the number of terms needed will be considerably greater than if sinusoidal basis functions had originally been chosen. Of course, since we have no *a priori* knowledge of $p(\mathbf{x})$ the basis functions must be chosen primarily for their simplicity of implementation. All we can say in general regarding the choice of basis functions is that, as long as they are linearly independent and under some mild conditions on $p(\mathbf{x})$, it can be shown that $\hat{p}(\mathbf{x}) \to p(\mathbf{x})$ as $m \to \infty$ and $N \to \infty$. It is noted that orthogonality is a special case of linear independence.

Example: Consider the pattern classes shown in Fig. 4.6. It is desired to design a Bayes classifier for these classes by employing probability density functions which have been directly estimated from the training samples. We may approximate these functions by an expansion of the form shown in Eq. (4.6–48):

$$\hat{p}(\mathbf{x}/\omega_i) = \sum_{j=1}^{m} c_{ij}\varphi_j(\mathbf{x})$$

where the first subscript on the coefficients denotes class ω_i.

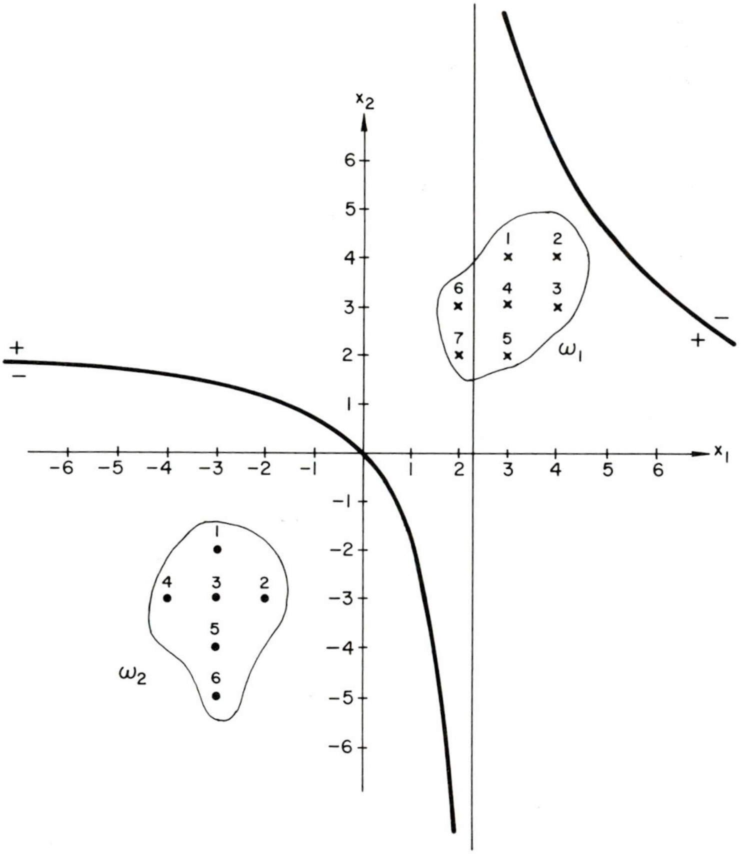

Figure 4.6. Bayes decision boundary determined by functional approximation

As indicated in Eq. (4.6–54), the functions $\{\varphi_j(\mathbf{x})\}$ are assumed to be orthogonal over the region of definition of the patterns. The Hermite polynomial functions discussed in Section 2.7 are particularly easy to apply since their region of orthogonality is the interval $(-\infty, \infty)$. In the one-dimensional case these functions are given by the recursive relation

$$H_{l+1}(x) - 2xH_l(x) + 2lH_{l-1}(x) = 0$$

as indicated in Eq. (2.7–18). The first few terms of $H(x)$ are as follows:

$$H_0(x) = 1, \qquad H_1(x) = 2x$$

$$H_2(x) = 4x^2 - 2, \qquad H_3(x) = 8x^3 - 12x$$

$$H_4(x) = 16x^4 - 48x^2 + 12$$

These functions are orthogonal. As discussed in Section 2.7.3, the orthonormal functions are given by

$$\phi_l(x) = \frac{\exp(-x^2/2)}{\sqrt{2^l l! \sqrt{\pi}}} H_l(x)$$

where the term multiplying $H_l(x)$ is an orthonormalization factor. For the purpose of illustration we will treat orthogonal functions as if they were orthonormal. This is in general a good practice which avoids computational difficulties for large k in Eq. (4.6–55). For example, if $k = 50$, $A_k \approx 6.07 \times 10^{79}$ for Hermite polynomials.

A two-dimensional orthogonal set of functions is easily obtained by forming arbitrary pairwise combinations of the one-dimensional functions. Suppose that we let $m = 4$.† The four lowest-order terms of the two-dimensional orthogonal set are given by

$$\varphi_1(\mathbf{x}) = \varphi_1(x_1, x_2) = H_0(x_1)H_0(x_2) = 1$$

$$\varphi_2(\mathbf{x}) = \varphi_2(x_1, x_2) = H_1(x_1)H_0(x_2) = 2x_1$$

$$\varphi_3(\mathbf{x}) = \varphi_3(x_1, x_2) = H_0(x_1)H_1(x_2) = 2x_2$$

$$\varphi_4(\mathbf{x}) = \varphi_4(x_1, x_2) = H_1(x_1)H_1(x_2) = 4x_1x_2$$

It should be clear that there is nothing unique about the order in which the above terms were formed. Any pairwise combination is acceptable for

† This value has been arbitrarily chosen as a reasonable approximation for illustrative purposes. In general, an acceptable value for m must be determined by direct trial.

any of the $\varphi(\mathbf{x})$'s. Any other choice of $H_l(\mathbf{x})$ would have simply yielded more complex terms.

The problem now is to determine the coefficients c_{ij} for use in the expansion of $p(\mathbf{x}/\omega_i)$. Treating the functions as if they were orthonormal, these coefficients may be computed as follows from Eq. (4.6–56). For class ω_1,

$$c_{1k} = \frac{1}{N_1}\sum_{j=1}^{N_1} \varphi_k(\mathbf{x}_{1j})$$

where N_1 is the number of patterns in class ω_1, and k ranges from 1 to m. Using the patterns of class ω_1 shown in Fig. 4.6 yields the following results:

$$c_{11} = \tfrac{1}{7}[\varphi_1(\mathbf{x}_{11}) + \varphi_1(\mathbf{x}_{12}) + \varphi_1(\mathbf{x}_{13}) + \cdots + \varphi_1(\mathbf{x}_{17})]$$

where the first subscript on the patterns indicates class ω_1. Since $\varphi_1(\mathbf{x}) = 1$, we obtain

$$c_{11} = \tfrac{1}{7}(1 + 1 + 1 + \cdots + 1) = 1$$

The next coefficient is given by

$$c_{12} = \tfrac{1}{7}[\varphi_2(\mathbf{x}_{11}) + \varphi_2(\mathbf{x}_{12}) + \varphi_2(\mathbf{x}_{13}) + \cdots + \varphi_2(\mathbf{x}_{17})]$$

and, since $\varphi_2(\mathbf{x})$ is equal to twice the first component of $\mathbf{x}$,

$$c_{12} = \tfrac{2}{7}(3 + 4 + 4 + 3 + 3 + 2 + 2) = 6$$

Similarly,

$$\begin{aligned} c_{13} &= \tfrac{1}{7}[\varphi_3(\mathbf{x}_{11}) + \varphi_3(\mathbf{x}_{12}) + \varphi_3(\mathbf{x}_{13}) + \cdots + \varphi_3(\mathbf{x}_{17})] \\ &= 6 \\ c_{14} &= \tfrac{1}{7}[\varphi_4(\mathbf{x}_{11}) + \varphi_4(\mathbf{x}_{12}) + \varphi_4(\mathbf{x}_{13}) + \cdots + \varphi_4(\mathbf{x}_{17})] \\ &= 37.1 \end{aligned}$$

Following the same procedure for the patterns of ω_2 results in the following coefficients for this class:

$$c_{21} = 1, \qquad c_{22} = -6, \qquad c_{23} = -6.7, \qquad c_{24} = 40$$

Therefore, according to Eq. (4.6–48), the approximations to $p(\mathbf{x}/\omega_i)$ are

$$\begin{aligned} \hat{p}(\mathbf{x}/\omega_1) &= c_{11}\varphi_1(\mathbf{x}) + c_{12}\varphi_2(\mathbf{x}) + c_{13}\varphi_3(\mathbf{x}) + c_{14}\varphi_4(\mathbf{x}) \\ &= 1 + 12x_1 + 12x_2 + 148.4x_1x_2 \end{aligned}$$

$$\hat{p}(\mathbf{x}/\omega_2) = c_{21}\varphi_1(\mathbf{x}) + c_{22}\varphi_2(\mathbf{x}) + c_{23}\varphi_3(\mathbf{x}) + c_{24}\varphi_4(\mathbf{x})$$
$$= 1 - 12x_1 - 13.4x_2 + 160x_1x_2$$

The decision functions for this problem are then given by

$$d_1(\mathbf{x}) = \hat{p}(\mathbf{x}/\omega_1)p(\omega_1)$$
$$d_2(\mathbf{x}) = \hat{p}(\mathbf{x}/\omega_2)p(\omega_2)$$

If it is assumed that $p(\omega_1) = p(\omega_2) = \frac{1}{2}$, we obtain

$$d_1(\mathbf{x}) = \tfrac{1}{2} + 6x_1 + 6x_2 + 74.2x_1x_2$$
$$d_2(\mathbf{x}) = \tfrac{1}{2} - 6x_1 - 6.7x_2 + 80x_1x_2$$

The equation of the decision boundary is then given by

$$d_1(\mathbf{x}) - d_2(\mathbf{x}) = 12x_1 + 12.7x_2 - 5.8x_1x_2 = 0$$

This decision boundary is shown in Fig. 4.6. Since this is a two-class problem, $d_1(\mathbf{x}) - d_2(\mathbf{x})$ represents the decision function for classification. It is also worth noting that, in this case, a linear approximation to $p(\mathbf{x}/\omega_1)$ and $p(\mathbf{x}/\omega_2)$ would have worked equally well. This can be seen by setting the nonlinear term in the above expression equal to zero. Although we started with a nonlinear decision function to fully illustrate the procedure, it should be evident that in most problems one normally starts with a linear approximation. Only when unacceptable results are obtained is the complexity of the approximation increased. ●

An important special case of functional approximation is the estimation of the probability density functions of binary patterns. When $\mathbf{x} = (x_1, x_2, \ldots, x_k, \ldots, x_n)'$ and $x_k = 1$ or 0, there are 2^n possible distinct patterns, each pattern being a vertex point of the unit n-cube. Instead of calculating a continuous density function, we are then interested in the discrete probability function $p(\mathbf{x} = \mathbf{x}_j)$, where j ranges from 1 to 2^n; that is, we are interested in the probability of occurrence of each of the 2^n possible pattern vectors. The results derived earlier in this section are easily applied to this problem by properly choosing the basis functions $\{\varphi(\mathbf{x})\}$. The Rademacher-Walsh polynomial functions, which are often used in the expansion of discrete functions, may be employed for this purpose. This set contains 2^n terms and is formed by taking products of *distinct* terms of the form $(2x_k - 1)$ none at a time, one at a time, two at a time, three at a time, and so forth until the product of n terms is formed. The procedure is illustrated in Table 4.1.

TABLE 4.1. *Formation of the Rademacher-Walsh Polynomials*

j	$\varphi_j(\mathbf{x})$
1	1
2	$2x_1 - 1$
3	$2x_2 - 1$
$\vdots$	$\vdots$
$n + 1$	$2x_n - 1$
$n + 2$	$(2x_1 - 1)(2x_2 - 1)$
$n + 3$	$(2x_1 - 1)(2x_3 - 1)$
$\vdots$	$\vdots$
$n + 2 + n - 1$	$(2x_1 - 1)(2x_n - 1)$
$n + 3 + n - 1$	$(2x_2 - 1)(2x_3 - 1)$
$n + 4 + n - 1$	$(2x_2 - 1)(2x_4 - 1)$
$\vdots$	$\vdots$
$n + 2 + n(n - 1)/2$	$(2x_{n-1} - 1)(2x_n - 1)$
$n + 3 + n(n - 1)/2$	$(2x_1 - 1)(2x_2 - 1)(2x_3 - 1)$
$\vdots$	$\vdots$
$n + 3 + n(n - 1)/2 + n(n - 1)(n - 2)/6$	$(2x_{n-2} - 1)(2x_{n-1} - 1)(2x_n - 1)$
$\vdots$	$\vdots$
2^n	$(2x_1 - 1)(2x_2 - 1) \cdots (2x_n - 1)$

These discrete polynomial functions are orthogonal with respect to the weighting function $u(\mathbf{x}) = 1$ (see Sec. 2.7.1) since

$$\sum_{\mathbf{x}} \varphi_j(\mathbf{x})\varphi_k(\mathbf{x}) = \begin{cases} 2^n & \text{if } j = k \\ 0 & \text{if } j \neq k \end{cases} \tag{4.6–58}$$

where the summation is taken over all 2^n values of the binary vectors $\mathbf{x}$.

If only m basis functions are used in the expansion, the approximation of the *discrete* probability density function $p(\mathbf{x})$ is, from Eq. (4.6–48),

$$\hat{p}(\mathbf{x}) = \sum_{j=1}^{m} c_j\varphi_j(\mathbf{x})$$

where the coefficients are determined using Eq. (4.6–55) with $A_k = 2^n$ and $u(\mathbf{x}) = 1$, that is,

$$c_k = \frac{1}{2^n N} \sum_{i=1}^{N} \varphi_k(\mathbf{x}_i) \tag{4.6–59}$$

The relation for orthonormal functions is given by Eq. (4.6–56).

Since, in this case, a complete set of basis functions consists of 2^n terms, convergence of $\hat{p}(\mathbf{x})$ to $p(\mathbf{x})$ is assured when $m = 2^n$ and N equals 2^n distinct binary patterns.

Example: As an illustration of discrete functional approximation, consider again the patterns shown in Fig. 4.3. The pattern classes are ω_1: $\{(0, 0, 0)', (1, 0, 1)', (1, 0, 0)', (1, 1, 0)'\}$ and ω_2: $\{(0, 0, 1)', (0, 1, 1)', (0, 1, 0)', (1, 1, 1)'\}$.

Choosing a linear approximation to $p(\mathbf{x})$, we have, from Table 4.1,

$$\varphi_1(\mathbf{x}) = 1, \qquad \varphi_2(\mathbf{x}) = 2x_1 - 1, \qquad \varphi_3(\mathbf{x}) = 2x_2 - 1, \qquad \varphi_4(\mathbf{x}) = 2x_3 - 1$$

where each x_i is either 0 or 1.

The coefficients for class ω_1 are, from Eq. (4.6–59),

$$c_{1k} = \frac{1}{2^n N_1} \sum_{i=1}^{N_1} \varphi_k(\mathbf{x}_{1i})$$

where N_1 represents the number of patterns in class ω_1, and $n = 3$. Carrying out the summation over the patterns of class ω_1 yields

$$\begin{aligned} c_{11} &= \frac{1}{32} \sum_{i=1}^{4} \varphi_1(\mathbf{x}_{1i}) \\ &= \tfrac{1}{32}(1 + 1 + 1 + 1) = \tfrac{1}{8} \\ c_{12} &= \frac{1}{32} \sum_{i=1}^{4} \varphi_2(\mathbf{x}_{1i}) \\ &= \tfrac{1}{32}(-1 + 1 + 1 + 1) = \tfrac{1}{16} \\ c_{13} &= \frac{1}{32} \sum_{i=1}^{4} \varphi_3(\mathbf{x}_{1i}) \\ &= \tfrac{1}{32}(-1 - 1 - 1 + 1) = -\tfrac{1}{16} \\ c_{14} &= \frac{1}{32} \sum_{i=1}^{4} \varphi_4(\mathbf{x}_{1i}) \\ &= \tfrac{1}{32}(-1 + 1 - 1 - 1) = -\tfrac{1}{16} \end{aligned}$$

Following the same procedure with the patterns of ω_2 yields

$$c_{21} = \tfrac{1}{8}, \qquad c_{22} = -\tfrac{1}{16}, \qquad c_{23} = \tfrac{1}{16}, \qquad c_{24} = \tfrac{1}{16}$$

The approximate density functions are, then,

$$\begin{aligned}\hat{p}(\mathbf{x}/\omega_1) &= \sum_{j=1}^{4} c_{1j}\varphi_j(\mathbf{x}) \\ &= \tfrac{1}{8} + \tfrac{1}{16}(2x_1 - 1) - \tfrac{1}{16}(2x_2 - 1) - \tfrac{1}{16}(2x_3 - 1)\end{aligned}$$

$$\begin{aligned}\hat{p}(\mathbf{x}/\omega_2) &= \sum_{j=1}^{4} c_{2j}\varphi_j(\mathbf{x}) \\ &= \tfrac{1}{8} - \tfrac{1}{16}(2x_1 - 1) + \tfrac{1}{16}(2x_2 - 1) + \tfrac{1}{16}(2x_3 - 1)\end{aligned}$$

If we assume $p(\omega_1) = p(\omega_2) = \frac{1}{2}$, the decision functions are as follows:

$$d_1(\mathbf{x}) = \hat{p}(\mathbf{x}/\omega_1)p(\omega_1) = \tfrac{1}{16} + \tfrac{1}{32}(2x_1 - 1) - \tfrac{1}{32}(2x_2 - 1) - \tfrac{1}{32}(2x_3 - 1)$$

$$d_2(\mathbf{x}) = \hat{p}(\mathbf{x}/\omega_2)p(\omega_2) = \tfrac{1}{16} - \tfrac{1}{32}(2x_1 - 1) + \tfrac{1}{32}(2x_2 - 1) + \tfrac{1}{32}(2x_3 - 1)$$

A single decision function for both classes is obtained by defining $d(\mathbf{x}) = d_1(\mathbf{x}) - d_2(\mathbf{x})$. Thus,

$$d(\mathbf{x}) = \tfrac{1}{16}(2x_1 - 1) - \tfrac{1}{16}(2x_2 - 1) - \tfrac{1}{16}(2x_3 - 1)$$

which, after multiplication by 16, becomes

$$d(\mathbf{x}) = (2x_1 - 1) - (2x_2 - 1) - (2x_3 - 1)$$

It is easily verified that $d(\mathbf{x}) > 0$ for all patterns of ω_1 and $d(\mathbf{x}) < 0$ for all patterns of ω_2. Equivalent results are obtained using orthonormal functions.

It should be noted that $d(\mathbf{x})$ is valid only for binary values of $\mathbf{x}$. Consequently, it makes no sense in this case to talk about a decision surface in the manner previously discussed. The function $d(\mathbf{x})$ assumes only eight values—one for each of the eight possible binary patterns in three dimensions. ●

4.7 CONCLUDING REMARKS

The principal development in this chapter has been the derivation of the Bayes classification rule from elementary statistical decision theory. In terms of pattern recognition, the special case derived under the assumption of a zero-one loss function establishes the upper limit of performance that any classifier based on the decision function concept can achieve on an average basis. This important theoretical result is applicable, therefore, to all the classification schemes derived in Chapters 3 through 6.

Since the implementation of a Bayes classifier requires knowledge of the probability density function characterizing each of the pattern classes, it is evident that estimation of these densities is the central problem underlying the application of this classification scheme. Making use of the principle of maximum entropy, we showed that it is reasonable to choose a normal density when the mean and variance are the only known parameters. Since this represents a problem of practical as well as theoretical importance, considerable effort was devoted to methods for estimating these parameters. When parametric estimation is not sufficient, the method of direct functional approximation of probability densities may be employed. As indicated in the preceding section, the true probability density function can be approached with an arbitrary degree of closeness by increasing the number of terms used in the expansion, as well as the number of patterns employed in the determination of the coefficients.

In Chapter 6 we will return to the problem of the functional approximation of probability densities from a different point of view. It is worth noting that, although we have been discussing statistical decision functions, these functions fall within the general framework established in Chapter 2. Examples of this were evident in the development of a Bayes classifier for normal patterns and for patterns characterized the Pearson Type VII density function. The same is also true of the more general functional approximation technique described in Section 4.6.4. Clearly, once an approximation to a density function has been expanded in a set of basis functions (e.g., polynomial functions), there would be no difference in form between the resulting statistical decision function and a decision function of the same type established by deterministic means. Of course, the *performances* of these decision functions depend on the method chosen for their calculation.

REFERENCES

The field of statistical games and decision theory is well documented in the literature. The book by Blackwell and Girshick [1954] is an excellent reference in this area. It is possible to arrive at the results developed in Section 4.2 from a communication theory point of view. The books by Reza [1961], Van Trees [1968], and by Helstrom [1968] develop the Bayes classification rule by considering the problem from an engineering standpoint.

Bayes classification of normal patterns is also a topic which has received ample coverage in the literature. Additional references in this area are Cooper [1967], Anderson and Bahadur [1962], Fukunaga [1972], Patrick [1972], Tou [1969a], Kanal and Randall [1964], Nilsson [1965], Duda and Hart [1973], Fu [1968], and Meisel [1972].

Early work on the Bayesian approach to learning the mean vector and covariance matrix can be found in the papers by Abramson and Braverman [1962] and Keehn [1965]. However, this problem is treated in varying degrees of detail in almost all books dealing with statistical pattern recognition. The books by Patrick, Fukunaga, and Duda and Hart are oriented toward statistical pattern recognition and thus provide excellent supplementary reading for the material presented in this chapter. Complementary material on the functional approximation problem may be found in Tou [1969a, 1969b], and Meisel [1972].

PROBLEMS

4.1 Consider an M-class, one-dimensional pattern recognition problem in which each class is characterized by a Rayleigh probability density function:

$$p(x/\omega_i) = \begin{cases} \dfrac{x}{\sigma_i^2} \exp\left(\dfrac{-x^2}{2\sigma_i^2}\right), & x \geqslant 0 \\ 0, & x < 0 \end{cases}$$

Derive the Bayes decision functions for this problem, assuming a zero-one loss function. Let $p(\omega_i) = 1/M$.

4.2 (a) Repeat Problem 4.1 using the normal density:

$$p(x/\omega_i) = \frac{1}{\sqrt{2\pi}\sigma_i} \exp\left[\frac{-(x-m_i)^2}{2\sigma_i^2}\right]$$

(b) Sketch the density functions for a two-class problem in which $\sigma_1 = \sigma_2 = 2$, $m_1 = 0$, and $m_2 = 2$. Where is the decision boundary located?

4.3 Two one-dimensional pattern classes are governed by the following probability density functions:

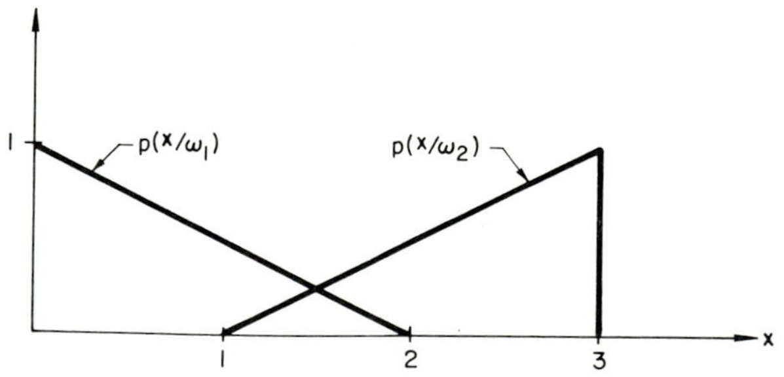

(a) Derive the Bayes decision functions, assuming a zero-one loss function and equal *a priori* probabilities.

(b) Find the location of the decision boundary.

4.4 Assume that the following pattern classes have normal probability density functions: ω_1: $\{(0, 0)', (2, 0)', (2, 2)', (0, 2)'\}$ and ω_2: $\{(4, 4)', (6, 4)', (6, 6)', (4, 6)'\}$.

(a) Assuming $p(\omega_1) = p(\omega_2) = \frac{1}{2}$, obtain the equation of the Bayes decision boundary between these two classes.

(b) Sketch the boundary.

4.5 Repeat Problem 4.4 using the following pattern classes: ω_1: $\{(-1, 0)', (0, -1)', (1, 0)', (0, 1)'\}$ and ω_2: $\{(-2, 0)', (0, -2)', (2, 0)', (0, 2)'\}$. Observe that these classes are not linearly separable.

4.6 (a) Obtain an equation for the Bayes decision boundary between two pattern classes characterized by Pearson Type II density functions with equal values of k.

(b) Discuss the properties of the decision boundary obtained in part (a) for equal and unequal weight matrices.

4.7 (a) Use the method of functional approximation to obtain estimates of $p(\mathbf{x}/\omega_1)$ and $p(\mathbf{x}/\omega_2)$ for the following pattern classes: ω_1: $\{(-5, -5)', (-5, -4)', (-4, -5)', (-5, -6)', (-6, -5)'\}$ and ω_2: $\{(5, 5)', (5, 6)', (6, 5)', (5, 4)', (4, 5)'\}$. Use the first four two-dimensional Hermite polynomial functions in their orthogonal form, and use Eq. (4.6–55) to compute the coefficients. Note from Eqs. (2.7–7) and (2.7–19) that $A_k = 2^k k! \sqrt{\pi}$. Assume for convenience that $\mu(\mathbf{x}) = 1$.

(b) Repeat part (a) with the orthogonal functions, but use Eq. (4.6–56) to compute the coefficients.

(c) Assuming $p(\omega_1) = p(\omega_2) = \frac{1}{2}$, obtain the Bayes decision functions for parts (a) and (b).

(d) Sketch the decision boundaries obtained in part (c).

(e) Repeat parts (b) through (d) using the orthonormal Hermite polynomials, and compare.

4.8 The decision functions $d_i(\mathbf{x}) = p(\mathbf{x}/\omega_i)p(\omega_i)$ were derived using a zero-one loss function. Prove that these decision functions minimize the probability of error. *Hint*: The probability of error $p(e)$ is $1 - p(c)$, where $p(c)$ is the probability of being correct. For a given pattern $\mathbf{x}$ belonging to class ω_i, $p(c/\mathbf{x}) = p(\omega_i/\mathbf{x})$. Use this to find $p(c)$ and show that $p(c)$ is maximum [$p(e)$ minimum] when $p(\mathbf{x}/\omega_i)p(\omega_i)$ is maximum.

5

TRAINABLE PATTERN CLASSIFIERS—THE DETERMINISTIC APPROACH

5.1 INTRODUCTION

Thus far, our approaches to the design of pattern classifiers have been based on direct computations in the sense that the decision boundaries generated by these approaches are derived from sample patterns which determine the coefficients via direct calculation. We have examples of this kind in Chapter 3, where it is necessary to estimate cluster centers or standard patterns before a classifier can be specified, and again in Chapter 4, where the structure of the Bayes classifier for normal patterns is completely fixed by the determination of the mean vector and covariance matrix of each class.

In this chapter we begin the study of classifiers whose decision functions are generated from training patterns by means of iterative, "learning" algorithms. As was pointed out in Chapter 2, once a type of decision function has been specified, the problem is the determination of the coefficients. The algorithms presented in this chapter are capable of learning the solution coefficients from the training sets whenever these training pattern sets are separable by the specified decision functions.

It was pointed out in Section 2.4 that the solution of a two-class problem is equivalent to the solution of a system of linear inequalities. Thus, if we are given two sets of patterns belonging, respectively, to classes ω_1 and ω_2, it is desired to find a solution weight vector $\mathbf{w}$ with the property that $\mathbf{w}'\mathbf{x} > 0$ for all patterns of ω_1 and $\mathbf{w}'\mathbf{x} < 0$ for all patterns of ω_2. If the patterns of ω_2 are multiplied by -1, we obtain the equivalent condition $\mathbf{w}'\mathbf{x} > 0$

for all patterns. Letting N represent the total number of augmented sample patterns (see Chapter 2) in both classes, we may express the problem as one of finding a vector $\mathbf{w}$ such that the system of inequalities

$$\mathbf{X}\mathbf{w} > \mathbf{0} \tag{5.1–1}$$

is satisfied, where

$$\mathbf{X} = \begin{pmatrix} \mathbf{x}_1' \\ \mathbf{x}_2' \\ \vdots \\ \mathbf{x}_N' \end{pmatrix} \tag{5.1–2}$$

$\mathbf{w} = (w_1, w_2, \ldots, w_n, w_{n+1})'$, and $\mathbf{0}$ is the zero vector. If the patterns are well distributed, as defined in Chapter 2, $\mathbf{X}$ satisfies the Haar condition, that is, every $(n + 1) \times (n + 1)$ submatrix of $\mathbf{X}$ is of rank $n + 1$ (Cheney [1966]).

If there exists a $\mathbf{w}$ which satisfies expression (5.1–1), the inequalities are said to be *consistent*; otherwise, they are *inconsistent*. In pattern recognition terminology we say that the classes are separable or inseparable, respectively. The reader should keep clearly in mind that the formulation given in expression (5.1–1) assumes that all the patterns of one class have been multiplied by -1, and also that all patterns have been augmented, as discussed in Chapter 2.

Basically, we can take either a *deterministic* or a *statistical* approach to the solution of (5.1–1). The deterministic approach forms the basis for the algorithms developed in this chapter. As the name implies, these algorithms are developed without making any assumptions concerning the statistical properties of the pattern classes. On the other hand, the statistical algorithms developed in Chapter 6 attempt to approximate the density functions $p(\omega_i/\mathbf{x})$, which can then be used as Bayes decision functions, as indicated in Eq. (4.2–23). As will be seen when the study of the two approaches is completed, however, the statistical and deterministic algorithms are surprisingly similar in form.

5.2 THE PERCEPTRON APPROACH

The origin of the pattern classification algorithm to be presented in this section may be traced to early efforts in the field of *bionics* (the application of biological concepts to electronic machines), which were concerned with problems in animal and machine learning. During the mid 1950's and early 1960's a class of machines, originated by Rosenblatt [1957] and frequently called *perceptrons,* seemed to offer what many researchers thought was a natural and powerful model of machine learning. Although it is now generally agreed that the hopes and expectations in regard to perceptron performance were overoptimistic, the mathematical concepts which resulted from the development of perceptrons continue to play a central role in pattern recognition theory.

The basic model of a perceptron capable of classifying a pattern into one of two classes is shown in Fig. 5.1. The machine consists of an array S of *sensory units* which are randomly connected to a second array A of *associative units.* Each of these units produces an output only if enough of the sensory

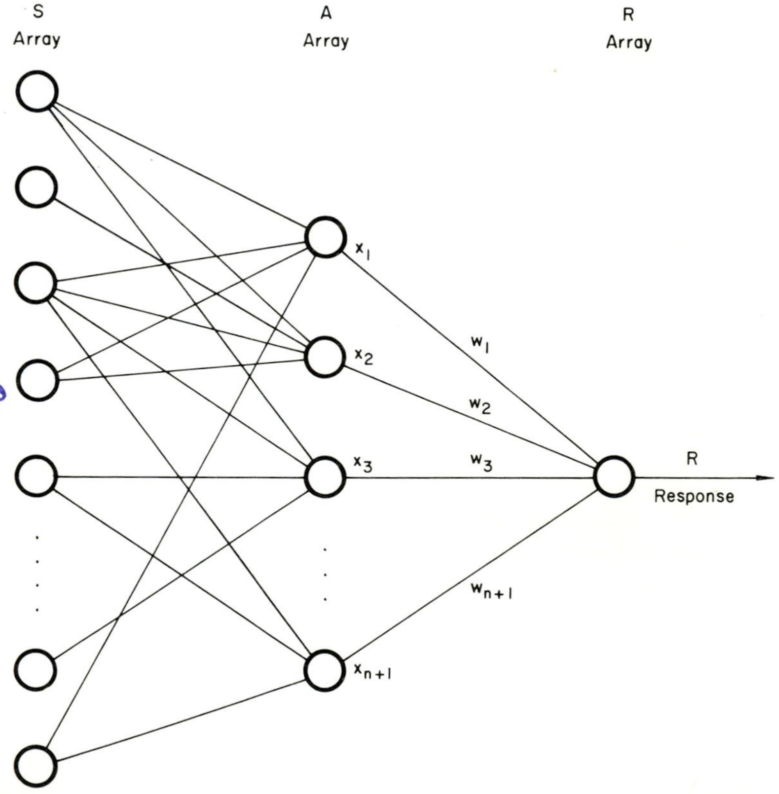

Figure 5.1. A basic perceptron model

units which are connected to it are activated. We may view these sensory units as the means by which the machine receives stimuli from its external environment, that is, its measurement devices, and the associative units as the first stage or input to the machine.

The response of the machine is proportional to the weighted sum of the associative array responses; that is, if we let x_i denote the response of the ith associative unit and w_i the corresponding weight, the response is given by

$$R = \sum_{i=1}^{n+1} w_i x_i = \mathbf{w}'\mathbf{x} \tag{5.2-1}$$

If $R > 0$, we say that the pattern observed by the sensory units belongs to class ω_1; if $R < 0$, it belongs to ω_2. This description agrees with our established concepts of classification, and, except for the sensory array, the basic perceptron model is seen to be nothing more than an implementation of a linear decision function.

Figure 5.1 can be easily extended to the multiclass case by increasing the number of units in the R array. For example, multiclass Case **3** in Section 2.2 can be implemented by adding M units to the R array, where M is the number of classes. Classification is accomplished in the usual manner: responses $R_1, R_2, \ldots, R_M$ are observed, and the pattern is assigned to class ω_i if $R_i > R_j$ for all $j \neq i$. The basic model can also be easily extended to nonlinear decision functions by inserting the appropriate nonlinear preprocessor between the A and R arrays. The reader will recall from Section 2.3, however, that all discussions may be limited to linear decision functions without loss of generality since nonlinear decision functions may be treated as linear functions in an augmented space.

5.2.1 The Reward-Punishment Concept

The training algorithm for the perceptron machine of Fig. 5.1 is a simple scheme for the iterative determination of the weight vector $\mathbf{w}$. This scheme, which is frequently called the *perceptron algorithm*, may be succinctly stated as follows:

Given two training sets belonging to pattern classes ω_1 and ω_2, respectively, let $\mathbf{w}(1)$ represent the initial weight vector, which may be arbitrarily chosen. Then, at the kth training step:

If $\mathbf{x}(k) \in \omega_1$ and $\mathbf{w}'(k)\mathbf{x}(k) \leq 0$, replace $\mathbf{w}(k)$ by

$$\mathbf{w}(k+1) = \mathbf{w}(k) + c\mathbf{x}(k) \tag{5.2-2}$$

where c is a correction increment.

If $\mathbf{x}(k) \in \omega_2$ and $\mathbf{w}'(k)\mathbf{x}(k) \geqslant 0$, replace $\mathbf{w}(k)$ by

$$\mathbf{w}(k+1) = \mathbf{w}(k) - c\mathbf{x}(k) \tag{5.2–3}$$

Otherwise, leave $\mathbf{w}(k)$ unchanged, that is,

$$\mathbf{w}(k+1) = \mathbf{w}(k) \tag{5.2–4}$$

Simply stated, the algorithm makes a change in $\mathbf{w}$ if and only if the pattern being considered at the kth training step is misclassified by the weight vector at this step. The correction increment c must be positive and is assumed, for now, to be constant.

The perceptron algorithm is clearly a reward-and-punishment procedure where, admittedly, the reward for correctly classified patterns is really the absence of punishment; that is, if the pattern is classified correctly, the machine is rewarded by the fact that no change is made in $\mathbf{w}$. On the other hand, if the pattern is misclassified and $\mathbf{w}'(k)\mathbf{x}(k)$ is less than zero when it should have been greater than zero, the machine is "punished" by increasing the value of $\mathbf{w}(k)$ an amount proportional to $\mathbf{x}(k)$. Similarly, if $\mathbf{w}'(k)\mathbf{x}(k)$ is greater than zero when it should have been less than zero, the machine is punished in the opposite mode.

Convergence of the algorithm occurs when a weight vector classifies all patterns correctly. It is shown in the next section that the perceptron algorithm converges in a finite number of iterations if the classes under consideration are linearly separable. Before proceeding with the proof, however, it will be instructive to consider in detail a simple numerical example.

Example: Consider the patterns shown in Fig. 5.2(a). It is desired to apply the perceptron algorithm to these patterns in an attempt to find a solution weight vector. We see by inspection that, since the two pattern classes are linearly separable, the algorithm will be successful.

Before the algorithm is applied, all patterns are augmented. The classes then become ω_1: $\{(0, 0, 1)', (0, 1, 1)'\}$ and ω_2: $\{(1, 0, 1)', (1, 1, 1)'\}$. Letting $c = 1$ and $\mathbf{w}(1) = \mathbf{0}$, and presenting the patterns in the above order, results in the following sequence of steps:

$$\mathbf{w}'(1)\mathbf{x}(1) = (0, 0, 0)\begin{pmatrix}0\\0\\1\end{pmatrix} = 0, \qquad \mathbf{w}(2) = \mathbf{w}(1) + \mathbf{x}(1) = \begin{pmatrix}0\\0\\1\end{pmatrix}$$

$$\mathbf{w}'(2)\mathbf{x}(2) = (0, 0, 1)\begin{pmatrix}0\\1\\1\end{pmatrix} = 1, \qquad \mathbf{w}(3) = \mathbf{w}(2) = \begin{pmatrix}0\\0\\1\end{pmatrix}$$

$$\mathbf{w}'(3)\mathbf{x}(3) = (0, 0, 1)\begin{pmatrix}1\\0\\1\end{pmatrix} = 1, \qquad \mathbf{w}(4) = \mathbf{w}(3) - \mathbf{x}(3) = \begin{pmatrix}-1\\0\\0\end{pmatrix}$$

$$\mathbf{w}'(4)\mathbf{x}(4) = (-1, 0, 0)\begin{pmatrix}1\\1\\1\end{pmatrix} = -1, \quad \mathbf{w}(5) = \mathbf{w}(4) = \begin{pmatrix}-1\\0\\0\end{pmatrix}$$

where corrections on the weight vector were made in the first and third steps because of misclassification, as indicated in Eqs. (5.2–2) and (5.2–3). Since a solution has been obtained only when the algorithm yields a complete, error-free iteration through all patterns, the training set must be presented

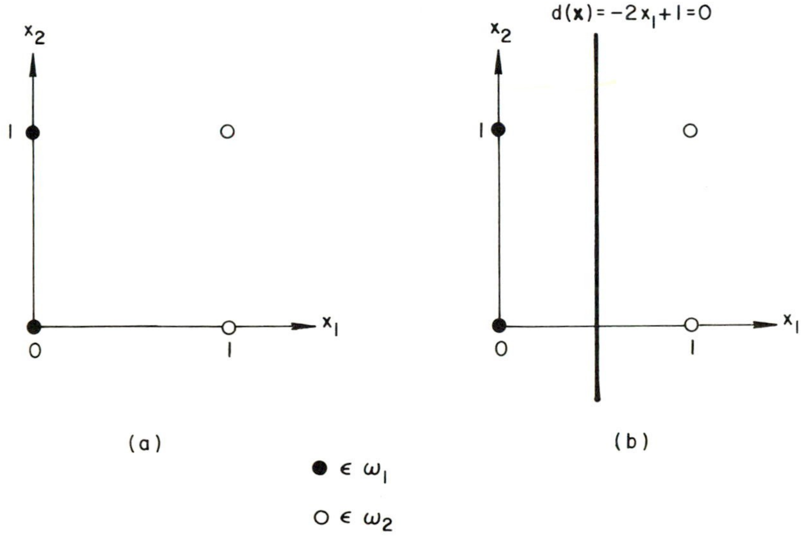

Figure 5.2. Illustration of the perceptron algorithm. (a) Patterns belonging to two classes. (b) Decision boundary determined by training

again. The machine learning process is continued by letting $\mathbf{x}(5) = \mathbf{x}(1)$, $\mathbf{x}(6) = \mathbf{x}(2)$, $\mathbf{x}(7) = \mathbf{x}(3)$, and $\mathbf{x}(8) = \mathbf{x}(4)$. The second iteration through the patterns yields:

$$\mathbf{w}'(5)\mathbf{x}(5) = 0, \qquad \mathbf{w}(6) = \mathbf{w}(5) + \mathbf{x}(5) = \begin{pmatrix} -1 \\ 0 \\ 1 \end{pmatrix}$$

$$\mathbf{w}'(6)\mathbf{x}(6) = 1, \qquad \mathbf{w}(7) = \mathbf{w}(6) = \begin{pmatrix} -1 \\ 0 \\ 1 \end{pmatrix}$$

$$\mathbf{w}'(7)\mathbf{x}(7) = 0, \qquad \mathbf{w}(8) = \mathbf{w}(7) - \mathbf{x}(7) = \begin{pmatrix} -2 \\ 0 \\ 0 \end{pmatrix}$$

$$\mathbf{w}'(8)\mathbf{x}(8) = -2, \quad \mathbf{w}(9) = \mathbf{w}(8) = \begin{pmatrix} -2 \\ 0 \\ 0 \end{pmatrix}$$

Since two errors occurred in this iteration, the patterns are presented again:

$$\mathbf{w}'(9)\mathbf{x}(9) = 0, \qquad \mathbf{w}(10) = \mathbf{w}(9) + \mathbf{x}(9) = \begin{pmatrix} -2 \\ 0 \\ 1 \end{pmatrix}$$

$$\mathbf{w}'(10)\mathbf{x}(10) = 1, \qquad \mathbf{w}(11) = \mathbf{w}(10) = \begin{pmatrix} -2 \\ 0 \\ 1 \end{pmatrix}$$

$$\mathbf{w}'(11)\mathbf{x}(11) = -1, \quad \mathbf{w}(12) = \mathbf{w}(11) = \begin{pmatrix} -2 \\ 0 \\ 1 \end{pmatrix}$$

$$\mathbf{w}'(12)\mathbf{x}(12) = -1, \quad \mathbf{w}(13) = \mathbf{w}(12) = \begin{pmatrix} -2 \\ 0 \\ 1 \end{pmatrix}$$

It is easily verified that in the next iteration all patterns are classified correctly. The solution vector is, therefore, $\mathbf{w} = (-2, 0, 1)'$. The corresponding decision function is $d(\mathbf{x}) = -2x_1 + 1$, which, when set equal to zero, becomes the equation of the decision boundary shown in Fig. 5.2(b). ●

According to the discussion in Section 5.1, we may express the perceptron algorithm in an equivalent form by multiplying the augmented patterns of one class by -1. Thus, arbitrarily multiplying the patterns of ω_2 by -1, we can write the perceptron algorithm as

$$\mathbf{w}(k+1) = \begin{cases} \mathbf{w}(k) & \text{if} \quad \mathbf{w}'(k)\mathbf{x}(k) > 0 \\ \mathbf{w}(k) + c\mathbf{x}(k) & \text{if} \quad \mathbf{w}'(k)\mathbf{x}(k) \leqslant 0 \end{cases} \qquad (5.2\text{--}5)$$

where c is a positive correction increment. We will use this equivalent formulation throughout the rest of this chapter.

5.2.2 Proof of Convergence

In this section it will be shown that, if the pattern classes under consideration are linearly separable, the algorithm presented in the preceding section yields a solution weight vector in a finite number of steps. Before proceeding with the proof, however, it will be convenient to summarize the statement of the problem in a notation designed to simplify the presentation of the proof.

Let $\mathbf{x}_1, \mathbf{x}_2, \ldots, \mathbf{x}_N$ represent a set of training patterns belonging to two classes, where the patterns of class ω_2 have been multiplied by -1. It is stipulated that if the pattern classes are linearly separable the learning algorithm of Eq. (5.2–5) yields a solution weight vector $\mathbf{w}^*$ with the property

$$\mathbf{w}^{*\prime}\mathbf{x}_i > 0, \quad i = 1, 2, \ldots, N \qquad (5.2\text{--}6)$$

It is possible to generalize expression (5.2–6) slightly by introducing a non-negative threshold T such that, if the classes are linearly separable,

$$\mathbf{w}^{*\prime}\mathbf{x}_i > T, \quad i = 1, 2, \ldots, N \qquad (5.2\text{--}7)$$

Under these conditions the algorithm of Eq. (5.2–5) becomes

$$\mathbf{w}(k+1) = \begin{cases} \mathbf{w}(k) & \text{if} \quad \mathbf{w}'(k)\mathbf{x}_i(k) > T \\ \mathbf{w}(k) + \mathbf{x}_i(k) & \text{if} \quad \mathbf{w}'(k)\mathbf{x}_i(k) \leqslant T \end{cases} \qquad (5.2\text{--}8)$$

where $\mathbf{w}(1)$ is arbitrary. For simplicity it is assumed that $c = 1$. This assumption is made without loss of generality since any other value of c could be absorbed in the pattern vectors as a normalizing constant. From the geometrical discussion of Section 2.4 and from Fig. 2.5, we see that the threshold T establishes a buffer region on each side of the hyperplane $\mathbf{w}'(k)\mathbf{x}(k) = 0$. Any pattern in this region is incorrectly classified. Referring to Fig. 2.5(c),

divide all vectors by c — retains separation

we note also that increasing T has the net effect of reducing the volume of the solution cone.

On the assumption that each pattern is presented as many times as necessary, the assertion is that, if the classes are linearly separable, the algorithm of Eq. (5.2–8) will terminate after a finite number of steps. In addition to using the above notation, the proof is greatly facilitated by considering only the indices k for which a correction takes place during training. In other words, if we leave out the values of k which correspond to correctly classified patterns, then, readapting the index notation, we may write

$$\mathbf{w}(k+1) = \mathbf{w}(k) + \mathbf{x}_i(k) \tag{5.2–9}$$

and

$$\mathbf{w}'(k)\mathbf{x}_i(k) \leqslant T \tag{5.2–10}$$

for all values of k in the training sequence where a correction took place. Convergence of the algorithm really means that, after some finite index value k_m,

$$\mathbf{w}(k_m) = \mathbf{w}(k_m + 1) = \mathbf{w}(k_m + 2) = \cdots$$

With the foregoing simplifications in mind, the proof of convergence is as follows. From Eq. (5.2–9),

$$\mathbf{w}(k+1) = \mathbf{w}(1) + \mathbf{x}_i(1) + \mathbf{x}_i(2) + \cdots + \mathbf{x}_i(k) \tag{5.2–11}$$

Taking the inner product of $\mathbf{w}^*$ with both sides of Eq. (5.2–11) yields

$$\mathbf{w}'(k+1)\mathbf{w}^* = \mathbf{w}'(1)\mathbf{w}^* + \mathbf{x}_i'(1)\mathbf{w}^* + \cdots + \mathbf{x}_i'(k)\mathbf{w}^* \tag{5.2–12}$$

Since, from expression (5.2–7), each term $\mathbf{x}_i'(j)\mathbf{w}^*$, $j = 1, \ldots, k$, is less than T, then

$$\mathbf{w}'(k+1)\mathbf{w}^* \geqslant \mathbf{w}'(1)\mathbf{w}^* + kT \tag{5.2–13}$$

Using the Cauchy-Schwartz inequality, $||\mathbf{a}||^2||\mathbf{b}||^2 \geqslant (\mathbf{a}'\mathbf{b})^2$, results in

$$[\mathbf{w}'(k+1)\mathbf{w}^*]^2 \leqslant ||\mathbf{w}(k+1)||^2||\mathbf{w}^*||^2 \tag{5.2–14}$$

where, for example, $||\mathbf{a}||^2$ indicates the magnitude of $\mathbf{a}$ squared. Expression (5.2–14) may be written in the form

$$||\mathbf{w}(k+1)||^2 \geqslant \frac{[\mathbf{w}'(k+1)\mathbf{w}^*]^2}{||\mathbf{w}^*||^2} \tag{5.2–15}$$

Substituting expression (5.2–13) into (5.2–15) yields

$$||\mathbf{w}(k+1)||^2 \geqslant \frac{[\mathbf{w}'(1)\mathbf{w}^* + kT]^2}{||\mathbf{w}^*||^2} \tag{5.2–16}$$

An alternative line of reasoning leads to a contradiction regarding $||\mathbf{w}(k+1)||^2$. From Eq. (5.2–9),

$$||\mathbf{w}(j+1)||^2 = ||\mathbf{w}(j)||^2 + 2\mathbf{w}'(j)\mathbf{x}_i(j) + ||\mathbf{x}_i(j)||^2 \tag{5.2–17}$$

or

$$||\mathbf{w}(j+1)||^2 - ||\mathbf{w}(j)||^2 = 2\mathbf{w}'(j)\mathbf{x}_i(j) + ||\mathbf{x}_i(j)||^2 \tag{5.2–18}$$

Using expression (5.2–10) and letting $Q = \max_i ||\mathbf{x}_i(j)||^2$ results in

$$||\mathbf{w}(j+1)||^2 - ||\mathbf{w}(j)||^2 \leqslant 2T + Q \tag{5.2–19}$$

Adding these inequalities for $j = 1, 2, \ldots, k$ yields the inequality

$$||\mathbf{w}(k+1)||^2 \leqslant ||\mathbf{w}(1)||^2 + (2T + Q)k \tag{5.2–20}$$

Comparing expressions (5.2–16) and (5.2–20), we see that these inequalities establish conflicting bounds on $||\mathbf{w}(k+1)||^2$ for sufficiently large k. In fact, k can be no larger than k_m, which is a solution to the equation

$$\frac{[\mathbf{w}'(1)\mathbf{w}^* + k_m T]^2}{||\mathbf{w}^*||^2} = ||\mathbf{w}(1)||^2 + (2T + Q)k_m \tag{5.2–21}$$

According to Eq. (5.2–21), k_m is finite, implying that the perceptron algorithm converges in a finite number of steps, provided that the classes are linearly separable. This completes the proof.

Remarks: The special case with $T = 0$ is proved in a slightly different manner. Under this condition, expression (5.2–13) becomes

$$\mathbf{w}'(k+1)\mathbf{w}^* \geqslant \mathbf{w}'(1)\mathbf{w}^* + ka \tag{5.2–22}$$

where

$$a = \min_i \, [\mathbf{x}_i'(j)\mathbf{w}^*] \tag{5.2–23}$$

Since $\mathbf{w}^*$ is, by hypothesis, a solution vector, a is greater than 0. Also, since $\mathbf{w}'(j)\mathbf{x}_i(j) \leqslant 0$, expression (5.2–19) becomes

$$\begin{aligned}||\mathbf{w}(j+1)||^2 - ||\mathbf{w}(j)||^2 &\leqslant ||\mathbf{x}_i(j)||^2 \\ &\leqslant Q \end{aligned} \tag{5.2–24}$$

The rest of the proof remains the same. The bound on the number of steps required for convergence when $T = 0$ is given by the solution of the equation

$$\frac{[\mathbf{w}'(1)\mathbf{w}^* + k_m a]^2}{||\mathbf{w}^*||^2} = ||\mathbf{w}(1)||^2 + Qk_m \tag{5.2–25}$$

Observe that, although Eqs. (5.2–21) and (5.2–25) establish a bound on k_m, these equations cannot be used to determine the number of steps required for convergence since they depend on knowledge of the solution vector $\mathbf{w}^*$. Notice that k_m also depends on the initial weight vector $\mathbf{w}(1)$. Convergence of the perceptron algorithm can be proved in a variety of ways. The proof presented above, however, is one of the most concise.

5.2.3 Variations of the Perceptron Approach

Several variations of the perceptron algorithm can be formulated, depending on how the value of the correction increment c is selected. Among the commonly used training algorithms are the *fixed-increment algorithm*, the *absolute-correction algorithm*, and the *fractional-correction algorithm*. In the fixed-increment algorithm c is a constant greater than zero. An example of the application of this algorithm was given in Section 5.2.1 with $c = 1$.

In the absolute-correction algorithm c is chosen to be just large enough to guarantee that the pattern is correctly classified after a weight adjustment. In other words, if $\mathbf{w}'(k)\mathbf{x}(k) \leqslant 0$, the coefficient c is chosen so that

$$\mathbf{w}'(k+1)\mathbf{x}(k) = [\mathbf{w}(k) + c\mathbf{x}(k)]'\mathbf{x}(k) > 0 \tag{5.2–26}$$

It is noted that, according to the formulation of Eq. (5.2–5), an error is committed only when $\mathbf{w}'(k)\mathbf{x}(k)$ is less than or equal to zero. One way to satisfy Eq. (5.2–26) is to choose c as the smallest integer greater than $|\mathbf{w}'(k)\mathbf{x}(k)|/\mathbf{x}'(k)\mathbf{x}(k)$.

In the fractional-correction algorithm c is chosen so that the quantity $|\mathbf{w}'(k)\mathbf{x}(k) - \mathbf{w}'(k+1)\mathbf{x}(k)|$ is a certain positive fraction λ of $|\mathbf{w}'(k)\mathbf{x}(k)|$, that is,

$$|\mathbf{w}'(k)\mathbf{x}(k) - \mathbf{w}'(k+1)\mathbf{x}(k)| = \lambda|\mathbf{w}'(k)\mathbf{x}(k)| \tag{5.2–27}$$

Substituting $\mathbf{w}(k+1) = \mathbf{w}(k) + c\mathbf{x}(k)$ into Eq. (5.2–27) yields

$$c = \lambda \frac{|\mathbf{w}'(k)\mathbf{x}(k)|}{\mathbf{x}'(k)\mathbf{x}(k)} \tag{5.2–28}$$

Clearly, this algorithm requires that the starting weight vector be different from $\mathbf{0}$. From the geometrical discussion of Section 2.5.1 we see that λ is the ratio of the distance between the old weight vector $\mathbf{w}(k)$ and the new weight vector $\mathbf{w}(k+1)$ to the normal Euclidean distance from $\mathbf{w}(k)$ to the pattern hyperplane in the weight space. If $\lambda > 1$, the pattern is correctly classified after each weight adjustment. It can be shown that this algorithm converges for $0 < \lambda < 2$.

5.3 DERIVATION OF PATTERN CLASSIFICATION ALGORITHMS

It was indicated in Section 5.2 that the development of the perceptron algorithm was originally based on the concept of adaptation by reward and punishment. In this section we take a more general approach to the problem of generating pattern classification algorithms. It will be shown that the perceptron algorithm is just one of a family of iterative schemes which may be easily derived by utilizing the well-known gradient concept.

5.3.1 The Gradient Technique

Basically, gradient schemes provide a tool for finding the minimum of a function. The reader will recall from vector analysis that the gradient of a function $f(\mathbf{y})$ with respect to the vector $\mathbf{y} = (y_1, y_2, \ldots, y_n)'$ is defined as

$$\text{grad}\, f(\mathbf{y}) = \frac{df(\mathbf{y})}{d\mathbf{y}} = \begin{pmatrix} \dfrac{\partial f}{\partial y_1} \\ \dfrac{\partial f}{\partial y_2} \\ \vdots \\ \dfrac{\partial f}{\partial y_n} \end{pmatrix} \tag{5.3–1}$$

We see from this equation that the gradient of a scalar function of a vector argument is a vector and that each component of the gradient gives the rate of change of the function in the direction of that component.

One of the most important properties of the gradient vector is that it points in the direction of the maximum rate of increase of the function f when the argument increases. Conversely, the negative of the gradient points in the direction of the maximum rate of decrease of f. On the basis of this property, we can devise iterative schemes for finding the minimum of a function. In the following discussions, only functions with a unique minimum will be considered. If the function is chosen so that it achieves its minimum value whenever $\mathbf{w}'\mathbf{x}_i > 0$, where $\mathbf{x}_i$ is the ith row of the $N \times (n+1)$ matrix $\mathbf{X}$ of the system of inequalities given in expression (5.1–1), then finding the minimum of the function for all i, $i = 1, 2, \ldots, N$, is equivalent to solving the given system of linear inequalities. For example, consider the criterion function

$$J(\mathbf{w}, \mathbf{x}) = (|\mathbf{w}'\mathbf{x}| - \mathbf{w}'\mathbf{x}) \tag{5.3–2}$$

where $|\mathbf{w}'\mathbf{x}|$ is the absolute value of $\mathbf{w}'\mathbf{x}$. It is evident that the minimum of this function is $J(\mathbf{w}, \mathbf{x}) = 0$ and that this minimum results when $\mathbf{w}'\mathbf{x} > 0$. We are excluding, of course, the trivial case in which $\mathbf{w} = \mathbf{0}$.

The approach employed below consists of incrementing $\mathbf{w}$ in the direction of the negative gradient of $J(\mathbf{w}, \mathbf{x})$ in order to seek the minimum of the function. In other words, if we let $\mathbf{w}(k)$ represent the value of $\mathbf{w}$ at the kth step, the general gradient descent algorithm may be written as

$$\mathbf{w}(k+1) = \mathbf{w}(k) - c\left\{\frac{\partial J(\mathbf{w}, \mathbf{x})}{\partial \mathbf{w}}\right\}_{\mathbf{w}=\mathbf{w}(k)} \tag{5.3–3}$$

where $\mathbf{w}(k+1)$ represents the new value of $\mathbf{w}$, and $c > 0$ dictates the magnitude of the correction. It is noted that no corrections are made on $\mathbf{w}$ when $(\partial J/\partial \mathbf{w}) = \mathbf{0}$, which is the condition for a minimum.

Equation (5.3–3) may be interpreted geometrically with the aid of Fig. 5.3. We see from this simple scalar case that, if $(\partial J/\partial w)$ is negative at the kth step, w is incremented in the direction of the minimum of J. It is evident from the figure that this descent scheme will eventually lead to a positive w and, consequently, to the minimum value of J. It should also be noted that Fig. 5.3 is a plot of Eq. (5.3–2) for $x = 1$. Clearly, there are as many curves as there are patterns in a problem.

If the inequalities are consistent and a proper $J(\mathbf{w}, \mathbf{x})$ is chosen, the algorithm of Eq. (5.3–3) will result in a solution. Otherwise, it will simply oscillate until the procedure is stopped. In the next section specific algorithms are derived by specifying criterion functions $J(\mathbf{w}, \mathbf{x})$ and substituting these functions into the general descent scheme given by Eq. (5.3–3).

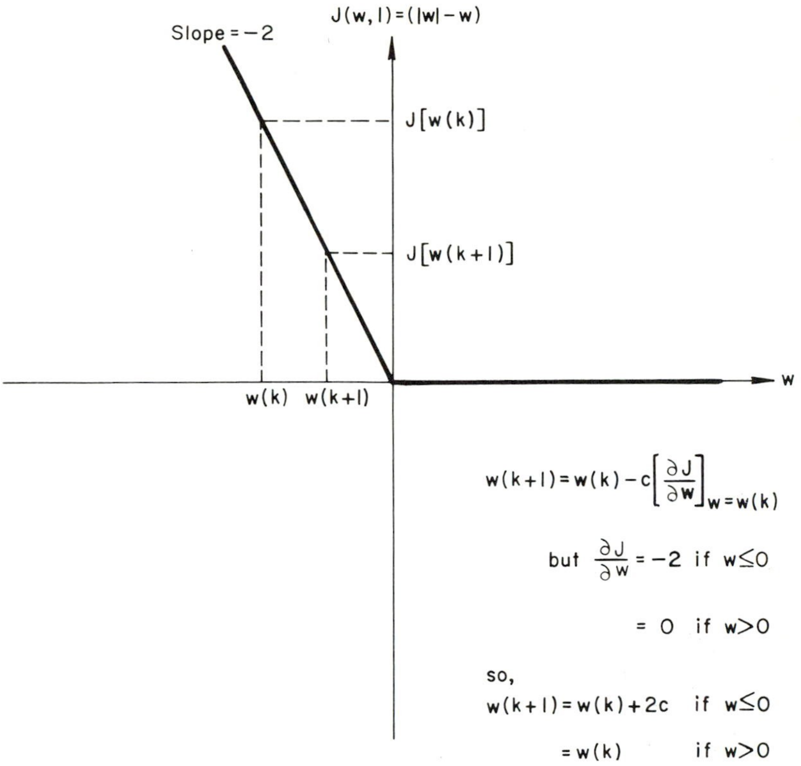

Figure 5.3. Geometrical illustration of the gradient descent algorithm

5.3.2 Perceptron Algorithm

The perceptron algorithm was introduced in Section 5.2.1 as a reward-and-punishment iterative scheme. In this section it is shown that this algorithm is derivable from Eq. (5.3–3) by properly choosing $J(\mathbf{w}, \mathbf{x})$. Let this criterion function be

$$J(\mathbf{w}, \mathbf{x}) = \tfrac{1}{2}(|\mathbf{w}'\mathbf{x}| - \mathbf{w}'\mathbf{x}) \tag{5.3–4}$$

The partial derivative of J with respect to $\mathbf{w}$ is given by

$$\frac{\partial J}{\partial \mathbf{w}} = \tfrac{1}{2}[\mathbf{x}\,\mathrm{sgn}(\mathbf{w}'\mathbf{x}) - \mathbf{x}] \tag{5.3–5}$$

where, by definition,

$$\operatorname{sgn}(\mathbf{w}'\mathbf{x}) = \begin{cases} 1 & \text{if} \quad \mathbf{w}'\mathbf{x} > 0 \\ -1 & \text{if} \quad \mathbf{w}'\mathbf{x} \leqslant 0 \end{cases} \tag{5.3–6}$$

It is noted from Eq. (5.3–6) that the occurrence of $\mathbf{w}'\mathbf{x} = 0$ is grouped with the condition for $\mathbf{w}'\mathbf{x} < 0$. This, of course, reflects the fact that we wish to make a correction on the weight vector $\mathbf{w}$ whenever $\mathbf{w}'\mathbf{x} \leqslant 0$, according to the formulation given in Eq. (5.2–5).

Substituting Eq. (5.3–5) into Eq. (5.3–3) yields

$$\mathbf{w}(k+1) = \mathbf{w}(k) + \frac{c}{2}\{\mathbf{x}(k) - \mathbf{x}(k)\operatorname{sgn}[\mathbf{w}'(k)\mathbf{x}(k)]\} \tag{5.3–7}$$

where $\mathbf{x}(k)$ represents the training pattern being considered at the kth iterative step.

Substituting Eq. (5.3–6) into Eq. (5.3–7) results in the algorithm

$$\mathbf{w}(k+1) = \mathbf{w}(k) + c\begin{cases} \mathbf{0} & \text{if} \quad \mathbf{w}'(k)\mathbf{x}(k) > 0 \\ \mathbf{x}(k) & \text{if} \quad \mathbf{w}'(k)\mathbf{x}(k) \leqslant 0 \end{cases} \tag{5.3–8}$$

where $c > 0$ and $\mathbf{w}(1)$ is arbitrary. This algorithm is clearly the perceptron algorithm as expressed in Eq. (5.2–5).

The variations given in Section 5.2.3 are also easily derivable from the general algorithm of Eq. (5.3–3). For example, consider the criterion function

$$J(\mathbf{w}, \mathbf{x}) = \frac{1}{4\mathbf{x}'\mathbf{x}}(|\mathbf{w}'\mathbf{x}|^2 - |\mathbf{w}'\mathbf{x}|\mathbf{w}'\mathbf{x}) \tag{5.3–9}$$

The partial derivative of J with respect to $\mathbf{w}$ is given by

$$\frac{\partial J}{\partial \mathbf{w}} = \frac{1}{4\mathbf{x}'\mathbf{x}}[2|\mathbf{w}'\mathbf{x}|\mathbf{x}\operatorname{sgn}(\mathbf{w}'\mathbf{x}) - |\mathbf{w}'\mathbf{x}|\mathbf{x} - (\mathbf{w}'\mathbf{x})\mathbf{x}\operatorname{sgn}(\mathbf{w}'\mathbf{x})]$$

where $\operatorname{sgn}(\mathbf{w}'\mathbf{x})$ is defined in Eq. (5.3–6). It can be easily shown that the above equation may be expressed in the equivalent form

$$\frac{\partial J}{\partial \mathbf{w}} = \frac{1}{2\mathbf{x}'\mathbf{x}}[|\mathbf{w}'\mathbf{x}|\mathbf{x}\operatorname{sgn}(\mathbf{w}'\mathbf{x}) - |\mathbf{w}'\mathbf{x}|\mathbf{x}] \tag{5.3–10}$$

Substituting Eq. (5.3–10) into Eq. (5.3–3) yields the algorithm

$$\mathbf{w}(k+1) = \mathbf{w}(k) + \frac{\lambda|\mathbf{w}'(k)\mathbf{x}(k)|}{2\mathbf{x}'(k)\mathbf{x}(k)}\{\mathbf{x}(k) - \mathbf{x}(k)\operatorname{sgn}[\mathbf{w}'(k)\mathbf{x}(k)]\} \tag{5.3–11}$$

where, in order to avoid confusion in the comparison to be made below, the correction increment c in Eq. (5.3–3) has been temporarily replaced by λ.

Using Eq. (5.3–6), we obtain

$$\mathbf{w}(k+1) = \mathbf{w}(k) + \frac{\lambda|\mathbf{w}'(k)\mathbf{x}(k)|}{\mathbf{x}'(k)\mathbf{x}(k)} \begin{cases} \mathbf{0} & \text{if } \mathbf{w}'(k)\mathbf{x}(k) > 0 \\ \mathbf{x}(k) & \text{if } \mathbf{w}'(k)\mathbf{x}(k) \leqslant 0 \end{cases} \tag{5.3–12}$$

Comparing Eq. (5.3–12) with Eq. (5.2–28), we see that we have derived the fractional-correction algorithm. In the next section we again use these basic concepts to derive an algorithm which possesses some very important properties.

5.3.3 A Least-Mean-Square-Error Algorithm

The perceptron algorithm and its variations converge when the classes under consideration are separable by the specified decision surface. In nonseparable situations, however, these algorithms simply oscillate for as long as they are allowed to execute. Since it is not possible to precompute the number of steps required for convergence in a separable situation, one can seldom be sure whether or not a long training sequence implies that the classes are not linearly separable.

The algorithm derived in this section, in addition to being convergent for separable classes, also indicates in the course of its operation that the classes under consideration are not separable, if this is indeed the case. This unique property makes this algorithm a valuable tool for the design of pattern classifiers.

In the following derivation we shall use the formulation given in expression (5.1–1). Instead of stating the problem as that of finding a vector $\mathbf{w}$ such that $\mathbf{X}\mathbf{w} > \mathbf{0}$ is satisfied, we will instead search for vectors $\mathbf{w}$ and $\mathbf{b}$ such that

$$\mathbf{X}\mathbf{w} = \mathbf{b} \tag{5.3–13}$$

where the components of $\mathbf{b} = (b_1, b_2, \ldots, b_N)'$ are all positive. Clearly, the two formulations are mutually equivalent.

Consider the criterion function

$$J(\mathbf{w}, \mathbf{x}, \mathbf{b}) = \frac{1}{2} \sum_{j=1}^{N} (\mathbf{w}'\mathbf{x}_j - b_j)^2 = \tfrac{1}{2}||\mathbf{X}\mathbf{w} - \mathbf{b}||^2 \tag{5.3–14}$$

where $||\mathbf{X}\mathbf{w} - \mathbf{b}||$ indicates the magnitude of the vector $(\mathbf{X}\mathbf{w} - \mathbf{b})$. The function $J(\mathbf{w}, \mathbf{x}, \mathbf{b})$ achieves its minimum value whenever Eq. (5.3–13) is satisfied.

Since this function depends on $\mathbf{w}$ and $\mathbf{b}$, there is no reason why both variables cannot be used in the minimization procedure, thus providing more degrees of freedom. One can hope in this manner to improve the convergence rate of the algorithm. Observe that the term $(\mathbf{w}'\mathbf{x}_j - \mathbf{b}_j)^2$ or $||\mathbf{X}\mathbf{w} - \mathbf{b}||^2$ expresses the squared error between the two quantities in the argument. Since the summation of these errors is proportional to an average or mean value, and since we are attempting to minimize this summation, the resulting algorithm is appropriately called the *least-mean-square-error* (LMSE) algorithm. This procedure is sometimes referred to as the Ho-Kashyap algorithm.

In view of the fact that J will be minimized with respect to both $\mathbf{w}$ and $\mathbf{b}$, the approach taken must necessarily differ slightly from the general algorithm of Eq. (5.3–3). The gradients associated with this problem are

$$\frac{\partial J}{\partial \mathbf{w}} = \mathbf{X}'(\mathbf{X}\mathbf{w} - \mathbf{b}) \tag{5.3–15}$$

and

$$\frac{\partial J}{\partial \mathbf{b}} = -\ (\mathbf{X}\mathbf{w} - \mathbf{b}) \tag{5.3–16}$$

Since $\mathbf{w}$ is not constrained in any way, we can set $\partial J/\partial \mathbf{w} = \mathbf{0}$ and obtain

$$\mathbf{w} = (\mathbf{X}'\mathbf{X})^{-1}\mathbf{X}'\mathbf{b} = \mathbf{X}^{\#}\mathbf{b} \tag{5.3–17}$$

where $\mathbf{X}^{\#}$ is often called the *generalized inverse* of $\mathbf{X}$. Since all the components of $\mathbf{b}$ are constrained to be positive, this vector must be varied in such a manner as never to violate this constraint. This can be accomplished by letting

$$\mathbf{b}(k+1) = \mathbf{b}(k) + \delta\mathbf{b}(k) \tag{5.3–18}$$

where

$$\delta b_i(k) = \begin{cases} 2c[\mathbf{X}\mathbf{w}(k) - \mathbf{b}(k)]_i & \text{if} \quad [\mathbf{X}\mathbf{w}(k) - \mathbf{b}(k)]_i > 0 \\ 0 & \text{if} \quad [\mathbf{X}\mathbf{w}(k) - \mathbf{b}(k)]_i \leqslant 0 \end{cases} \tag{5.3–19}$$

In Eqs. (5.3–18) and (5.3–19), k denotes the iteration index, i is the index of the vector components, and c is a positive correction increment to be determined below.

Equation (5.3–19) may be written in vector form as follows:

$$\delta\mathbf{b}(k) = c[\mathbf{X}\mathbf{w}(k) - \mathbf{b}(k) + |\mathbf{X}\mathbf{w}(k) - \mathbf{b}(k)|] \tag{5.3–20}$$

where $|\mathbf{X}\mathbf{w}(k) - \mathbf{b}(k)|$ indicates the absolute value of each component of the vector $[\mathbf{X}\mathbf{w}(k) - \mathbf{b}(k)]$. From Eqs. (5.3–17) and (5.3–18), we obtain

$$\begin{aligned} \mathbf{w}(k+1) &= \mathbf{X}^{\#}\mathbf{b}(k+1) \\ &= \mathbf{X}^{\#}[\mathbf{b}(k) + \delta\mathbf{b}(k)] \\ &= \mathbf{X}^{\#}\mathbf{b}(k) + \mathbf{X}^{\#}\,\delta\mathbf{b}(k) \\ &= \mathbf{w}(k) + \mathbf{X}^{\#}\,\delta\mathbf{b}(k) \end{aligned} \tag{5.3–21}$$

By letting

$$\mathbf{e}(k) = \mathbf{X}\mathbf{w}(k) - \mathbf{b}(k) \tag{5.3–22}$$

we have the following algorithm:

$$\begin{aligned} \mathbf{w}(1) &= \mathbf{X}^{\#}\mathbf{b}(1), \quad \mathbf{b}(1) > 0, \text{ but otherwise arbitrary} \\ \mathbf{e}(k) &= \mathbf{X}\mathbf{w}(k) - \mathbf{b}(k) \\ \mathbf{w}(k+1) &= \mathbf{w}(k) + c\mathbf{X}^{\#}[\mathbf{e}(k) + |\mathbf{e}(k)|] \\ \mathbf{b}(k+1) &= \mathbf{b}(k) + c[\mathbf{e}(k) + |\mathbf{e}(k)|] \end{aligned} \tag{5.3–23}$$

In Eqs. (5.3–23), $|\mathbf{e}(k)|$ denotes the vector whose components are the absolute value of the components of $\mathbf{e}(k)$. It is noted that $\mathbf{w}(k+1)$ can also be calculated using the relation $\mathbf{w}(k+1) = \mathbf{X}^{\#}\mathbf{b}(k+1)$.

When the inequalities $\mathbf{X}\mathbf{w} > \mathbf{0}$ have a solution this algorithm converges for $0 < c \leqslant 1$. Furthermore, if *all* the components of $\mathbf{e}(k)$ cease to be positive (but are not all zero) at any iteration step, this indicates that the classes are not separable by the specified decision boundary. Of course, if $\mathbf{e}(k) \geqslant \mathbf{0}$, we have that $\mathbf{w}(k)$ is a solution since this would imply that $\mathbf{X}\mathbf{w}(k) \geqslant \mathbf{b}(k)$ and $\mathbf{b}(k)$ is a positive vector. This *test of separability* is an important feature of the algorithm, as was mentioned earlier.

Example: (a) Consider again the pattern classes ω_1: $\{(0, 0)', (0, 1)'\}$ and ω_2: $\{(1, 0)', (1, 1)'\}$. Augmenting the patterns and multiplying the patterns of class ω_2 by -1 results in the matrix

$$\mathbf{X} = \begin{pmatrix} 0 & 0 & 1 \\ 0 & 1 & 1 \\ -1 & 0 & -1 \\ -1 & -1 & -1 \end{pmatrix}$$

The generalized inverse $\mathbf{X}^{\#} = (\mathbf{X}'\mathbf{X})^{-1}\mathbf{X}'$ is

$$\mathbf{X}^{\#} = \frac{1}{2}\begin{pmatrix} -1 & -1 & -1 & -1 \\ -1 & 1 & 1 & -1 \\ \frac{3}{2} & \frac{1}{2} & -\frac{1}{2} & \frac{1}{2} \end{pmatrix}$$

Letting $\mathbf{b}(1) = (1, 1, 1, 1)'$ and $c = 1$, and applying the algorithm of Eqs. (5.3–23), we obtain

$$\mathbf{w}(1) = \mathbf{X}^{\#}\mathbf{b}(1) = \begin{pmatrix} -2 \\ 0 \\ 1 \end{pmatrix}$$

Since

$$\mathbf{X}\mathbf{w}(1) = \begin{pmatrix} 1 \\ 1 \\ 1 \\ 1 \end{pmatrix}$$

we see, according to Eq. (5.3–13), that $\mathbf{w}(1)$ is a solution. In practice, we say that a solution has been achieved whenever $\mathbf{X}\mathbf{w} > \mathbf{0}$.

(b) Consider now the classes ω_1: $\{(0, 0)', (1, 1)'\}$ and ω_2: $\{(0, 1)', (1, 0)'\}$, which are not linearly separable. Letting $c = 1$ and $\mathbf{b}(1) = (1, 1, 1, 1)'$, we obtain

$$\mathbf{X} = \begin{pmatrix} 0 & 0 & 1 \\ 1 & 1 & 1 \\ 0 & -1 & -1 \\ -1 & 0 & -1 \end{pmatrix}$$

$$\mathbf{X}^{\#} = (\mathbf{X}'\mathbf{X})^{-1}\mathbf{X}' = \frac{1}{2}\begin{pmatrix} -1 & 1 & 1 & -1 \\ -1 & 1 & -1 & 1 \\ \frac{3}{2} & -\frac{1}{2} & -\frac{1}{2} & -\frac{1}{2} \end{pmatrix}$$

$$\mathbf{w}(1) = \mathbf{X}^{\#}\mathbf{b}(1) = \begin{pmatrix} 0 \\ 0 \\ 0 \end{pmatrix}$$

$$\mathbf{e}(1) = \mathbf{X}\mathbf{w}(1) - \mathbf{b}(1) = \begin{pmatrix} -1 \\ -1 \\ -1 \\ -1 \end{pmatrix}$$

The fact that $\mathbf{e}(1)$ is a negative vector indicates that $\mathbf{X}\mathbf{w} > \mathbf{0}$ has no solution.

The speed of convergence which characterizes the LMSE algorithm is due to the facts that (1) modifications with respect to both $\mathbf{w}$ and $\mathbf{b}$ take place at each step, and (2) the procedure is a *many-pattern-adaptation* scheme which involves all the patterns of both classes at each iterative step.

The only apparent disadvantage in the application of the LMSE algorithm involves the inversion of the matrix $(\mathbf{X}'\mathbf{X})$. Unless the patterns are of very high dimensionality, however, this does not present a serious difficulty since the matrix needs to be inverted only once per problem. In addition, the inverse matrix $(\mathbf{X}'\mathbf{X})^{-1}$ can be recursively updated as new rows (i.e., patterns) are added to $\mathbf{X}$ (Bodewig [1956]).

It has been assumed throughout that $(\mathbf{X}'\mathbf{X})$ possesses an inverse, a condition which is met whenever $\mathbf{X}$ is of rank $n + 1$. Since this matrix is formed from the augmented patterns, it is clear that whether or not $(\mathbf{X}'\mathbf{X})$ is singular is determined not only by the pattern populations, but also by the decision function chosen. Note that if at least $n + 1$ of the patterns used in forming $\mathbf{X}$ are well distributed, as defined in Chapter 2, $\mathbf{X}$ is guaranteed to be of rank $n + 1$.

It is possible to derive other algorithms in addition to the ones presented above. In fact, the number of algorithms that can be derived using the gradient technique is limited only by the number of meaningful criterion functions that can be specified. However, many of these algorithms, although different in form, do not differ greatly in capability. This was evident when two cases of the perceptron algorithm were derived by starting with different criterion functions.

The two basic algorithms derived in this chapter span the spectrum of the types of algorithms that can be derived using the gradient technique. They are important for different reasons, however. The perceptron algorithm is attractive because of its relative simplicity of implementation and, as will be seen in Section 5.4, its straightforward extension to the multiclass case. The LMSE algorithm, on the other hand, offers the separability-test feature in the two-class case. Of course, we pay for this feature by added complexity.

Although speed of convergence is an important consideration, it is difficult to assign a figure of merit to an algorithm based on this factor For example, although the LMSE algorithm generally converges to a solution in fewer iterations than the perceptron algorithm, it must be taken into consideration that the former is a more complex procedure requiring more operations per iteration plus a matrix inversion. Also, the fact that these schemes depend on the geometry of the situation and the starting weight vectors makes absolute comparisons almost impossible to formulate.

5.3.4 Convergence Proof of the LMSE Algorithm

In this section we prove the convergence of the LMSE algorithm when the classes are linearly separable and the correction increment satisfies the condition $0 < c \leqslant 1$. The key to proving convergence is to show that the error vector $\mathbf{e}(k) = \mathbf{X}\mathbf{w}(k) - \mathbf{b}(k)$ becomes $\mathbf{0}$ in the limit. Since, from Eq. (5.3–23), $\mathbf{b}(k)$ starts out with all positive components and its components never decrease, it is clear that, if $\mathbf{e}(k) = \mathbf{0}$ for some k, we have $\mathbf{X}\mathbf{w}(k) = \mathbf{b}(k) > \mathbf{0}$, indicating a solution to Eq. (5.3–13).

From Eq. (5.3–23) we have

$$\mathbf{e}(k) = \mathbf{X}\mathbf{w}(k) - \mathbf{b}(k)$$

However, since $\mathbf{w}(k) = \mathbf{X}^{\#}\mathbf{b}(k)$, this equation may be expressed in the form

$$\mathbf{e}(k) = (\mathbf{X}\mathbf{X}^{\#} - \mathbf{I})\mathbf{b}(k) \tag{5.3–24}$$

It then follows that

$$\mathbf{e}(k+1) = (\mathbf{X}\mathbf{X}^{\#} - \mathbf{I})\mathbf{b}(k+1) \tag{5.3–25}$$

Using the expression $\mathbf{b}(k+1) = \mathbf{b}(k) + c[\mathbf{e}(k) + |\mathbf{e}(k)|]$ yields

$$\begin{aligned}\mathbf{e}(k+1) &= (\mathbf{X}\mathbf{X}^{\#} - \mathbf{I})\{\mathbf{b}(k) + c[\mathbf{e}(k) + |\mathbf{e}(k)|]\} \\ &= \mathbf{e}(k) + c(\mathbf{X}\mathbf{X}^{\#} - \mathbf{I})[\mathbf{e}(k) + |\mathbf{e}(k)|]\end{aligned} \tag{5.3–26}$$

From this equation we obtain

$$\begin{aligned}||\mathbf{e}(k+1)||^2 = ||\mathbf{e}(k)||^2 &+ 2c\mathbf{e}'(k)(\mathbf{X}\mathbf{X}^{\#} - \mathbf{I})[\mathbf{e}(k) + |\mathbf{e}(k)|] \\ &+ ||c(\mathbf{X}\mathbf{X}^{\#} - \mathbf{I})[\mathbf{e}(k) + |\mathbf{e}(k)|]||^2\end{aligned} \tag{5.3–27}$$

The notation in Eq. (5.3–27) may be clarified by defining

$$\mathbf{e}^*(k) = \mathbf{e}(k) + |\mathbf{e}(k)| \tag{5.3–28}$$

Then, Eq. (5.3–27) becomes

$$||\mathbf{e}(k+1)||^2 = ||\mathbf{e}(k)||^2 + 2c\mathbf{e}'(k)(\mathbf{X}\mathbf{X}^{\#} - \mathbf{I})\mathbf{e}^*(k) + ||c(\mathbf{X}\mathbf{X}^{\#} - \mathbf{I})\mathbf{e}^*(k)||^2 \tag{5.3–29}$$

This equation may be simplified considerably. First we note that $(\mathbf{X}\mathbf{X}^{\#})'(\mathbf{X}\mathbf{X}^{\#}) = \mathbf{X}\mathbf{X}^{\#}$ and $\mathbf{w}(k) = \mathbf{X}^{\#}\mathbf{b}(k)$. Therefore,

$$\begin{aligned}\mathbf{X}\mathbf{X}^{\#}\mathbf{e}(k) &= \mathbf{X}\mathbf{X}^{\#}[\mathbf{X}\mathbf{w}(k) - \mathbf{b}(k)] \\ &= \mathbf{X}\mathbf{X}^{\#}[\mathbf{X}\mathbf{X}^{\#}\mathbf{b}(k) - \mathbf{b}(k)] \\ &= \mathbf{0}\end{aligned}$$

Since $\mathbf{X}\mathbf{X}^{\#}$ is symmetric, it follows that $\mathbf{e}'(k)\mathbf{X}\mathbf{X}^{\#} = \mathbf{0}$. Therefore, Eq. (5.3–29) becomes

$$||\mathbf{e}(k+1)||^2 = ||\mathbf{e}(k)||^2 - 2c\mathbf{e}'(k)\mathbf{e}^*(k) + ||c(\mathbf{X}\mathbf{X}^{\#} - \mathbf{I})\mathbf{e}^*(k)||^2 \tag{5.3–30}$$

However, $\mathbf{e}'(k)\mathbf{e}^*(k) = \frac{1}{2}||\mathbf{e}^*(k)||^2$, so we have

$$||\mathbf{e}(k+1)||^2 = ||\mathbf{e}(k)||^2 - c||\mathbf{e}^*(k)||^2 + ||c(\mathbf{X}\mathbf{X}^{\#} - \mathbf{I})\mathbf{e}^*(k)||^2 \tag{5.3–31}$$

Since $\mathbf{X}\mathbf{X}^{\#}$ is symmetric and $(\mathbf{X}\mathbf{X}^{\#})'(\mathbf{X}\mathbf{X}^{\#}) = \mathbf{X}\mathbf{X}^{\#}$, the last term in Eq. (5.3–31) may be expressed in the form

$$\begin{aligned}||c(\mathbf{X}\mathbf{X}^{\#} - \mathbf{I})\mathbf{e}^*(k)||^2 &= c^2\mathbf{e}^{*\prime}(k)(\mathbf{X}\mathbf{X}^{\#} - \mathbf{I})'(\mathbf{X}\mathbf{X}^{\#} - \mathbf{I})\mathbf{e}^*(k) \\ &= c^2||\mathbf{e}^*(k)||^2 - c^2\mathbf{e}^{*\prime}(k)\mathbf{X}\mathbf{X}^{\#}\mathbf{e}^*(k)\end{aligned}$$

Substituting this relation in Eq. (5.3–31) yields

$$||\mathbf{e}(k)||^2 - ||\mathbf{e}(k+1)||^2 = c(1-c)||\mathbf{e}^*(k)||^2 + c^2\mathbf{e}^{*\prime}(k)\mathbf{X}\mathbf{X}^{\#}\mathbf{e}^*(k) \tag{5.3–32}$$

From this equation we can prove convergence in the separable case. First we note that, since $\mathbf{X}\mathbf{X}^{\#}$ is positive semidefinite, we have $c^2\mathbf{e}^{*\prime}(k)\mathbf{X}\mathbf{X}^{\#}\mathbf{e}^*(k) \geqslant 0$. Therefore, if $0 < c \leqslant 1$, the right-hand side of Eq. (5.3–32) is greater than or equal to zero. Therefore,

$$||\mathbf{e}(k)||^2 \geqslant ||\mathbf{e}(k+1)||^2 \tag{5.3–33}$$

and the sequence $||\mathbf{e}(1)||^2, ||\mathbf{e}(2)||^2, \ldots$ is monotonically decreasing. With a little thought we arrive at the conclusion that the only way in which

$||\mathbf{e}(k+1)||^2 = ||\mathbf{e}(k)||^2$ can occur for *all* values of k past some point in the sequence is for all the components of the error vector to become less than or equal to zero. If, for some k, $\mathbf{e}(k) = \mathbf{0}$ we have a solution since the components of $\mathbf{b}(k)$ are always positive and $\mathbf{e}(k) = \mathbf{X}\mathbf{w}(k) - \mathbf{b}(k)$. If $\mathbf{e}(k) = \mathbf{0}$, it is clear that the algorithm will cease to make corrections. However, this will also occur if all components of $\mathbf{e}(k)$ become nonpositive. Therefore, it remains to be shown that this condition cannot occur in the separable case. We can easily show this by contradiction. If the classes are linearly separable, there exists a $\hat{\mathbf{w}}$ and a $\hat{\mathbf{b}} > \mathbf{0}$ such that $\mathbf{X}\hat{\mathbf{w}} = \hat{\mathbf{b}}$. If we hypothesize that there exists an $\mathbf{e}(k)$ whose components are all nonpositive, then

$$\mathbf{e}'(k)\,\hat{\mathbf{b}} < 0 \tag{5.3–34}$$

since all the components of $\hat{\mathbf{b}}$ are positive. Now,

$$\begin{aligned}\mathbf{X}'\mathbf{e}(k) &= \mathbf{X}'[\mathbf{X}\mathbf{w}(k) - \mathbf{b}(k)] \\ &= \mathbf{X}'(\mathbf{X}\mathbf{X}^{\#} - \mathbf{I})\mathbf{b}(k) \\ &= (\mathbf{X}' - \mathbf{X}')\mathbf{b}(k) = \mathbf{0}\end{aligned}$$

where the last step follows from the fact that $\mathbf{X}'\mathbf{X}\mathbf{X}^{\#} = \mathbf{X}'\mathbf{X}(\mathbf{X}'\mathbf{X})^{-1}\mathbf{X}' = \mathbf{X}'$ if $(\mathbf{X}'\mathbf{X})^{-1}$ exists. The conditions for the existence of this inverse were discussed in Section 5.3.3.

If $\mathbf{X}'\mathbf{e}(k) = \mathbf{0}$, it follows that $(\mathbf{X}\hat{\mathbf{w}})'\mathbf{e}(k) = \hat{\mathbf{w}}'\mathbf{X}'\mathbf{e}(k) = 0$. However, since $\mathbf{X}\hat{\mathbf{w}} = \hat{\mathbf{b}}$, we must also have $\hat{\mathbf{b}}'\mathbf{e}(k) = \mathbf{e}'(k)\,\hat{\mathbf{b}} = 0$. This contradicts Eq. (5.3–34); hence $\mathbf{e}(k)$ cannot have all nonpositive components in the separable case. Therefore, the occurrence of a nonpositive error vector is a clear indication that the classes under consideration are not linearly separable.

Returning now to the monotonically decreasing sequence $||\mathbf{e}(1)||^2$, $||\mathbf{e}(2)||^2, \ldots$, we note from the foregoing discussion that the algorithm will not terminate in the separable case until $\mathbf{e}(k)$ becomes $\mathbf{0}$. From Lyapunov's stability theorem for discrete systems we know that

$$\lim_{k\to\infty} ||\mathbf{e}(k)||^2 = 0 \tag{5.3–35}$$

Therefore, this proves convergence of the algorithm in the separable case for infinite k. To show convergence for finite k, we note that $\mathbf{X}\mathbf{w}(k) = \mathbf{b}(k) + \mathbf{e}(k)$. Letting $b_{\min}$ denote the minimum component of $\mathbf{b}(1)$, and recalling that $\mathbf{b}(k)$ never decreases, we see that, if $\mathbf{e}(k)$ converges to $\mathbf{0}$ for infinite k, it must enter the hypersphere $||\mathbf{e}(k)|| = b_{\min}$ in finite k, at which point $\mathbf{X}\mathbf{w}(k) > \mathbf{0}$. This completes the proof.

The above proof gives no indication of the exact number of steps required for convergence. In implementing the algorithm, therefore, it is necessary to monitor the procedure for the occurrence of a solution. One way to do this is to examine $\mathbf{Xw}(k)$ and the error vector after each iteration. If $\mathbf{Xw}(k) > \mathbf{0}$ or $\mathbf{e}(k)$ becomes $\mathbf{0}$, a solution has been obtained. On the other hand, if $\mathbf{e}(k)$ becomes nonpositive, the classes are not linearly separable and the algorithm is terminated. It is noted that there is no bound on the number of steps required to disclose nonseparability of the pattern classes.

5.4 MULTICATEGORY CLASSIFICATION

In Section 2.2 three multiclass configurations were considered. In the first case, each of the M pattern classes is separable from the rest by a single decision surface. It is clear that each of the M decision functions required to solve this problem may be determined with the aid of any of the training algorithms already discussed in this chapter. For example, to determine the decision function for the ith pattern class we simply consider the two-class problem ω_i and $\bar{\omega}_i$, where $\bar{\omega}_i$ denotes all classes except ω_i.

In the second case, each class is separable from each other class. Here, the problem consists of determining $M(M-1)/2$ decision functions. These functions may be determined by applying any of the algorithms previously presented to every pair of the pattern classes under consideration.

In the third case, it is assumed that there exist M decision functions with the property that, if $\mathbf{x} \in \omega_i$, then

$$d_i(\mathbf{x}) > d_j(\mathbf{x}) \quad \text{for all} \quad j \neq i \tag{5.4–1}$$

In this section, an algorithm is presented which can be used to determine the decision functions of Case 3 directly. This algorithm, which is a generalization of the perceptron algorithm, may be described as follows.

Consider M pattern classes $\omega_1, \omega_2, \ldots, \omega_M$. Assume that, at the kth iterative step during training, a pattern $\mathbf{x}(k)$ belonging to class ω_i is presented to the machine. The M decision functions $d_j[\mathbf{x}(k)] = \mathbf{w}_j'(k)\mathbf{x}(k)$, $j = 1, 2, \ldots, M$, are evaluated. Then, if

$$d_i[\mathbf{x}(k)] > d_j[\mathbf{x}(k)] \quad j = 1, 2, \ldots, M; \quad j \neq i \tag{5.4–2}$$

the weight vectors are not adjusted, that is,

$$\mathbf{w}_j(k+1) = \mathbf{w}_j(k), \quad j = 1, 2, \ldots, M \tag{5.4–3}$$

On the other hand, assume that for some l

$$d_i[\mathbf{x}(k)] \leqslant d_l[\mathbf{x}(k)] \tag{5.4–4}$$

Under this condition the following weight adjustments are made:

$$\begin{aligned}
\mathbf{w}_i(k+1) &= \mathbf{w}_i(k) + c\mathbf{x}(k) \\
\mathbf{w}_l(k+1) &= \mathbf{w}_l(k) - c\mathbf{x}(k) \\
\mathbf{w}_j(k+1) &= \mathbf{w}_j(k), \quad j = 1, 2, \ldots, M; \quad j \neq i, \quad j \neq l
\end{aligned} \tag{5.4–5}$$

where c is a positive constant. If the classes are separable under Case 3, it can be shown that this algorithm converges in a finite number of iterations for arbitrary initial weight vectors $\mathbf{w}_i(1)$, $i = 1, 2, \ldots, M$. The procedure is illustrated by the following example.

Example: Consider the following pattern classes in which each class contains a single pattern: ω_1: $\{(0, 0)'\}$, ω_2: $\{(1, 1)'\}$, and ω_3: $\{(-1, 1)'\}$. In order to apply the generalized perceptron algorithm to these classes we first augment the patterns: $(0, 0, 1)'$, $(1, 1, 1)'$, and $(-1, 1, 1)'$. It is noted that none of the patterns is multiplied by -1. Starting with $\mathbf{w}_1(1) = \mathbf{w}_2(1) = \mathbf{w}_3(1) = (0, 0, 0)'$, letting $c = 1$, and presenting the patterns in the above order yields the following sequence of steps:

$$\begin{aligned}
d_1[\mathbf{x}(1)] &= \mathbf{w}_1'(1)\mathbf{x}(1) = 0 \\
d_2[\mathbf{x}(1)] &= \mathbf{w}_2'(1)\mathbf{x}(1) = 0 \\
d_3[\mathbf{x}(1)] &= \mathbf{w}_3'(1)\mathbf{x}(1) = 0
\end{aligned}$$

Since $\mathbf{x}(1) \in \omega_1$ and $d_1[\mathbf{x}(1)] = d_2[\mathbf{x}(1)] = d_3[\mathbf{x}(1)]$, the first weight vector is increased, while the other two are decreased, as indicated in Eq. (5.4–5), that is,

$$\mathbf{w}_1(2) = \mathbf{w}_1(1) + \mathbf{x}(1) = \begin{pmatrix} 0 \\ 0 \\ 1 \end{pmatrix}$$

$$\mathbf{w}_2(2) = \mathbf{w}_2(1) - \mathbf{x}(1) = \begin{pmatrix} 0 \\ 0 \\ -1 \end{pmatrix}$$

$$\mathbf{w}_3(2) = \mathbf{w}_3(1) - \mathbf{x}(1) = \begin{pmatrix} 0 \\ 0 \\ -1 \end{pmatrix}$$

The next pattern, $\mathbf{x}(2) = (1, 1, 1)'$, belongs to ω_2, and we have

$$\mathbf{w}_1'(2)\mathbf{x}(2) = 1$$

$$\mathbf{w}_2'(2)\mathbf{x}(2) = -1$$

$$\mathbf{w}_3'(2)\mathbf{x}(2) = -1$$

Since all products were either greater than or equal to $\mathbf{w}_2'(2)\mathbf{x}(2)$, the following adjustments are made:

$$\mathbf{w}_1(3) = \mathbf{w}_1(2) - \mathbf{x}(2) = \begin{pmatrix} -1 \\ -1 \\ 0 \end{pmatrix}$$

$$\mathbf{w}_2(3) = \mathbf{w}_2(2) + \mathbf{x}(2) = \begin{pmatrix} 1 \\ 1 \\ 0 \end{pmatrix}$$

$$\mathbf{w}_3(3) = \mathbf{w}_3(2) - \mathbf{x}(2) = \begin{pmatrix} -1 \\ -1 \\ -2 \end{pmatrix}$$

The next pattern, $\mathbf{x}(3) = (-1, 1, 1)'$, belongs to ω_3, and we have

$$\mathbf{w}_1'(3)\mathbf{x}(3) = 0$$

$$\mathbf{w}_2'(3)\mathbf{x}(3) = 0$$

$$\mathbf{w}_3'(3)\mathbf{x}(3) = -2$$

All three products are again incorrect; therefore, the following adjustments are made:

$$\mathbf{w}_1(4) = \mathbf{w}_1(3) - \mathbf{x}(3) = \begin{pmatrix} 0 \\ -2 \\ -1 \end{pmatrix}$$

$$\mathbf{w}_2(4) = \mathbf{w}_2(3) - \mathbf{x}(3) = \begin{pmatrix} 2 \\ 0 \\ -1 \end{pmatrix}$$

$$\mathbf{w}_3(4) = \mathbf{w}_3(3) + \mathbf{x}(3) = \begin{pmatrix} -2 \\ 0 \\ -1 \end{pmatrix}$$

Since a complete, error-free iteration through all patterns has not been obtained, the patterns must be recycled. Letting $\mathbf{x}(4) = \mathbf{x}(1)$, $\mathbf{x}(5) = \mathbf{x}(2)$, and $\mathbf{x}(6) = \mathbf{x}(3)$, we obtain

$$\mathbf{w}_1'(4)\mathbf{x}(4) = -1$$

$$\mathbf{w}_2'(4)\mathbf{x}(4) = -1$$

$$\mathbf{w}_3'(4)\mathbf{x}(4) = -1$$

Since $\mathbf{x}(4)$ belongs to ω_1, all products are incorrect. Therefore,

$$\mathbf{w}_1(5) = \mathbf{w}_1(4) + \mathbf{x}(4) = \begin{pmatrix} 0 \\ -2 \\ 0 \end{pmatrix}$$

$$\mathbf{w}_2(5) = \mathbf{w}_2(4) - \mathbf{x}(4) = \begin{pmatrix} 2 \\ 0 \\ -2 \end{pmatrix}$$

$$\mathbf{w}_3(5) = \mathbf{w}_3(4) - \mathbf{x}(4) = \begin{pmatrix} -2 \\ 0 \\ -2 \end{pmatrix}$$

The next pattern, $\mathbf{x}(5) = (1, 1, 1)'$, belongs to ω_2. Performing the required inner products yields

$$\mathbf{w}_1'(5)\mathbf{x}(5) = -2$$

$$\mathbf{w}_2'(5)\mathbf{x}(5) = 0$$

$$\mathbf{w}_3'(5)\mathbf{x}(5) = -4$$

We note that $\mathbf{x}(5)$ has been correctly classified. Therefore,

$$\mathbf{w}_1(6) = \mathbf{w}_1(5) = \begin{pmatrix} 0 \\ -2 \\ 0 \end{pmatrix}$$

$$\mathbf{w}_2(6) = \mathbf{w}_2(5) = \begin{pmatrix} 2 \\ 0 \\ -2 \end{pmatrix}$$

$$\mathbf{w}_3(6) = \mathbf{w}_3(5) = \begin{pmatrix} -2 \\ 0 \\ -2 \end{pmatrix}$$

The pattern $\mathbf{x}(6) = (-1, 1, 1)'$ belongs to ω_3, and we have

$$\mathbf{w}_1'(6)\mathbf{x}(6) = -2$$

$$\mathbf{w}_2'(6)\mathbf{x}(6) = -4$$

$$\mathbf{w}_3'(6)\mathbf{x}(6) = 0$$

This pattern has also been correctly classified, so no changes are necessary, that is,

$$\mathbf{w}_1(7) = \mathbf{w}_1(6) = \begin{pmatrix} 0 \\ -2 \\ 0 \end{pmatrix}$$

$$\mathbf{w}_2(7) = \mathbf{w}_2(6) = \begin{pmatrix} 2 \\ 0 \\ -2 \end{pmatrix}$$

$$\mathbf{w}_3(7) = \mathbf{w}_3(6) = \begin{pmatrix} -2 \\ 0 \\ -2 \end{pmatrix}$$

Continuing the training process with $\mathbf{x}(7) = (0, 0, 1)'$, which belongs to ω_1, yields

$$\mathbf{w}_1'(7)\mathbf{x}(7) = 0$$

$$\mathbf{w}_2'(7)\mathbf{x}(7) = -2$$

$$\mathbf{w}_3'(7)\mathbf{x}(7) = -2$$

This represents a complete, error-free iteration through all patterns. The solution weight vectors are, therefore,

$$\mathbf{w}_1(8) = \mathbf{w}_1(7) = \begin{pmatrix} 0 \\ -2 \\ 0 \end{pmatrix}$$

$$\mathbf{w}_2(8) = \mathbf{w}_2(7) = \begin{pmatrix} 2 \\ 0 \\ -2 \end{pmatrix}$$

$$\mathbf{w}_3(8) = \mathbf{w}_3(7) = \begin{pmatrix} -2 \\ 0 \\ -2 \end{pmatrix}$$

Using these weight vectors yields the following decision functions:

$$\begin{aligned} d_1(\mathbf{x}) &= \quad 0x_1 - 2x_2 + 0 = -2x_2 \\ d_2(\mathbf{x}) &= \quad 2x_1 + 0x_2 - 2 = -2x_1 - 2 \\ d_3(\mathbf{x}) &= -2x_1 + 0x_2 - 2 = -2x_1 - 2 \end{aligned}$$

5.5 LEARNING AND GENERALIZATION

All the algorithms presented in this chapter employ sample patterns to generate the coefficients of decision functions. As was previously mentioned, this is called the *learning* or *training* phase of a pattern classifier design. The *generalization* properties of a given classifier are tested when the classifier is confronted with data not used in the training phase. Clearly, a well-designed classifier is derived from data which are reasonably representative of the "field" data.

One important question still needs to be discussed: How many training patterns should one choose in order to obtain good generalization properties in the resulting classifier? Intuitively the answer is simple: Choose as many samples as possible. In practice, however, the question of economics will usually place a constraint on the number of samples that can be gathered for training, as well as the computer time available for the training phase.

Very few analytical results exist which can be used as a guide in pattern selection. However, in the absence of any probabilistic information, Cover [1965] has shown that the total number of patterns chosen for a two-class problem must be at least equal to twice the dimensionality of the pattern vectors for algorithms of the type discussed in this chapter to yield results with meaningful generalization properties. This is the *dichotomization capacity* concept, $C_K = 2(K + 1)$, defined in Eq. (2.5–14), where $K + 1$ is the number of weights in the decision function.

Basically, the dichotomization capacity tells us that, if the number N of training patterns which are well distributed is less than C_K, the probability of correctly dichotomizing the training set is low. However, if $N > C_K$ and we are able to classify the training set correctly, a high degree of confidence can be placed in the solution and its generalization properties. In practice, a good rule of thumb is to choose N in the order of ten times C_K.

When the two classes under consideration are not separable by the specified decision surface, it is of interest to know the maximum number of training patterns that can be correctly classified by that surface. If the probability density of each pattern population is known, the Bayes classifier discussed in Section 4.2 can be implemented to yield the lowest average probability of error. For the deterministic case, a minimum-error algorithm which guarantees an optimal classifier has been derived (Warmack and Gonzalez [1972, 1973]). This procedure has some important properties worth mentioning in this context. When the patterns are well distributed, the algorithm yields *all* optimal solutions.† If the classes are separable, there exists of course a unique solution. When the classes are not separable, however, the presence of more than one optimal solution indicates that either the training set is not representative of the true pattern population or the complexity of the chosen decision functions is inadequate, or both. This follows from the fact that, according to the Bayes classification rule, the optimal classifier must be unique. Although the algorithm is deterministic, this does not alter the fact that the absolute limit on classification performance is determined by the Bayes classification rule. Therefore, this algorithm provides a tool for designing a meaningful optimal pattern classifier in nonseparable situations.

5.6 THE POTENTIAL FUNCTION APPROACH

The discussions in the preceding sections point out that the analytical design of automatic pattern classification systems consists primarily in the determination of the decision functions which generate the partition boundaries in the pattern space to separate patterns of one class from another. We have examined several basic concepts for pattern classification and training algorithms for generating decision functions. Several weight-adjustment training algorithms are reviewed, which provide useful procedures for the determination of partition boundaries using sample patterns known to belong to one of the M admissible classes. In this section, we discuss an

† In this discussion two solutions are considered different only if they satisfy different patterns.

approach to the determination of decision functions and partition boundaries by use of the potential function concept.

Suppose that we want to distinguish between two pattern classes, ω_1 and ω_2. Sample patterns of both classes are represented by vectors or points in the n-dimensional pattern space. If these sample pattern points are likened to some kind of energy source, the potential at any of these points attains a peak value and then decreases rapidly at any point away from the sample pattern point, $\mathbf{x}_k$. Using this analogy, we may visualize the presence of equipotential contours which are described by a potential function $K(\mathbf{x}, \mathbf{x}_k)$. For pattern class ω_1, we may imagine that the cluster of sample patterns forms a "plateau" with the sample points located at the peaks of a group of hills. A similar geometrical interpretation may be visualized for pattern class ω_2. These two "plateaus" are separated by a "valley" in which the potential is said to drop to zero. This intuitive argument leads to the determination of decision functions for pattern classification by the potential function method.

5.6.1 Generation of Decision Functions†

The decision functions for pattern classification can be generated from the potential functions for sample pattern vectors $\mathbf{x}_k$, $k = 1, 2, 3, \ldots,$ in the pattern space. The potential function for any sample pattern point $\mathbf{x}_k$ can be characterized by the expression

$$K(\mathbf{x}, \mathbf{x}_k) = \sum_{i=1}^{\infty} \lambda_i^2 \varphi_i(\mathbf{x}) \varphi_i(\mathbf{x}_k) \tag{5.6-1}$$

where $\varphi_i(\mathbf{x})$, $i = 1, 2, \ldots,$ are assumed for convenience to be orthonormal functions, and λ_i, $i = 1, 2, \ldots,$ are real numbers different from zero chosen in such a way that the potential function $K(\mathbf{x}, \mathbf{x}_k)$ is bounded for $\mathbf{x}_k \in \omega_1 \cup \omega_2$. The problem of how to select appropriate potential functions is discussed in the next section.

The decision function $d(\mathbf{x})$ can be constructed from the sequence of potential functions $K(\mathbf{x}, \mathbf{x}_1)$, $K(\mathbf{x}, \mathbf{x}_2), \ldots,$ corresponding to the sequence of training sample patterns $\mathbf{x}_1, \mathbf{x}_2, \ldots,$ which are presented to the machine during the training process. The decision function $d(\mathbf{x})$ is related to the potential functions $K(\mathbf{x}, \mathbf{x}_k)$ by the set of orthonormal functions $\varphi_i(\mathbf{x})$, and may be represented by the series expansion

† The discussions in this section are based on Chapter 4, *Advances in Information Systems Science,* Volume 1, Plenum Press.

$$d(\mathbf{x}) = \sum_{i=1}^{\infty} c_i \varphi_i(\mathbf{x}) \tag{5.6–2}$$

In Eq. (5.6–2), the coefficients c_i, $i = 1, 2, \ldots$, are unknown and can be determined iteratively from the training sample patterns. The function $d(\mathbf{x})$ is a relatively smooth function which does not have many extrema in a small region. Its values at nearby points differ slightly.

It will be shown below that the decision function of Eq. (5.6–2) is related to the potential function given in Eq. (5.6–1) by the following iterative relation:

$$d_{k+1}(\mathbf{x}) = d_k(\mathbf{x}) + r_{k+1} K(\mathbf{x}, \mathbf{x}_{k+1}) \tag{5.6–3}$$

where k represents the iterative step and r_{k+1} is a coefficient to be discussed below. The important point to keep in mind now is that the decision function $d(\mathbf{x})$ can be directly obtained from the potential functions. Therefore, the following discussion will be focused initially on the determination of potential functions.

In the training phase, the sample patterns are presented to the machine, which computes the corresponding potential functions successively. The *cumulative potential* at the kth iterative step will be determined by the aggregate of individual potential functions. This cumulative potential, which will be denoted by $K_k(\mathbf{x})$, is determined in such a way that, if the training sample pattern $\mathbf{x}_{k+1}$ is incorrectly classified, the cumulative potential is modified. If this pattern is classified correctly, however, the cumulative potential remains unchanged at this step. The determination of the cumulative potential is explained as follows.

At the beginning of the training phase, the initial cumulative potential $K_0(\mathbf{x})$ is assumed for notational convenience to be zero. When the first training sample pattern, $\mathbf{x}_1$, is presented, the cumulative potential is updated according to the relation

$$K_1(\mathbf{x}) = \begin{cases} K_0(\mathbf{x}) + K(\mathbf{x}, \mathbf{x}_1) & \text{if} \quad \mathbf{x}_1 \in \omega_1 \\ K_0(\mathbf{x}) - K(\mathbf{x}, \mathbf{x}_1) & \text{if} \quad \mathbf{x}_1 \in \omega_2 \end{cases} \tag{5.6–4}$$

However, since $K_0(\mathbf{x}) = 0$, we may express the first computed value of the cumulative potential as

$$K_1(\mathbf{x}) = \begin{cases} K(\mathbf{x}, \mathbf{x}_1) & \text{if} \quad \mathbf{x}_1 \in \omega_1 \\ -K(\mathbf{x}, \mathbf{x}_1) & \text{if} \quad \mathbf{x}_1 \in \omega_2 \end{cases} \tag{5.6–5}$$

In this situation, the cumulative potential is simply equal to the potential function for sample pattern $\mathbf{x}_1$. The potential is assumed to be positive for patterns belonging to class ω_1 and negative for patterns belonging to class ω_2. At this stage, the cumulative potential $K_1(\mathbf{x})$ describes the initial partition boundary.

When the second training sample pattern, $\mathbf{x}_2$, is presented, the cumulative potential is determined in the following manner.

1. If $\mathbf{x}_2 \in \omega_1$ and $K_1(\mathbf{x}_2) > 0$, or if $\mathbf{x}_2 \in \omega_2$ and $K_1(\mathbf{x}_2) < 0$, then

$$K_2(\mathbf{x}) = K_1(\mathbf{x}) \tag{5.6-6}$$

This situation implies that the cumulative potential remains unchanged if the sample pattern point lies on the correct side of the partition boundary defined by the cumulative potential $K_1(\mathbf{x})$.

2. If $\mathbf{x}_2 \in \omega_1$ and $K_1(\mathbf{x}_2) \leqslant 0$, then

$$\begin{aligned} K_2(\mathbf{x}) &= K_1(\mathbf{x}) + K(\mathbf{x}, \mathbf{x}_2) \\ &= \pm K(\mathbf{x}, \mathbf{x}_1) + K(\mathbf{x}, \mathbf{x}_2) \end{aligned} \tag{5.6-7}$$

3. If $\mathbf{x}_2 \in \omega_2$ and $K_1(\mathbf{x}_2) \geqslant 0$, then

$$\begin{aligned} K_2(\mathbf{x}) &= K_1(\mathbf{x}) - K(\mathbf{x}, \mathbf{x}_2) \\ &= \pm K(\mathbf{x}, \mathbf{x}_1) - K(\mathbf{x}, \mathbf{x}_2) \end{aligned} \tag{5.6-8}$$

These two situations indicate that, if sample pattern point $\mathbf{x}_2$ lies on the wrong side of the partition boundary defined by $K_1(\mathbf{x})$, the cumulative potential is increased by $K(\mathbf{x}, \mathbf{x}_2)$ for $\mathbf{x}_2 \in \omega_1$ and is decreased by $K(\mathbf{x}, \mathbf{x}_2)$ for $\mathbf{x}_2 \in \omega_2$.

When the third training sample pattern, $\mathbf{x}_3$, is presented, the cumulative potential is determined in a similar manner.

1. If $\mathbf{x}_3 \in \omega_1$ and $K_2(\mathbf{x}_3) > 0$, or $\mathbf{x}_3 \in \omega_2$ and $K_2(\mathbf{x}_3) < 0$, then

$$K_3(\mathbf{x}) = K_2(\mathbf{x}) \tag{5.6-9}$$

In other words, when the partition boundary defined by $K_2(\mathbf{x})$ makes a correct classification, the cumulative potential remains unchanged.

2. If $\mathbf{x}_3 \in \omega_1$ and $K_2(\mathbf{x}_3) \leqslant 0$, then

$$\begin{aligned} K_3(\mathbf{x}) &= K_2(\mathbf{x}) + K(\mathbf{x}, \mathbf{x}_3) \\ &= \pm K(\mathbf{x}, \mathbf{x}_1) \pm K(\mathbf{x}, \mathbf{x}_2) + K(\mathbf{x}, \mathbf{x}_3) \end{aligned} \tag{5.6-10}$$

3. If $\mathbf{x}_3 \in \omega_2$ and $K_2(\mathbf{x}_3) \geqslant 0$, then

$$\begin{aligned} K_3(\mathbf{x}) &= K_2(\mathbf{x}) - K(\mathbf{x}, \mathbf{x}_3) \\ &= \pm K(\mathbf{x}, \mathbf{x}_1) \pm K(\mathbf{x}, \mathbf{x}_2) - K(\mathbf{x}, \mathbf{x}_3) \end{aligned} \tag{5.6–11}$$

In other words, when the partition boundary defined by $K_2(\mathbf{x})$ makes a wrong classification, the cumulative potential is increased or decreased by $K(\mathbf{x}, \mathbf{x}_3)$, depending on whether sample pattern $\mathbf{x}_3$ belongs to class ω_1 or class ω_2. The term $K(\mathbf{x}, \mathbf{x}_2)$ in Eqs. (5.6–10) and (5.6–11) will, of course, not be present if $\mathbf{x}_2$ is classified correctly.

Now, let $K_k(\mathbf{x})$ be the cumulative potential after the presentation of k training sample patterns $\mathbf{x}_1, \mathbf{x}_2, \ldots, \mathbf{x}_k$. Then the cumulative potential $K_{k+1}(\mathbf{x})$ following the presentation of the $(k + 1)$th sample pattern is determined as follows:

1. If $\mathbf{x}_{k+1} \in \omega_1$ and $K_k(\mathbf{x}_{k+1}) > 0$, or $\mathbf{x}_{k+1} \in \omega_2$ and $K_k(\mathbf{x}_{k+1}) < 0$, then

$$K_{k+1}(\mathbf{x}) = K_k(\mathbf{x}) \tag{5.6–12}$$

2. If $\mathbf{x}_{k+1} \in \omega_1$ and $K_k(\mathbf{x}_{k+1}) \leqslant 0$, then

$$K_{k+1}(\mathbf{x}) = K_k(\mathbf{x}) + K(\mathbf{x}, \mathbf{x}_{k+1}) \tag{5.6–13}$$

3. If $\mathbf{x}_{k+1} \in \omega_2$ and $K_k(\mathbf{x}_{k+1}) \geqslant 0$, then

$$K_{k+1}(\mathbf{x}) = K_k(\mathbf{x}) - K(\mathbf{x}, \mathbf{x}_{k+1}) \tag{5.6–14}$$

Equations (5.6–12) through (5.6–14) provide an algorithm for the iterative determination of the cumulative potential. This algorithm may be written as

$$K_{k+1}(\mathbf{x}) = K_k(\mathbf{x}) + r_{k+1} K(\mathbf{x}, \mathbf{x}_{k+1}) \tag{5.6–15}$$

where the coefficient r_{k+1} of the correction term is given by

$$r_{k+1} = \begin{cases} 0 & \text{for} \quad \mathbf{x}_{k+1} \in \omega_1 \quad \text{and} \quad K_k(\mathbf{x}_{k+1}) > 0 \\ 0 & \text{for} \quad \mathbf{x}_{k+1} \in \omega_2 \quad \text{and} \quad K_k(\mathbf{x}_{k+1}) < 0 \\ 1 & \text{for} \quad \mathbf{x}_{k+1} \in \omega_1 \quad \text{and} \quad K_k(\mathbf{x}_{k+1}) \leqslant 0 \\ -1 & \text{for} \quad \mathbf{x}_{k+1} \in \omega_2 \quad \text{and} \quad K_k(\mathbf{x}_{k+1}) \geqslant 0 \end{cases} \tag{5.6–16}$$

When the algorithm makes a correct classification, the coefficient $r_{k+1} = 0$. On the other hand, when the algorithm makes a wrong classification, the coefficient $r_{k+1} = +1$ or -1, depending on whether the sample pattern belongs to class ω_1 or class ω_2.

From the given training sequence $\{\mathbf{x}_1, \mathbf{x}_2, \ldots, \mathbf{x}_k, \ldots\}$, we may form a sequence $\{\hat{\mathbf{x}}_1, \hat{\mathbf{x}}_2, \ldots, \hat{\mathbf{x}}_j, \ldots\}$ by omitting the sample patterns for which the cumulative potentials remain unchanged, that is, for which $K_j(\mathbf{x}_{j+1}) > 0$ if $\mathbf{x}_{j+1} \in \omega_1$ or $K_j(\mathbf{x}_{j+1}) < 0$ if $\mathbf{x}_{j+1} \in \omega_2$. The elements of this reduced training sequence are the error-correction sample patterns. Then it follows from Eqs. (5.6–13) and (5.6–14) by iteration that the cumulative potential $K_{k+1}(\mathbf{x})$ after the presentation of training sample patterns is given by

$$K_{k+1}(\mathbf{x}) = \sum_{\hat{\mathbf{x}}_j} a_j K(\mathbf{x}, \hat{\mathbf{x}}_j) \tag{5.6–17}$$

where

$$a_j = \begin{cases} +1 & \text{for} \quad \hat{\mathbf{x}}_j \in \omega_1 \\ -1 & \text{for} \quad \hat{\mathbf{x}}_j \in \omega_2 \end{cases} \tag{5.6–18}$$

The coefficient a_j is referred to as the *category index*, which designates to which class sample pattern $\hat{\mathbf{x}}_j$ belongs. Equations (5.6–17) and (5.6–18) point out that the cumulative potential generated by a sequence of $k + 1$ training sample patterns is equal to the difference between the total potential due to error-correction samples of class ω_1 and the total potential due to error-correction samples of class ω_2.

It is evident from the potential function algorithm that the cumulative potential plays the role of a decision function. In other words, if $K_k(\mathbf{x}_{k+1})$ is greater than zero when $\mathbf{x}_{k+1}$ belongs to ω_1 or less than zero when $\mathbf{x}_{k+1}$ belongs to ω_2, the cumulative potential is not modified. On the other hand, misclassification of a pattern results in a change in the potential function during training. Consequently, the potential function algorithm provides an iterative procedure for the direct determination of a decision function for classes ω_1 and ω_2; that is, letting $d(\mathbf{x}) = K(\mathbf{x})$, we obtain from Eq. (5.6–15)

$$d_{k+1}(\mathbf{x}) = d_k(\mathbf{x}) + r_{k+1} K(\mathbf{x}, \mathbf{x}_{k+1}) \tag{5.6–19}$$

as indicated in Eq. (5.6–3).

The condition for the determination of the coefficient r_{k+1} may be restated in compact form as

$$r_{k+1} = \tfrac{1}{2} a_{k+1} \{1 - a_{k+1} \operatorname{sgn}[d_k(\mathbf{x}_{k+1})]\} \tag{5.6–20}$$

where a_{k+1} is given by Eq. (5.6–18), and $\operatorname{sgn}[d_k(\mathbf{x}_{k+1})]$ is defined in this particular case as $\operatorname{sgn}[d(\mathbf{x}_{k+1})] = 1$ or -1, depending on whether $d_k(\mathbf{x}_{k+1})$

is greater than zero, or less than or equal to zero, respectively. If the decision function $d_k(\mathbf{x})$ classifies the pattern $\mathbf{x}_{k+1}$ correctly, then $r_k = 0$, implying no change in the cumulative potential. It can readily be seen that Eq. (5.6–20) covers all other classification conditions.

From Eq. (5.6–2), we can express Eq. (5.6–19) in the alternative recursive form

$$d_{k+1}(\mathbf{x}) = \sum_{i=1}^{\infty} c_i(k+1)\varphi_i(\mathbf{x}) \tag{5.6–21}$$

where the coefficients $c_i(k+1)$ depend on the number of iterations in the training process. It follows from this equation and the above discussion that the cumulative potential may also be expressed in the form

$$K_{k+1}(\mathbf{x}) = \sum_{i=1}^{\infty} c_i(k+1)\varphi_i(\mathbf{x}) \tag{5.6–22}$$

Combining Eqs. (5.6–19) and (5.6–21) with Eq. (5.6–1) results in the relation

$$c_i(k+1) = c_i(k) + r_{k+1}\lambda_i^2\varphi_i(\mathbf{x}_{k+1}) \tag{5.6–23}$$

which can be used for the iterative evaluation of the expansion coefficients.

5.6.2 Selection of Potential Functions

The general form of the potential function $K(\mathbf{x}, \mathbf{x}_k)$ was given in Eq. (5.6–1). Although an infinite series expansion is often employed in mathematical discussions of potential function algorithms, it clearly is of no practical usefulness. There are two basic methods for the practical construction of potential functions.

The first is to use a truncated series of the form

$$K(\mathbf{x}, \mathbf{x}_k) = \sum_{i=1}^{m} \varphi_i(\mathbf{x})\varphi_i(\mathbf{x}_k) \tag{5.6–24}$$

where the $\{\varphi_i(\mathbf{x})\}$ are orthonormal functions over the region of definition of the patterns. This assumption does not represent any real practical restriction since orthonormal functions are easily obtainable, as discussed in Section 2.7. The λ_i factors used in the general representation given in Eq. (5.6–1) are related to boundedness of the potential functions and can be omitted for the type of functions which we will consider. Functions obtained by using Eq. (5.6–24) will be referred to as *potential functions of Type 1*.

The second method consists of selecting a symmetrical function of two variables, $\mathbf{x}$ and $\mathbf{x}_k$, and using it as a potential function. The symmetry condition is imposed so that the resulting potential functions will be consistent with the general form given in Eq. (5.6–1). We see from this equation that, in fact, $K(\mathbf{x}, \mathbf{x}_k) = K(\mathbf{x}_k, \mathbf{x})$. It is further required that the chosen functions be mathematically expandable in an infinite series. This requirement is also consistent with the general form given in Eq. (5.6–1). Functions which satisfy these conditions will be referred to as *potential functions of Type 2.* Examples of commonly used potential functions of Type 2 are

$$K(\mathbf{x}, \mathbf{x}_k) = \exp\{-\alpha||\mathbf{x} - \mathbf{x}_k||^2\} \tag{5.6–25}$$

$$K(\mathbf{x}, \mathbf{x}_k) = \frac{1}{1 + \alpha||\mathbf{x} - \mathbf{x}_k||^2} \tag{5.6–26}$$

$$K(\mathbf{x}, \mathbf{x}_k) = \left|\frac{\sin \alpha||\mathbf{x} - \mathbf{x}_k||^2}{\alpha||\mathbf{x} - \mathbf{x}_k||^2}\right| \tag{5.6–27}$$

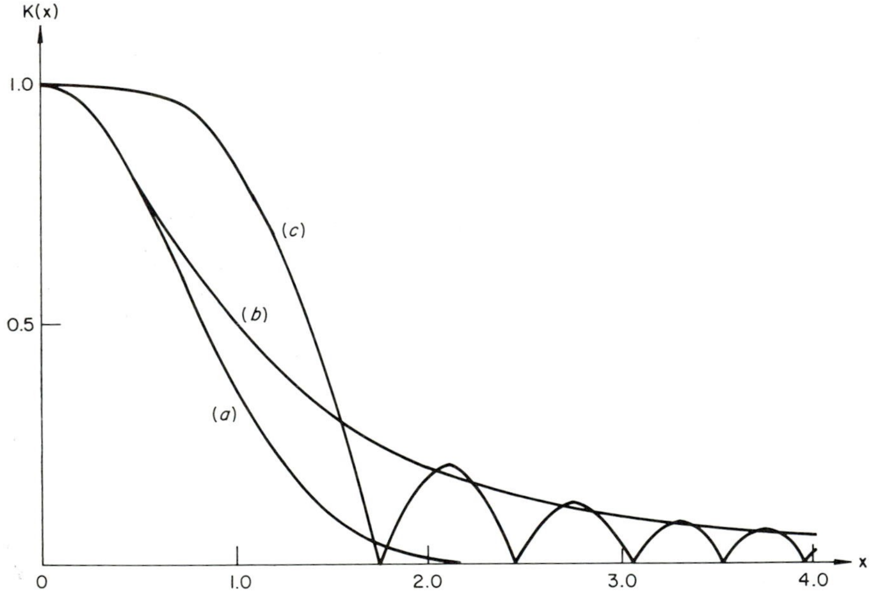

Figure 5.4. Examples of one-dimensional potential functions: (a) plot of Eq. (5.6–25); (b) plot of Eq. (5.6–26); (c) plot of Eq. (5.6–27). In all three cases $\alpha = 1$ and $x_k = 0$

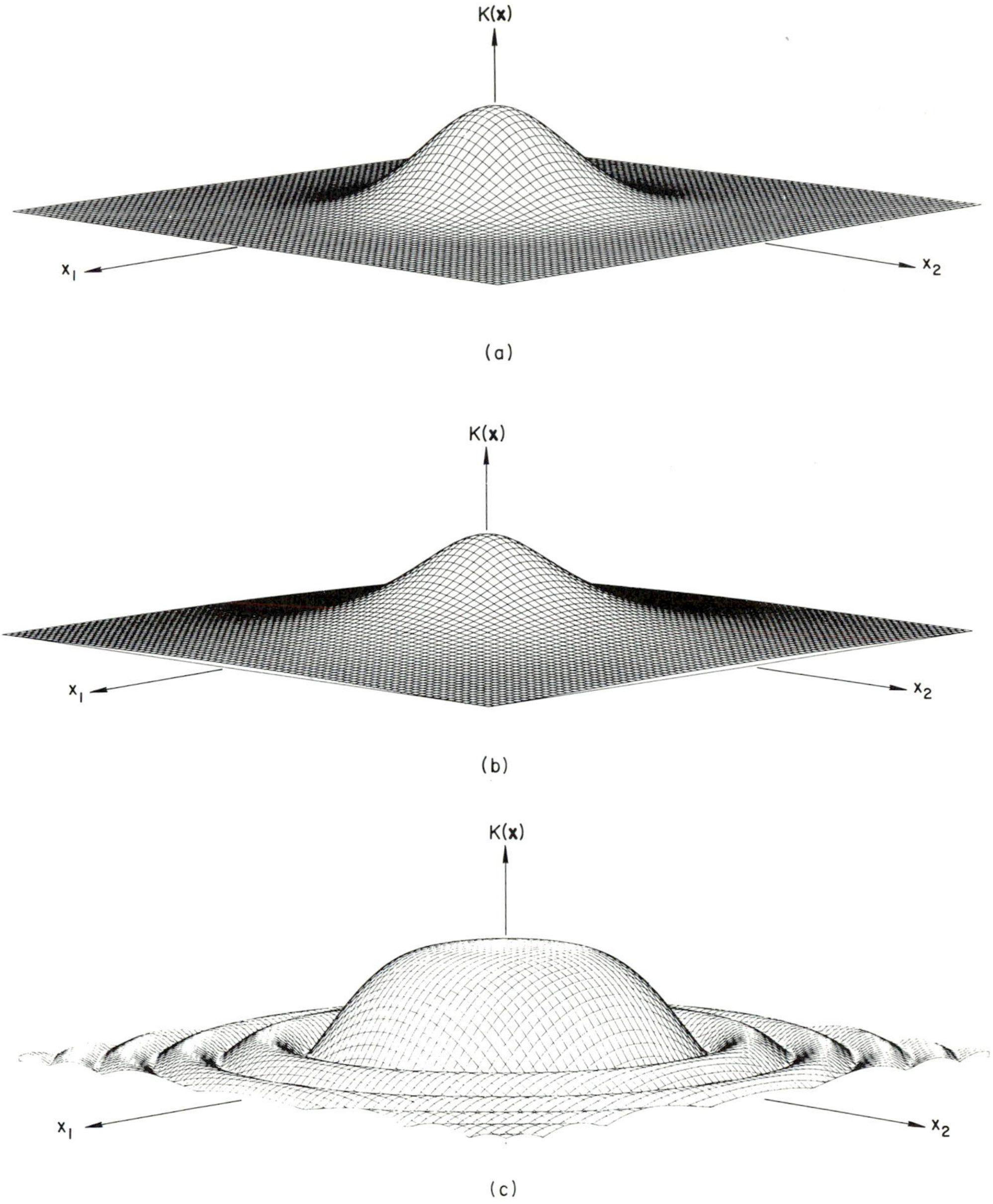

Figure 5.5. Two-dimensional potential functions: (a) plot of Eq. (5.6–25); (b) plot of Eq. (5.6–26); (c) plot of Eq. (5.6–27). In all three cases the range on the coordinates of $\mathbf{x} = (x_1, x_2)'$ is from -3 to 3, $\alpha = 1$, and $\mathbf{x}_k = \mathbf{0}$

where α is a positive constant, and $||\mathbf{x} - \mathbf{x}_k||$ is the norm of the vector $(\mathbf{x} - \mathbf{x}_k)$. It is worth noting that these functions are inversely proportional to the squared distance measure, $D^2 = ||\mathbf{x} - \mathbf{x}_k||^2$, which is also a characteristic, for example, of the force in a gravitational potential field. The above functions are plotted in Fig. 5.4 for one-dimensional patterns and in Fig. 5.5 for the two-dimensional case.

Example 1: Let us apply the method of potential functions to the patterns shown in Fig. 5.6, using potential functions of Type 1. The first thing we

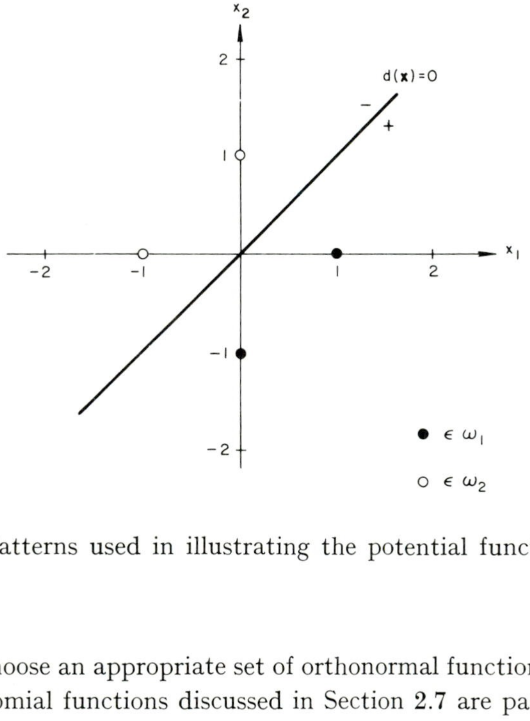

Figure 5.6. Patterns used in illustrating the potential function algorithm

must do is to choose an appropriate set of orthonormal functions $\{\varphi_i(\mathbf{x})\}$. The Hermite polynomial functions discussed in Section 2.7 are particularly easy to apply since their region of orthonormality is the interval $(-\infty, \infty)$. In the one-dimensional case these functions are given by

$$\varphi_l(x) = \frac{\exp(-x^2/2)}{\sqrt{2^l l! \sqrt{\pi}}} H_l(x)$$

where the term multiplying $H_l(x)$ is an orthonormalization factor. The first few terms of $H_l(x)$ are

$$H_0(x) = 1, \qquad H_1(x) = 2x$$

$$H_2(x) = 4x^2 - 2, \qquad H_3(x) = 8x^3 - 12x$$

$$H_4(x) = 16x^4 - 48x^2 + 12$$

For the purpose of illustration, let us use these orthogonal functions instead of their more numerically complex orthonormal counterparts. As was indicated in Section 2.7, equivalent results are often obtained with the orthogonal functions. Letting $m = 4$ as a first approximation, and following the discussion in Section 2.7 for the construction of multidimensional orthogonal functions from a single-variable orthogonal set yields

$$\varphi_1(\mathbf{x}) = \varphi_1(x_1, x_2) = H_0(x_1)H_0(x_2) = 1$$

$$\varphi_2(\mathbf{x}) = \varphi_2(x_1, x_2) = H_1(x_1)H_0(x_2) = 2x_1$$

$$\varphi_3(\mathbf{x}) = \varphi_3(x_1, x_2) = H_0(x_1)H_1(x_2) = 2x_2$$

$$\varphi_4(\mathbf{x}) = \varphi_4(x_1, x_2) = H_1(x_1)H_1(x_2) = 4x_1x_2$$

Using now Eq. (5.6–24), we may form the potential function $K(\mathbf{x}, \mathbf{x}_k)$ as follows:

$$K(\mathbf{x}, \mathbf{x}_k) = \sum_{i=1}^{4} \varphi_i(\mathbf{x})\varphi_i(\mathbf{x}_k)$$

$$= 1 + 4x_1x_{k1} + 4x_2x_{k2} + 16x_1x_2x_{k1}x_{k2}$$

where x_{k1} and x_{k2} are the components of $\mathbf{x}_k$. The patterns of class ω_1 are $\{(1, 0)', (0, -1)'\}$ and, of ω_2, $\{(-1, 0)', (0, 1)'\}$. Using the potential function training algorithm of Eq. (5.6–15) yields the following sequence of steps.

Let $\mathbf{x}_1 = (1, 0)'$ be the first pattern presented. Since it belongs to class ω_1, the cumulative potential is given by

$$K_1(\mathbf{x}) = K(\mathbf{x}, \mathbf{x}_1) = 1 + 4x_1(1) + 4x_2(0) + 16x_1x_2(1)(0)$$

$$= 1 + 4x_1$$

Pattern $\mathbf{x}_2 = (0, -1)'$ belongs to ω_1. Evaluating $K_1(\mathbf{x}_2)$ yields

$$K_1(\mathbf{x}_2) = 1 + 4(0) = 1$$

Since $K_1(\mathbf{x}_2) > 0$ and $\mathbf{x}_2 \in \omega_1$, we let

$$K_2(\mathbf{x}) = K_1(\mathbf{x}) = 1 + 4x_1$$

The next pattern, $\mathbf{x}_3 = (-1, 0)'$, belongs to ω_2, and since

$$K_2(\mathbf{x}_3) = 1 + 4(-1) = -3$$

is less than zero, we let

$$K_3(\mathbf{x}) = K_2(\mathbf{x}) = 1 + 4x_1$$

The fourth training pattern, $\mathbf{x}_4 = (0, 1)'$, belongs to ω_2, and since

$$K_3(\mathbf{x}_4) = 1 + 4(0) = 1$$

is greater than zero, the following adjustment must be made:

$$\begin{aligned} K_4(\mathbf{x}) &= K_3(\mathbf{x}) - K(\mathbf{x}, \mathbf{x}_4) \\ &= 1 + 4x_1 - (1 + 4x_2) \\ &= 4x_1 - 4x_2 \end{aligned}$$

Iterating through the patterns again yields

$$\mathbf{x}_5 = \begin{pmatrix} 1 \\ 0 \end{pmatrix} \in \omega_1, \qquad K_4(\mathbf{x}_5) = 4$$

$$K_5(\mathbf{x}) = K_4(\mathbf{x}) = 4x_1 - 4x_2$$

$$\mathbf{x}_6 = \begin{pmatrix} 0 \\ -1 \end{pmatrix} \in \omega_1, \qquad K_5(\mathbf{x}_6) = 4$$

$$K_6(\mathbf{x}) = K_5(\mathbf{x}) = 4x_1 - 4x_2$$

$$\mathbf{x}_7 = \begin{pmatrix} -1 \\ 0 \end{pmatrix} \in \omega_2, \qquad K_6(\mathbf{x}_7) = -4$$

$$K_7(\mathbf{x}) = K_6(\mathbf{x}) = 4x_1 - 4x_2$$

$$\mathbf{x}_8 = \begin{pmatrix} 0 \\ 1 \end{pmatrix} \in \omega_2, \qquad K_7(\mathbf{x}_8) = -4$$

$$K_8(\mathbf{x}) = K_7(\mathbf{x}) = 4x_1 - 4x_2$$

Since a complete, error-free iteration through all patterns has taken place, the algorithm has converged to the decision function

$$d(\mathbf{x}) = K_8(\mathbf{x}) = 4x_1 - 4x_2$$

The decision boundary determined by this function is shown in Fig. 5.6. ●

Example 2: Let us now illustrate the use of potential functions of Type 2 with the aid of the patterns shown in Fig. 5.7(a). Choosing for this example the exponential form given in Eq. (5.6–25) with $\alpha = 1$ yields, for the two-dimensional case under consideration,

$$K(\mathbf{x}, \mathbf{x}_k) = \exp\{-\,||\mathbf{x} - \mathbf{x}_k||^2\} = \exp\{-\,[(x_1 - x_{k1})^2 + (x_2 - x_{k2})^2]\}$$

The patterns of ω_1 are $\{(0, 0)', (2, 0)'\}$, while those of ω_2 are $\{(1, 1)', (1, -1)'\}$. It is noted that these two classes are not linearly separable. Applying the potential function algorithm to these patterns yields the following steps.

Let $\mathbf{x}_1 = (0, 0)'$ be the first training pattern. Since it belongs to ω_1,

$$K_1(\mathbf{x}) = K(\mathbf{x}, \mathbf{x}_1) = \exp\{-\,[(x_1 - 0)^2 + (x_2 - 0)^2]\}$$
$$= \exp\{-\,(x_1^2 + x_2^2)\}$$

Training pattern $\mathbf{x}_2 = (2, 0)'$ belongs to ω_1. Evaluating $K_1(\mathbf{x}_2)$ yields

$$K_1(\mathbf{x}_2) = e^{-(4+0)} = e^{-4} > 0$$

Therefore, we let

$$K_2(\mathbf{x}) = K_1(\mathbf{x}) = \exp\{-\,(x_1^2 + x_2^2)\}$$

Presenting now $\mathbf{x}_3 = (1, 1)'$, which belongs to ω_2, and evaluating $K_2(\mathbf{x}_3)$ yields

$$K_2(\mathbf{x}_3) = e^{-(1+1)} = e^{-2} > 0$$

Since $K_2(\mathbf{x}_3)$ should have been less than zero, the following adjustment is made:

$$K_3(\mathbf{x}) = K_2(\mathbf{x}) - K(\mathbf{x}, \mathbf{x}_3)$$
$$= \exp\{-\,(x_1^2 + x_2^2)\} - \exp\{-\,[(x_1 - 1)^2 + (x_2 - 1)^2]\}$$

The next pattern, $\mathbf{x}_4 = (1, -1)'$, belongs to ω_2. Substituting $\mathbf{x}_4$ into $K_3(\mathbf{x})$ yields:

$$K_3(\mathbf{x}_4) = e^{-(1+1)} - e^{-(0+4)} = e^{-2} - e^{-4} > 0$$

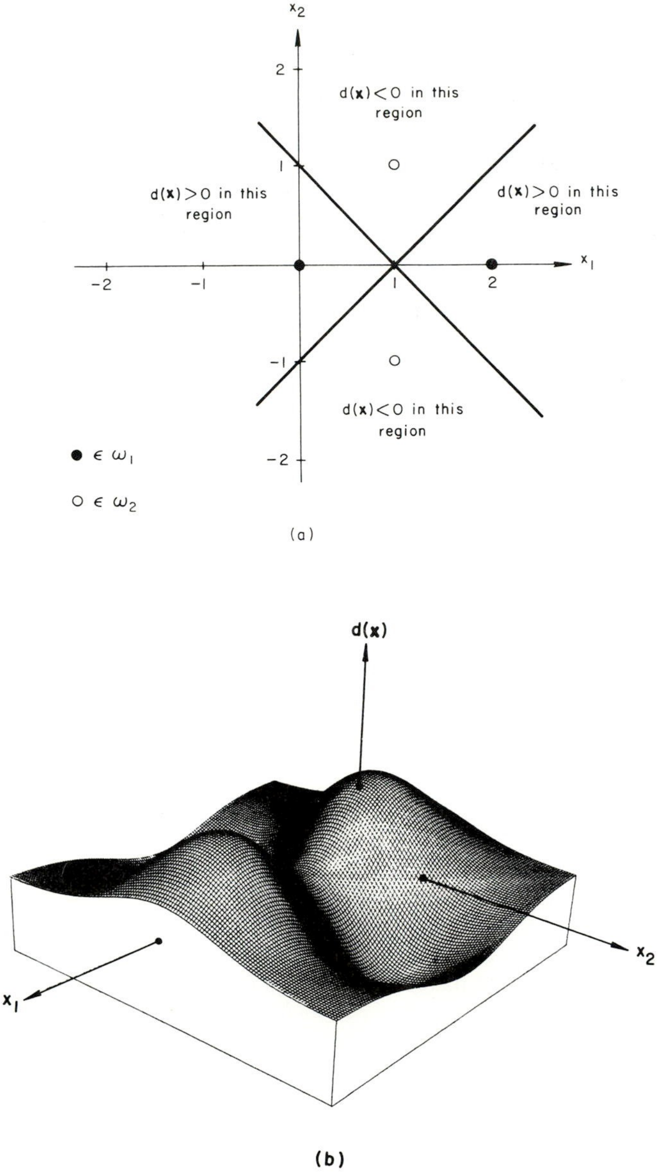

Figure 5.7. Patterns used in illustrating the potential function algorithm. (a) Patterns and decision surface. (b) Plot of $d(\mathbf{x})$ in the range $-1 \leqslant x_1 \leqslant 3$ and $-2 \leqslant x_2 \leqslant 2$

Since $K_3(\mathbf{x}_4)$ should have been less than zero, the cumulative potential is adjusted:

$$\begin{aligned} K_4(\mathbf{x}) &= K_3(\mathbf{x}) - K(\mathbf{x}, \mathbf{x}_4) \\ &= \exp\{-(x_1^2 + x_2^2)\} - \exp\{-[(x_1 - 1)^2 + (x_2 - 1)^2]\} \\ &\quad - \exp\{-[(x_1 - 1)^2 + (x_2 + 1)^2]\} \end{aligned}$$

It can be easily verified that this function cannot classify all training patterns correctly. Therefore, the patterns must be recycled:

$$\mathbf{x}_5 = \begin{pmatrix} 0 \\ 0 \end{pmatrix} \in \omega_1, \qquad K_4(\mathbf{x}_5) = e^{-0} - e^{-2} - e^{-2} > 0$$

$$K_5(\mathbf{x}) = K_4(\mathbf{x})$$

$$\mathbf{x}_6 = \begin{pmatrix} 2 \\ 0 \end{pmatrix} \in \omega_1, \qquad K_5(\mathbf{x}_6) = e^{-4} - e^{-2} - e^{-2} < 0$$

$$\begin{aligned} K_6(\mathbf{x}) &= K_5(\mathbf{x}) + K(\mathbf{x}, \mathbf{x}_6) \\ &= \exp[-(x_1^2 + x_2^2)] \\ &\quad - \exp\{-[(x_1 - 1)^2 + (x_2 - 1)^2]\} \\ &\quad - \exp\{-[(x_1 - 1)^2 + (x_2 + 1)^2]\} \\ &\quad + \exp\{-[(x_1 - 2)^2 + x_2^2]\} \end{aligned}$$

$$\mathbf{x}_7 = \begin{pmatrix} 1 \\ 1 \end{pmatrix} \in \omega_2, \qquad K_6(\mathbf{x}_7) = e^{-2} - e^{0} - e^{-4} + e^{-2} < 0$$

$$K_7(\mathbf{x}) = K_6(\mathbf{x})$$

$$\mathbf{x}_8 = \begin{pmatrix} 1 \\ -1 \end{pmatrix} \in \omega_2, \qquad K_7(\mathbf{x}_8) = e^{-2} - e^{-2} - e^{0} + e^{-2} < 0$$

$$K_8(\mathbf{x}) = K_7(\mathbf{x})$$

$$\mathbf{x}_9 = \begin{pmatrix} 0 \\ 0 \end{pmatrix} \in \omega_1, \qquad K_8(\mathbf{x}_9) = e^{0} - e^{-2} - e^{-2} + e^{-4} > 0$$

$$K_9(\mathbf{x}) = K_8(\mathbf{x})$$

$$\mathbf{x}_{10} = \begin{pmatrix} 2 \\ 0 \end{pmatrix} \in \omega_1, \qquad K_9(\mathbf{x}_{10}) = e^{-4} - e^{-2} - e^{-2} + e^0 > 0$$

$$K_{10}(\mathbf{x}) = K_9(\mathbf{x})$$

Since we have completed an entire iteration through the patterns without committing an error, the algorithm has converged to the decision function:

$$d(\mathbf{x}) = K_{10}(\mathbf{x}) = \exp[-(x_1^2 + x_2^2)] - \exp\{-[(x_1 - 1)^2 + (x_2 - 1)^2]\}$$
$$- \exp\{-[(x_1 - 1)^2 + (x_2 + 1)^2]\} + \exp\{-[(x_1 - 2)^2 + x_2^2]\}$$

The decision boundary obtained by setting $d(\mathbf{x}) = 0$ is shown in Fig. 5.7(a). A plot of the potential function $d(\mathbf{x}) = K_{10}(\mathbf{x})$ in the range $-1 \leqslant x_1 \leqslant 3$ and $-2 \leqslant x_2 \leqslant 2$ is shown in Fig. 5.7(b). ●

It is of interest to compare the two examples given above. Once a specific potential function of Type 1 has been selected, it is evident from the first example that the resulting algorithm is very similar to the perceptron algorithm in the sense that the final form of the decision function is predetermined. In the first example, the general form of the selected decision function was quadratic. The coefficients were then computed during training.

If potential functions of Type 2 are chosen, it is evident from the second example that the form of the decision function depends on the number of corrections made on the cumulative potential. The reason for this is, of course, that every time a correction on a pattern is made, a term is added to the potential function. It is conceivable that the resulting decision function could contain as many terms as there are different patterns in the training set, as was the case in Example 2 above. Generally, potential functions of Type 2 present computational storage problems when the training set is large because of the substantial number of terms that must be stored. Of course, it should not be overlooked that the addition of new terms during training adds considerable classification power to this method.

5.6.3 Geometrical Interpretation and Weight Adjustment†

In this section we present a geometrical interpretation of the potential function method and the generation of the decision function through the

† This section is adapted from Chapter 4 in *Advances in Information Systems Science*, Volume 1, Plenum Press.

adjustment of the weight vector. By letting

$$z_i = \lambda_i \varphi_i(\mathbf{x}) \tag{5.6–28}$$

and

$$u_i = \lambda_i \varphi_i(\mathbf{y}) \tag{5.6–29}$$

where $i = 1, 2, \ldots, m$, and the variable $\mathbf{y}$ is identified with the sample patterns presented during the training process, the potential function defined in Eq. (5.6–24) becomes

$$K(\mathbf{x}, \mathbf{y}) = \mathbf{z}'\mathbf{u} \tag{5.6–30}$$

In Eq. (5.6–30) the vectors $\mathbf{z}$ and $\mathbf{u}$ are given by

$$\mathbf{z} = \begin{pmatrix} z_1 \\ z_2 \\ \vdots \\ z_i \\ \vdots \\ z_m \end{pmatrix} \tag{5.6–31}$$

and

$$\mathbf{u} = \begin{pmatrix} u_1 \\ u_2 \\ \vdots \\ u_i \\ \vdots \\ u_m \end{pmatrix} \tag{5.6–32}$$

The decision function $d_k(\mathbf{x})$ at the kth step is then

$$\begin{aligned} d_k(\mathbf{x}) &= \sum_{i=1}^{m} w_i(k) z_i \\ &= \mathbf{z}'\mathbf{w}(k) \end{aligned} \tag{5.6–33}$$

where

$$\mathbf{w}(k) = \begin{pmatrix} w_1(k) \\ w_2(k) \\ \vdots \\ w_i(k) \\ \vdots \\ w_m(k) \end{pmatrix} \tag{5.6–34}$$

is a weight vector with the weights $w_i(k)$ given by

$$w_i(k) = \frac{c_i(k)}{\lambda_i} \tag{5.6–35}$$

The transformation from the X-domain to the Z-domain by Eq. (5.6–28) linearizes the decision function. The partition boundary in the Z-domain becomes the hyperplane

$$\mathbf{z}'\mathbf{w}(k) = 0 \tag{5.6–36}$$

which passes through the origin with normal vector $\mathbf{w}$, as shown in Fig. 5.8. Then $\mathbf{z}'\mathbf{w}(k) > 0$ if $\mathbf{x} \in \omega_1$, and $\mathbf{z}'\mathbf{w}(k) < 0$ if $\mathbf{x} \in \omega_2$.

Let $T_1 \in \omega_1$ and $T_2 \in \omega_2$ be the two sets of training sample patterns, which are known to lie on the opposite sides of a partition hyperplane, as illustrated in Fig. 5.8. The problem now reduces to the generation of an algorithm for

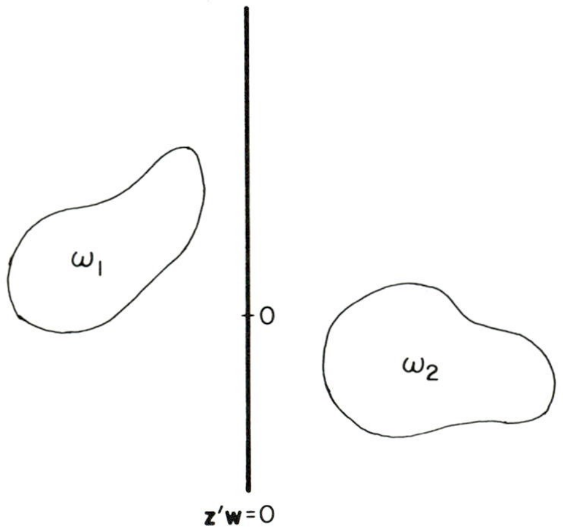

Figure 5.8. Disjoint pattern classes

the determination of the weight vector $\mathbf{w}(k)$ through successive presentation of sample patterns, so that, for all patterns belonging to training set T_1,

$$\mathbf{z}'\mathbf{w}(k) > 0 \tag{5.6–37}$$

and, for all patterns belonging to training set T_2,

$$\mathbf{z}'\mathbf{w}(k) < 0 \tag{5.6–38}$$

If we reflect training set T_2 symmetrically about the origin to form set T_2^*, the condition for separability of sets T_1 and T_2^* by a hyperplane with normal vector $\mathbf{w}(k)$ is simply

$$\mathbf{z}'\mathbf{w}(k) > 0 \quad \text{for} \quad \mathbf{z} \in T_1 \cup T_2^* \tag{5.6–39}$$

In other words, training sets T_1 and T_2^* are separated by this hyperplane if all the training sample pattern points lie to one side of the plane, as shown in Fig. 5.9.

Let the training set be $\{\mathbf{z}_1, \mathbf{z}_2, \ldots, \mathbf{z}_j, \ldots\}$, and the sequence of error-correction sample patterns be represented by $\hat{\mathbf{z}}_1, \hat{\mathbf{z}}_2, \ldots, \hat{\mathbf{z}}_i, \ldots$. The cumulative potential in the Z-domain at the kth step is

$$\begin{aligned} K_k(\mathbf{z}) &= \sum_i (\mathbf{z}'\hat{\mathbf{z}}_i) \\ &= \mathbf{z}'(\sum_i \hat{\mathbf{z}}_i) \end{aligned} \tag{5.6–40}$$

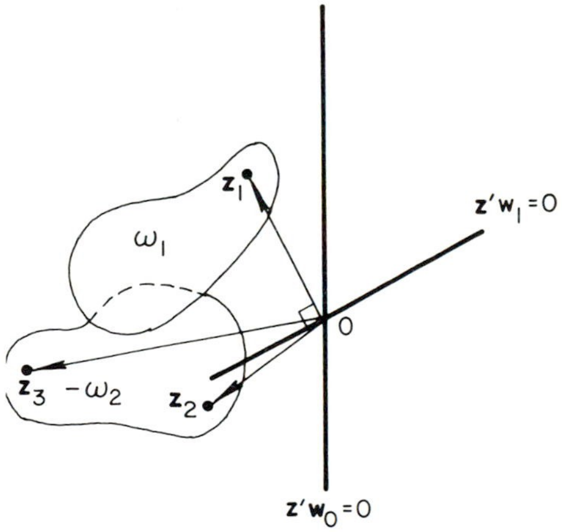

Figure 5.9. Reflected pattern classes

At the beginning of the training phase, the potential $K_0(\mathbf{z})$ is assumed to be zero and the initial decision boundary is

$$K_0(\mathbf{z}) = \mathbf{z}'\mathbf{w}(0) = 0 \tag{5.6–41}$$

When the first training sample pattern, $\mathbf{z}_1$, is presented, the cumulative potential is

$$\begin{aligned} K_1(\mathbf{z}) &= K(\mathbf{z}, \mathbf{z}_1) \\ &= \mathbf{z}'\hat{\mathbf{z}}_1 \end{aligned} \tag{5.6–42}$$

The decision boundary is given by

$$\mathbf{z}'\mathbf{w}(1) = 0 \tag{5.6–43}$$

The weight vector $\mathbf{w}(1)$ is so determined that sample pattern vector $\mathbf{z}_1$ is perpendicular to the hyperplane defined by Eq. (5.6–43). Hence,

$$\mathbf{w}(1) = \hat{\mathbf{z}}_1 \tag{5.6–44}$$

It is noted that on the decision boundary the potential drops to zero. This condition also leads to Eq. (5.6–44).

When the second training sample pattern, $\mathbf{z}_2$, is presented, if $K_1(\mathbf{z}_2) = \mathbf{z}_2'\mathbf{z}_1 > 0$ the cumulative potential is

$$K_2(\mathbf{z}) = K_1(\mathbf{z}) = \mathbf{z}'\hat{\mathbf{z}}_1 \tag{5.6–45}$$

and if $K_1(\mathbf{z}_2) = \mathbf{z}_2'\mathbf{z}_1 < 0$ it is increased to

$$\begin{aligned} K_2(\mathbf{z}) &= K_1(\mathbf{z}) + K(\mathbf{z}, \hat{\mathbf{z}}_2) \\ &= \mathbf{z}'(\hat{\mathbf{z}}_1 + \hat{\mathbf{z}}_2) \end{aligned} \tag{5.6–46}$$

The decision boundary is

$$\mathbf{z}'\mathbf{w}(2) = 0 \tag{5.6–47}$$

The weight vector $\mathbf{w}(2)$ is determined in such a way that the resultant of sample pattern vectors $\mathbf{z}_1$ and $\mathbf{z}_2$ is perpendicular to the hyperplane defined by Eq. (5.6–47). Thus,

$$\begin{aligned} \mathbf{w}(2) &= \hat{\mathbf{z}}_1 + \hat{\mathbf{z}}_2 \\ &= \mathbf{w}(1) + \hat{\mathbf{z}}_2 \end{aligned} \tag{5.6–48}$$

When the third training sample pattern, $\mathbf{z}_3$, is presented, if $K_2(\mathbf{z}_3) > 0$ the cumulative potential is

$$K_3(\mathbf{z}) = K_2(\mathbf{z}) \tag{5.6–49}$$

and if $K_2(\mathbf{z}_3) < 0$ it is increased to

$$\begin{aligned} K_3(\mathbf{z}) &= K_2(\mathbf{z}) + K(\mathbf{z}, \mathbf{z}_3) \\ &= \mathbf{z}'(\hat{\mathbf{z}}_1 + \hat{\mathbf{z}}_2 + \hat{\mathbf{z}}_3) \end{aligned} \tag{5.6–50}$$

The weight vector is then given by

$$\begin{aligned} \mathbf{w}(3) &= \hat{\mathbf{z}}_1 + \hat{\mathbf{z}}_2 + \hat{\mathbf{z}}_3 \\ &= \mathbf{w}(2) + \hat{\mathbf{z}}_3 \end{aligned} \tag{5.6–51}$$

The construction of the successive decision boundaries is illustrated in Fig. 5.10. If sample pattern vector $\mathbf{z}_3$ lies on the positive side of the hyperplane, $\mathbf{z}'\mathbf{w}(2) = 0$, the decision boundary remains unchanged and $\mathbf{w}(3) = \mathbf{w}(2) = \hat{\mathbf{z}}_1 + \hat{\mathbf{z}}_2$. If pattern vector $\mathbf{z}_3$ lies on the negative side of the hyperplane $\mathbf{z}'\mathbf{w}(2) = 0$, the decision boundary is shifted to the hyperplane $\mathbf{z}'\mathbf{w}(3) = 0$ and $\mathbf{w}(3) = \hat{\mathbf{z}}_1 + \hat{\mathbf{z}}_2 + \hat{\mathbf{z}}_3$.

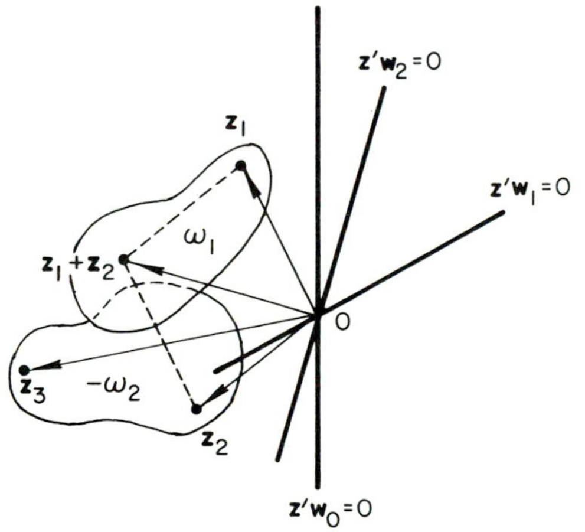

Figure 5.10. Generation of decision boundaries

Now, let $K_k(\mathbf{z})$ be the cumulative potential after the presentation of k training sample patterns $\mathbf{z}_1, \mathbf{z}_2, \ldots, \mathbf{z}_k$. Then, if $K_k(\mathbf{z}_{k+1}) > 0$, the cumulative potential $K_{k+1}(\mathbf{z})$ after the presentation of sample pattern $\mathbf{z}_{k+1}$ is

$$K_{k+1}(\mathbf{z}) = K_k(\mathbf{z}) \tag{5.6–52}$$

and, if $K_k(\mathbf{z}_{k+1}) < 0$, it is increased to

$$\begin{aligned} K_{k+1}(\mathbf{z}) &= K_k(\mathbf{z}) + K(\mathbf{z}, \hat{\mathbf{z}}_{k+1}) \\ &= \mathbf{z}'(\sum_i \hat{\mathbf{z}}_i) \end{aligned} \tag{5.6–53}$$

The weight vector $\mathbf{w}(k+1)$ is found to be

$$\begin{aligned} \mathbf{w}(k+1) &= \sum_{i=1}^{k} \hat{\mathbf{z}}_i \\ &= \mathbf{w}(k) + \hat{\mathbf{z}}_{k+1} \end{aligned} \tag{5.6–54}$$

where $\hat{\mathbf{z}}_{k+1} \in T_1 \cup T_2^*$. Using Eqs. (5.6–28) yields the following recursive relationship for the weights $w_i(k+1)$:

$$w_i(k+1) = w_i(k) + \lambda_i \varphi_i(\hat{\mathbf{x}}_{k+1}) \tag{5.6–55}$$

Equations (5.6–54) and (5.6–55) provide the algorithms for training the pattern recognition machine through iterative weight adjustment upon receiving error-correction sample patterns. The reader should note the similarity between Eq. (5.6–55) and the perceptron algorithm.

5.6.4 Convergence of Training Algorithms

In this section we state some useful theorems about the training algorithms discussed in Sections 5.6.1 and 5.6.2. Theorems on the convergence, the rate of convergence, and the conditions for termination of the algorithm are examined. These theorems play a fundamental role in pattern classification by potential functions.

Theorem 1: This theorem is concerned with the convergence properties of the algorithm. Suppose that the pattern vectors $\mathbf{x}$ in the pattern space satisfy the following conditions.

1. The potential function

$$K(\mathbf{x}, \mathbf{x}_j) = \sum_{i=1}^{\infty} \lambda_i^2 \varphi_i(\mathbf{x}) \varphi_i(\mathbf{x}_j) \tag{5.6–56}$$

is bounded for $\mathbf{x} \in T_1 \cup T_2$.

2. There exists a decision function representable by the expansion

$$d(\mathbf{x}) = \sum_{i=1}^{m} c_i \varphi_i(\mathbf{x}) \tag{5.6–57}$$

such that

$$d(\mathbf{x}) \begin{cases} > \varepsilon & \text{if} \quad \mathbf{x} \in \omega_1 \\ < -\varepsilon & \text{if} \quad \mathbf{x} \in \omega_2 \end{cases} \tag{5.6–58}$$

where $\varepsilon > 0$.

3. The training sample patterns possess the following statistical properties: (a) the sample patterns of the training sequence appear independently, and (b) at the kth step of the training algorithm, if complete correct classification of the patterns $\mathbf{x}_1, \mathbf{x}_2, \ldots, \mathbf{x}_k$ by the decision function $d_k(\mathbf{x})$ has not been achieved, there is a strictly positive probability of occurrence of pattern $\mathbf{x}_{k+1}$ to correct misclassification. Then it is possible to find with probability 1 a finite number of steps, R, such that the cumulative potential is

$$K_R(\mathbf{x}) \begin{cases} > 0 & \text{for} \quad \mathbf{x} \in \omega_1 \\ < 0 & \text{for} \quad \mathbf{x} \in \omega_2 \end{cases} \tag{5.6–59}$$

In other words, the approximate decision function $d_k(\mathbf{x})$ converges with probability 1 to the decision function $d(\mathbf{x})$ with a finite number of training samples; that is, the separation of class ω_1 and class ω_2 can be realized in a finite number of steps with probability 1.

Theorem 2: This theorem is concerned with the rate of convergence of the algorithm. Let

$$S_{\mathbf{x}} = \{\mathbf{x}_1, \mathbf{x}_2, \ldots, \mathbf{x}_k, \ldots\} \tag{5.6–60}$$

be an infinite sequence of training samples taken from the training set $T = T_1 \cup T_2$, with $T_1 \in \omega_1$ and $T_2 \in \omega_2$. Assume that the potential function $K(\mathbf{x}, \mathbf{x}_j)$ is bounded for $\mathbf{x} \in T_1 \cup T_2$, and that there exists a decision function representable by the expansion given in Eq. (5.6–57) and satisfying the condition of Eq. (5.6–58). Then there exists an integer R:

$$R = \sum_{i=1}^{\infty} \left(\frac{c_i}{\lambda_i}\right)^2 \left(\frac{\sup_{\mathbf{x} \in T} K(\mathbf{x}, \mathbf{x}_j)}{\inf_{\mathbf{x} \in T} d^2(\mathbf{x})}\right) \tag{5.6–61}$$

which is independent of the choice of the training sequence $S_{\mathbf{x}}$ so that, in using the algorithms in Sections 5.6.1 and 5.6.2, the number of corrections does not exceed R.

We will prove this theorem in order to illustrate the typical methodology followed in proving the other theorems in this section. First, we make a transformation from the X-domain to the Z-domain using Eq. (5.6–28). Training set T_2 is symmetrically reflected about the origin to form set T_2^*. Now, let

$$\alpha = \inf_{\mathbf{z} \in T_{\mathbf{z}}} \frac{\mathbf{z}'\mathbf{w}}{||\mathbf{w}||} \tag{5.6–62}$$

and

$$\beta = \sup_{\mathbf{z} \in T_{\mathbf{z}}} ||\mathbf{z}|| \tag{5.6–63}$$

In geometrical language, α is a positive quantity representing the minimum distance from the hyperplane $\mathbf{z}'\mathbf{w} = 0$ to the set of training samples $T_1 \cup T_2^*$, and the quantity β is the distance from the origin to the *furthest* point of the region $T_1 \cup T_2^*$. In view of the property that the normal Euclidean distance from the hyperplane to an arbitrary point $\mathbf{z}$ is equal to $\mathbf{z}'\mathbf{w}/||\mathbf{w}||$, the quantity α is the minimum normal distance. Since, by definition, $||\mathbf{z}||$ is the distance from the origin to the set $T_{\mathbf{z}} = T_1 \cup T_2^*$, the quantity β is the maximum distance.

It follows from Eq. (5.6–62) that, for any pattern $\mathbf{z}_i \in T_1 \cup T_2^*$,

$$\mathbf{z}_i'\mathbf{w} \geqslant \alpha||\mathbf{w}|| \tag{5.6–64}$$

From Eq. (5.6–63) we have

$$||\mathbf{z}_i|| \leqslant \beta \tag{5.6–65}$$

We want to show that there is an upper limit on k for which the weight vector $\mathbf{w}(k)$ will not be changed by a training sample pattern. After k training sample patterns of the error-correction pattern sequence:

$$S_{\hat{\mathbf{z}}} = \{\hat{\mathbf{z}}_1, \hat{\mathbf{z}}_2, \ldots, \hat{\mathbf{z}}_i, \ldots\} \tag{5.6–66}$$

have been presented to the machine, the weight vector becomes

$$\mathbf{w}(k) = \sum_{i=1}^{k} \hat{\mathbf{z}}_i \tag{5.6–67}$$

This weight vector is the normal of the hyperplane $\mathbf{z}'\mathbf{w}(k) = 0$ after k steps. The theorem can be proved by showing that the sequence $S_{\hat{\mathbf{z}}}$ is a finite sequence.

From Eqs. (5.6–64) and (5.6–67), we obtain

$$\mathbf{w}'(k)\mathbf{w} \geqslant \alpha k \|\mathbf{w}\| \qquad (5.6\text{–}68)$$

Applying the Cauchy-Schwarz inequality yields

$$|\mathbf{w}'(k)\mathbf{w}| \leqslant \|\mathbf{w}(k)\| \, \|\mathbf{w}\| \qquad (5.6\text{–}69)$$

From Eqs. (5.6–68) and (5.6–69), we have

$$\|\mathbf{w}(k)\| \geqslant \alpha k \qquad (5.6\text{–}70)$$

In view of Eq. (5.6–54), we derive

$$\|\mathbf{w}(k)\|^2 = \|\mathbf{w}(k-1)\|^2 + 2\hat{\mathbf{z}}_k{}'\mathbf{w}(k-1) + \|\hat{\mathbf{z}}_k\|^2 \qquad (5.6\text{–}71)$$

Since $\|\hat{\mathbf{z}}_k\| \leqslant \beta$ and there is a $\hat{\mathbf{z}}_k$ satisfying the condition $\hat{\mathbf{z}}_k{}'\mathbf{w}(k-1) < 0$, Eq. (5.6–71) may be written as

$$\|\mathbf{w}(k)\|^2 \leqslant \|\mathbf{w}(k-1)\|^2 + \beta^2 \qquad (5.6\text{–}72)$$

By iteration and on the assumption that $\mathbf{w}(0) = \mathbf{0}$, we obtain

$$\|\mathbf{w}(k)\|^2 \leqslant k\beta^2 \qquad (5.6\text{–}73)$$

Combining expressions (5.6–70) and (5.6–73) yields

$$k \leqslant R = \frac{\beta^2}{\alpha^2} \qquad (5.6\text{–}74)$$

that is, the upper limit of k, the size of the error-correction pattern sequence $S_{\hat{\mathbf{z}}}$, is finite and equal to β^2/α^2.

In terms of the X-domain, we have

$$\alpha = \frac{\inf\limits_{\mathbf{x}\in T} \left| \sum_{i=1}^{\infty} c_i \varphi_i(\mathbf{x}) \right|}{\left[\sum_{i=1}^{\infty} (c_i^2/\lambda_i^2) \right]^{1/2}} = \frac{\inf\limits_{\mathbf{x}\in T} |d(\mathbf{x})|}{\left[\sum_{i=1}^{\infty} (c_i^2/\lambda_i^2) \right]^{1/2}} \qquad (5.6\text{–}75)$$

$$\beta = \sup_{\mathbf{x}\in T} \sqrt{K(\mathbf{x}, \mathbf{x}_j)} \qquad (5.6\text{–}76)$$

Then the upper limit of k as given in Eq. (5.6–61) is obtained. Since $K(\mathbf{x}, \mathbf{x}_j)$ is bounded and $|d(\mathbf{x})|$ is nonzero, the constant k is finite if

$$\sum_{i=1}^{\infty} \left(\frac{c_i}{\lambda_i} \right)^2 < \infty \qquad (5.6\text{–}77)$$

This series is known to converge if, for $i > m$, all the coefficients c_i are zero.

The foregoing discussions reveal that R is smaller if the minimum of the decision function $d(\mathbf{x})$ is made larger with the other conditions remaining the same. Since R is inversely proportional to $\inf_{\mathbf{x}\in T} d^2(\mathbf{x})$, the size of the error-correction training sequence can be decreased by increasing the minimum of $|d(\mathbf{x})|$. This implies that the error-correction sequence size decreases as the training sample patterns in $T_1 \cup T_2^*$ are farther from the decision boundary $d(\mathbf{x}) = 0$, that is, as they are farther from each other. This result is in agreement with intuitive observation.

Theorem 3: This theorem is concerned with the conditions for termination of the algorithm and is stated as follows. Assume that the training process terminates if after k corrections of misclassifications no further corrections occur during the subsequent L_0 presentations of sample patterns. In other words, the training process terminates after L_k sample patterns have been presented, where L_k is given by

$$L_k = L_0 + k \tag{5.6–78}$$

Thus, the total number of observations for termination increases by 1 after each correction of misclassification. The problem is to determine the number of test sample patterns L_0 so as to guarantee the specified quality of the training procedure. Let $p_{L_k}(e)$ be the probability of error after L_k training sample patterns have been presented to the machine. Then, for any $\varepsilon > 0$ and $\delta > 0$, the probability that $p_{L_k}(e) < \varepsilon$ is greater than $1 - \delta$ if

$$L_0 > \frac{\log \varepsilon\delta}{\log (1 - \varepsilon)} \tag{5.6–79}$$

It is noted that choice of the number of test sample patterns according to the above inequality depends only on the prespecified values of ε and δ characterizing the quality of the training procedure. The selection of L_0 is independent of the forms of the pattern classes ω_1 and ω_2 and the sample pattern statistics.

5.6.5 Multiclass Generalization

Like the perceptron algorithm, the potential function algorithm is easily generalized to cover any of the three multiclass cases discussed in Section 2.2. The first two cases can, of course, be handled by successive applications of the two-class algorithm discussed above. For multiclass Case 3, the potential function algorithm follows the straightforward generalization used for the perceptron scheme in Section 5.4. Thus, the potential function algorithm given in Eqs. (5.6–12) through (5.6–14) may be generalized as follows.

At the beginning of the training phase, the initial cumulative potentials $K_0^{(1)}(\mathbf{x}), K_0^{(2)}(\mathbf{x}), \ldots, K_0^{(M)}(\mathbf{x})$ are assumed to be zero for notational convenience. The superscripts on these potentials indicate the class membership. Suppose that at the $(k+1)$th iterative step a sample pattern $\mathbf{x}_{k+1}$ belonging to class ω_i is presented. If

$$K_k^{(i)}(\mathbf{x}_{k+1}) > K_k^{(j)}(\mathbf{x}_{k+1}) \quad \text{for all} \quad j \neq i \tag{5.6–80}$$

the potentials are not changed, that is,

$$K_{k+1}^{(i)}(\mathbf{x}) = K_k^{(i)}(\mathbf{x}), \quad i = 1, 2, \ldots, M \tag{5.6–81}$$

However, if $\mathbf{x}_{k+1} \in \omega_i$ and for some l

$$K_k^{(i)}(\mathbf{x}_{k+1}) \leqslant K_k^{(l)}(\mathbf{x}_{k+1}) \tag{5.6–82}$$

the following corrections are made:

$$\begin{aligned} K_{k+1}^{(i)}(\mathbf{x}) &= K_k^{(i)}(\mathbf{x}) + K(\mathbf{x}, \mathbf{x}_{k+1}) \\ K_{k+1}^{(l)}(\mathbf{x}) &= K_k^{(l)}(\mathbf{x}) - K(\mathbf{x}, \mathbf{x}_{k+1}) \\ K_{k+1}^{(j)}(\mathbf{x}) &= K_k^{(j)}(\mathbf{x}), \quad j = 1, 2, \ldots, M; \quad j \neq i, \quad j \neq l \end{aligned} \tag{5.6–83}$$

Since the decision functions $d^{(i)}(\mathbf{x})$ are equal to the cumulative potentials $K^{(i)}(\mathbf{x})$, it follows that the equivalent algorithm given in Eq. (5.6–21) can be expressed in the multiclass case simply be replacing $K^{(i)}(\mathbf{x})$ by $d^{(i)}(\mathbf{x})$ in Eqs. (5.6–80) through (5.6–83).

5.7 CONCLUDING REMARKS

In this chapter several basic concepts underlying pattern classification by deterministic training algorithms are presented. Starting with a general gradient technique, we derive three different algorithms. It is pointed out that, although these algorithms are not exhaustive, they do represent the spectrum of available schemes. The salient features of the perceptron and LSME algorithms are also compared.

The basic problem in the application of these three algorithms is the selection of an appropriate set of decision functions. In a sense, this is a trial-and-error situation since the only way to ascertain the performance of a given set of decision functions is by direct trial. When the pattern classes under consideration do not share identical patterns, it is always possible to determine a set of decision functions which will correctly classify all patterns of the training set, although these functions may be quite complex. The attitude that should be taken in solving most problems of practical significance, however, is that a certain number of misclassifications must be tolerated because of economic and computational considerations. Once a certain percentage of tolerable misclassifications has been decided upon, the design of the classifier is guided to meet this goal. In many cases the specified percentage is not achievable within the complexity constraints placed on the classifier. Under these conditions, either the percentage of acceptable misclassifications must be raised, the complexity of the classifier increased, or an alternative method of classification chosen.

This chapter concludes with a discussion of pattern classification by potential functions. The training of a pattern classifier is accomplished through successive modifications of the cumulative potential instead of iterative adjustment of weight vectors. Two methods for the construction of potential functions are presented. The first method specifies the form of the decision functions, while the second allows the decision functions to grow in classification power as training proceeds. The first method does not differ greatly from training with the perceptron algorithm, as is evident from the examples given in Section 5.6.2. It is also clear from these examples that the second method will, in general, present computational difficulties when applied to relatively large pattern sets.

In the next chapter attention is focused on the statistical approach to classification. As will be seen, the concept of a decision function still holds in the statistical case with the exception, of course, that the generation of these functions involves probabilistic, rather than deterministic, concepts. It is worth mentioning before leaving this chapter, however, that the algorithms presented here are not the only approaches to the solution of systems of linear inequalities of the form shown in expression (5.1–1). Linear programming methods have been used for a long time to solve linear inequalities (Simonnard [1966]). In terms of pattern recognition, however, linear programming has little to offer since simpler algorithms, such as the ones developed in this chapter, are certainly capable of equal performance.

REFERENCES

Some of the original work on perceptrons can be found in several papers by Rosenblatt [1957, 1960, 1961]. Early work on linear classifiers is also contained in the representative papers by Highleyman [1961] and by Block

[1962]. The simple proof of convergence of the perceptron algorithm given in this chapter is due to Novikoff [1963]; other proofs have been presented by Rosenblatt [1960], Block [1962], Joseph [1960], Singleton [1962], and Charnes [1964].

Efforts on the application of the gradient approach to the generation of pattern classification algorithms are found in the report by Blaydon [1967] and in the papers by Devyaterikov, Pripoi, and Tsypkin [1967], and by Ho and Kashyap [1965], among others. The algorithm presented in Section 5.3.3 is due to Ho and Kashyap [1965]. A proof of convergence of the algorithm presented in Section 5.4 can be found in the book by Nilsson [1965].

Much of the early work on potential functions is reported in the Russian literature. Fundamental papers in this area are due to Aizerman, Braverman, and Rozonoer [1964a, 1964b, 1965]. Some of the material presented in Section 5.6 has been adapted from Tou [1969a].

PROBLEMS

5.1 Apply the absolute-correction algorithm to the patterns of the example given in Section 5.2.1.

5.2 Repeat Problem 5.1 using the fractional-correction algorithm.

5.3 Show that Eq. (5.2–25) is satisfied by the results of the example given in Section 5.2.1.

5.4 Use Eq. (5.3–3) and the criterion function

$$J(\mathbf{w}, \mathbf{x}, b) = \frac{1}{8\|\mathbf{x}\|^2}[(\mathbf{w}'\mathbf{x} - b) - |\mathbf{w}'\mathbf{x} - b|]^2$$

where $b > 0$, to derive a two-class pattern classification algorithm.

5.5 (a) Let $c = b = 1$ and apply the algorithm obtained in Problem 5.4 to the patterns of Problem 5.1.

(b) Discuss the effect of increasing b on the convergence of the algorithm for linearly separable pattern classes. *Hint*: Refer to Section 2.4.

5.6 Prove that the algorithm of Problem 5.4 converges in the separable case for $0 < c < 2$.

5.7 Apply the perceptron algorithm to the following pattern classes: ω_1: $\{(0, 0, 0)', (1, 0, 0)', (1, 0, 1)', (1, 1, 0)'\}$ and ω_2: $\{(0, 0, 1)', (0, 1, 1)', (0, 1, 0)', (1, 1, 1)'\}$. Let $\mathbf{w}(1) = (-1, -2, -2, 0)'$.

5.8 Sketch the decision surface obtained in Problem 5.7. Show the patterns, and indicate the positive side of the separating surface.

5.9 (a) Specify an appropriate decision function for the one-dimensional pattern classes ω_1: {0, 2} and ω_2: {1, 3}, and use the perceptron algorithm to determine the coefficients. Note that the classes are not linearly separable. It is suggested that a computer be used for this problem.

(b) Sketch $d(x)$ versus x.

5.10 Use the LMSE algorithm with $c = 1$ and $\mathbf{b}(1) = (1, 1)'$ to generate a decision boundary for the following simple one-dimensional pattern classes ω_1: {1} and ω_2: {0}.

5.11 Repeat Problem 5.7 using the LMSE algorithm.

5.12 Test the following pattern classes for linear separability using the LMSE algorithm: ω_1: $\{(-1, -1)', (0, 0)', (1, 1)'\}$ and ω_2: $\{(-1, 1)', (1, -1)'\}$.

5.13 Apply the potential function algorithm to the following pattern classes: ω_1: $\{(0, 1)', (0, -1)'\}$ and ω_2: $\{(1, 0)', (-1, 0)'\}$. Use a second-degree decision function expressible in the form given in Eq. (5.6–24).

5.14 Repeat Problem 5.13 using a potential function of the type given in Eq. (5.6–25).

5.15 Apply the multiclass perceptron algorithm to the following pattern classes: ω_1: $\{(-1, -1)'\}$, ω_2: $\{(0, 0)'\}$, and ω_3: $\{(1, 1)'\}$.

5.16 Repeat Problem 5.15 using potential functions of Type 1 with linear terms only.

6

TRAINABLE PATTERN CLASSIFIERS–THE STATISTICAL APPROACH

6.1 INTRODUCTION

The pattern classification algorithms derived in Chapter 5 are deterministic approaches since the statistical properties of the pattern classes did not play a role in either the formulation or the derivation of these algorithms. By contrast, all the algorithms derived in this chapter are the result of statistical considerations.

Since the Bayes classification rule sets the standard of optimum classification performance, it is logical that a statistical formulation of pattern classification algorithms should be centered on this rule. It was shown in Chapter 4 that the Bayes decision functions

$$d_i(\mathbf{x}) = p(\mathbf{x}/\omega_i)p(\omega_i), \quad i = 1, 2, \ldots, M \tag{6.1–1}$$

minimize the average cost of misclassification as well as yielding the lowest probability of error.

When the relation $p(\mathbf{x}/\omega_i) = p(\omega_i/\mathbf{x})p(\mathbf{x})/p(\omega_i)$ is used, Eq. (6.1–1) becomes $d_i(\mathbf{x}) = p(\omega_i/\mathbf{x})p(\mathbf{x})$. However, since the term $p(\mathbf{x})$ does not depend on i, it may be dropped, yielding the equivalent Bayes decision functions

$$d_i(\mathbf{x}) = p(\omega_i/\mathbf{x}), \quad i = 1, 2, \ldots, M \tag{6.1–2}$$

In the two-class case the decision boundary is given by $d_1(\mathbf{x}) - d_2(\mathbf{x}) = 0$. Thus, we may derive the equivalent decision boundary function

$$\begin{aligned} d(\mathbf{x}) &= d_1(\mathbf{x}) - d_2(\mathbf{x}) \\ &= p(\omega_1/\mathbf{x}) - p(\omega_2/\mathbf{x}) \\ &= p(\omega_1/\mathbf{x}) - [1 - p(\omega_1/\mathbf{x})] \\ &= 2p(\omega_1/\mathbf{x}) - 1 \end{aligned} \tag{6.1–3}$$

With this equivalent formulation we classify patterns according to the following rule: $\mathbf{x} \in \omega_1$ if $d(\mathbf{x}) > 0$ and $\mathbf{x} \in \omega_2$ if $d(\mathbf{x}) < 0$, which, in view of Eq. (6.1–3), may be expressed in the form

$$\begin{aligned} &\text{if} \quad p(\omega_1/\mathbf{x}) > \tfrac{1}{2}, \quad \text{assign } \mathbf{x} \text{ to } \omega_1 \\ &\text{if} \quad p(\omega_1/\mathbf{x}) < \tfrac{1}{2}, \quad \text{assign } \mathbf{x} \text{ to } \omega_2 \end{aligned} \tag{6.1–4}$$

Chapter 4 is devoted to the decision functions of Eq. (6.1–1). In this chapter attention will be focused on the functions of Eq. (6.1–2). Before proceeding with the discussion, however, it is important that the fundamental difference between the two approaches be clearly understood.

The key problem in the implementation of the functions of Eq. (6.1–1) is the estimation of the probability density function of each class, $p(\mathbf{x}/\omega_i)$. As was indicated in Chapter 4, only the patterns of class ω_i are considered in the estimation of $p(\mathbf{x}/\omega_i)$. Therefore, no learning, in the sense discussed in Chapter 5, takes place since patterns of other classes do not influence the estimation process.

As will be seen in the following sections, estimation of the densities $p(\omega_i/\mathbf{x})$ for the implementation of the decision functions of Eq. (6.1–2) can be formulated in an interactive learning framework. The result of this formulation will be training algorithms very similar in form to those discussed in Chapter 5.

6.2 STOCHASTIC APPROXIMATION METHODS

Before proceeding with the study of statistical pattern classification algorithms, it is necessary to introduce some concepts which will allow the development of these algorithms in a consistent manner. The methods which will be employed in this chapter are very similar to the gradient techniques discussed in Chapter 5. Instead of dealing with deterministic criterion functions, however, we are now faced with statistical functions which statisticians normally call *regression functions*. We will employ the so-called stochastic approximation methods to find the root of a regression function. If this regression function represents the derivative of a properly formulated criterion function, finding the root of this derivative function yields the minimum of the criterion function. By selecting certain types of criterion functions, it is possible to generate iterative learning algorithms capable of yielding an approximation in some specified sense to the Bayes classifier. In order to simplify the following developments, attention is initially focused on one-dimensional problems. The results are then extended to the multidimensional case.

6.2.1 The Robbins-Monro Algorithm

Let $g(w)$ be a function of w having a single root $\hat{w}$ so that $g(\hat{w}) = 0$. Assume that $g(w)$ is negative for all values of w less than $\hat{w}$ and positive for all values of w greater than $\hat{w}$. This is assumed with little loss of generality since most functions of a single root not satisfying this condition can be made to do so by multiplying the function by -1.

Suppose that instead of being able to observe $g(w)$ directly we are able to observe only *noisy* values of $g(w)$. These random observations will be denoted by $h(w)$. The error between the true value and the noisy observation at any point w is given by $g(w) - h(w)$, as shown in Fig. 6.1.

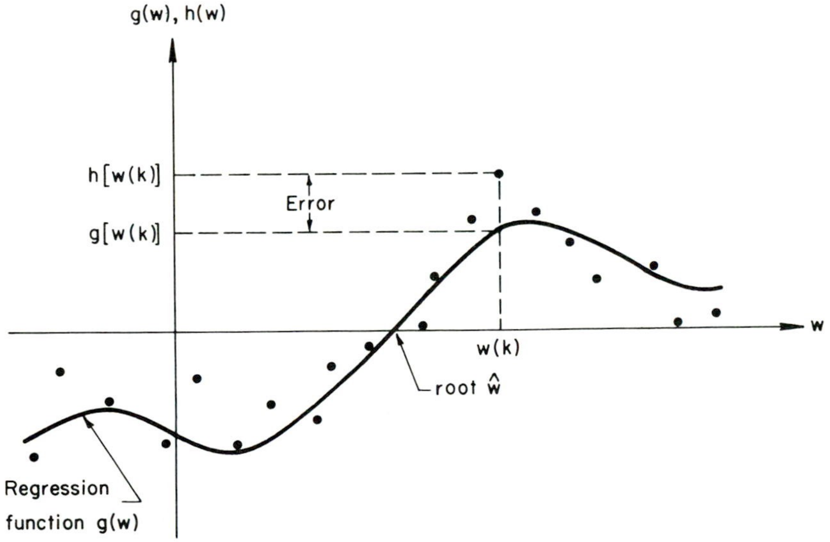

Figure 6.1. Noisy observations of a regression function

Two mild assumptions must be made concerning the random variables $h(w)$. First, it is assumed that they are *unbiased*, that is,

$$E\{h(w)\} = g(w) \tag{6.2–1}$$

This equation simply says that, if w were fixed and numerous observations $h(w)$ were taken at that value of w, the average of these observations, denoted by the expected value, should approach $g(w)$ at that point as the sample size increases.

A second basic assumption is that the variance of the observations $h(w)$ from $g(w)$ should be finite for all values of w. In other words, denoting this variance by

$$\sigma^2(w) = E\{[g(w) - h(w)]^2\} \tag{6.2–2}$$

it is assumed that

$$\sigma^2(w) < L \tag{6.2–3}$$

for all w, where L is a finite, positive constant. This assumption precludes observations so far from the true values of $g(w)$ that the root-seeking procedure would never be able to recover. Physically, this condition requires the noisy observations to be reasonably well behaved.

If it is assumed that the mild conditions of Eqs. (6.2–1) and (6.2–2) are satisfied, the algorithm due to Robbins and Monro can be used to iteratively seek the root $\hat{w}$ of the function $g(w)$. If $w(1)$ represents the initial, arbitrary estimate of $\hat{w}$, and $w(k)$ the estimate at the kth iterative step, the Robbins-Monro (R-M) algorithm updates the estimate according to the relation

$$w(k+1) = w(k) - \alpha_k h[w(k)] \tag{6.2–4}$$

where α_k is a member of a sequence of positive numbers which satisfy the following conditions:

$$\lim_{k \to \infty} \alpha_k = 0 \tag{6.2–5a}$$

$$\sum_{k=1}^{\infty} \alpha_k = \infty \tag{6.2–5b}$$

$$\sum_{k=1}^{\infty} \alpha_k^2 < \infty \tag{6.2–5c}$$

An example of a sequence satisfying these conditions is the harmonic sequence $\{1/k\} = \{1, \frac{1}{2}, \frac{1}{3}, \ldots\}$.

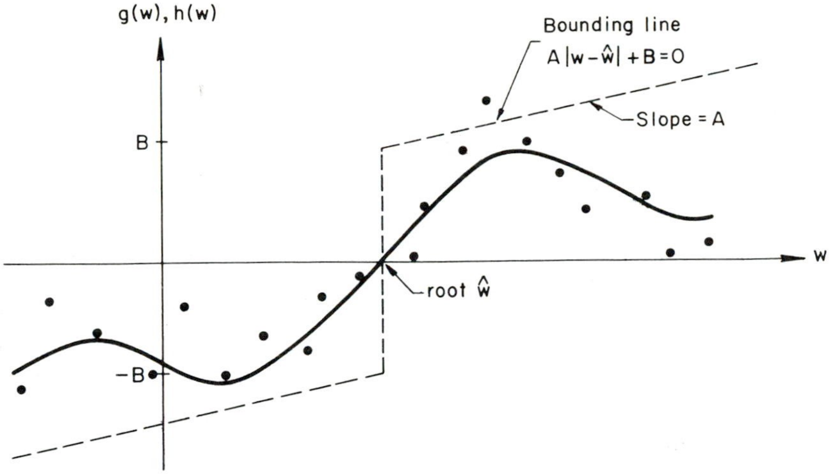

Figure 6.2. Bounding condition of the Robbins-Monro algorithm

It is noted that the R-M algorithm makes corrections on the estimates which are proportional to the previous observation $h[w(k)]$. In order to prevent large overcorrections it is assumed that $g(w)$ is bounded by a straight line on either side of the root, as shown in Fig. 6.2. This bounding function is assumed because of its simplicity and can be expressed by the relation

$$|g(w)| < A|w - \hat{w}| + B < \infty \tag{6.2–6}$$

where A is the slope of the lines and $\pm B$ are the values of $g(w)$ just to the right and the left of $\hat{w}$, respectively. This assumption is not as restrictive as it may seem since the values of A and B need not be known to prove the validity of the algorithm. Also, it is evident from Fig. 6.2 that, as long as the root lies in some finite interval, the existence of an A and B which will satisfy expression (6.2–6) can always be assumed.

If the conditions given in expressions (6.2–1), (6.2–3), (6.2–5), and (6.2–6) are satisfied, Robbins and Monro [1951] have shown that the algorithm of Eq. (6.2–4) converges to $\hat{w}$ in the *mean-square sense*, that is,

$$\lim_{k \to \infty} \{E[(w(k) - \hat{w})^2]\} = 0 \tag{6.2–7}$$

Simply stated, this equation says that, as the number of iterations approaches infinity, the variance of the estimates $w(k)$ from the root $\hat{w}$ will approach zero.

Shortly after the appearance of the R-M algorithm, Blum [1954a] established an even stronger form of convergence, which states, if the above conditions are satisfied, $w(k)$ will approach $\hat{w}$ with probability 1 as $k \to \infty$, that is,

$$\text{Prob}\,\{\lim_{k\to\infty} w(k) = \hat{w}\} = 1 \tag{6.2–8}$$

This relation indicates that, in the limit, it is *guaranteed* that $w(k)$ will equal $\hat{w}$.

Interestingly, the proofs due to Robbins and Monro and to Blum are special cases of a more general theorem established later by Aryeh Dvoretzky [1956]. Dvoretzky was able to show that *both* the convergence criteria of Eqs. (6.2–7) and (6.2–8) hold for *any* stochastic approximation procedure satisfying the conditions of his theorem. Although an explanation of the Dvoretzky conditions and their relation to the R-M algorithm is outside the mainstream of our discussion, the reader will find the original paper by this author interesting and informative.

Example: Let us consider a simple illustration of the R-M algorithm. It is desired to use the algorithm to find the root of the function $g(w) = \tanh(w)$ shown in Fig. 6.3. However, instead of being able to observe the function itself, we are able to observe only noisy values of the function, indicated by $h(w)$. It is assumed for illustrative purposes that the noise consists of random $\pm$ 0.1's added to $g(w)$ with equal probability.

The algorithm is initiated by choosing an arbitrary first guess at the root and an appropriate sequence $\{\alpha_k\}$. Let $w(1) = 1.0$ and $\alpha_k = 1/k$. Assume that the noise for the first observation is -0.1. Then $h[w(1)] = g[w(1)] - 0.1 = \tanh(1) - 0.1 = 0.662$. By invoking the R-M algorithm, the estimate of the root is updated according to the relation

$$\begin{aligned} w(2) &= w(1) - \alpha_1 h[w(1)] \\ &= 1.000 - 0.662 = 0.338 \end{aligned}$$

The updated estimate is shown in Fig. 6.3. If the noise at this new value is $+0.1$, then $h[w(2)] = g[w(2)] + 0.1 = 0.426$. Therefore,

$$\begin{aligned} w(3) &= w(2) - \alpha_2 h[w(2)] \\ &= 0.338 - \tfrac{1}{2}(0.426) = 0.125 \end{aligned}$$

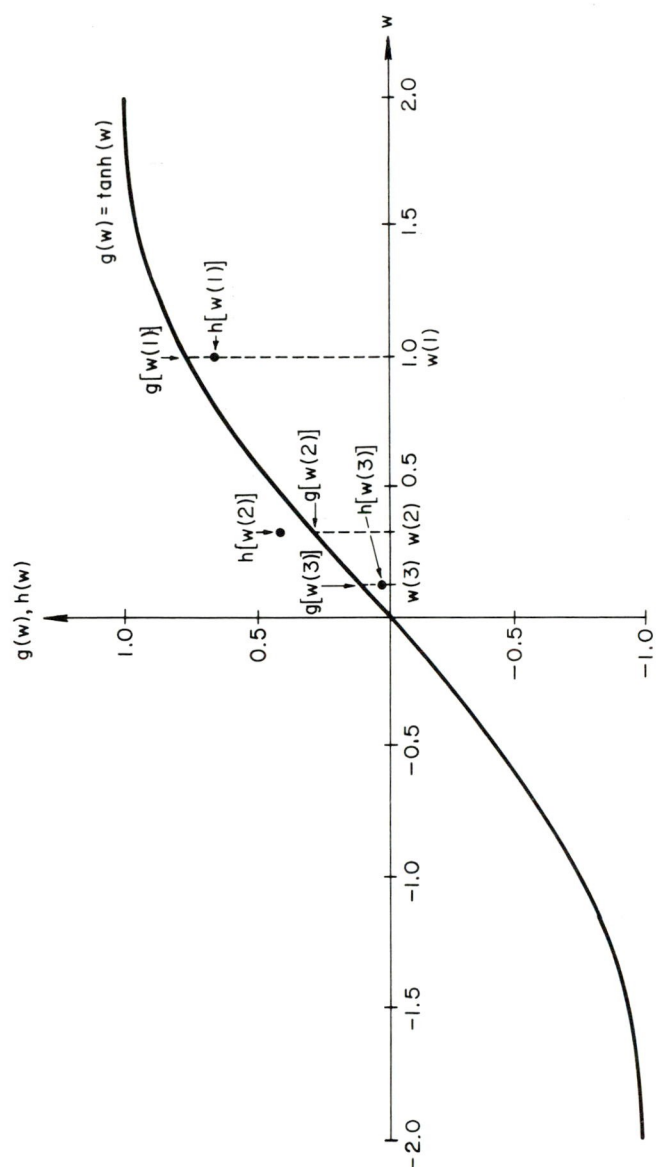

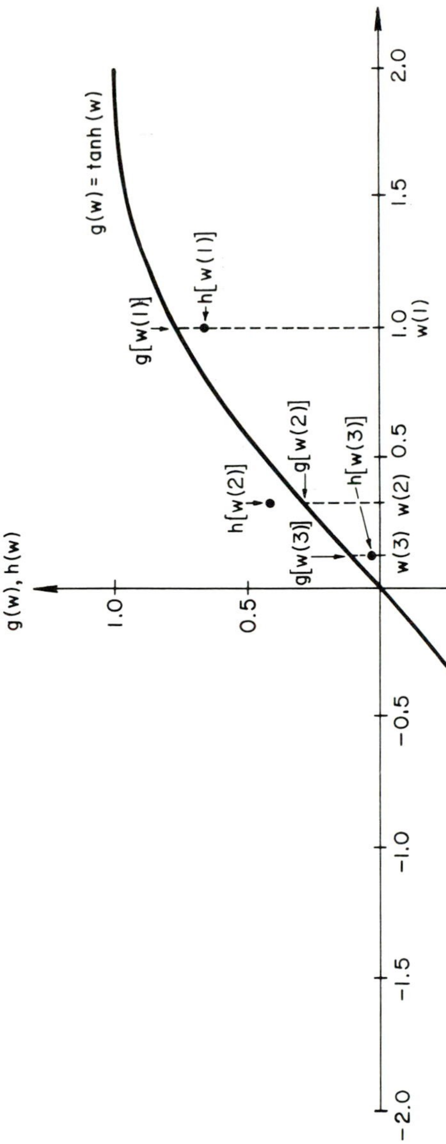

Figure 6.3. Illustration of the Robbins-Monro algorithm

This value is clearly closer to the root $\hat{w} = 0.0$. A sample of the successive values of the estimate for up to $k = 50$ is shown in the accompanying table, where η_k represents the noise factor at the kth step.

k	$w(k)$	$g[w(k)]$	α_k	η_k	$h[w(k)]$	$w(k+1)$
1	1.000	0.762	1.000	− 0.100	0.662	0.338
2	0.338	0.326	0.500	+ 0.100	0.426	0.125
3	0.125	0.125	0.333	− 0.100	0.025	0.117
4	0.117	0.117	0.250	+ 0.100	0.217	0.063
5	0.063	0.063	0.200	− 0.100	− 0.037	0.070
10	0.039	0.039	0.100	− 0.100	− 0.061	0.045
20	0.029	0.029	0.050	− 0.100	− 0.071	0.033
30	0.026	0.026	0.033	+ 0.100	0.126	0.022
40	0.014	0.014	0.025	− 0.100	− 0.086	0.016
50	0.015	0.015	0.020	+ 0.100	0.115	0.013

It is noted that the root is quickly approached in the first few iterations and that the rate of approach decreases with increasing k. There are two reasons for this. First, α_k loses its corrective power as k increases, since $\alpha_k = 1/k$. Second, it is evident that the noise factor dominates $g(w)$ for values of w near the root. This makes the approach to the root in this region dependent to a greater degree on the randomness of the noise. ●

6.2.2 Speed of Convergence

Although the R-M algorithm converged toward the root rather quickly in the preceding example, this will not always be the case. As k increases, the decreasing significance of the correction factors α_k has the effect of decreasing the magnitude of the adjustments with successive iterations. Since any sequence $\{\alpha_k\}$ satisfying Eqs. (6.2–5) must decrease with increasing k, the R-M algorithm, as well as other similar stochastic approximation schemes, is generally slow to converge.

A very effective method of accelerating convergence of the R-M algorithm consists of keeping α_k constant during steps in which $h[w(k)]$ has the same sign. This method is based on the fact that changes in the sign of $h[w(k)]$ tend to occur more often in the vicinity of the root $\hat{w}$. For points away from the root large corrections are desired, whereas these corrections should be smaller and smaller as the root is approached. The technique is illustrated in Table 6.1 for $\alpha_k = 1/k$.

TABLE 6.1. *Illustration of the Convergence Acceleration Technique for* $\alpha_k = 1/k$

k:	1	2	3	4	5	6	7	8	9	10
Sign of $h[w(k)]$:	+	+	+	−	−	+	−	+	−	−
Normal α_k:	1	$\frac{1}{2}$	$\frac{1}{3}$	$\frac{1}{4}$	$\frac{1}{5}$	$\frac{1}{6}$	$\frac{1}{7}$	$\frac{1}{8}$	$\frac{1}{9}$	$\frac{1}{10}$
Accelerated α_k:	1	1	1	$\frac{1}{2}$	$\frac{1}{2}$	$\frac{1}{3}$	$\frac{1}{4}$	$\frac{1}{5}$	$\frac{1}{6}$	$\frac{1}{6}$

6.2.3 Multidimensional Extension

The Robbins-Monro algorithm is directly extendable to the multidimensional case. Using the vector notation of earlier discussions, we have that $\mathbf{w} = (w_1, w_2, \ldots, w_n, w_{n+1})'$, and it is desired to find the root of a regression function $g(\mathbf{w})$ from the noisy observations $h(\mathbf{w})$. In other words, with $\mathbf{w}(1)$ representing the initial (arbitrary) estimate of the root $\hat{\mathbf{w}}$, and $\mathbf{w}(k)$ the estimate at the kth iterative step, the multidimensional R-M algorithm updates the estimate according to the relation

$$\mathbf{w}(k+1) = \mathbf{w}(k) - \alpha_k h[\mathbf{w}(k)] \tag{6.2–9}$$

where α_k is a member of a sequence of positive numbers satisfying the conditions stated in Eqs. (6.2–5). If, in addition, the vector equivalents of Eqs. (6.2–1), (6.2–3), and (6.2–6) are satisfied, convergence of the multidimensional R-M algorithm is guaranteed both in the mean-square sense and with probability 1; that is, if the noisy observations are unbiased, their variance from $g(\mathbf{w})$ is finite, and the regression function is itself bounded, then Eq. (6.2–9), with a sequence $\{\alpha_k\}$ satisfying Eqs. (6.2–5), can be shown to converge in the sense that

$$\lim_{k\to\infty} E\{\|\mathbf{w}(k) - \hat{\mathbf{w}}\|^2\} = 0 \tag{6.2–10}$$

and

$$\text{Prob}\,\{\lim_{k\to\infty} \mathbf{w}(k) = \hat{\mathbf{w}}\} = 1 \tag{6.2–11}$$

where $\|\mathbf{w}(k) - \hat{\mathbf{w}}\|^2$ is the magnitude squared of the vector $[\mathbf{w}(k) - \hat{\mathbf{w}}]$.

In the multidimensional case it is very difficult to formulate rules for accelerating convergence. Although specialized combinations of stochastic approximation and other well-known optimization methods have been proposed for accelerating convergence, the resulting algorithms generally do not warrant the extra effort because of their complexity. Therefore, our attention will be focused on the R-M algorithm in its original form as given in Eq. (6.2–9). It is important to keep in mind that this algorithm is characterized by the typical slow convergence properties exhibited by all stochastic approximation algorithms.

6.3 DERIVATION OF PATTERN CLASSIFICATION ALGORITHMS

This section follows the same format as Section 5.3, where deterministic algorithms were derived. Section 6.3.1 establishes the method of stochastic approximation as a general approach to the derivation of statistical pattern classification algorithms. A general algorithm similar to the gradient algorithm of Eq. (5.3–3) is derived, and the two algorithms are compared.

By using the results of Section 6.3.1, a statistical algorithm which resembles the perceptron algorithm is derived in Section 6.3.2. Similarly, a statistical least-mean-square-error algorithm is derived in Section 6.3.3. As was true in Chapter 5, the derivation of statistical algorithms by the general methods developed below is limited only by one's ability to specify meaningful criterion functions.

6.3.1 Estimation of Optimum Decision Functions by Stochastic Approximation Methods

As was indicated in Section 6.1, the main theme of this chapter is the estimation from training patterns of the densities $p(\omega_i/\mathbf{x})$ for the implementation of the Bayes decision functions $d_i(\mathbf{x}) = p(\omega_i/\mathbf{x})$, $i = 1, 2, \ldots, M$. The approach which will be taken is to expand these functions in a set of known basis functions according to the relation

$$d_i(\mathbf{x}) = p(\omega_i/\mathbf{x}) \approx \sum_{j=1}^{K+1} w_{ij}\varphi_j(\mathbf{x}) = \mathbf{w}_i'\boldsymbol{\varphi}(\mathbf{x}) \tag{6.3–1}$$

where $\mathbf{w}_i = (w_{i1}, w_{i2}, \ldots, w_{iK}, w_{i,K+1})'$ is the weight vector of the ith pattern class, and $\boldsymbol{\varphi}(\mathbf{x}) = [\varphi_1(\mathbf{x}), \varphi_2(\mathbf{x}), \ldots, \varphi_K(\mathbf{x}), 1]'$. This expansion is identical to the one used in Eq. (2.3–1) in connection with generalized decision functions. According to the concepts developed in Section 2.3, therefore, we may without loss of generality devote all further discussions to the linear approximations

$$p(\omega_i/\mathbf{x}) \approx \mathbf{w}_i'\mathbf{x} \tag{6.3–2}$$

where $\mathbf{w}_i = (w_{i1}, w_{i2}, \ldots, w_{in}, w_{i,n+1})'$ and $\mathbf{x} = (x_1, x_2, \ldots, x_n, 1)'$.

Ideally, we would like to observe values of $p(\omega_i/\mathbf{x})$ during the training or estimation phase. Unfortunately, however, it is impossible to measure or observe this probability density function. The only information that is available during training is the class membership of each pattern vector. In order to take this fact into account, and to formulate the problem in a manner that will allow the utilization of the concepts developed in Section 6.2, we will make use of a slightly artificial manipulation. For each class, let us define a *random classification variable*, $r_i(\mathbf{x})$, with the following property:

$$r_i(\mathbf{x}) = \begin{cases} 1 & \text{if } \mathbf{x} \in \omega_i \\ 0 & \text{otherwise} \end{cases} \tag{6.3–3}$$

The choice of values 1 and 0 for $r_i(\mathbf{x})$ is arbitrary. Other values may be used, as long as they are distinct.

Although we cannot observe $p(\omega_i/\mathbf{x})$ during training, we certainly know the values of $r_i(\mathbf{x})$ during this phase since the class membership of each pattern is known. Therefore, since we desire knowledge of $p(\omega_i/\mathbf{x})$ only for classification purposes, let us interpret $r_i(\mathbf{x})$ as being a *noisy* observation of $p(\omega_i/\mathbf{x})$, that is,

$$r_i(\mathbf{x}) = p(\omega_i/\mathbf{x}) + \eta \tag{6.3–4}$$

where η is a noise factor which is assumed to have zero expected value, so that $E\{r_i(\mathbf{x})\} = E\{p(\omega_i/\mathbf{x})\}$. This is not an unreasonable assumption since if the noise did not have zero average value it could certainly be forced to satisfy this condition by proper normalization. Another way to interpret the classification variable $r_i(\mathbf{x})$ is to consider it an approximation to $p(\omega_i/\mathbf{x})$ in the sense that $p[r_i(\mathbf{x}) = 1/\mathbf{x}] \approx p(\omega_i/\mathbf{x})$ and $p[r_i(\mathbf{x}) = 0/\mathbf{x}] \approx p(\bar{\omega}_i/\mathbf{x})$, where $\bar{\omega}_i$ denotes "not" class ω_i. What we propose to do is to seek an approximation to $p(\omega_i/\mathbf{x})$ of the form $\mathbf{w}_i'\mathbf{x}$ by observing values of $r_i(\mathbf{x})$.

In Chapter 5 we employed deterministic criterion functions which were substituted in a general gradient algorithm to obtain classification algorithms. Here we will follow the same approach, except that the criterion functions will be statistical and the general algorithm will be the R-M algorithm. As an introduction to this approach, consider the criterion function $J(\mathbf{w}_i, \mathbf{x}) = E\{|r_i(\mathbf{x}) - \mathbf{w}_i'\mathbf{x}|\}$, The minimum of this function is zero, and it occurs when $\mathbf{w}_i'\mathbf{x} = r_i(\mathbf{x})$. In other words, the minimum occurs when the pattern $\mathbf{x}$ is classified correctly. This follows from the fact that $r_i(\mathbf{x})$ is a known classification variable during training. Therefore, if $\mathbf{w}_i'\mathbf{x} = r_i(\mathbf{x})$ for all patterns of the training set, $\mathbf{w}_i$ is capable of classifying all these patterns correctly.

Since it is assumed that $E\{r_i(\mathbf{x})\} = E\{p(\omega_i/\mathbf{x})\}$, $J(\mathbf{w}_i, \mathbf{x})$ can also be expressed as $J(\mathbf{w}_i, \mathbf{x}) = E\{|p(\omega_i/\mathbf{x}) - \mathbf{w}_i'\mathbf{x}|\}$. This equation clearly states that finding the minimum of $J(\mathbf{w}_i, \mathbf{x})$ corresponds to finding an *average* approximation to $p(\omega_i/\mathbf{x})$. In other words, the approximation is such that the expected value of the absolute difference between the function $p(\omega_i/\mathbf{x})$ and its approximation is zero.

In order to find the minimum of a function we find the root of its derivative. In the present situation, we are interested in finding the minimum of a function $J(\mathbf{w}, \mathbf{x})$ which is the expected value of some other function $f(\mathbf{w}, \mathbf{x})$, that is,

$$J(\mathbf{w}, \mathbf{x}) = E\{f(\mathbf{w}, \mathbf{x})\} \tag{6.3–5}$$

Taking the partial derivative of $J(\mathbf{w}, \mathbf{x})$ with respect to $\mathbf{w}$, we obtain

$$\frac{\partial J(\mathbf{w}, \mathbf{x})}{\partial \mathbf{w}} = E\left\{\frac{\partial f(\mathbf{w}, \mathbf{x})}{\partial \mathbf{w}}\right\} \tag{6.3–6}$$

The root of $\partial J(\mathbf{w}, \mathbf{x})/\partial \mathbf{w}$ can now be successively estimated by invoking the R-M algorithm with

$$h[\mathbf{w}(k)] = \left\{\frac{\partial f(\mathbf{w}, \mathbf{x})}{\partial \mathbf{w}}\right\}_{\mathbf{w}=\mathbf{w}(k)} \tag{6.3–7}$$

Using Eq. (6.2–9), we obtain

$$\mathbf{w}(k+1) = \mathbf{w}(k) - \alpha_k \left\{\frac{\partial f(\mathbf{w}, \mathbf{x})}{\partial \mathbf{w}}\right\}_{\mathbf{w}=\mathbf{w}(k)} \tag{6.3–8}$$

where $\mathbf{w}(1)$ may be arbitrarily chosen.

It is interesting to compare this result with the general deterministic gradient algorithm given in Eq. (5.3–3):

$$\mathbf{w}(k+1) = \mathbf{w}(k) - c \left\{\frac{\partial J(\mathbf{w}, \mathbf{x})}{\partial \mathbf{w}}\right\}_{\mathbf{w}=\mathbf{w}(k)} \tag{5.3–3}$$

Several differences are evident between these two equations. Obvious differences are seen in the nature of the correction increments α_k and c and in the partial derivative terms. It is noted that the criterion function $J(\mathbf{w}, \mathbf{x})$ appears directly in the deterministic algorithm. This is due to the fact that $J(\mathbf{w}, \mathbf{x})$ is directly observable in the deterministic case. On the other hand, since $J(\mathbf{w}, \mathbf{x})$ is not directly observable in the statistical case, the algorithm of Eq. (6.3–8) employs the observable function $f(\mathbf{w}, \mathbf{x})$. Another important difference is the fact that the statistical algorithm will seek an approximation to the Bayes classifier, whereas its deterministic counterpart does not have this capability. It is also worth emphasizing that the statistical algorithm will converge to the approximation regardless of whether or not the classes are strictly separable, while the deterministic algorithm simply oscillates in nonseparable situations. The price that we pay for the guaranteed convergence of the statistical algorithm is, indeed, the slowness with which it generally achieves this convergence.

In the rest of this chapter attention is focused on the use of Eq. (6.3–8) for the derivation of pattern classification algorithms. It is suggested that this material be carefully compared with the corresponding analysis in Chapter 5.

6.3.2 Increment-Correction Algorithm

An algorithm similar to the perceptron algorithm may be derived by considering the criterion function introduced in the preceding section:

$$J(\mathbf{w}_i, \mathbf{x}) = E\{|r_i(\mathbf{x}) - \mathbf{w}_i'\mathbf{x}|\} \tag{6.3–9}$$

where, as before,

$$r_i(\mathbf{x}) = \begin{cases} 1 & \text{if} \quad \mathbf{x} \in \omega_i \\ 0 & \text{otherwise} \end{cases}$$

The minimum of $J(\mathbf{w}_i, \mathbf{x})$ with respect to $\mathbf{w}_i$ is achieved when the patterns are classified correctly, as was previously mentioned.

We need the partial derivative of J with respect to $\mathbf{w}_i$, which is given by

$$\frac{\partial J}{\partial \mathbf{w}_i} = E\{-\mathbf{x}\,\mathrm{sgn}[r_i(\mathbf{x}) - \mathbf{w}_i'\mathbf{x}]\} \tag{6.3–10}$$

where $\mathrm{sgn}(\cdot) = 1$ if the argument is greater than zero and -1 otherwise.

Letting $h(\mathbf{w}_i) = -\mathbf{x}\,\mathrm{sgn}[r_i(\mathbf{x}) - \mathbf{w}_i'\mathbf{x}]$ and substituting in the general algorithm of Eq. (6.3–8) yields

$$\mathbf{w}_i(k+1) = \mathbf{w}_i(k) + \alpha_k \mathbf{x}(k)\,\mathrm{sgn}\{r_i[\mathbf{x}(k)] - \mathbf{w}_i'(k)\mathbf{x}(k)\} \tag{6.3–11}$$

where $\mathbf{w}_i(1)$ may be arbitrarily chosen. Using the definition of the sgn function given above, we may express Eq. (6.3–11) in the equivalent form

$$\mathbf{w}_i(k+1) = \begin{cases} \mathbf{w}_i(k) + \alpha_k \mathbf{x}(k) & \text{if} \quad \mathbf{w}_i'(k)\mathbf{x}(k) < r_i[\mathbf{x}(k)] \\ \mathbf{w}_i(k) - \alpha_k \mathbf{x}(k) & \text{if} \quad \mathbf{w}_i'(k)\mathbf{x}(k) \geqslant r_i[\mathbf{x}(k)] \end{cases} \tag{6.3–12}$$

It is interesting to note that this algorithm makes an adjustment on the weight vector at every step. This is in contrast with the perceptron algorithm, where a correction is made only when a pattern is misclassified. The algorithm of Eq. (6.3–11) or (6.3–12) derives its name from the fact that the corrections are proportional to the increment α_k.

The iterative procedure of Eq. (6.3–11) or (6.3–12) is said to have converged to an error-free solution when all training patterns of ω_i, $i = 1, 2, \ldots, M$, have been correctly classified. In the strictest sense this means that $\mathbf{w}_i'\mathbf{x} = r_i(\mathbf{x})$, that is, $\mathbf{w}_i'\mathbf{x} = 1$ if $\mathbf{x} \in \omega_i$ and $\mathbf{w}_i'\mathbf{x} = 0$ otherwise. However, in terms of correct recognition, it is sufficient to require that, for all patterns of class ω_i,

$$d_i(\mathbf{x}) > d_j(\mathbf{x}) \quad \text{for all} \quad j \neq i \tag{6.3–13}$$

where $d_i(\mathbf{x}) = \mathbf{w}_i'\mathbf{x}$ and $d_j(\mathbf{x}) = \mathbf{w}_j'\mathbf{x}$. This is recognized as the multiclass Case 3 discussed in Section 2.2. It should be noted that the multiclass algorithm was derived directly, in contrast with the method followed in Chapter 5, where the two-class case was considered first.

When the classes under consideration are not strictly separable with the specified decision functions, we are assured that, in the limit, the solution will converge to the absolute-value approximation of $p(\omega_i/\mathbf{x})$, as indicated by the criterion function chosen in Eq. (6.3–9). Since the Bayes decision functions are identically equal to these probability density functions, we are therefore guaranteed an absolute-value approximation to the Bayes classifier.

In the two-class case, the weight vector of the separating surface can be evaluated directly. In this case, Eq. (6.3–11) becomes

$$\mathbf{w}(k+1) = \mathbf{w}(k) + \alpha_k \mathbf{x}(k) \operatorname{sgn}\{r[\mathbf{x}(k)] - \mathbf{w}'(k)\mathbf{x}(k)\} \tag{6.3–14}$$

where $\mathbf{w}(1)$ is arbitrary. When using Eq. (6.3–14) the assumption is made that $\mathbf{w}$ is the weight vector of class ω_1, so that $r[\mathbf{x}(k)] = 1$ if $\mathbf{x}(k)$ belongs to ω_1 and $r[\mathbf{x}(k)] = 0$ if $\mathbf{x}(k)$ belongs to ω_2. From Eq. (6.1–4) we then have the decision rule

$$\begin{aligned} &\text{if} \quad p(\omega_1/\mathbf{x}) = \mathbf{w}'\mathbf{x} > \tfrac{1}{2}, \quad \text{assign } \mathbf{x} \text{ to } \omega_1 \\ &\text{if} \quad p(\omega_1/\mathbf{x}) = \mathbf{w}'\mathbf{x} < \tfrac{1}{2}, \quad \text{assign } \mathbf{x} \text{ to } \omega_2 \end{aligned} \tag{6.3–15}$$

since $\mathbf{w}'\mathbf{x}$ represents an approximation to $p(\omega_1/\mathbf{x})$. The algorithm of Eq. (6.3–14) is easily expressible in the form of Eq. (6.3–12).

From expression (6.3–15) we see that the two-class algorithm has converged to an error-free solution when $\mathbf{w}'\mathbf{x} > \frac{1}{2}$ for all patterns of ω_1 and $\mathbf{w}'\mathbf{x} < \frac{1}{2}$ for all patterns of ω_2. Of course, it is also perfectly valid in this case to use the multiclass algorithm to obtain two decision functions, $d_1(\mathbf{x}) = \mathbf{w}_1'\mathbf{x}$ and $d_2(\mathbf{x}) = \mathbf{w}_2'\mathbf{x}$. A single decision function can then be obtained by defining $d(\mathbf{x}) = d_1(\mathbf{x}) - d_2(\mathbf{x})$, as has been previously explained.

Example: In Chapter 4 the Bayes decision functions $d_i(\mathbf{x}) = p(\mathbf{x}/\omega_i)p(\omega_i)$ were determined for the patterns shown in Fig. 6.4. It is of interest to apply the increment-correction algorithm derived in this section to the estimation of the alternative decision functions $d_i(\mathbf{x}) = p(\omega_i/\mathbf{x})$ for the same pattern classes. Augmenting the patterns yields the classes ω_1: $\{(0, 0, 0, 1)', (1, 0, 0, 1)', (1, 0, 1, 1)', (1, 1, 0, 1)'\}$ and ω_2: $\{(0, 0, 1, 1)', (0, 1, 0, 1)', (0, 1, 1, 1)', (1, 1, 1, 1)'\}$. It is noted that the patterns of neither class are multiplied by -1 as was done in Chapter 5 for the two-class case.

Letting $\mathbf{w}(1) = \mathbf{0}$, $\alpha_k = 1/k$, and $\mathbf{x}(1) = (0, 0, 0, 1)'$, and invoking the increment-correction algorithm, we obtain

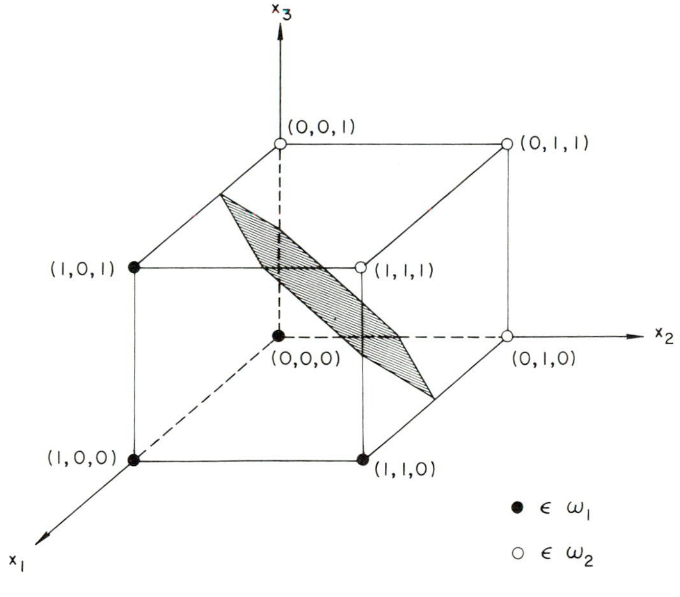

Figure 6.4. Decision boundary determined by the increment-correction algorithm

$$\mathbf{w}(2) = \mathbf{w}(1) + \alpha_1 \mathbf{x}(1)\,\text{sgn}\{r[\mathbf{x}(1)] - \mathbf{w}'(1)\mathbf{x}(1)\}$$

$$= \mathbf{0} + \mathbf{x}(1) = \begin{pmatrix} 0 \\ 0 \\ 0 \\ 1 \end{pmatrix}$$

In the next step, $\mathbf{x}(2) = (1, 0, 0, 1)'$, $\alpha_2 = \frac{1}{2}$, and, since $\mathbf{x}(2)$ also belongs to ω_1, $r[\mathbf{x}(2)] = 1$. Therefore,

$$\mathbf{w}(3) = \mathbf{w}(2) + \alpha_2 \mathbf{x}(2)\,\text{sgn}\{r[\mathbf{x}(2)] - \mathbf{w}'(2)\mathbf{x}(2)\}$$

$$= \begin{pmatrix} 0 \\ 0 \\ 0 \\ 1 \end{pmatrix} + \frac{1}{2}\begin{pmatrix} 1 \\ 0 \\ 0 \\ 1 \end{pmatrix} \text{sgn}\{0\}$$

$$= \begin{pmatrix} 0 \\ 0 \\ 0 \\ 1 \end{pmatrix} - \frac{1}{2}\begin{pmatrix} 1 \\ 0 \\ 0 \\ 1 \end{pmatrix} = \begin{pmatrix} -\frac{1}{2} \\ 0 \\ 0 \\ \frac{1}{2} \end{pmatrix}$$

Next, $\mathbf{x}(3) = (1, 0, 1, 1)'$, $\alpha_3 = \frac{1}{3}$, and $r[\mathbf{x}(3)] = 1$, so that

$$\mathbf{w}(4) = \mathbf{w}(3) + \tfrac{1}{3}\mathbf{x}(3)\,\text{sgn}\{1\}$$

$$= \begin{pmatrix} -\frac{1}{2} \\ 0 \\ 0 \\ \frac{1}{2} \end{pmatrix} + \begin{pmatrix} \frac{1}{3} \\ 0 \\ \frac{1}{3} \\ \frac{1}{3} \end{pmatrix} = \begin{pmatrix} -\frac{1}{6} \\ 0 \\ \frac{1}{3} \\ \frac{5}{6} \end{pmatrix}$$

Continuing in this manner and testing after each iterative step to see whether the new weight vector correctly classifies all patterns, we find that the algorithm converges to a solution for $k = 15$, yielding the weight vector

$$\mathbf{w} = \begin{pmatrix} 0.233 \\ -0.239 \\ -0.216 \\ 0.619 \end{pmatrix}$$

In order to calculate the equation of the decision boundary it must be kept in mind that decisions are made according to the rule $\mathbf{w}'\mathbf{x} > 0.5$ or $\mathbf{w}'\mathbf{x} < 0.5$. Thus, the boundary is given by $\mathbf{w}'\mathbf{x} = 0.5$ or $\mathbf{w}'\mathbf{x} - 0.5 = 0$, which, using the above weight vector, yields

$$0.233x_1 - 0.239x_2 - 0.216x_3 + 0.119 = 0$$

This decision boundary is shown in Fig. 6.4. ●

6.3.3 Least-Mean-Square-Error Algorithm

The algorithm developed in Section 6.3.2 seeks an approximation to $p(\omega_i/\mathbf{x})$ in absolute value. The criterion of a least-mean-square-error (LMSE) fit can also be conveniently employed to derive another training algorithm. Consider the criterion function

$$J(\mathbf{w}_i, \mathbf{x}) = \tfrac{1}{2}E\{[r_i(\mathbf{x}) - \mathbf{w}_i'\mathbf{x}]^2\} \tag{6.3–16}$$

This function also achieves its minimum upon correct classification of the patterns, as required.

Taking the partial derivative of J with respect to $\mathbf{w}_i$ yields

$$\frac{\partial J}{\partial \mathbf{w}_i} = E\{-\,\mathbf{x}[r_i(\mathbf{x}) - \mathbf{w}_i'\mathbf{x}]\} \tag{6.3–17}$$

Letting $h(\mathbf{w}_i) = -\,\mathbf{x}[r_i(\mathbf{x}) - \mathbf{w}_i'\mathbf{x}]$ and substituting in the general algorithm of Eq. (6.3–8) we obtain

$$\mathbf{w}_i(k+1) = \mathbf{w}_i(k) + \alpha_k \mathbf{x}(k)\{r_i[\mathbf{x}(k)] - \mathbf{w}_i'(k)\mathbf{x}(k)\} \tag{6.3–18}$$

where $\mathbf{w}_i(1)$ is arbitrary and $r_i[\mathbf{x}(k)] = 1$ or 0, depending on whether or not $\mathbf{x}(k)$ belongs to class ω_i. We note that this algorithm also makes a correction on $\mathbf{w}_i$ at every iterative step, and that the magnitudes of the corrections differ from those of the algorithm derived in Section 6.3.2 by the factors $\{r_i[\mathbf{x}(k)] - \mathbf{w}_i'(k)\mathbf{x}(k)\}$. The LMSE algorithm converges to a solution which minimizes Eq. (6.3–16) if the following conditions are satisfied (Blaydon [1967]):

1. α_k satisfies Eq. (6.2–5).
2. $E\{\mathbf{x}\mathbf{x}'\}$ and $E\{(\mathbf{x}\mathbf{x}')^2\}$ must exist and be positive definite.
3. $E\{\mathbf{x}p(\omega_i/\mathbf{x})\}$ and $E\{\mathbf{x}\mathbf{x}'\mathbf{x}p(\omega_i/\mathbf{x})\}$ must exist.

In the two-class case we may express Eq. (6.3–18) in the form

$$\mathbf{w}(k+1) = \mathbf{w}(k) + \alpha_k \mathbf{x}(k)\{r[\mathbf{x}(k)] - \mathbf{w}'(k)\mathbf{x}(k)\} \tag{6.3–19}$$

where $\mathbf{w}(1)$ is arbitrary. It should be kept in mind that, when using this formulation, decisions are made according to the rule $\mathbf{w}'\mathbf{x} > \frac{1}{2}$ and $\mathbf{w}'\mathbf{x} < \frac{1}{2}$, as indicated in expression (6.3–15).

Example: Let us repeat the example of Section 6.3.2 using the LMSE algorithm. The augmented patterns are ω_1: $\{(0, 0, 0, 1)', (1, 0, 0, 1)', (1, 0, 1, 1)', (1, 1, 0, 1)'\}$ and ω_2: $\{(0, 0, 1, 1)', (0, 1, 0, 1)', (0, 1, 1, 1)', (1, 1, 1, 1)'\}$.

Letting $\mathbf{w}(1) = \mathbf{0}$, $\alpha_k = 1/k$, and $\mathbf{x}(1) = (0, 0, 0, 1)'$ and using the algorithm of Eq. (6.3–19) yields

$$\mathbf{w}(2) = \mathbf{w}(1) + \alpha_1 \mathbf{x}(1)[1 - \mathbf{w}'(1)\mathbf{x}(1)]$$

$$= \mathbf{0} + \mathbf{x}(1) = \begin{pmatrix} 0 \\ 0 \\ 0 \\ 1 \end{pmatrix}$$

In the next step $\mathbf{x}(2) = (1, 0, 0, 1)'$, $\alpha_2 = \frac{1}{2}$, and $r[\mathbf{x}(2)] = 1$. Therefore,

$$\mathbf{w}(3) = \mathbf{w}(2) + \alpha_2 \mathbf{x}(2)[1 - \mathbf{w}'(2)\mathbf{x}(2)]$$

$$= \begin{pmatrix} 0 \\ 0 \\ 0 \\ 1 \end{pmatrix} + \frac{0}{2}\begin{pmatrix} 1 \\ 0 \\ 0 \\ 1 \end{pmatrix}$$

$$= \begin{pmatrix} 0 \\ 0 \\ 0 \\ 1 \end{pmatrix}$$

It can be easily verified that $\mathbf{w}(5) = \mathbf{w}(4) = \mathbf{w}(3)$. In the next step, $\mathbf{x}(5) = (0, 0, 1, 1)'$, $\alpha_5 = \frac{1}{5}$, and, since $\mathbf{x}(5)$ belongs to ω_2, $r[\mathbf{x}(5)] = 0$, so that

$$\mathbf{w}(6) = \mathbf{w}(5) + \alpha_5 \mathbf{x}(5)[0 - \mathbf{w}'(5)\mathbf{x}(5)]$$

$$= \begin{pmatrix} 0 \\ 0 \\ 0 \\ 1 \end{pmatrix} - \frac{1}{5}\begin{pmatrix} 0 \\ 0 \\ 1 \\ 1 \end{pmatrix}$$

$$= \begin{pmatrix} 0 \\ 0 \\ -\frac{1}{5} \\ \frac{4}{5} \end{pmatrix}$$

Continuing in this manner and testing after each iterative step to see whether the new weight vector correctly classifies all patterns, we find that the LMSE algorithm converges to a solution for $k = 19$, yielding the weight vector

$$\mathbf{w} = \begin{pmatrix} 0.135 \\ -0.238 \\ -0.305 \\ 0.721 \end{pmatrix}$$

As in the example in the preceding section, the decision boundary is given by the equation $\mathbf{w}'\mathbf{x} - 0.5 = 0$, or

$$0.135x_1 - 0.238x_2 - 0.305x_3 + 0.221 = 0$$

The patterns and their decision surface are shown in Fig. 6.5. ●

6.4 THE METHOD OF POTENTIAL FUNCTIONS

The potential function approach was introduced in Section 5.6, where the assumption was made that the training sample patterns taken from different pattern classes form disjoint sets. The observed data belong to either class ω_i or class ω_j, but cannot belong to both. In view of this assumption, partition boundaries can be generated to categorize the pattern classes. The major problem of pattern classification lies in the generation of partition boundaries on the basis of the observed sample patterns known to belong to a certain class.

In many practical situations, this assumption may not be valid. Examples exist in abundance. In a radar detection system, the observable pattern on the radar screen can correspond to the presence and the absence of the object being sought. In the case of medical diagnosis, clinical data generally do not provide a basis for a unique recognition of a disease. Because of the presence of noise and the lack of complete information in the measured pattern vectors, the observed data can belong to both of the classes ω_i and

$\bar{\omega}_i$ at different times, where $\bar{\omega}_i$ denotes patterns which do not belong to class ω_i. In other words, sample patterns taken from different pattern classes do not form disjoint sets. Consequently, no partition boundaries can be generated to completely separate the pattern classes. For each observed pattern, only a probability can be determined for assignment to class ω_i or to class $\bar{\omega}_i$. The patterns are derived from ω_i or $\bar{\omega}_i$ with these probabilities. The problem of probabilistic pattern classification lies in training the machine to determine correctly the probability that new patterns belong to a particular pattern class, on the basis of individual observations during the training process when the association of the sample patterns and the corresponding classes is given *a priori*.

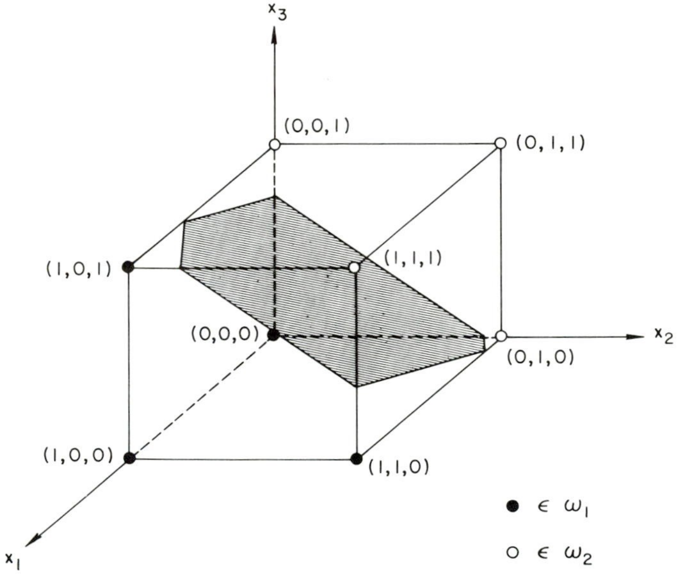

Figure 6.5. Decision boundary determined by the LMSE algorithm

Under the stochastic situation, the classification of new patterns is based on the set of conditional probabilities $p(\omega_i/\mathbf{x})$, $i = 1, 2, \ldots, M$, which are in effect the recognition functions. If $p(\omega_i/\mathbf{x}) > p(\omega_j/\mathbf{x})$ for all $j \neq i$, the new pattern $\mathbf{x}$ is assigned to pattern class ω_i. The recognition function $p(\omega_i/\mathbf{x})$ can be estimated iteratively from the training sample patterns by application of the potential function method. Let the recognition function $p(\omega_i/\mathbf{x})$ be approximated by $\tilde{f}_k(\mathbf{x})$. The function $\tilde{f}_k(\mathbf{x})$, which lies between zero and one, is defined by

$$\tilde{f}_k(\mathbf{x}) = \begin{cases} 0 & \text{if} \quad -\infty < \hat{f}_k(\mathbf{x}) < 0 \\ \hat{f}_k(\mathbf{x}) & \text{if} \quad 0 \leqslant \hat{f}_k(\mathbf{x}) \leqslant 1 \\ 0 & \text{if} \quad 1 < \hat{f}_k(\mathbf{x}) < \infty \end{cases} \tag{6.4–1}$$

where the function $\hat{f}_k(\mathbf{x})$ can be represented by the expansion

$$\hat{f}_k(\mathbf{x}) = \sum_{j=1}^{m} c_j(k)\varphi_j(\mathbf{x}) \tag{6.4–2}$$

In this expansion, the functions $\varphi_j(\mathbf{x})$ are given, and $c_j(k)$ are unknown coefficients. The potential function associated with any pattern point $\mathbf{x}_k$ is given by Eq. (5.6–24) and is repeated here:

$$K(\mathbf{x}, \mathbf{x}_k) = \sum_{j=1}^{m} \lambda_j^2\varphi_j(\mathbf{x})\varphi_j(\mathbf{x}_k) \tag{6.4–3}$$

The recursive algorithm for the determination of the approximation function $\hat{f}_k(\mathbf{x})$ may be stated as follows. Starting with $\hat{f}_0(\mathbf{x}) = 0$, when a sample pattern $\mathbf{x}_1$ is presented to the machine, the potential function associated with $\mathbf{x}_1$ is $K(\mathbf{x}, \mathbf{x}_1)$, and three situations may arise:

1. If $\mathbf{x}_1 \in \omega_i$ and $\hat{f}_0(\mathbf{x}_1) > 0$, or $\mathbf{x}_1 \notin \omega_i$ and $\hat{f}_0(\mathbf{x}_1) < 0$, then $\hat{f}_1(\mathbf{x}) = \hat{f}_0(\mathbf{x})$. In other words, if the machine makes a correct classification for pattern $\mathbf{x}_1$, $\hat{f}_0(\mathbf{x})$ remains unchanged.

2. If $\mathbf{x}_1 \in \omega_i$ and $\hat{f}_0(\mathbf{x}_1) < 0$, then $\hat{f}_1(\mathbf{x}) = \hat{f}_0(\mathbf{x}) + \gamma_1 K(\mathbf{x}, \mathbf{x}_1)$. In other words, if the machine makes a misclassification for $\mathbf{x}_1$, which is known to belong to class ω_i, the function $\hat{f}_0(\mathbf{x})$ is increased by $\gamma_1 K(\mathbf{x}, \mathbf{x}_1)$ to yield $\hat{f}_1(\mathbf{x})$.

3. If $\mathbf{x}_1 \notin \omega_i$ and $\hat{f}_0(\mathbf{x}_1) > 0$, then $\hat{f}_1(\mathbf{x}) = \hat{f}_0(\mathbf{x}) - \gamma_1 K(\mathbf{x}, \mathbf{x}_1)$. In other words, if the machine makes a misclassification for $\mathbf{x}_1$, which is known not to belong to ω_i, the function $\hat{f}_0(\mathbf{x})$ is decreased by $\gamma_1 K(\mathbf{x}, \mathbf{x}_1)$ to form $\hat{f}_1(\mathbf{x})$.

The coefficient γ_1 is a correction factor whose properties will be discussed below.

When a second sample pattern $\mathbf{x}_2$ is presented, the corresponding potential function is $K(\mathbf{x}, \mathbf{x}_2)$. If $\mathbf{x}_2 \in \omega_i$ and $\hat{f}_1(\mathbf{x}_2) > 0$, or $\mathbf{x}_2 \notin \omega_i$ and $\hat{f}_1(\mathbf{x}_2) < 0$, then $\hat{f}_2(\mathbf{x}) = \hat{f}_1(\mathbf{x})$. If $\mathbf{x}_2 \in \omega_i$ and $\hat{f}_1(\mathbf{x}_2) < 0$, then $\hat{f}_2(\mathbf{x}) = \hat{f}_1(\mathbf{x}) + \gamma_2 K(\mathbf{x}, \mathbf{x}_2)$. If $\mathbf{x}_2 \notin \omega_i$ and $\hat{f}_1(\mathbf{x}_2) > 0$, then $\hat{f}_2(\mathbf{x}) = \hat{f}_1(\mathbf{x}) - \gamma_2 K(\mathbf{x}, \mathbf{x}_2)$.

After the presentation of the sample pattern $\mathbf{x}_{k+1}$ to the machine, the potential function associated with $\mathbf{x}_{k+1}$ is $K(\mathbf{x}, \mathbf{x}_{k+1})$. If $\mathbf{x}_{k+1} \in \omega_i$ and $\hat{f}_k(\mathbf{x}_{k+1}) > 0$, or $\mathbf{x}_{k+1} \notin \omega_i$ and $\hat{f}_k(\mathbf{x}_{k+1}) < 0$, then

$$\hat{f}_{k+1}(\mathbf{x}) = \hat{f}_k(\mathbf{x}) \tag{6.4–4}$$

If $\mathbf{x}_{k+1} \in \omega_i$ and $\hat{f}_k(\mathbf{x}_{k+1}) < 0$, then

$$\hat{f}_{k+1}(\mathbf{x}) = \hat{f}_k(\mathbf{x}) + \gamma_{k+1}K(\mathbf{x}, \mathbf{x}_{k+1}) \tag{6.4–5}$$

If $\mathbf{x}_{k+1} \notin \omega_i$ and $\hat{f}_k(\mathbf{x}_{k+1}) > 0$, then

$$\hat{f}_{k+1}(\mathbf{x}) = \hat{f}_k(\mathbf{x}) - \gamma_{k+1}K(\mathbf{x}, \mathbf{x}_{k+1}) \tag{6.4–6}$$

The coefficients γ_k, $k = 1, 2, \ldots$, form a sequence of positive numbers satisfying the conditions

$$\lim_{k\to\infty} \gamma_k = 0 \tag{6.4–7}$$

$$\sum_{k=1}^{\infty} \gamma_k = \infty \tag{6.4–8}$$

and

$$\sum_{k=1}^{\infty} \gamma_k^2 < \infty \tag{6.4–9}$$

The harmonic sequence $\{1/k\} = \{1, \frac{1}{2}, \frac{1}{3}, \ldots\}$ satisfies these conditions and can be used for the coefficients γ_k.

Since the generation of the function $\hat{f}_k(\mathbf{x})$ involves the training sample patterns $\mathbf{x}_k$, which appear at random and which may come randomly from class ω_i or any other class under consideration, the function $\hat{f}_k(\mathbf{x})$ is a random function. For the range from zero to one, the function $\hat{f}_k(\mathbf{x})$ converges to the recognition function $p(\omega_i/\mathbf{x})$ with increasing k. It can be shown that by virtue of the above algorithm the function $\hat{f}(\mathbf{x})$ defined in Eq. (6.4–1) converges in the mean to the recognition function $p(\omega_i/\mathbf{x})$, that is,

$$\lim_{k\to\infty} \int_{\mathbf{x}} [\hat{f}_k(\mathbf{x}) - p(\omega_i/\mathbf{x})]^2 p(\mathbf{x})\, d\mathbf{x} = 0 \tag{6.4–10}$$

The above version of the algorithm requires the storage of the functions $\hat{f}_{k+1}(\mathbf{x})$, $k = 1, 2, \ldots$, over the entire X-domain. This problem can be circumvented by making use of the cumulative potential. From Eqs. (6.4–5) and (6.4–6), we obtain by iteration

$$\hat{f}_{k+1}(\mathbf{x}) = \sum_{\mathbf{x}_a \in \omega_i} \gamma_a K(\mathbf{x}, \hat{\mathbf{x}}_a) - \sum_{\mathbf{x}_b \in \omega_i} \gamma_b K(\mathbf{x}, \hat{\mathbf{x}}_b) \tag{6.4–11}$$

where the observed sample patterns belong to the error-correction training sequence. Consequently, it is sufficient to store only two sequences of numbers in the computer memory. They are the error-correction training sequence $\hat{\mathbf{x}}_1, \hat{\mathbf{x}}_2, \ldots, \hat{\mathbf{x}}_{k+1}$, and the corresponding sequence of coefficients $\gamma_1, \gamma_2, \ldots, \gamma_{k+1}$. When a new pattern $\mathbf{x}^*$ occurs, the machine computes the quantity $\hat{f}_{k+1}(\mathbf{x}^*)$ according to Eq. (6.4–11), from which an estimation of the recognition function $p(\omega_i/\mathbf{x}^*)$ is obtained. The recognition functions for other pattern classes may be determined in like manner.

An alternative algorithm can be derived by the substitution of Eqs. (6.4–2) and (6.4–3). It follows from Eqs. (6.4–5), (6.4–6), and (6.4–3) that

$$\hat{f}_{k+1}(\mathbf{x}) = \hat{f}_k(\mathbf{x}) \pm \gamma_{k+1} \sum_{j=1}^{m} \lambda_j^2 \varphi_j(\hat{\mathbf{x}}_{k+1}) \varphi_j(\mathbf{x}) \tag{6.4–12}$$

Making use of Eq. (6.4–2), we obtain

$$\sum_{j=1}^{m} c_j(k+1)\varphi_j(\mathbf{x}) = \sum_{j=1}^{m} [c_j(k) \pm \gamma_{k+1}\lambda_j^2 \varphi_j(\hat{\mathbf{x}}_{k+1})]\varphi_j(\mathbf{x}) \tag{6.4–13}$$

Hence, when the machine makes a correct classification for the sample pattern $\mathbf{x}_{k+1}$,

$$c_j(k+1) = c_j(k) \tag{6.4–14}$$

When the machine makes a misclassification for the sample pattern $\mathbf{x}_{k+1}$, if $\mathbf{x}_{k+1} \in \omega_i$,

$$c_j(k+1) = c_j(k) + \gamma_{k+1}\lambda_j^2 \varphi_j(\mathbf{x}_{k+1}) \tag{6.4–15}$$

and, if $\mathbf{x}_{k+1} \notin \omega_i$,

$$c_j(k+1) = c_j(k) - \gamma_{k+1}\lambda_j^2 \varphi_j(\mathbf{x}_{k+1}) \tag{6.4–16}$$

In the realization of this algorithm, it is not necessary to memorize the training sample patterns $\mathbf{x}_i$, $i = 1, 2, \ldots$. At the ith iteration the machine stores the sequence $c_1(i), c_2(i), \ldots, c_m(i)$. At the $(i+1)$th iteration, the machine determines the coefficients $c_j(i+1)$, $j = 1, 2, \ldots, m$, from the above algorithm. The values of $c_j(i+1)$ are then stored in place of $c_j(i)$. At the completion of the training phase, an estimation of the recognition function $p(\omega_i/\mathbf{x})$ for each pattern class is obtained from Eqs. (6.4–1) and (6.4–2).

6.5 CONCLUDING REMARKS

In this chapter the basic concepts underlying pattern classification by statistical training algorithms are presented. As was done in Chapter 5, several algorithms are derived from a general iterative scheme by properly choosing different criterion functions. Other algorithms in addition to the ones presented here can easily be derived. The ones given in this chapter, however, are representative of the spectrum of available schemes.

As is true with deterministic approaches, the quality of the decision functions generated by statistical methods is, in general, strongly dependent on the complexity of the approximation chosen for these decision functions. Unlike their deterministic counterparts, however, the statistical algorithms developed in this chapter converge in the limit to an approximation of the Bayes classifier. It is worth noting that the poor convergence rates of statistical classifiers tend to overshadow their potential for optimum performance. For this reason, the algorithms derived in Chapter 5 are certainly competitive with the schemes developed here.

The material in this chapter represents the conclusion of our study of pattern classification by decision functions. The study has progressed from the minimum-distance and likelihood function concepts to the training algorithms developed in this chapter and the preceding one. Once again it is of interest to compare the diversity of approaches in these methods. A broad look at Chapters 3–5 reveals that the methods of Chapters 3 and 4 are not based on the interactive, training framework which has been established in Chapter 5 and the present chapter. Also, it is evident that the techniques developed in these chapters have been clearly based on either deterministic or statistical concepts. The effectiveness of a given technique is strongly dependent on both the data and the intended application. The pattern classification methods presented thus far, however, represent a varied and powerful set of tools capable of handling a large variety of problems of practical significance. In the following chapter we begin the study of feature selection and extraction techniques. As will be seen, these techniques are very useful in the preprocessing stages of a pattern recognition system.

REFERENCES

The method of stochastic approximation developed in Section 6.2 is due to Robbins and Monro [1951]. The Robbins-Monro algorithm was extended to the multidimensional case by Blum [1954b]. A general discussion on the convergence properties of the stochastic approximation algorithm is given by Dvoretzky [1956]. The book by Wilde [1964] contains a lucid introduction to stochastic approximation methods.

The application of stochastic approximation techniques to pattern recognition dates back to the early 1960's. Interestingly, many early papers in this field are contributions relating the methods of potential functions and stochastic approximation. A series of papers by Aizerman, Braverman, and Rozonoer [1964a, 1964b, 1965] describes the method of potential functions and stochastic approximation, and establishes much of the fundamental theory related to the pattern recognition aspects of these methods. Additional references in this area are the papers by Braverman [1965], Blaydon [1967], and Ho and Agrawala [1968], and the books by Fu [1968], Tou [1969a], Fukunaga [1972], Patrick [1972], Meisel [1972], and Duda and Hart [1973].

PROBLEMS

6.1 Use the Robbins-Monro algorithm to find the root of the regression function

$$g(w) = \frac{4w}{w^2 + 1}$$

starting with $w(1) = 1$ and letting $\alpha_k = 1/k$. To simulate experimental error, flip a coin at each step and let

$$h[w(k)] = g[w(k)] + \eta_k$$

where

$$\eta_k = \begin{cases} 0.1 & \text{if coin reads "heads"} \\ -0.1 & \text{if coin reads "tails"} \end{cases}$$

Carry out the algorithm up to $k = 10$.

6.2 Repeat Problem 6.1 using the accelerated sequence described in Section 6.2.2 and compare the results.

6.3 Assuming that $h[w(k)] = g[w(k)] + \eta_k$, where η_k is given in Problem 6.1, would you expect the R-M algorithm to converge to the root of the function $g(w) = w^3 + w$ for arbitrary $w(1)$? Explain.

6.4 Formulate a meaningful criterion function, and use the methods of Section 6.3 to derive a pattern classification algorithm. Keep in mind that the criterion function must have a unique minimum and that this minimum must be achieved upon correct classification of the patterns.

6.5 Apply the algorithm derived in Problem 6.4 to the following pattern classes: ω_1: $\{(0, 0)', (1, 0)'\}$ and ω_2: $\{(0, 1)', (1, 1)'\}$.

6.6 Apply the increment-correction algorithm to the patterns of Problem 6.5.

6.7 Apply the LMSE algorithm to the patterns of Problem 6.5.

6.8 Choose an appropriate potential function (see Section 5.6.2), and apply the potential function algorithm to the patterns of Problem 6.5.

6.9 Repeat Problem 6.8 for the pattern classes ω_1: $\{(0, 0)', (2, 0)'\}$ and ω_2: $\{(1, -1)', (1, 1)'\}$. Note that these classes are not linearly separable.

7

PATTERN PREPROCESSING AND FEATURE SELECTION

7.1 INTRODUCTION

Thus far we have been concerned with a study of various techniques for pattern classification. Before a pattern recognizer can be properly designed, however, it is necessary to consider the feature extraction and data reduction problems. Although these problems should be considered before a classifier is designed, it has been our experience that this material is better understood and appreciated when these two topics are presented in the reverse order, as has been done in this book.

Any object or pattern which can be recognized and classified possesses a number of discriminatory properties or features. The first step in any recognition process, performed either by a machine or by a human being, is to consider the problem of what discriminatory features to select and how to extract (measure) these features. It is evident that the number of features needed to successfully perform a given recognition task depends on the discriminatory qualities of the chosen features. However, the problem of feature selection is usually complicated by the fact that the most important features are not necessarily easily measurable, or, in many cases, their measurement is inhibited by economic considerations.

Consider, for example, the handwritten character recognition problem discussed in Chapter 1. The more important discriminatory features are the sequence of strokes, the directions of strokes, the arrangement of strokes, and the interrelation between strokes, which are generally not easy to measure by physical devices. On the other hand, the conversion of a character into a zero-one matrix or an equivalent n-dimensional measurement vector by a scanning device can readily be accomplished. However, the measured values do not necessarily carry much discriminatory information. Such measured data may even complicate the subsequent classification scheme because they contain insufficient discriminatory information. When such a situation arises, we naturally wish to extract more significant features from the measurement vectors in order to realize a more efficient and accurate pattern classification system. This operation is often referred to as preprocessing for feature extraction.

As a second example, we consider oil prospecting, which may be treated as a two-class pattern recognition problem. In this case, it is desired to categorize a given geographical region as either containing or lacking an acceptable quantity of oil. Clearly, the classification of a region into one of these two classes can be accomplished by drilling oil wells throughout the region until either oil is found or the number of dry or semidry oil wells approaches a quantity large enough to indicate that the region is, in fact, oilless for all practical purposes. These measurements will yield the most significant features for this particular problem. As any oil industry official would testify, however, it would not be long before the foregoing approach would lead a firm into bankruptcy. Because of the high cost of drilling, oil industry scientists and engineers must settle for features which, though conveying less information, are more economical to obtain. These features usually take the form of seismic events obtained from low-frequency reflection waves caused, for example, by discharging dynamite into the earth's surface at several points throughout the region in question. In this manner a local map of the earth's inner crust is obtained, and the region can be classified as having or lacking the *potential* for holding oil. Thus, in this problem, a necessary compromise in feature selection results in a classification process which is considerably far from optimum. Unfortunately, this trade-off between feature selection and classification performance is a constraint present in most pattern recognition problems of practical significance.

From the above observations, it is evident that feature selection and extraction plays a central role in pattern recognition. In fact, the selection of an appropriate set of features which take into account the difficulties present in the extraction or selection process, and at the same time result in acceptable performance, is one of the most difficult tasks in the design of pattern recognition systems. To facilitate the analysis of this problem, features will be classified into three categories: (1) physical features, (2) structural features, and (3) mathematical features.

Physical and structural features are commonly used by human beings in the recognition of patterns because these features are easily detected by touch or by the eye or other sensory organs. When we distinguish between oranges and bananas, we usually consider such features as color and shape. To distinguish between lemons and bananas, however, color is no longer an effective feature. In distinguishing between Florida and California oranges, neither color nor shape are useful properties; instead, other features such as fragrance and skin texture must be employed. Color and fragrance are examples of physical features. Shape, texture, and other geometrical properties of patterns are considered structural features. Although it could be argued that structural features are also physical features, the reader should keep in mind that the distinctions being made here are simply for the purpose of convenience and that they are, in a sense, arbitrary.

Since sensory organs are trained to recognize physical and structural features, it is natural for human beings to use these features as the basis for classification and recognition. However, when machines are designed to recognize patterns, the effectiveness of these features in the recognition process may be sharply reduced since the capabilities of human sensory organs are generally difficult to imitate in most practical situations. On the other hand, machines can be designed to extract mathematical features of patterns which a human being may have some difficulty in determining without mechanical aid. Examples of these types of features are statistical means, correlation coefficients, eigenvalues and eigenvectors of covariance matrices, and other invariant properties.

In automatic pattern recognition, physical and structural features are used primarily in the area of image processing. These features are strongly problem-oriented in the sense that their use involves the development of specialized algorithms which fit the situation at hand. For instance, if one were trying to identify crops by means of aerial photography, the selection of physical features (e.g., color) would be meaningful. On the other hand, the identification of objects such as trucks, buildings, and highways would have to be based on structural feature analysis. The important point to keep in mind is that it is almost impossible to formulate general guidelines regarding the selection of physical and structural features.

In this book we will be concerned only with structural and mathematical features. Structural features will play a significant role in the topics covered in the next chapter. In this chapter attention is focused on the selection and extraction of mathematical features from training patterns. These features exhibit two principal advantages over structural features: (1) they are more general in scope, and (2) they lend themselves readily to machine implementation.

In the mathematical approach to preprocessing and data reduction, the feature extraction problem plays a central role. It will be seen that this problem consists of determining certain invariant attributes of the pattern classes under consideration. These attributes are then used, for example, to reduce the dimensionality of the pattern vectors by means of a linear transformation. Once a set of attributes has been selected, the extraction process consists simply of extracting these attributes from the patterns under consideration. In the following sections, numerous procedures are developed which deal with mathematical feature selection and extraction. Although most of these methods cover a broad class of problems, it is important to recognize that the superiority of any one procedure is ultimately determined by the problem at hand.

Pattern preprocessing generally involves two major tasks: clustering transformation and feature selection. A central problem in pattern recognition is the development of decision functions from sets of finite sample patterns of the classes so that the functions will partition the measurement space into regions each of which contains the sample pattern points belonging to one class. This argument leads to the concept of clustering transformation, which is made on the measurement space in order to cluster the points representing samples of the class. Such a transformation will maximize the interset distance, while minimizing the intraset distance. The interset distance is defined as the mean-square distance between pattern points that belong to two different classes. The intraset distance is the mean-square distance between pattern points of the same class.

Through selection of the most effective features, the dimensionality of the measurement vector can be reduced. Feature selection may be accomplished independently of the performance of the classification scheme. Optimum feature selection is dictated by the maximization or minimization of a criterion function. Such an approach may be referred to as absolute feature selection. An alternative approach is performance-dependent feature selection, the effectiveness of which is directly related to the performance of the classification system, usually in terms of the probability of correct recognition. When the feature distribution for each pattern class is known, we may use divergence or entropy function in effecting feature selection. When the feature distribution for each pattern class is unknown, nonparametric feature selection based on direct estimation of the error probability may be used.

7.2 DISTANCE MEASURES

In processing pattern information, distance measures are a fundamental concept. This section is devoted to a discussion of the distance measures which are applied to preprocessing and feature extraction. We begin with point-to-point distances and extend these concepts to point-to-set as well as set-to-set distances.

(a) Point-to-Point Distance

In Euclidean n-dimensional space, the distance between two points $\mathbf{a}$ and $\mathbf{b}$ is given by

$$\begin{aligned} D(\mathbf{a}, \mathbf{b}) &= \|\mathbf{a} - \mathbf{b}\| \\ &= \sqrt{(\mathbf{a} - \mathbf{b})'(\mathbf{a} - \mathbf{b})} \\ &= \sqrt{\sum_{k=1}^{n} (a_k - b_k)^2} \end{aligned} \tag{7.2–1}$$

where $\mathbf{a}$ and $\mathbf{b}$ are n-dimensional vectors with the kth components equal to a_k and b_k, respectively.

(b) Point-to-Set Distance

The distance between a pattern point $\mathbf{x}$ and a set of pattern points $\{\mathbf{a}^i\}$ which represent a class of K patterns is defined as the mean-square distance between the point $\mathbf{x}$ and the K members of the set $\{\mathbf{a}^i\}$. The squared distance between $\mathbf{x}$ and $\mathbf{a}^i$ is

$$\begin{aligned} D^2(\mathbf{x}, \mathbf{a}^i) &= (\mathbf{x} - \mathbf{a}^i)'(\mathbf{x} - \mathbf{a}^i) \\ &= \sum_{k=1}^{n} (x_k - a_k{}^i)^2 \end{aligned} \tag{7.2–2}$$

The mean-square distance is then given by

$$\begin{aligned} \overline{D^2(\mathbf{x}, \{\mathbf{a}^i\})} &= \frac{1}{K} \sum_{i=1}^{K} D^2(\mathbf{x}, \mathbf{a}^i) \\ &= \frac{1}{K} \sum_{i=1}^{K} \sum_{k=1}^{n} (x_k - a_k{}^i)^2 \end{aligned} \tag{7.2–3}$$

(c) Intraset Distance

The intraset distance for a set of pattern points $\{\mathbf{a}^i, i = 1, 2, \ldots, K\}$ is given by

$$\overline{D^2(\{\mathbf{a}^j\}, \{\mathbf{a}^i\})}, \quad i, j = 1, 2, \ldots, K-1; \quad i \neq j \tag{7.2–4}$$

From Eq. (7.2–2), we have

$$D^2(\mathbf{a}^j, \mathbf{a}^i) = \sum_{k=1}^{n} (a_k{}^j - a_k{}^i)^2 \tag{7.2–5}$$

For fixed $\mathbf{a}^j$ and with $\mathbf{a}^i$ ranging over all of the $K - 1$ other points in the set $\{\mathbf{a}^i\}$, the partial average follows from Eq. (7.2–3) with $\mathbf{x}$ replaced by $\mathbf{a}^j$. Thus,

$$\overline{D^2(\mathbf{a}^j, \{\mathbf{a}^i\})} = \frac{1}{K-1} \sum_{i=1}^{K} \sum_{k=1}^{n} (a_k{}^j - a_k{}^i)^2 \tag{7.2–6}$$

It is noted that the contribution for $i = j$ is zero and may harmlessly be left in the expression. There are K terms, but only $K - 1$ nonzero terms.

Following the same line of reasoning, we then take the average over all K points in set $\{\mathbf{a}^j\}$ to express the intraset distance as

$$\begin{aligned}\overline{D^2(\{\mathbf{a}^j\}, \{\mathbf{a}^i\})} &= \frac{1}{K} \sum_{j=1}^{K} \left[\frac{1}{K-1} \sum_{i=1}^{K} \sum_{k=1}^{n} (a_k{}^j - a_k{}^i)^2 \right] \\ &= \frac{1}{K(K-1)} \sum_{j=1}^{K} \sum_{i=1}^{K} \sum_{k=1}^{n} (a_k{}^j - a_k{}^i)^2 \end{aligned} \tag{7.2–7}$$

The intraset distance may also be expressed in terms of the variances associated with the components of the pattern points. Rearranging, we may write Eq. (7.2–7) as

$$\begin{aligned}\overline{D^2} &= \frac{K}{K-1} \sum_{k=1}^{n} \left[\frac{1}{K^2} \sum_{j=1}^{K} \sum_{i=1}^{K} (a_k{}^j - a_k{}^i)^2 \right] \\ &= \frac{K}{K-1} \sum_{k=1}^{n} \left[\frac{1}{K^2} \sum_{j=1}^{K} \sum_{i=1}^{K} (a_k{}^j)^2 - \frac{2}{K^2} \sum_{j=1}^{K} \sum_{i=1}^{K} a_k{}^j a_k{}^i + \frac{1}{K^2} \sum_{j=1}^{K} \sum_{i=1}^{K} (a_k{}^i)^2 \right] \\ &= \frac{K}{K-1} \sum_{k=1}^{n} \left[\frac{1}{K} \sum_{i=1}^{K} \overline{(a_k{}^j)^2} - 2\overline{(a_k{}^j)}\ \overline{(a_k{}^i)} + \frac{1}{K} \sum_{j=1}^{K} \overline{(a_k{}^i)^2} \right] \\ &= \frac{2K}{K-1} \sum_{k=1}^{n} [\overline{(a_k{}^i)^2} - \overline{(a_k{}^i)}^2] \end{aligned} \tag{7.2–8}$$

The last step follows from the fact that $\overline{(a_k^{\,j})^2} = \overline{(a_k^{\,i})^2}$ since we are referring to the same sample set. Also, it is noted that

$$\frac{1}{K}\sum_{i=1}^{K}\overline{(a_k^{\,j})^2} = \overline{(a_k^{\,j})^2} \quad \text{and} \quad \frac{1}{K}\sum_{j=1}^{K}\overline{(a_k^{\,i})^2} = \overline{(a_k^{\,i})^2}$$

Since

$$\overline{(a_k^{\,i})^2} - \overline{(a_k^{\,i})}^2 = (\sigma_k^{\,*})^2 \tag{7.2–9}$$

is the biased sample variance of the kth component of the K pattern points in $\{\mathbf{a}^i\}$, the intraset distance is given by

$$\overline{D^2} = \frac{2K}{K-1}\sum_{k=1}^{n}(\sigma_k^{\,*})^2 \tag{7.2–10}$$

Since the biased variance is

$$(\sigma_k^{\,*})^2 = \frac{1}{K}\sum_{i=1}^{K}(a_k^{\,i} - \overline{a_k^{\,i}})^2 \tag{7.2–11}$$

and the unbiased variance is

$$(\sigma_k)^2 = \frac{1}{K-1}\sum_{i=1}^{K}(a_k^{\,i} - \overline{a_k^{\,i}})^2 \tag{7.2–12}$$

we obtain from these two equations

$$(\sigma_k)^2 = \frac{K}{K-1}(\sigma_k^{\,*})^2 \tag{7.2–13}$$

Hence, using the unbiased sample variance, we have the intraset distance:

$$\overline{D^2} = 2\sum_{k=1}^{n}(\sigma_k)^2 \tag{7.2–14}$$

This distance measure will be used in the following sections in the study of clustering transformation and feature ordering.

(d) Interset Distance

The interset distance between sets $\{\mathbf{a}^i\}$ and $\{\mathbf{b}^j\}$ containing K_a and K_b samples, respectively, is given by

$$\overline{D^2(\{\mathbf{a}^i\}, \{\mathbf{b}^j\})}, \quad i = 1, 2, \ldots, K_a; \quad j = 1, 2, \ldots, K_b \tag{7.2–15}$$

However, this expression is not easily reduced to a simple closed form in terms of statistical properties. An alternative way to measure interset distances is to use the distance between the centroids of the two sets under consideration or to use the Mahalanobis distance concept discussed in Chapter 4.

7.3 CLUSTERING TRANSFORMATIONS AND FEATURE ORDERING

The measurements of a pattern which are represented by the different coordinate axes x_k are not all equally important in influencing the definition of the category to which similar patterns belong. In comparing two patterns feature by feature, measurements with decreasing significance should be assigned decreasing weights. The process of feature weighting may be realized through a linear transformation, which will cluster most highly the transformed pattern points in the new space.

Consider the pattern vectors $\mathbf{a}$ and $\mathbf{b}$, which are transformed to pattern vectors $\mathbf{a}^*$ and $\mathbf{b}^*$ through a transformation $\mathbf{W}$. Then

$$\mathbf{a}^* = \mathbf{W}\mathbf{a} \qquad \text{and} \qquad \mathbf{b}^* = \mathbf{W}\mathbf{b}$$

where

$$\mathbf{W} = \begin{pmatrix} w_{11} & w_{12} & \cdots & w_{1n} \\ w_{21} & w_{22} & \cdots & w_{2n} \\ \vdots & \vdots & & \vdots \\ w_{n1} & w_{n2} & \cdots & w_{nn} \end{pmatrix}$$

in which w_{kj} are the weighting coefficients.

Thus, we have

$$a_k^* - b_k^* = \sum_{j=1}^{n} w_{kj}(a_j - b_j)$$

Each element of the transformed pattern vector is a linear combination of the elements of the original pattern vector. The Euclidean distance between $\mathbf{a}^*$ and $\mathbf{b}^*$ in the new space is then given by

$$D(\mathbf{a}^*, \mathbf{b}^*) = \sqrt{\sum_{k=1}^{n} (a_k^* - b_k^*)^2}$$

$$= \sqrt{\sum_{k=1}^{n} \left[\sum_{j=1}^{n} w_{kj}(a_j - b_j) \right]^2}. \tag{7.3–1}$$

When the linear transformation involves only scale-factor changes of the coordinates, we may let $\mathbf{W}$ be a diagonal matrix with only the elements on the main diagonal nonzero. Thus, the Euclidean distance reduces to

$$D(\mathbf{a}^*, \mathbf{b}^*) = \sqrt{\sum_{k=1}^{n} w_{kk}^2 (a_k - b_k)^2} \tag{7.3–2}$$

where w_{kk} represent the feature-weighting coefficients. The clustering transformation problem is to determine the coefficients w_{kk} so that the intraset distance between $\{\mathbf{a}^i, i = 1, 2, \ldots, K\}$ and $\{\mathbf{a}^j, j = 1, 2, \ldots, K\}$ is minimized, subject to a specified constraint on w_{kk}.

It follows from the preceding section that the intraset distance for pattern points in the new space is

$$\overline{D^2} = 2 \sum_{k=1}^{n} (w_{kk}\sigma_k)^2 \tag{7.3–3}$$

where σ_k^2 is the unbiased sample variance of the components along the x_k coordinate direction. In carrying out the minimization procedure, we will consider two cases.

Case 1. Constraint: $\sum_{k=1}^{n} w_{kk} = 1$.

Minimizing $\overline{D^2}$ subject to this constraint is equivalent to minimizing

$$S_1 = 2 \sum_{k=1}^{n} (w_{kk}\sigma_k)^2 - \rho_1 \left(\sum_{k=1}^{n} w_{kk} - 1 \right) \tag{7.3–4}$$

Taking the partial derivative of Eq. (7.3–4) with respect to w_{kk} and equating it to zero yields, upon simplification,

$$w_{kk} = \frac{\rho_1}{4\sigma_k^2} \tag{7.3–5}$$

where ρ_1 is the Lagrange multiplier, given by

$$\rho_1 = \frac{4}{\sum_{k=1}^{n} \sigma_k^{-2}} \tag{7.3–6}$$

Thus, the feature-weighting coefficient is

$$w_{kk} = \frac{1}{\sigma_k{}^2 \sum_{k=1}^{n} (1/\sigma_k{}^2)} \tag{7.3–7}$$

From Eq. (7.3–5), it is noted that w_{kk} is small if $\sigma_k{}^2$ is large. This implies that in the distance measure a small weight is to be assigned to a feature of large variation. On the other hand, if $\sigma_k{}^2$ is small, the corresponding feature should be weighted heavily.

In the above analysis, the clustering transformation is accomplished by feature weighting. Intuitively, a small $\sigma_k{}^2$ implies that the kth measurement is more reliable; a large $\sigma_k{}^2$, that the kth measurement is less reliable. The more reliable measurements are more heavily weighted.

Case 2. Constraint: $\prod_{k=1}^{n} w_{kk} = 1$.

Minimization of $\overline{D^2}$ subject to this constraint is equivalent to minimization of

$$S_2 = 2\sum_{k=1}^{n} (w_{kk}\sigma_k)^2 - \rho_2\left(\prod_{k=1}^{n} w_{kk} - 1\right) \tag{7.3–8}$$

Taking the partial derivative of Eq. (7.3–8) with respect to w_{kk} and equating it to zero yields

$$w_{kk} = \frac{\sqrt{\rho_2}}{2\sigma_k} \tag{7.3–9}$$

where the Lagrange multiplier ρ_2 is given by

$$\rho_2 = 4\left(\prod_{k=1}^{n} \sigma_k\right)^{2/n} \tag{7.3–10}$$

Thus, the featuring-weighting coefficient is

$$w_{kk} = \frac{1}{\sigma_k}\left(\prod_{j=1}^{n} \sigma_j\right)^{1/n} \tag{7.3–11}$$

which is inversely proportional to the standard deviation of the kth measurement.

Equations (7.3–7) and (7.3–11) determine the transformation matrix $\mathbf{W}$ under the constraints specified above. If the pattern vectors are transformed from space X to space X^* by the transformation

$$\mathbf{x}^* = \mathbf{W}\mathbf{x} \tag{7.3–12}$$

the intraset distance in space X^* is minimized. Now, we want to perform a second transformation:

$$\mathbf{x}^{**} = \mathbf{A}\mathbf{x}^*$$

in order to make apparent which components have small (or large) variances, thus enabling the ordering and selection of features. Such a transformation will make the covariance matrix of the pattern points in space X^{**} a diagonal matrix. Furthermore, the transformation matrix $\mathbf{A}$ is to be chosen as orthonormal so as to keep the distances unchanged.

The problem is to determine an expression for $\mathbf{A}$ in terms of the eigenvectors of the covariance matrix which is known. Let $\mathbf{C}$ be the covariance matrix for pattern points in space X, and $\mathbf{C}^*$ and $\mathbf{C}^{**}$ be the corresponding covariance matrices in spaces X^* and X^{**}, respectively. Let $\mathbf{m}$ be the mean vector for the pattern points in space X, and $\mathbf{m}^*$ and $\mathbf{m}^{**}$ be the corresponding mean vectors in spaces X^* and X^{**}, respectively. Then we have

$$\mathbf{m}^* = \mathbf{W}\mathbf{m} \tag{7.3–13}$$

and

$$\mathbf{x}^* - \mathbf{m}^* = \mathbf{W}(\mathbf{x} - \mathbf{m}) = \mathbf{W}\mathbf{z} \tag{7.3–14}$$

where

$$\mathbf{m}^* = E\{\mathbf{x}^*\} \qquad \text{and} \qquad \mathbf{z} = \mathbf{x} - \mathbf{m}$$

Here E is the expectation operator. The covariance matrix in space X^* is given by

$$\begin{aligned}\mathbf{C}^* &= E\{(\mathbf{x}^* - \mathbf{m}^*)(\mathbf{x}^* - \mathbf{m}^*)'\} \\ &= E\{\mathbf{W}\mathbf{z}\mathbf{z}'\mathbf{W}\} \\ &= \mathbf{W}\mathbf{C}\mathbf{W}' \end{aligned} \tag{7.3–15}$$

since $\mathbf{C} = E\{\mathbf{z}\mathbf{z}'\}$.

Similarly, it can readily be shown that

$$\begin{aligned} C^{**} &= \mathbf{A}\mathbf{C}^*\mathbf{A}' \\ &= \mathbf{A}\mathbf{W}\mathbf{C}\mathbf{W}'\mathbf{A}' \end{aligned} \tag{7.3–16}$$

Since $\mathbf{A}$ is orthonormal,

$$\mathbf{A}\mathbf{A}' = \mathbf{I} \qquad \text{and} \qquad \mathbf{A}' = \mathbf{A}^{-1}$$

Then we have

$$\mathbf{C}^{**} = \mathbf{A}\mathbf{C}^{*}\mathbf{A}^{-1} \tag{7.3–17}$$

which is a similarity transformation.

It is well known that for a similarity transformation the matrix $\mathbf{C}^{**}$ will be diagonal if $\mathbf{A}^{-1}$ is chosen as the modal matrix of $\mathbf{C}^{*}$, that is, the columns of $\mathbf{A}^{-1}$ are the eigenvectors of $\mathbf{C}^{*}$, or the rows of $\mathbf{A}$ are the eigenvectors of $\mathbf{C}^{*}$. Thus, the rows of $\mathbf{A}$ are the eigenvectors of $\mathbf{C}^{*} = \mathbf{W}\mathbf{C}\mathbf{W}'$. This transformation, which is a congruent rather than a similarity transformation, does not allow easy expression of the eigenvectors of $\mathbf{W}\mathbf{C}\mathbf{W}'$ in terms of those of $\mathbf{C}$.

Let $\mathbf{e}_k$, $k = 1, 2, \ldots, n$, be the normalized eigenvectors of $\mathbf{C}^{*}$, and λ_k, $k = 1, 2, \ldots, n$, be the corresponding eigenvalues. Then

$$\mathbf{C}^{*}\mathbf{e}_k = \lambda_k \mathbf{e}_k \tag{7.3–18}$$

and

$$(\mathbf{C}^{*} - \lambda_k \mathbf{I})\mathbf{e}_k = \mathbf{0} \tag{7.3–19}$$

We choose $\mathbf{A}$ so that

$$\mathbf{A} = \begin{pmatrix} \mathbf{e}_1' \\ \mathbf{e}_2' \\ \vdots \\ \mathbf{e}_n' \end{pmatrix}, \qquad \mathbf{A}^{-1} = (\mathbf{e}_1\ \mathbf{e}_2 \cdots \mathbf{e}_n)$$

and, since the eigenvectors form an orthonormal set, $\mathbf{A}\mathbf{A}' = \mathbf{I}$. Then

$$\begin{aligned} C^{**} &= \mathbf{A}\mathbf{C}^{*}\mathbf{A}^{-1} \\ &= \begin{pmatrix} \mathbf{e}_1' \\ \mathbf{e}_2' \\ \vdots \\ \mathbf{e}_n' \end{pmatrix} \mathbf{C}^{*}(\mathbf{e}_1\ \mathbf{e}_2 \cdots \mathbf{e}_n) \end{aligned}$$

Making use of Eq. (7.3–18), we can write

$$\mathbf{C}^{**} = \begin{pmatrix} \lambda_1\mathbf{e}_1'\mathbf{e}_1 & \lambda_2\mathbf{e}_1'\mathbf{e}_2 & \cdots & \lambda_n\mathbf{e}_1'\mathbf{e}_n \\ \lambda_1\mathbf{e}_2'\mathbf{e}_1 & \lambda_2\mathbf{e}_2'\mathbf{e}_2 & \cdots & \lambda_n\mathbf{e}_2'\mathbf{e}_n \\ \vdots & \vdots & & \vdots \\ \lambda_1\mathbf{e}_n'\mathbf{e}_1 & \lambda_2\mathbf{e}_n'\mathbf{e}_2 & \cdots & \lambda_n\mathbf{e}_n'\mathbf{e}_n \end{pmatrix}$$

$$= \begin{pmatrix} \lambda_1 & 0 & \cdots & 0 \\ 0 & \lambda_2 & \cdots & 0 \\ \vdots & \vdots & \ddots & \vdots \\ 0 & 0 & \cdots & \lambda_n \end{pmatrix} \tag{7.3–20}$$

since $\mathbf{e}_k'\mathbf{e}_k = 1$ and $\mathbf{e}_k'\mathbf{e}_j = 0$ for $k \neq j$. It can be shown that

$$\lambda_k = \sigma_k^2 \tag{7.3–21}$$

The transformation matrix **A** converts the covariance matrix **C*** into a diagonal matrix in terms of the unbiased sample variances. The measurements corresponding to small variances are more reliable and can be considered as more important features.

The above procedure for decoupling the covariance matrix does not allow an easy expression of the eigenvectors of **WCW**′ in terms of those of the original covariance matrix **C**. However, if the sequence of the operations (**W**, **A**) is reversed, a simple expression for the rows of **A** in terms of the original covariance matrix can be found. We choose an orthonormal matrix **A** whose rows are the eigenvectors of the covariance matrix **C**. Matrix **A** converts matrix **C** into a diagonal matrix **C***. We then require that **W** be a diagonal matrix which minimizes the intraset distance in space X^{**} subject to a specified constraint. If the constraint

$$\prod_{k=1}^{n} w_{kk} = 1$$

is chosen, it is found that

$$w_{kk} = \left(\prod_{j=1}^{n} \sigma_j \right)^{1/n} \frac{1}{\sigma_k} \tag{7.3–22}$$

where σ_k^2 are the elements of the diagonalized covariance matrix **C***:

$$\sigma_k^2 = c_{kk}^*$$

The covariance matrix after the clustering transformation will be

$$\mathbf{C}^{**} = \mathbf{W}\mathbf{C}^*\mathbf{W}' = \mathbf{W}\mathbf{A}\mathbf{C}\mathbf{A}'\mathbf{W}' \tag{7.3–23}$$

Since **W**, **C***, and **W**′ are each diagonal matrices and since the product of diagonal matrices is always a diagonal matrix, it follows that **C**** will be diagonal, as desired.

Mean-Square Distance Versus Likelihood Ratio

In the following discussions we establish the relationship between the likelihood ratio presented in Chapter 4 and the mean-square distance measure by making use of the transformations described in the preceding paragraphs. Consider the normal probability density function:

$$p(\mathbf{x}) = \frac{1}{(2\pi)^{n/2}|\mathbf{C}|^{1/2}} \exp[-\tfrac{1}{2}(\mathbf{x} - \mathbf{m})'\mathbf{C}^{-1}(\mathbf{x} - \mathbf{m})] \tag{7.3–24}$$

where $\mathbf{C}$ is the covariance matrix, and $\mathbf{m}$ is the mean vector of a pattern class in space X. It is noted that contours of constant probability density occur for values of $\mathbf{x}$ for which the argument of the exponential is constant.

To decouple the covariance matrix, we perform an orthonormal transformation:

$$\mathbf{x}^* = \mathbf{A}\mathbf{x} \tag{7.3–25}$$

where the rows of $\mathbf{A}$ are the normalized eigenvectors of the covariance matrix $\mathbf{C}$. This transformation will facilitate the establishment of the relation between the likelihood ratio and the mean-square distance measure. After the transformation, the mean vector and the covariance matrix are given by

$$\mathbf{m}^* = \mathbf{A}\mathbf{m} \tag{7.3–26}$$

and

$$\mathbf{C}^* = \mathbf{A}\mathbf{C}\mathbf{A}' \tag{7.3–27}$$

respectively.

Let $\mathbf{e}_k$ be the eigenvectors of $\mathbf{C}$, and λ_k be the corresponding eigenvalues. Then it follows from Eq. (7.3–27) that

$$\mathbf{C}^* = \begin{pmatrix} \lambda_1 & 0 & \cdots & 0 \\ 0 & \lambda_2 & \cdots & 0 \\ \vdots & \vdots & \ddots & \vdots \\ 0 & 0 & \cdots & \lambda_n \end{pmatrix} = \mathbf{\Lambda} \tag{7.3–28}$$

From Eqs. (7.3–27) and (7.3–28), we have

$$\mathbf{C} = \mathbf{A}'\mathbf{\Lambda}\mathbf{A} \tag{7.3–29}$$

and

$$\mathbf{C}^{-1} = \mathbf{A}'\mathbf{\Lambda}^{-1}\mathbf{A} \tag{7.3–30}$$

Thus, the probability density function in space X^* is given by

$$p(\mathbf{x}^*) = \frac{1}{(2\pi)^{n/2}|\mathbf{\Lambda}|^{1/2}} \exp[-\tfrac{1}{2}(\mathbf{x}^* - \mathbf{m}^*)'\mathbf{\Lambda}^{-1}(\mathbf{x}^* - \mathbf{m}^*)] \tag{7.3–31}$$

The above density function points out that the contours of constant probability density are ellipsoids with centers at $\mathbf{m}^*$. The directions of the principal axes are along the eigenvectors of the covariance matrix, and the diameters are proportional to the square roots of the corresponding eigenvalues or standard deviations since $\sqrt{\lambda_k} = \sigma_k$. This becomes more evident when the exponent is expanded:

$$(\mathbf{x}^* - \mathbf{m}^*)'\mathbf{\Lambda}^{-1}(\mathbf{x}^* - \mathbf{m}^*) = \sum_{k=1}^{n} \frac{(x_k^* - m_k^*)^2}{\lambda_k} \tag{7.3–32}$$

where x_k^* is the coordinate of $\mathbf{x}^*$ in the direction of the kth eigenvector, and m_k^* is the mean of the ensemble in the same direction.

The mean-square distance between an arbitrary pattern point $\mathbf{x}$ and members of the pattern set $\{\mathbf{g}_j, j = 1, 2, \ldots, N\}$ is

$$\overline{D^2(\mathbf{x}, \{\mathbf{g}_j\})} = \overline{(\mathbf{x} - \mathbf{g}_j)'(\mathbf{x} - \mathbf{g}_j)} \tag{7.3–33}$$

The average is taken over all the N pattern points in the specified set. We first perform the orthonormal transformation with the eigenvectors of the covariance matrix forming the rows of the $\mathbf{A}$ matrix:

$$\begin{aligned} \overline{D^2(\mathbf{x}^*, \{\mathbf{g}_j^*\})} &= \overline{(\mathbf{x}^* - \mathbf{g}_j^*)'(\mathbf{x}^* - \mathbf{g}_j^*)} \\ &= \overline{(\mathbf{x} - \mathbf{g}_j)'\mathbf{A}'\mathbf{A}(\mathbf{x} - \mathbf{g}_j)} \\ &= \overline{(\mathbf{x} - \mathbf{g}_j)'(\mathbf{x} - \mathbf{g}_j)} \end{aligned} \tag{7.3–34}$$

since $\mathbf{A}$ is orthonormal and $\mathbf{A}'\mathbf{A} = \mathbf{I}$. The distance remains unchanged under this transformation.

If we perform the clustering transformation:

$$\mathbf{x}^{**} = \mathbf{W}\mathbf{x}^* \tag{7.3–35}$$

the mean-square distance becomes

$$\begin{aligned} \overline{D^2(\mathbf{x}^{**}, \{\mathbf{g}_j^{**}\})} &= \overline{(\mathbf{x}^{**} - \mathbf{g}_j^{**})'(\mathbf{x}^{**} - \mathbf{g}_j^{**})} \\ &= \overline{(\mathbf{x}^* - \mathbf{g}_j^*)'\mathbf{W}'\mathbf{W}(\mathbf{x}^* - \mathbf{g}_j^*)} \end{aligned} \tag{7.3–36}$$

The matrix **W** chosen is a diagonal matrix with the elements equal to the reciprocal standard deviations of the pattern set $\{\mathbf{g}_j^*, j = 1, 2, \ldots, N\}$ in the directions of the eigenvectors. It has been shown that such a transformation minimizes the intraset distance of the pattern set.

The matrix $\mathbf{W}'\mathbf{W}$ is a diagonal matrix with elements equal to the reciprocal variances of the pattern set $\{\mathbf{g}_j, j = 1, 2, \ldots, N\}$. Since the variances are equal to the corresponding eigenvalues, that is, $\sigma_k^2 = \lambda_k$, we have

$$\mathbf{W}'\mathbf{W} = \mathbf{\Lambda}^{-1} \tag{7.3–37}$$

Hence, the mean-square distance is

$$\overline{D^2(\mathbf{x}^{**}, \{\mathbf{g}_j^{**}\})} = \overline{(\mathbf{x}^* - \mathbf{g}_j^*)'\mathbf{\Lambda}^{-1}(\mathbf{x}^* - \mathbf{g}_j^*)} \tag{7.3–38}$$

which, upon expansion, may be expressed as

$$\overline{D^2} = \overline{\sum_{k=1}^{n} \frac{(x_k^* - g_{jk}^*)^2}{\lambda_k}} \tag{7.3–39}$$

Since the average is taken over all the N points in the pattern set, it is independent of the summation process. Thus, Eq. (7.3–39) reduces to

$$\begin{aligned} \overline{D^2} &= \sum_{k=1}^{n} \frac{\overline{(x_k^* - g_{jk}^*)^2}}{\lambda_k} \\ &= \sum_{k=1}^{n} \frac{(x_k^* - m_k^*)^2 + \overline{(g_{jk}^*)^2} - (\overline{g_{jk}^*})^2}{\lambda_k} \end{aligned} \tag{7.3–40}$$

where $m_k^* = \overline{g_{jk}^*}$ over all $j = 1, 2, \ldots, N$. Since

$$\overline{(g_{jk}^*)^2} - (\overline{g_{jk}^*})^2 = \sigma_k^2 = \lambda_k \tag{7.3–41}$$

Eq. (7.3–40) becomes

$$\overline{D^2} = \sum_{k=1}^{n} \frac{(x_k^* - m_k^*)^2}{\lambda_k} + n \tag{7.3–42}$$

Thus, when the constant n is dropped, the mean-square distance for pattern class ω_i is given by

$$\overline{D_i^2} = (\mathbf{x}^* - \mathbf{m}_i^*)'\mathbf{\Lambda}_i^{-1}(\mathbf{x}^* - \mathbf{m}_i^*) \tag{7.3–43}$$

and similarly, for pattern class ω_j, the mean-square distance is

$$\overline{D_j^2} = (\mathbf{x}^* - \mathbf{m}_j^*)'\mathbf{\Lambda}_j^{-1}(\mathbf{x}^* - \mathbf{m}_j^*) \tag{7.3–44}$$

We may derive a decision rule on the basis of the distance concept as $\mathbf{x} \in \omega_i$ if and only if

$$\overline{D_j^2} - \overline{D_i^2} > \theta, \text{ where } \theta \text{ is a threshold}$$

For normal patterns, the probability density or likelihood function for class ω_i is

$$p(\mathbf{x}/\omega_i) = (2\pi)^{-n/2}|\mathbf{C}_i|^{-1/2} \exp[-\tfrac{1}{2}(\mathbf{x} - \mathbf{m}_i)'\mathbf{C}_i^{-1}(\mathbf{x} - \mathbf{m}_i)] \quad (7.3\text{–}45)$$

After the orthonormal transformation, Eq. (7.3–45) becomes

$$p(\mathbf{x}^*/\omega_i) = (2\pi)^{-n/2}|\mathbf{\Lambda}_i|^{-1/2} \exp[-\tfrac{1}{2}(\mathbf{x}^* - \mathbf{m}_i^*)'\mathbf{\Lambda}_i^{-1}(\mathbf{x}^* - \mathbf{m}_i^*)] \quad (7.3\text{–}46)$$

Similarly, for class ω_j the density function is

$$p(\mathbf{x}^*/\omega_j) = (2\pi)^{-n/2}|\mathbf{\Lambda}_j|^{-1/2} \exp[-\tfrac{1}{2}(\mathbf{x}^* - \mathbf{m}_j^*)'\mathbf{\Lambda}_j^{-1}(\mathbf{x}^* - \mathbf{m}_j^*)] \quad (7.3\text{–}47)$$

Taking the logarithm of these functions and dropping the constant term yields

$$d_i = (\mathbf{x}^* - \mathbf{m}_i^*)'\mathbf{\Lambda}_i^{-1}(\mathbf{x}^* - \mathbf{m}_i^*) \quad (7.3\text{–}48)$$

and

$$d_j = (\mathbf{x}^* - \mathbf{m}_j^*)'\mathbf{\Lambda}_j^{-1}(\mathbf{x}^* - \mathbf{m}_j^*) \quad (7.3\text{–}49)$$

Then the decision rule based on these two functions is that $\mathbf{x} \in \omega_i$ if and only if $d_j - d_i > \theta$, where θ is a threshold.

From the above analysis, we may draw the conclusion that fitting normal probability densities to the sets of observed samples of the pattern classes is equivalent to measuring the mean-square distances of the class after clustering transformation of the measurement space.

7.4 CLUSTERING IN FEATURE SELECTION

Intraset feature selection may be studied as a clustering problem. A linear transformation is used to cluster pattern points belonging to the same class and to reduce the dimensionality of the measurement space. In this section we derive a set of optimum features through a clustering transformation. These feature vectors are then used to form the orthogonal transformation matrix.

Consider a pattern class characterized by a multivariate population. One of its normalized members, say $\mathbf{z}_1$, is arbitrarily selected as a reference in forming the sequence of all distances from adjacent normalized pattern vectors $\mathbf{z}$. The choice of pattern vector $\mathbf{z}_1$ is assumed to be independent of the selection of the other pattern vectors $\mathbf{z}$. Thus,

$$p(\mathbf{z}, \mathbf{z}_1) = p(\mathbf{z})p(\mathbf{z}_1) \tag{7.4–1}$$

Denoting $p(\mathbf{z})$ by p and $p(\mathbf{z}_1)$ by p_1, we have as the intraset distance of the multivariate population

$$\overline{D^2} = E_{p_1 p}\{||\mathbf{z} - \mathbf{z}_1||^2\} \tag{7.4–2}$$

which may be written as

$$\overline{D^2} = E_{p_1 p}\{(\mathbf{z} - \mathbf{z}_1)'(\mathbf{z} - \mathbf{z}_1)\} \tag{7.4–3}$$

Simplifying Eq. (7.4–3) yields

$$\begin{aligned}\overline{D^2} &= E_p\{\mathbf{z}'\mathbf{z}\} + E_{p_1}\{\mathbf{z}_1'\mathbf{z}_1\} \\ &= 2E_p(\mathbf{z}'\mathbf{z})\end{aligned} \tag{7.4–4}$$

Expressed in terms of the covariance matrix

$$\mathbf{C}_\mathbf{z} = E_p\{\mathbf{z}\mathbf{z}'\} \tag{7.4–5}$$

Eq. (7.4–4) may be written as

$$\overline{D^2} = 2E_p\{\text{tr } \mathbf{z}\mathbf{z}'\} = 2 \text{ tr } \mathbf{C}_\mathbf{z} \tag{7.4–6}$$

Introducing the orthogonal transformation $\mathbf{A}$ and the diagonal transformation $\mathbf{W}$, we have the covariance matrix in the transformed space, given by

$$\mathbf{C}_\mathbf{z}^{**} = \mathbf{W}\mathbf{A}\mathbf{C}_\mathbf{z}\mathbf{A}'\mathbf{W}' \tag{7.4–7}$$

Then the intraset distance in the transformed space is

$$\overline{D^2} = 2 \text{ tr } (\mathbf{W}\mathbf{A}\mathbf{C}_\mathbf{z}\mathbf{A}'\mathbf{W}') \tag{7.4–8}$$

Let $\mathbf{e}_1, \mathbf{e}_2, \ldots, \mathbf{e}_n$ be the eigenvectors of covariance matrix $\mathbf{C}_\mathbf{z}$, and $\lambda_1, \lambda_2, \ldots, \lambda_n$ be the corresponding eigenvalues. Then

$$\mathbf{C}_\mathbf{z}\mathbf{e}_k = \lambda_k\mathbf{e}_k \tag{7.4–9}$$

The elements of the orthogonal transformation $\mathbf{A}$ are chosen so that the covariance matrix in the transformed space is diagonalized. This can be accomplished by choosing m of the n transposed eigenvectors of $\mathbf{C_z}$ as the rows of orthogonal matrix $\mathbf{A}$. Thus,

$$\mathbf{A} = \begin{pmatrix} \mathbf{e}' \\ \mathbf{e}_2' \\ \vdots \\ \mathbf{e}_m' \end{pmatrix} \tag{7.4–10}$$

The dimensionality of the transformed space is reduced to m. It follows from Eqs. (7.4–9) and (7.4–10) that

$$\mathbf{C_z A}' = (\lambda_1 \mathbf{e}_1 \quad \lambda_2 \mathbf{e}_2 \quad \cdots \quad \lambda_m \mathbf{e}_m) \tag{7.4–11}$$

In view of the orthonormality conditions, the matrix $\mathbf{AC_zA}'$ reduces to a diagonal matrix:

$$\mathbf{AC_zA}' = \begin{pmatrix} \lambda_1 & 0 & \cdots & 0 \\ 0 & \lambda_2 & \cdots & 0 \\ \vdots & \vdots & \ddots & \vdots \\ 0 & 0 & \cdots & \lambda_m \end{pmatrix} = \mathbf{\Lambda} \tag{7.4–12}$$

Hence the intraset distance may be written as

$$\overline{D^2} = 2 \operatorname{tr} (\mathbf{W \Lambda W}') \tag{7.4–13a}$$

$$= 2 \sum_{k=1}^{m} \lambda_k w_{kk}^2 \tag{7.4–13b}$$

Now, we want to determine the weighting matrix $\mathbf{W}$ so that $\overline{D^2}$ is an extremum under a certain specified constraint. Two cases will be studied.

First, let us consider the constraint $\prod_{k=1}^{m} w_{kk} = 1$. This constraint may be written as $|\mathbf{W}| - 1 = 0$, which is chosen to avoid the trivial solution $\mathbf{W} = \mathbf{0}$. Minimizing $\overline{D^2}$ subject to the above constraint is equivalent to minimizing

$$S = 2 \sum_{k=1}^{m} \lambda_k w_{kk}^2 - \gamma \left(\prod_{k=1}^{m} w_{kk} - 1 \right) \tag{7.4–14}$$

Taking the partial derivative of Eq. (7.4–14) with respect to w_{kk} and equating it to zero yields, upon simplification,

$$w_{kk} = \pm \frac{\sqrt{\gamma}}{2\sqrt{\lambda_k}} \tag{7.4–15}$$

where the Lagrange multiplier γ is given by

$$\gamma = 4\left(\prod_{k=1}^{m} \sqrt{\lambda_k}\right)^{2/m} \tag{7.4–16}$$

Combining Eqs. (7.4–15) and (7.4–16) yields

$$w_{kk} = \frac{1}{\sqrt{\lambda_k}}\left(\prod_{j=1}^{m} \sqrt{\lambda_j}\right)^{1/m} \tag{7.4–17}$$

Thus, the weighting matrix $\mathbf{W}$ is given by

$$\mathbf{W} = \left(\prod_{j=1}^{m} \lambda_j\right)^{1/2m} \begin{pmatrix} \lambda_1^{-1/2} & 0 & \cdots & 0 \\ 0 & \lambda_2^{-1/2} & \cdots & 0 \\ \vdots & \vdots & \ddots & \vdots \\ 0 & 0 & \cdots & \lambda_m^{-1/2} \end{pmatrix} \tag{7.4–18}$$

Substituting Eq. (7.4–17) into Eq. (7.4–13) yields the minimum intraset distance as

$$\overline{D^2} = 2m\left(\prod_{k=1}^{m} \lambda_k\right)^{1/m} \tag{7.4–19}$$

This equation implies that $\overline{D^2}$ will be a global minimum if the m smallest eigenvalues are used. Hence, if we want to minimize the intraset distance, the eigenvectors corresponding to the smallest eigenvalues of the covariance matrix $\mathbf{C}_\mathbf{z}$ must be chosen as the feature vectors.

On the other hand, when the constraint $\sum_{k=1}^{m} w_{kk} = 1$ is used, it can be shown that the weighting coefficients are

$$w_{kk} = \left(\sum_{j=1}^{m} \frac{1}{\lambda_j}\right)^{-1} \frac{1}{\lambda_k} \tag{7.4–20}$$

and the minimum intraset distance is given by

$$\overline{D^2} = 2\left(\sum_{j=1}^{m} \frac{1}{\lambda_j}\right)^{-1} \tag{7.4–21}$$

Thus, $\overline{D^2}$ will assume a global minimum when the eigenvalues λ_j are chosen as the m smallest of the n eigenvalues of the covariance matrix $\mathbf{C}_\mathbf{z}$, and the transformation matrix $\mathbf{A}$ is constructed with the corresponding m eigenvectors.

7.5 FEATURE SELECTION THROUGH ENTROPY MINIMIZATION

Entropy is a statistical measure of uncertainty. For a given ensemble of pattern vectors, a good measure of intraset dispersion is the population entropy, given by

$$H = -E_p\{\ln p\} \tag{7.5–1}$$

where p is the probability density of the pattern population, and E_p is the expectation operator with respect to p. The entropy concept can be used as a suitable criterion in the design of optimum feature selection. Features which reduce the uncertainty of a given situation are considered more informative than those which have the opposite effect. Thus, if one views entropy as a measure of uncertainty, a meaningful feature selection criterion is to choose the features which minimize the entropy of the pattern classes under consideration. Since this criterion is equivalent to minimizing the dispersion of the various pattern populations, it is reasonable to expect that the resulting procedure will have clustering properties.

Consider M pattern classes whose populations are governed by the probability densities $p(\mathbf{x}/\omega_1), p(\mathbf{x}/\omega_2), \ldots, p(\mathbf{x}/\omega_M)$. The entropy of the ith population of patterns is, from Eq. (7.5–1), given by

$$H_i = -\int_{\mathbf{x}} p(\mathbf{x}/\omega_i) \ln p(\mathbf{x}/\omega_i)\, d\mathbf{x} \tag{7.5–2}$$

where the integration is taken over the pattern space. It is observed that, if $p(\mathbf{x}/\omega_i) = 1$, indicating no uncertainty, $H_i = 0$, in agreement with the previous interpretation of the entropy concept.

In the following discussion it will be assumed that each of the M pattern populations is characterized by a normal probability density function, $p(\mathbf{x}/\omega_i) \sim N(\mathbf{m}_i, \mathbf{C}_i)$, where $\mathbf{m}_i$ and $\mathbf{C}_i$ are the mean vector and covariance matrix, respectively, of the ith population as discussed in Chapter 4. In addition, it will be assumed that the M covariance matrices describing the statistics of the M pattern classes are identical. This situation arises when each pattern belonging to a class is a random vector formed by the superposition of a random vector on a nonrandom vector. The superimposed random vectors are drawn from the same normal distribution, a situation which arises in many practical applications.

With these assumptions in mind, the basic idea underlying the developments of this section consists of determining a linear transformation matrix

A, which operates on the pattern vectors to yield new vectors of lower dimensionality. This transformation may be written as

$$\mathbf{y} = \mathbf{A}\mathbf{x} \tag{7.5–3}$$

where the transformation matrix is determined by minimizing the population entropies of the various pattern classes under consideration. In Eq. (7.5–3) **x** is an n-vector, **y** is an image m-vector of lower dimensionality than **x**, and **A** is an $m \times n$ matrix. The *rows* of the matrix **A** consist of the selected m feature vectors $\mathbf{a}_1', \mathbf{a}_2', \ldots, \mathbf{a}_k', \ldots, \mathbf{a}_m'$, which are row vectors. Thus, the matrix **A** is given by

$$\mathbf{A} = \begin{pmatrix} \mathbf{a}_1' \\ \mathbf{a}_2' \\ \vdots \\ \mathbf{a}_m' \end{pmatrix} \tag{7.5–4}$$

The problem is how to select the m feature vectors so that the measurement vector **x** is transformed to the image vector **y** while minimizing the entropy function defined by Eq. (7.5–2).

A multivariate normal distribution is completely characterized by its mean vector and covariance matrix. This matrix is, in turn, characterized by its eigenvalues and eigenvectors. The eigenvectors may be regarded as the property vectors of the patterns under consideration. Some of the property vectors carry less information in the pattern recognition sense than others and may therefore be ignored. This phenomenon suggests a feature selection procedure whereby the most significant property vectors are chosen as feature vectors. These feature vectors can then be used to construct the transformation matrix **A**. One approach to the selection of feature vectors making use of the minimum-entropy concept is as follows.

Recalling the assumption that all covariance matrices are equal, and letting $\mathbf{C}_1 = \mathbf{C}_2 = \cdots = \mathbf{C}_M = \mathbf{C}$, we can write the normal probability density of the ith pattern class as

$$p(\mathbf{x}/\omega_i) = \frac{1}{(2\pi)^{n/2}|\mathbf{C}|^{1/2}} \exp[-\tfrac{1}{2}(\mathbf{x} - \mathbf{m}_i)'\mathbf{C}^{-1}(\mathbf{x} - \mathbf{m}_i)] \tag{7.5–5}$$

The mean vector for the image patterns **y**, denoted by $\mathbf{m}_i^*$, is, from Eq. (7.5–3),

$$\mathbf{m}_i^* = \mathbf{A}\mathbf{m}_i \tag{7.5–6}$$

Letting $\mathbf{z} = \mathbf{x} - \mathbf{m}_i$, we obtain from Eq. (7.5–6)

$$\mathbf{y} - \mathbf{m}_i^* = A(\mathbf{x} - \mathbf{m}_i) = A\mathbf{z} \tag{7.5–7}$$

The covariance matrix for the image vectors is then

$$\mathbf{C}^* = E\{(\mathbf{y} - \mathbf{m}_i^*)(\mathbf{y} - \mathbf{m}_i^*)'\} \tag{7.5–8}$$

$$= \mathbf{A}E\{\mathbf{z}\mathbf{z}'\}\mathbf{A}' = \mathbf{A}\mathbf{C}\mathbf{A}' \tag{7.5–9}$$

since $E\{\mathbf{z}\mathbf{z}'\} = E\{(\mathbf{x} - \mathbf{m}_i)(\mathbf{x} - \mathbf{m}_i)'\} = \mathbf{C}$.

From Eqs. (7.5–6) and (7.5–9) the probability density of the image patterns is

$$p(\mathbf{y}/\omega_i) = \frac{1}{(2\pi)^{m/2}|\mathbf{A}\mathbf{C}\mathbf{A}'|^{1/2}} \exp[-\tfrac{1}{2}(\mathbf{y} - \mathbf{m}_i^*)'(\mathbf{A}\mathbf{C}\mathbf{A}')^{-1}(\mathbf{y} - \mathbf{m}_i^*)] \tag{7.5–10}$$

The entropy of the image patterns is then

$$H_i^* = -\int_{\mathbf{y}} p(\mathbf{y}/\omega_i) \ln p(\mathbf{y}/\omega_i)\, d\mathbf{y} \tag{7.5–11}$$

Substituting Eq. (7.5–10) into Eq. (7.5–11) and minimizing with respect to the eigenvectors of $\mathbf{C}$ yields the following result:†

> The entropy function H_i^* is minimized by forming the transformation matrix $\mathbf{A}$ from the m normalized eigenvectors associated with the smallest eigenvalues of the covariance matrix $\mathbf{C}$.

In applying the foregoing result to the formation of the matrix $\mathbf{A}$, the number of vectors utilized should be large enough for the image patterns to carry sufficient discriminatory information.

The difference between feature selection and extraction should be kept clearly in mind. In this section, the selection procedure consists of choosing as features the m eigenvectors of $\mathbf{C}$ which satisfy the above-stated conditions, whereas the extraction procedure consists of determining the eigenvalues and eigenvectors of $\mathbf{C}$ from the training data.

Example: The foregoing procedure will now be illustrated with the aid of a simple example. Assume that the patterns shown in Fig. 7.1(a) are to

† The proof of this result spans several pages of moderately complicated algebra. With our assurance that the omission of this proof will in no way affect his basic understanding of pattern recognition concepts, the interested reader is referred to Tou and Heydorn [1967] for a detailed proof of the above result.

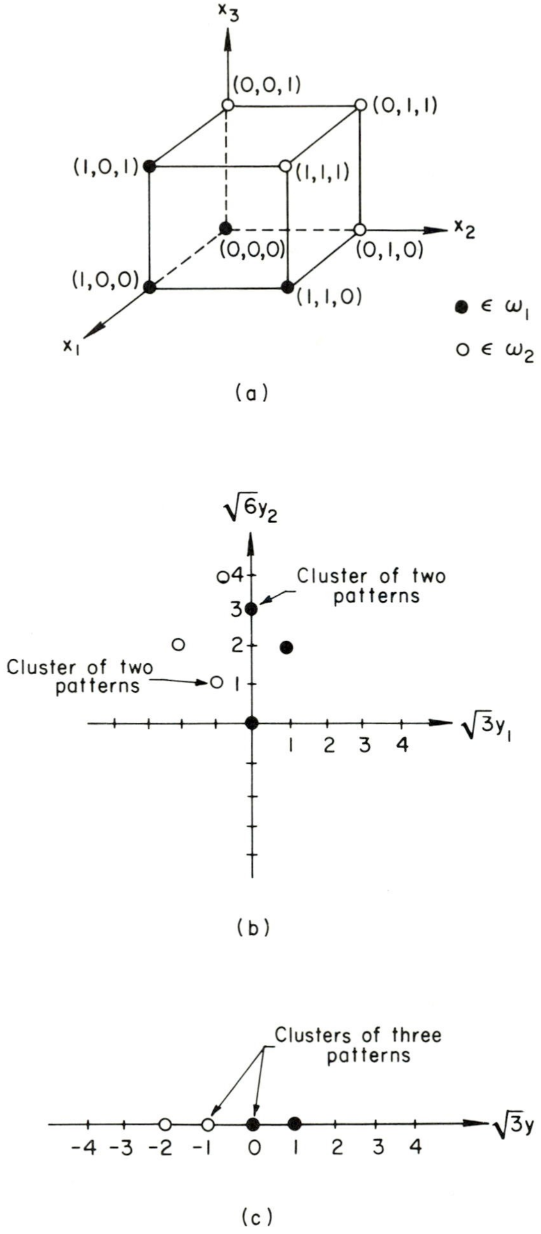

Figure 7.1. Illustration of the minimum-entropy concept. (a) Original patterns. (b) Result of the first transformation. (c) Result of the second transformation

be reduced in dimensionality by means of the minimum-entropy transformation. The patterns of each class are as follows:

$$
\begin{array}{cc}
\omega_1 & \omega_2 \\
\mathbf{x}_{11} = \begin{pmatrix} 0 \\ 0 \\ 0 \end{pmatrix} & \mathbf{x}_{21} = \begin{pmatrix} 0 \\ 0 \\ 1 \end{pmatrix} \\
\mathbf{x}_{12} = \begin{pmatrix} 1 \\ 0 \\ 0 \end{pmatrix} & \mathbf{x}_{22} = \begin{pmatrix} 0 \\ 1 \\ 0 \end{pmatrix} \\
\mathbf{x}_{13} = \begin{pmatrix} 1 \\ 0 \\ 1 \end{pmatrix} & \mathbf{x}_{23} = \begin{pmatrix} 0 \\ 1 \\ 1 \end{pmatrix} \\
\mathbf{x}_{14} = \begin{pmatrix} 1 \\ 1 \\ 0 \end{pmatrix} & \mathbf{x}_{24} = \begin{pmatrix} 1 \\ 1 \\ 1 \end{pmatrix}
\end{array}
$$

where the first number in the subscripts indicates class ω_1 or ω_2.

The reader will recall from Section 4.6 that the estimates of the mean vector and covariance matrix are given by

$$\mathbf{m}_i = \frac{1}{N_i} \sum_{j=1}^{N_i} \mathbf{x}_{ij}$$

and

$$\mathbf{C}_i = \frac{1}{N_i} \sum_{j=1}^{N_i} \mathbf{x}_{ij}\mathbf{x}_{ij}' - \mathbf{m}_i\mathbf{m}_i'$$

where N_i denotes the number of training samples from class ω_i. From these two equations we obtain

$$\mathbf{m}_1 = \frac{1}{4}\begin{pmatrix} 3 \\ 1 \\ 1 \end{pmatrix}, \qquad \mathbf{m}_2 = \frac{1}{4}\begin{pmatrix} 1 \\ 3 \\ 3 \end{pmatrix}$$

and

$$\mathbf{C} = \mathbf{C}_1 = \mathbf{C}_2 = \frac{1}{16}\begin{pmatrix} 3 & 1 & 1 \\ 1 & 3 & -1 \\ 1 & -1 & 3 \end{pmatrix}$$

The eigenvalues of $\mathbf{C}$ are

$$\lambda_1 = \tfrac{1}{16}, \qquad \lambda_2 = \lambda_3 = \tfrac{1}{4}$$

Since the covariance matrix is symmetrical, it is always possible to find a set of real orthogonal eigenvectors, regardless of the multiplicity of the eigenvalues. The normalized eigenvectors corresponding to these eigenvalues are as follows:

$$\mathbf{e}_1 = \frac{1}{\sqrt{3}}\begin{pmatrix} 1 \\ -1 \\ -1 \end{pmatrix}, \qquad \mathbf{e}_2 = \frac{1}{\sqrt{6}}\begin{pmatrix} 2 \\ 1 \\ 1 \end{pmatrix}, \qquad \mathbf{e}_3 = \frac{1}{\sqrt{2}}\begin{pmatrix} 0 \\ 1 \\ -1 \end{pmatrix}$$

where $\mathbf{e}_1$, $\mathbf{e}_2$, and $\mathbf{e}_3$ correspond to λ_1, λ_2, and λ_3, respectively. Choosing $\mathbf{e}_1$ and $\mathbf{e}_2$ yields the following transformation matrix:

$$\mathbf{A} = \begin{pmatrix} \mathbf{e}_1' \\ \mathbf{e}_2' \end{pmatrix} = \begin{pmatrix} 1/\sqrt{3} & -1/\sqrt{3} & -1/\sqrt{3} \\ 2/\sqrt{6} & 1/\sqrt{6} & 1/\sqrt{6} \end{pmatrix}$$

Choosing $\mathbf{e}_1$ and $\mathbf{e}_3$ would have been equally valid since $\mathbf{e}_2$ and $\mathbf{e}_3$ correspond to identical eigenvalues.

The image patterns obtained from $\mathbf{y} = \mathbf{A}\mathbf{x}$ are

$$\begin{array}{cc} \omega_1 & \omega_2 \\ \mathbf{y}_{11} = \begin{pmatrix} 0 \\ 0 \end{pmatrix} & \mathbf{y}_{21} = \begin{pmatrix} -1/\sqrt{3} \\ 1/\sqrt{6} \end{pmatrix} \\ \mathbf{y}_{12} = \begin{pmatrix} 1/\sqrt{3} \\ 2/\sqrt{6} \end{pmatrix} & \mathbf{y}_{22} = \begin{pmatrix} -1/\sqrt{3} \\ 1/\sqrt{6} \end{pmatrix} \\ \mathbf{y}_{13} = \begin{pmatrix} 0 \\ 3/\sqrt{6} \end{pmatrix} & \mathbf{y}_{23} = \begin{pmatrix} -2/\sqrt{3} \\ 2/\sqrt{6} \end{pmatrix} \\ \mathbf{y}_{14} = \begin{pmatrix} 0 \\ 3/\sqrt{6} \end{pmatrix} & \mathbf{y}_{24} = \begin{pmatrix} -1/\sqrt{3} \\ 4/\sqrt{6} \end{pmatrix} \end{array}$$

The reduced patterns are shown in Fig. 7.1(b). It is interesting to observe the clustering effect produced by the transformation. The reader may easily verify that the same basic results are obtained if $\mathbf{e}_1$ and $\mathbf{e}_2$ are reversed in $\mathbf{A}$. The only effect is that the components of the vector $\mathbf{y}$ are also reversed.

Further reductions are possible if $\mathbf{A}$ is formed by considering only the eigenvector $\mathbf{e}_1$:

$$\mathbf{A} = \mathbf{e}_1' = \frac{1}{\sqrt{3}} \begin{pmatrix} 1 \\ -1 \\ -1 \end{pmatrix}'$$

Applying this transformation to the original patterns yields the new image patterns:

ω_1	ω_2
$y_{11} = 0$	$y_{21} = -1/\sqrt{3}$
$y_{12} = 1/\sqrt{3}$	$y_{22} = -1/\sqrt{3}$
$y_{13} = 0$	$y_{23} = -2/\sqrt{3}$
$y_{14} = 0$	$y_{24} = -1/\sqrt{3}$

The reduced patterns are shown in Fig. 7.1(c). The clustering effect produced by the minimum-entropy transformation is again evident in this figure. ●

7.6 FEATURE SELECTION THROUGH ORTHOGONAL EXPANSIONS

The minimum-entropy concept developed in the preceding section is based on the assumption that the pattern classes under consideration are normally distributed. When this assumption is not valid, the method of orthogonal expansion offers an alternative approach to the feature selection problem. We will make use of the Karhunen-Loève (K-L) expansion in carrying out feature selection. The principal advantage of this expansion is that it does not require knowledge of the various probability densities. In addition, the K-L expansion possesses two optimal properties which make it a meaningful criterion for feature selection, as will be seen below.

Before discussing the K-L expansion, we give a brief review of the Fourier series expansion to point out the analogies. The K-L expansion is presented first in terms of continuous patterns and then extended to cover the more useful discrete case. Attention is focused on the latter case because of its significance in terms of digital computation and pattern recognition.

7.6.1 Review of the Fourier Series Expansion

A stationary periodic random process with period T can be expanded in a Fourier series:

$$x(t) = \sum_{n=-\infty}^{\infty} x_n \exp(jn\omega_0 t) \tag{7.6–1}$$

where $\omega_0 = 2\pi/T$ is the angular frequency, and

$$x_n = \frac{1}{T} \int_0^T x(t) \exp(-jn\omega_0 t)\, dt \tag{7.6–2}$$

are the Fourier coefficients, which are random variables. For different sample functions, Eq. (7.6–2) yields, in general, different values for x_n. If the whole ensemble of sample functions is considered, Eq. (7.6–2) defines x_n as a random variable. The integral in Eq. (7.6–2) exists with probability 1. It can be shown that

$$x(t) = \lim_{N\to\infty} \left(\sum_{k=-N}^{N} x_k \exp(jk\omega_0 t) \right)$$

The requirement for the random process to be periodic guarantees that x_n and x_m, $n \neq m$, are uncorrelated. Using Eq. (7.6–2), we have

$$E\{x_n \tilde{x}_m\} = \frac{1}{T^2} E\left\{ \int_0^T \int_0^T x(t)\tilde{x}(s) \exp(-jn\omega_0 t) \exp(jm\omega_0 s)\, ds\, dt \right\}$$

$$= \frac{1}{T^2} \int_0^T \int_0^T R(t-s) \exp[j\omega_0(ms - nt)]\, ds\, dt \tag{7.6–3}$$

where $\tilde{x}$ denotes the complex conjugate of x, and

$$R(t-s) = E\{x(t)\tilde{x}(s)\}$$

is the correlation function. Since $R(\tau)$, where $\tau = t - s$, is periodic, it can be written as

$$R(\tau) = \sum_{k=-\infty}^{\infty} b_k \exp(jk\omega_0 \tau) \tag{7.6–4}$$

From Eqs. (7.6–3) and (7.6–4),

$$E\{x_n \tilde{x}_m\} = \frac{1}{T^2} \int_0^T \int_0^T \sum_{k=-\infty}^{\infty} b_k \exp[jk\omega_0(t-s)] \exp[j\omega_0(ms - nt)]\, ds\, dt$$

$$= \frac{1}{T^2} \sum_{k=-\infty}^{\infty} b_k \int_0^T \exp[j\omega_0(m-k)s]\, ds \int_0^T \exp[j\omega_0(k-n)t]\, dt$$

$$= \begin{cases} b_n & \text{if} \quad n = m \\ 0 & \text{if} \quad n \neq m \end{cases} \tag{7.6–5}$$

Equation (7.6–5) points out not only that x_n and x_m are uncorrelated for $n \neq m$, but also that the nth Fourier coefficient of the correlation function $R(\tau)$ is equal to the variance of the nth random Fourier coefficient of $x(t)$. This is analogous to the situation in the deterministic case. For a periodic function $x(t)$, the nth coefficient of its correlation function $R(\tau)$ is equal to the square of the nth Fourier coefficient of $x(t)$.

If the stationary process is periodic, the random Fourier coefficients x_n and x_m, $n \neq m$, are uncorrelated. Conversely, it can be shown that, in order for the coefficients to be uncorrelated, the process must be periodic. If the given random process is not periodic, the correlation function cannot be written so simply in terms of the variances of the Fourier coefficient of $x(t)$.

7.6.2 Karhunen-Loève Expansion

A nonperiodic random process cannot be expressed as a Fourier series with uncorrelated random coefficients, but it can be expanded in a series of orthogonal functions $\phi_n(t)$ with uncorrelated coefficients. This operation is often referred to as the Karhunen-Loève expansion.

A nonperiodic random process $x(t)$ in an interval $[a, b]$ may be expanded into

$$x(t) = \sum_{n=1}^{\infty} \gamma_n x_n \phi_n(t), \quad a \leqslant t \leqslant b \tag{7.6–6}$$

where

$$\int_a^b \phi_n(t)\tilde{\phi}_m(t)\, dt = \begin{cases} 1 & \text{if} \quad m = n \\ 0 & \text{if} \quad m \neq n \end{cases} \tag{7.6–7}$$

$$E\{x_n \tilde{x}_m\} = \begin{cases} 1 & \text{if} \quad m = n \\ 0 & \text{if} \quad m \neq n \end{cases} \tag{7.6–8}$$

and the γ_n are real or complex numbers. This is called an orthogonal expansion of the random process in the given interval. For a stationary periodic process, such an expansion is given with $\phi_n(t) = (1/T)\exp(jn\omega_0 t)$ and $\gamma_n x_n$ equal to the corresponding random Fourier coefficients. If the periodicity condition is dropped, Eq. (7.6–8) is no longer true with $\phi_n(t) = (1/T)\exp(jn\omega_0 t)$.

The orthogonal functions $\phi_n(t)$ and the numbers γ_n are determined as follows. Suppose that Eqs. (7.6–6) through (7.6–8) are satisfied for some set of functions $\phi_n(t)$, some set of numbers γ_n, and some set of random variables x_n. Then the correlation function $R(t, s)$ is given by

$$\begin{aligned} R(t, s) &= E\{x(t)x(s)\} \\ &= E\{\sum_n \gamma_n x_n \phi_n(t) \sum_k \tilde{\gamma}_k \tilde{x}_k \tilde{\phi}_k(s)\} \\ &= \sum_n |\gamma_n|^2 \phi_n(t)\tilde{\phi}_n(t) \end{aligned} \tag{7.6–9}$$

where t and s are in the interval $[a, b]$. It is noted that, since the random process is assumed to be nonperiodic, we can no longer express the correlation function as $R(t - s)$.

Using Eq. (7.6–9), we obtain

$$\int_a^b R(t, s)\phi_k(s)\, ds = \sum_n |\gamma_n|^2 \phi_n(t) \int_a^b \phi_k(s)\tilde{\phi}_n(s)\, ds \tag{7.6–10}$$

Making use of Eq. (7.6–7) gives

$$\int_a^b R(t, s)\phi_k(s)\, ds = |\gamma_k|^2 \phi_k(t) \tag{7.6–11}$$

In the language of integral equations, the numbers $|\gamma_k|^2$ are the eigenvalues and the functions $\phi_k(t)$ are the eigenfunctions of the familiar integral equation whose general form is

$$\int_a^b R(t, s)\phi(s)\, ds = \lambda\phi(t) \tag{7.6–12}$$

where $a \leqslant t \leqslant b$. Determination of γ_n and $\phi_n(t)$ requires the solution of this integral equation. Conversely, we can construct an orthogonal expansion, valid over any given interval $a \leqslant t \leqslant b$, for a random process with a continuous correlation function by using for the γ's and $\phi(t)$'s of Eqs. (7.6–6) through (7.6–8) the positive square roots of eigenvalues and the eigenfunctions of Eq. (7.6–12).

We now apply the above concepts to pattern recognition work. Consider M pattern classes $\omega_1, \omega_2, \ldots, \omega_M$, where the patterns are real, continuous random functions, and let $x_i(t)$, $T_1 \leqslant t \leqslant T_2$, $i = 1, 2, \ldots, M$, represent observations from any one of these M classes. Then $x_i(t)$ can be expanded as a linear combination of known basis functions $\phi_j(t)$ as follows:

$$x_i(t) = \sum_{j=1}^{\infty} c_{ij}\phi_j(t), \quad T_1 \leqslant t \leqslant T_2, \quad i = 1, 2, \ldots, M \qquad (7.6\text{–}13)$$

where the c_{ij}'s are *random* coefficients satisfying the condition $E\{c_{ij}\} = 0$. The practical implications of this assumption will be discussed in the next section. The basis functions $\phi_j(t)$ are assumed to be a set of deterministic orthonormal functions over the interval $T_1 \leqslant t \leqslant T_2$.

The autocorrelation function over the M pattern classes is defined as

$$R(t, s) = \sum_{i=1}^{M} p(\omega_i)E\{x_i(t)\, x_i(s)\} \qquad (7.6\text{–}14)$$

where $p(\omega_i)$ is the *a priori* probability of occurrence of the ith pattern class, and $E\{x_i(t)x_i(s)\}$ indicates the expectation operator over *all* observations from this class. Since the quantity $E\{x_i(t)x_i(s)\}$ is recognized as the usual definition of the autocorrelation function, it is seen that Eq. (7.6–14) represents an "average" autocorrelation function which takes into account the fact that the random functions $x_i(t)$ may arise from more than one source, that is, there are M sources or classes from which these functions can originate. It has been shown that both formulations of the autocorrelation function lead to the same optimal properties (to be discussed below) of the K-L expansion. From a pattern recognition point of view, however, only the formulation given by Eq. (7.6–14) is considered meaningful since it takes into account the existence of more than one pattern class, whereas the quantity $E\{x_i(t)x_i(s)\}$ is confined to random functions of a unique origin in the pattern recognition sense.

Substitution of Eq. (7.6–13) into Eq. (7.6–14) yields the relation

$$R(t, s) = \sum_{i=1}^{M} p(\omega_i)E\left\{\sum_{j=1}^{\infty} c_{ij}\phi_j(t) \sum_{k=1}^{\infty} c_{ik}\phi_k(s)\right\} \qquad (7.6\text{–}15)$$

Observe the change of index in the expansion of $x_i(s)$. Since the basis functions are deterministic, Eq. (7.6–15) may be written as

$$R(t, s) = \sum_{i=1}^{M} p(\omega_i) \sum_{j=1}^{\infty} \sum_{k=1}^{\infty} \phi_j(t)\phi_k(s)E\{c_{ij}c_{ik}\}$$

$$= \sum_{j=1}^{\infty} \sum_{k=1}^{\infty} \phi_j(t)\phi_k(s) \sum_{i=1}^{M} p(\omega_i)E\{c_{ij}c_{ik}\} \tag{7.6–16}$$

Assume that the random coefficients are statistically independent in the sense that

$$\sum_{i=1}^{M} p(\omega_i)E\{c_{ij}c_{ik}\} = \begin{cases} \lambda_j & \text{if } j = k \\ 0 & \text{if } j \neq k \end{cases} \tag{7.6–17}$$

where λ_j is a constant greater than zero. Under these conditions, Eq. (7.6–16) becomes

$$R(t, s) = \sum_{j=1}^{\infty} \lambda_j \phi_j(t)\, \phi_j(s) \tag{7.6–18}$$

Multiplying both sides of Eq. (7.6–18) by $\phi_k(s)$ and integrating over the interval of orthonormality yields

$$\int_{T_1}^{T_2} R(t, s)\phi_k(s)\, ds = \int_{T_1}^{T_2} \sum_{j=1}^{\infty} \lambda_j \phi_j(t)\, \phi_j(s)\, \phi_k(s)\, ds \tag{7.6–19}$$

Interchanging the order of summation and integration yields

$$\int_{T_1}^{T_2} R(t, s)\phi_k(s)\, ds = \sum_{j=1}^{\infty} \lambda_j \phi_j(t) \int_{T_1}^{T_2} \phi_j(s)\, \phi_k(s)\, ds \tag{7.6–20}$$

In view of the assumed orthonormality of the basis functions, Eq. (7.6–20) reduces to the integral equation

$$\int_{T_1}^{T_2} R(t, s)\phi_k(s)\, ds = \lambda_k \phi_k(t) \tag{7.6–21}$$

The expansion given in Eq. (7.6–13), where the basis functions are determined from (7.6–20) or (7.6–21) and the autocorrelation function is calculated according to (7.6–14), is known as the *generalized* K-L *expansion*. The term "generalized" is used to indicate that $R(t, s)$ is calculated from Eq. (7.6–14) rather than from $E\{x_i(t)x_i(s)\}$, which is the normal definition of the autocorrelation function.

The K-L expansion possesses the following optimal properties: (1) it minimizes the mean-square error when only a finite number of basis functions are used in the expansion given in Eq. (7.6–13), and (2) it minimizes the entropy function defined in terms of the average squared coefficients used in the expansion. The first property is important because it guarantees that no other expansion will yield a lower approximation error in the mean-square sense. The significance of the second property is that it associates with the coefficients of the expansion a measure of minimum entropy or dispersion. As will be seen in the following discussion, these coefficients play the role of components of image vectors similar to the **y**-vectors of the transformation $\mathbf{y} = \mathbf{Ax}$ discussed in Section 7.5. Therefore, because of its minimum-entropy property, we expect the K-L expansion to be characterized by clustering transformational properties.

The Discrete Case

If the functions $x_i(t)$ are uniformly sampled in the interval $T_1 \leqslant t \leqslant T_2$, they may be represented in the following vector form:

$$\mathbf{x}_i = \begin{pmatrix} x_i(t_1) \\ x_i(t_2) \\ \vdots \\ x_i(t_n) \end{pmatrix} \tag{7.6–22}$$

where n is the number of samples taken in the interval of definition of $x_i(t)$. Equation (7.6–13) then becomes the finite sum

$$\mathbf{x}_i = \sum_{j=1}^{n} c_{ij}\boldsymbol{\phi}_j \tag{7.6–23}$$

where the coefficients are assumed to satisfy $E\{c_{ij}\} = 0$, and $\boldsymbol{\phi}_j$ is the vector

$$\boldsymbol{\phi}_j = \begin{pmatrix} \phi_j(t_1) \\ \phi_j(t_2) \\ \vdots \\ \phi_j(t_n) \end{pmatrix} \tag{7.6–24}$$

If the coefficients are represented in the following vector form:

$$\mathbf{c}_i = \begin{pmatrix} c_{i1} \\ c_{i2} \\ \vdots \\ c_{ij} \\ \vdots \\ c_{in} \end{pmatrix} \tag{7.6–25}$$

where $E\{\mathbf{c}_i\} = \mathbf{0}$, Eq. (7.6–23) may be expressed in the more convenient matrix notation,

$$\mathbf{x}_i = \mathbf{\Phi c}_i \tag{7.6–26}$$

where $\mathbf{\Phi}$ is the matrix

$$\mathbf{\Phi} = (\boldsymbol{\phi}_1 \quad \boldsymbol{\phi}_2 \quad \cdots \quad \boldsymbol{\phi}_n) \tag{7.6–27}$$

The discrete analog of the autocorrelation function of Eq. (7.6–14) is the autocorrelation matrix, defined as

$$\mathbf{R} = \sum_{i=1}^{M} p(\omega_i) E\{\mathbf{x}_i \mathbf{x}_i'\} \tag{7.6–28}$$

Substituting Eq. (7.6–26) for $\mathbf{x}_i$ yields

$$\begin{aligned} \mathbf{R} &= \sum_{i=1}^{M} p(\omega_i) E\{\mathbf{\Phi c}_i \mathbf{c}_i' \mathbf{\Phi}'\} \\ &= \mathbf{\Phi} \left(\sum_{i=1}^{M} p(\omega_i) E\{\mathbf{c}_i \mathbf{c}_i'\} \right) \mathbf{\Phi}' \end{aligned} \tag{7.6–29}$$

where the second step follows from the deterministic nature of the matrix $\mathbf{\Phi}$.

If we now require that

$$\sum_{i=1}^{M} p(\omega_i) E\{\mathbf{c}_i \mathbf{c}_i'\} = \mathbf{D}_\lambda \tag{7.6–30}$$

where $\mathbf{D}_\lambda$ is the diagonal matrix

$$\mathbf{D}_\lambda = \begin{pmatrix} \lambda_1 & 0 & \cdots & 0 \\ 0 & \lambda_2 & \cdots & 0 \\ \vdots & \vdots & \ddots & \vdots \\ 0 & 0 & \cdots & \lambda_n \end{pmatrix} \tag{7.6–31}$$

then Eq. (7.6–29) reduces to

$$\mathbf{R} = \mathbf{\Phi D}_\lambda \mathbf{\Phi}' \tag{7.6–32}$$

If the basis vectors $\boldsymbol{\phi}_j$ are assumed to be orthonormal, postmultiplying Eq. (7.6–32) by the matrix $\mathbf{\Phi}$ yields

$$\begin{aligned} \mathbf{R\Phi} &= \mathbf{\Phi D}_\lambda \mathbf{\Phi}'\mathbf{\Phi} \\ &= \mathbf{\Phi D}_\lambda \end{aligned} \tag{7.6–33}$$

since $\mathbf{\Phi}'\mathbf{\Phi} = \mathbf{I}$ because of the assumed orthonormality of the basis vectors composing $\mathbf{\Phi}$.

In view of Eq. (7.6–33), it is evident that

$$\mathbf{R}\boldsymbol{\phi}_j = \lambda_j \boldsymbol{\phi}_j \tag{7.6–34}$$

which is the discrete analog of (7.6–21).

From Eq. (7.6–34) and the definition of eigenvalues and eigenvectors, we see that the jth basis vector used in the expansion given in Eq. (7.6–23) is simply the eigenvector of the correlation matrix corresponding to the jth eigenvalue. Since the basis vectors are the eigenvectors of a real symmetric matrix, they are mutually orthogonal. If, in addition, they are orthonormalized, then

$$\boldsymbol{\phi}_j'\boldsymbol{\phi}_k = \begin{cases} 1 & \text{if} \quad j = k \\ 0 & \text{if} \quad j \neq k \end{cases} \tag{7.6–35}$$

which was the condition leading to Eq. (7.6–33). On the basis of this property, the coefficients of the expansion may be obtained as follows:

$$\mathbf{\Phi c}_i = \mathbf{x}_i, \qquad \mathbf{\Phi}'\mathbf{\Phi c}_i = \mathbf{\Phi}'\mathbf{x}_i, \qquad \mathbf{c}_i = \mathbf{\Phi}'\mathbf{x}_i \tag{7.6–36}$$

It can be verified by direct substitution that these coefficients satisfy the condition stated in Eq. (7.6–30). In addition, we see from Eq. (7.6–36) that the condition $E\{\mathbf{c}_i\} = \mathbf{0}$ has the alternative interpretation

$$E\{\mathbf{c}_i\} = E\{\mathbf{\Phi}'\mathbf{x}_i\} = \mathbf{\Phi}'E\{\mathbf{x}_i\} = \mathbf{0} \tag{7.6–37}$$

which indicates that the assumption $E\{\mathbf{c}_i\} = \mathbf{0}$ is automatically satisfied if the various pattern populations are characterized by zero statistical means.

The discrete version of the generalized K-L expansion consists of Eq. (7.6–23) or (7.6–26), where the basis vectors are the orthonormal eigenvectors of the correlation matrix given in Eq. (7.6–28). The coefficients of the expansion are determined from Eq. (7.6–36). The application of these concepts to feature selection is discussed in the next section.

Application of the Discrete K-L Expansion to Feature Selection

The motivations for using the discrete K-L expansion as a tool for feature selection are based on the optimum properties discussed earlier. In the discrete case, the least-mean-square-error property implies that the K-L expansion minimizes the approximation error when fewer than n basis vectors are used in the expansion given by Eq. (7.6–23) or (7.6–26).† The minimum-entropy property has the desirable clustering effects observed in the method developed in the Section 7.5.

The application of the discrete K-L expansion to feature selection may be viewed as a linear transformation. If we consider

$$\mathbf{\Phi} = (\boldsymbol{\phi}_1 \quad \boldsymbol{\phi}_2 \quad \cdots \quad \boldsymbol{\phi}_m), \quad m < n \tag{7.6–38}$$

to be the transformation matrix, then, from Eqs. (7.6–36), the image patterns are the *coefficients* of the K-L expansion, that is, for any pattern $\mathbf{x}_i$ of class ω_i we know from Eqs. (7.6–36) that

$$\mathbf{c}_i = \mathbf{\Phi}'\mathbf{x}_i$$

Since $\mathbf{\Phi}'$ is an $m \times n$ matrix and $\mathbf{x}$ is an n-vector, we see that, if $m < n$, the $\mathbf{c}_i$ are image vectors of lower dimensionality.

It can be shown that the optimum properties of the K-L expansion are satisfied if the *columns* of the transformation matrix $\mathbf{\Phi}$ are chosen as the m *normalized* eigenvectors corresponding to the largest eigenvalues of the correlation matrix $\mathbf{R}$.

The above notation can be expressed in the same form as that developed in Section 7.5 simply by defining a matrix

$$\mathbf{A} = \mathbf{\Phi}' = \begin{pmatrix} \boldsymbol{\phi}_1' \\ \boldsymbol{\phi}_2' \\ \vdots \\ \boldsymbol{\phi}_m' \end{pmatrix} \tag{7.6–39}$$

where the *rows* of $\mathbf{A}$ are now the normalized eigenvectors corresponding to

---

† This error is given by

$$\mathbf{e} = \mathbf{x}_i - \sum_{j=1}^{m} c_{ij}\boldsymbol{\phi}_j$$

where, in general, $m < n$. We see from Eq. (7.6–23) that, if $m = n$, the error is zero.

the largest eigenvalues of $\mathbf{R}$. If we let $\mathbf{y} = \mathbf{c}$, then, for any vector $\mathbf{x}$, the reduced image vectors are given by

$$\mathbf{y} = \mathbf{A}\mathbf{x}$$

as before.

The foregoing results may be summarized as follows:

1. Compute the correlation matrix $\mathbf{R}$ from the patterns of the training set, as indicated in Eq. (7.6–28).
2. Obtain the eigenvalues and corresponding eigenvectors of $\mathbf{R}$. Normalize the eigenvectors.
3. Form the transformation matrix $\mathbf{\Phi}$ from the m eigenvectors corresponding to the largest eigenvalues of $\mathbf{R}$, as indicated in Eq. (7.6–38).
4. Compute the coefficients of the expansion from Eq. (7.6–36). These coefficients represent the reduced image patterns.

The condition $E\{\mathbf{c}_i\} = \mathbf{0}$ or its equivalent, $E\{\mathbf{x}_i\} = \mathbf{0}$, must be satisfied for the K-L expansion to yield optimal results. As was previously mentioned, this condition is automatically satisfied if the various pattern classes are characterized by zero means. If this is not the case, only suboptimum results may be expected from the K-L expansion. Although it may appear at first that this problem can be circumvented by centralizing the patterns of each class about their respective means, the reader is reminded that in a pattern recognition problem the origin of patterns (except, generally, during the training phase) is not known. Although it is true that the patterns of the training set could be centralized before being used to estimate the correlation matrix, this approach would be meaningless since it would imply altering the characteristics of the pattern classes under consideration. Of course, the special case in which all pattern classes possess identical means presents no difficulties since all patterns, regardless of their origin, would be centralized about the same mean during both the training and the recognition phases.

Although the assumption that all pattern populations must share identical means is certainly a limitation of the K-L expansion, one should not conclude that this approach to feature selection is without merit. Assumptions such as this are characteristic of most statistical methods of analysis. The success of any given method depends simply on how closely the data under consideration conform to the basic assumptions underlying the development of the statistical technique.

Example: As a simple illustration of the use of the discrete K-L expansion, consider the patterns shown in Fig. 7.2:

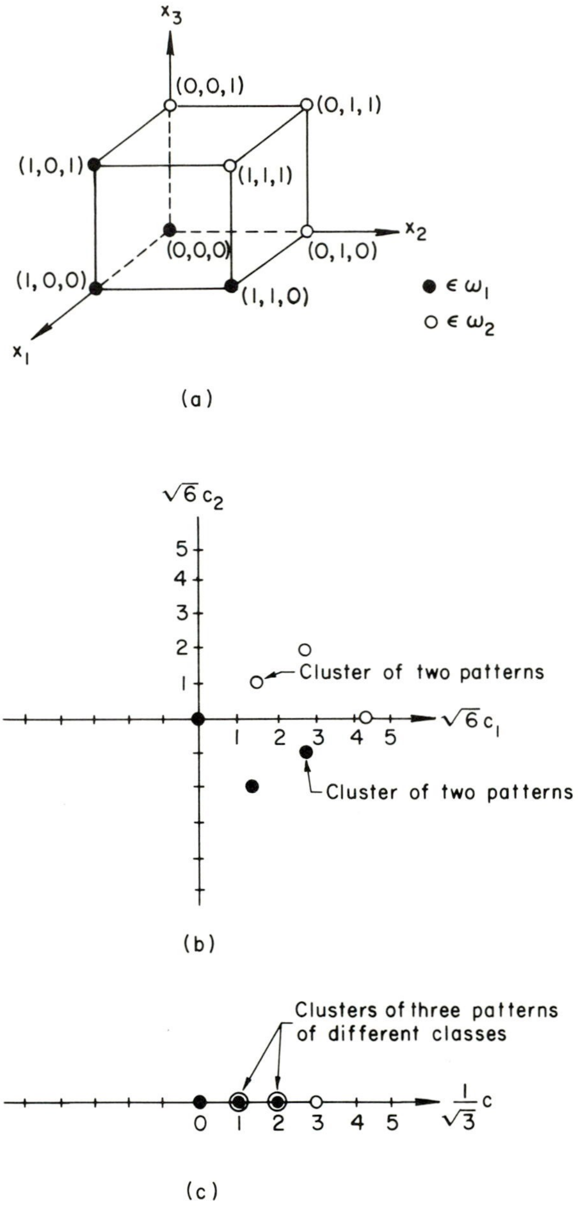

Figure 7.2. Illustration of the K-L expansion. (a) Original patterns. (b) Patterns reduced to two dimensions. (c) Patterns reduced to one dimension

$$\begin{array}{cc} \omega_1 & \omega_2 \\ \mathbf{x}_{11} = \begin{pmatrix}0\\0\\0\end{pmatrix} & \mathbf{x}_{21} = \begin{pmatrix}0\\0\\1\end{pmatrix} \\ \mathbf{x}_{12} = \begin{pmatrix}1\\0\\0\end{pmatrix} & \mathbf{x}_{22} = \begin{pmatrix}0\\1\\0\end{pmatrix} \\ \mathbf{x}_{13} = \begin{pmatrix}1\\0\\1\end{pmatrix} & \mathbf{x}_{23} = \begin{pmatrix}0\\1\\1\end{pmatrix} \\ \mathbf{x}_{14} = \begin{pmatrix}1\\1\\0\end{pmatrix} & \mathbf{x}_{24} = \begin{pmatrix}1\\1\\1\end{pmatrix} \end{array}$$

where the first subscript identifies the class, and the second the pattern number. Assuming $p(\omega_1) = p(\omega_2) = \frac{1}{2}$, we have

$$\mathbf{R} = \sum_{i=1}^{2} p(\omega_i) E\{\mathbf{x}_i \mathbf{x}_i'\}$$

$$= \tfrac{1}{2} E\{\mathbf{x}_1 \mathbf{x}_1'\} + \tfrac{1}{2} E\{\mathbf{x}_2 \mathbf{x}_2'\}$$

where $E\{\mathbf{x}_1\mathbf{x}_1'\}$ and $E\{\mathbf{x}_2\mathbf{x}_2'\}$ indicate expectations over all patterns of classes ω_1 and ω_2, respectively. Carrying out these operations as discussed in Section 4.6 yields

$$R = \frac{1}{8} \sum_{j=1}^{4} \mathbf{x}_{1j}\mathbf{x}_{1j}' + \frac{1}{8} \sum_{j=1}^{4} \mathbf{x}_{2j}\mathbf{x}_{2j}'$$

$$= \frac{1}{8}\begin{pmatrix}3 & 1 & 1\\ 1 & 1 & 0\\ 1 & 0 & 1\end{pmatrix} + \frac{1}{8}\begin{pmatrix}1 & 1 & 1\\ 1 & 3 & 2\\ 1 & 2 & 3\end{pmatrix}$$

$$= \frac{1}{4}\begin{pmatrix}2 & 1 & 1\\ 1 & 2 & 1\\ 1 & 1 & 2\end{pmatrix}$$

The eigenvalues and corresponding normalized eigenvectors of $\mathbf{R}$ are

$$\lambda_1 = 1, \qquad \mathbf{e}_1 = \frac{1}{\sqrt{3}}\begin{pmatrix} 1 \\ 1 \\ 1 \end{pmatrix}$$

$$\lambda_2 = \tfrac{1}{4}, \qquad \mathbf{e}_2 = \frac{1}{\sqrt{6}}\begin{pmatrix} -2 \\ 1 \\ 1 \end{pmatrix}$$

$$\lambda_3 = \tfrac{1}{4}, \qquad \mathbf{e}_3 = \frac{1}{\sqrt{2}}\begin{pmatrix} 0 \\ 1 \\ -1 \end{pmatrix}$$

Choosing $\mathbf{e}_1$ and $\mathbf{e}_2$, which correspond to the largest eigenvalues, results in the following transformation matrix:

$$\mathbf{\Phi} = \begin{pmatrix} 1/\sqrt{3} & -2/\sqrt{6} \\ 1/\sqrt{3} & 1/\sqrt{6} \\ 1/\sqrt{3} & 1/\sqrt{6} \end{pmatrix}$$

Using the transformation $\mathbf{c} = \mathbf{\Phi}'\mathbf{x}$, we obtain the image patterns:

$$\begin{array}{ll} \omega_1 & \omega_2 \\ \mathbf{c}_{11} = \begin{pmatrix} 0 \\ 0 \end{pmatrix} & \mathbf{c}_{21} = \frac{1}{\sqrt{6}}\begin{pmatrix} \sqrt{2} \\ 1 \end{pmatrix} \\ \mathbf{c}_{12} = \frac{1}{\sqrt{6}}\begin{pmatrix} \sqrt{2} \\ -2 \end{pmatrix} & \mathbf{c}_{22} = \frac{1}{\sqrt{6}}\begin{pmatrix} \sqrt{2} \\ 1 \end{pmatrix} \\ \mathbf{c}_{13} = \frac{1}{\sqrt{6}}\begin{pmatrix} 2\sqrt{2} \\ -1 \end{pmatrix} & \mathbf{c}_{23} = \frac{1}{\sqrt{6}}\begin{pmatrix} 2\sqrt{2} \\ 2 \end{pmatrix} \\ \mathbf{c}_{14} = \frac{1}{\sqrt{6}}\begin{pmatrix} 2\sqrt{2} \\ -1 \end{pmatrix} & \mathbf{c}_{24} = \frac{1}{\sqrt{6}}\begin{pmatrix} 3\sqrt{2} \\ 0 \end{pmatrix} \end{array}$$

These image patterns are shown in Fig. 7.2(b). Observe the clustering effect and also the fact that the linear separability of the patterns has not been affected.

If the patterns are reduced to one dimension by using the transformation matrix with the eigenvector corresponding to the largest eigenvalue,

$$\mathbf{\Phi} = \frac{1}{\sqrt{3}}\begin{pmatrix}1\\1\\1\end{pmatrix}$$

we obtain the image points:

$$\begin{array}{ll} \omega_1 & \omega_2 \\ c_{11} = 0 & c_{21} = \sqrt{3} \\ c_{12} = \sqrt{3} & c_{22} = \sqrt{3} \\ c_{13} = 2\sqrt{3} & c_{23} = 2\sqrt{3} \\ c_{14} = 2\sqrt{3} & c_{24} = 3\sqrt{3} \end{array}$$

These patterns are shown in Fig. 7.2(c). We see in this figure that several patterns of different classes overlap, a condition which makes the last transformation undesirable.

It is interesting to note that the minimum-entropy transformation was considerably more successful in this case than the K-L expansion transformation. This comparison again underscores the important fact that the merits of a given feature selection technique are determined by the problem under consideration. ●

7.7 FEATURE SELECTION THROUGH FUNCTIONAL APPROXIMATION

If the features of a pattern class can be characterized by a function $f(\mathbf{x})$ which is determined on the basis of observed data, the process of feature selection can be viewed as a problem of functional approximation. During the training phase we obtain the values of the feature function $f(\mathbf{x})$ at the sample pattern points $\mathbf{x}_1, \mathbf{x}_2, \ldots, \mathbf{x}_N$. We wish to seek an approximation $\hat{f}(\mathbf{x})$ to $f(\mathbf{x})$ such that a certain performance criterion is optimized. There are various methods for the determination of functional approximations. In this section we introduce the method of functional expansion, the method of stochastic approximation, and the method of kernel approximation for the determination of approximate feature functions.

7.7.1 Functional Expansion

Given M pattern classes, let $f_i(\mathbf{x})$ represent the feature function of the ith class. In the determination of an approximation function $\hat{f}_i(\mathbf{x})$, a meaningful performance criterion is that the weighted sum of the squares of the errors at these observed points be a minimum. This error criterion may be written as

$$e_i = \sum_{k=1}^{N_i} \{u_i(\mathbf{x}_{ik})[f_i(\mathbf{x}_{ik}) - \hat{f}_i(\mathbf{x}_{ik})]^2\}, \quad i = 1, 2, \ldots, M \tag{7.7–1}$$

where $\mathbf{x}_{ik}$ represents the kth pattern from the ith class, N_i is the number of patterns in this class, and $u_i(\mathbf{x}_{ik})$ are some positive weights associated with the pattern vectors $\mathbf{x}_{ik}$. Now the problem becomes the determination of an approximate feature function $\hat{f}_i(\mathbf{x})$ for each pattern class such that the M error functions in Eq. (7.7–1) are minimized.

The approximation function $\hat{f}_i(\mathbf{x})$ may be expressed as a linear combination of basis functions in the form

$$\hat{f}_i(\mathbf{x}) = \sum_{j=1}^{m_i} c_{ij}\phi_{ij}(\mathbf{x}) = \mathbf{c}_i'\boldsymbol{\phi}_i(\mathbf{x}) \tag{7.7–2}$$

In this equation,

$$\boldsymbol{\phi}_i(\mathbf{x}) = \begin{pmatrix} \phi_{i1}(\mathbf{x}) \\ \phi_{i2}(\mathbf{x}) \\ \vdots \\ \phi_{ij}(\mathbf{x}) \\ \vdots \\ \phi_{im_i}(\mathbf{x}) \end{pmatrix} \tag{7.7–3}$$

and

$$\mathbf{c}_i = \begin{pmatrix} c_{i1} \\ c_{i2} \\ \vdots \\ c_{ij} \\ \vdots \\ c_{im_i} \end{pmatrix} \tag{7.7–4}$$

where m_i is the number of terms used in the approximation of the ith feature function, and the $\{\phi_{ij}(\mathbf{x})\}$ are linearly independent functions over the discrete observations $\mathbf{x}_{i1}, \mathbf{x}_{i2}, \ldots, \mathbf{x}_{iN_i}$. In view of Eq. (7.7–2), the approximate functional value $\hat{f}_i(\mathbf{x}_{ik})$ depends on the coefficients c_{ij}, $j = 1, 2, \ldots, m_i$, with $m_i < N_i$. If m_i equaled N_i, the error would be reduced to zero, but then the number of terms in the expansion would equal the number of patterns in class ω_i. The minimum of e_i may be determined by taking the partial derivatives with respect to c_{ij}. The conditions for a minimum:

$$\frac{\partial e_i}{\partial c_{ij}} = 0, \quad i = 1, 2, \ldots, M; \quad j = 1, 2, \ldots, m_i \tag{7.7–5}$$

provide a set of algebraic equations for the determination of the expansion coefficients. Once the functions $\phi_{ij}(\mathbf{x})$ are preselected and the coefficients computed, the approximate feature function $\hat{f}_i(\mathbf{x})$ follows from Eq. (7.7–1).

Substituting Eq. (7.7–2) into (7.7–1) and carrying out the partial differentiation yields

$$\frac{\partial e_i}{\partial c_{ij}} = -\sum_{k=1}^{N_i}\left\{2u_i(\mathbf{x}_{ik})\left[f_i(\mathbf{x}_{ik}) - \sum_{j=1}^{m_i} c_{ij}\phi_{ij}(\mathbf{x}_{ik})\right]\phi_{ij}(\mathbf{x}_{ik})\right\} \tag{7.7–6}$$

Equating the partial derivative to zero and simplifying yields

$$\sum_{k=1}^{N_i} u_i(\mathbf{x}_{ik})\phi_{ij}(\mathbf{x}_{ik})\left[\sum_{j=1}^{m_i} c_{ij}\phi_{ij}(\mathbf{x}_{ik})\right] = \sum_{k=1}^{N_i} u_i(\mathbf{x}_{ik})\phi_{ij}(\mathbf{x}_{ik})f_i(\mathbf{x}_{ik}), \qquad i = 1, 2, \ldots, M \tag{7.7–7}$$

Expressing Eq. (7.7–7) in matrix form results in the following condition for a minimum:

$$\mathbf{B}_i\mathbf{c}_i = \mathbf{v}_i \tag{7.7–8}$$

where $\mathbf{B}_i$ is an $m_i \times m_i$ positive-definite symmetric matrix with elements

$$b_{lq} = \sum_{k=1}^{N_i} u_i(\mathbf{x}_{ik})\phi_{il}(\mathbf{x}_{ik})\phi_{iq}(\mathbf{x}_{ik}) \tag{7.7–9}$$

and $\mathbf{v}_i$ is an m_i-vector with components

$$v_{il} = \sum_{k=1}^{N_i} u_i(\mathbf{x}_{ik})\phi_{il}(\mathbf{x}_{ik})f_i(\mathbf{x}_{ik}) \tag{7.7–10}$$

Since it has been assumed that the basis functions $\phi_{ij}(\mathbf{x})$ are linearly independent over the patterns of class ω_i, to show that $\mathbf{B}_i$ possesses an inverse is not difficult. Therefore, the coefficients of the expansion are given by

$$\mathbf{c}_i = \mathbf{B}_i^{-1}\mathbf{v}_i, \quad i = 1, 2, \ldots, M \tag{7.7–11}$$

The computation of these coefficients may be simplified by choosing the functions $\phi_{ij}(\mathbf{x})$ so that they are orthogonal with respect to the weight factors $u_i(\mathbf{x}_{ik})$. Then these functions satisfy the conditions

$$\sum_{k=1}^{N_i} u_i(\mathbf{x}_{ik})\phi_{il}(\mathbf{x}_{ik})\phi_{iq}(\mathbf{x}_{ik}) = 0, \quad l \neq q \tag{7.7–12}$$

and the matrix $\mathbf{B}_i$ is therefore reduced to diagonal form, considerably simplifying the calculation of $\mathbf{B}_i^{-1}$. Under the condition expressed in Eq. (7.7–12), the coefficients of the expansion become

$$c_{ij} = \frac{\sum_{k=1}^{N_i} u_i(\mathbf{x}_{ik})\phi_{ij}(\mathbf{x}_{ik})f_i(\mathbf{x}_{ik})}{\sum_{k=1}^{N_i} u_i(\mathbf{x}_{ik})\phi_{ij}^2(\mathbf{x}_{ik})} \tag{7.7–13}$$

or, in vector form,

$$\mathbf{c}_i = \mathbf{B}_{iD}^{-1}\mathbf{v}_i \tag{7.7–14}$$

where $\mathbf{B}_{iD}$ is a diagonal matrix with elements

$$b_{ll} = \frac{1}{\sum_{k=1}^{N_i} u_i(\mathbf{x}_{ik})\phi_{il}^2(\mathbf{x}_{ik})} \tag{7.7–15}$$

If, in addition, the functions $\phi_{ij}(\mathbf{x})$ are chosen to be orthonormal with respect to the weight factors, then

$$c_{ij} = \sum_{k=1}^{N_i} u_i(\mathbf{x}_{ik})\phi_{ij}(\mathbf{x}_{ik})f_i(\mathbf{x}_{ik}) \tag{7.7–16}$$

and, since $\mathbf{B} = \mathbf{I}$ under this condition, we have from Eq. (7.7–11) that

$$\mathbf{c}_i = \mathbf{I}\mathbf{v}_i = \mathbf{v}_i \tag{7.7–17}$$

The above approach to feature selection is motivated by the Weierstrass approximation theorem, which, as indicated in Section 2.7.3, states that any function which is continuous in a closed interval can be uniformly approximated within any prescribed tolerance over that interval by some polynomial. In this case, the features of each class are simply the coefficient vectors $\mathbf{c}_i$, $i = 1, 2, \ldots, M$. The selection process consists of choosing enough coefficients so that the errors defined in Eq. (7.7–1) are sufficiently small. Referring to Eq. (7.7–13) or (7.7–16), we note that the coefficients are independent of the dimensionality of the vectors $\boldsymbol{\phi}_i(\mathbf{x})$. Consequently, if the sum of the square of the errors at the observed pattern points is not small enough, we may obtain a higher-order approximation by introducing an extra term $c_{i,m_i+1}\phi_{i,m_i+1}(\mathbf{x})$, where $\phi_{i,m_i+1}(\mathbf{x})$ is another orthogonal or orthonormal function. Furthermore, all the previously determined coefficients $c_{i1}, c_{i2}, \ldots, c_{im_i}$ remain unchanged. We merely add the new term to the approximation.

Example: Consider the following observations of the feature functions of two classes at the sample points indicated:

ω_1		ω_2	
$\mathbf{x}_{11} = \begin{pmatrix} 1 \\ 0 \end{pmatrix}$,	$f_1(\mathbf{x}_{11}) = 1$	$\mathbf{x}_{22} = \begin{pmatrix} 1 \\ 2 \end{pmatrix}$,	$f_2(\mathbf{x}_{21}) = -2$
$\mathbf{x}_{12} = \begin{pmatrix} 2 \\ -5 \end{pmatrix}$,	$f_1(\mathbf{x}_{12}) = 2$	$\mathbf{x}_{22} = \begin{pmatrix} 2 \\ 3 \end{pmatrix}$,	$f_2(\mathbf{x}_{22}) = -1$
$\mathbf{x}_{13} = \begin{pmatrix} 5 \\ 2 \end{pmatrix}$,	$f_1(\mathbf{x}_{13}) = 0$	$\mathbf{x}_{23} = \begin{pmatrix} -4 \\ 2 \end{pmatrix}$,	$f_3(\mathbf{x}_{23}) = -1$

It is desired to obtain the approximate feature functions $\hat{f}_1(\mathbf{x})$ and $\hat{f}_2(\mathbf{x})$ by the methods of this section.

The first step in the solution of this problem consists of selecting an appropriate set of basis functions. Letting x_1 and x_2 represent the first and second components of the general vector $\mathbf{x} = (x_1, x_2)'$, we can easily verify that the following basis functions:

$$\phi_{11}(\mathbf{x}) = \phi_{21}(\mathbf{x}) = x_1, \qquad \phi_{12}(\mathbf{x}) = \phi_{22}(\mathbf{x}) = x_2$$

are orthogonal with respect to weighting coefficients $u_i(\mathbf{x}_{ik}) = 1$ for all values of k in each class. Observe that, in this case, the basis functions for each class are identical, and that they are equal in number. This need not be the case in general, as is evident from the previous development. The basis functions used here are purely for demonstration purposes.

The coefficients of the expansion are given by Eq. (7.7–13) since no effort has been made to orthogonalize the basis functions. Using this equation with $u_i(\mathbf{x}_{ik}) = 1$ results in the following expansion coefficients:

$$c_{11} = \frac{\sum_{k=1}^{3} \phi_{11}(\mathbf{x}_{1k}) f_1(\mathbf{x}_{1k})}{\sum_{k=1}^{3} \phi_{11}(\mathbf{x}_{1k})} = \frac{1}{6}$$

$$c_{12} = -\frac{10}{29}, \qquad c_{21} = 0, \qquad c_{22} = -\frac{9}{17}$$

where, for example, $\phi_{11}(\mathbf{x}_{11})$ is numerically equal to the first component of $\mathbf{x}_{11}$, according to the definition of this basis function.

The approximate feature functions are given by Eq. (7.7–2):

$$\hat{f}_1(\mathbf{x}) = c_{11}\phi_{11}(\mathbf{x}) + c_{12}\phi_{12}(\mathbf{x}) = \tfrac{1}{6}x_1 - \tfrac{10}{29}x_2$$

$$\hat{f}_2(\mathbf{x}) = c_{21}\phi_{21}(\mathbf{x}) + c_{22}\phi_{22}(\mathbf{x}) = -\tfrac{9}{17}x_2$$

Observe that these functions still retain the property that $\hat{f}_1(\mathbf{x})$ is nonnegative upon substitution of any pattern from class ω_1 and that $\hat{f}_2(\mathbf{x})$ assumes negative values upon substitution of patterns from class ω_2.

The error introduced by using less than three basis functions for each pattern class can be obtained from Eq. (7.7–1). It should be pointed out, however, that the approximation error does not provide a direct index by which to measure the performance of the resulting feature functions. In many situations, relatively large errors can be tolerated in the approximations without introducing any degeneracy in the performance of the pattern recognition system. ●

7.7.2 Stochastic Approximation Formulation

When the observed values of the feature functions $f_i(\mathbf{x})$ at the sample points $\mathbf{x}_{ik}$, $k = 1, 2, \ldots, n_i$, are random variables characterized by the probability density functions $p_i(\mathbf{x}) = p(\mathbf{x}/\omega_i)$, we cannot use the error criterion given in Eq. (7.7–1) to determine the approximation functions $\hat{f}_i(\mathbf{x})$. In this situation a convenient criterion to choose is the expected value of some convex function of the deviation of $\hat{f}_i(\mathbf{x})$ from $f_i(\mathbf{x})$. Such an error criterion may be expressed as

$$e_i = \int_{\mathbf{x}\in\omega_i} G_i[f_i(\mathbf{x}) - \hat{f}_i(\mathbf{x})]p(\mathbf{x}/\omega_i)\,d\mathbf{x}, \quad i = 1, 2, \ldots, M \qquad (7.7\text{–}18)$$

where $G_i[f_i(\mathbf{x}) - \hat{f}_i(\mathbf{x})]$ are convex functions, such as $|f_i(\mathbf{x}) - \hat{f}_i(\mathbf{x})|$ and $[f_i(\mathbf{x}) - \hat{f}_i(\mathbf{x})]^2$. The problem of feature selection becomes the determination of the best approximation $\hat{f}_i(\mathbf{x})$, which minimizes the error criterion given in Eq. (7.7–18).

If $f_i(\mathbf{x})$ is expressed as a linear combination of basis functions, substitution of Eq. (7.7–2) into (7.7–18) yields

$$e_i = \int_{\mathbf{x}\in\omega_i} G_i[f_i(\mathbf{x}) - \mathbf{c}_i'\boldsymbol{\phi}_i(\mathbf{x})]p(\mathbf{x}/\omega_i)\,d\mathbf{x}, \quad i = 1, 2, \ldots, M \qquad (7.7\text{–}19)$$

Carrying out the minimization procedure with respect to the coefficients yields the relation

$$\frac{\partial e_i}{\partial c_{ij}} = \int_{\mathbf{x}\in\omega_i} g_i[f_i(\mathbf{x}) - \mathbf{c}_i'\boldsymbol{\phi}_i(\mathbf{x})]\phi_{ij}(\mathbf{x})p(\mathbf{x}/\omega_i)\,d\mathbf{x} = 0$$

$$i = 1, 2, \ldots, M; \quad j = 1, 2, \ldots, m_i \tag{7.7–20}$$

where

$$g_i[f_i(\mathbf{x}) - \mathbf{c}_i'\boldsymbol{\phi}_i(\mathbf{x})] = \frac{\partial}{\partial c_{ij}} G_i[f_i(\mathbf{x}) - \mathbf{c}_i'\boldsymbol{\phi}_i(\mathbf{x})].$$

For a given value of i, Eq. (7.7–20) provides a system of m_i equations for the determination of the coefficients c_{ij}. Since Eq. (7.7–20) involves an unknown probability density, the solution can be obtained by the method of stochastic approximation discussed in Chapter 6.

Invoking the method of stochastic approximation, we obtain the solution to Eq. (7.7–20), given by the following recursive algorithm:

$$c_{ij}(k+1) = c_{ij}(k) + \alpha_k g_i[f_i(\mathbf{x}_k) - \mathbf{c}_i'(k)\boldsymbol{\phi}_i(\mathbf{x}_k)]\phi_{ij}(\mathbf{x}_k)$$

$$i = 1, 2, \ldots, M; \quad j = 1, 2, \ldots, m_i \tag{7.7–21}$$

where $c_{ij}(k)$ is the value of the coefficient c_{ij} at the kth iteration, $\mathbf{c}_i(k)$ is the coefficient vector at the kth iteration, and α_k is a member of the sequence $\{\alpha_k, k = 1, 2, \ldots\}$, which satisfies the conditions

$$\alpha_k > 0, \quad \sum_{k=1}^{\infty} \alpha_k = \infty, \quad \sum_{k=1}^{\infty} \alpha_k^2 < \infty \tag{7.7–22}$$

as was indicated in Eq. (6.2–5). The algorithm given by Eq. (7.7–21) provides a procedure for making successive experiments in such a way that the coefficients will tend toward the solution of Eq. (7.7–20) in probability if the number of iterations approaches infinity. In other words, if we let the solution coefficients be represented by c_{ij}^*, $i = 1, 2, \ldots, M$; $j = 1, 2, \ldots, m_i$, then

$$\lim_{k\to\infty} \{E[c_{ij}(k) - c_{ij}^*]^2\} = 0 \tag{7.7–23}$$

and

$$\text{Prob}\,\{\lim_{k\to\infty} c_{ij}(k) = c_{ij}^*\} = 1 \tag{7.7–24}$$

The initial values of the coefficients used in initiating the recursive algorithm are chosen arbitrarily.

As a specific case of Eq. (7.7–21), assume that the absolute value of the deviation of $\hat{f}_i(\mathbf{x})$ from $f_i(\mathbf{x})$ is chosen as the function for G_i, that is,

$$G_i[f_i(\mathbf{x}) - \hat{f}_i(\mathbf{x})] = |f_i(\mathbf{x}) - \mathbf{c}_i'\boldsymbol{\phi}_i(\mathbf{x})| \tag{7.7–25}$$

Then, since

$$\frac{\partial}{\partial c_{ij}} G_i[f_i(\mathbf{x}) - \mathbf{c}_i'\boldsymbol{\phi}_i(\mathbf{x})] = \operatorname{sgn}[f_i(\mathbf{x}_{ik}) - \mathbf{c}_i'(k)\boldsymbol{\phi}_i(\mathbf{x}_{ik})] \tag{7.7–26}$$

the recursive algorithm becomes

$$c_{ij}(k+1) = c_{ij}(k) + \alpha_k \operatorname{sgn}[\mathbf{c}_i'(k)\boldsymbol{\phi}_i(\mathbf{x}_{ik}) - f_i(\mathbf{x}_{ik})]\phi_{ij}(\mathbf{x}_{ik}) \tag{7.7–27}$$

If the square of the deviation of $\hat{f}_i(\mathbf{x})$ from $f_i(\mathbf{x})$ is chosen for G_i, then

$$G_i[f_i(\mathbf{x}) - \hat{f}_i(\mathbf{x})] = [f_i(\mathbf{x}) - \mathbf{c}_i'\boldsymbol{\phi}_i(\mathbf{x})]^2 \tag{7.7–28}$$

and the recursive algorithm is given by

$$c_{ij}(k+1) = c_{ij}(k) + 2\alpha_k[f_i(\mathbf{x}_{ik}) - \mathbf{c}_i'(k)\boldsymbol{\phi}_i(\mathbf{x}_{ik})]\phi_{ij}(\mathbf{x}_{ik}) \tag{7.7–29}$$

These recursive algorithms provide a convenient scheme for the determination of the approximate statistical feature functions from observed pattern samples.

7.7.3 Kernel Approximation

Statistical feature functions may be determined from the observed pattern samples by the method of kernel approximation. It can be shown that an approximation $\hat{f}_i(\mathbf{x})$ to the statistical feature function $f_i(\mathbf{x})$ is given by

$$\hat{f}_i(\mathbf{x}) = \int_{\mathbf{y}\in\omega_i} K_{in}(\mathbf{x}, \mathbf{y}) f(\mathbf{y})\, d\mathbf{y} \tag{7.7–30}$$

where $K_{in}(\mathbf{x}, \mathbf{y})$ is a known kernel which satisfies the following conditions:

(a) $$\int_a^b K_{in}(\mathbf{x}, \mathbf{y})\, d\mathbf{y} = 1$$

(b) $$\lim_{n\to\infty} K_{in}(\mathbf{x}, \mathbf{y}) = \delta(\mathbf{x}, \mathbf{y}) \text{ (Kronecker delta)}$$

(c) $$K_{in}(\mathbf{x}, \mathbf{y}) \geqslant 0$$

(d) $$K_{in}(\mathbf{x}, \mathbf{y}) = K_{in}(\mathbf{y}, \mathbf{x}) \tag{7.7–31}$$

Among the kernels which satisfy these conditions are the Fejer kernel, the Jackson kernel, and the Weierstrass kernel. By the strong law of large numbers the approximation functions $\hat{f}_i(\mathbf{x})$ can be estimated from the independent pattern samples by using the relationship

$$\hat{f}_{ik}(\mathbf{x}) = \frac{1}{k} \sum_{j=1}^{k} K_{in}(\mathbf{x}, \mathbf{x}_j) \tag{7.7–32}$$

where $\hat{f}_{ik}(\mathbf{x})$ converges to $\hat{f}_i(\mathbf{x})$ with probability 1 as k approaches infinity, and $\hat{f}_i(\mathbf{x})$ converges to $f_i(\mathbf{x})$ uniformly as n approaches infinity.

The quality of approximation given by Eq. (7.7–30) depends on the nature of the kernels $K_{in}(\mathbf{x}, \mathbf{y})$. For high-quality approximations $K_{in}(\mathbf{x}, \mathbf{y})$ must be "tuned" to the value of $f_i(\mathbf{y})$ for $\mathbf{y} = \mathbf{x}$. The three kernels mentioned above possess this type of behavior.

7.7.4 Use of Feature Functions in Classification

The functions $\hat{f}_i(\mathbf{x})$, $i = 1, 2, \ldots, M$, obtained by any of the methods discussed above, can serve as the basis for classification and recognition. Once the feature functions have been determined from the training data, a simple classification scheme can be mechanized as follows: For an unknown pattern $\mathbf{x}^*$, the functions $\hat{f}_i(\mathbf{x}^*)$, $i = 1, 2, \ldots, M$, are computed and the unknown is assigned to the class whose feature function yields the largest value. The success of this scheme depends on the relative distribution of the various pattern classes and, of course, on the number of terms used to approximate the feature functions.

7.8 DIVERGENCE CONCEPT

Divergence is a measure of "distance" or dissimilarity between two classes. It can be used to determine feature ranking and to evaluate the effectiveness of class discrimination. In this section we present the concept of divergence and discuss its application in determining the effectiveness of feature selection and ordering.

Let the probability of occurrence of pattern $\mathbf{x}$, given that it belongs to class ω_i, be $p_i(\mathbf{x}) = p(\mathbf{x}/\omega_i)$, and the probability of occurrence of pattern $\mathbf{x}$, given that it belongs to class ω_j, be $p_j(\mathbf{x}) = p(\mathbf{x}/\omega_j)$. Then the discriminating information for class ω_i versus class ω_j may be measured by the logarithm of the likelihood ratio

$$u_{ij} = \ln \frac{p_i(\mathbf{x})}{p_j(\mathbf{x})} \tag{7.8–1}$$

The average discriminating information for class ω_i is then given by

$$I(i, j) = \int_{\mathbf{x}} p_i(\mathbf{x}) \ln \frac{p_i(\mathbf{x})}{p_j(\mathbf{x})} \, d\mathbf{x} \tag{7.8–2}$$

The discriminating information for class ω_j versus class ω_i may be measured by the logarithm of the likelihood ratio

$$u_{ji} = \ln \frac{p_j(\mathbf{x})}{p_i(\mathbf{x})} \tag{7.8–3}$$

The average discriminating information for class ω_j is given by

$$I(j, i) = \int_{\mathbf{x}} p_j(\mathbf{x}) \ln \frac{p_j(\mathbf{x})}{p_i(\mathbf{x})} \, d\mathbf{x} \tag{7.8–4}$$

The total average information for discriminating class ω_i from class ω_j is often referred to as *divergence*, which is given by

$$\begin{aligned} J_{ij} &= I(i, j) + I(j, i) \\ &= \int_{\mathbf{x}} [p_i(\mathbf{x}) - p_j(\mathbf{x})] \ln \frac{p_i(\mathbf{x})}{p_j(\mathbf{x})} \, d\mathbf{x} \end{aligned} \tag{7.8–5}$$

Suppose that we have two pattern classes characterized by two n-variate normal populations

$$N(\mathbf{m}_i, \mathbf{C}_i) \qquad \text{and} \qquad N(\mathbf{m}_j, \mathbf{C}_j)$$

where $\mathbf{m}_i$ and $\mathbf{m}_j$ are the mean vectors, and $\mathbf{C}_i$ and $\mathbf{C}_j$ are $n \times n$ covariance matrices. The population densities are

$$p_i(\mathbf{x}) = \frac{1}{(2\pi)^{n/2}|\mathbf{C}_i|^{1/2}} \exp[-\tfrac{1}{2}(\mathbf{x} - \mathbf{m}_i)'\mathbf{C}_i^{-1}(\mathbf{x} - \mathbf{m}_i)] \tag{7.8–6}$$

and

$$p_j(x) = \frac{1}{(2\pi)^{n/2}|\mathbf{C}_j|^{1/2}} \exp[-\tfrac{1}{2}(\mathbf{x} - \mathbf{m}_j)'\mathbf{C}_j^{-1}(\mathbf{x} - \mathbf{m}_j)] \tag{7.8–7}$$

from which we obtain the logarithm of the likelihood ratio as

$$u_{ij} = \tfrac{1}{2} \ln \frac{|\mathbf{C}_j|}{|\mathbf{C}_i|} - \tfrac{1}{2} \operatorname{tr} [\mathbf{C}_i^{-1}(\mathbf{x} - \mathbf{m}_i)(\mathbf{x} - \mathbf{m}_i)']$$

$$+ \tfrac{1}{2} \operatorname{tr} [\mathbf{C}_j^{-1}(\mathbf{x} - \mathbf{m}_j)(\mathbf{x} - \mathbf{m}_j)'] \tag{7.8–8}$$

The average information for discrimination between these two classes is

$$I(i, j) = \int_{\mathbf{X}} p_i(x_1, x_2, \ldots, x_n) \ln \frac{p_i(x_1, x_2, \ldots, x_n)}{p_j(x_1, x_2, \ldots, x_n)} \, dx_1 \, dx_2 \cdots dx_n$$

$$= \tfrac{1}{2} \ln \frac{|\mathbf{C}_j|}{|\mathbf{C}_i|} + \tfrac{1}{2} \operatorname{tr} [\mathbf{C}_i(\mathbf{C}_j^{-1} - \mathbf{C}_i^{-1})]$$

$$+ \tfrac{1}{2} \operatorname{tr} [\mathbf{C}_j^{-1}(\mathbf{m}_i - \mathbf{m}_j)(\mathbf{m}_i - \mathbf{m}_j)'] \tag{7.8–9}$$

Hence, the divergence for these two classes is

$$J_{ij} = \int_{\mathbf{X}} [p_i(x_1, x_2, \ldots, x_n) - p_j(x_1, x_2, \ldots, x_n)] \ln \frac{p_i(x_1, x_2, \ldots, x_n)}{p_j(x_1, x_2, \ldots, x_n)} \, dx_1 \, dx_2 \cdots dx_n$$

$$= \tfrac{1}{2} \operatorname{tr} [(\mathbf{C}_i - \mathbf{C}_j)(\mathbf{C}_j^{-1} - \mathbf{C}_i^{-1})]$$

$$+ \tfrac{1}{2} \operatorname{tr} [(\mathbf{C}_i^{-1} + \mathbf{C}_j^{-1})(\mathbf{m}_i - \mathbf{m}_j)(\mathbf{m}_i - \mathbf{m}_j)'] \tag{7.8–10}$$

Two special cases are of particular interest.

Case 1. Equal covariance matrices: $\mathbf{C}_i = \mathbf{C}_j = \mathbf{C}$.
It follows from Eq. (7.8–9) that

$$I(i, j) = \tfrac{1}{2} \operatorname{tr} [\mathbf{C}^{-1}(\mathbf{m}_i - \mathbf{m}_j)(\mathbf{m}_i - \mathbf{m}_j)']$$

$$= \tfrac{1}{2} \operatorname{tr} (\mathbf{C}^{-1}\boldsymbol{\delta}\boldsymbol{\delta}')$$

$$= \tfrac{1}{2}\boldsymbol{\delta}'\mathbf{C}^{-1}\boldsymbol{\delta} \tag{7.8–11}$$

and

$$J_{ij} = \operatorname{tr} [\mathbf{C}^{-1}(\mathbf{m}_i - \mathbf{m}_j)(\mathbf{m}_i - \mathbf{m}_j)']$$

$$= \boldsymbol{\delta}'\mathbf{C}^{-1}\boldsymbol{\delta} \tag{7.8–12}$$

where $\boldsymbol{\delta} = \mathbf{m}_i - \mathbf{m}_j$. It is noted that $\boldsymbol{\delta}'\mathbf{C}^{-1}\boldsymbol{\delta}$ is a Mahalanobis generalized distance.

For a univariate normal population, $n = 1$,

$$I(i, j) = \frac{1}{2} \frac{(\mu_i - \mu_j)^2}{\sigma^2}$$

and

$$J_{ij} = \frac{(\mu_i - \mu_j)^2}{\sigma^2}$$

in which μ_i and μ_j are the means, and σ^2 is the variance.

Case 2. Equal population means: $\mathbf{m}_i = \mathbf{m}_j$, $\boldsymbol{\delta} = \mathbf{0}$.

The average information for discrimination and the divergence are given by

$$I(i, j) = \tfrac{1}{2}\ln\frac{|\mathbf{C}_j|}{|\mathbf{C}_i|} + \tfrac{1}{2}\,\mathrm{tr}\,[\mathbf{C}_i(\mathbf{C}_j^{-1} - \mathbf{C}_i^{-1})]$$

$$= \tfrac{1}{2}\ln\frac{|\mathbf{C}_j|}{|\mathbf{C}_i|} + \tfrac{1}{2}\,\mathrm{tr}\,(\mathbf{C}_i\mathbf{C}_j^{-1}) - \frac{n}{2} \tag{7.8-13}$$

and

$$J_{ij} = \tfrac{1}{2}\,\mathrm{tr}\,[(\mathbf{C}_i - \mathbf{C}_j)(\mathbf{C}_j^{-1} - \mathbf{C}_i^{-1})]$$

$$= \tfrac{1}{2}\,\mathrm{tr}\,[\mathbf{C}_i\mathbf{C}_j^{-1}] + \mathrm{tr}\,[\mathbf{C}_j\mathbf{C}_i^{-1}] - n \tag{7.8-14}$$

respectively.

The divergence possesses the following useful properties.

1. $J_{ij} > 0$ for $i \neq j$.
2. $J_{ij} = 0$ for $i = j$.
3. $J_{ij} = J_{ji}$.
4. J_{ij} is additive for independent measurements:

$$J_{ij}(x_1, x_2, \ldots, x_m) = \sum_{k=1}^{m} J_{ij}(x_k)$$

5. Adding a new measurement never decreases the divergence:

$$J_{ij}(x_1, x_2, \ldots, x_m) \leqslant J_{ij}(x_1, x_2, \ldots, x_m, x_{m+1})$$

The additive property of divergence implies that, if the measurements are independent, the divergence based on m measurements is equal to the sum of the m divergences based on each measurement separately. This property may be utilized to determine the relative importance of each of the various features to be selected. The features which will lead to a large divergence are more important ones, since they carry more discriminatory information. Thus, we may rank the importance of each feature according to its associated divergence. Any feature that makes a small contribution to the total divergence may be discarded. The divergence concept provides us with a convenient way to order and select features.

In the following discussions, we make use of the divergence concept to study the effect of feature selection on recognition system performance. We first establish the relationship between error probability and divergence and then derive recursive expressions for selecting features to meet the minimum divergence requirement for a specified error probability.

It was shown in Chapter 4 that when a zero-one loss function is chosen the condition for a pattern $\mathbf{x}$ to belong to class ω_i in the sense of minimum probability of misclassification is

$$p(\omega_i)p(\mathbf{x}/\omega_i) > p(\omega_j)p(\mathbf{x}/\omega_j) \tag{7.8–15}$$

for all $j \neq i$. For the case of equal *a priori* probabilities of occurrence of patterns from both classes, the decision boundary is defined by

$$p_i(\mathbf{x}) = p_j(\mathbf{x}) \tag{7.8–16}$$

For a normal distribution with equal covariance matrices, we obtain from Eq. (7.8–8) the decision boundary

$$u_{ij} = \mathbf{x}'\mathbf{C}^{-1}(\mathbf{m}_i - \mathbf{m}_j) - \tfrac{1}{2}(\mathbf{m}_i + \mathbf{m}_j)'\mathbf{C}^{-1}(\mathbf{m}_i - \mathbf{m}_j) = 0 \tag{7.8–17}$$

The decision rules are $\mathbf{x} \in \omega_i$ if $u_{ij} > 0$, and $\mathbf{x} \in \omega_j$ if $u_{ij} < 0$.

The error probability is given by

$$e_{ij} = \tfrac{1}{2}p(u_{ij} > 0/\omega_j) + \tfrac{1}{2}p(u_{ij} < 0/\omega_i) \tag{7.8–18}$$

It has also been shown in Chapter 4 that

$$e_{ij} = p(e) = \int_{(1/2)\sqrt{r_{ij}}}^{\infty} \frac{1}{\sqrt{2\pi}} \exp\left(-\frac{y^2}{2}\right) dy \tag{7.8–19}$$

where

$$\begin{aligned} r_{ij} &= (\mathbf{m}_i - \mathbf{m}_j)'\mathbf{C}^{-1}(\mathbf{m}_i - \mathbf{m}_j) \\ &= \boldsymbol{\delta}'\mathbf{C}^{-1}\boldsymbol{\delta} \end{aligned} \tag{7.8–20}$$

denotes the Mahalanobis distance between two probability densities, $p_i(\mathbf{x})$ and $p_j(\mathbf{x})$. Comparing Eqs. (7.8–12) and (7.8–20), we have, for equal covariances,

$$r_{ij} = J_{ij} \tag{7.8–21}$$

which is the divergence for classes ω_i and ω_j. Hence, the divergence is an appropriate "distance" between pairs of normal distributions and is a measure of the difficulty of discriminating between two classes. When the covariance matrix $\mathbf{C}$ is the identity matrix, J_{ij} represents the squared distance between the means of $p_i(\mathbf{x})$ and $p_j(\mathbf{x})$. From Eq. (7.8–19), we observe that the error probability e_{ij} is a monotonically decreasing function of r_{ij}, and that the function which relates r_{ij} to e_{ij} is the univariate normal distribution with zero mean and unit variance.

When m features are selected, the effectiveness measure may be determined by $r_{ij}(m)$. With an additional feature taken, the effectiveness measure is given by $r_{ij}(m + 1)$. Then the incremental effectiveness due to the addition of a feature is

$$r_{ij}(m + 1) - r_{ij}(m)$$

Let the additional feature variable be x_{m+1}, which has mean μ_i or μ_j and variance σ^2; and let $\mathbf{v}$ be the vector covariance between x_{m+1} and the elements of $\mathbf{x}$. Then the new mean vectors and new covariance matrix are

$$\mathbf{m}_i^{\mathrm{v}} = \begin{pmatrix} \mathbf{m}_i \\ \mu_i \end{pmatrix} \tag{7.8–22}$$

$$\mathbf{m}_j^{\mathrm{v}} = \begin{pmatrix} \mathbf{m}_j \\ \mu_j \end{pmatrix} \tag{7.8–23}$$

and

$$\mathbf{C}_{\mathrm{v}} = \begin{pmatrix} \mathbf{C} & \mathbf{v} \\ \mathbf{v}' & \sigma^2 \end{pmatrix} \tag{7.8–24}$$

The inverse of the new covariance matrix is

$$\mathbf{C}_{\mathrm{v}}^{-1} = \begin{pmatrix} \mathbf{C}^{-1} + \boldsymbol{\beta}\theta^{-1}\boldsymbol{\beta}' & -\boldsymbol{\beta}\theta^{-1} \\ -\theta^{-1}\boldsymbol{\beta}' & \theta^{-1} \end{pmatrix} \tag{7.8–25}$$

where

$$\boldsymbol{\beta} = \mathbf{C}^{-1}\mathbf{v}, \qquad \theta = \sigma^2 - \mathbf{v}'\boldsymbol{\beta} = \sigma^2 - \mathbf{v}'\mathbf{C}^{-1}\mathbf{v}$$

The new effectiveness measure $r_{ij}(m + 1)$ is

$$\begin{aligned} r_{ij}(m + 1) &= (\mathbf{m}_i^{\mathrm{v}} - \mathbf{m}_j^{\mathrm{v}})'\mathbf{C}_{\mathrm{v}}^{-1}(\mathbf{m}_i^{\mathrm{v}} - \mathbf{m}_j^{\mathrm{v}}) \\ &= [(\mathbf{m}_i - \mathbf{m}_j)'(\mu_i - \mu_j)] \begin{pmatrix} \mathbf{C}^{-1} + \boldsymbol{\beta}\theta^{-1}\boldsymbol{\beta}' & -\boldsymbol{\beta}\theta^{-1} \\ -\theta^{-1}\boldsymbol{\beta}' & \theta^{-1} \end{pmatrix} \begin{pmatrix} \mathbf{m}_i - \mathbf{m}_j \\ \mu_i - \mu_j \end{pmatrix} \end{aligned} \tag{7.8–26}$$

which, upon simplification, reduces to

$$r_{ij}(m+1) = r_{ij}(m) + \frac{1}{\theta}[(\mu_i - \mu_j) - (\mathbf{m}_i - \mathbf{m}_j)'\boldsymbol{\beta}]^2 \tag{7.8-27}$$

Hence, the incremental effectiveness is

$$r_{ij}(m+1) - r_{ij}(m) = \frac{[(\mu_i - \mu_j) - (\mathbf{m}_i - \mathbf{m}_j)'\mathbf{C}^{-1}\mathbf{v}]^2}{\sigma^2 - \mathbf{v}'\mathbf{C}^{-1}\mathbf{v}} \tag{7.8-28}$$

When the additional feature x_{m+1} is uncorrelated with the other selected features $x_1, x_2, \ldots, x_m$, we have $\mathbf{v} = \mathbf{0}$ and

$$r_{ij}(m+1) - r_{ij}(m) = \frac{(\mu_i - \mu_j)^2}{\sigma^2} \tag{7.8-29}$$

In the preceding sections, the value of m is assumed to be known. On the basis of the above analysis, a recursive expression for evaluating m to meet an error probability specification may be derived as follows. The transformation matrix $\mathbf{A}$ is

$$\mathbf{A} = \begin{pmatrix} \mathbf{e}_1' \\ \mathbf{e}_2' \\ \vdots \\ \mathbf{e}_m' \end{pmatrix}$$

where $\mathbf{e}_1, \mathbf{e}_2, \ldots, \mathbf{e}_m$ are the orthogonal eigenvectors associated with the m smallest eigenvalues, $\lambda_1, \lambda_2, \ldots, \lambda_m$, of covariance matrix $\mathbf{C}$. It has been shown that

$$\mathbf{m}^* = \mathbf{A}\mathbf{m}$$

$$\mathbf{C}^* = \mathbf{A}\mathbf{C}\mathbf{A}' = \begin{pmatrix} \lambda_1 & 0 & \cdots & 0 \\ 0 & \lambda_2 & \cdots & 0 \\ \vdots & \vdots & \ddots & \vdots \\ 0 & 0 & \cdots & \lambda_m \end{pmatrix}$$

Thus,

$$\begin{aligned} r_{ij}(m) &= (\mathbf{m}_i^* - \mathbf{m}_j^*)(\mathbf{C}^*)^{-1}(\mathbf{m}_i^* - \mathbf{m}_j^*) \\ &= \sum_{k=1}^{m} \frac{(m_{ik}^* - m_{jk}^*)^2}{\sigma_k} \end{aligned} \tag{7.8-30}$$

where m_{ik}^* and m_{jk}^* are the elements of the transformed mean vectors $\mathbf{m}_i^*$ and $\mathbf{m}_j^*$, respectively. From Eq. (7.8–30), we have

$$r_{ij}(m+1) - r_{ij}(m) = \frac{[m_{i(m+1)}^* - m_{j(m+1)}^*]^2}{\sigma_{m+1}^2} \tag{7.8–31}$$

Since

$$m_{i(m+1)}^* = \mathbf{e}_{m+1}'\mathbf{m}_i \qquad \text{and} \qquad m_{j(m+1)}^* = \mathbf{e}_{m+1}'\mathbf{m}_j$$

we obtain

$$\begin{aligned}[m_{i(m+1)}^* - m_{j(m+1)}^*]^2 &= \mathbf{e}_{m+1}'(\mathbf{m}_i - \mathbf{m}_j)(\mathbf{m}_i - \mathbf{m}_j)'\mathbf{e}_{m+1} \\ &= \mathbf{e}_{m+1}'\boldsymbol{\delta}\boldsymbol{\delta}'\mathbf{e}_{m+1}\end{aligned} \tag{7.8–32}$$

Hence, the recursive expression is

$$r_{ij}(m+1) - r_{ij}(m) = \frac{\mathbf{e}_{m+1}'\boldsymbol{\delta}\boldsymbol{\delta}'\mathbf{e}_{m+1}}{\lambda_{m+1}} \tag{7.8–33}$$

with

$$r_{ij}(1) = \frac{\mathbf{e}_1'\boldsymbol{\delta}\boldsymbol{\delta}'\mathbf{e}_1}{\lambda_1} \tag{7.8–34}$$

where $\mathbf{e}_1$ is the eigenvector associated with the smallest eigenvalue of covariance matrix $\mathbf{C}$. Starting with the effectiveness measure for the most significant feature, we can use Eq. (7.8–33) iteratively to determine the effectiveness measures for additional features which will fulfill the error probability specification. In determining the effectiveness measure we make use of the curve in Fig. 4.4 which describes the relationship between error probability and distance measure.

7.9 FEATURE SELECTION THROUGH DIVERGENCE MAXIMIZATION†

A suitable approach to feature extraction consists of generating a set of features which will tend to maximize the separation between classes. If one can derive a set of features which, upon combining with the patterns of two or more pattern populations by a suitable transformation, will generate a set of image patterns that exhibit an increase in separation as measured between

† The material in this section has been adapted from *Computer and Information Sciences–II*, J. T. Tou, ed., Academic Press, New York, 1967.

populations, these features can be interpreted as being representative of the dissimilarities between populations. Such a problem has been considered from the point of view of utilizing a matrix transformation to generate images which maximize the interset distance while keeping the intraset distance or the sum of the interset and intraset distances constant. The separation of pattern classes can be measured in terms of quantities other than a Euclidean distance, however. A more abstract concept of distance is the divergence between two pattern classes, discussed in Section 7.8.

Consider two populations of patterns, ω_1 and ω_2, governed by probability density functions $p_1(\mathbf{x}) = p(\mathbf{x}/\omega_1)$ and $p_2(\mathbf{x}) = p(\mathbf{x}/\omega_2)$, respectively. The divergence between the two classes is given by

$$J_{12} = \int_{\mathbf{x}} [p_1(\mathbf{x}) - p_2(\mathbf{x})] \ln \frac{p_1(\mathbf{x})}{p_2(\mathbf{x})} \, d\mathbf{x} \tag{7.9–1}$$

The divergence is to be used as a criterion function for generating an optimum set of features. As in Section 7.5, we are seeking a transformation matrix $\mathbf{A}$ which yields image patterns of lower dimensionality. The image patterns are given by

$$\mathbf{y} = \mathbf{A}\mathbf{x} \tag{7.9–2}$$

where $\mathbf{y}$ is an m-vector, $\mathbf{x}$ is an n-vector, and $\mathbf{A}$ is an $m \times n$ matrix whose rows are the linearly independent vectors $\mathbf{a}_k$, $k = 1, 2, \ldots, m < n$. The divergence of the image patterns is given by

$$J_{12}^* = \int_{\mathbf{y}} [p_1(\mathbf{y}) - p_2(\mathbf{y})] \ln \frac{p_1(\mathbf{y})}{p_2(\mathbf{y})} \, d\mathbf{y} \tag{7.9–3}$$

Assume that the classes ω_1 and ω_2 are normally distributed according to $N(\mathbf{m}_1, \mathbf{C}_1)$ and $N(\mathbf{m}_2, \mathbf{C}_2)$, respectively. From Eqs. (7.5–6) and (7.5–9), the mean vectors of the image are given by

$$\mathbf{m}_1^* = \mathbf{A}\mathbf{m}_1, \qquad \mathbf{m}_2^* = \mathbf{A}\mathbf{m}_2 \tag{7.9–4}$$

and the covariance matrices are

$$\mathbf{C}_1^* = \mathbf{A}\mathbf{C}_1\mathbf{A}', \qquad \mathbf{C}_2^* = \mathbf{A}\mathbf{C}_2\mathbf{A}' \tag{7.9–5}$$

Under these conditions the divergence of the image populations is given by

$$J_{12}^* = \tfrac{1}{2} \operatorname{tr} [(\mathbf{C}_2^*)^{-1}\mathbf{C}_1^* + (\mathbf{C}_1^*)^{-1}\mathbf{C}_2^*] - m + \tfrac{1}{2} \operatorname{tr} \{[(\mathbf{C}_1^*)^{-1} + (\mathbf{C}_2^*)^{-1}]\boldsymbol{\delta}^*(\boldsymbol{\delta}^*)'\} \tag{7.9–6}$$

where

$$\boldsymbol{\delta}^* = \mathbf{A}\boldsymbol{\delta} = \mathbf{A}(\mathbf{m}_1 - \mathbf{m}_2) = \mathbf{m}_1^* - \mathbf{m}_2^* \tag{7.9–7}$$

Since the trace of a matrix is equal to the sum of its eigenvalues, we have

$$J_{12}^* = \frac{1}{2}\sum_{k=1}^{m} (\lambda_k + \lambda_k^{-1}) - m + \frac{1}{2}\lambda_{m+1} + \frac{1}{2}\lambda_{m+2} \tag{7.9–8}$$

where λ_k are the eigenvalues of $(\mathbf{C}_2^*)^{-1}(\mathbf{C}_1^*)$, λ_{m+1} are the eigenvalues of $(\mathbf{C}_1^*)^{-1}\boldsymbol{\delta}^*(\boldsymbol{\delta}^*)'$, and λ_{m+2} are the eigenvalues of $(\mathbf{C}_2^*)^{-1}\boldsymbol{\delta}^*(\boldsymbol{\delta}^*)'$.

The differential of Eq. (7.9–8) is

$$dJ_{12}^* = \frac{1}{2}\sum_{k=1}^{m} (1 - \lambda_k^{-1})\, d\lambda_k + \frac{1}{2}d\lambda_{m+1} + \frac{1}{2}d\lambda_{m+2} \tag{7.9–9}$$

Since λ_k are the eigenvalues of $(\mathbf{C}_2^*)^{-1}(\mathbf{C}_1^*)$, they satisfy the following relation:

$$(\mathbf{A}\mathbf{C}_2\mathbf{A}')^{-1}(\mathbf{A}\mathbf{C}_1\mathbf{A}')\mathbf{e}_k = \lambda_k\mathbf{e}_k \tag{7.9–10}$$

or

$$(\mathbf{A}\mathbf{C}_1\mathbf{A}')\mathbf{e}_k = \lambda_k(\mathbf{A}\mathbf{C}_2\mathbf{A}')\mathbf{e}_k \tag{7.9–11}$$

where $\mathbf{e}_k$ is the eigenvector of $(\mathbf{C}_2^*)^{-1}(\mathbf{C}_1^*)$ associated with λ_k. Taking the differential of (7.9–11) yields

$$\begin{aligned}(d\mathbf{A})(\mathbf{C}_1\mathbf{A}' - \lambda_k\mathbf{C}_2\mathbf{A}')\mathbf{e}_k + (\mathbf{A}\mathbf{C}_1 - \lambda_k\mathbf{A}\mathbf{C}_2)(d\mathbf{A}')\lambda_k \\ = -(\mathbf{A}\mathbf{C}_1\mathbf{A}' - \lambda_k\mathbf{A}\mathbf{C}_2\mathbf{A}')\, d\mathbf{e}_k + (d\lambda_k)\mathbf{A}\mathbf{C}_2\mathbf{A}'\mathbf{e}_k\end{aligned} \tag{7.9–12}$$

Since the matrices $\mathbf{C}_1^*$ and $\mathbf{C}_2^*$ are symmetrical, the eigenvectors will be mutually orthogonal with respect to $\mathbf{C}_2^*$. We can find a complete set of eigenvectors, and $d\mathbf{e}_k$ may be written as

$$d\mathbf{e}_k = \sum_{j=1}^{m} c_{jk}\mathbf{e}_j \tag{7.9–13}$$

where the eigenvectors $\mathbf{e}_j$ are normalized with respect to $\mathbf{C}_2^*$, that is, $\mathbf{e}_j'\mathbf{C}_2^*\mathbf{e}_j = 1$.

Substituting Eq. (7.9–13) into Eq. (7.9–12) yields

$$\begin{aligned}(d\mathbf{A})(\mathbf{C}_1\mathbf{A}' - \lambda_k\mathbf{C}_2\mathbf{A}')\mathbf{e}_k + (\mathbf{A}\mathbf{C}_1 - \lambda_k\mathbf{A}\mathbf{C}_2)(d\mathbf{A}')\mathbf{e}_k \\ = \sum_{j=1}^{m} c_{jk}(\lambda_j - \lambda_k)\mathbf{A}\mathbf{C}_2\mathbf{A}'\mathbf{e}_j + \mathbf{A}\mathbf{C}_2\mathbf{A}'\mathbf{e}_k(d\lambda_k)\end{aligned} \tag{7.9–14}$$

Premultiplying Eq. (7.9–14) by $\mathbf{e}_k'$ and making use of the conditions that

$$\mathbf{e}_k'\mathbf{A}\mathbf{C}_2\mathbf{A}'\mathbf{e}_k = 1, \qquad \mathbf{e}_j'\mathbf{A}\mathbf{C}_2\mathbf{A}'\mathbf{e}_k = 0, \quad j \neq k \tag{7.9–15}$$

results in

$$\begin{aligned} d\lambda_k &= \mathbf{e}_k'(d\mathbf{A})(\mathbf{C}_1\mathbf{A}' - \lambda_k\mathbf{C}_2\mathbf{A}')\mathbf{e}_k + \mathbf{e}_k'(\mathbf{A}\mathbf{C}_1 - \lambda_k\mathbf{A}\mathbf{C}_2)(d\mathbf{A}')\mathbf{e}_k \\ &= 2\mathbf{e}_k'(d\mathbf{A})(\mathbf{C}_1\mathbf{A}' - \lambda_k\mathbf{C}_2\mathbf{A}')\mathbf{e}_k \end{aligned} \tag{7.9–16}$$

The differentials $d\lambda_{m+1}$ and $d\lambda_{m+2}$ can be determined in a similar manner. Since λ_{m+1} is an eigenvalue of $(\mathbf{C}_1^*)^{-1}\boldsymbol{\delta}^*(\boldsymbol{\delta}^*)'$, it satisfies the relation

$$(\mathbf{A}\boldsymbol{\delta}\boldsymbol{\delta}'\mathbf{A}')\mathbf{e}_{m+1} = \lambda_{m+1}(\mathbf{A}\mathbf{C}_1\mathbf{A}')\mathbf{e}_{m+1} \tag{7.9–17}$$

Taking the differential of Eq. (7.9–17) yields

$$\begin{aligned} &(d\mathbf{A})(\boldsymbol{\delta}\boldsymbol{\delta}'\mathbf{A}' - \lambda_{m+1}\mathbf{C}_1\mathbf{A}')\mathbf{e}_{m+1} + (\mathbf{A}\boldsymbol{\delta}\boldsymbol{\delta}' - \lambda_{m+1}\mathbf{A}\mathbf{C}_1)(d\mathbf{A}')\mathbf{e}_{m+1} \\ &\quad = -(\mathbf{A}\boldsymbol{\delta}\boldsymbol{\delta}'\mathbf{A}' - \lambda_{m+1}\mathbf{A}\mathbf{C}_1\mathbf{A}')\, d\mathbf{e}_{m+1} + \mathbf{A}\mathbf{C}_1\mathbf{A}'\mathbf{e}_{m+1}(d\lambda_{m+1}) \end{aligned} \tag{7.9–18}$$

Since the matrices $\mathbf{C}_1^*$ and $[\boldsymbol{\delta}^*(\boldsymbol{\delta}^*)']$ are symmetrical, all of the eigenvectors are mutually orthogonal with respect to $\mathbf{C}_1^*$. We note, however, that $[\boldsymbol{\delta}^*(\boldsymbol{\delta}^*)']$ is of rank 1 and thus $(\mathbf{C}_1^*)^{-1}[\boldsymbol{\delta}^*(\boldsymbol{\delta}^*)']$ is also of rank 1. We can find a complete set of eigenvectors $\mathbf{e}_{m+1}, \boldsymbol{\gamma}_{21}, \ldots, \boldsymbol{\gamma}_{m1}$ of the matrix $(\mathbf{C}_1^*)^{-1}[\boldsymbol{\delta}^*(\boldsymbol{\delta}^*)']$. These eigenvectors are orthogonal with respect to $\mathbf{C}_1^*$, such that

$$\left.\begin{aligned} \boldsymbol{\gamma}_{j1}'\mathbf{C}_1^*\boldsymbol{\gamma}_{k1} &= 0 \\ \mathbf{e}_{m+1}'\mathbf{C}_1^*\boldsymbol{\gamma}_{k1} &= 0 \\ \boldsymbol{\gamma}_{j1}'\mathbf{C}_1^*\boldsymbol{\gamma}_{j1} &= 1 \\ \mathbf{e}_{m+1}'\mathbf{C}_1^*\mathbf{e}_{m+1} &= 1 \end{aligned}\right\}, \quad j \neq k; \quad k = 2, 3, \ldots, m; \quad j = 2, 3, \ldots, m \tag{7.9–19}$$

The eigenvalues of $(\mathbf{C}_1^*)^{-1}[\boldsymbol{\delta}^*(\boldsymbol{\delta}^*)']$ corresponding to the augmented eigenvectors $\boldsymbol{\gamma}_{k1}$, $k = 2, 3, \ldots, m$, are equal to zero. Thus, we may express $d\mathbf{e}_{m+1}$ as

$$d\mathbf{e}_{m+1} = c_1\mathbf{e}_{m+1} + \sum_{k=2}^{m} c_k\boldsymbol{\gamma}_{k1} \tag{7.9–20}$$

Substituting Eq. (7.9–20) into Eq. (7.9–18) and simplifying yields

$$\begin{aligned} &(d\mathbf{A})(\boldsymbol{\delta}\boldsymbol{\delta}'\mathbf{A}' - \lambda_{m+1}\mathbf{C}_1\mathbf{A}')\mathbf{e}_{m+1} + (\mathbf{A}\boldsymbol{\delta}\boldsymbol{\delta}' - \lambda_{m+1}\mathbf{A}\mathbf{C}_1)(d\mathbf{A}')\mathbf{e}_{m+1} \\ &\quad = -\left(\sum_{k=2}^{m} c_k\lambda_{m+1}\mathbf{A}\mathbf{C}_1\mathbf{A}'\boldsymbol{\gamma}_{k1}\right) + \mathbf{A}\mathbf{C}_1\mathbf{A}'\mathbf{e}_{m+1}(d\lambda_{m+1}) \end{aligned} \tag{7.9–21}$$

In arriving at Eq. (7.9–21) use has been made of Eq. (7.9–17) and the fact that the eigenvalues corresponding to $\boldsymbol{\gamma}_{k1}$ are zero. Premultiplying Eq. (7.9–21) by $\mathbf{e}_{m+1}$ and utilizing Eq. (7.9–19) yields

$$\begin{aligned} d\lambda_{m+1} &= \mathbf{e}'_{m+1}(d\mathbf{A})(\boldsymbol{\delta}\boldsymbol{\delta}'\mathbf{A}' - \lambda_{m+1}\mathbf{C}_1\mathbf{A}')\mathbf{e}_{m+1} \\ &\quad + \mathbf{e}'_{m+1}(\mathbf{A}\boldsymbol{\delta}\boldsymbol{\delta}' - \lambda_{m+1}\mathbf{A}\mathbf{C}_1)(d\mathbf{A}')\mathbf{e}_{m+1} \\ &= 2\mathbf{e}_{m+1}(d\mathbf{A})(\boldsymbol{\delta}\boldsymbol{\delta}'\mathbf{A}' - \lambda_{m+1}\mathbf{C}_1\mathbf{A}')\mathbf{e}_{m+1} \end{aligned} \tag{7.9–22}$$

Similarly, we obtain

$$d\lambda_{m+2} = 2\mathbf{e}'_{m+2}(d\mathbf{A})(\boldsymbol{\delta}\boldsymbol{\delta}'\mathbf{A}' - \lambda_{m+2}\mathbf{C}_2\mathbf{A}')\mathbf{e}_{m+2} \tag{7.9–23}$$

Inserting Eqs. (7.9–23), (7.9–22), and (7.9–16) into Eq. (7.9–9) yields

$$\begin{aligned} dJ^*_{12} &= \sum_{k=1}^{m} (1 - \lambda_k^{-2})\mathbf{e}_k'(d\mathbf{A})(\mathbf{C}_1\mathbf{A}' - \lambda_k\mathbf{C}_2\mathbf{A}')\mathbf{e}_k \\ &\quad + \mathbf{e}'_{m+1}(d\mathbf{A})(\boldsymbol{\delta}\boldsymbol{\delta}'\mathbf{A}' - \lambda_{m+1}\mathbf{C}_1\mathbf{A}')\mathbf{e}_{m+1} \\ &= \mathbf{e}'_{m+1}(d\mathbf{A})(\boldsymbol{\delta}\boldsymbol{\delta}'\mathbf{A}' - \lambda_{m+2}\mathbf{C}_2\mathbf{A}')\mathbf{e}_{m+2} \end{aligned} \tag{7.9–24}$$

Expressing Eq. (7.9–24) in terms of the trace yields

$$dJ^*_{12} = \operatorname{tr}[(d\mathbf{A})\mathbf{G}] \tag{7.9–25}$$

where

$$\begin{aligned} \mathbf{G} &= \sum_{k=1}^{m} (1 - \lambda_k^{-2})(\mathbf{C}_1\mathbf{A}' - \lambda_k\mathbf{C}_2\mathbf{A}')\mathbf{e}_k\mathbf{e}_k' \\ &\quad + (\boldsymbol{\delta}\boldsymbol{\delta}'\mathbf{A}' - \lambda_{m+1}\mathbf{C}_1\mathbf{A}')\mathbf{e}_{m+1}\mathbf{e}'_{m+1} + (\boldsymbol{\delta}\boldsymbol{\delta}'\mathbf{A}' - \lambda_{m+2}\mathbf{C}_2\mathbf{A}')\mathbf{e}_{m+2}\mathbf{e}'_{m+2} \end{aligned} \tag{7.9–26}$$

Since $d\mathbf{A}$ is arbitrary, a necessary condition for J^*_{12} to be an extremum is that the matrix $\mathbf{G}$ be equal to the zero matrix. The foregoing results may be summarized as follows:

If two pattern populations ω_1 and ω_2 are normally distributed according to $N(\mathbf{m}_1, \mathbf{C}_1)$ and $N(\mathbf{m}_2, \mathbf{C}_2)$, respectively, and if the patterns are mapped into a space of lower dimensionality by the transformation $\mathbf{y} = \mathbf{A}\mathbf{x}$, where $\mathbf{y}$ is an m-vector, $\mathbf{x}$ is an n-vector, m is less than n, and $\mathbf{A}$ is an $m \times n$ matrix whose rows are the linearly independent feature vectors $\mathbf{a}_k$, a necessary condition for the divergence J_{12}^* to be an extremum is that the matrix **A** satisfy the relation

$$\sum_{k=1}^{m} (1 - \lambda_k^{-2})(\mathbf{C}_1\mathbf{A}' - \lambda_k\mathbf{C}_2\mathbf{A}')\mathbf{e}_k\mathbf{e}_k'$$

$$+ (\boldsymbol{\delta}\boldsymbol{\delta}'\mathbf{A}' - \lambda_{m+1}\mathbf{C}_1\mathbf{A}')\mathbf{e}_{m+1}\mathbf{e}_{m+1}' + (\boldsymbol{\delta}\boldsymbol{\delta}'\mathbf{A}' - \lambda_{m+2}\mathbf{C}_2\mathbf{A}')\mathbf{e}_{m+2}\mathbf{e}_{m+2}' = 0$$

where λ_k and $\mathbf{e}_k$ are the eigenvalues and eigenvectors of $(\mathbf{A}\mathbf{C}_2\mathbf{A}')^{-1}(\mathbf{A}\mathbf{C}_1\mathbf{A}')$; λ_{m+1}, $\mathbf{e}_{m+1}$ and λ_{m+2}, $\mathbf{e}_{m+2}$ are the eigenvalues of $(\mathbf{C}_1^*)^{-1}(\mathbf{A}\boldsymbol{\delta}\boldsymbol{\delta}'\mathbf{A}')$ and $(\mathbf{C}_2^*)^{-1}(\mathbf{A}\boldsymbol{\delta}\boldsymbol{\delta}'\mathbf{A}')$, respectively; and $\boldsymbol{\delta} = \mathbf{m}_1 - \mathbf{m}_2$.

Three different cases are discussed below.

Case 1. $\mathbf{C}_1 = \mathbf{C}_2 = \mathbf{C}$ and $\mathbf{m}_1 \neq \mathbf{m}_2$.
When the covariance matrices $\mathbf{C}_1$ and $\mathbf{C}_2$ are equal, Eq. (7.9–11) reduces to

$$\mathbf{A}\mathbf{C}\mathbf{A}'(\mathbf{I} - \lambda_k\mathbf{I})\mathbf{e}_k = 0 \tag{7.9–27}$$

which implies that $\lambda_k = 0$. Under this condition, Eq. (7.9–26) reduces to

$$\mathbf{G} = 2(\boldsymbol{\delta}\boldsymbol{\delta}'\mathbf{A}' - \lambda_{m+1}\mathbf{C}\mathbf{A}')\mathbf{e}_{m+1}\mathbf{e}_{m+1}' \tag{7.9–28}$$

By choosing $m = 1$ and letting $\mathbf{A}' = \mathbf{a}$, we can reduce vector $\mathbf{e}_{m+1}$ to a scalar e and Eq. (7.9–28) becomes

$$\mathbf{G} = 2(\boldsymbol{\delta}\boldsymbol{\delta}'\mathbf{a} - \lambda_{m+1}\mathbf{C}\mathbf{a})e^2 \tag{7.9–29}$$

In view of Eq. (7.9–17), it can be shown that

$$\lambda_{m+1} = \frac{\mathbf{a}'\boldsymbol{\delta}\boldsymbol{\delta}'\mathbf{a}}{\mathbf{a}'\mathbf{C}\mathbf{a}} \tag{7.9–30}$$

Therefore,

$$\mathbf{G} = 2\left[\boldsymbol{\delta}\boldsymbol{\delta}'\mathbf{a} - \left(\frac{\mathbf{a}'\boldsymbol{\delta}\boldsymbol{\delta}'\mathbf{a}}{\mathbf{a}'\mathbf{C}\mathbf{a}}\right)\mathbf{C}\mathbf{a}\right]e^2 \tag{7.9–31}$$

and the necessary condition for the divergence to be an extremum is that

$$\boldsymbol{\delta}\boldsymbol{\delta}'\mathbf{a} = \left(\frac{\mathbf{a}'\boldsymbol{\delta}\boldsymbol{\delta}'\mathbf{a}}{\mathbf{a}'\mathbf{C}\mathbf{a}}\right)\mathbf{C}\mathbf{a} \tag{7.9–32}$$

or

$$(\mathbf{C}^{-1}\boldsymbol{\delta}\boldsymbol{\delta}')\mathbf{a} = \left(\frac{\mathbf{a}'\boldsymbol{\delta}\boldsymbol{\delta}'\mathbf{a}}{\mathbf{a}'\mathbf{C}\mathbf{a}}\right)\mathbf{a} \tag{7.9–33}$$

which implies that $\mathbf{a}$ is an eigenvector of $\mathbf{C}^{-1}\boldsymbol{\delta}\boldsymbol{\delta}'$ with the corresponding eigenvalue equal to $(\mathbf{a}'\boldsymbol{\delta}\boldsymbol{\delta}'\mathbf{a})/(\mathbf{a}'\mathbf{C}\mathbf{a})$. Hence, in order to make the divergence an extremum, we let $\mathbf{A}' = \mathbf{a}$, which is an eigenvector of $\mathbf{C}^{-1}\boldsymbol{\delta}\boldsymbol{\delta}'$. The corresponding divergence is

$$\begin{aligned} J_{12} &= \tfrac{1}{2}\,\mathrm{tr}\,(\mathbf{C}_1^{-1}\mathbf{C}_2 + \mathbf{C}_2^{-1}\mathbf{C}_1) - n + \tfrac{1}{2}(\mathbf{C}_1^{-1} + \mathbf{C}_2^{-1})\boldsymbol{\delta}\boldsymbol{\delta}' \\ &= \mathrm{tr}\,(\mathbf{C}^{-1}\boldsymbol{\delta}\boldsymbol{\delta}') \end{aligned} \tag{7.9–34}$$

which is equal to the nonzero eigenvalue of the matrix $\mathbf{C}^{-1}\boldsymbol{\delta}\boldsymbol{\delta}'$. In view of Eq. (7.9–6), we have for the transformed case

$$J_{12}^{*} = \lambda_{m+1} \tag{7.9–35}$$

which, according to Eq. (7.9–30), is equal to the nonzero eigenvalue of $\mathbf{C}^{-1}\boldsymbol{\delta}\boldsymbol{\delta}'$. Hence, in this special case, the transformation from the vectors $\mathbf{x}$ to the vectors $\mathbf{y}$ causes no loss of information since $J_{12} = J_{12}^{*}$.

Case 2. $\mathbf{C}_1 \neq \mathbf{C}_2$ and $\mathbf{m}_1 = \mathbf{m}_2$.

When the mean vectors are equal, $\boldsymbol{\delta} = 0$ and $\lambda_{m+1} = \lambda_{m+2} = 0$. Thus, Eq. (7.9–26) reduces to

$$\mathbf{G} = \sum_{k=1}^{m} (1 - \lambda_1^{-2})(\mathbf{C}_1\mathbf{A}' - \lambda_k\mathbf{C}_2\mathbf{A}')\mathbf{e}_k\mathbf{e}_k' \tag{7.9–36}$$

If we let the rows of $\mathbf{A}$ be the eigenvectors of $\mathbf{C}_2^{-1}\mathbf{C}_1$ normalized with respect to $\mathbf{C}_2$, it can be shown that

$$\mathbf{A}\mathbf{C}_1\mathbf{A}' = \begin{pmatrix} \alpha_1 & 0 & \cdots & & 0 \\ 0 & \alpha_2 & \cdots & & 0 \\ & & \ddots & & \\ \vdots & \vdots & & \alpha_k & \vdots \\ & & & \ddots & \\ 0 & 0 & \cdots & & \alpha_m \end{pmatrix} \tag{7.9–37}$$

and

$$\mathbf{A}\mathbf{C}_2\mathbf{A}' = \mathbf{I} \tag{7.9–38}$$

where α_k, $k = 1, 2, \ldots, m$, are the m eigenvalues of $\mathbf{C}_2^{-1}\mathbf{C}_1$. Then Eq. (7.9–11) becomes

$$\begin{pmatrix} \alpha_1 & 0 & \cdots & 0 \\ 0 & \alpha_2 & \cdots & 0 \\ \vdots & \vdots & \ddots & \vdots \\ 0 & 0 & \cdots & \alpha_m \end{pmatrix} \mathbf{e}_k = \lambda_k \mathbf{I}\mathbf{e}_k \tag{7.9–39}$$

Therefore,

$$\lambda_k = \alpha_k, \quad k = 1, 2, \ldots, m \tag{7.9–40}$$

and, in addition,

$$\mathbf{e}_k = \begin{pmatrix} 0 \\ 0 \\ \vdots \\ 1 \\ \vdots \\ 0 \end{pmatrix} \tag{7.9–41}$$

where the 1 occurs in the kth element. From this property of the eigenvectors $\mathbf{e}_k$ we have

$$\mathbf{A}'\mathbf{e}_k = \mathbf{a}_k \tag{7.9–42}$$

where $\mathbf{a}_k$ is the kth column of $\mathbf{A}'$. Equation (7.9–36) now becomes

$$\mathbf{G} = \sum_{k=1}^{m} (1 - \lambda_k^{-2})(\mathbf{C}_1\mathbf{a}_k - \lambda_k\mathbf{C}_2\mathbf{a}_k)\mathbf{e}_k \tag{7.9–43}$$

Since $\lambda_k = \alpha_k$ and $\mathbf{a}_k$ satisfy the relation $\mathbf{C}_1\mathbf{a}_k = \lambda_k\mathbf{C}_2\mathbf{a}_k$, we see that $\mathbf{G}$ is the zero matrix and the condition for an extremum is satisfied. In view of Eq. (7.9–8), the divergence J_{12}^* is maximized if the eigenvectors of $\mathbf{C}_2^{-1}\mathbf{C}_1$ corresponding to the eigenvalues α_k for which

$$(\alpha_k + \alpha_k^{-1}) \geqslant (\alpha_j + \alpha_j^{-1}), \quad j = 1, 2, \ldots, n; \quad k = 1, 2, \ldots, m; \quad j \neq k \tag{7.9–44}$$

are chosen as the rows of the transformation matrix $\mathbf{A}$.

Case 3. $\mathbf{C}_1 \neq \mathbf{C}_2$ and $\mathbf{m}_1 \neq \mathbf{m}_2$.

In the general case, the solution of the equation $\mathbf{G} = \mathbf{0}$ is considerably more difficult. From Eq. (7.9–25),

$$\begin{aligned} dJ_{12}^* &= \operatorname{tr}[(d\mathbf{A})\mathbf{G}] = \sum_{k=1}^{m} d\mathbf{a}_k'\mathbf{g}_k \\ &= (d\mathbf{a}_1' \, d\mathbf{a}_2' \cdots d\mathbf{a}_m') \begin{pmatrix} \mathbf{g}_1 \\ \mathbf{g}_2 \\ \vdots \\ \mathbf{g}_m \end{pmatrix} \end{aligned} \tag{7.9–45}$$

Thus, $(\mathbf{g}_1', \mathbf{g}_2', \ldots, \mathbf{g}_m')$ is the gradient of J_{12}^* with respect to the features $\mathbf{a}_k$, $k = 1, \ldots, m$. Therefore, if we increment $\mathbf{A}$ by $\theta\mathbf{G}$, where θ is some suitable convergence factor, J_{12}^* will increase. We can consider a steepest-ascent approach in which we solve the following set of difference equations:

$$\mathbf{A}(s+1) = \mathbf{A}(s) + \theta\mathbf{G}(s) \tag{7.9–46}$$

where s is an iteration index.

Example: As a simple illustration of the results derived in this section, consider the patterns of Fig. 7.1. Case 1 applies to these patterns since they satisfy the conditions $\mathbf{C}_1 = \mathbf{C}_2 = \mathbf{C}$ and $\mathbf{m}_1 \neq \mathbf{m}_2$.

Referring to Section 7.5, we obtain

$$\mathbf{m}_1 = \frac{1}{4}\begin{pmatrix} 3 \\ 1 \\ 1 \end{pmatrix}, \qquad \mathbf{m}_2 = \frac{1}{4}\begin{pmatrix} 1 \\ 3 \\ 3 \end{pmatrix}$$

Therefore,

$$\boldsymbol{\delta} = \mathbf{m}_1 - \mathbf{m}_2 = \frac{1}{4}\begin{pmatrix} 2 \\ -2 \\ -2 \end{pmatrix}$$

The covariance matrix is

$$\mathbf{C} = \frac{1}{16}\begin{pmatrix} 3 & 1 & 1 \\ 1 & 3 & -1 \\ 1 & -1 & 3 \end{pmatrix}$$

with inverse

$$\mathbf{C}^{-1} = \begin{pmatrix} 8 & -4 & -4 \\ -4 & 8 & 4 \\ -4 & 4 & 8 \end{pmatrix}$$

The matrix $\mathbf{C}^{-1}\boldsymbol{\delta}\boldsymbol{\delta}'$ is then

$$\mathbf{C}^{-1}\boldsymbol{\delta}\boldsymbol{\delta}' = \frac{1}{4}\begin{pmatrix} 1 & -1 & -1 \\ -1 & 1 & 1 \\ -1 & 1 & 1 \end{pmatrix}$$

The nonzero eigenvalue and corresponding eigenvector of $\mathbf{C}^{-1}\boldsymbol{\delta}\boldsymbol{\delta}'$ are

$$\lambda = \tfrac{3}{4}, \qquad \mathbf{e} = \begin{pmatrix} -1 \\ 1 \\ 1 \end{pmatrix}$$

The transformation matrix is formed from this eigenvector:

$$\mathbf{A} = (-1 \quad 1 \quad 1)$$

Applying the transformation $\mathbf{y} = \mathbf{A}\mathbf{x}$ to the patterns results in the following one-dimensional image patterns:

ω_1	ω_2
$y_{11} = 0$	$y_{21} = 1$
$y_{12} = -1$	$y_{22} = 1$
$y_{13} = 0$	$y_{23} = 2$
$y_{14} = 0$	$y_{24} = 1$

These patterns exhibit the same clustering properties as were found in Section 7.5. In addition, we observe that the transformation did not cause any two patterns of different classes to overlap. ●

7.10 BINARY FEATURE SELECTION

The features resulting from the selection techniques of the preceding sections are, in general, quantities which assume any real value. In this section, the problem of extracting and selecting binary features from patterns which are also binary is discussed.

Unlike the situation with the methods previously derived, the more useful aspects of binary feature selection do not deal with dimensionality reduction. Instead, the basic problem is to select a minimum set of binary features of the same dimensionality as the patterns which will be sufficient to reconstruct the original patterns, with the fewest possible errors. Although this problem has not been solved in general, the following algorithms represent a reasonable (but not always completely successful) approach to generating useful binary features. As will be seen below, these algorithms attempt to determine a minimum set of features which are common to a group of patterns.

7.10.1 A Sequential Algorithm

The algorithm presented in this section generates one binary feature for each iteration through the given patterns. Basically, the procedure consists of establishing a variable threshold and altering the feature being generated during a given iteration whenever the threshold is exceeded. The algorithm is introduced with the aid of the following example.

Consider the three binary patterns shown in Fig. 7.3(a), where a shaded square indicates a binary 1 and a blank square a 0. This representation is adopted purely for convenience in the following explanation. If desired, the patterns can be expressed in vector form by arranging the elements of the binary matrices in a consistent manner. Since these patterns will be considered as sets in the following discussion, they will be represented by the symbols P_i rather than the familiar vector notation $\mathbf{x}_i$.

The procedure is initiated by selecting an arbitrary threshold θ, to be discussed below, and features which are composed entirely of 1's, as shown

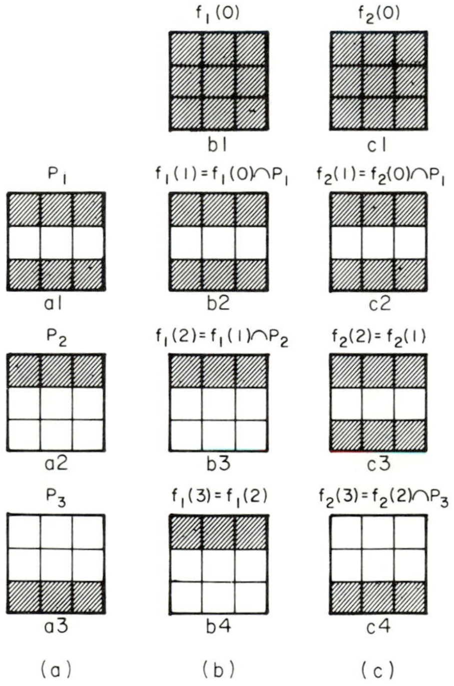

Figure 7.3. Illustration of the sequential algorithm

in Figs. 7.3(b1) and (c1). Feature f_1 is generated during the first iteration through the patterns, f_2 during the second iteration, f_k during the kth iteration, and so on.

The generation of the first feature proceeds as follows. Let $f_1(0)$ represent the initial value of feature f_1, and let $||f_1(0) \cap P_1||$ represent the "distance" between $f_1(0)$ and P_1, which is defined as the number of 1's in the intersection of $f_1(0)$ and pattern P_1. Then, if $||f_1(0) \cap P_1|| \geqslant \theta$, we let $f_1(1) = f_1(0) \cap P_1$; otherwise $f_1(1) = f_1(0)$. Letting θ be equal to 3 in this case, we see from Figs. 7.3(a1) and (b1) that $||f_1(0) \cap P_1|| = 6 > \theta$. Therefore, we let $f_1(1) = f_1(0) \cap P_1$, as shown in Fig. 7.3(b2). Since the intersection of $f_1(1)$ with P_2 yields $||f_1(1) \cap P_2|| = 3 = \theta$, we let $f_1(2) = f_1(1) \cap P_2$ as indicated in Fig. 7.3(b3). In the next step it is clear that $||f_1(2) \cap P_3|| = 0 < \theta$; hence, the feature is not changed, that is, $f_1(3) = f_1(2)$, as shown in Fig. 7.3(b4). This figure represents the final value of feature f_1 since all the patterns have been considered.

To determine f_2 the procedure is repeated, with the exception that the threshold is recomputed before making each comparison, as follows. The first new value of the threshold is given by $\theta^* = \theta + ||f_1(3) \cap [f_2(0) \cap P_1]||$, where $f_1(3)$ indicates the final value of f_1. Then, if $||f_2(0) \cap P_1|| \geqslant \theta^*$, we let $f_2(1) = f_2(0) \cap P_1$; otherwise we let $f_2(1) = f_2(0)$. In this case, $\theta^* = 3 + 3 = 6$; and, since $||f_2(0) \cap P_1|| = 6 = \theta^*$, we let $f_2(1) = f_2(0) \cap P_1$, as shown in Fig. 7.3(c2). The basic idea behind raising the threshold in this manner is that duplication of features is avoided. The threshold must be recomputed before a new comparison is made. Using the updated value of f_2, we obtain for the new threshold $\theta^* = \theta + ||f_1(3) \cap [f_2(1) \cap P_2]|| = 3 + 3 = 6$. Since $||f_2(1) \cap P_2|| = 3 < \theta^*$, we let $f_2(2) = f_2(1)$, as shown in Fig. 7.3(c3). Finally, $\theta^* = \theta + ||f_1(3) \cap [f_2(2) \cap P_3]|| = 3 + 0 = 3$; and, since $||f_2(2) \cap P_3|| = 3 = \theta^*$, we let $f_2(3) = f_2(2) \cap P_3$, as indicated in Fig. 7.3(c4). It can be verified by inspection that the f_1 and f_2 determined by the foregoing procedure represent the minimum set of features necessary for the errorfree reconstruction of the given patterns.

The sequential algorithm may be formalized as follows. For N binary patterns $P_1, P_2, \ldots, P_N$, the feature at the ith step in the kth iteration through the patterns is given by

$$f_k(i) = \begin{cases} f_k(i-1) \cap P_i & \text{if } ||f_k(i-1) \cap P_i|| \geqslant \theta^* \\ f_k(i-1) & \text{otherwise} \end{cases}, \quad i = 1, 2, \ldots, N \tag{7.10–1}$$

where

$$\theta^* = \theta + \|f_1(M) \cap [f_k(i-1) \cap P_i]\| + \|f_2(M) \cap [f_k(i-1) \cap P_i]\| + \cdots + \|f_{k-1}(M) \cap [f_k(i-1) \cap P_i]\| \tag{7.10–2}$$

Two questions remain to be answered in connection with this algorithm: (1) How do we select the threshold θ, and (2) how many features need to be generated? Unfortunately neither question can, at this time, be answered in general. Since the real problem centers about the selection of θ, however, it is often practical to repeat the procedure for several values of θ and to choose the threshold which yields the best results.

7.10.2 A Parallel Algorithm

Instead of determining one feature per iteration, it is possible to determine several features at the same time in a parallel manner. The parallel algorithm to be presented below starts with a single feature as before, but it introduces new features whenever they are needed to reconstruct a pattern at a given step. After a pattern has been presented and the changes in the features have been carried out, a test is made to see whether the union of the new features is sufficient to reconstruct the pattern under consideration. If it is, the next pattern is presented. If it is not, a new feature, identically equal to the pattern being considered, is created, and then the next pattern is presented. Since the parallel algorithm is somewhat more complicated than its sequential counterpart, it will be advantageous first to present it in general terms and then to illustrate the mechanics by an example.

Consider N binary patterns $P_1, P_2, \ldots, P_N$ and assume that in the ith step of the iteration through the patterns j features, $f_1(i), f_2(i), \ldots, f_j(i)$, are being considered. When pattern P_{i+1} is presented, the new features are determined as follows:

1. $f_1(i+1) = f_1(i) \cap P_{i+1}$ if $\|f_1(i) \cap P_{i+1}\| \geqslant \theta$. Otherwise $f_1(i+1) = f_1(i)$.
2. $f_2(i+1) = f_2(i) \cap P_{i+1}$ if $\|f_2(i) \cap P_{i+1}\| \geqslant \theta + \theta_2$. Otherwise $f_2(i+1) = f_2(i)$. The parameter θ_2 is given by $\theta_2 = \|f_1(i+1)\|$ if (a) $\|f_1(i) \cap P_{i+1}\| \geqslant \theta$, *and* (b) $f_1(i+1)$ is contained in $f_2(i)$, that is, $f_1(i+1) \subseteq f_2(i)$. Otherwise $\theta_2 = 0$.
3. In general, $f_l(i+1) = f_l(i) \cap P_{i+1}$ if $\|f_l(i) \cap P_{i+1}\| \geqslant \theta + \theta_l$. Otherwise $f_l(i+1) = f_l(i)$. The parameter θ_l is given by $\theta_l = \sum_k \|f_k(i+1)\|$ (for $k < l$), where a term $\|f_k(i+1)\|$ is included in the summation only if (a) $\|f_k(i) \cap P_{i+1}\| \geqslant \theta + \theta_k$, *and* (b) $f_k(i+1) \subseteq f_l(i)$.

After the j new features have been computed, the union of the features *which were changed* is formed. If this union yields the pattern P_{i+1}, the next

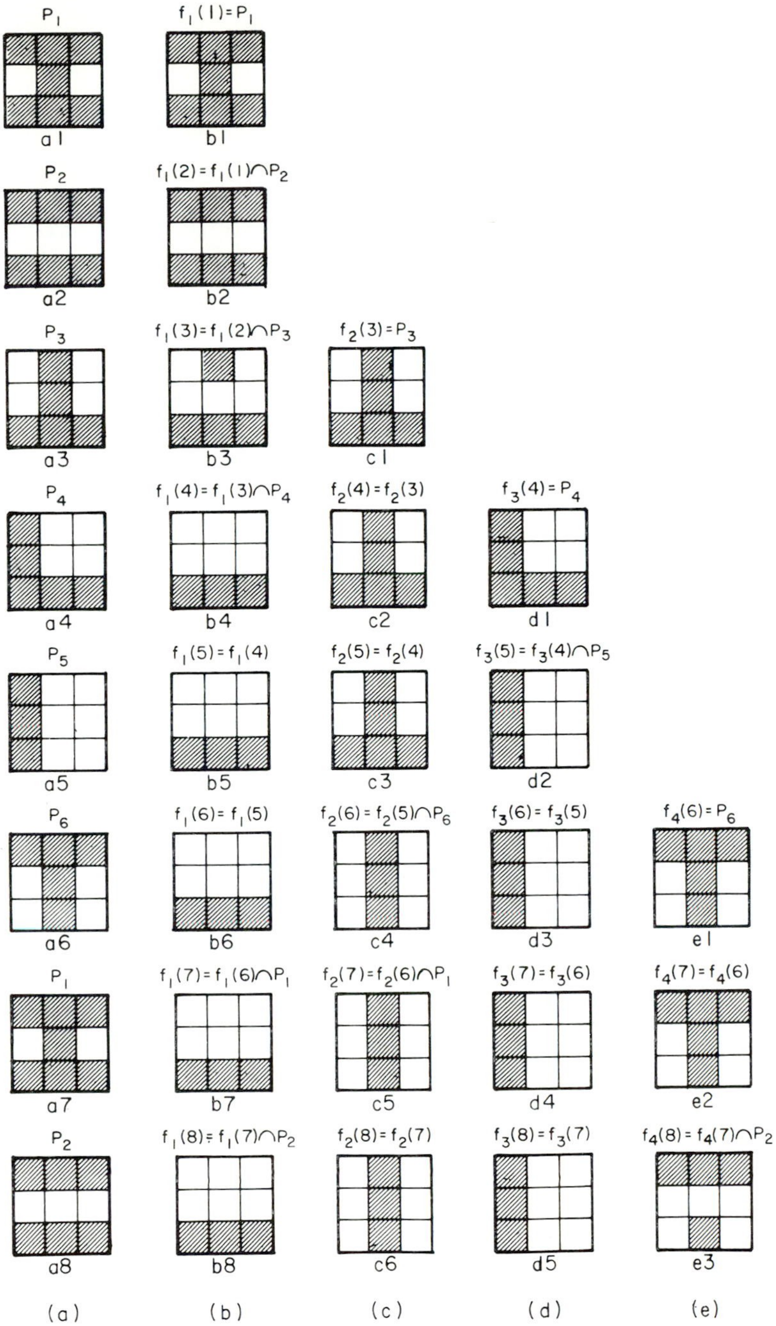

Figure 7.4. Illustration of the parallel algorithm

pattern is presented. If it does not, a new feature, $f_{j+1} = P_{i+1}$, is created and then the next pattern is presented.

This algorithm can be illustrated with the aid of the patterns shown in Fig. 7.4(a). Assuming that θ is equal to 3, we initiate the procedure by letting $f_1(1) = P_1$. Next, P_2 is presented; and, since $||f_1(1) \cap P_2|| = 6 > \theta$, we let $f_1(2) = f_1(1) \cap P_2$, as shown in Fig. 7.4(b2). Since this feature is sufficient to reconstruct P_2, the next pattern is presented. Since $||f_1(2) \cap P_3|| = 4 > \theta$, we let $f_1(3) = f_1(2) \cap P_3$, as shown in Fig. 7.4(b3). However, P_3 cannot be reconstructed from $f_1(3)$ alone; hence, a new feature, $f_2(3) = P_3$, is created, as indicated in Fig. 7.4(c1). Next, we see that $||f_1(3) \cap P_4|| = 3 = \theta$, so we let $f_1(4) = f_1(3) \cap P_4$. Since $||f_1(3) \cap P_4|| = \theta$ and $f_1(4) \subseteq f_2(3)$, the threshold for f_2 is raised to $\theta + \theta_2 = \theta + ||f_1(4)|| = 3 + 3 = 6$. As can be seen in Fig. 7.4, this prevents $f_2(4)$ from becoming identical to $f_1(4)$. We see that $||f_2(3) \cap P_4|| = 3 < (\theta + \theta_2)$, so $f_2(4) = f_2(3)$. The only feature which changed in this step is $f_1(4)$. Since P_4 cannot be reconstructed from this feature alone, a new feature, $f_3(4) = P_4$, is created. Presenting pattern P_5, we see that $f_1(5) = f_1(4)$ since $||f_1(4) \cap P_5|| < \theta$. Consequently, the threshold for f_2 is not changed. However, $||f_2(4) \cap P_5|| < \theta$; hence, $f_2(5) = f_2(4)$. From these two events we see that the threshold for f_3 is not raised either; and, since $||f_3(4) \cap P_5|| = 3 = \theta$, we let $f_3(5) = f_3(4) \cap P_5$. Pattern P_5 can be reconstructed from $f_3(5)$ (the only feature that changed); therefore, it is not necessary to create a new feature in this step. The features resulting from the next step are shown in Fig. 7.4. Since these features are not sufficient to reconstruct all six patterns, however, a new iteration through the patterns must be undertaken.

Presenting P_1 again, we see that $||f_1(6) \cap P_1|| = 3 = \theta$, so $f_1(7) = f_1(6) \cap P_1$. Since $f_1(7)$ is not contained in $f_2(6)$, the threshold for f_2 is not raised. Therefore, $f_2(7) = f_2(6) \cap P_1$ since $||f_2(6) \cap P_1|| = 3 = \theta$. The remaining features are obtained in the same manner. The procedure terminates in the next step since, as can be seen in Fig. 7.4, the resulting features are sufficient to reconstruct the six patterns under consideration. For instance, P_1 is given by $f_1 \cap f_2 \cap f_4$, P_2 by $f_1 \cap f_4$, P_3 by $f_1 \cap f_2$, and so on.

The parallel algorithm often yields a set of features in a fewer number of iterations than the sequential algorithm. This speed is gained by creating new features before old ones have been completely determined. This complicates the threshold-raising mechanism, however, and frequently leads to the determination of more features than are needed for reconstruction. As was the case with the sequential algorithm, the only way to obtain an acceptable set of features is, in general, by running the algorithm with various values of θ and choosing the best results.

7.11 CONCLUDING REMARKS

This chapter introduces in some detail various techniques for the mathematical ordering, selection, and extraction of features. The expressions for the set-to-set distance measure are derived in terms of variances, which are used in the study of clustering transformation and feature ordering through intraset distance minimization and diagonalization of the covariance matrix. The measurements corresponding to small variances are more reliable and can be considered as more important features. Through a clustering transformation, we demonstrate that fitting normal probability densities to the sets of observed samples of the pattern classes is equivalent to measuring the mean-square distances of the class after clustering transformation of the measurement space. The concept of clustering transformation is further extended to reduce the dimensionality of the measurement space and to generate a set of optimum features. These feature vectors are used in orthogonal transformations for reducing the dimensionality of pattern vectors.

The concept of entropy is used as an alternative way to derive a transformation which reduces the dimensionality of the pattern vectors. The derivation of this transformation is based on the assumption that all pattern classes are normally distributed and possess equal covariance matrices. When this assumption cannot be justified, the discrete version of the generalized Karhunen-Loève expansion offers an alternative approach to feature selection. The K-L expansion is derived under the assumption that all classes are characterized by zero or identical means. As is shown in Section 7.6, this requirement plays an important role in the application of the K-L expansion.

When the features of a pattern class can be characterized by a function which is determined on the basis of observed data, the methods of functional approximation introduced in Section 7.7 are applicable. Three basic methods are covered in this section. The method of functional expansion is applicable to deterministic data. The methods of stochastic and kernel approximation are the result of statistical considerations.

The concept of divergence is presented as an appropriate "distance" measure between pairs of arbitrary distributions and as a measure of the difficulty in discriminating between two populations. For two normal distributions with equal covariances, the divergence is equal to the Mahalanobis distance between these two distributions. The divergence concept is applied in feature ordering and in the determination of the number of measurements required to meet an error probability specification. An interset feature selection criterion based on divergence maximization is presented. The procedure is limited to two classes, although a similar approach based on the consideration of a "mean" divergence has been attempted for the multiclass case.

Finally, the problem of binary feature selection is considered. Although this problem has not been solved in general, the algorithms presented in Section 7.10 probably indicate the most serious effort in this area.

REFERENCES

Supplementary reading for Section 7.2 can be found in Sebestyen [1962], Cooper [1964], and Babu [1973]. Additional references for Sections 7.3 and 7.4 are Sebestyen [1962], Tou [1968b, 1969a, 1970], Fu [1968], Bodewig [1956], Kovelevsky [1970], and Watanabe [1970]. The minimum-entropy approach to feature selection given in Section 7.5 is due to Tou and Heydorn [1967]. Some results in the application of this concept to binary patterns can be found in the paper by Gonzalez and Tou [1968].

An early reference for the K-L expansion presented in Section 7.6 is the paper by Karhunen [1947]. This concept was subsequently applied to pattern recognition by Watanabe [1965]. The generalized K-L expansion is due to Chien and Fu [1967]. References for Section 7.7 are Loginov [1966], Rice [1964], and Tou [1969a]. Supplementary reading for Sections 7.8 and 7.9 consists of Kullback [1958], Reza [1961], and Tou and Heydorn [1967]. The binary feature selection algorithms presented in Section 7.10 are due to Block, Nilsson, and Duda [1964].

PROBLEMS

7.1 Show that Eq. (7.3–21) is valid.

7.2 Show that Eq. (7.4–20) is valid.

7.3 Consider two pattern classes, ω_1 and ω_2. The autocorrelation matrix for class ω_1 is $\mathbf{R}_1$, and that for class ω_2 is $\mathbf{R}_2$. Find a transformation matrix $\mathbf{A}$, $\mathbf{y} = \mathbf{A}\mathbf{x}$, such that

$$\mathbf{A}(\mathbf{R}_1 + \mathbf{R}_2)\mathbf{A}' = \mathbf{I}$$

Such a transformation is useful in interset feature selection.

7.4 Reduce the following patterns to one dimension by means of the minimum-entropy transformation discussed in Section 7.5: ω_1: $\{(-5, -5)', (-5, -4)', (-4, -5)', (-5, -6)', (-6, -5)'\}$ and ω_2: $\{(5, 5)', (5, 6)', (6, 5)', (5, 4)', (4, 5)'\}$.

7.5 Repeat Problem 7.4 using the K-L expansion transformation.

7.6 Make a comparative study of dimensionality reduction of pattern vectors by clustering transformation and by entropy minimization.

7.7 Show that the entropy function H_i^* given in Eq. (7.5–11) is minimized by forming the transformation matrix **A** from the m orthogonal eigenvectors associated with the smallest eigenvalues of the covariance matrix of the ith population (see Tou and Heydorn [1967]).

7.8 Derive Eq. (7.7–21) from stochastic approximation methods.

7.9 Repeat Problem 7.4 using the divergence transformation discussed in Section 7.9.

7.10 Apply the sequential binary feature selection algorithm to the patterns of Fig. 7.4.

7.11 Apply the parallel binary feature selection algorithm to the patterns of Fig. 7.3.

8

SYNTACTIC PATTERN RECOGNITION

8.1 INTRODUCTION

In the preceding chapters we were concerned with a mathematical approach to pattern recognition. In this chapter we explore a relatively new and promising approach based on the utilization of concepts from formal language theory. This approach is frequently referred to as *syntactic pattern recognition*, although terms such as linguistic pattern recognition, grammatical pattern recognition, and structural pattern recognition are often found in the literature.

The basic difference between syntactic pattern recognition and the approaches discussed thus far is that the former explicitly utilizes the structure of patterns in the recognition process. Analytical approaches, on the other hand, deal with patterns on a strictly quantitative basis, thus largely ignoring interrelationships between the components of a pattern. Of course, the existence of a recognizable "structure" is essential for the success of the syntactic approach. For this reason, syntactic pattern recognition research has been largely confined thus far to pictorial patterns which are characterized by recognizable shapes, such as characters, chromosomes, and particle collision photographs.

The interest in syntactic pattern recognition may be traced to the early 1960's, although research in this area did not gain momentum until later in that decade. Even today, however, many of the major problems associated with the design of a syntactic pattern recognition system have been only partially solved. For example, no general training algorithms for syntactic systems have yet been discovered.

After the introduction of some concepts from formal language theory, attention is focused in the following sections on the basic problems encountered in applying these concepts to syntactic pattern recognition. This material represents the fundamental framework from which much of the present research in this field is evolving.

8.2 CONCEPTS FROM FORMAL LANGUAGE THEORY

The origin of formal language theory may be traced to the middle 1950's with the development by Noam Chomsky of mathematical models of grammars related to his work in natural languages. One of the original goals of the work of linguists working in this area was to develop computational grammars capable of describing natural languages such as English. The hope was that, if this could be done, it would be a relatively simple matter to "teach" computers to interpret natural languages for the purposes of translation and problem solving. Although it is generally agreed that these expectations have been unrealized thus far, spin-offs of research in this area have had significant impact on other fields such as compiler design, computer languages, automata theory, and, more recently, pattern recognition. In this section we are concerned with the development of the essential ideas from formal language theory, as related to problems in syntactic pattern recognition and machine learning.

8.2.1 Definitions

The concepts defined below play a central role in the study of formal language theory. Although some of these concepts are readily identifiable with concepts from natural languages, the reader is cautioned against carrying such comparisons too far.

An *alphabet* is any finite set of symbols.

A *sentence* over an alphabet is any string of finite length composed of symbols from the alphabet. For example, given the alphabet $\{0, 1\}$, the following are valid sentences: $\{0, 1, 00, 01, 10, \ldots\}$. The terms *string* and *word* are also commonly used to denote a sentence.

The sentence with no symbols is called the *empty sentence*. The empty sentence will be denoted by s_0. For any alphabet V, we will use V^* to denote the set of all sentences composed of symbols from V, including the empty sentence. The symbol V^+ will denote the set of sentences $V^* - s_o$. For example, given the alphabet $V = \{a, b\}$, we have $V^* = \{s_o, a, b, aa, ab, bb, \ldots\}$ and $V^+ = \{a, b, aa, ab, bb, \ldots\}$.

A *language* is any set (not necessarily finite) of sentences over an alphabet.

As is true in natural languages, a serious study of formal language theory must be focused on grammars and their properties. We define a *grammar* as a fourtuple:

$$G = (V_N, V_T, P, S) \tag{8.2–1}$$

where

V_N is a set of *nonterminals* (variables);
V_T is a set of *terminals* (constants);
P is a set of *productions* or rewriting rules;
S is the *start* or *root* symbol.

It is assumed that S belongs to the set V_N and that V_N and V_T are disjoint sets. The alphabet V is the union of sets V_N and V_T.

It will be useful at this point to compare the above definition of a formal grammar with familiar concepts from English grammar. This comparison will help the reader to gain some feeling for the notation and terminology. Consider the simple sentence "The boy runs." The tree structure of this sentence is shown in Fig. 8.1. The generation of the sentence is seen to proceed as follows. We start with an abstract concept which we call ⟨sentence⟩. At this point ⟨sentence⟩ is nothing more than a syntactic concept which represents all correct sentences in the English language. We then replace ⟨sentence⟩ by ⟨noun phrase⟩ plus ⟨verb phrase⟩. In formal language theory we always start from the symbol S described above. The *productions* of the grammar G in Eq. (8.2–1) correspond in English to the replacement of, for example, ⟨sentence⟩ by ⟨noun phrase⟩ plus ⟨verb phrase⟩. We see in Fig. 8.1 that by further application of productions or rewriting rules ⟨noun phrase⟩ is reduced to ⟨article⟩ plus ⟨noun⟩, and ⟨verb phrase⟩ is reduced to ⟨intransitive verb⟩. Finally, applying the productions which map ⟨article⟩ into "the," ⟨noun⟩ into "boy," and ⟨intransitive verb⟩ into "runs" results in the desired sentence. The *nonterminals* of G correspond to the syntactic categories ⟨noun phrase⟩, ⟨verb phrase⟩, ⟨article⟩, ⟨noun⟩, and so forth, while the *terminals* correspond to the words "the," "boy," and "runs." In other words, nonterminals play the role of variables; terminals, the role of constants.

The *language* generated by G, denoted by $L(G)$, is the set of strings which satisfy two conditions: (1) each string is composed only of terminals (i.e., each

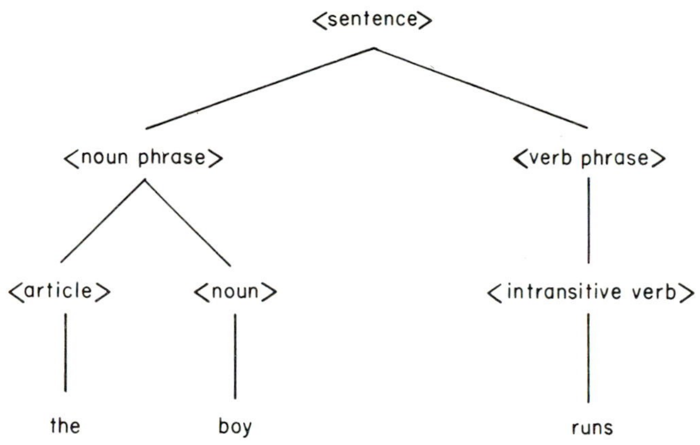

<sentence> → <noun phrase> <verb phrase>

<noun phrase> → <article> <noun>

<verb phrase> → <intransitive verb>

<article> → the

<noun> → boy

<intransitive verb> → runs

Figure 8.1. Productions used in the generation of the sentence "The boy runs" and corresponding semantic tree

string is a *terminal sentence*), and (2) each string can be derived from S by suitable applications of productions from the set P.

The following notation will be used throughout this chapter. Nonterminals will be denoted by capital letters: $S, A, B, C, \ldots$. Lower-case letters at the beginning of the alphabet will be used for terminals: $a, b, c, \ldots$. Strings of terminals will be denoted by lower-case letters toward the end of the alphabet: $v, w, x, \ldots$. Strings of mixed terminals and nonterminals will be represented by lower-case Greek letters: $\alpha, \beta, \gamma, \delta, \ldots$.

The set P of productions consists of expressions of the form $\alpha \to \beta$, where α is a string in V^+ and β is a string in V^*. In other words, the symbol $\to$ indicates replacement of the string α by the string β. The symbol $\underset{G}{\Rightarrow}$ will be used to indicate operations of the form $\gamma\alpha\delta \underset{G}{\Rightarrow} \gamma\beta\delta$ in the grammar G, that is, $\underset{G}{\Rightarrow}$ indicates the replacement of α by β by means of the production $\alpha \rightarrow \beta$, γ and δ being left unchanged. It is customary to drop the G and simply use the symbol $\Rightarrow$ when it is clear which grammar is being considered.

Example: Consider the grammar $G = (V_N, V_T, P, S)$, where $V_N = \{S\}$, $V_T = \{a, b\}$, and $P = \{S \rightarrow aSb, S \rightarrow ab\}$. If the first production is applied $m - 1$ times, we obtain

$$S \Rightarrow aSb \Rightarrow aaSbb \Rightarrow a^3Sb^3 \Rightarrow \cdots a^{m-1}Sb^{m-1}$$

Applying now the second production results in the string

$$a^{m-1}Sb^{m-1} \Rightarrow a^m b^m$$

The language generated by this grammar is seen to consist solely of strings of this type, where the length of a particular string depends on m. We may express $L(G)$ in the form $L(G) = \{a^m b^m | m \geqslant 1\}$. It is worth noticing that the simple grammar of this example is capable of producing a language with an infinite number of strings or sentences. ●

8.2.2 Types of Grammars

In this section we consider grammars which are specific examples of Eq. (8.2–1). These grammars are all of the form $G = (V_N, V_T, P, S)$, differing only in the type of productions allowed in each.

An *unrestricted grammar* has productions of the form $\alpha \rightarrow \beta$, where α is a string in V^+ and β is a string in V^*.

A *context-sensitive grammar* has productions of the form $\alpha_1 A \alpha_2 \rightarrow \alpha_1 \beta \alpha_2$, where α_1 and α_2 are in V^*, β is in V^+, and A is in V_N. This grammar allows replacement of the nonterminal A by the string β only when A appears in the context $\alpha_1 A \alpha_2$ of strings α_1 and α_2. An alternative definition is $\alpha \rightarrow \beta$, with both α and β in V^+ and the length of α not exceeding that of β.

A *context-free grammar* has productions of the form $A \rightarrow \beta$, where A is in V_N and β is in V^+. The name context free arises from the fact that the variable A may be replaced by a string β regardless of the context in which A appears.

Finally, a *regular* (or *finite-state*) *grammar* is one with productions of the form $A \rightarrow aB$ or $A \rightarrow a$, where A and B are variables in V_N and a is a terminal in V_T. Alternative valid productions are $A \to Ba$ and $A \to a$. However, once one of the two types has been chosen, the other set must be excluded.

These grammars are sometimes called *type* 0, 1, 2, and 3 *grammars*, respectively. They are also often referred to as *phrase-structure grammars*.

If every production of a context-free grammar is of the form $A \to xBw$ or $A \to w$, where A and B are nonterminals and x and w are terminal strings, the grammar is said to be *linear*.

It is interesting to note that all regular grammars are context free, all context-free grammars are context sensitive, and all context-sensitive grammars are unrestricted.

Example: The mechanics of the above discussion are illustrated by the following simple grammars.

(a) The unrestricted grammar

$$G = (V_N, V_T, P, S)$$

with

$$V_N = \{S, A, B\}, \qquad V_T = \{a, b, c\}$$

$$P: \quad S \to aAbc$$

$$Ab \to bA$$

$$Ac \to Bbcc$$

$$bB \to Bb$$

$$aB \to aaA$$

$$aB \to s_o$$

generates sentences of the form $x = a^n b^{n+2} c^{n+2}$, where $n \geqslant 0$ indicates the length of a string of symbols. For example, to generate $x = a^0 b^2 c^2 = bbcc$, we apply the first four productions followed by the last, that is,

$$S \Rightarrow aAbc \Rightarrow abAc \Rightarrow abBbcc \Rightarrow aBbbcc \Rightarrow bbcc$$

Note that the last production is allowed only in unrestricted grammars.

(b) The context-sensitive (using the second definition given above) grammar

$$G = (V_N, V_T, P, S)$$

with

$$V_N = \{S, A, B\}, \qquad V_T = \{a, b, c\}$$

$$\begin{aligned} P\colon\quad S &\to abc \\ S &\to aAbc \\ Ab &\to bA \\ Ac &\to Bbcc \\ bB &\to Bb \\ aB &\to aaA \\ aB &\to aa \end{aligned}$$

generates sentences of the form $x = a^n b^n c^n$, where $n \geqslant 1$.

(c) The context-free grammar

$$G = (V_N, V_T, P, S)$$

with

$$V_N = \{S\}, \qquad V_T = \{a, b\}$$

$$\begin{aligned} P\colon\ S &\to ab \\ S &\to aSb \end{aligned}$$

generates strings of the form $x = a^n b^n$, where $n \geqslant 1$.

(d) The regular grammar

$$G = (V_N, V_T, P, S)$$

with

$$V_N = \{S\}, \qquad V_T = \{a, b\}$$

$$\begin{aligned} P\colon\ S &\to a \\ S &\to b \end{aligned}$$

$$S \rightarrow aS$$

$$S \rightarrow bS$$

generates strings of a's and b's.

As expected, unrestricted grammars are considerably more powerful than the other three types. However, their generality presents some serious difficulties in the theoretical and practical applications of these grammars. This is also true of context-sensitive grammars. ●

Although other grammatical structures are often found in the literature, the grammars defined in this section constitute the foundation for most of the research in this area. In the following sections we will be concerned with the extension of these concepts and their application to pattern recognition.

8.3 FORMULATION OF THE SYNTACTIC PATTERN RECOGNITION PROBLEM

The concepts presented in Section 8.2 can be related to pattern recognition in the following manner. Suppose that we have two pattern classes, ω_1 and ω_2. Let the patterns of these classes be composed of features from some finite set. We call the features *terminals* and denote the set of terminals by V_T, in agreement with the notation introduced in Section 8.2. The term *primitives* is also often used in syntactic pattern recognition terminology to denote terminals. Each pattern may be considered as a string or sentence since it is composed of terminals from the set V_T. Assume that there exists a grammar G with the property that the language it generates consists of sentences (patterns) which belong exclusively to one of the pattern classes, say ω_1. This grammar can clearly be used for pattern classification since a given pattern of unknown origin can be classified as belonging to ω_1 if it is a sentence of $L(G)$. Otherwise the pattern is assigned to ω_2. For example, the context-free grammar $G = (V_N, V_T, P, S)$ with $V_N = \{S\}$, $V_T = \{a, b\}$, and production set $P = \{S \rightarrow aaSb, S \rightarrow aab\}$, is capable of generating only sentences which contain twice as many a's as b's. If we formulate a hypothetical two-class pattern recognition problem in which the patterns of class ω_1 are strings of forms *aab*, *aaaabb*, and so forth, while the patterns of ω_2 contain equal numbers of a's and b's (i.e., *ab*, *aabb*, etc.), it is clear that classification of a given pattern string can be accomplished simply by determining whether the given string can be generated by the grammar G discussed above. If it can, the pattern belongs to ω_1. If it cannot, it is automatically assigned to ω_2. The procedure used to determine whether or not a string represents a sentence which is grammatically correct with respect to a given language is called *parsing*. We will have more to say about parsing methods later on in this chapter.

The above classification scheme assigns a pattern into class ω_2 strictly by default. If a pattern is found to be an incorrect sentence over G, it is assumed that the pattern must belong to ω_2. However, it is entirely possible that the pattern does not belong to ω_2 either. It may represent a noisy or distorted string which is best rejected. In order to provide a rejection capability it is necessary to determine two grammars, G_1 and G_2, which generate languages $L(G_1)$ and $L(G_2)$. A pattern is assigned to the class over whose language it represents a grammatically correct sentence. If the pattern is found to belong to both classes it may be arbitrarily assigned to either class. If it is not a sentence of either $L(G_1)$ or $L(G_2)$, the pattern is rejected.

In the M-class case we consider M grammars and their associated languages $L(G_i)$, $i = 1, 2, \ldots, M$. An unknown pattern is classified into class ω_i if and only if it is a sentence of $L(G_i)$. If the pattern belongs to more than one language, or if it does not belong to any of the languages, it may be rejected or arbitrarily assigned to one of the ambiguous classes.

Several fundamental questions associated with the above approach to pattern recognition come immediately to mind. (1) How are the patterns best described for classification by this technique? (2) How are the recognition grammars selected? (3) Any problem of practical significance is normally corrupted by random variables such as measurement noise; how can statistical considerations be incorporated into the syntactic approach to account for these random variables? (4) One of the most important characteristics of the previously-discussed approaches to pattern recognition is the ability to derive decision functions by iterative training procedures; can the concept of learning from training samples be extended to the syntactic approach? These questions are individually considered in the following sections.

8.4 SYNTACTIC PATTERN DESCRIPTION

The patterns which have been considered thus far in this chapter have been strings of symbols. If we are to make real use of the structural properties associated with syntactic pattern recognition, the concept of a string must be generalized to two dimensions. As was pointed out in Section 8.1, we are primarily concerned in this chapter with two-dimensional patterns.

The productions of string grammars are simply juxtapositions[†] of strings to form new strings. Juxtaposition of two-dimensional structures is not a straightforward problem, however. The reader can prove this for himself by examining the variety of structures that result from two-dimensional juxtapositions of the simple primitives | and —. A direct attack on this problem involves the concept of two-dimensional position on a fairly general level. For example, consider the positional descriptors ABOVE (a, b) to indicate that the structure represented by a is above the structure represented by b, and LEFT (a, b) to indicate that a is to the left of b. With these descriptors, the square structure □ composed of the primitives | and — would be described by the statement ABOVE (—, ABOVE (LEFT (|,|), —)). The main difficulty with this approach is the characterization of the descriptors ABOVE and LEFT. For example, the structure | |‾_ also satisfies the foregoing description of a square. Whether or not this is a valid pattern depends on the application. However, it should be evident that general positional descriptors are difficult to specify. What is often done is to constrain the relationship between structures. For instance, for the descriptor ABOVE (a, b), a reasonable restriction is to require that at least part of a be above b. In this case the structure | |‾_ would not be a valid square since ‾ is not above | | and the latter structure is not above _.

The idea of constraining the rules for juxtaposition can be carried one step further with considerable simplifications resulting in the grammatical formalisms required for pattern description and recognition. A simple scheme which has been employed in the most successful experiments with syntactic pattern recognition consists of requiring that structures be joined only at prespecified points. One way to accomplish this is to require that each structure have two distinguished points and, furthermore, that juxtapositions of structures take place only at these points. We will consider later a syntactic pattern recognition system which employs this approach. The two distinguished points in this system are interpreted as the *head* and *tail* of an arrow defined by these two points, as shown in Fig. 8.2(a). Typical valid rules for juxtapositions in this system are shown in Fig. 8.2(b). It is evident

† The term concatenation is also often used. There is a difference, however, between these two terms. Juxtapositioning two objects means simply placing the objects together, with each object maintaining its individual identity. Concatenation, on the other hand, involves spatial rearrangement as well as a loss of identity on the part of the individual objects. An important difference here is that any concatenation of objects is also an object, whereas the juxtaposition of objects may, but need not, be considered as a single object. Since the ability to retain identity often plays a crucial role in pattern description, we will use the term juxtaposition throughout this chapter. The reader should be aware, however, that these two terms are often used interchangeably in the literature.

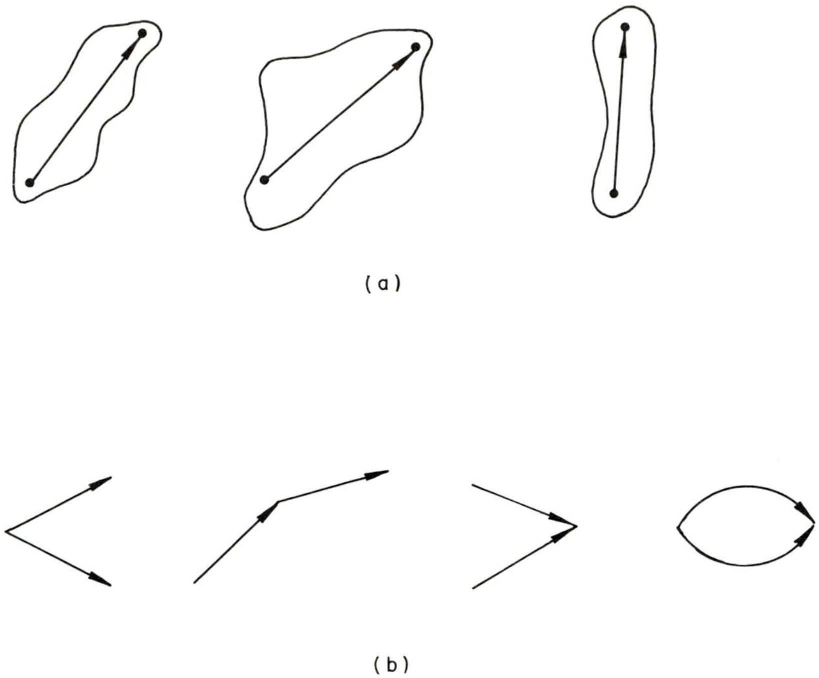

Figure 8.2. Reduction of the juxtaposition problem to one dimension by abstracting patterns as directed line segments. (a) Sample patterns. (b) Typical valid rules of juxtaposition for the abstracted patterns

that this approach effectively reduces the two-dimensional juxtaposition problem to equivalent string manipulations, which can be handled by the familiar string grammars previously discussed.

Another useful technique for describing two-dimensional relationships is based on tree structures. A *tree* is a finite set T of one or more nodes such that (1) there is one especially designated node called the *root* of the tree; and (2) the remaining nodes (excluding the root) are partitioned into $m \geqslant 0$ disjoint sets $T_1, T_2, \ldots, T_m$, where each of these sets is in turn a tree. The trees $T_1, T_2, \ldots, T_m$ are called *subtrees* of the root. The number of subtrees of a node is called the *degree* of that node. A node of degree zero is called a *leaf*, while a node of higher degree is called a *branch node*. Finally, the tree representation of a pattern is called a *pattern tree*.

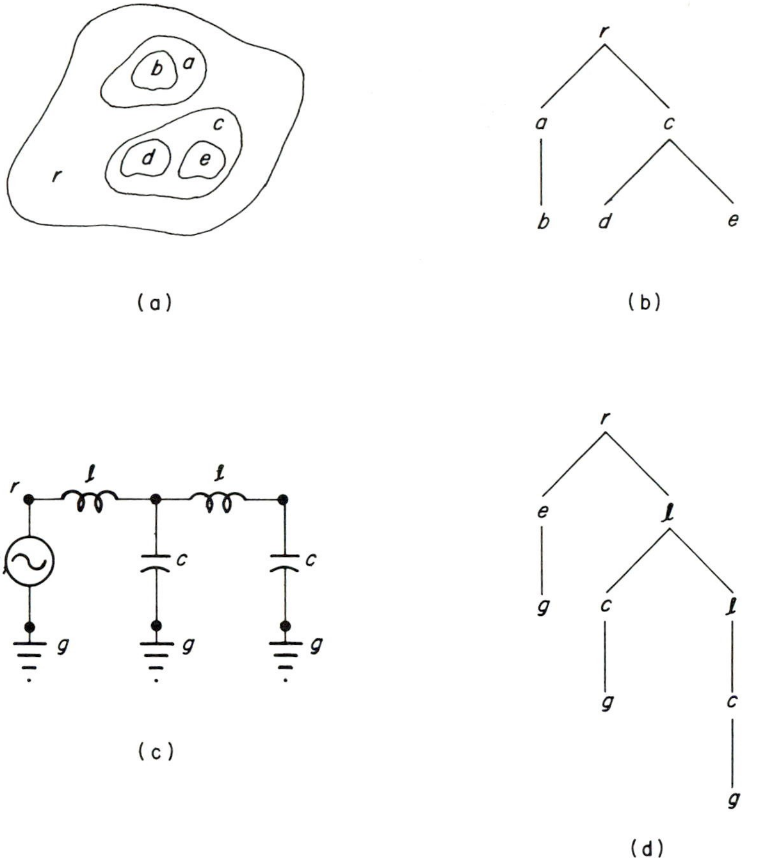

Figure 8.3. Tree representation of patterns

The use of trees for describing higher-dimensional structures is straightforward. Basically, any hierarchical ordering scheme leads to a tree representation. Two examples of this are shown in Fig. 8.3. In Fig. 8.3(a) the ordering consists of nested regions where, for example, region b is contained in region a, which is in turn contained in region r. If we denote the root of a tree by r, the tree structure shown in Fig. 8.3(b) follows naturally from the above ordering scheme. A second example is shown in Fig. 8.3(c). In this case, the connectivity of the various circuit components determines the resulting two-dimensional pattern. The corresponding pattern tree is shown in Fig. 8.3(d). It is noted that each tree node represents a node in the circuit, and also that the root of the pattern tree is arbitrarily defined as the leftmost upper node in the pattern.

8.5 RECOGNITION GRAMMARS

In this section we consider the problem of recognizing patterns by the syntactic approach. The mechanics for determining whether or not a pattern can be generated by a particular grammar are discussed in Section 8.5.1. Section 8.5.2 deals with the recognition of two-dimensional patterns which can be reduced to an equivalent string representation. This simplification plays an important role in the design of syntactic pattern recognition systems since it allows the utilization of well-established concepts from string grammars. Finally, in Section 8.5.3 we consider the recognition of patterns which are expressed as tree structures. These structures are handled by tree grammars, which are an extension of the results discussed thus far in this chapter.

8.5.1 Syntax-Directed Recognition

It was indicated in Section 8.3 that formal grammars can be used for pattern recognition by determining whether a given pattern represents a terminal sentence which can be generated by any of the grammars under consideration for a specific problem. Once the grammars are known, the basic problem is the development of a procedure for determining whether or not a given pattern represents a valid sentence. The procedure used in formal language theory to accomplish this is called *parsing*. Basically, we consider two types of parsing techniques: *top-down* and *bottom-up*. These names make more sense if viewed in terms of a semantic tree such as the one shown in Fig. 8.1. The top or *root* of the (inverted) tree is the start symbol S. The terminal sentences (patterns) represent the bottom or leaves of the tree. The top-down technique starts with the root symbol S and, through repeated applications of the productions of the grammar, attempts to arrive at the given terminal sentence. The bottom-up approach, on the other hand, starts with the given sentence and attempts to arrive at the symbol S by applying the productions in reverse. In either case, if the parse fails, the given pattern represents an incorrect sentence and is therefore rejected.

It is evident that the parsing schemes described above are inherently inefficient since they involve essentially an exhaustive search in the applications of the productions of the grammar. However, it is seldom necessary to carry a sequence of productions all the way through, since partial results can be checked against the desired goal in order to determine whether a given sequence of productions has the potential to produce a successful parse.

The parsing process can be further improved by employing the rules of *syntax* of the grammar. Syntax is defined as the juxtaposition and concatenation of objects. A *rule of syntax* states some permissible (or prohibited) relations between objects. For example, the juxtaposition *qqq* never occurs in the English language. In this terminology, a grammar is nothing more than a set of rules of syntax which define the permissible or desired relations between objects. A *syntax-directed* parser, therefore, employs the syntax of the grammar in the parsing process. The following example should further clarify these concepts.

Example: Let us return to the square-like structures used in illustrating the developments of the preceding section. The primitives are a horizontal and a vertical line of fixed length, denoted by a_1 and a_2, respectively, as shown in Fig. 8.4(a). A context-free grammar capable of generating squares is given by $G = (V_N, V_T, P, S)$ with

$$V_T = \{a_1, a_2\}, \qquad V_N = \{S, O_1, O_2\}$$

$$P\colon\ S \to A(a_1, O_2),$$

$$O_2 \to A(O_1, a_1),$$

$$O_1 \to L(a_2, a_2)$$

where $A(x, y)$ and $L(x, y)$ read "x is above y" and "x is to the left of y," respectively. It is important to point out again that in order to handle pictorial patterns we must be able to generalize the productions of the grammar to handle two-dimensional juxtapositions. In this simple example we consider the positional descriptor $A(x, y)$ to be valid only if part of y is directly below x, and the descriptor $L(x, y)$ to be valid only if part of y is directly to the right of x.

The square-like structures shown in Fig. 8.4(b) are generated by the following sequence of productions:

$$S \to A(a_1, O_2)$$

This production replaces the start symbol by primitive a_1 located above some object O_2, not yet defined. The production

$$O_2 \to A(O_1, a_1)$$

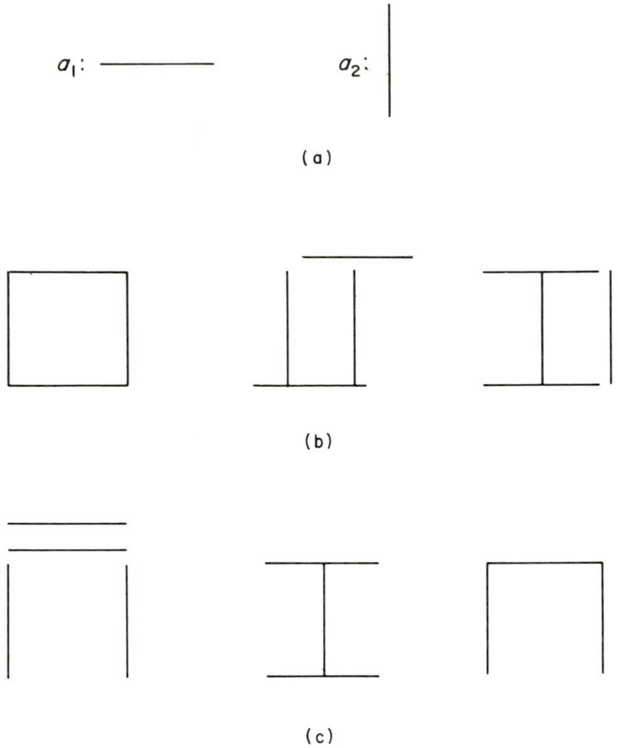

Figure 8.4. Patterns used in the illustration of syntax-directed parsing. (a) Pattern primitives. (b) Patterns that would parse correctly. (c) Patterns that would fail the parse

replaces the undefined object O_2 by another object O_1, not yet defined, located above a horizontal segment a_1. Finally, O_1 is replaced by two vertical primitives by use of the production

$$O_1 \rightarrow L(a_2, a_2)$$

Simply stated, the construction of these structures is started with a horizontal segment, followed by another horizontal segment below it, and completed by placing two vertical segments in between. The variability of the structures can be controlled by the constraints placed on the positional descriptors $A(x, y)$ and $L(x, y)$. It is also worth noting that the above grammar is capable only of generating square-like structures and that only the sequence of productions illustrated above is allowed.

Parsing in this simple system is a straightforward procedure since there is only one possible sequence of productions. For example, suppose that it is desired to determine whether or not a given structure belongs to the class of patterns generated by the above grammar. A syntax-directed, top-down parse would proceed as follows. Starting from S, the first production says to look for some object O_2 below a primitive a_1. If no object is found below some a_1, the parse fails at this point and the pattern is rejected. If this production is satisfied, we next look for some object O_1 above a different primitive a_1. The first a_1 is not considered a part of O_1. If O_1 is found, the parse proceeds; otherwise the pattern is rejected. Finally, the object O_1 found in the preceding step must resolve into two a_2 primitives satisfying the condition $L(a_2, a_2)$ if the pattern is to be accepted. The structures shown in Fig. 8.4(b) would satisfy this parsing scheme, whereas those in Fig. 8.4(c) would be rejected.

A syntax-directed, bottom-up parse, which consists of applying the productions in reverse, would proceed as follows. First we attempt to find O_1 by determining whether the given pattern contains a_2 to the left of a_2. If this search is successful, the procedure is continued; otherwise the pattern is rejected. It is noted that, since the bottom-up parse starts with the terminal sentence, the productions yielding only terminals must be considered first. To continue the parse it is necessary to produce O_2 next; this consists of O_1 above a primitive a_1. If this step is successful, we attempt to produce the start symbol S by looking for a_1 above O_2. If S can be produced, the pattern is accepted; otherwise it is rejected at this step. The patterns shown in Fig. 8.4(b) would parse correctly, whereas those in Fig. 8.4(c) would be rejected at some point in the parsing process. ●

8.5.2 Recognition of Graph-Like Patterns

Although the foregoing example certainly illustrates the principles of the syntactic approach, we recognize that it is considerably idealized, particularly since the grammar is capable of executing only one sequence of productions. There is, however, one important problem which is evident in this example. It should be clear that scanning for the primitives or substructures of interest in a two-dimensional situation can represent a formidable task for a machine. Although this problem was discussed in the preceding section, it is worth mentioning again since it constitutes one of the principal obstacles in the way of a truly general syntactic pattern recognition system. To date, most suc-

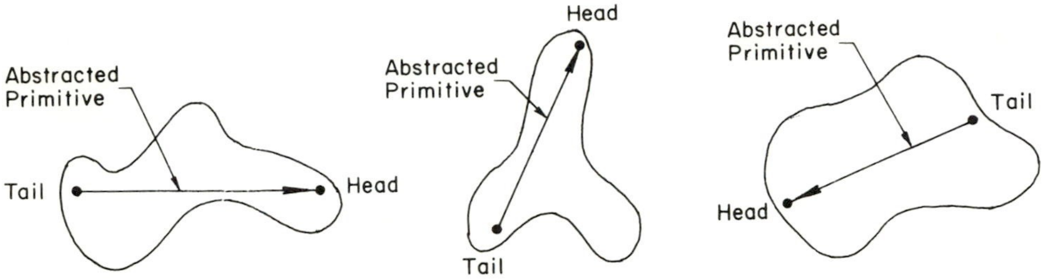

Figure 8.5. Abstraction of pattern structures by directed line segments for use in PDL

cessful attempts in this area have involved patterns which can be reduced to graph-like structures. In this section, we discuss several of these approaches in order to illustrate the basic concepts followed in the syntactic recognition of graph-like patterns.

An interesting application of linguistic concepts to pattern recognition is the Picture Description Language (PDL) proposed by Shaw [1970]. A primitive in PDL is any n-dimensional structure with two distinguished points, a *tail* and a *head*, as shown in Fig. 8.5 for two-dimensional structures. Observe that a fairly general structure can be abstracted as a directed line segment since there are only two points of definition.

A primitive can be linked to other primitives *only* at its tail and/or head. On the basis of this permissible form of juxtapositioning, and because of the fact that each primitive is abstracted as a directed line segment, it is evident that the structures of PDL are directed graphs, and also that these structures can be handled by string grammars.

The principal rules for the juxtaposition of abstracted primitives are shown in Fig. 8.6. It is important to point out that *blank* primitives may be used to generate seemingly disjoint structures while preserving the rules of connectivity. Also, it is often useful to consider a *null point* primitive having identical head and tail.

The mechanics of PDL are best illustrated by an example. Consider the following simple PDL grammar:

$$G = (V_N, V_T, P, S)$$

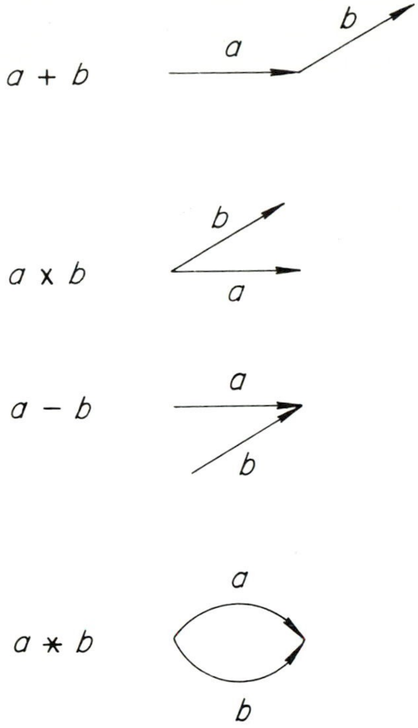

Figure 8.6. Rules of juxtaposition in PDL

with

$$V_N = \{S, A_1, A_2, A_3, A_4, A_5\}$$

$$V_T = \{a\nearrow, b\searrow, c\rightarrow, d\downarrow\}$$

$$P:\quad S \rightarrow d + A_1$$

$$A_1 \rightarrow c + A_2$$

$$A_2 \rightarrow \sim d * A_3$$

$$A_3 \rightarrow a + A_4$$

$$A_4 \rightarrow b * A_5$$

$$A_5 \rightarrow c$$

where $(\sim d)$ indicates the primitive d with its direction reversed.

Application of the first production yields a primitive d followed by a variable not yet defined. All we know at this point is that the tail of the structure represented by A_1 will be connected to the head of d because this primitive is followed by the "+" operator. The variable A_1 resolves into $c + A_2$, where A_2 is not yet defined. Similarly, A_2 resolves into $\sim d * A_3$. The results of applying the first three productions are shown in Figs. 8.7(a), (b), and (c). From the definition of the operator "$*$" we know that when A_3 is resolved it will be connected to the composite structure shown in Fig. 8.7(c) in a tail-to-tail and head-to-head fashion. The final result obtained by applying all the productions is shown in Fig. 8.7(f).

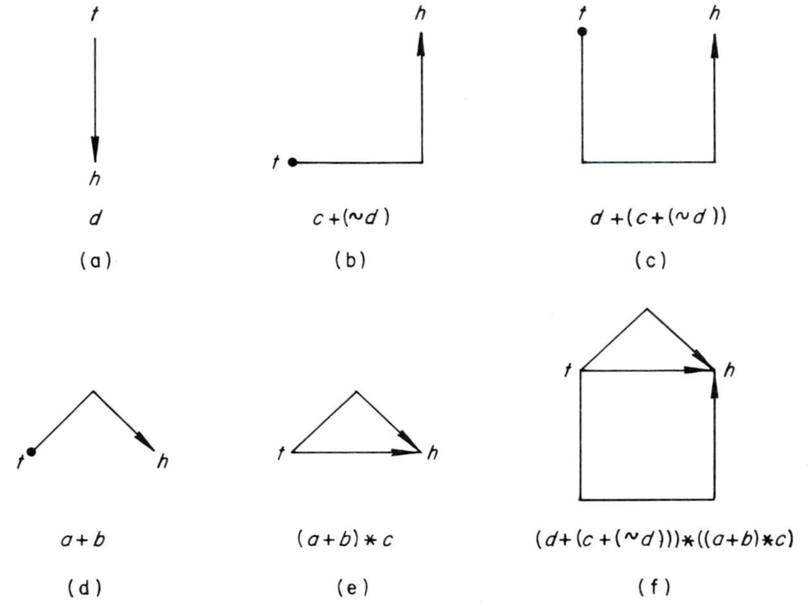

Figure 8.7. Steps in the construction of a PDL structure. Note the heads and tails of composite substructures

The PDL grammar described above can generate only one structure. However, the scope of structures generated by this grammar can be extended by introducing recursiveness—the capability of a variable to replace itself—into the productions. For example, suppose that we define the following productions:

$$S \rightarrow d + A_1$$

$$A_1 \rightarrow c + A_1$$

$$A_1 \rightarrow \sim d * A_2$$

$$A_2 \rightarrow a + A_2$$

$$A_2 \rightarrow b * A_2$$

$$A_2 \rightarrow c$$

If these productions were applied in the order shown, they would produce Fig. 8.7(f). However, this new set of productions allows, for instance, the application of the first production followed by the third, completely omitting the second production. If the remaining productions were applied in order, we would obtain a triangular structure. Furthermore, these productions allow the generation of infinite structures by repeated substitutions of a variable by itself. The variety of structures generated by the above grammar can be increased further by letting A_1 and A_2 equal S. This substitution would yield the maximum capability of this grammar. It should be noted, however, that increasing the generating capability of a grammar is not always desirable. This is particularly true in syntactic pattern recognition applications where more than one grammar is required. In this case, excessive variability reduces the discriminatory power of the grammars involved.

The parsing of structures using the above grammar is, in principle, straightforward. For example, suppose that the pattern of Fig. 8.7(f) is presented for recognition and that the second set of productions is used. A top-down parsing sequence would proceed as follows. Let us assume that the pattern in question has been scanned to produce its terminal representation $(d + (c + (\sim d))) * ((a + b) * c)$. As was mentioned earlier, the scanning process generally is not a trivial procedure. A top-down parser starts with S and attempts to produce the pattern in question by applying the productions from the grammar. In this case, S calls for $d + A_1$. The terminal d followed by "+" is found, so the parse continues by trying to resolve A_1. Here we have two choices since A_1 can be resolved by using either the second or third production. The second production is successful since a c follows the first "+" in the pattern. The third production does not meet this requirement. In order to resolve the A_1 following the "+" after c, we must find a production of the form $A_1 \rightarrow \sim d$ which is followed by "$*$." The third production satisfies this condition. Continuing with this procedure, it is evident that the given pattern would parse correctly. When two or more grammars are present, the parsing is carried out for each grammar until a match is found or the grammars are exhausted, in which case the pattern is rejected.

Another interesting application of syntactic pattern recognition is the work of Ledley [1964, 1965] dealing with the automatic classification of chromosomes. The following context-free grammar is capable of classifying a chromosome as being either *submedian* or *telocentric*:

$$V_T = \{a, b, c, d, e\}$$

$$V_N = \{S, T, Bottom, Side, Armpair, Rightpart, Leftpart, Arm\}$$

$$
\begin{aligned}
P: \qquad S &\rightarrow Armpair \cdot Armpair \\
T &\rightarrow Bottom \cdot Armpair \\
Armpair &\rightarrow Side \cdot Armpair \\
Armpair &\rightarrow Armpair \cdot Side \\
Armpair &\rightarrow Arm \cdot Rightpart \\
Armpair &\rightarrow Leftpart \cdot Arm \\
Leftpart &\rightarrow Arm \cdot c \\
Rightpart &\rightarrow c \cdot Arm \\
Bottom &\rightarrow b \cdot Bottom \\
Bottom &\rightarrow Bottom \cdot b \\
Bottom &\rightarrow e \\
Side &\rightarrow b \cdot Side \\
Side &\rightarrow Side \cdot b \\
Side &\rightarrow b \\
Side &\rightarrow d \\
Arm &\rightarrow b \cdot Arm \\
Arm &\rightarrow Arm \cdot b \\
Arm &\rightarrow a
\end{aligned}
$$

The primitives $\{a, b, c, d, e\}$ are shown in Fig. 8.8(a); typical submedian and telocentric chromosomes, in Fig. 8.8(b). In terms of these figures, we interpret the operator "·" as describing simple connectivity of parts as a chromosome boundary is tracked in the clockwise direction. The starting symbols S and T represent submedian and telocentric chromosomes, respectively. It is interesting to note that a single grammar with two starting symbols is used here to perform classification into two classes. If, for example, a bottom-up parse arrives at T, the chromosome is said to be telocentric.

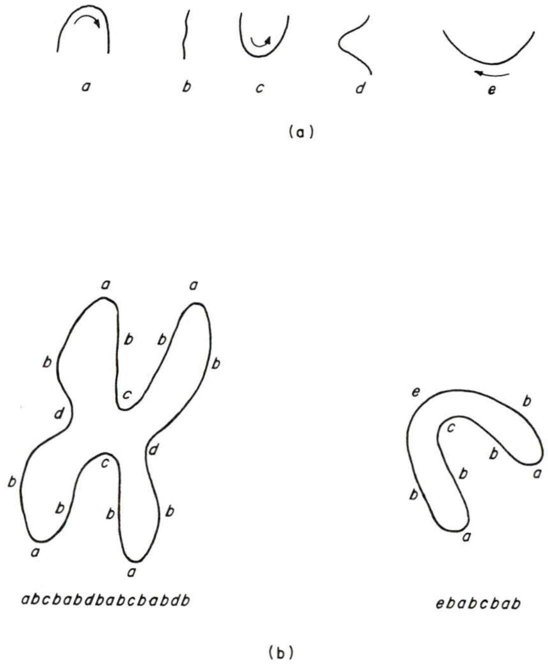

Figure 8.8. (a) Primitives of a chromosome grammar. (b) Submedian and telocentric chromosomes and corresponding terminal sentences. From R. S. Ledley, "High-Speed Automatic Analysis of Biomedical Pictures," *Science*, vol. 146, No. 3641, 1964

If the parse arrives at S, it is classified as a submedian chromosome. Of course, if the parse fails, the chromosome is rejected. It should be clear that using a single grammar for classification is really nothing more than uniting two classification grammars with different starting symbols. This can always be done, but it makes sense only when the grammars are sufficiently alike, since nothing would be gained by uniting vastly distinct grammars.

Let us illustrate the bottom-up approach by considering in some detail how this scheme can be employed in conjunction with the above chromosome grammar. For a given digitized image of a chromosome, the first step in the recognition process is to find a boundary point on the chromosome and then to track this boundary in the clockwise direction. As the boundary is tracked, a set of recognition routines detects the primitive elements $\{a, b, c, d, e\}$. At the end of the tracking stage, a chromosome has been effectively reduced to a string of primitives to form a terminal sentence, as shown in Fig. 8.8(b).

The syntactic recognition process commences after a chromosome has been reduced to a terminal sentence. Consider, for example, the sentence resulting from the submedian chromosome shown in Fig. 8.8(b). A bottom-up parser would start by applying the productions of the grammar in reverse. Let us follow the order of the productions *in reverse*, starting with $Arm \rightarrow a$. Thus, if the parser finds a, it returns the nonterminal *Arm*. As shown in Fig. 8.9, a is found four times, thus producing four nonterminals *Arm* at the first level of search counting from the bottom. The next productions combine *Arm* with b. As can be seen in the tree, only *Arms* are produced at the next level. Following a prespecified, ordered sequence can reduce the number of attempts in the parsing process. The "best" order is found by experimentation. The next productions of interest deal with the generation of *Side*. Three of these nonterminals are produced, two by the d's and one by the only b left. In the next two levels we see the combination of *Arm* with c to produce *Rightpart*, and of *Rightpart* with *Arm* to produce *Armpair*. Finally, the combination of *Armpairs* with *Sides* produces two *Armpairs*, which are then combined to produce S and thus terminate the bottom-up parse. Therefore, the chromosome has been properly classified as submedian.

It should be noted that, because of the way in which the chromosomes are tracked, the resulting symbol strings are not always in the correct order for parsing. This difficulty is easily resolved, however, by realizing that the beginning and the end of a string are in reality adjacent since, after all, a string is produced by a complete revolution around the chromosome boundary. For example, if the string of Fig. 8.8(b) had instead been *bcbabdbabcbabdba*, the first b would have been combined with the last a to form *Arm*.

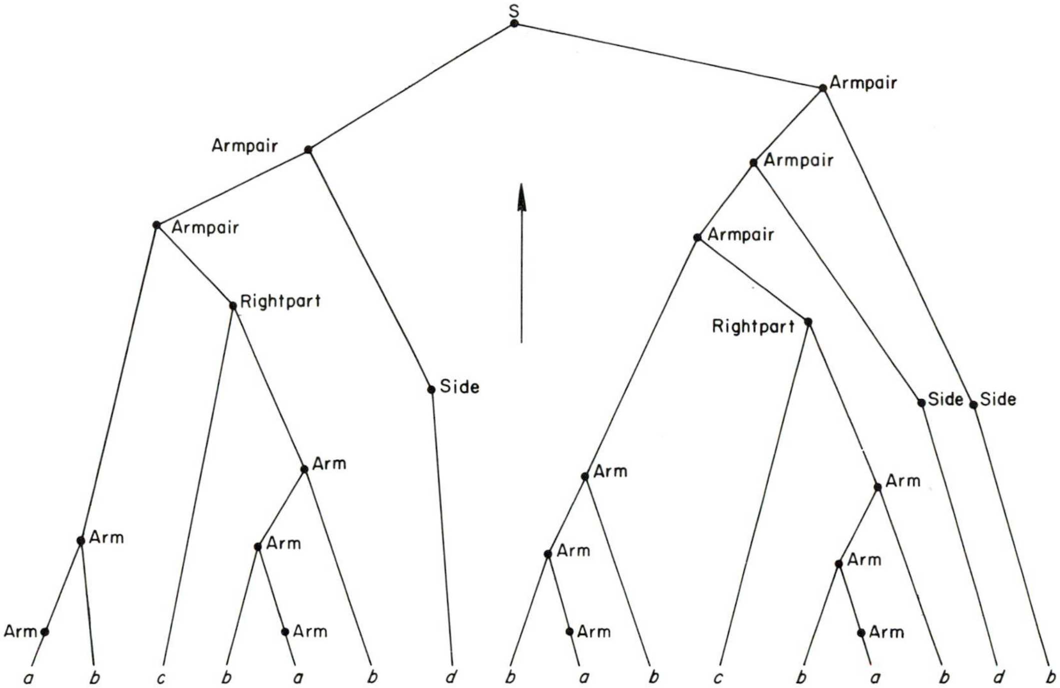

Figure 8.9. Bottom-up parsing of the chromosome sentence *abcbabdbabcbabdb*

The parse shown here was successful in the first pass. This, of course, is not true in general since frequent back-ups are usually necessary. These back-ups can be minimized, however, by the ordering previously mentioned and also by building heuristic rules into the search process which tell the parser which way to proceed in situations where more than one action can be taken.

8.5.3 Recognition of Tree Structures

In order to handle tree structures it is necessary to modify slightly our concept of a grammar. A *tree grammar* is defined as a quintuple

$$G = (V_N, V_T, P, R, S) \tag{8.5–1}$$

where V_N and V_T are, as before, sets of nonterminals and terminals, respectively; S is the start symbol which can, in general, be a tree; P is a set of productions of the form $\Omega \to \Psi$, where Ω and Ψ are trees; and R is a *ranking function* which denotes the number of direct descendants of a node whose label is a terminal in the grammar.

As an example of a tree grammar, consider the electric circuit shown in Fig. 8.3(c). A grammar for this pattern consists of the following elements:

$$V_N = \{A, S\}, \qquad V_T = \{r, e, l, c, g\}$$

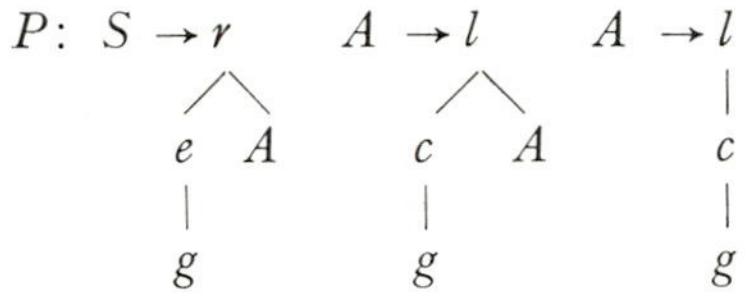

$$R(r) = 2$$

$$R(l) = \{2, 1\}$$

$$R(e) = 1$$

$$R(g) = 0$$

$$R(c) = 1$$

In order to generate a particular pattern, it is required that all nonterminal nodes be rewritten to yield a tree in which all nodes are labeled as terminals.

The recognition of tree structures can be accomplished by the techniques discussed earlier in this section with the exception, of course, that the productions must be of a tree nature, as specified in the tree grammar.

8.6 STATISTICAL CONSIDERATIONS

Statistical concepts and methodologies must be called upon to describe and characterize variables in a random environment. In pattern recognition, this randomness is generally due to two principal factors: measurement noise, and lack of complete knowledge about the characteristics of the pattern classes. In this section, attention is focused on the generalization of the basic formal grammar model $G = (V_N, V_T, P, S)$ to encompass a statistical framework. The resulting *stochastic* model of the grammar can then be made to absorb statistical considerations in the recognition process.

8.6.1 Stochastic Grammars and Languages

A very meaningful way to incorporate statistics into our grammatical formulations is to let the productions of a grammar be nondeterministic and to assign a certain probability measure to each of these productions. On the basis of this idea, we define a *stochastic grammar* as follows:

$$G = (V_N, V_T, P, Q, S) \tag{8.6–1}$$

where V_N, V_T, P, and S are, as before, sets of nonterminals, terminals, productions, and the start symbol, respectively, and Q is a set of probability assignments over the productions of P. The basic definitions of unrestricted, context-sensitive, context-free, and regular grammars given in Section 8.2.2 hold also for stochastic grammars. As before, the type of grammar depends on the type of productions allowed in the set P.

Consider the following generation of a terminal string x starting from S:

$$S \overset{r_1}{\Rightarrow} \alpha_1 \overset{r_2}{\Rightarrow} \alpha_2 \Rightarrow \cdots \overset{r_m}{\Rightarrow} \alpha_m = x \tag{8.6–2}$$

where $\{r_1, r_2, \ldots, r_m\}$ represent *any m* productions from P, and $\alpha_1, \alpha_2, \ldots, \alpha_{m-1}$ are intermediate strings. Let the various productions have probabilities of being applied which are given by $p(r_1), p(r_2), \ldots, p(r_m)$. Then, the *probability of generation* of x is given by

$$p(x) = p(r_1)p(r_2/r_1)p(r_3/r_1r_2)\cdots p(r_m/r_1r_2\cdots r_{m-1}) \tag{8.6–3}$$

where $p(r_j/r_1r_2\cdots r_{j-1})$ is the conditional probability associated with production r_j, given that productions $r_1, r_2, \ldots, r_{j-1}$ have previously been applied.

If $p(r_j/r_1r_2\cdots r_{j-1}) = p(r_j)$, the probability assignment associated with production r_j is said to be *unrestricted*; Q is unrestricted if all its probability assignments are unrestricted. A stochastic grammar is said to be *ambiguous* if there are n distinct generations of x with probabilities $p_1(x), p_2(x), \ldots, p_n(x)$, $n > 1$. Thus, for an ambiguous stochastic grammar, the probability of generation of x is given by

$$p(x) = \sum_{i=1}^{n} p_i(x) \tag{8.6–4}$$

The set Q is *consistent* if

$$\sum_{x \in L(G)} p(x) = 1 \tag{8.6–5}$$

A *stochastic language* $L(G)$ is the language generated by a stochastic grammar G. Each terminal string x in $L(G)$ must have a probability of generation

$p(x)$ associated with it. We may formally define the stochastic language generated by a stochastic grammar G as follows:

$$L(G) = \left\{[x, p(x)] \mid x \in V_T^+, S \overset{*}{\Rightarrow} x, p(x) = \sum_{i=1}^{n} p_i(x)\right\} \qquad (8.6\text{–}6)$$

where V_T^+ is the set of all terminal strings, excluding the empty string, generated by G, and $S \overset{*}{\Rightarrow} x$ is used to indicate that x is derivable from S by suitable applications of productions from P. Simply stated, Eq. (8.6–6) indicates that a stochastic language is the set of all terminal strings, where each string has a probability of generation associated with it, and all strings are derivable from S. The probability of generation $p(x)$ is given by the sum of all distinct probabilities of generation of x. It is noted, however, that if $n > 1$ the stochastic language is ambiguous. The above concepts are illustrated by the following example.

Example: Consider the stochastic, context-free grammar given by

$$G = (V_N, V_T, P, Q, S)$$

where

$$V_T = \{a, b\}, \qquad V_N = \{S\}$$

$$P, Q: \; S \overset{p}{\rightarrow} aSb$$

$$S \overset{1-p}{\rightarrow} ab$$

It is noted that each production has a probability associated with it. In this case, the first production has probability p, while the second has probability $1 - p$.

Applying the first production twice, followed by the second production, yields

$$S \Rightarrow aSb \Rightarrow aaSbb \Rightarrow aaabbb$$

Letting x represent the terminal string $aaabbb$ and using Eq. (8.6–3), we have

$$p(x) = (p)(p)(1 - p) = p^2(1 - p)$$

The language generated by G is given in this case by

$$L(G) = \{[a^t b^t, p^{t-1}(1 - p)] \mid t \geqslant 1\}$$

We see that each string $a^t b^t$ has a probability $p^{t-1}(1 - p)$ associated with it. It is also noted that this stochastic grammar is not ambiguous since the sequence of productions leading to each terminal string is unique. It is left as an exercise at the end of this chapter to show that the set Q is consistent in this case. ●

Parsing methods for stochastic languages are the same as those illustrated in the preceding section. However, knowledge of the production probabilities can be used to reduce the parsing effort. For example, suppose that at a certain step in a bottom-up parsing procedure there are several candidate productions, one of which must be used next. It is clear that the production which offers the highest probability of success is the one with the highest probability of having been applied in the generation of the terminal sentence being parsed. In general, then, the production probabilities should be used in the parsing process in order to increase the speed of recognition of a stochastic system.

8.6.2 Learning the Production Probabilities

The transition from deterministic to stochastic grammars has been relatively simple. The only difference between these two types of grammars lies simply in the presence or absence of a set of production probabilities Q. Clearly, if we wish to utilize stochastic grammars, we must have at our disposal some mechanism for estimating these production probabilities.

Consider an M-class problem characterized by the stochastic grammars

$$G_q = (V_{N_q}, V_{T_q}, P_q, Q_q, S_q), \quad q = 1, 2, \ldots, M \tag{8.6–7}$$

It is assumed that V_{N_q}, V_{T_q}, P_q, and S_q are known and that the grammars are unambiguous. Since, as of this writing, there still exist many unsolved problems related to learning the production probabilities, we will focus attention on context-free and regular grammars. With this assumption in mind, it is desired to estimate the production probabilities of Q_q, $q = 1, 2, \ldots, M$, from a set of sample terminal strings

$$T = \{x_1, x_2, \ldots, x_m\} \tag{8.6–8}$$

where each string belongs to the language generated by one of the stochastic grammars of Eq. (8.6–7).

When all strings have been gathered, we count them and denote by $n(x_h)$ the number of times that string x_h occurs. Each string is also subjected to the parser of each grammar, and we let $N_{qij}(x_h)$ represent the number of times that a production $A_i \rightarrow \beta_j$ of grammar G_q is used in the parsing of string x_h. Although we do not know the production probabilities of the grammars given in Eq. (8.6–7), the productions themselves are assumed to be known, so that a parse is possible.

The expected number of times n_{qij} that the production $A_i \rightarrow \beta_j$ of grammar G_q is used in parsing a given string can be approximated by

$$n_{qij} = \sum_{x_h \in T} n(x_h) p(G_q/x_h) N_{qij}(x_h) \tag{8.6–9}$$

where $p(G_q/x_h)$ is the probability that a given string x_h was generated by grammar G_q. This probability must be provided for each string during training.

The probability p_{qij} associated with the production $A_i \rightarrow \beta_j$ in grammar G_q can now be approximated by means of the relation

$$\hat{p}_{qij} = \frac{n_{qij}}{\sum_k n_{qik}} \tag{8.6–10}$$

where $\hat{p}_{qij}$ represents an estimate of p_{qij}, and the summation in the denominator of Eq. (8.6–10) is carried out over all productions in G_q of the form $A_i \rightarrow \beta_k$, that is, over all productions in G_q that have the same left-part nonterminal A_i.

It has been shown by Lee and Fu [1972] that the estimate $\hat{p}_{qij}$ approaches the true production probability p_{qij} as the number of strings in T approaches infinity, if the following conditions are satisfied:

1. T is representative of the languages $L(G_q)$, $q = 1, 2, \ldots, M$, in the sense that $T \rightarrow L$, where L is the union of the languages, that is, $L = \bigcup_{q=1}^{M} L(G_q)$.
2. The estimate of the probability of string x_h occurring in T, given by

$$\hat{p}(x_h) = \frac{n(x_h)}{\sum_{x_k \in L} n(x_k)} \tag{8.6–11}$$

approaches the true probability $p(x_h)$.

3. The probability $p(G_q/x_h)$ can be specified for each string x_h during the learning process.

The probability $p(G_q/x_h)$ that a given string x_h belongs to class ω_q can usually be provided without difficulty during the learning phase. If it is known with certainty that a given string belongs exclusively to class ω_q, then $p(G_q/x_h) = 1$. Similarly, if it is known that x_h cannot belong to ω_q, then $p(G_q/x_h) = 0$. Often, however, because of the conditions discussed at the beginning of this section, some strings may belong to more than one class. In this case, we can obtain a simple estimate of the probabilities $p(G_q/x_h)$, $q = 1, 2, \ldots, M$, for these strings by noting the relative frequency with which they occur in each class. Of course, it is required that

$$\sum_{q=1}^{M} p(G_q/x_h) = 1 \tag{8.6–12}$$

When it is not possible to observe the relative number of times that ambiguous strings occur in a particular class, usually a reasonable assumption is to let $p(G_q/x_h) = 1/M$ for these strings.

Example: Let us illustrate the concepts developed in this section by means of a simple numerical example. Consider the stochastic grammars

$$G_1 = (V_N, V_T, P, Q_1, S)$$
$$G_2 = (V_N, V_T, P, Q_2, S)$$

where, for both grammars,

$$V_T = \{a, b\}, \qquad V_N = \{S\}$$

The productions and corresponding probabilities are as follows:

		Q_1	Q_2
P:	$S \to aS$	p_{11}	p_{21}
	$S \to a$	p_{12}	p_{22}
	$S \to bS$	p_{13}	p_{23}
	$S \to b$	p_{14}	p_{24}

It is desired to learn the probabilities of Q_1 and Q_2.

In order to conform with our previous notation, we may change the above symbology as follows:

		Q_1	Q_2
P:	$A_1 \to \beta_1$	p_{111}	p_{211}
	$A_1 \to \beta_2$	p_{112}	p_{212}
	$A_1 \to \beta_3$	p_{113}	p_{213}
	$A_1 \to \beta_4$	p_{114}	p_{214}

where we have let $S = A_1$, $\beta_1 = aS$, $\beta_2 = a$, $\beta_3 = bS$, and $\beta_4 = b$. The subscripts on the probabilities are interpreted as before, that is, the first subscript represents the class, the second stands for the subscript of the left-hand side of the production, and the third indicates the subscript of the right-hand side of the production. In this case all left-hand sides are identical.

Let us hypothesize for illustrative purposes that class ω_1 consists solely of strings of a's, and class ω_2 of strings of b's. However, because of noise corruption, mixed strings may sometimes occur. Note that, although G_1 and G_2 can both produce mixed strings, it is postulated in this example that G_1 is used only to produce strings of a's and G_2 is used only to produce strings of b's. Let us further assume that 100 pattern strings are gathered for the purposes of training with the following results:

String	*Number of Times That It Occurred*
a	30
aa	20
$aabbb$	5
bb	25
b	20

Denoting the first string type by x_1, the second by x_2, and so forth, we obtain

$$n(x_1) = 30, \qquad n(x_2) = 20, \qquad n(x_3) = 5$$

$$n(x_4) = 25, \qquad n(x_5) = 20$$

In order to estimate the probabilities p_{qij} using Eq. (8.6–10), we must first compute the quantities n_{qij}. From Eq. (8.6–9),

$$n_{qij} = \sum_{x_h \in T} n(x_h) p(G_q/x_h) N_{qij}(x_h)$$

where T consists of 30 strings x_1, 20 strings x_2, and so forth. Using this equation, we obtain for class ω_1

$$\begin{aligned} n_{111} = {} & n(x_1)p(G_1/x_1)N_{111}(x_1) + n(x_2)p(G_1/x_2)N_{111}(x_2) \\ & + n(x_3)p(G_1/x_3)N_{111}(x_3) + n(x_4)p(G_1/x_4)N_{111}(x_4) \\ & + n(x_5)p(G_1/x_5)N_{111}(x_5) \end{aligned}$$

Let us analyze these terms in some detail. The quantity $n(x_1)$ is known, and $p(G_1/x_1)$ is the probability that x_1 belongs to class ω_1. We may assume that this probability is 1 since x_1 consists only of a's. The term $N_{111}(x_1)$ is the number of times that $A_1 \rightarrow \beta_1$ is used in parsing x_1. It can be determined by inspection that this production is not used in parsing x_1, so we have that $N_{111}(x_1) = 0$. The second term is similarly computed. The third string contains both a's and b's and therefore can belong to either class. Assuming that it is equally likely to belong to ω_1 or ω_2, we may let $p(G_1/x_3) = 0.5$. In general, these probabilities can be meaningfully specified by having some knowledge of the problem, as was previously discussed. In the fourth and fifth terms, we assume that strings x_4 and x_5 belong to ω_2 since they consist solely of b's. It is also noted that $N_{111}(x_4) = N_{111}(x_5) = 0$ since $A_1 \rightarrow \beta_1$ is not used in the parse of these strings. With these considerations in mind we obtain

$$\begin{aligned} n_{111} &= (30)(1)(0) + (20)(1)(1) + (5)(0.5)(2) + (25)(0)(0) + (20)(0)(0) \\ &= 25 \end{aligned}$$

Using a simple top-down parsing scheme, we obtain the following values of $N_{1ij}(x_h)$:

x_h	$N_{111}(x_h)$	$N_{112}(x_h)$	$N_{113}(x_h)$	$N_{114}(x_h)$
x_1	0	1	0	0
x_2	1	1	0	0
x_3	2	0	2	1
x_4	0	0	1	1
x_5	0	0	0	1

With these values, computation of the remaining n_{qij} yields

$$\begin{aligned} n_{112} &= (30)(1)(1) + (20)(1)(1) + (5)(0.5)(0) + (25)(0)(0) + (20)(0)(0) \\ &= 50 \end{aligned}$$

$$\begin{aligned} n_{113} &= (30)(1)(0) + (20)(1)(0) + (5)(0.5)(2) + (25)(0)(1) + (20)(0)(0) \\ &= 5 \end{aligned}$$

$$\begin{aligned} n_{114} &= (30)(1)(0) + (20)(1)(0) + (5)(0.5)(1) + (25)(0)(1) + (20)(0)(1) \\ &= 2.5 \end{aligned}$$

We may now compute all the probabilities of class ω_1, using the relation

$$\hat{p}_{1ij} = \frac{n_{1ij}}{\sum_k n_{1ik}}$$

where the summation is taken over all productions of G_1 having the same left-part nonterminal A_i. In this example all left-hand productions are identical. Therefore,

$$\hat{p}_{111} = \frac{n_{111}}{\sum_k n_{11k}} = \frac{n_{111}}{n_{111} + n_{112} + n_{113} + n_{114}}$$

$$= \frac{25.0}{82.5} = 0.303$$

$$\hat{p}_{112} = \frac{n_{112}}{\sum_k n_{11k}} = \frac{50.0}{82.5} = 0.606$$

$$\hat{p}_{113} = \frac{n_{113}}{\sum_k n_{11k}} = \frac{5.0}{82.5} = 0.061$$

$$\hat{p}_{114} = \frac{n_{114}}{\sum_k n_{11k}} = \frac{2.5}{82.5} = 0.030$$

As expected, the productions of class ω_1 related to the generation of strings of *a*'s have a higher probability.

The computation of the production probabilities for class ω_2 is similar to the above procedure. Since the two grammars have identical productions, it follows that $N_{2ij}(x_h) = N_{1ij}(x_h)$. Using the values previously tabulated for these quantities yields the following n_{2ij}'s:

$$n_{211} = n(x_1)p(G_2/x_1)N_{211}(x_1) + n(x_2)p(G_2/x_2)N_{211}(x_2)$$
$$+ n(x_3)p(G_2/x_3)N_{211}(x_3) + n(x_4)p(G_2/x_4)N_{211}(x_4)$$
$$+ n(x_5)p(G_2/x_5)N_{211}(x_5)$$

In this case x_1 and x_2 clearly belong to class ω_1, and therefore we may assume that $p(G_2/x_1) = p(G_2/x_2) = 0$. Similarly, $p(G_2/x_4) = p(G_2/x_5) = 1$. Also, since we are assuming strictly a two-class problem, it follows that $p(G_2/x_3) = 1 - p(G_1/x_3) = 0.5$. Using these probabilities and the quantities previously tabulated, we obtain

$$n_{211} = (30)(0)(0) + (20)(0)(1) + (5)(0.5)(2) + (25)(1)(0) + (20)(1)(0)$$
$$= 5$$

$$n_{212} = (30)(0)(1) + (20)(0)(1) + (5)(0.5)(0) + (25)(1)(0) + (20)(1)(0)$$
$$= 0$$
$$n_{213} = (30)(0)(0) + (20)(0)(0) + (5)(0.5)(2) + (25)(1)(1) + (20)(1)(0)$$
$$= 30$$
$$n_{214} = (30)(0)(0) + (20)(0)(0) + (5)(0.5)(1) + (25)(1)(1) + (20)(1)(1)$$
$$= 47.5$$

The production probabilities can now be computed using the relation

$$p_{2ij} = \frac{n_{2ij}}{\sum_k n_{2ik}}$$

where, as before, the summation is taken over all productions of G_2 having the same left-part nonterminal A_i—in this case, this is true for all productions. Using the above relation yields

$$\hat{p}_{211} = \frac{n_{211}}{\sum_k n_{21k}} = \frac{n_{211}}{n_{211} + n_{212} + n_{213} + n_{214}}$$
$$= \frac{5}{82.5} = 0.061$$
$$\hat{p}_{212} = \frac{n_{212}}{\sum_k n_{21k}} = \frac{0}{82.5} = 0$$
$$\hat{p}_{213} = \frac{n_{213}}{\sum_k n_{21k}} = \frac{30.0}{82.5} = 0.364$$
$$\hat{p}_{214} = \frac{n_{214}}{\sum_k n_{21k}} = \frac{47.5}{82.5} = 0.576$$

Having computed all production probabilities from sample strings, we may now completely specify the stochastic grammar of this example as follows:

$$G_1 = (V_N, V_T, P, Q_1, S)$$
$$G_2 = (V_N, V_T, P, Q_2, S)$$

where, for both grammars,

$$V_T = \{a, b\}, \qquad V_N = \{S\}$$

and

		Q_1	Q_2
P:	$S \to aS$	0.303	0.061
	$S \to a$	0.606	0
	$S \to bS$	0.061	0.364
	$S \to b$	0.030	0.576

8.7 LEARNING AND GRAMMATICAL INFERENCE

Chapters 3 through 6 were largely concerned with the problem of learning decision functions from training patterns. In this chapter, however, this problem has thus far been conveniently ignored. In the terminology of linguistics, learning from sample patterns is easily interpreted as the problem of learning a grammar from a set of sample sentences. This procedure, commonly referred to as *grammatical inference,* is an important subject in the study of syntactic pattern recognition because of its automatic learning implications. As will be evident in the following discussions, however, the area of grammatical inference is still in its infancy in relation to learning capabilities which would be considered acceptable as a general tool for syntactic pattern recognition system design.

This section is largely concerned with the introduction of grammatical inference concepts from two points of view. In Section 8.7.1 an algorithm for the inference of certain classes of string grammars is developed. Then, in Section 8.7.2, the problem of inferring two-dimensional grammars is treated in some detail. Although tree grammars are quickly becoming an important topic of research in syntactic pattern recognition, algorithms for the inference of these grammars are, in our opinion, not yet in a form suitable for inclusion in a textbook. The interested reader can consult the work of Gonzalez and Thomason [1974b] as an introduction to this area.

8.7.1 Inference of String Grammars

A model for the inference of string grammars is shown in Fig. 8.10. The problem depicted in this figure is one of feeding a set of sample terminal strings $\{x_i\}$ into an adaptive, learning algorithm, represented by the box, whose eventual output is a grammar G which is *compatible* with the given

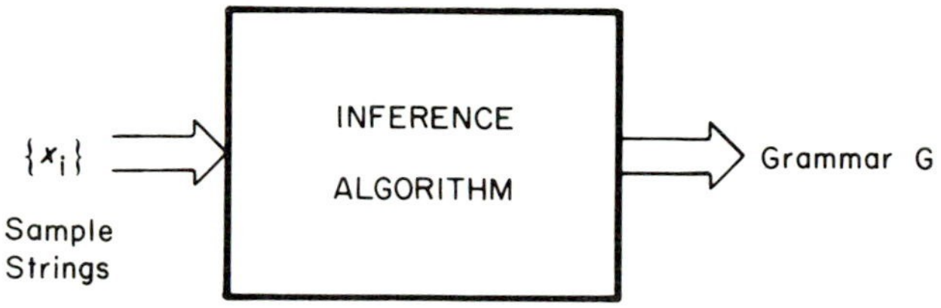

Figure 8.10. Inference of string grammars

strings, that is, the strings $\{x_i\}$ are a subset of $L(G)$. Unfortunately, no known scheme is capable of attacking this problem in the general form shown in Fig. 8.10. Instead, numerous algorithms for the inference of restricted grammars have been proposed. The algorithm presented in this section is typical in many ways of results in this area. This algorithm, which is adapted from a procedure due to Feldman [1967, 1969], infers a finite-state grammar for the given set of terminal strings. The basic strategy of Feldman's method is first to construct a nonrecursive grammar that generates exactly the given strings, and then to merge nonterminals to obtain a simpler, recursive grammar that generates an infinite number of strings. The algorithm may be divided into three parts. The first part forms the nonrecursive grammar. The second part converts the result to a recursive grammar. This grammar is then simplified in the third part. The procedure is best explained by means of an example.

Consider the sample set of terminal strings $\{caaab, bbaab, caab, bbab, cab, bbb, cb\}$. It is desired to obtain a finite-state grammar capable of generating these strings. The steps followed by the algorithm in the construction of the grammar are as follows.

Part 1. A nonrecursive grammar that generates exactly the given sample set is constructed. Sample strings are processed in order of decreasing length. Productions are constructed and added to the grammar as they are needed to generate each sample string. The final production used to generate the longest sample strings is a *residue production* with a right side of length 2. A residue production of length n has the form

$$A \rightarrow a_1 a_2 \cdots a_n$$

where A is a nonterminal and $a_1, a_2, \ldots, a_n$ are terminals. It is assumed that the residue of each string of maximum length is the suffix (tail end) of some shorter string. If this condition is not met for some residue, a string equal to the residue is added to the sample set. It will be evident from the following discussion that the choice of residues of length 2 is not a limiting factor in the algorithm. Longer residues may be chosen, but this requires a more complete sample set because of the condition that each residue must be the suffix of some shorter string.

In this example, the first string of maximum length in the sample set is *caaab*. The following productions are constructed to generate this string:

$$S \to cA_1$$
$$A_1 \to aA_2$$
$$A_2 \to aA_3$$
$$A_3 \to ab$$

where A_3 is a residue production. The second string is *bbaab*. The following productions are added to the grammar to generate this string:

$$S \to bA_4$$
$$A_4 \to bA_5$$
$$A_5 \to aA_6$$
$$A_6 \to ab$$

A residue production of length 2 is required since *bbaab* is of the same length as the previous string. We also note that the first part of the algorithm results in some redundant productions. For example, the second string could have been equally well accounted for by introducing the productions $S \to bA_4$, $A_4 \to bA_2$. However, in the first part we are interested only in determining a set of productions which will generate exactly the sample set, without regard to redundancy. In complex situations, it is difficult to keep track of this condition and also to reduce the number of productions required. Scanning the established productions from left to right to see if they will generate a new string without paying attention to minimizing the number of productions is an easier procedure to implement. Redundancy is then taken care of in Part 3 of the algorithm.

To generate the third string, *caab*, we need only to add the following production to the grammar:

$$A_3 \to b$$

Considering the rest of the strings in the sample set, we see that the final set of productions constructed to generate the sample set is

$$
\begin{array}{ll}
S \rightarrow cA_1 & A_3 \rightarrow ab \\
S \rightarrow bA_4 & A_4 \rightarrow bA_5 \\
A_1 \rightarrow b & A_5 \rightarrow b \\
A_1 \rightarrow aA_2 & A_5 \rightarrow aA_6 \\
A_2 \rightarrow b & A_6 \rightarrow b \\
A_2 \rightarrow aA_3 & A_6 \rightarrow ab \\
A_3 \rightarrow b &
\end{array}
$$

Part 2. In this part, a recursive finite-state grammar is obtained by merging each residue production of length 2 with a nonresidue production of the grammar. This is accomplished by merging each residue nonterminal with a nonresidue nonterminal which can generate the residue. Thus, if A_r is a residue nonterminal of the form $A_r \rightarrow a_1a_2$, and A_n is a nonresidue nonterminal of the form $A_n \rightarrow a_1A_m$, where $A_m \rightarrow a_2$, we replace all occurrences of A_r by A_n, and delete the production $A_r \rightarrow a_1a_2$. This technique produces a finite-state grammar which can generate the given sample set, and also has the generalization power to generate an infinite set of other strings.

In the present example, A_6 can be merged with A_5, and A_3 can be merged with A_2, yielding the productions

$$
\begin{array}{ll}
S \rightarrow cA_1 & A_2 \rightarrow b \\
S \rightarrow bA_4 & A_4 \rightarrow bA_5 \\
A_1 \rightarrow b & A_5 \rightarrow b \\
A_1 \rightarrow aA_2 & A_5 \rightarrow aA_5 \\
A_2 \rightarrow b & A_5 \rightarrow b \\
A_2 \rightarrow aA_2 &
\end{array}
$$

The recursive productions are $A_2 \rightarrow aA_2$, and $A_5 \rightarrow aA_5$.

Part 3. In this part the grammar from Part 2 is simplified by merging equivalent productions. Two productions with left parts A_i and A_j are equivalent if the following condition is satisfied. Suppose that we start with

A_i and are able to generate a set of strings $\{x\}_i$. Similarly, suppose that we start with A_j and are able to generate set $\{x\}_j$. If $\{x\}_i \equiv \{x\}_j$, the two productions are equivalent and every occurrence of A_j can be replaced by A_i without affecting the language generated by the grammar. Formally, the two productions are equivalent if $\{x | A_i \overset{*}{\Rightarrow} x\} \equiv \{x | A_j \overset{*}{\Rightarrow} x\}$, where $A_i \overset{*}{\Rightarrow} x$ is used to indicate that string x is derivable from A_i by a suitable application of productions.

In the above example, the productions with left parts A_1 and A_2 are equivalent. After merging A_1 and A_2, we obtain:

$$\begin{array}{ll} S \rightarrow cA_1 & A_4 \rightarrow bA_5 \\ S \rightarrow bA_4 & A_5 \rightarrow b \\ A_1 \rightarrow b & A_5 \rightarrow aA_5 \\ A_1 \rightarrow aA_1 & \end{array}$$

where multiple occurrences of the same production have been deleted. Similarly, we see that A_1 and A_5 are equivalent, yielding

$$\begin{array}{ll} S \rightarrow cA_1 & A_1 \rightarrow aA_1 \\ S \rightarrow bA_4 & A_4 \rightarrow bA_1 \\ A_1 \rightarrow b & \end{array}$$

No further mergings are possible. Therefore, the algorithm has learned the following finite-state grammar:

$$G = (V_N, V_T, P, S)$$

where

$$V_N = \{S, A, B\}, \qquad V_T = \{a, b, c\}$$

$$\begin{array}{ll} P: & S \rightarrow cA \\ & S \rightarrow bB \\ & A \rightarrow aA \\ & B \rightarrow bA \\ & A \rightarrow b \end{array}$$

It is easily verified that this grammar can generate the sample set used in the inference process.

8.7.2 Inference of Two-Dimensional Grammars

The problems associated with two-dimensional recognition grammars were discussed in detail in Sections 8.4 and 8.5. Basically, the principal problem with these grammars lies in the specification of two-dimensional juxtaposition rules. In this section we present a simple algorithm, due to Evans [1971], which illustrates direct learning of two-dimensional grammars. The algorithm assumes that appropriate two-dimensional positional descriptors have been provided by the trainer. Essentially, the algorithm is based on the following procedure. Given a set of primitives and positional descriptors, we start with the primitives and, through application of the descriptors, build up more complex structures. When the process is completed, we derive a grammar, using the steps followed in building the structures. This scheme is best illustrated by an example.

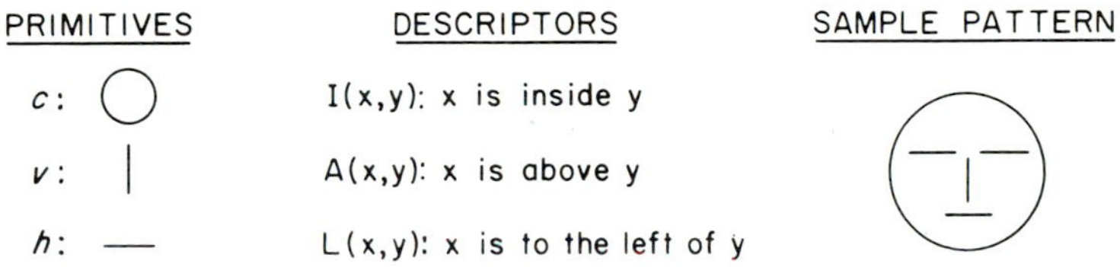

Figure 8.11. Elements of a two-dimensional grammar

Consider the simple primitives, positional descriptors, and sample pattern illustrated in Fig. 8.11. The sample pattern is clearly a combination of primitives. To simplify the notation, let us call the circle in the sample pattern "Object 1," the left eye "Object 2," the right eye "Object 3," the nose "Object 4," and the mouth "Object 5." We may build various complex objects, starting with the primitives and successively applying the descriptors. The sample pattern is used to guide the process until a total description of this pattern is obtained. The first complex object is

$$\text{Object 6: } I(2, 1)$$

which is simply Object 2 inside Object 1. This condition is satisfied by the sample pattern. It is easily verified that the following objects are also satisfied by the sample pattern:

Object 7: $I(3, 1)$ Object 10: $L(2, 3)$

Object 8: $I(4, 1)$ Object 11: $A(4, 5)$

Object 9: $I(5, 1)$

Clearly, there are other combinations which will also be satisfied by the sample pattern, but for the moment let us proceed with the ones listed above.

In the next pass, more complex structures are built with the objects previously generated:

Object 12: $I(10, 1)$ Object 14: $A(10, 5)$

Object 13: $A(10, 4)$ Object 15: $A(10, 11)$

The next level of complexity is obtained by further combinations of previously generated objects:

Object 16: $I(13, 1)$ Object 18: $I(15, 1)$

Object 17: $I(14, 1)$ Object 19: $A(13, 5)$

It is noted that Object 18 is a complete terminal description of the input pattern, that is, Object 18 is Object 15 inside Object 1, which is the circle. Object 15 is, in turn, Object 10 above 11. Object 10, on the other hand, is one eye to the left of another, while Object 11 is the nose above the mouth. Thus, Object 18 is the desired face.

A grammar to generate the sample pattern is easily constructed by considering the steps which lead to the construction of the object. Thus, a grammar for this example is as follows:

$$G = (V_N, V_T, P, S)$$

where

$$V_N = \{S, B, C, D\}, \qquad V_T = \{h, v, c\}$$

$$\begin{aligned} P\colon\ S &\to I(B, c) \\ B &\to A(C, D) \\ C &\to L(h, h) \\ D &\to A(v, h) \end{aligned}$$

It is noted that the set of productions is, in effect, a set of rules for constructing the pattern. If we let S represent the face, the production rules simply indicate the following. A face is some object B inside a circle. This object B is some object C above another object D, where C is a horizontal segment to the left of another horizontal segment (the eyes), and D is a vertical segment above a horizontal segment (the nose and mouth).

When several samples are available, a grammar is derived for each sample. Then the grammars are united, and equivalent productions combined. The resulting grammar is capable of generating the entire sample set. This procedure is seen to be similar to the merging scheme discussed in the preceding section.

Several points need further clarification. It was indicated above that the intermediate objects generated in the illustration are not exhaustive. Although it is not difficult to specify an algorithm which generates all valid combinations for the given descriptors and sample pattern, the principal goal of this procedure is the generation of one or more sets of construction steps which, starting with the primitives, result in the sample pattern. The specification of the pattern grammar is then a straightforward matter. With this goal in mind, it is clearly desirable to generate the fewest possible intermediate objects. Of course, this may involve more than one trial. If one views the algorithm from an interactive standpoint, however, this shortcoming need not be a serious drawback of the procedure. This is particularly true, for example, if the algorithm is implemented in an interactive display system. Another point which is worth emphasizing once again is the problem of specifying the positional descriptors. The success of any two-dimensional linguistic scheme is ultimately dependent on one's ability to specify properly the rules for the two-dimensional juxtaposition of structures.

Many of the presently known techniques for grammatical inference are heuristic in nature. This is particularly true of the two-dimensional case. The approaches discussed in this section should have served the purpose of giving the reader a sound idea of some of the techniques used and the problems encountered in this branch of pattern recognition.

8.8 AUTOMATA AS PATTERN RECOGNIZERS

The grammars studied in the preceding sections are largely string-generating schemes. In this section we enter briefly the area of automata theory and introduce the concept of an automaton as a string recognizer. The connection between this theory and pattern recognition is clear since, as was shown in preceding sections, it is often possible to express patterns in the form of terminal strings. Although a comprehensive study of automata is well outside our present scope, we will consider in some detail a specific type of automaton, the finite automaton, and show that it is capable of recognizing finite-state (type 3) languages.

A *finite automaton* $\mathscr{A}$ over an alphabet Σ is defined as

$$\mathscr{A} = (K, \Sigma, \delta, q_0, F) \tag{8.8–1}$$

where K is a finite, nonempty set of *states*, Σ is a finite *input alphabet*, δ is a *mapping* of $K \times \Sigma$ into K, q_0 in K is the *initial state*, and $F \subseteq K$ is the set of *final states*. The terminology and notation associated with Eq. (8.8–1) are best illustrated by an example.

Example: Consider the automaton characterized by Eq. (8.8–1), where

$$\Sigma = \{0, 1\}$$

$$K = \{q_0, q_1, q_2\}$$

$$F = \{q_0\}$$

and the mapping δ of $K \times \Sigma$ into K is given by

$$\delta(q_0, 0) = q_2 \qquad \delta(q_0, 1) = q_1$$

$$\delta(q_1, 0) = q_2 \qquad \delta(q_1, 1) = q_0$$

$$\delta(q_2, 0) = q_0 \qquad \delta(q_2, 1) = q_1$$

If, for example, the automaton is in state q_0 and a 0 is applied, its state changes to q_2. If a 1 is applied next, the automaton moves to state q_1, and so forth. It is noted that the final state is, in this case, equal to the initial state.

A *state diagram* for this automaton is shown in Fig. 8.12. The state diagram consists of a node for each possible state and a directed line connecting states which are mutually accessible. In this case, if state q_1 were not accessible from q_2, and vice versa, no path would be shown between these two states in the diagram. Each path is labeled with the corresponding symbol from Σ which will cause it to change to the indicated state.

Suppose that the automaton is in state q_0 and that the string $x = 00110011$ is applied to it. The automaton scans the string from left to right, one symbol at a time. Upon encountering the first 0, the automaton changes to state q_2.

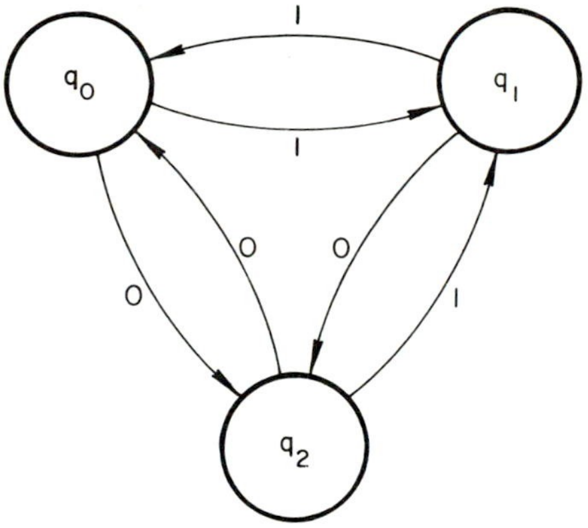

Figure 8.12. A finite automaton

The next 0 makes it return to state q_0. Similarly, the next symbol, which is a 1, changes the state to q_1, and the second 1 resets it to q_0. The rest of the procedure is self-explanatory. It is obvious that the automaton will be in state q_0 after x is read. ●

A string or sentence x is said to be *accepted* by $\mathscr{A}$ if the automaton rests in one of its possible final states after reading x. The set of all x accepted by $\mathscr{A}$ is designated by $T(\mathscr{A})$, that is,

$$T(\mathscr{A}) = \{x \mid \delta(q, x) \text{ is in } F\} \tag{8.8–2}$$

where $\delta(q, x)$ designates the state of the automaton after having read x.

If the strings $\{x\}$ represent patterns, we may conveniently think of a finite automaton as a two-class classifier, where a string is assigned to class ω_1 if it is accepted and to class ω_2 if it is rejected by the automaton.

It can be shown that, if $G = (V_N, V_T, P, S)$ is a finite-state grammar, there exists a finite automaton $\mathscr{A} = (K, V_T, \delta, S, F)$ with $T(\mathscr{A}) = L(G)$. Conversely, for a given finite automaton $\mathscr{A}$, there exists a finite-state grammar G such that $L(G) = T(\mathscr{A})$.

A study of automata theory would reveal that unrestricted, context-sensitive, and context-free grammars can be recognized by other types of automata. Unrestricted languages are accepted by Turing machines; context-sensitive languages, by linear bounded automata; and context-free languages by push-down automata. In addition, automata theory is easily expressed in a statistical framework, as illustrated by Fu [1970]. The resulting stochastic automata may be used for the recognition of stochastic languages. It is also possible to formulate automata which accept tree structures rather than strings. The reader interested in gaining further insight into this topic can consult, for example, Fu and Bhargava [1973], Thatcher [1973], and Gonzalez and Thomason [1974a].

8.9 CONCLUDING REMARKS

The material in this chapter exemplifies the principal ideas underlying the use of linguistic concepts for pattern recognition. Several key problems are identified and discussed. The primitive selection problem is directly related to the structural feature selection problem discussed in detail in Chapter 7. However, the primitives in this chapter are treated as the terminals of some grammar. This allows the interpretation of patterns as sentences from a corresponding language.

The selection of an appropriate two-dimensional grammar is complicated by the variability inherent in the juxtapositioning of two-dimensional structures. This problem can be somewhat circumvented by limiting the rules of juxtaposition in some predetermined fashion. Examples of this are given in Section 8.5.2, where two-dimensional patterns are effectively reduced to terminal strings. Another method for handling higher-dimensional patterns is to use tree grammars, as was indicated in Section 8.5.3.

It has been shown how recognition of syntactic structures can be accomplished by parsing. Top-down or bottom-up parsing schemes may be employed in the recognition process. Parsing efficiency can be improved considerably by using the syntax of the grammar in conjunction with the sentence being parsed.

Statistical considerations may be incorporated into a syntactic recognition framework by means of stochastic grammars. In these grammars, the productions are governed by probabilistic assignments. Therefore, the key problem in utilizing stochastic grammars lies in learning the production probabilities. The method illustrated in Section 8.6.2 indicates that it is possible to learn these probabilities from training samples.

The problem of grammatical inference is the linguistic equivalent of the learning algorithms developed in earlier chapters. As was previously stated, however, known grammatical inference schemes are still limited in scope. The algorithms presented in Section 8.7 are characteristic of the approaches which may be employed in learning grammars from sample sentences.

It is possible to associate syntactic pattern recognition with certain aspects of automata theory. The connection is briefly described in Section 8.8, where the finite automaton is shown to be an effective recognizer of finite-state languages. It is also mentioned in that section that other types of automata may be used as recognizers of unrestricted, context-sensitive, and context-free languages.

REFERENCES

A comprehensive introduction to formal languages can be found in the book by Hopcroft and Ullman [1969]. The literature on syntactic pattern recognition has been growing at a rapid rate since the middle 1960's. Early efforts in this field are those of Eden [1961], Narasimhan [1962], Kirsch [1964], and Ledley [1964, 1965]. The trend in syntactic pattern recognition may be appreciated by studying the review articles by Miller and Shaw [1968], Fu and Swain [1971], and Gonzalez [1972].

The picture description language described in Section 8.5.2 is due to Shaw [1970], while the chromosome grammar is the work of Ledley [1964, 1965]. A comprehensive coverage of parsing techniques can be found in Aho and Ullman [1972]. An excellent reference on tree systems is Knuth [1968]. Additional reading on tree grammars is given in Fu and Bhargava [1973], Thatcher [1973], and Gonzalez and Thomason [1974a]. References on stochastic grammars are Fu [1971a], Lee and Fu [1971, 1972], and Booth [1969]. The algorithm for string grammars presented in Section 8.7.1 is adapted from Feldman [1967, 1969], and the algorithm given in Section 8.7.2 is due to Evans [1971]. Additional references on grammatical inference are Feldman, Gips, Horning, and Reder [1969], Fu [1972], Gold [1967], Horning [1969], Pao [1969], and Crespi-Reghizzi [1971]. An introduction to the problem of inferring tree grammars can be found in Gonzalez and Thomason [1974b]. References for Section 8.8 are Hopcroft and Ullman [1969] and Fu [1970].

PROBLEMS

8.1 Give a context-free grammar with terminal set $V_T = \{a, b\}$ whose language is the set of strings composed of alternating a's and b's and alternating b's and a's, that is, $L(G) = \{ab, ba, aba, bab, abab, baba, \ldots\}$.

8.2 Is it possible to generate the language of Problem 8.1 with a finite-state grammar?

8.3 Using primitives similar to those associated with Fig. 8.7, construct a PDL grammar capable of generating the numerals from 0 through 5. It will be helpful to consider a common origin and to define one or more blank primitives.

8.4 Show the recognition process for the patterns in Problem 8.3 by using a syntax-directed, top-down parsing scheme.

8.5 Repeat Problem 8.4 for a bottom-up, syntax-directed parser.

8.6 Would Ledley's chromosome parser recognize the string *acabdabcabd* as a submedian or a telocentric chromosome?

8.7 Give a tree grammar for a cube whose edges are of unit length. Define the primitives as edges of the cube.

8.8 Show that the set Q in the example in Section 8.6.1 is consistent.

8.9 Consider the stochastic grammars $G_1 = (V_N, V_T, P, Q_1, S)$ and $G_2 = (V_N, V_T, P, Q_2, S)$, where $V_N = \{S\}$, $V_T = \{a, b, c\}$, and $P = \{S \rightarrow aS, S \rightarrow a, S \rightarrow bS, S \rightarrow b, S \rightarrow cS, S \rightarrow c\}$. The following strings were produced by the two pattern classes represented by these grammars in 200 observations.

String		*Number of Times That It Occurred*
x_1:	*aaccac*	50
x_2:	*aaacca*	40
x_3:	*aabcbc*	20
x_4:	*cbccbc*	50
x_5:	*bbbcbc*	40

It is known that $p(G_1/x_1) = 1.0$, $p(G_1/x_2) = 1.0$, $p(G_1/x_3) = 0.25$, $p(G_1/x_4) = 0$, $p(G_1/x_5) = 0$. Use the methods of Section 8.6.2 to learn the production probabilities.

8.10 Use the algorithm presented in Section 8.7.1 to learn a finite-state grammar capable of generating the following sample strings: $\{aaacc, aaacb, aacc, bacb, aaa, abc, bb, cc\}$.

8.11 Apply Evans' algorithm to learn a two-dimensional grammar for the pattern  . Use the primitives and descriptors shown in Fig. 8.11.

8.12 Give a finite automaton which will accept only strings composed of an even number of a's and/or an even number of b's.

BIBLIOGRAPHY

Abramson, N., and Braverman, D. [1962]. "Learning to Recognize Patterns in a Random Environment," *IRE Trans. Info. Theory*, vol. IT-8, no. 5, pp. S58–S63.

Agmon, S. [1954]. "The Relaxation Method for Linear Inequalities," *Can. J. Math.*, vol. 6, no. 3, pp. 382–392.

Aho, A. V., and Ullman, J. D. [1972]. *The Theory of Parsing, Translation and Compiling*, vol. 1, Prentice-Hall, Englewood Cliffs, N.J.

Aizerman, M. A., Braverman, E. M., and Rozonoer, L. I. [1964a]. "The Method of Potential Functions in the Problem of Determining the Characteristics of a Function Generator from Randomly Observed Points," *Automation and Remote Control*, vol. 25, no. 12, pp. 1546–1556.

Aizerman, M. A., Braverman, E. M., and Rozonoer, L. I. [1964b]. "Theoretical Foundations of the Potential Function Method in Pattern Recognition," *Automation and Remote Control*, vol. 25, no. 6, pp. 821–837.

Aizerman, M. A., Braverman, E. M., and Rozonoer, L. I. [1965]. "The Robbins-Monro Process and the Method of Potential Functions," *Automation and Remote Control*, vol. 26, no. 11, pp. 1882–1885.

Anderberg, M. R. [1973]. *Cluster Analysis for Applications*, Academic Press, New York.

Anderson, T. W. [1958]. *Introduction to Multivariate Statistics*, John Wiley & Sons, New York.

Anderson, T. W., and Bahadur, R. R. [1962]. "Classification into Two Multivariate Normal Distributions with Different Covariance Matrices," *Ann. Math. Stat.*, vol. 33, pp. 420–431.

Andrews, H. C. [1972]. *Introduction to Mathematical Techniques in Pattern Recognition*, John Wiley & Sons, New York.

Augustson, J. G., and Minker, J. [1970]. "An Analysis of Some Graph-Theoretical Cluster Techniques," *J. ACM* vol. 17, no. 4, pp. 571–588.

Babu, C, Chitti [1973]. "On the Application of Probabilistic Distance Measures for the Extraction of Features from Imperfectly Labeled Patterns," *Internat. J. Computer and Infor. Sci.*, vol. 2, no. 2, pp. 103–114.

Ball, G. H. [1965]. "Data Analysis in the Social Sciences: What about the Details?" *Proceedings of the Fall Joint Computer Conference*.

Ball, G. H., and Hall, D. J. [1965a]. "Isodata, an Iterative Method of Multivariate Analysis and Pattern Classification," *Proceedings of the IFIPS Congress*.

Ball, G. H., and Hall, D. J. [1965b]. "Isodata, a Novel Method of Data Analysis and Pattern Classification," *NTIS Rept.* AD699616.

Batchelor, B. G., and Wilkins, B. R. [1969]. "Method for Location of Clusters of Patterns to Initialize a Learning Machine," *Electronics Letters*, vol. 5, no. 20, pp. 481–483.

Blackwell, D., and Girshick, M. A. [1954]. *Theory of Games and Statistical Decision*, John Wiley & Sons, New York.

Blaydon, C. C. [1967]. "Recursive Algorithms for Pattern Classification," *Office Naval Res. Tech. Rept.* 520, Division of Engineering and Applied Physics, Harvard University, Cambridge, Mass.

Block, H. D. [1962]. "The Perceptron: A Model for Brain Functioning, I," *Rev. Mod. Phys.*, vol. 34, no. 1, pp. 123–135.

Block, H. D., Nilsson, N. J., and Duda, R. O. [1964]. "Determination and Detection of Features in Patterns," in *Computer and Information Sciences—I* (J. T. Tou and R. H. Wilcox, eds.), Spartan Books, Washington, D. C.

Blum, J. R. [1954a]. "Approximation Methods Which Converge with Probability One," *Ann. Math. Stat.*, vol. 25, pp. 382–386.

Blum, J. R. [1954b]. "Multidimensional Stochastic Approximation Methods," *Ann. Math. Stat.*, vol. 25, pp. 737–744.

Bodewig, E. [1956]. *Matrix Calculus*, Interscience Publishers, New York.

Bonner, R. E. [1964]. "On Some Clustering Techniques," *IBM J. Res. and Develop.*, vol. 8, no. 1, pp. 22–32.

Booth, T. L. [1969]. "Probabilistic Representation of Formal Languages," *IEEE Conference Record of the 10th Annual Symposium on Switching Automata.*

Braverman, E. M. [1965]. "On the Method of Potential Functions," *Automation and Remote Control*, vol. 26, no. 12, pp. 2130–2138.

Brown, R. [1963]. "Logical Properties of Adaptive Networks," *Stanford Electronics Lab. Quart. Res. Rev.*, no. 4, III-6–III-9.

Butt, E. B., et al. [1968]. "Studies in Visual Texture Manipulation and Synthesis," Tech. Rept. 68-64, Computer Science Center, University of Maryland, College Park.

Charnes, A. [1964]. "On Some Fundamental Theorems of Perceptron Theory and Their Geometry," in *Computer and Information Sciences—I* (J. T. Tou and R. Wilcox, eds.), Spartan Books, Washington, D. C.

Cheney, E. W. [1966]. *Introduction to Approximation Theory*, McGraw-Hill Book Co., New York.

Chien, Y. T., and Fu, K. S. [1967]. "On the Generalized Karhunen-Loève Expansion," *IEEE Trans. Info. Theory*, vol. IT-13, no. 3, pp. 518–520.

Chien, Y. T., and Ribak, R. [1971]. "Relationship Matrix as a Multi-Dimensional Data Base for Syntactic Pattern Generation and Recognition," *Proceedings of the Two-Dimensional Signal Processing Conference*, University of Missouri, Columbia.

Chomsky, Noam [1956]. "Three Models for the Description of Language," *PGIT*, vol. 2, no. 3, pp. 113–124.

Clowes, M. B. [1969]. "Transformational Grammars and the Organization of Pictures," in *Automatic Interpretation and Classification of Images* (A. Grasselli, ed.), Academic Press, New York.

Cofer, R. H. [1972]. "Picture Acquisition and Graphical Preprocessing System," *Proceedings of the 9th Annual IEEE Region III Convention*, Charlottesville, Va.

Cofer, R. H., and Tou, J. T. [1971]. "Preprocessing for Pictorial Pattern Recognition," *Proceedings of the 21st NATO Technical Symposium on Artificial Intelligence*, Italy.

Cofer, R. H., and Tou, J. T. [1972]. "Automated Map Reading and Analysis by Computer," *Proceedings of the Fall Joint Computer Conference.*

Cooper, P. W. [1964]. "Hyperplanes, Hyperspheres, and Hyperquadrics as Decision Boundaries," in *Computer and Information Sciences—I* (J. T. Tou and R. H. Wilcox, eds.), Spartan Books, Washington, D.C.

Cooper, P. W. [1967]. "Some Topics in Nonsupervised Adaptive Detection for Multivariate Normal Distributions," in *Computer and Information Sciences—II* (J. T. Tou, ed.), Academic Press, New York.

Cooper, D. R., and Cooper, P. W. [1964]. "Nonsupervised Adaptive Signal Detection and Pattern Recognition," *Info. and Control,* vol. 7, no. 3, pp. 416–444.

Courant, R., and Hilbert, D. [1955]. *Methods of Mathematical Physics,* vol. 1, Interscience Publishers, New York.

Cover, T. M. [1964]. "Classification and Generalization Capabilities of Linear Threshold Units," *Rome Air Develop. Center Tech. Doc. Rept.* RADC-TDR-64-32.

Cover, T. M. [1965]. "Geometrical and Statistical Properties of Systems of Linear Inequalities with Applications to Pattern Recognition," *IEEE Trans. Electronic Computers,* vol. EC-14, no. 3, pp. 326–334.

Cover, T. M. [1969]. "Learning in Pattern Recognition," in *Methodologies of Pattern Recognition* (S. Watanabe, ed.), Academic Press, New York.

Cover, T. M., and Hart, P. E. [1967]. "Nearest Neighbor Pattern Classification," *IEEE Trans. Info. Theory,* vol. IT-13, no. 1, pp. 21–27.

Cramer, H. [1961]. *Mathematical Methods of Statistics,* Princeton University Press, Princeton, N.J.

Crespi-Reghizzi, S. [1971]. "An Effective Model for Grammar Inference," *IFIP Congress-71,* Yugoslavia.

Devyaterikov, I. P., Pripoi, A. I., and Tsypkin, Y. Z. [1967]. "Iterative Learning Algorithms for Pattern Recognition," *Automation and Remote Control,* vol. 28, no. 1, pp. 108–117.

Diday, E. [1973]. "The Dynamic Clusters Method in Nonhierarchical Clustering," *Internat. J. Computer and Info. Sci.,* vol. 2, no. 1, pp. 61–88.

Duda, R. O., and Fossum, H. [1966]. "Pattern Classification by Iteratively Determined Linear and Piecewise Linear Discriminant Functions," *IEEE Trans. Electronic Computers,* vol. EC-15, no. 2, pp. 220–232.

Duda, R., and Hart, P. [1973]. *Pattern Classification and Scene Analysis,* John Wiley & Sons, New York.

Dvoretzky, A. [1956]. "On Stochastic Approximation," in *Proceedings of the 3rd Berkeley Symposium on Mathematical Statistics and Probability* (J. Neyman, ed.), University of California Press, Berkeley, pp. 39–55.

Eden, M. [1961]. "On the Formalization of Handwriting," in "Structure of Language and Its Mathematical Aspect," *Proceedings of the 12th Symposium on Applied Mathematics,* American Mathematical Society, Rhode Island, pp. 83–88.

Evans, T. G. [1971]. "Grammatical Inference Techniques in Pattern Analysis," in *Software Engineering* (J. T. Tou, ed.), Academic Press, New York.

Feldman, J. [1967]. "First Thoughts on Grammatical Inference," Artificial Intelligence Memo. 55, Computer Science Dept., Stanford University, Stanford, Calif.

Feldman, J. [1969]. "Some Decidability Results on Grammatical Inference and Complexity," Artificial Intelligence Memo. 93, Computer Science Dept., Stanford University, Stanford, Calif.

Feldman, J., Gips, J., Horning, J., and Reder, S. [1969]. "Grammatical Complexity and Inference," Artificial Intelligence Memo. 89, Computer Science Dept., Stanford University, Stanford, Calif.

Fischler, M. A. [1969]. "Machine Perception and Description of Pictorial Data," *Proceedings of the Joint International Conference on Artificial Intelligence*, Washington, D.C.

Fix, E., and Hodges, J. L., Jr. [1951]. "Discriminatory Analysis, Nonparametric Discrimination," Project 21-49-004, Rept. 4, USAF School of Aviation Medicine, Randolph Field, Texas (Contract AF41(128)-31).

Fu, K. S. [1968]. *Sequential Methods in Pattern Recognition and Machine Learning*, Academic Press, New York.

Fu, K. S. [1970]. "Stochastic Automata as Models of Learning Systems," in *Adaptive, Learning, and Pattern Recognition Systems* (J. M. Mendel and K. S. Fu, eds.), Academic Press, New York.

Fu, K. S. [1971a]. "On Syntactic Pattern Recognition and Stochastic Languages," Tech. Rept. TR-EE-71-21, School of Electrical Engineering, Purdue University, Lafayette, Ind.

Fu, K. S., ed. [1971b]. *Pattern Recognition and Machine Learning*, Plenum Press, New York.

Fu, K. S. [1972]. "A Survey of Grammatical Inference," Tech. Report TR-EE-72-18, School of Electrical Engineering, Purdue University, Lafayette, Ind.

Fu, K. S. [1974]. *Syntactic Methods in Pattern Recognition*, Academic Press, New York.

Fu, K. S., and Bhargava, B. K. [1973]. "Tree Systems for Syntactic Pattern Recognition," *IEEE Trans. Computers*, vol. C-22, no. 12, pp. 1087–1099.

Fu, K. S., and Swain, P. H. [1971]. "On Syntactic Pattern Recognition" in *Software Engineering* (J. T. Tou, ed.), Academic Press, New York.

Fukunaga, K. [1972]. *Introduction to Statistical Pattern Recognition*, Academic Press, New York.

Ginsburg, S. [1966]. *The Mathematical Theory of Context-Free Languages*, McGraw-Hill Book Co., New York.

Gold, E. M. [1967]. "Language Identification in the Limit," *Information and Control*, vol. 10, no. 5, pp. 447–474.

Gonzalez, R. C. [1972]. "Syntactic Pattern Recognition—Introduction and Survey," *Proceedings of the National Electronics Conference*, vol. 27, no. 1, pp. 27–32.

Gonzalez, R. C. [1973]. "Generation of Linguistic Filter Structures for Image Enhancement," *Proceedings of the ACM Conference*.

Gonzalez, R. C., Fry, D. N., and Kryter, R. C. [1974]. "Results in the Application of Pattern Recognition Methods to Nuclear Reactor Core Component Surveillance," *IEEE Trans. Nucl. Sci.*, vol. 21, no. 1, pp. 750–757.

Gonzalez, R. C., Lane, M. C., Bishop, A. O., Jr., and Wilson, W. P. [1972]. "Some Results in Automatic Sleep-State Classification," *Proceedings of the Fourth Southeastern Symposium on System Theory*.

Gonzalez, R. C., and Thomason, M. G. [1974a]. "Tree Grammars and Their Application to Pattern Recognition," Tech. Rept. TR-EE/CS-74-10, Electrical Engineering Dept., University of Tennessee, Knoxville.

Gonzalez, R. C., and Thomason, M. G. [1974b]. "Inference of Tree Grammars for Syntactic Pattern Recognition," Tech. Rept. TR-EE/CS-74-20, Electrical Engineering Dept., University of Tennessee, Knoxville.

Gonzalez, R. C., and Tou, J. T. [1968]. "Some Results in Minimum-Entropy Feature Extraction," *IEEE Convention Record—Region III.*

Guzman, A. [1967]. "Some Aspects of Pattern Recognition by Computer," Project MAC, Rept. MAC-TR-37, MIT.

Guzman, A. [1968]. "Decomposition of a Visual Scene into Three Dimensional Bodies," *Proceedings of the Fall Joint Computer Conference.*

Hankley, W. J., and Tou, J. T. [1968]. "Automatic Fingerprint Interpretation and Classification via Contextual Analysis and Topological Coding" in *Pictorial Pattern Recognition,* (G. C. Cheng, et al., eds.), Thompson Book Company, Washington, D.C.

Harary, F. [1969]. *Graph Theory,* Addison-Wesley Publishing Co., Reading, Mass.

Hawkins, J. K. [1970]. "Image Processing Principles and Techniques," in *Advances in Information Systems Science,* vol. 3 (J. T. Tou, ed.), Plenum Press, New York.

Helstrom, C. W. [1968]. *Statistical Theory of Signal Detection,* Pergamon Press, New York.

Highleyman, W. H. [1961]. "Linear Decision Functions with Applications to Pattern Recognition," Ph.D. Dissertation, Electrical Engineering Dept., Polytechnic Institute of Brooklyn, New York. (A summary bearing the same title may be found in *Proc. IRE,* vol. 50, no. 6, pp. 1501–1514, 1962.)

Ho, Y. C., and Agrawala, A. K. [1968]. "On Pattern Classification Algorithms—Introduction and Survey," *IEEE Proc.,* vol. 56, no. 12, pp. 2101–2114.

Ho, Y. C., and Kashyap, R. L. [1965]. "An Algorithm for Linear Inequalities and Its Applications," *IEEE Trans. Electronic Computers,* vol. EC-14, no. 5, pp. 683–688.

Hopcroft, J. E., and Ullman, J. D. [1969]. *Formal Languages and Their Relation to Automata,* Addison-Wesley Publishing Co., Reading, Mass.

Horning, J. J. [1969]. "A Study of Grammatical Inference," Tech. Report CS-139, Computer Science Dept., Stanford University, Stanford, Calif.

Horning, J. J. [1971]. "A Procedure for Grammatical Inference," *IFIP Congress-71,* Yugoslavia.

Jardine, N., and Sibson, R. [1968]. "The Construction of Hierarchic and Non-hierarchic Classifications," *Computer J.,* vol. 11, pp. 177–184.

Joseph, R. D. [1960]. "Contributions to Perceptron Theory," *Cornell Aeronaut. Lab. Rept.* VG-1196-G-7.

Kanal, L., ed. [1968]. *Pattern Recognition,* Thompson Book Co., Washington, D.C.

Kanal, L. N., and Randall, N. C. [1964]. "Recognition System Design by Statistical Analysis," *Proceedings of the 19th ACM National Conference.*

Karhunen, K. [1947]. "Über lineare Methoden in der Wahrscheinlichkeitsrechnung," *Ann. Acad. Sci. Fennicae,* Ser. A137 (translated by I. Selin in "On Linear Methods in Probability Theory," T-131, 1960, The RAND Corp., Santa Monica, Calif.)

Keehn, D. G. [1965]. "A Note on Learning for Gaussian Properties," *IEEE Trans. Info. Theory,* vol. IT-11, no. 1, pp. 126–132.

Kirsch, K. A. [1964]. "Computer Interpretation of English Text and Picture Patterns," *IEEE Trans. Electronic Computers,* vol. EC-13, no. 4, pp. 363–376.

Knuth, D. E. [1968]. *The Art of Computer Programming,* vol. 1, Addison-Wesley Publishing Co., Reading, Mass.

Koford, J. [1962]. "Adaptive Network Organization," *Stanford Electronics Lab.* Quart. Res. Rev., no. 3, III-6.

Kovelevsky, V. A. [1970]. "Pattern Recognition, Heuristics or Science?" in *Advances in Information Systems Science,* vol. 3 (J. T. Tou, ed.), Plenum Press, New York.

Kullback, S. [1958]. *Information Theory and Statistics*, John Wiley & Sons, New York.

Laboratory for Agricultural Remote Sensing, Annual Report, vol. 4, Agricultural Experiment Station, Res. Bull. 873, December 1970, Purdue University, Lafayette, Ind.

Ledley, R. S. [1964]. "High-Speed Automatic Analysis of Biomedical Pictures," *Science*, vol. 146, no. 3641, pp. 216–223.

Ledley, R. S., et al. [1965]. "FIDAC: Film Input to Digital Automatic Computer and Associated Syntax-Directed Pattern Recognition Programming System," in *Optical and Electro-Optical Information Processing Systems* (J. Tippet, D. Beckowitz, L. Clapp, C. Koester, and A. Vanderburgh, Jr., eds.), MIT Press, Cambridge, Mass., Chapter 33.

Lee, H. C., and Fu, K. S. [1971]. "A Stochastic Syntax Analysis Procedure and Its Application to Pattern Classification," *Proceedings of the Two-Dimensional Digital Signal Processing Conference*, University of Missouri, Columbia.

Lee, H. C., and Fu, K. S. [1972]. "A Syntactic Pattern Recognition System with Learning Capability," in *Information Systems—COINS-72* (J. T. Tou, ed.), Plenum Press, New York.

Lewis, P. M. [1962]. "The Characteristic Selection Problem in Recognition Systems," *IRE Trans. Info. Theory*, vol. IT-8, no. 2, pp. 161–171.

Loginov, N. V. [1966]. "Methods of Stochastic Approximation," *Automation and Remote Control*, vol. 27, no. 4, pp. 706–728.

MacQueen, J. [1967]. "Some Methods for Classification and Analysis of Multivariate Data," *Proceedings of the 5th Berkeley Symposium on Probability and Statistics*, University of California Press, Berkeley.

Marill, T., and Green, D. M. [1963]. "On the Effectiveness of Receptors in Recognition Systems," *IEEE Trans. Info. Theory*, vol. IT-9, no. 1, pp. 11–27.

Meisel, S. M. [1972]. *Computer-Oriented Approaches to Pattern Recognition*, Academic Press, New York.

McCarthy, J. [1963]. "A Basis for a Mathematical Theory of Computation," in *Computer Programming and Formal Systems* (P. Braffort and D. Hirschberg, eds.), North Holland, Amsterdam.

Miller, W. F., and Shaw, A. C. [1968]. "Linguistic Methods in Picture Processing—A Survey," *Proceedings of the Fall Joint Computer Conference*.

Minsky, M. L. [1961]. "Steps Toward Artificial Intelligence," *Proc. IRE*, vol. 49, no. 1, pp. 8–30.

Motzkin, T. S., and Schoenberg, I. J. [1954]. "The Relaxation Method for Linear Inequalities," *Can. J. Math.*, vol. 6, no. 3, pp. 393–404.

Nagy, G. [1968]. "State of the Art in Pattern Recognition," *Proc. IEEE*, vol. 56, no. 5, pp. 836–862.

Narasimhan, R. [1962]. "A Linguistic Approach to Pattern Recognition," Rept. 21, Digital Computer Laboratory, University of Illinois, Urbana.

Nilsson, N. J. [1965]. *Learning Machines*, McGraw-Hill Book Co., New York.

Novikoff, A. [1963]. "On Convergence Proofs for Perceptrons," *Symposium on Mathematical Theory of Automata*, Polytechnic Institute of Brooklyn, vol. 12, pp. 615–622.

Osteen, R. E., and Tou, J. T. [1973]. "A Clique Detection Algorithm Based on Neighborhoods in Graphs," *Internat. J. Computer Info. Sci.*, vol. 2, no. 4, pp. 257–268.

Pao, T. W. [1969]. "A Solution of the Syntactical Induction-Inference Problem for a Non-Trivial Subset of Context-Free Languages," Interim Tech. Rept. 78-19, Moore School of Electrical Engineering, University of Pennsylvania, Philadelphia.

Patrick, E. A. [1972]. *Fundamentals of Pattern Recognition*, Prentice-Hall, Englewood Cliffs, N.J.

Patterson, J. D., Wagner, T. J., and Womack, B. F. [1967]. "A Mean-Square Performance Criterion for Adaptive Pattern Classification," *IEEE Trans. Automatic Control*, vol. 12, no. 2, pp. 195–197.

Pfaltz, J. L., and Rosenfeld, A. [1969]. "Web Grammars," *Proceedings of the Joint International Conference on Artificial Intelligence*, Washington, D.C.

Reza, F. M. [1961]. *An Introduction to Information Theory*, McGraw-Hill Book Co., New York.

Rice, J. R. [1964]. *The Approximation of Functions*, Addison-Wesley Publishing Co., Reading, Mass.

Ridgway, W. C. [1962]. "An Adaptive Logic System with Generalizing Properties," *Stanford Electronics Lab. Tech. Rept.* 1556-1, Stanford University, Stanford, Calif.

Robbins, H., and Monro, S. [1951]. "A Stochastic Approximation Method," *Ann. Math. Stat.*, vol. 22, pp. 400–407.

Rogers, D., and Tanimoto, T. [1960]. "A Computer Program for Classifying Plants," *Science*, vol. 132, pp. 1115–1118.

Rosenblatt, F. [1957]. "The Perceptron: A Perceiving and Recognizing Automaton," Project PARA, *Cornell Aeronaut. Lab. Rept.* 85-460-1.

Rosenblatt, F. [1960]. "On the Convergence of Reinforcement Procedures in Simple Perceptrons," *Cornell Aeronaut. Lab. Rept.* VG-1196-G-4.

Rosenblatt, F. [1961]. *Principles of Neurodynamics: Perceptrons and the Theory of Brain Mechanisms*, Spartan Books, Washington, D.C.

Rosenfeld, A. [1969]. "Picture Processing by Computer," *Computing Surveys*, vol. 1, no. 3, pp. 147–176.

Sebestyen, G. S. [1962]. *Decision Making Processes in Pattern Recognition*, Macmillan, New York.

Shaw, A. C. [1970]. "Parsing of Graph-Representable Pictures," *J. ACM*, vol. 17, no. 3, pp. 453–481.

Simonnard, M. [1966]. *Linear Programming*, Prentice-Hall, Englewood Cliffs, N.J.

Singleton, R. C. [1962]. "A Test for Linear Separability as Applied to Self-Organizing Machines," in *Self-Organizing Systems-1962* (M. C. Yovits, G. T. Jacobi, and G. D. Goldstein, eds.), Spartan Books, Washington, D.C.

Skinner, C. W., and Gonzalez, R. C. [1973]. "On the Management and Processing of Earth Resources Information," *Proceedings of the Conference on Machine Processing of Remotely Sensed Data*, Purdue University, Lafayette, Ind.

Specht, D. F. [1967]. "Generation of Polynomial Discriminant Functions for Pattern Recognition," *IEEE Trans. Electronic Computers*, vol. EC-16, no. 3, pp. 308–319.

Spragins, J. [1966]. "Learning Without a Teacher," *IEEE Trans. Info. Theory*, IT-12, no. 2, pp. 223–230.

Swain, P. H. [1970]. "On Nonparametric and Linguistic Approaches to Pattern Recognition," Ph.D. Dissertation, Purdue University, Lafayette, Ind.

Thatcher, J. W. [1973]. "Tree Automata: An Informal Survey," in *Currents in the Theory of Computing* (A. V. Aho, ed.), Prentice-Hall, Englewood Cliffs, N.J.

Tou, J. T. [1968a]. "Information Theoretic Approach to Pattern Recognition," *IEEE International Convention Record*.

Tou, J. T. [1968b]. "Feature Extraction in Pattern Recognition," *Pattern Recognition*, vol. 1, no. 1, pp. 3–11.

Tou, J. T. [1969a]. "Engineering Principles of Pattern Recognition," in *Advances in Information Systems Science*, vol. 1 (J. T. Tou, ed.), Plenum Press, New York.

Tou, J. T. [1969b]. "On Feature Encoding in Picture Processing by Computer," *Proceedings of the Allerton Conference on Circuits and System Theory*, University of Illinois, Urbana.

Tou, J. T. [1969c]. "Feature Selection for Pattern Recognition Systems," in *Methodologies of Pattern Recognition* (S. Watanabe, ed.), Academic Press, New York.

Tou, J. T., ed. [1969d]. *Advances in Information Systems Science*, vol. 2, Plenum Press, New York.

Tou, J. T., ed. [1970]. *Advances in Information Systems Science*, vol. 3, Plenum Press, New York.

Tou, J. T. [1972a]. "Automatic Analysis of Blood Smear Micrographs," *Proceedings of the 1972 Computer Image Processing and Recognition Symposium*, University of Missouri, Columbia.

Tou, J. T. [1972b]. "CPA: A Cellular Picture Analyzer," paper presented at the IEEE Computer Society Workshop on Pattern Recognition, Hot Springs, Va.

Tou, J. T., and Gonzalez, R. C. [1971]. "A New Approach to Automatic Recognition of Handwritten Characters," *Proceedings of the Two-Dimensional Signal Processing Conference*, University of Missouri, Columbia.

Tou, J. T., and Gonzalez, R. C. [1972a]. "Automatic Recognition of Handwritten Characters via Feature Extraction and Multi-level Decision," *Internat. J. Computer and Info. Sci.*, vol. 1, no. 1, pp. 43–65.

Tou, J. T., and Gonzalez, R. C. [1972b]. "Recognition of Handwritten Characters by Topological Feature Extraction and Multilevel Categorization," *IEEE Trans. Computers*, vol. C-21, no. 7, pp. 776–785.

Tou, J. T., and Heydorn, R. P. [1967]. "Some Approaches to Optimum Feature Extraction," in *Computer and Information Sciences—II* (J. T. Tou, ed.), Academic Press, New York.

Tou, J. T., and Wilcox, R. H., eds. [1964]. *Computer and Information Sciences—I*, Spartan Books, Washington, D.C.

Tsypkin, Ya. Z. [1965]. "Establishing Characteristics of a Function Transformer from Randomly Observed Points," *Automation and Remote Control*, vol. 26, no. 11, pp. 1878–1882.

Uhr, L., ed. [1969]. *Pattern Recognition*, John Wiley & Sons, New York.

Uhr, L. [1971]. "Flexible Linguistic Pattern Recognition," *Pattern Recognition*, vol. 3, no. 4, pp. 363–383.

Ullman, J. R. [1973]. *Pattern Recognition Techniques*, Crane-Russak, New York.

Van Trees, H. L. [1968]. *Detection, Estimation, and Modulation Theory—Part I*, John Wiley & Sons, New York.

Warmack, R. E., and Gonzalez, R. C. [1972]. "Minimum-Error Pattern Recognition in Supervised Learning Environments," *IEEE Convention Record—Region III*.

Warmack, R. E., and Gonzalez, R. C. [1973]. "An Algorithm for the Optimal Solution of Linear Inequalities and Its Application to Pattern Recognition," *IEEE Trans. Computers*, vol. C-22, no. 12, pp. 1065–1075.

Watanabe, S. [1965]. "Karhunen-Loève Expansion and Factor Analysis-Theoretical Remarks and Applications," *Proceedings of the 4th Conference on Information Theory*, Prague.

Watanabe, S., ed. [1969]. *Methodologies of Pattern Recognition*, Academic Press, New York.

Watanabe, S. [1970]. "Feature Compression," in *Advances in Information Systems Science*, vol. 3 (J. T. Tou, ed.), Plenum Press, New York.

Watanabe, S. [1971a]. "Ungrammatical Grammar in Pattern Recognition," *Pattern Recognition*, vol. 3, no. 4, pp. 385–408.

Watanabe, S., ed. [1971b]. *Frontiers of Pattern Recognition*, Academic Press, New York.

Widrow, B. [1962]. "Generalization and Information Storage in Networks of Adaline Neurons," in *Self-Organizing Systems—1962* (M. C. Yovits, G. T. Jacobi, and G. D. Goldstein, eds.), Spartan Books, Washington, D.C.

Wilde, D. J. [1964]. *Optimum Seeking Methods*, Prentice-Hall, Englewood Cliffs, N.J.

Winder, R. O. [1962]. "Threshold Logic," Ph.D. Dissertation, Princeton University, Princeton, N.J.

Winder, R. O. [1963]. "Bounds on Threshold Gate Realizability," *IEEE Trans. Electronic Computers*, vol. EC-12, no. 5, pp. 561–564.

Winder, R. O. [1968]. "Fundamentals of Threshold Logic," in *Applied Automata Theory* (J. T. Tou, ed.), Academic Press, New York.

Young, T. Y., and Calvert, T. W. [1974]. *Classification, Estimation, and Pattern Recognition*, American Elsevier Publishing Co., New York.

Zahn, C. T. [1971]. "Graph-Theoretical Methods for Detecting and Describing Gestalt Clusters," *IEEE Trans. Computers*, vol. C-20, no. 1, pp. 68–86.

INDEX